History *of* Interior Design

History *of* In

erior Design

JEANNIE IRELAND
Missouri State University

Fairchild Books, Inc.
New York

Director of Sales and Acquisitions: Dana Meltzer-Berkowitz

Executive Editor: Olga T. Kontzias

Acquisitions Editor: Joseph Miranda

Senior Associate Acquisitions Editor: Jaclyn Bergeron

Senior Development Editor: Jennifer Crane

Development Editor: Rob Phelps

Assistant Development Editor: Blake Royer

Art Director: Adam B. Bohannon

Production Director: Ginger Hillman

Associate Production Editor: Jessica Rozler

Associate Art Director: Erin Fitzsimmons

Photo Researchers: Matthew and Ellen Dudley, Candlepants, Inc.,

Kushya Sugarman, and Erin Fitzsimmons

Cover Design: Erin Fitzsimmons

Cover Art: © Bildarchiv Monheim Gmbt/Alamy

Backcover Art: © George Hammerstein/Solus-Veer/Corbis

Text Design: Renato Stanisic Design

Page Composition: Barbara J. Barg

Library of Congress Catalog Card Number: 2007940934

ISBN: 978-1-56367-462-4

GST R 133004424

Printed in the United States of America

TP08

To my daughters, Stephanie and Heather,
the great joys of my life.

Contents

Extended Contents

Preface

Having taught history of design for more than 30 years, I've been disappointed in the texts on the market. Many cover history of architecture very well, although they typically concentrate on specific structures rather than general characteristics. Others cover interiors and furniture but typically concentrate on Renaissance design. There are few texts that combine architecture, interiors, and furniture over a broad spectrum of time, and those that do are rarely comprehensive. Because architecture is the basis for interior design as well as for furniture in most artistic periods, it is essential that students have a broad-based knowledge and be able to see the similarities among the three entities. While many texts cover ancient design in a few pages, classical forms have been revived throughout the subsequent ages and have affected design throughout history. Classical design forms the basis of much design and must therefore be thoroughly understood.

In addition, those of us in modern society often tend to believe that the technological developments that shape our world are recent innovations. It is, however, the ancient cultures that were called on to develop, over a period of hundreds of years, the basic forms for construction, space planning, the forms and design of ornament and interiors, and even functional furnishings. The post and lintel, arch, truss, and cantilever were developed very early, as were methods of turning corners, forming walls, and spanning space. The same techniques developed by early cultures are used today. The technological developments of the past 200 years have made it possible to build higher and wider than ever before with materials such as steel and prestressed concrete, but most of the basic techniques are ancient. Differences in buildings constructed for the rich, the middle class, and the poor are usually related to size and opulence rather than structural form.

The house has changed less over time than have public and religious structures. Cultural and religious developments dictated change, while the basic family unit and its needs remained relatively static. Fashions in architecture, interiors, and furnishings have also changed, but most changes have been a result of increasing knowledge of the world, differences among groups of people, and availability of materials.

Early buildings most often made use of local materials, although some important structures such as Stonehenge were constructed of materials brought long distances. Early buildings were built to suit the environment with materials that were at hand (and such buildings are still built in nonindustrialized areas today). In fact, most such buildings were more suited to local climatic conditions than are current-day green buildings. Buildings in hot, dry areas were typically constructed of adobe, a material that was readily available and that resulted in buildings that were warm at night when the outside air was cool and cool during the day when the outside air was hot. Today, buildings that have the appearance of adobe are constructed almost anywhere—usually of concrete. Most are air conditioned and heated, negating their advantages. Wooden structures have been typical in areas where forests abounded, but modern technology has made it possible to move wood from the forests to any building site. An individual who lives in the middle of a forest may even obtain building materials from forests hundreds of miles away!

Fashions change but are associated with culture, social mores, and economic conditions that have varied over time and among groups. The folk paintings on building exteriors in cultural pockets in Bavaria, onion domes covered with multicolored tiles in Russia, and movable rice paper walls in Oriental structures are differences that may not be understood by individuals in other cultures. Each, however, has been developed over a long period of time and reflects the habits and values of the people who built them. Today, skyscrapers in Hong Kong, New York, Berlin, or Bangkok are so similar that it would be difficult to determine from a photograph their locations. The world has become a global community and though much is the same, much is different. It is essential that designers understand differences across history and across the contemporary world. Only then can buildings suit the needs of their occupants. This text compares historic and contemporary buildings, interiors, and furnishings to better enable designers to complete their tasks successfully.

Acknowledgments

The unsung heroes of ancient cultures deserve much credit. Their patient development of the basic building blocks of architecture, interiors, and furniture ultimately led to this text. Who were these people? No one will ever know, but they were true heroes of their time. They experimented with materials and forms, sometimes giving their lives in the advancement of knowledge, which led to subsequent and more successful trials.

There are many, though, who are known and can be acknowledged as part of the creative process that led to this tome. First, and foremost, are the students who asked questions, stimulated thought, and motivated me to better understand history of design. It is my hope that through the laughter, toil, and seeking of solutions, they have gained an appreciation of what the world of design had to do to become what it is today.

My sister, Willa Gilliam, is the one who has stood by me over the years, encouraging me and inspiring my creativity. She taught me what it is to really live, to laugh when the world is falling around me, and to express joy unequivocally and unabashedly. My daughters, Stephanie and Heather, have kept me grounded, taught me patience, and heartened me as they blossomed into women of integrity, creativity, success, and above all, joy.

A number of my colleagues have made the process easy and enjoyable. Janet Leighton protected my door, ensuring that I was undisturbed, and offered insightful comments about the manuscript. Marciann Patton and Nancy Asay aided the process by volunteering for additional duties so this manuscript could become a reality. Pat Juncos gave me more pep talks than anyone should ever need, always bolstering my confidence and enthusiasm for the task at hand. Sandy Bailey and Jenifer Roberts made certain that I was on track, always showing interest and cheering me on.

The following reviewers examined the manuscript and made numerous suggestions that have improved the quality of the finished product: Mary Anne Beecher, University of Oregon; Christian Dugg, Auburn University; and Vibhavari Jani, Louisiana Tech University. Their comments were much appreciated, and I am grateful for the time and effort they expended. It is my hope that the resulting text is all they desired and more.

The Fairchild people, as always, have been wonderful to work with. Rob Phelps has made the entire process fun, engaging, and so very encouraging. He can turn a phrase into an absolute delight, stir immovable authors with his humor, and appreciate concepts and experiences in new ways. Adam Bohannon and Erin Fitzsimmons shared their enthusiasm for the art and worked tirelessly to make the book come alive with photos and drawings. I am also most appreciative of Executive Editor Olga Kontzias, Senior Development Editor Jennifer Crane, and Production Editor Jessica Rozler. I could not imagine a better team of people with whom to work.

Through it all, however, it has been my family who has given the free spirit within me wings to fly and space to soar. I have been most richly blessed.

History *of* Interior Design

Introduction to Design History

Technology, availability of materials, and tools may all play important roles in the design of structures, interiors, and furnishings. But design choices are shaped much more by the cultural needs and desires of people. (See Figure 1.1.) Substantial structures, even primitive ones, usually go beyond filling a need; therefore, they are affected by users' desires to enhance them aesthetically. Even mud buildings may have painted or incised designs on exterior or interior surfaces.

Culture often dictates the size of the structure, reserving the largest for the gods or individuals with higher status; the location of the structure in relation to topography, the sun, or the direction it faces; and the amount and type of decoration used. Furnishings provide comfort, serve utilitarian purposes, and often indicate status. Use of specific articles of furniture may also be dictated by cultural mores. For example, until the nineteenth century, whether an individual stood or sat on a cushion, stool, or chair was socially determined. Throughout history, the designs of structures, interiors, and furniture have changed, usually slowly, reflecting the society in which they were used. In order to understand these changes, it is necessary to put them into social and historic context. That is the focus of this text.

Technologies Associated with Buildings

Technologies necessary for building structures were developed out of necessity by prehistoric and ancient peoples. **Technology,** or the application of knowledge for a practical purpose, influences the building arts in very basic ways. (See Figure 1.2.) Building does not always mean enclosing space, but it does mean defining space. Structures such as those at Stonehenge and Avebury in England

FIGURE 1.1 Even primitive structures such as this Aboriginal windbreak in Australia perform a function, if only to provide shade or block the wind.

remain relative enigmas with their true functions unknown. It is evident, however, that technologies for moving and erecting great stones were used in their construction. Even primitive shelters require that their builders devise ways to utilize materials and enclose space successfully.

Building technology has developed over many centuries, albeit more slowly than other technologies such as warfare or agriculture. Innovations in building technology are predominantly reflected in monumental structures rather than in homes in part because a suitable form of shelter was developed very early and significant change was unnecessary. Other technologies, even those as basic as food getting, that are indirectly related to building have an impact on structural design as well.

Food-Getting Technology

Because satisfaction of the basic physiological need for food takes precedence over other needs, the methods by which people obtain food affect building arts. Anthropologists generally separate food-getting technologies into two major categories: hunting-gathering and agriculture. Herding, as a food-getting technology, falls between the two types but is not necessarily a transitional form. Hunter-gatherers and herders establish nomadic cultures, while agriculturalists set up more settled ones. With all food-getting technologies, there must be a sufficient number of people living in a group to defend against enemies and to provide mutual assistance in the search for or raising of food supplies.

Prior to the development of agriculture and before the domestication of animals, all people had to forage for food. Even in modern times, there are isolated cultures that have not gone beyond this technology. These societies subsist especially where herding or agriculture are not viable alternatives, such as in some arctic and tropic areas. In hunting-gathering technologies, only naturally occurring wild plants are gathered and wild animals are hunted. As the food supply is exhausted or as animals move on, the people must move.

Large territories are necessary for hunting-gathering cultures because this technology requires more land to support each individual than other food-getting technologies. Areas inhabited by hunter-gatherers are consequently sparsely populated. Groups are small and are generally based on the family. Typically, division of labor is based on gender. Hunting is done by men and gathering by women. In such cultures, the old and infirm may be left to die and infanticide may be culturally approved.

Groups foraging for food follow culturally established norms. Nomadic Australian aborigines camp several hundred feet away from the scarce water holes for two reasons: They do not want to frighten away game, and they do not want to cause strife with other bands waiting for game at the same water hole.

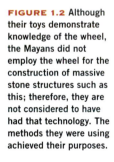

FIGURE 1.2 Although their toys demonstrate knowledge of the wheel, the Mayans did not employ the wheel for the construction of massive stone structures such as this; therefore, they are not considered to have had that technology. The methods they were using achieved their purposes.

Not all nomadic people are hunter-gatherers. Nomadic herders and pastoralists who maintain large herds of animals must follow a food supply. In this instance, the food supply is for the animals. In both groups, food supply is relatively constant, shelters are often made of animal hides or fibers and may be framed with their bones, and clothing is made with yarns woven from the fibers produced by animals or from their skins.

Nomadic herders follow wild animal herds, with only a few individuals actually staying with the animals as they migrate. When the animals have reached their seasonal feeding grounds, the remainder of the people follows and sets up camps. Lapps of northern Europe still follow herds of reindeer, satisfied with an age-old quality of life.

Pastoralists, on the other hand, herd domesticated animals and are more vigilant toward their animals than are nomadic herders. Rather than following herds to food supplies, pastoralists accept greater responsibility and locate food and provide protection for their herds.

The development of agriculture about 10,000 years ago made it possible for people to stop wandering in search of food and settle in one place. Successful agriculture requires that people remain in one place through a growing season or, in the case of orchards and vineyards, for years. The food supply is therefore relatively reliable and people are released to expend their energies making life more comfortable and enjoyable.

Agriculture also made living in larger groups possible, which improved security for the group and its food supplies. In fact, urban development depends on agricultural surplus. People first settled where wild grains were indigenous, and evidence points to villages above major river valleys long before the ancient civilizations established towns and cities in the valleys. Civilizations also depend on water supplies, and as groups became larger, movement into the river valleys ensured constant supplies. Four river valleys are known to have supported major ancient civilizations: the Tigris-Euphrates of Mesopotamia, the Nile River in Egypt, the Yellow River in China, and the Indus River in India.

Shelter is important to all, including hunter-gatherers, herders, and agriculturalists. Early building technologies used simple construction techniques for shelter, many of which are still used by primitive and nomadic cultures. No-madic people either carry their belongings with them or leave them behind. Shelters designed to be abandoned are quickly constructed of readily available materials in a new location. African Pygmies, who live in dense forests, erect hemispherical huts of flexible poles that are then covered with leaves. The huts can be quickly constructed, used for one or two nights, and abandoned without concern. Some nomads build transportable shelters, carrying them along as they travel. Such structures must be easily dismantled and erected and light in weight for portability. The **tipi** of the North American Plains Indians is an example. Because the Amerindians had to travel long distances to cut poles for their tipis, the poles had to be transported when moving to another site. Amerindians lashed them together to form a **travois**, which could carry other belongings. Originally, dogs were utilized to pull the travois. The Spanish brought the horse, an animal not indigenous to the Americas, and as the Indians were able to obtain some of these horses, their tipis could be larger because horses could pull longer poles.

The Navaho Indians approached the problem of shelter in a different manner. Becoming pastoralists after the Civil War, they were obliged to move seasonally to provide pasture for the animals. Two types of dwellings evolved for use by these herders. During the winter, they lived in a mud and log hogan. The summer shelter, called a **ramada**, was merely a roof of branches supported by posts. (See Figure 1.3.)

FIGURE 1.3 The Navaho ramada is a simple structure designed to provide shade and allow outdoor living.

FIGURE 1.4 Modern gers make use of lumber, but traditional examples used bent poles to form the framework that supports the felt covering. Until modern times, yaks, camels, and oxen transported gers when people moved.

Even nomadic peoples are concerned with aesthetics and may ornament their structures, especially when the shelter will be moved with them. The Mongol ger, or yurt, for example, is often decorated with traditional designs. (See Figure 1.4.) In an agricultural society, residences are more permanent and people have more leisure time to develop an aesthetically pleasing environment. Eventually, this leads to the development of arts and crafts and division of labor based on skill rather than gender. As agriculturists banded together and settled down in one place, building arts became more important. Not only could settled people build permanent homes for themselves but for their gods.

Probably the most difficult techniques to develop involved those of spanning space, or roofing a structure. In order to cover an open space, the weight of the roof must be supported. How that is accomplished is a function of the materials used as well as the structure of the roof itself. Ancient builders had to determine not only what materials were suitable but also how they could be incorporated into the structure.

SPANNING SPACE

Four methods are used for spanning space, all of which were well developed by the time of the ancient Greeks. These include the post and lintel; the arch; the truss; and the cantilever, or corbel. Each method is in use today, sometimes having been changed or improved over thousands of years but with no new basic techniques.

The **post and lintel** was the first device used to span space. This method makes use of two or more vertical supports, either posts or walls, bridged by horizontal lintels. When isolated freestanding posts are used for support, vertical members may be called posts or columns. Today, post-and-lintel construction is used for openings and as a basic support system for carrying the load of the entire roof. Early people used posts and lintels and may even have assigned them magical or ceremonial qualities. Ancient Egyptian temples employed this technique with so many supporting posts required that relatively little free space remained inside.

The **arch** was developed where large stones and heavy timbers were unavailable, thus making the simpler post-and-lintel device impractical. **Corbelled arches** are the simplest type, employing the cantilever. A **cantilever** is a horizontal projection that extends beyond the support beneath it. The corbelled arch was used in ancient India, Scotland, Ireland, Central America, and third-century AD Chinese tombs. The beehive houses of Italy's Apulia region are a more modern example of this space-spanning technology.

The arch employs a series of small blocks to span space. The true arch makes use of wedge-shaped members called **voussoirs** that push against each other to form a strong support. Each stone thrusts outward diagonally. Once the **keystone**, or the stone at the apex of the arch, is in, the arch becomes self-supporting. As weight is added, the arch becomes stronger as long as there is sufficient mass or another device such as an adjacent arch to provide counterthrust. (See Box 1.1.) The ancient Mesopotamians used arches for drains, tombs, and gates. But it was the Romans who frequently receive credit for the invention of the arch because they used it extensively and carried it throughout their Empire. Specific arch design tends to become identified with a specific historic period or cultural group. Pointed arches, for example, are characteristic of the Gothic period.

The **truss** is a triangular form that relies on the geometric principle that the length of any side cannot change without changing the angles at the corners. If even one angle is stable, the truss itself is stable. The truss can span very long distances, freeing up large interior spaces. The truss form was first extensively used in ancient Greece. As a result, in contrast to Egyptian post-and-lintel construction, Greek structures were more open, less massive in form, and more graceful in appearance.

FIGURE 1.5 Corbelled arches make use of individual units, usually stone or brick, laid so that each successive layer is cantilevered or extended beyond the one beneath it until the two sides meet at the top.

BOX 1.1 ARCH TERMINOLOGY

A **voussoir** is a truncated wedge-shaped unit designed to retain its position while resisting thrusts against it.

The **keystone** is the center voussoir at the top of the arch. The arch must be supported until the keystone is installed. Once the keystone is inserted, the arch is self-supporting.

The soffit, or interior curve, beneath the arch is the **intrados**.

The exterior curve of the arch is the **extrados**.

The point at which the curve of the arch begins is the **springpoint**.

The **springline** is an imaginary line drawn between the two springpoints of the arch.

The sideways pressure of one part of the arch against another is called **thrust**.

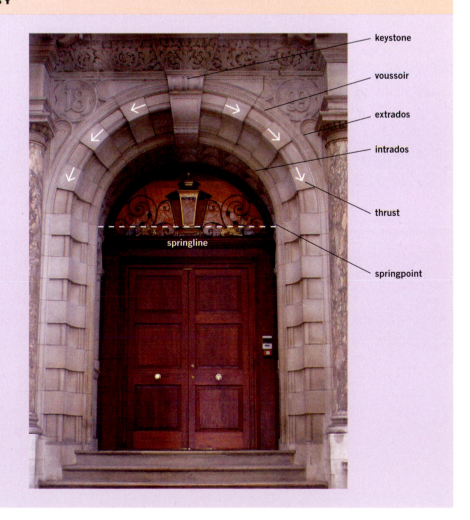

keystone

voussoir

extrados

intrados

thrust

springline

springpoint

FIGURE 1.6 While usually arranged in a curve, there are also flat arches. A flat arch makes use of voussoirs, but rather than forming a curve, the wedges form a straight line.

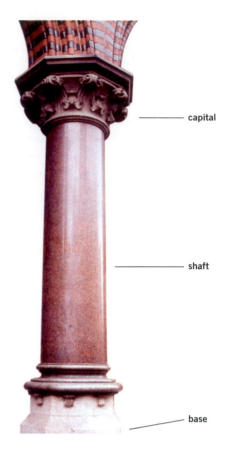

FIGURE 1.7 Three major components of the column.

COLUMNS

The column is a type of decorative post and has been used in every historic architectural period. Like the arch, its design is associated with a cultural group or historic era. Columns consist of three parts: the **base**, the **shaft**, and the **capital**. (See Figure 1.7.) The base is larger than the shaft and serves to spread the weight transmitted through the column over a larger area. Bases do not need to have the same shape footprint as the column shaft and are usually square or circular. The vertical shaft is cylindrical and may be plain or decorated. The capital at the top is larger than the shaft and is typically the most decorative part of the column. Most capitals are single, but there are a few instances when the capital is doubled, especially in Persia and during the Baroque period. Capitals may be purely decorative, educational, or symbolic. The lacy capitals of the Byzantine era served a decorative function only, but during the Medieval period when most individuals were illiterate, capitals were used to tell a story or make a point. The corn capitals in the U.S. Capitol building in Washington, D.C., were a way the architect Latrobe chose to "Americanize" the columns.

Columns used for support are freestanding, but through most of history, columns have also been used ornamentally. Decorative columns serve no structural function because they support no building weight. The Romans used decorative columns as bases for statues. Trajan's Column in Rome (113 AD) is an example although the Nelson Column in London's Trafalgar Square (1840–1843) is probably more familiar. The Romans and almost every Western culture since antiquity have employed columns against walls where, again, they serve a purely decorative function.

Architecture

While the post and lintel, arch, truss, and column are the basis of most architectural forms, architecture itself is a more complex idea. Marcus Vitruvius Pollio, a first-century BC Roman engineer, wrote the treatise *Ten Books on Architecture* that became the bible of architecture for centuries. Vitruvius decreed that a number of criteria were necessary for what he termed "well building." His criteria included order, arrangement, eurythmy, symmetry, propriety, and economy among others.

Order involves working with modules, which in ancient times were established from the building itself. Romans and Greeks used the diameter of the column as an architectural module and based all of a building's measurements on it. Modern Western architects use a module based on a system of measurement—usually 4 inches

FIGURE 1.8 Decorative columns may be a part of the wall structure of a building, projecting outward from a few inches to almost their entire diameters. A rounded column attached to a wall is an engaged column.

or 4 feet. In Vitruvius' tome, order incorporates the use of pleasing proportions as well. These proportions include not only the relative size of structural components but the relative scale of the building and its parts, its surroundings, and the human body. Increasing the scale of a structure relative to the human body makes the building seem daunting and results in a psychological feeling of humility. This technique is often used by rulers to intimidate citizens.

According to Vitruvius, arrangement was based on three types of drawings: ground plans, elevations, and perspectives. Vitruvius concluded that such drawings only come from careful thought that provides creative solutions to problems. The ground or floor plan illustrates symmetry, but its major purpose is to demonstrate flow, allowing individuals to read how the building will function. The elevation provides a frontal view and demonstrates the aesthetic components of a structure including rhythm, relative scale of building components, texture, and ornament. The perspective allows viewers to better visualize the final three-dimensional structure and how it appears in its surroundings.

Elements can be arranged in a variety of ways and are affected by placement and texture. (See Figure 1.10.) Texture can be used to emphasize

FIGURE 1.9 When an applied column is squared off, it is known as a pilaster.

FIGURE 1.10 Rhythm is a patterned repetition of elements such as columns, voids or spaces, and windows. In this instance, the steps have been repeated in a pattern. Rhythms can be static, allowing viewers to examine units leisurely, or they can be dynamic, leading the eye in a specific direction.

solidity or lightness or to contrast element surfaces. Renaissance architecture suggested impenetrable defenses by using **rusticated**, or highly textured, stone with emphasized joints on the first story of a building. Oriental buildings often use rice paper panels framed with light wood that give the buildings an ethereal aura.

Eurythmy[1] refers to pleasing aesthetics of the structure. What is pleasing to the eye is dependent on culture, historic period, and individual taste. The aesthetics of a structure include aspects of order, arrangement, and symmetry as discussed by Vitruvius but add ornament, line, color, and light. Ornament is the element that has been most vilified or embraced. Greek architects insisted that anything that was not necessary for the structure itself detracted from it. Gothic builders added ornament to almost every surface. Line refers to whether the building results in an overall vertical or horizontal impression. Modern skyscrapers reach for the sky and draw the eye upward. In some ways, these vertical lines manifest the ascent of humans up the ladder of corporate success. The verticality of Gothic cathedrals was a visual expression of the desire to reach a heavenly realm. A more horizontal orientation, such as that of the twentieth-century Prairie House and ancient city walls, implies security or contentment.

Symmetry refers to formal arrangement where elements on each side of a center point are balanced in size, shape, and position and may be mirror images. The aesthetic sense of a culture like that in which Vitruvius lived may insist on symmetry. In other times and places, asymmetry is appreciated.

Propriety includes functionality and healthfulness of both the site and the building. Theaters must be designed to temporarily house large numbers of people, provide for crowd flow, give quick and easy access to seats, and present a view of the stage from all seats. Vitruvius was also concerned with the healthfulness of the structure and its site. Modern building codes dictate standards to ensure that this criterion is met.

Economy denotes management, both monetary and physical, of materials and the building site. It also assumes durability of the structure. Until the advent of modern transportation methods, materials were usually obtained from sources near the building site. There are examples, however, where materials were carried long distances, increasing costs, time, and effort significantly. In almost every case, however, the structures in which the materials were to be used were significant, which allowed builders to override the importance of economy. The builders of Stonehenge brought bluestones from the Preseli Hills in Wales, about 240 miles away, and Egyptian temples and pyramids were constructed of stones ferried down the Nile. Interestingly, part of Vitruvius' definition of economy includes the ability to plan dwellings suitable for "ordinary householders" as well as those for the wealthy and prominent.[2] Sir Henry Wotton (1568–1639) later selected what he termed firmness (durability), commodity (function), and delight (aesthetics) from the writings of Vitruvius as requirements for architecture. Contemporary architecture must meet these criteria.

Defining Architecture

Modern definitions of **architecture** vary, but most agree that architecture:

- refers to contrived environments suitable for their functions
- involves preplanning
- has inherent structural stability
- deliberately attempts to create pleasing aesthetic effects

While structures often enclose space, this is not a restricting characteristic. Architecture defines boundaries—not necessarily walls—that separate arranged spaces from their natural surroundings. Outdoor spaces have been an important part of architecture since ancient times when they frequently included processional pathways and courtyards. The fora of Rome, the cloisters of medieval Europe, and the open spaces between structures in Beijing's Imperial City are all considered courtyards. Modern variations of architectural outdoor spaces include parks and golf courses.

The fact that architectural forms are expressive of the contemporary political, social, economic, scientific, technological, and intellectual climate of the times in which they were built makes them historically significant. This is only true, however, if all types of structures are considered. Deriving an impression of a civilization by reading its monumental structures results in a one-sided view. For these reasons, this text assumes a broad definition of architecture and includes, where possible, information about indigenous housing.

CONDITIONS OF ARCHITECTURE

While the underlying principles of construction must be understood and properly used, architecture is more than mere building technology. Without the element of aesthetic concern, any

structural form that was planned in advance and durable could be considered architecture. History of architecture often excludes humble structures, including homes, partly because many of them have disappeared over time, but also because professionals often do not consider relatively simple structures architecture. The exclusion of humble structures as architecture assumes that they are untouched by aesthetic concerns, yet even primitive people incorporate decorative devices purely for aesthetic purposes in their structures. A central pole may be imbued with significance and be highly decorated, or designs may be molded into or scratched or painted on surfaces, even mud walls. Excluding such structures as architecture implies that only the wealthy, who can afford more lavish manifestations of beauty, have an aesthetic sense.

DURABILITY

Durability implies strength and safety. Appropriate wall construction and space spanning techniques must be incorporated to ensure that loads are safely transmitted to the ground. This requires the knowledge and use of certain engineering principles, including those of ensuring that underlying soil is capable of support and that foundations are suitable.

It has only been since the nineteenth century that accurate load calculations could be made

FIGURE 1.11 The medieval town square in Munich, Germany, is a well-defined planned space for gathering. Its boundaries are defined by the structures that face it.

FIGURE 1.12 The Leaning Tower of Pisa, started in the eleventh century, began to lean during construction. Rather than abandon it, architects tried to compensate for the lean by raising the height of one side of successive layers.

with the subsequent specification of appropriate materials or building forms. In medieval Europe, people of one city were often obsessed with building cathedrals with heights or spans that exceeded those in rival cities. For lack of adequate knowledge of engineering principles, innovations in building design were tested by trial and error. As a result, many roofs and towers collapsed, causing injury and death as well as construction delays and increased costs. Even in 1981 when strict building codes were in place and the science of structural engineering was well advanced, part of the Hyatt Regency in Kansas City, Missouri, collapsed.

How long a physical structure should last, or its durability, depends on social expectations. The nomadic hunter who constructs a branch and leaf hut expects it to last the few days it will be used, but there are numerous ancient structures that retain their structural integrity after thousands of years.

FUNCTION

The maxim "form follows function" is not new. Throughout history, designing structures suitable for their functions has been the rule. Forms of interaction differ according to time and culture and affect the size and shape of required spaces. Religious and civic structures must often provide spaces for ritual functions and ceremonies. The activities carried out in ancient Roman circuses and modern stadiums are similar, as are the structures provided for them even though

2,000 years separate them. While the basic function of religious edifices has remained constant—worship of gods—significant differences in rituals and ceremonies affect building form. Ancient Greek temples were designed to house a cult statue and were not entered by anyone other than those serving as priests.[3] Christian worshippers gather in large groups, requiring religious edifices that have appropriate spaces for mass participation in rituals and ceremonies. Buddhist temples provide numerous icons for worship and allow participants to circulate, contemplate, and worship individually rather than as a group.

A second aspect of functionality is efficiency. In homes, this means well-designed kitchens, workshops, and laundry areas—the places where most tasks are performed. Work efficiency becomes even more critical in the evaluation of businesses and manufacturing environments. Efficient means of entry and egress and crowd movement are especially important in public structures.

According to Vitruvius, a functional building is also one that meets budgetary needs and makes efficient use of materials and the site. Good use of space (i.e., serving the requirements of function and aesthetics while controlling costs) is critical where budgetary requirements must be considered. More than one ruler has become unpopular because of high building costs for palaces and public structures. Ludwig II of Bavaria (1845–1886) bankrupted the country because he did not consider costs while building castles for himself. Unfortunately, it has been historically common to have significant cost overruns when building public structures. (See Figure 1.13.)

AESTHETICS

Vitruvius insisted on the use of proportions that please, but cultural dictates affect what is discerned as pleasing. The ancient Greeks considered the human body the ideal form and based their proportions on it. The Egyptian seqt, the Golden Mean, and the Golden Rectangle are also based on the human form. The proportions of the ideal human body when divided horizontally at the navel are 1:1.618, with the torso used as the basis of measurement. Thus, ideally, the lower part of the body should be 1.618 times the height of the torso. These ratios have been transferred to buildings for centuries. The appearance of a

FIGURE 1.13 The Sydney Opera House designed by the Danish architect Jørn Utzon was initially expected to cost $7 million. By the time it was completed in 1973, the cost amounted to $102 million.

structure, however, is not only affected by technology and its design but by social factors.

SIGNIFICANCE OF ARCHITECTURE

As a reflection of social history, architecture defines the source of power in a society. Government buildings are often built to impress or control populations. Roman triumphal arches, the government buildings in Washington, D.C., and Beijing's Forbidden City were all designed specifically for that purpose.

Architecture may also be conceived to inspire a sense of awe. This is most frequently accomplished by impressive size or extravagance of decoration. (See Figure 1.14.) Places of worship often use this technique to corroborate the power of the gods. The soaring space and expanses of stained glass in Gothic cathedrals, gold leaf mosaics of Byzantine churches, and Mayan stepped pyramids help to establish that sense of awe and wonder.

The Seven Wonders of the Ancient World were expressions of pride in their civilizations and as such, designed to impress. Some architectural examples become national icons and serve the same purpose: India's Taj Mahal (1631–1648), the Eiffel Tower (1887–1889), and the Great Pyramid of Egypt (2589–2566 BC) are recognizable buildings that bring to mind the locations in which they are sited.

FIGURE 1.14 The 1964 monument *To the Conquerors of Space* in Moscow is awe-inspiring. Its paraboloid leads the eye upward to the spacecraft soaring into the sky.

FIGURE 1.15 In tropical areas, buildings often employ walls or roofs made of vegetative materials that breathe.

EXTERNAL INFLUENCES ON ARCHITECTURAL DESIGN

In addition to designing according to the basic tenets of architecture, there are external influences that must be considered. The use of locally available materials for structures is common in many cultures because it is inexpensive and convenient. However, the choice of building materials depends not only on availability but on sociocultural values and economic conditions. In ancient Egypt, for example, various types of stone were readily accessible and were used to build temples, palaces, and tombs. However, houses, even those for people of noble rank, were constructed of mud rather than stone. The Egyptians, assuming that the soul lived on after death, believed that permanent structures were more appropriate for sheltering the soul than the living body. The Greeks had to adapt their architecture because the forested hillsides from which they obtained large trees for early structures were denuded. They chose, instead, the rich stores of marble available on the Aegean islands.

Both temperature and the amount and type of moisture affect building style as well. In hot climates, buildings may be more spread out, with outdoor living areas such as courtyards a prominent component. In colder climates, buildings are more compact in form with living areas inside. Where there is plenty of rainfall, steep roofs are necessary. Where water tables are high, buildings may be raised above grade.

Unrelated technological developments can have a significant impact on buildings. When gunpowder made cannons possible, fortified walls could no longer provide protection and castles became obsolete. The development of the jigsaw made it possible for Victorian buildings to have a significant amount of decorative wood trim, which affected design.

Social concerns and mores are often expressed in architecture. In Moslem countries, **jali**, or pierced screens, and the location of doors on opposite sides of the street in alternating positions

FIGURE 1.16 Jali not only allow those behind to view the proceedings outdoors but allow breezes to enter and cool the room.

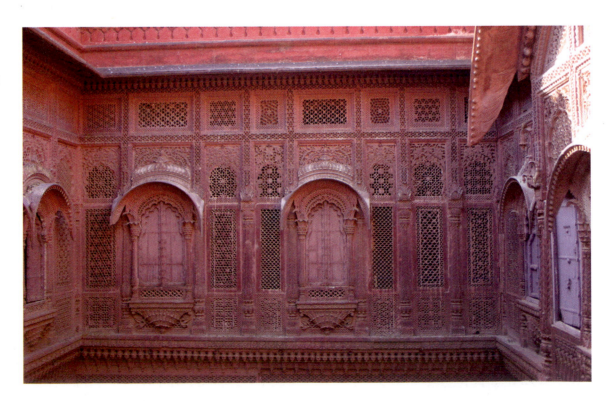

protect women from prying eyes. (See Figure 1.16.) Medieval churches had special places for nonbelievers, who were not allowed into the **nave,** or main worship area.

Religious beliefs may play a key role in the design of a structure. In Japanese homes, small rooms reserved for worship require space in the floor plan. In Asia, curved-up roofs were originally designed so that the spirits who were believed to live in the surrounding area could slide down the roof and head back up instead of landing beside the building.

Tombs also serve a religious function. Belief in an afterlife has led people to provide worldly goods and comforts to carry over into the next life. Ancient Egyptian pyramids served the same function as tombs in Manila's Chinese cemetery. There, the cemetery has the appearance of a small town with lighted streets and regular spacing of buildings that have the appearance of homes. Music emanates from some of the buildings; some are air-conditioned and even have functional toilets.

Exposure to other cultures affects architecture and design. It is difficult to determine, for example, which of the ancient civilizations developed the column first, but all used it. Its widespread use was most likely a result of cultural exchange. The establishment of the Portuguese colony at Macao (1557) opened up trade with China and Chinese porcelain and other goods became popular in Europe. The Portuguese colony at Goa (1510) in India led to the extensive use of ivory in furniture. The importation of mahogany from the West Indies during the Renaissance changed furniture construction because large planks became available for use.

ARCHITECTURAL STYLE

Architectural styles are affected by changes over a period of time and evolve gradually unless there is a significant technological development. In 1853, Elijah Otis developed the elevator braking system still used today. The Bessemer process was introduced for the manufacture of steel in 1855; this reduced the time required for production and the costs of the material, making it affordable for building. These two innovations were quickly embraced and changed the face of urban landscapes as skyscrapers became more feasible.

What are termed "historic" styles gradually evolved from their beginnings in ancient Meso-potamia and Egypt, influencing the subsequent styles of Greece and Rome, and continued to evolve as they were carried throughout Eastern and Western Europe and eventually to the Americas. Some architectural styles have little effect on architecture in distant regions. Ancient American architecture of the Incas, Mayans, Aztecs, and the farmers of the Pueblo cultures; the architecture of India; African sub-Saharan structures; and Saracenic buildings have all had small, if any, influence on architectural styles of other areas. Oriental styles have had more influence on mainstream architectural styles but only during certain periods. Western architecture has had more influence on Oriental architecture in the last 100 years than vice versa.

The development of architectural styles usually follows a pattern. In the beginning stages, the style incorporates simple forms. Gradually, the design is improved to best fit required functions. Once the design of the structure has been perfected, there is a gradual addition of ornament to the structural form. This leads to further increases in ornamentation and the strictly ornamental use of structural forms. By this time, another style has probably begun to develop and overlaps the use of the original style. Over time, structures may be adapted to meet new demands and the additions or changes to a structure may conceal its original design. Styles may be revived but almost always with adaptations for more modern techniques, materials, and processes. Revivals are often far removed from their original locus of influence, and resulting structures have attributes that make them suitable for the places and times in which they occur.

Interior Design

The term **interior design** implies that some effort has been made to enhance the quality of interiors, to improve function of spaces, and to treat interior areas in an aesthetically pleasing manner. Interiors have been thoughtfully contrived since drawings and paintings were done on the walls of caves. Like architecture, interiors are treated to make them more functional, as in the arrangement of furniture, and to make them beautiful. Surfaces are treated, furnishings and accessories included, and design motifs employed to ensure that the sum of the parts results in a pleasing whole. Interiors often incorporate architectural features such as columns, pediments over doorways, and moldings to delimit structural components.

Until the twentieth century, interiors were usually completed by the architects of the buildings and, as such, complemented the structure. Indeed, since the structure serves as the background for the design of the interior, creating a pleasing interior is simplified when the structure itself is pleasing.

Historically, interiors have been designed to conform to social mores that affect other aspects of design. There is little ornamentation and furniture is simple in Quaker homes, keeping with the beliefs of their inhabitants. In Renaissance palaces of Europe, interiors were lavish, as were the lifestyles and the types of entertainment of the people.

Furniture

Furniture and accessories add to the comfort or functionality of a building. Furniture must function in one of two ways: It must support objects or store them. Accessories such as mirrors, lighting units, and works of art perform other functions and may be purely decorative.

Like architecture, furniture reveals habits and social mores of a civilization. In much of the Orient, beds consist of mats that are rolled out when needed, allowing the space to be otherwise used during the day. By contrast, in Western cultures, the bed often occupies a space in a separate room requiring permanent space in the home. The seat-back angle of chairs has changed over time. A 90-degree angle requires users to sit upright. For many centuries, it was a way to preserve an individual's dignity (and sometimes to avoid disturbing one's wig). Most modern chairs have a 105-degree seat-back angle, and some adjust beyond that. Individuals lean against the back of the chair in an informal manner reflective of modern society. In addition, modern chairs are larger than previous models, making it easy to change positions and accommodating the fidgety nature of modern individuals.

Social status can also be expressed through furniture. Throughout much of history, only the wealthy were privileged to sit on chairs, while peasants squatted or sat on stools. Chairs with arms were often reserved for the most important person and many households did not even have one. Height of furniture has also been an indication of status, visually demonstrating elevated social position—the higher the furniture off the floor, the more important the personage in the bed or on the chair. Often footstools or steps have been necessary to mount the chair or bed of a particularly important individual. Raising the furniture on a dais is another technique used to indicate status. Even today, the "head table" at a formal event is located on a dais where occupants are visible from every part of the room.

Ornament

Ornamentation is the decorative treatment of a surface, creating a contrast to the surface itself. The ornament used for interiors and on furniture is often derived from that used on architecture, so an understanding of those forms is necessary. Regardless of its location, ornamentation can be achieved by applying a color or pattern to a surface, changing surface depth, or piercing.

APPLICATION OF COLOR OR PATTERN

Of the techniques used for ornamentation, the application of color is the most widespread. A single color may be applied to an entire surface such as a wall, or multiple colors may be applied in a pattern. Paint may also be used to conceal what may be considered undesirable. The various Windsor chairs of the eighteenth century were often painted to hide the fact that a variety of woods were used for construction. This is not to say that the design inherent in wood has not been appreciated. The reddish-purple color of the Dalbergia tree, often called rosewood or kingwood,[4] has been highly valued since the mid-eighteenth century in Europe, where it was imported from South America and the West Indies. Ebony, citrus, and other woods have been prized during various historic periods and their natural coloring and grain enhanced by polishing or the application of uncolored finishes.

Whitewashing, or the use of a lime-based coloring medium, has been a common technique for coloring a surface. When open fires were present in the home, surfaces were whitewashed every spring to cover the accumulated soot. **Stain** changes the color of wood and, depending on opacity, allows the grain to show to varying degrees. Stains are often used on inexpensive woods to give them the same coloring as more expensive species, although the pattern of the grain is usually dissimilar.

Lacquering is a more complicated technique used to apply color. This technique was well developed by the Chinese as early as the fourth century BC. Lacquer is made from the sap of a tree (*rhus vernicifera*) indigenous to China. When exposed to air, the molecular structure of the sap changes to form a plastic substance. The thickened liquid may or may not be colored before application on an object made of almost any material. Lacquer is waterproof and resistant to heat and the effects of acids and alkalis. It is applied in multiple coats, sometimes hundreds, and is so hard it can be carved. In fact, in the Orient, different-colored layers of lacquer are used so that the final carved product has multiple colors. European artisans often imitated the carving of lacquer products by using a mixture of sawdust and gum arabic to create raised designs. The object was then coated and sometimes gilded with metal dust. Many of these objects were much more colorful than their lacquered counterparts. Ornament is often added to lacquered products by the use of inlays of precious and semiprecious stones, precious metals, ivory, and mother-of-pearl. The technique of lacquering was carried to Japan, and much of the finer-quality lacquered goods imported to Europe in the sixteenth century originated there. Japanese lacquering often featured a black ground with gilded decoration.

Japanning is an imitation of the lacquering technique and was much used in Europe from the seventeenth through the nineteenth centuries. A secretion on trees deposited by the lac beetle is dissolved in alcohol, which can then be applied to a surface as **shellac.** When used for japanning, black or red coloring was often added to shellac. Shellac is not as waterproof as lacquer.

Veneering employs thin sheets of rare or expensive materials laminated to a less expensive material. Often, exotic woods are used to cover more common woods. In this way, good use can be made of expensive materials. The veneer sheet can consist of a single material or of shaped pieces of a variety of materials fit together to form a design. In the latter case, the technique is known as **marquetry** or **intarsia.**[5] Ivory, mother-of-pearl, brass, and tortoiseshell have been used in this way. Regardless of the technique used, veneering requires a relatively smooth overall surface.

When a space is gouged out of a material and another material is shaped to fit the space, the technique is known as **inlay.** (See Figure 1.17.) This technique has been used since ancient times to incorporate semiprecious stones and other ma-

FIGURE 1.17 This screen in Westminster Cathedral in London has mother-of-pearl inlay.

terials, especially in furniture. Egyptian stools for members of the priesthood were inlaid with ivory to give the appearance of leopard skin, a material reserved for priests and pharaohs.

Gilding is the application of thin sheets of gold to a surface. Very thin sheets are known as gold leaf; slightly thicker sheets are called foil. Because of the malleability of gold, gilding can be made to conform to the intricacies of an object's surface, or the surface can be patterned by tooling the gold. Over time, the gold wears off. Currently, eleven American state capitol buildings and numerous religious edifices have gold leaf on their domes. The dome on the Colorado state capitol building was re-gilded in 1991 with 47.5 ounces of gold.

Textiles, leather, and paper can be applied to provide colors or patterns on interior surfaces and furnishings. Tapestries and leather were hung on the stone walls of medieval and Renaissance castles and palaces not only for decorative interest but to minimize cold drafts from the walls. Wallpaper as it is known today began to be available in 1675, although the Chinese had glued rice paper on walls as early as 200 BC.

CHANGES IN SURFACE DEPTH

Ornamentation can be achieved by the addition or subtraction of materials to alter the depth of the surface, resulting in a three-dimensional appearance. The addition of materials includes embroidery and appliqué. Carving removes materials, leaving the design exposed.

Adding Materials to a Surface Appliqué may refer to a textile of a different color or texture applied to a second textile product, or it may refer to the addition of materials to furniture and structural surfaces that results in a three-dimensional effect. Mesopotamian builders applied cones to building surfaces; during the Georgian period (1720–1840), molded plaster designs were attached to ceilings; and modern artisans apply pressed or carved wood decoration to furniture, doors, panels, walls, and ceilings.

Subtracting Materials from a Surface Carving removes parts of surface materials. Both incised and relief carvings have long been common. With **incised carving**, a pattern is cut below the surface. Types of incised carving include scratch carving, chip carving, and gouge carving. **Scratch carving** uses lines incised on the surface to form the outline of a design. The lines are below the surface of the material, leaving the surfaces inside the lines flat. Spaces between the lines may or may not be filled with color. (See Figure 1.19.) Until the eighteenth century, scratch carving was commonly used on provincial furniture. In **chip carving**, small chips are removed from a surface, typically in geometric patterns. (See Figure 1.20.)

FIGURE 1.18 Embroidery uses yarns of various colors to form a raised design on textile products. This technique has been used for upholstery materials, tapestries, rugs, and other decorative fabrics.

FIGURE 1.19 Scratch carving has been used since the earliest times as on this Russian piece. The lines identify features much like in a coloring book.

FIGURE 1.20 Chip carving, popular on medieval chests, is common on Pennsylvania Dutch furniture, and is still frequently used in traditional rural areas in Eastern Europe and in Asia.

The tools used for **gouge carving** are shaped like a scoop and form shallow curved depressions. Gouge carving was used extensively in the sixteenth and seventeenth centuries.

In **relief carving**, the background surface is removed and the design projects above the finished surface. **Low-relief**, or **bas-relief**, carving differs from high relief carving in that low relief uses designs that are cut from the top only. (See Figure 1.21.) In **high-relief**, or **alto-relief**, carving, the design is undercut, forming a three-dimensional effect on the underside as well as the top of the design.

Molding is a type of relief carving. Sharp edges of furniture tops and chair seats, or at the angles of case furniture may be modified along their length to soften their lines, to simulate wear, or for safety. The technique may also be used to modify the surface of long boards that will be used as crown, base, picture, and other moldings on walls and ceilings.

Molding, however, has another connotation that is unrelated to carving. Materials may be shaped during manufacture to have three-dimensional surfaces. Ancient Mesopotamians molded brick and tile to create surface designs.

The term **shaping** also relates to subtracting material from a surface. The outside edges of objects can be shaped to make them conform to specific designs. In the Mycenaean Treasury of Atreus (1250 BC), stone edges are shaped to form a circle. The vertical surfaces beneath table edges or beneath case furniture are often shaped. (See Figure 1.22.)

Piercing is another form of shaping and is usually done in a pattern rather than randomly. Originally, piercing was a way to provide ventilation and was, therefore, utilitarian. Medieval food cupboards were pierced, facilitating the storage of food items in the bedroom for use as a midnight snack. In other instances, there is no utilitarian function and piercing is purely decorative. The jali in Figure 1.16 is pierced.

Turning is another method of subtracting surface material. Cutting of the design is accomplished while the material is rotating, usually on a tool called a lathe. Early lathes were powered by humans; modern lathes are generally electric. Balusters, spindles, and furniture legs are often turned. (See Figure 1.23.)

FIGURE 1.21 Parts of this stone plaque in Beijing's Imperial City are carved in low relief. Heads and some other parts of the dragons are carved in high relief.

FIGURE 1.22 This Mid-European example has shaped edges that employ a variety of curves.

FIGURE 1.23 To create a turning, a sharp tool is held against the rotating piece of material while it turns, resulting in an identical carved shape through 360 degrees.

ORNAMENTAL MOTIFS

Regardless of the methods used, the design of the ornament itself is typical of an historic period or group of people. Motifs are usually based on geometric forms, free-form curves, natural objects, or miscellaneous forms. Motifs maybe formed into a **pattern**, or orderly arrangement.

GEOMETRIC FORMS

Geometric designs use lines, angles, and curves. By themselves, lines are used fairly infrequently. (See Figure 1.24.) The **chevron** is a line motif that uses either a single V-shape or a series of them and has often been used to signify water or lightning. Native Americans of the Southwest and the medieval Normans made extensive use of this device.

Geometric Shapes Lines and angles are used to form other geometric motifs including polygons. Those most commonly used in motifs include the triangle, square, rectangle, octagon, and hexagon.

The triangle played a major role in Greek architecture and subsequent buildings as the shape that predominated at the ends of roofs.

FIGURE 1.24 Lines are used to form the symbol for the Mayan god Chac. This diagonal series of lines represent lightning.

The square is frequently used for building footprints and appears in a number of recurring motifs. Square blocks were separated by spaces to form **dentil** molding in ancient Greece and Rome; medieval battlements employed square, rectangular, or trapezoidal forms for the protection of those fighting on the ramparts; and checkerboard patterns have been used since at least ancient Roman times.

The rectangle is the most frequently used form for building footprints and has been used during all historic periods.

When people believed the earth was flat, they also assumed it was square. From any point on the earth, however, the heavens appeared as a circular dome. An octagon results when the square and circle are combined and the curves changed to angles. The octagon has been especially imbued with symbolism for this reason. The form was used by Charlemagne (c. 742–814 AD) to indicate his status as a liaison between the heavens (God) and the earth (humankind). His ninth century chapel at Aachen, Germany, illustrates this symbolism.

The hexagon was used for motifs but rarely for buildings.

Circles and Curves The curves used in ornamentation include mechanical, mathematical, and free form.

Mechanical curves are based on a circle, include any portions of circles, and are drawn with a compass. Circular designs include spheres, two-dimensional round forms, and partial circles. Spheres are symbolic of the pearl of wisdom in Chinese motifs. As globes, they were used as decorative devices during the Renaissance. Two-dimensional round forms have been used for footprints in a few buildings from ancient Greece to the present. The major use of circles, however, is as design motifs, often representative of the sun, as in the Egyptian winged disk. During the Gothic period, round rose windows graced buildings. Wheel forms and **rosettes**, or circles with designs that radiate from the center and have the appearance of stylized flowers, have been common since ancient times. The circle is the basis of both the arch shape and the individual curved foils in both medieval and Islamic designs. Semicircular arches were common in ancient Rome and derivative periods and are still frequently incorporated in buildings today. An

FIGURE 1.25 Here at the Vatican Museum in Rome, the staircase spirals inward toward the bottom.

arch formed by a portion of a circle greater than 180 degrees is a horseshoe arch and is extensively used in India and in Islamic architecture. Segmental curves, in which the curve is less than 180 degrees, are less frequently used but common in Regency and Baroque designs.

Mathematical curves are derived from conical sections with the degree of curvature dependant on the length of the curve. Ellipses, spirals, and helixes are mathematical curves. Ellipses are ovals, but not all ovals are ellipses. The egg and dart of the ancient Greeks and Romans, room footprints and design motifs of the Rococo period, and fanlights of the Georgian period all incorporate ovals or ellipses.

Spirals begin with a rather sharp curve that lessens as it progresses. While they may eventually have little curvature, they do not become straight lines. Both the **helix** and spiral wind about a center: the helix remains the same distance from the center but the spiral increases its distance from the center as it progresses. The helix is the basis of the thread of a screw. The Mayans used the spiral as a symbol for the wind, and both the impressive spiral ramp of the Vatican Museum (1932) and the structure of the Guggenheim Museum in New York City (1959) use this form. (See Figure 1.25.)

Free-form curves are drawn by hand and were especially popular during the Rococo period when asymmetrical scrolls and elongated S- and C-curves predominated.

Cross Forms A variety of cross forms are used for the design of both building footprints and as decorative motifs.

The **Latin cross**, which has four arms, three of which are equal in length and one that is extended, was used for floor plans, especially in medieval churches. The **Greek cross** consists of four arms of equal length, a footprint that adapts well to the form of worship in Greek and Russian Orthodox churches.

The **Maltese cross** has four arms radiating around a center point. Each arm is V-shaped, with the widest part on the outside edge. The width of each arm also has a wide V-shaped indentation. This cross form appears on the wall of the Krak de Chevaliers in Tartus, Syria, the castle of the Knights Hospitaliers (1144–1271).

The **swastika** is an ancient decorative form found in prehistoric Asia, pre-Columbian South America, ancient Mediterranean countries, and parts of Western Europe. A cross form, it has four equal arms that intersect at right angles in the center. Each arm has an additional 90-degree angle halfway along its length. Both clockwise and counterclockwise[6] swastikas have been used. The term derives from the ancient Sanskrit *svasti,* meaning well-being. The swastika has been used

FIGURE 1.26 Carved from wood, this rose is an example of a naturalistic motif. While the rose has the same form as a natural one, color, texture, and size are incorrect.

as a symbol of prosperity and good luck, as symbolic of the sun, and in early Christianity as a symbol of the resurrection.

Other Geometric Motifs Other geometric motifs include stars, lozenges, and lunettes. Star patterns may have any number of points. Medieval heraldic devices used a number of types of stars, vaulting in Gothic buildings often incorporated star motifs, and during the early years of independence, American design made extensive use of star patterns. The lozenge or diamond-shaped pattern has often been used as a background for other motifs, as well as in vaulting, heraldry, and strapwork. The **lunette**, which ranges from a very narrow crescent shape to a full half circle, is a fa-

miliar form in Islamic design and was common during the European Renaissance (1400–1643) and Baroque (1563–1760) periods.

FORMS DERIVED FROM NATURE

Forms derived from nature are inspired by natural forms, usually real or imaginary plants and animals and are either naturalistic or stylized. **Naturalistic** designs have an appearance that is as natural as possible within the limits of the material used. A naturalistic flower has details subordinated to the overall impression. A natural-appearing flower printed on wallpaper, woven into a textile product, or carved in a material that is obviously not its natural medium are examples. (See Figure 1.26.) A flower made of silk and other fibers may be so realistic that it is mistaken for the actual object. This type of form is an **imitation**. **Stylized** forms are inspired by natural ones but simplified to an extent that their origins may be difficult to determine. Paisley is a stylized plant form thought to have come variously from the pinecone or from the palm, almond, or cypress tree.

Typical plant forms include vines, flowers, leaves, fruits, and nuts. Pinecones and pineapples have also recurred as decorative motifs. Ancient Assyrian (c. 1200–612 BC) designs used pinecones; Jacobean (1603–1649) and Art Nouveau (1892–1910) designs incorporated stylized plant forms; and the English carver Grinling Gibbons

FIGURE 1.27 This jaguar at Chichen Itza holds a human heart in its paws, exemplifying the symbolism used by Mayans.

(1648–1721) was famous for carved fruits, nuts, and leaves.

Animals and animal parts are also popular design inspiration. The eagle has recurred as a symbol of power: ancient Rome, the Hapsburg Empire, Poland, France under Napoleon, Nazi Germany, Russia, the Toltecs, and the United States have all used this form. The bull, lion, ram, jaguar, swan, and other animals have been fashionable in various regions and historic periods. Sometimes, animal parts such as the head, legs, wings, skulls, scales, hooves, or claws are used alone. A number of chair leg styles through history have incorporated stylized animal legs.

The entire human form is featured in the paintings and other decorative mediums of a number of cultures. The three-dimensional human forms used by Greeks and Romans as columns often supported a load, but most human forms are depicted in everyday activities that range from Egyptian figures enjoying the hunt to the winners of games in Mayan ball courts. As with animal forms, sometimes only a part of the human body is used for design. Torsos are frequent, as are heads, but other parts may be used as well. Even heart and kidney forms have recurred. Medieval gargoyles and grotesques often featured some obvious human characteristics.

Imaginary animal forms emerge in some designs. Most of these are combinations of actual animals. The sphinx is a combination of a lion's body with a human head and the mermaid merges a human torso with the body of a fish. Totally imaginary animal forms such as the dragon, unicorn, and winged horses were especially common during the Middle Ages and are still used in the Orient.

MISCELLANEOUS FORMS

Miscellaneous forms include those derived from something other than natural sources. Representations of man-made objects and abstract forms are examples. Shield forms probably stem from the use of the shield in battle and the subsequent personalization of shield emblems emblazoned with identifying crests. Shields were often used during the Medieval period as ornamentation on both interior and exterior walls and on furniture. Shield-back chairs designed by George Hepplewhite (d. 1786) were popular during the Neoclassic period. The cornucopia has been used since ancient times as a symbol of abundance; musical instruments, especially the lyre and the trumpet, appear with some regularity; and initials are frequently used, especially on dower chests.

PATTERNS

The basic pattern types include bands, diapers, and panels. **Band patterns** are linear and may go in any direction, and they are unlimited in length, although their width is static. Bands may use repeated single or multiple motifs and are found on moldings, frames, linear forms, and around columns. The wave pattern is a typical band pattern symbolizing ocean waves. Band patterns have been used in all historic design periods and in almost all media.

Diaper[7] **patterns** employ motifs repeated in any direction to cover all or part of a surface. Wallpaper and textiles often employ diaper patterns. **Counterchange patterns** are diaper patterns that incorporate two alternating colors or textures with the same shapes. The checkerboard is an example. (See Figure 1.28.)

Panels are nonrepeating discontinuous patterns that cover a fixed area and are therefore difficult to extend in either direction. Panel patterns include rinceaux, arabesques, and grotesques. A **rinceau** is a linear decoration that incorporates foliage in curving lines. Often, it is symmetrical from a center point. **Arabesques** may have originated in Saracenic decoration used in Venice mostly on metal objects. They make use of interlaced scrolling foliage often in ogival patterns at design element intersections. Because lines intersect, the resulting shapes are often geometric in

FIGURE 1.28 A *gyronny* is a counterchange pattern that makes use of triangular shapes. It has been used in Roman mosaics, tiling, and heraldry.

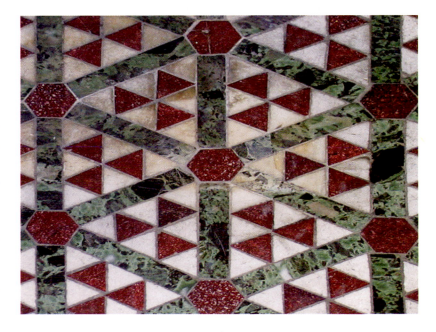

BOX 1.2 EXAMPLES OF BAND PATTERNS

form. **Grotesques** are similar to arabesques but add figures of birds, animals, and humans.

Drawing from the Past

Most of the technologies and design features discussed in this book were developed hundreds or even thousands of years ago. Each culture or historic period, however, interprets design elements differently, and for this reason, design choices can reveal much about the people. Even the choices made by prehistoric and primitive peoples provide clues to their cultures. Interpreting those clues can lead to a better understanding of the past, furnish a greater appreciation for the present, and inform the very future of design.

In the Beginning

Part One

In the Beginning

Camulodunum

Londinium

Koln

Treverorum

Lutetia

Atlantic

Ocean

Appenine Mountains

Arelate

Masillia

Felathri

Arretium

Curtun

Ankon

Clevsin

Perusna

Elba

Puplina

Velzna

Vetulonia

Corsica

Tarquinii

Veio

Caisra

Rome

Iberian Peninsula

Balearic Islands

Kapue

Neapolis

Pompeii

T

Herculaneum

Paestum

Sardinia

MAGNA GRAECIA

Su

PORTUGAL

Tyrrhenian Sea

Adriatic

SICILY

Akragas

Syracuse

Mediterranean S

TUNISIA

AFRICA

Sahara Desert

MALI

SONGHAI

Inset (top left — Greece/Aegean):

Troy
Pergamon
Aegean Sea
Delphi
Mt. Pentelicus
Marathon
Corinth
Athens
Mt. Olympus
Mycenae
Priene
Argos
Tiryns
Miletus
Sparta
Mt. Parpessa
RHODES
Ionian Sea
Knossos
Mallia
Phaestus
Zagros

Inset (top right — China):

Gobi Desert
Great Wall of China
CHINA

Main map:

Black Sea
Caspian Sea
Byzantium
Hattusas
ANATOLIA
Armenian Highlands
Çatal Hüyük
HITTITES
Tigris River
CYPRUS
Euphrates River
Byblos
SYRIA
PERSIA
Jordan River
ASSYRIA
CHALDEANS
Cyrene
Jericho
Dead Sea
SUMERIA
Gaza
Babylon
Nippur
Naucratis
Lagash
Giza
BABYLON
Säqqara
Memphis
al 'Ubaid
Ur
SINAI
Persian Gulf
Tell el-Amarna
Nile River
Red Sea
Luxor
Karnak
Valley of the Kings
N
LOWER NUBIA
Abu Simbel
Second cataract
Third cataract
Fourth cataract
Fifth cataract
UPPER NUBIA
Kingdom of Meroe
Kingdom of Axum

0   500 Miles

0   500 Km

All dates BC unless otherwise noted

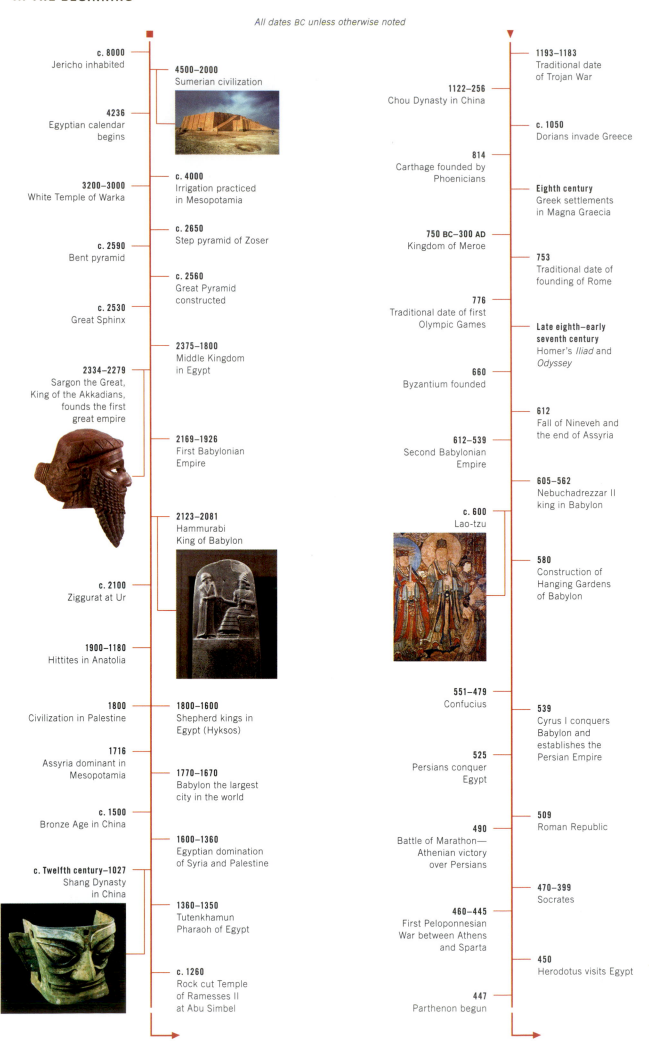

c. 8000
Jericho inhabited

4500–2000
Sumerian civilization

4236
Egyptian calendar
begins

c. 4000
Irrigation practiced
in Mesopotamia

3200–3000
White Temple of Warka

c. 2650
Step pyramid of Zoser

c. 2590
Bent pyramid

c. 2560
Great Pyramid
constructed

c. 2530
Great Sphinx

2375–1800
Middle Kingdom
in Egypt

2334–2279
Sargon the Great,
King of the Akkadians,
founds the first
great empire

2169–1926
First Babylonian
Empire

2123–2081
Hammurabi
King of Babylon

c. 2100
Ziggurat at Ur

1900–1180
Hittites in Anatolia

1800
Civilization in Palestine

1800–1600
Shepherd kings in
Egypt (Hyksos)

1716
Assyria dominant in
Mesopotamia

1770–1670
Babylon the largest
city in the world

c. 1500
Bronze Age in China

1600–1360
Egyptian domination
of Syria and Palestine

c. Twelfth century–1027
Shang Dynasty
in China

1360–1350
Tutenkhamun
Pharaoh of Egypt

c. 1260
Rock cut Temple
of Ramesses II
at Abu Simbel

1193–1183
Traditional date
of Trojan War

1122–256
Chou Dynasty in China

c. 1050
Dorians invade Greece

814
Carthage founded by
Phoenicians

Eighth century
Greek settlements
in Magna Graecia

750 BC–300 AD
Kingdom of Meroe

753
Traditional date of
founding of Rome

776
Traditional date of first
Olympic Games

**Late eighth–early
seventh century**
Homer's *Iliad* and
Odyssey

660
Byzantium founded

612
Fall of Nineveh and
the end of Assyria

612–539
Second Babylonian
Empire

605–562
Nebuchadrezzar II
king in Babylon

c. 600
Lao-tzu

580
Construction of
Hanging Gardens
of Babylon

551–479
Confucius

539
Cyrus I conquers
Babylon and
establishes the
Persian Empire

525
Persians conquer
Egypt

509
Roman Republic

490
Battle of Marathon—
Athenian victory
over Persians

470–399
Socrates

460–445
First Peloponnesian
War between Athens
and Sparta

450
Herodotus visits Egypt

447
Parthenon begun

All dates BC unless otherwise noted

443–429
Golden Age of Greece
under Pericles
(495–429)

431–404
Second
Peloponnesian War

c. 429–347
Plato

384–322
Aristotle

338
Philip II of Macedon
(382–336)
invades Greece

332
Alexander the Great
conquers Egypt and
establishes Alexandria

329
Alexander the Great
campaigns in India

312
Appian Way begun

283
Romans occupy most
of Magna Graecia

241
Sicily becomes a
Roman province

238
Corsica and Sardinia
added to Roman
territory

221–206
Ch'in Dynasty in
China and Great Wall
constructed

218
Hannibal crosses
the Alps and defeats
Roman armies in two
battles

206–9 AD; 25–220
Han Dynasty in China

212
Romans captured
Syracuse (Sicily)

201
Spain becomes a
Roman province

146
Rome destroys
Carthage and
occupies Greece

63 BC–14 AD
Roman Empire or
Imperial Period

58–50 AD
Julius Caesar
conquers Gaul

44 AD
Julius Caesar
assassinated

30 AD
Egypt added to
Roman Empire

64 AD
Burning of Rome and
first persecution of
Roman Christian

70 AD
Colosseum begun

77–84 AD
Roman conquest
of Britain

113 AD
Column of Trajan
constructed

79 AD
Eruption of Vesuvius
buries Pompeii and
Herculaneum

122 AD
Construction of
Hadrian's Wall
in England

200–600 AD
Kingdom of Axum

285 AD
Emperor Diocletian
divides Roman Empire

306–337 AD
Constantine I,
Roman Emperor

311 AD
Christianity legalized

312 AD
Battle of
Mulvian Bridge

313 AD
Edict of Milan
promotes Christianity
to official favor

315 AD
Arch of Constantine

330 AD
Constantinople
made capital of
Roman Empire

370 AD
Huns invade Europe

410 AD
Goths sack Rome

451–452 AD
Attila invades
Gaul and Italy

476 AD
Fall of Rome and
Western Roman
Empire

618–907 AD
T'ang Dynasty in China

900–1400 AD
Ethiopian rock-cut
churches

969–1279 AD
Song Dynasty in China

c. 1250–1629 AD
Empire of Great
Zimbabwe
(Matupa Empire)

c. 1200–1300 AD
Kingdom of Ghana

1235–1645 AD
Kingdom of Mali

1280–1367 AD
Yuan Dynasty in China

1368–1644 AD
Ming Dynasty in China

c. 1400–1600 AD
Kingdom of Songhai

Ancient Mesopotamian, Persian, and Egyptian Design

Western scholars have given too little credit to the contributions of two of the world's earliest large-scale civilizations. Both Mesopotamia and Egypt were instrumental in developing many of the most essential features of society such as agriculture, irrigation, political structures, laws, and writing.

Both civilizations were located in warm climates where the land was relatively flat. Because rainfall was limited and unpredictable, and the life-giving rivers periodically flooded, the land called for irrigation and dikes to hold back floodwaters. The people of these regions practiced irrigation as early as 4000 BC. Control of the water supply probably led to the development of central political structures as well as to writing. Aided by the plow, the seed drill, and a thresher—all of which had to be developed by these civilizations—crops were grown in sufficient quantities for feeding the populations of cities as well as for trade. Sailboats plied the rivers, and in Mesopotamia, the first solid-wheeled vehicles rolled across the plains, transporting grain and other goods.

Each year, priests surveyed the lands, assigned fields to specific farmers, and determined which crops would be planted and how the crops would later be distributed. Maintaining such a complex system necessitated recording the de-

tails. For this purpose, a system of pictographic writing was devised by 3600 BC, when stone was used as a writing surface. Over the centuries, pictographic writing developed into signs that represented ideas. By 3000 BC, the Sumerians wrote on wet clay tablets using a reed stylus, which left a wedge-shaped mark. This writing is called cuneiform, from the Latin "cuneus" meaning wedge (See Figure 2.1). Like Mesopotamian writing, Egyptian text was at first pictographic. Egyptian

FIGURE 2.1 Until c. 2700 BC, Mesopotamian writing was used for business and accounting. Later, writing was employed for relating royal deeds, love songs and poetry, and laws. The most famous of the epic poems of Sumeria is the Epic of Gilgamesh (c. 2000 BC), which describes the heroic deeds of Gilgamesh—probably an early king.

scribes first used stone, but by the Old Kingdom had learned to make papyrus from layered strips of papyrus stalks. Mesopotamian cuneiform writing never got beyond the stage of communicating ideas, while Egyptian writing evolved into signs known as hieroglyphics that communicated ideas, later sounds, and finally syllables.

Mesopotamia (4500–539 BC)

It was in the area between the Tigris and Euphrates rivers in modern Iraq that the earliest civilizations[1] developed. Mesopotamia had no natural boundaries, making it difficult to define geographically. Situated at the head of the Persian Gulf, the region stretched at times north to the highlands of Armenia, east to the foothills of Persia, as far west as Syria, and south toward the Arabian Desert. Political domination was mostly of one or more cities with their surrounding territories, although over several millennia, some far-reaching empires were established. With few exceptions, the major cities were located in the Tigris and Euphrates River valleys and along their tributaries. The lack of natural boundaries made the Mesopotamian cities accessible for trade but vulnerable to attack so city walls were necessary for defense and warfare was a constant possibility.

Mesopotamia was inhabited by several groups, each dominating for a period then being conquered by others. Each made significant advances in technology. The agricultural villages of Sumeria (4500–2000 BC) occupied the southern area of the Mesopotamian valley and by 3500 BC had become cities with a well-organized social and political structure. Sumerian civilization dominated the area for a millennium, followed by the Akkadians, the Babylonians, the Assyrians, and the Chaldeans although each was influenced by Sumerian social structure, religion, and art. The civilization of Sumeria itself was forgotten but lived on in legends. By 250 BC, the Babylonian Berosus wrote only of a race of monsters who introduced agriculture, writing, and metallurgy to the region.

The religions of Mesopotamia concentrated on life in the present. The afterlife was thought of as a dreary existence when only the gods would be happy. For this reason, there were only a few monumental tombs. Most people were either buried under the floors of their houses or cremated.

The gods were usually identified with natural phenomena such as the sun and moon, the sky, storms, and lightning, and each city had its favorites. The gods differed from humans only in that they were more powerful and, of course, immortal. Through sacrifices, magic, and prayer, the gods could be manipulated although this required certain rituals and expert knowledge. A powerful priesthood developed to interpret the movement of heavenly bodies as well as the internal organs of sacrificial animals for signs from the gods. Each of the dozen city-states of Sumeria was led by a priest-king—indicative of the importance of religion in their culture. Both political and religious powers were centered in the king, who was considered a representative of the gods and later, a deity himself.

The Babylonians (2169–1926 BC) were by far the best astronomers of their time, although astrology was of higher significance than astronomy. It was the Babylonians who initially divided the heavens into the 12 signs of the zodiac. The Babylonian king Hammurabi (reigned 2123–2081 BC) established a single code of laws that replaced those of individual cities. These laws demanded exact retribution—an eye for an eye was literal. If a house collapsed and the owner was killed, the life of the builder was demanded. If the owner's son was killed when the house collapsed, the builder's son was executed. Equivalent retaliation, however, was demanded only for free citizens. If a citizen blinded someone else's slave, only half of the slave's value was due to the owner.

INFLUENCE 2.1

The Greeks learned much from the Babylonians. Not only were Greek city-states similar to those of Babylon but also Greek mathematics, medicine, and philosophy owed much to these antecedents.

The Assyrians (c. 1200–612 BC) established an empire that ruled from North Africa to parts of Persia. Technological advances included the spoked wheel, more advanced plows, and glazed pottery. At least one Assyrian city, its capital, Nineveh, had an aqueduct that supplied water long before such structures were used in Rome.

Babylon once again rose to power in 612 BC as the Chaldean Empire. It was this Babylonian Empire that first produced glazed brick and tile, marble streets wide enough for two chariots, and the Hanging Gardens—one of the Seven Wonders of the Ancient World. The area was significantly influenced in its latter stages by the Hittites in Anatolia (modern Turkey) and by the Persians.

MESOPOTAMIAN ARTS AND DESIGN TECHNIQUES

Mesopotamian art forms were similar and showed gradual changes from simple stylized designs to more natural depictions. Early Mesopotamians carved low relief figures in stone; seventh-century BC Babylonians also carved figures in adobe brick prior to firing. Many of these bricks were glazed. The chemicals used created different colors and fused with the brick during the firing process, resulting in a durable, water-resistant product.

INFLUENCE 2.2

Molding in brick to create three-dimensional designs has been revived and is used in high-end décor today.

In paintings, figures were represented on ground lines and depicted with their heads and legs in profile and with their shoulders and an eye shown frontally. Mesopotamian artists did not use perspective but overlapped figures to es-

tablish a sense of depth. Sculpture in the round exhibited rigid forms either without any spaces between limbs and the body or with those spaces filled in. Arms were carved close to the body and elaborate beards and hair filled spaces around the neck. The eyes of Sumerian figures were emphasized by making them exceedingly large and inlaying them with shells.

Mesopotamian artisans were skilled at inlay work using shell, **lapis lazuli** (a natural blue stone), limestone, and other materials. The Standard of Ur—a box probably intended to be mounted on a pole—illustrates third-millennium BC artistic forms. (See Figure 2.3)

FIGURE 2.2 A brick design might cover numerous bricks, so its final installation required careful planning. Such figures were used on Babylon's Ishtar Gate, where relief dragons representing the god Marduk and lions representing the goddess Ishtar invoked the power of the deities for the protection of the city.

FIGURE 2.3 The activities depicted on the two sides of the Standard of Ur differ. On one side are scenes from war. In the peaceful scenes on this side, the king (inset) is larger than other figures, indicating his elevated status.

FIGURE 2.4 The black, red, white, or tan enameled bases of cone-like units were applied in patterns on a surface that was sometimes prepared by whitewashing.

Among the animals found in the various decorative arts were the ibex (wild goat), lion, bull, bear, deer, wolf, eagle, and horse each associated with a deity. Animals were often featured standing on their hind legs and participating in human activities such as carrying objects and serving food. **Griffins** (mythical creatures with a lion's body, an eagle's head and wings, and in some instances, the tail of a snake), winged lions and bulls, and winged human figures were all incorporated in Mesopotamian designs. Motifs were often derived from nature and geometric forms such as the zigzag and chevron, or V-shape, were common. Counterchange and gyronny patterns were also used. See Box 2.1.

About 3000 BC, the Sumerians were creating cone mosaics by embedding thousands of thin, fired clay cones in adobe walls and columns so only the circular bases of the cones were visible. The fired cones were set closely together and improved the durability of adobe structures. Cone mosaics were used for temple walls and other structures and were adopted by the later Babylonians.

MESOPOTAMIAN ARCHITECTURE

Because the southern part of the region lacked good building stone, this material was used sparingly and reserved for carved reliefs on the lower parts of palace walls, thresholds, foundations, and some pavements. Most buildings, regardless of culture, were constructed of adobe brick—a form that first had to be developed. The brick, like stone, was used in **load-bearing construction**, meaning that each part of the wall supported the weight above it; this limited the size of openings and required that walls be thick. Alternating projections and recesses in the walls recalled early reed structures from the marshes (See Figure 2.5) with the projections serving as **buttresses**, or areas of reinforcement, to provide support and stability.

At al 'Ubaid, (6000–4000 BC) a few fired bricks were found—a significant technological innovation. The lack of wood for fuel, however, made fired brick expensive and it continued to

FIGURE 2.5 Modern houses in the marshes of Iraq are strikingly similar to the reed structures depicted in ancient drawings and reliefs. Bundles of reeds are tied together to form a framework. Reed mats or wattle and daub may fill the spaces between the bundles. This alternation of projections and recesses recalls ancient wall construction.

be used sparingly throughout Mesopotamia. Because there was little timber or stone for roof construction, fired bricks were employed in vaults and arches and possibly domes. There are numerous representations of buildings with domical roofs although the material used is not known. Clay was plastered on adobe surfaces to smooth them, and later, the Assyrians used stone slabs and Chaldeans used a layer of glazed brick for facing important buildings.

In northern areas of Mesopotamia, where there was indigenous stone, the true arch, or that which employs wedge-shaped voussoirs, was first used. The royal tombs at Ur and the more than 5,000-year-old drains in Nippur are examples of these ancient arches and vaults and Herodotus reported that the Hanging Gardens of Babylon were supported on an **arcade**, or a series of side-by-side arches. The Mesopotamian use of columns and engaged columns preceded their use in Egypt by 500 years.

MONUMENTAL ARCHITECTURE

Walls surrounded the cities, and access was through gates flanked by towers. Both walls and gates had **crenellated battlements** with stepped parapet projections. A battlement included the walkway along the top of a wall with crenellations or alternating vertical recesses (**crenels**) and projections (**merlons**). Soldiers on the wall could shoot an arrow from the crenel and retreat behind the merlon for protection. (See Figure 2.6.) Gateways and city walls not only served a protective function, but were intended to impress visitors and to display the prosperity of the city.

The Babylon of Nebuchadnezzar (c. 605–562 BC) exhibited the first urban planning with a raised paved processional way, or **dromos**, that

began at the Ishtar Gate and led to the palace and the temples. The dromos was flanked with walls faced with fired brick with low-relief lions. The Ishtar Gate is one of the few remaining examples of Babylonian architecture and features a semicircular arch and glazed brick with reliefs.

The earliest type of public building was the temple—the focus not only of religion but of administration. The city and its people were there to serve the gods. Like humans, the gods required shelter and a constant supply of food, servants, concubines, and money.

Temple corners were oriented toward the cardinal points. Early temples were constructed on a solid **battered** (sloped) brick platform to raise the temple above the level of the houses of mortals. These adobe structures deteriorated and others were built on top of the remains eventually resulting in the **ziggurat**, or stepped tower. The White Temple of Warka (3200–3000 BC) was composed of successive platforms that were stepped back from those below and painted a different color. Remains of one ziggurat show circular designs in its sides formed by the bottoms of pottery jars embedded in the walls and others were decorated with cone mosaics (See Figure 2.7).

FIGURE 2.6 The Mesopotamian stepped merlons were vertical copies of the horizontal projections and recesses of the walls.

FIGURE 2.7 Formal staircases led to the top of the ziggurat, where the temple itself was located. Stairways might be straight, multiple stairways might ascend to a gateway from which a single stairway proceeded, or the stairway might wind around the ziggurat.

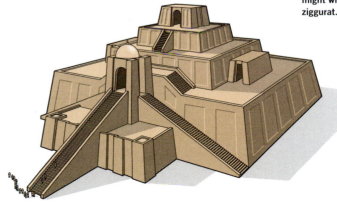

Box 2.1 Mesopotamian Motifs

The **palmette** had radiating fronds, each of which might have a central stem and diagonal lines representing individual leaves. The fronds radiated from a central curved motif and fanned outward. A pair of volutes or sometimes fruits or cones completed the design at its base. The palmette was sometimes used as a terminal device at the top of a stele or other trunklike form.

The fir cone of the Mesopotamians was pointed and was frequently used at the base of furniture legs in an inverted form.

A **rosette** is a flower-like motif formed by adding radiating petals to a circular form. The Mesopotamian rosette was sometimes enclosed within a circle or within concentric circles.

The tree of life motif incorporated a number of palmettes connected by curving "ribbons" or bands.

The **guilloche** was formed by interlacing curved lines or bands. Most civilizations have used the guilloche, and its form varies considerably.

The flower of the lotus plant was easily stylized and was used by a number of ancient civilizations as a motif. Most likely, the Mesopotamian civilizations copied the lotus from the Egyptians, where the plant was native. Pointed petals characterized the lotus flower, the number of petals and sepals varied, and it was frequently alternated with the fir cone or with a lotus bud.

Imbricated, or scale, ornament was used as a diaper pattern.

The Mesopotamian tree motif has the appearance of an evergreen.

Geometric forms were typical of Mesopotamian designs, and frequently bands of patterns or radiating patterns were incorporated within a square or rectangle.

FIGURE 2.8 The Lamassu was the most memorable Mesopotamian anthropomorphic form. This human-headed bull had five legs, wings, and was designed to be seen from both the front and the side.

Two types of temple developed: the house of the god (usually located near the ziggurat) and the summit temple. The house of god temple was

built like a dwelling and had a courtyard surrounded by a wall. It was in this courtyard that most of the religious ceremonies took place. The two doors were staggered so they were not in line with one another, avoiding a straight axis—a typical Mesopotamian feature. Summit temples were entered from the side rather than through the imposing gateways at the ends that were reserved for use by the gods.

The exteriors of temples were decorated with glazed brick or cone mosaics. Walls of the central sanctuary rose above those of the side rooms, allowing clerestory openings to penetrate the wall. The decorations at the top of the temple and over doorways might be worked in copper or semiprecious stones.

Statuary representing animals, gods, and heroes were housed in temple rooms. **Anthropomorphic** forms were common and combined features of an animal with a human head. (See Figure 2.8.) See Box 2.2 for a summary of Mesopotamian architectural characteristics.

The Hittites (1900–1180 BC) were an Indo-European people who immigrated to Asia Minor and controlled the area of Anatolia in modern Turkey. By the fourteenth century BC, the Hittites mined iron, which they may have been the first to process by smelting. They used the cuneiform script of the Babylonians and in trading with Crete taught them to use clay tablets.

The Hittites' access to more stone and to timbers resulted in differences in architectural style from the Tigris-Euphrates region. Rather than adobe brick buildings, those with timber frames and brick infill were more common, although temples were constructed of stone. Hittite arched gateways were guarded by monumental sculptured beasts long before such sculptures were used in Mesopotamia. Friezes of stone with relief sculptures lined the lower part of the gateway walls. **Colonnades**, or rows of columns, bordered courtyards. While columns were often of wood, they were set on bases of stone, some relatively simple and cushion shaped, others reclining beasts that supported the columns on their backs.

INFLUENCE 2.6

During the Medieval period in Western Europe and into the Renaissance, columns were sometimes placed on the backs of reclining beasts.

DOMESTIC ARCHITECTURE

While early dwellings employed bundles of reeds for supports, as do those in contemporary Mesopotamian marshlands, homes in urban areas were constructed of adobe brick, with a flat roof constructed of wood beams covered with mud and sometimes used for sleeping. Doors were wooden and pivoted on pegs set into stone sockets. There are few remains of ordinary dwellings.

The Assyrians were the first to emphasize the palace, which was built by wealthy citizens as well as by members of royalty. Palaces were built on artificial hills as high as 40 feet—an early use of height as an indication of status. These walled complexes were entered through narrow gateways guarded by colossal figures. The eighth-century BC palace of Khorsabad was entered through an arch that sprang from the backs of Lamassu, while basalt lions guarded the palace of Nebuchadnezzar in Babylon. Guards concealed in recesses that flanked the entrance further protected the entrances. Private apartments had extra guards, and temples were constructed on palace grounds—sometimes on a small ziggurat—to decrease the necessity for kings and nobles to leave the security of the palace.

The long rectangular throne room was accessed from the court of honor courtyard. Behind this was another courtyard around which the palace rooms were constructed, although there was little overall planning and separate buildings tended to be located without regard to symmetry. A large reception room, a kitchen, bedrooms, and other necessary spaces were incorporated along the inner courtyard. In multistoried structures, there was probably an exterior gallery that provided access to private upstairs family rooms and shaded the courtyard below.

MESOPOTAMIAN INTERIORS

Mesopotamian floors were often simply compressed earth; stone flooring was typical of more opulent dwellings. Walls were plastered and divided horizontally into decorative bands. Stone slabs with relief carvings formed a **dado**, or lower part of an interior wall (when finished differently from the remainder of the wall). Frescoes covered much of the wall surface. (See Figure 2.9.) Materials and decorative techniques used for walls might also include cedar or cypress, alabaster, or marble paneling or inlays of semiprecious stones including agate and onyx, mother-of-pearl, and precious metals. The walls of the palace of Nebuchadnezzar in Babylon featured yellow brick and blue glazed tiles with reliefs.

Palace ceilings were probably timber-framed and mud-covered or vaulted with fired brick.

MESOPOTAMIAN FURNITURE

Little Mesopotamian furniture survived the ravages of time. Archaeologists must rely on illustrations of furniture rather than actual examples.

FIGURE 2.9 Scenes were painted above the stone lining on plastered walls. At the top, a further horizontal wall division, or frieze, often had another set of paintings—sometimes scenes from a religious ritual, sometimes band or diaper patterns.

FIGURE 2.10 This bronze anthropomorphic form was used as a mount beneath an arm of an Urartian throne, as shown in the inset drawing. As on Assyrian furniture, bulbous feet that decreased almost to a point at the bottom raised the chair above the floor and may have represented a fir cone. (Urartu was a little-known kingdom in the Mesopotamian region that is now southeastern Turkey.)

Height as an indication of status was followed from the earliest times in Oriental cultures, and Mesopotamian chair seats were often high enough to require the use of a footstool. See the seat of the king on the Standard of Ur in Figure 2.3. Records exist of furniture constructed of expensive woods and inlaid with precious metals

FIGURE 2.11 Here the sun god is seated on a stool with a stretcher on the floor. His seat is shaded by an awning, which is supported by columns. The table or altar on which an image of the sun is depicted has turned legs with a stretcher above the feet. The much smaller Babylonian king approaches the god from the left.

and stones. Some Assyrian furniture legs were evidently turned on a lathe—an important invention that made it possible for pieces of wood to be carved while being turned, ensuring that the pattern was identical through 360 degrees.

Furniture legs were connected with **stretchers** near the floor. Stretchers attached the legs to one another between the floor and the body of a furniture piece and kept the legs from splaying outward. The legs often terminated in animal feet. Some of the bands that appear in depictions of furniture appear to represent the method by which one piece was attached to another. Other bands appear to be decorative. Furnishings were raised above the floor on turned or carved supports.

INFLUENCE 2.7

The popularity of animal feet as furniture supports continued throughout all of the ancient periods, and they were again used from the eighteenth century on—especially the lion's paw.

The Mesopotamians used stools, chairs, footstools, chests, tables, and beds. Beds might be simple built-in platforms or more elaborate models used not only for sleeping but for dining. Seating units such as stools and chairs were used by royalty or reserved for deities, with attendants standing.

INFLUENCE 2.8

One relief depicts a Babylonian king (Asurbanipal; reign, 668–627 BC) dining from a small table near his high bed or couch—a custom that was adopted by the Greeks, the Etruscans, and later the Romans.

The Persian Empire
(559 BC–c. 1600 AD)

The ancient Persian Empire was actually a series of empires that ruled what is now Iran for a thousand years. The later Achaemenid Empire was founded by the Persian Cyrus the Great (c. 580–529 BC) when he conquered the territories of the Medes, Babylonians, and others in the Near East. At its greatest extent, Persia included an area from the Indus River in India through North Africa.

Achaemenid architecture was based on the column, a form vastly different from its Mesopotamian neighbors who used bearing wall construction. Persian columns often had double capitals differing significantly from those of Egypt, Greece, and Rome. An **impost**, or block, was mounted on the lower column capital and featured an additional capital. The impost capital most frequently had **addorsed**, or back to back, animal forms such as lions or horses (See Figure 2.12). Slender and graceful, columns sometimes had a 1:12 diameter to height ratio, possible because flat timber roofs were employed. For the same reason, they could be widely spaced. In the **apadana**, or audience hall, at Persepolis, the 65-feet-high columns were over 28 feet apart. Stone columns were used for major halls, but residential areas had wood columns that were covered with plaster and then painted. In fact, most of the carved relief figures were painted as well. For very large buildings, the Persians used adobe brick walls on the exterior with the ceiling supported on rows of columns inside; some structures were open on all sides and employed no exterior walls.

Although stone was readily available in some areas, its use was generally limited to columns, relief sculpture, surrounds for openings, and platforms. When used, stone was cut into large blocks, smoothly dressed, and reinforced with metal clamps rather than with mortar. Like the Greeks, Persians sometimes used the truss form

FIGURE 2.12 The opening formed over the animals' backs on Persian capitals formed a seat to support a wooden beam.

as exemplified in the Tomb of Cyrus the Great (555–529 BC), which was raised on a platform composed of six steps.

Persian architecture borrowed from neighboring cultures, and artisans from surrounding areas

FIGURE 2.13 By the Seleucid period (323–60 BC), the Persians began to substitute the iwan, or open-fronted hall, for the columned hall. The iwan was typically constructed of mosaic brickwork or faced with glazed tiles. This example is from India to where Persian influence spread.

were employed to do much of the construction. Egyptian moldings, Babylonian glazed brick and parapet walls with stepped battlements, Assyrian sculptured monsters, and Greek-influenced columns were standard features of Persian buildings. Plans were square and concentric with smaller squares placed within larger ones. Important buildings were raised on platforms. The Palace of Persepolis (518–460 BC) was constructed on a stone-faced platform raised above the surrounding area about 50 feet and was accessed by a series of shallow steps designed so that horses could easily ascend. A procession of low relief figures permanently ascended the stairs. Stone Lamassu, or bulls with human heads, guarded a gatehouse.

INFLUENCE 2.9

Persian design was to have a significant effect on later Islamic, Byzantine, and Moghul design.

One of the most important structures in the Palace of Persepolis complex was its 250-square-feet **apadana**. Raised an additional 12 feet above the platform, the apadana had double colonnaded porticoes on three sides and four towers. The throne hall was called the Hall of the Hundred Columns. Columns that supported the cedar roof were 37 feet high.

Under the Sassanians, palace architecture remained the most important. Domed halls were constructed for the major buildings. As these were square halls roofed by round domes, the Sassanians had to connect the round structure to the square. The later Byzantines would solve this problem with the pendentive. The Persians employed the **squinch,** or a support that connected two adjacent walls at an angle essentially creating an octagon from the square. The dome then rested on the octagon.

Over the centuries, the Persians adapted building components and designs from cultures with which they came in contact. After the seventh century, Islamic influences were incorporated; the exchange was mutual, with Persian designs affecting those of Moslem structures as well.

Egypt (3500–1100 BC)

Ancient Egypt consisted only of the land along the Nile and the area that it flooded. In fact, except for a little rain in the delta area, there is no rain in Egypt, and the civilization that developed along the banks of the Nile depended on its water for survival. Without the river, the land would become desert. From the first cataract, the Nile flows through 500 miles of narrow cliff-lined valleys that reach 12 miles in width at their widest point. The valley widens near Memphis,[2] about 175 miles before reaching the Mediterranean, and spreads into a delta stretching to 115 miles in width. It was in the river delta where the silt deposited by the river enriched the soil that farming began in the area during the fifth millennium BC.

Egyptian artistic periods are named for the historic periods. The Archaic period (3300–2649 BC)[3] includes the first two ruling dynasties about which little is known. The Archaic period represented the formative years of the Egyptian civilization. After the unification of Egypt possibly under Narmer, artistic creations became more regular and structured and the conventions that underlined Egyptian art for the next 3000 years were established. Little Archaic art remains—only a few statuettes, engravings, and some stelae. The Old Kingdom (c. 3500–2631 BC) capital was at Memphis, a city located on the border between Upper and Lower Egypt near modern Cairo. The Old Kingdom broke down when centralized control was lost. During the succeeding First Intermediate Period, areas were controlled by local leaders. The Middle Kingdom (c. 2375–c. 1800 BC) began when an Eleventh Dynasty pharaoh was able to wrest control from the nobles. The capital of both the Middle and New Kingdoms was at Thebes, some distance south of Memphis. A Second Intermediate Period followed when Egypt was ruled by the Hyksos from Western Asia. The Hyksos invaded with horse-drawn chariots and compound bows for which the Egyptian army on foot and using the longbow was no match. The New Kingdom (c. 1580–1100 BC) encompassed the reigns of some of the most powerful pharaohs. Rameses III was the last strong native ruler of Egypt. Subsequent to his reign, the deterioration that had already begun accelerated. Shortly thereafter, Egypt was conquered by foreign armies who succeeded one another until Egypt finally succumbed to Roman rule after the death of Cleopatra in 31 BC. After the rule of Rameses III, ancient Egyptian art and design become enmeshed with that of foreign powers. In this text, only the art of Egypt through the New Kingdom is considered as it is most consistent with Egyptian influences.

Egyptian History

Egypt was bordered by the Mediterranean Sea on the north and by large expanses of desert elsewhere, creating natural boundaries that provided some security, made it unnecessary for cities to be walled, and led to the unification of the area. Prehistoric Egypt was divided into two parts: Upper Egypt in the south and Lower Egypt in the north.

Egyptian rulers were known as pharaohs, a title that means "great house," and kingship was based on divine right. The future pharaoh was considered a child of the sun god Ra and, upon coronation, was deified as the god Horus. On his death, the pharaoh became the god Osiris, the god of the dead, who had it in his power to grant immortality to his subjects. As a god, the ruler had absolute power. More than one usurper invented a tale of divine origins to strengthen claims to the throne.

The pharaoh owned all of the land, although control was assigned to administrators, distributing wealth and ensuring the loyalty of powerful individuals. Peasants were attached to the land, and the majority of the harvest belonged to the pharaoh. During the flood stage of the Nile, when farming was not possible, most peasants were required to work for the pharaoh—essentially paying a tax. This large labor force enabled the Egyptians to undertake huge building and engineering projects. Peasants were not slaves, however, and evidence at one site indicates they lived relatively comfortably.

EGYPTIAN RELIGION

The Egyptian religion included more than 2,000 known gods. Animals were often deified, such as Sekhmet, the lioness; Anubis, the jackal; Hathor the cow; and Seth, the hippopotamus. Because Egypt depended on good harvests, there were gods associated with agriculture. Ra, the sun god, Osiris, the god of vegetation (and of death and resurrection), and Isis, the goddess who ensured fecundity are a few important examples. Animal gods were often combined in anthropomorphic fashion, with their heads on human bodies and vice versa. None of the gods were considered so powerful they could not be controlled with the right words or offerings; this effectively ensured a powerful priesthood.

The Egyptian attitude toward death affected life on earth and the design of a large number of objects. Life was considered temporary and the afterlife eternal; hence, it was most important to prepare for the afterlife. The Egyptians believed that the individual had both a body and a spirit. It was essential to preserve the body by mummification, although in order to ensure that the Ka, or spirit, could recognize the body in the event the mummy deteriorated beyond recognition, images in the form of drawings or sculpture were left in the tomb and name signs, or **cartouches**, were located in numerous places. (See Figure 2.15.) Surely one of these would suffice. The Ka would live better if the body was provided with the accoutrements of life as well, and images or models sufficed. Housing both the body and the material possessions of the dead required tombs constructed of durable materials.

EGYPTIAN ARTS AND DESIGN TECHNIQUES

Egypt's location gave it some measure of protection, allowing the arts to develop over a period of many years but also affecting design. Since art served religion and most craft schools were attached to temples, deviation from standard forms was unlikely. While the art of most of ancient Egyptian

FIGURE 2.14 The falcon represented the god Horus, who was associated with the living pharaoh and was thus a symbol of royalty.

FIGURE 2.15 The oval of the cartouche probably originally represented the sun on the horizon. The cartouche illustrated here is the name sign of Thutmosis II.

history is formal, there was one short interlude when art became more informal and realistic. When Amenhotep, the son of a foreign queen and an Egyptian pharaoh, came to the throne, he tried to establish a monotheistic religion—replacing traditional gods. He even changed his name to Akhenaten to reflect his beliefs. The resulting art period is known as the Amarna style because the pharaoh moved the capital of Egypt to Tell el-Amarna. After his early death, his son-in-law Tutankhamen reestablished the old religion, and art forms followed. The period of experimentation was over.

The Egyptians covered most interior and exterior surfaces with some type of decoration—often scenes that were either painted or carved in low relief and subsequently painted blue, green, yellow, and red. When painting on dry plastered walls, the Egyptians used **fresco secco**, although it was subject to flaking and much has been lost. In the New Kingdom, **cavo relievo** was sometimes used. In this technique, the artisan carves a silhouette into the surface rather than removing the background, making it less time-consuming and less expensive. The human silhoutte in Figure 2.16 is an example of cavo relievo. These works represented general daily activities such as hunting, fishing, planting, and harvesting. In the New Kingdom, scenes associated with the lives of individuals were added. In religious structures, the scenes often depicted festivals associated with the gods or interactions between the gods and pharaohs. Any representation of an activity or object in tombs was considered equal to reality in the afterlife. Hieroglyphics that told a story or extolled the deeds or virtues of individuals were also used decoratively.

The Egyptians did not use perspective, and figures were represented above or below others to indicate their positions in the background or foreground. Most figures stood on a ground line rather than being suspended in space. Relative size of figures denoted their importance, not their distance from one another. The pharaoh was established by relative size as the most important individual depicted. Men were drawn larger than women, and in sculptures a wife was sometimes carved in smaller form in front of her husband. Slaves were depicted smaller yet. Scribes were shown sitting on the floor with their legs crossed and a papyrus scroll in their laps. Nudity indicated inferiority and was reserved for prisoners or slaves.

FIGURE 2.16 While the head was shown in profile, the eye was shown frontally. The shoulders, too, were frontal, allowing both arms to be shown. Fingers were curved and all were of the same length. While the legs were drawn in profile, on men the hips were often turned to enable the navel to be shown. Usually, the back leg was slightly forward, serving as a means of displaying gender. The big toes were both drawn on the same side, eliminating the need for perspective.

Like the face being represented ideally without signs of aging, the body was also represented with ideal proportions and form. (See Figure 2.16.) Figures representing pharaohs often depicted the false beard and wig or crown. Males were drawn with reddish brown skin, women with lighter yellowish brown skin. Birds, fish, and most other animals were shown in profile although it was important to represent distinguishing features. Horned animals had their faces turned forward, making it possible to draw the curvature of both horns. Owls were shown frontally. Small animals such as insects and snakes, however, were usually depicted from above.

The earliest known Egyptian sculptures were intended to ensure the immortality of the individual was represented and to serve as a dwelling place for the Ka. Mistaken identity was precluded by including a name cartouche. Sculptures were usually worked in hard stones so detailing was fairly simple and they were often executed

FIGURE 2.17 Here the block from which the sculpture was carved is obvious. Such sculptures were not designed to be seen from all sides. There are, however, some examples of large sculpture in the round.

in block form—the most obvious of which is the seated individual with knees raised, arms crossed over the knees, and a cloak wrapped around the body. Other statues were carved to be seen only from the front. Prior to the late Middle Kingdom, statues were usually painted. (See Figure 2.17.)

Sphinxes combined the body of a lion with the head of either a human or another animal—most typically the ram. Human-headed sphinxes, or **androsphinxes**, such as the Great Sphinx at Giza (2990 BC) illustrated the monarch as a conqueror and most often featured the false beard and headdress of the pharaoh. (See Figure 2.18.) Influences from Mesopotamia gave some later sphinx forms wings.

Cartonnage developed from the use of plaster to refine objects made of other materials. In this technique, plaster was reinforced with alternating layers of linen that can be applied to any shape. When dry, it retained its shape and could be gilded or painted. Cartonnage was often used for coffin cases because it could be easily conformed to the contours of the body. Face masks could also be made to emulate the gold masks of the wealthy.

Developments in glass and pottery led to the discovery that when powdered quartz was mixed with certain agents, a paste was formed that could be worked much like clay and molded or thrown to form any shape. Glaze was applied and then the body was fired to produce a glazed product known as **faïence**. Faïence was used for beads, statuettes, tiles, game pieces, and containers. Egyptian faïence was finer than the clay-based forms of the fifteenth century.

Egyptian artisans soldered wire to a metal base plate forming **cloisons**, or enclosed two-dimensional spaces, into which glass or semiprecious stones were glued. The Egyptians also did embossing, **repoussé**, and **chased** work to make jewelry. Repoussé and chasing were techniques used by hammering out a design on metal. Repoussé designs were hammered out from the back, raising the design on the front. Chased designs were hammered out from the front leaving the design recessed. See Box 2.3 for typical Egyptian motifs.

INFLUENCE 2.10

Napoleon adopted several of the Egyptian motifs and architectural forms for use in furniture. Josephine used the Egyptian bee (which was probably actually a wasp) as a personal symbol. These forms greatly affected the Empire Style, which began in France and spread to England and America.

FIGURE 2.18 Ram-headed sphinxes—or cryosphinxes—were also used and were symbolic of royalty.

Box 2.3 Egyptian Motifs

Most motifs used had some religious symbolism, so imbued with religion was Egyptian society. The sun disk, representing Ra, the sun god, was the most consistent, as it befitted an agrarian culture. Several band patterns were common: the guilloche, palmette, lotus, papyrus, wave, and spiral. Most of these were also used in diaper patterns filling entire walls or ceilings.

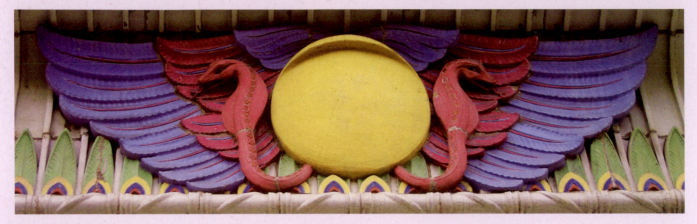

Here the sun disk is shown combined with the outstretched wings of the vulture as was typical.

The human eye and eyebrow, to which were added the markings from a falcon's head, was the **udjat** eye and symbolized filial piety, was thought to restore life, and protected against illness.

The **ankh** symbolized life, and its shape was often used for mirrors.

The bee was part of the title of the Pharaoh: "He of the sedge and the bee," which indicated the dual nature—human and divine—of the Pharaoh. This symbol was frequently used in reference to a pharaoh.

The Egyptians used gold five-pointed stars on a dark blue background on ceilings.

The symbol of Lower Egypt was the papyrus plant.

The cobra, or uraeus, sometimes winged, was a royal symbol associated with wisdom and life.

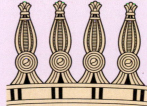

Decorative khekhers were used as band patterns, and the hieroglyphic sign for khekhers came to mean ornament.

The symbol of Upper Egypt was the lotus—a blue water lily. When used with the papyrus, they symbolized the unification of Egypt.

The scarab (dung beetle) symbolized eternal life, and here is shown in a cartouche.

EGYPTIAN ARCHITECTURE

Ancient Egypt had more wood than does the modern country. Tamarisk,[4] sidder,[5] dom[6] and date palms, acacia, and sycamore-fig were indigenous. Cedar was imported from Byblos, ebony from Nubia, and myrtle and other woods from the Land of Punt. One hieroglyphic temple inscription boasts of cedar flagstaffs covered with copper and tipped with **electrum** and doors of the best cedar lined with copper and inlaid with gold. (Electrum is a natural alloy of gold with a significant percentage of silver—up to 50 percent—and sometimes copper.) Gold and electrum were used in massive quantities, but refined silver had to be imported so it was less used.

Stone was available in large quantities. The pharaoh owned the quarries where granite, basalt, diorite, quartzite, sandstone, and limestone were roughly finished before being transported to building sites. Limestone and sandstone were more easily cut than other stones and were used for interiors, in places where they would be covered with a more durable stone, and even for the exterior of some structures without additional covering. Granite was used mostly for exterior surfaces, especially the tops of pyramids and obelisks, although some rooms in tombs were lined with it. Other hard stones were carved into bowls, coffins, and statuary.

Hippopotamus ivory (from the teeth of the animal) was used for amulets, but imported elephant ivory from Nubia and Syria during the New Kingdom was used for containers, jewelry, figurines, handles for mirrors and fans, and combs. Bone was sometimes used in less expensive articles to emulate ivory.

The Egyptian system of measurement was based on the human body, which was considered the ideal form. The major unit of measurement was based on the length of the arm from the elbow to the tip of the thumb and known as the royal cubit (about 20½ inches), and other practical measurements were based on the palm and the breadth of a finger. The short cubit was about 17 inches. Using these measurements, they were able to accurately construct large buildings. The **seqt**, with a ratio of 1:1.618 and later known as the Golden Rectangle, was the basis of proportions. It, too, was based on human proportions.

Egyptian builders employed post or column and lintel construction and bearing wall construction for solid walls. For buildings without eternal significance, adobe brick and wood were used until the downfall of Egypt. Stone was not used for structures until the Third Dynasty, when the architect Imhotep used stone for the Step Pyramid of Zoser (2650 BC). He has been recognized as the first builder in stone and was deified by the Egyptians for that accomplishment.

The Egyptians used the arch infrequently and then in structures where there was substantial abutment. Some tombs had vaulted ceilings, and underground drains employed the arch. Arches were either constructed of mud brick or covered with the brick. There are several instances where a vaulted room was carved out of a rock cliff where it would have been unnecessary to add the brick but one or two layers were applied to cover the rock.

Almost without exception, Egyptian architecture was **axial** in plan, meaning that buildings were organized in a longitudinal direction. In Egyptian monumental structures, there was a linear progression from the public entry to the most sacred portions of the building near the back. Although individual buildings were axially arranged, the buildings within a complex might not be so obviously organized.

MONUMENTAL ARCHITECTURE

Monumental architecture was reserved exclusively for the military, deities, and the dead, with temples and tombs the most important structures. Early fortresses incorporated walls of alternating projections and recesses like those in Mesopotamia and gates were protected by flanking towers with straight sides. These characteristics were also incorporated in temple and tomb complexes. Neither, however, was built in isolation, and most often, the complexes were enclosed with a perimeter wall, and entrance was through a series of gateways. The wall enclosed the **temenos**, or sacred area, separating it from the profane. Tombs had associated temples or, later, chapels. Tombs had most of the same features, although they were smaller and less complex and the sarcophagus room replaced the sanctuary. Gardens in which olives, dates, and other foods could be produced and either pools of water or a waterside quay were part of both types of complexes. The column was freely employed in all of these structures.

Columns In the earliest stone structures, columns were engaged but later structures made use of freestanding columns. The first columns and those used in dwellings were probably tree trunks—most likely palm trees. Egyptians probably also used bundles of reeds as columns as evidenced by later reeded stone columns. **Reeding** is a series of convex curves that recalled the appearance of a bundle of reeds tied together. Stone columns were usually sandstone or limestone. Unlike obelisks, columns were not monoliths but were composed of a number of stones fitted together. Smoothing was done after the stones were in place.

Column shafts were treated in three basic ways: round, in which case they were usually covered with hieroglyphics; polygonal with as many as 32 sides; and reeded. Fluted shafts are more associated with Persian or Greek column shafts and their derivatives, but there were a few fluted columns used in Egypt. Fluted columns continued to be used south of Egypt in Nubia. Also representing a bundle of reeds, Egyptian fluted columns had no capital other than a square stone or **abacus** at the top. It was probably this form that led to the use of polygonal shafts. For their height, Egyptian columns have a relatively large diameter, making them appear more massive than the graceful columns of the Greeks and the Persians.

Typical of many Egyptian columns, a slight inward curvature at the bottom of the shaft made some of the columns appear weaker. This cur-

vature, however, represented the way in which plants grew, and indeed, there was often a painted or carved depiction of the stalk sheath at the bottom of such column shafts.

Column type depends on the capital, but all have a square abacus at the top sized to fit the beam above. The most frequently used Egyptian column types included the tent pole, campaniform, palmate, papyriform, lotiform, and Hathor. Osiride pillars were human forms used in front of piers. Most were brightly painted. Square or rectangular pillars topped with capitals were also used. (See Box 2.4.)

INFLUENCE 2.11

After the 1922 discovery of King Tutenkhamon's tomb, Egyptian influence once again came to the forefront. During the Art Deco period of the early twentieth century, theaters were especially graced with Egyptian forms.

Temples Temple complexes were approached by a dromos, usually lined with sphinxes. (See Figure 2.20.) Pairs of pylons flanked a single lower square-headed opening leading into the complex, which often featured the winged sun disk on the top molding or on the door itself. Pylons were quadrangular structures with battered walls that slope inward. This feature began of necessity. Adobe brick walls had to be wide

FIGURE 2.19 Stone was used to ensure durability, but stone is limited to a relatively short free span, resulting in closely spaced columns.

BOX 2.4 EGYPTIAN COLUMNS

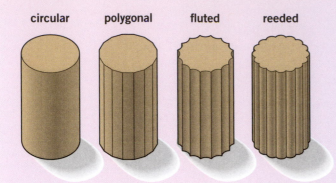

circular   polygonal   fluted   reeded

Campaniform capitals have a bell shape that spreads out at the top. Both the palmate and open papyriform capitals used this basic shape. There are, however, a number of examples of this form without other decoration—hence the campaniform column. Usually the shaft is cylindrical. The abacus can be seen at the top of the column.

Palmate columns were used by the Fifth Dynasty but rarely after that. The shaft is plain and cylindrical and may or may not have rested on a base. A band or series of bands appear to hold the eight palm fronds of the capital to the shaft. The palm fronds curve outward at the top and are incised with lines to represent individual divisions of the fronds.

The **tent pole column** was so named because it was thought these columns were derived from the tent poles used to support small structures such as military tents. The only surviving examples are at Karnak. Tent pole columns have a circular base and a cylindrical shaft with a series of horizontal bands near the top. The capital is decorated with the calyx of a plant. An inverted bell- or campaniform-shaped capital forms a ridge separating the shaft from the capital. Some remnants of the original colors can still be seen in the example.

Papyriform columns have either a circular or reeded shaft, bands used at the top of the shaft, and either a bud or open form capital. Both types of capitals have representations of the flower calyx, and a leaf design is added at the base. Remnants of color can still be seen on the representation of the calyx.

The **Osiride pillar** is fronted by a sculpted representation of the pharaoh recognizable by crossed arms. The term Osiride is used because numerous examples were in the form of a mummy—a form used to depict the god Osiris.

Lotiform columns were used in all dynastic periods but less frequently during the New Kingdom. They employ the lotus bud and have four or eight "stalks" and a closed-flower capital. During the Ptolemaic period, a few examples of an open flower form were used for capitals. Lotiform columns were often placed on the southern side of a hall or courtyard juxtaposed with papyriform columns on the northern side—symbolic of the relative positions of Upper and Lower Egypt. A band or series of bands separate the capital from the shaft.

Hathor columns were used only in temples dedicated to goddess Hathor. The capital consisted of two parts: the head of Hathor, which has cow's ears, surmounted by a **sistrum**, or rattle, in the form of a temple that was used by women. The Hathor head was usually carved on all four sides of the square capital.

FIGURE 2.20 Sphinxes line the dromos, the paved pathway, leading to the main gateway to the temple at Luxor. Each sphinx protects a statue of the king.

at the bottom, but to decrease the weight of the wall, brick was laid so the wall was thinner at the top. A conventional structural type, battering was transferred to stone construction and became a characteristic of Egyptian architecture. Interior walls were plumb. Pylons were generally constructed of a rubble stone core with a facing of regular stone blocks.

INFLUENCE 2.12

The Egyptian Revival style (1840–1850) affected the construction of Masonic Lodges, prisons, and monuments. Because Egyptian culture revolved around a cult of the dead, the greatest influence of the style, however, was on cemetery architecture. The pylon, obelisk, and Egyptian column were especially popular. A number of obelisks were erected during the nineteenth century as a result of the Egyptian influence fostered by Napoleon. Actual Egyptian obelisks were raised in a number of European cities, and other obelisks such as the Washington Monument (1848–1885) were newly constructed.

During the New Kingdom, a pair of colossal statues of the pharaoh was often placed in front of the pylons. Standards bearing flags were mounted in recesses on the front of the pylons with brackets toward the top for additional support. At the top, the pylon had a **cavetto** molding,

or a molding with a horizontal concave curve. The cavetto was a convention inherited from earlier structures of mud and reeds when the weight of a flat mud roof pushed down the tops of reed walls or from structures framed with bundled reeds with their khekher finials. A **torus**, or convex molding, was located at the edges of the pylon walls. The walls of pylons were covered with reliefs. (See Figure 2.21.)

In Old and Middle Kingdom temples, an **obelisk** was located at the rear of complexes dedicated to sun worship. In New Kingdom temples, a pair of obelisks was located in front of the pylons. Obelisks were four-sided tapered pillars with a square plan rising nine or ten times the width of their bases. They were topped with a small pyramid shape—the **pyramidion**—that was faced with gold, electrum, or copper. High above the walls, it was the pyramidion that was first touched by the sun each morning. Not surprisingly, these granite monoliths were symbolic of the sun god Ra. The sides of the obelisks were covered with hieroglyphics extolling the greatness of the monarch who ordered them.

Generally, a wall just inside the gateway hid activities behind it from view and forced a circuitous path to the temple. The temple complex was considered a house for the god, not a gathering place for crowds, who were typically restricted to the first courtyard. The largest and

FIGURE 2.21 This pylon has remnants of the cavetto molding at the top and the torus at its sides.

most impressive structures and courtyards were sited near the entrance and, as a celebrant proceeded through the complex, became smaller. In addition, floors were raised and ceilings lowered in subsequent structures on the major axis. **Peristyle** courtyards, or those with columns on two or more sides, had offering tables or altars. Multiple courtyards were common, each preceded by a formal entrance. In fact, any of the features of the temple complex might be repeated either along the main axis or sited laterally.

There was no single plan, but most temples included a dromos, at least one gateway protected by **pylons**, one or more courtyards, a **pronaos**, a **hypostyle hall**, and a sanctuary, or **naos**. The pronaos was either an exterior covered columnar porch or an interior vestibule. Beyond the pronaos was the hypostyle hall—a structure with many closely spaced columns. The central section of the hypostyle hall was raised above the roofs of the adjacent sections. There, stone grilles between these pillars allowed filtered light to enter the space. (See Figure 2.22.) In later temples, the hypostyle hall was often of uniform height rather than having a taller central space.

Beyond the hypostyle hall was the naos, which functioned as a sanctuary that held a statue of the god and sometimes the sacred barge used for ceremonial occasions. This narrow, deep, and dark space was surrounded by small chambers honoring minor gods or used for storage, treasuries, or slaughter areas. The only light came from a slit in

FIGURE 2.22 These stone grilles are located between pillars on the exterior walls of the center section of a hypostyle hall.

INFLUENCE 2.13

Gothic cathedrals used the same technique of layering to provide clerestory windows above the side aisles to bring light into the structure.

the ceiling through which a beam of light shown on the statue.

To the Egyptians, the temple was a model of the cosmos and this attitude was reflected in the interiors. Walls were covered with scenes of daily activities and the ceiling was often painted to represent the stars in the night sky.

A sacred lake was often included in the temenos and used by the priests for their daily ablutions and on festival occasions when barges were used in sacred ceremonies. The temenos often had other structures including resting places used by images of the gods and sacred barges during festivals. Some of these smaller buildings were temples—simply a roof supported by columns, an arrangement known as a **baldachin**. The same type of structure was located on the sacred barge to provide shade for the body of a deceased pharaoh as it was ferried down the Nile.

Temples associated with tombs were smaller and less complex than other types of temples and were one of two types: the valley temple and the mortuary temple. Later, these were condensed to a chapel. Valley temples were located parallel to the Nile and had T-shaped pools connecting to the river allowing the barge bearing the body to dock. A dromos led from the valley temple to the mortuary temple closer to the burial site where funerary ceremonies were performed.

Tombs Since the afterlife was most important to the Egyptians, it was their tombs that were built to last for eternity, and it is those structures that have remained most intact until modern times. Since the afterlife was perceived to be a replica of life on earth, the Egyptians assumed the spirit would need the same things it enjoyed in life—food, furnishings, servants for doing manual labor, and the ability to participate in activities such as hunting and fishing. Paintings, models, and sculptures could magically become real and provide all the needs of the deceased. Paintings depicted successful hunts and other activities, **shawabty** figures (substitutes for laborers) accomplished any necessary work such as harvesting, and models of homes and tools substituted for the actual objects.

Before the unification of Egypt, in Lower Egypt, the dead were buried beneath their houses. In Upper Egypt, the dead were buried in the sand beyond the reach of Nile floods. By the first dynasties, the mound of sand that covered desert graves had been replaced by a **mastaba**, or rectangular, flat-topped structure of adobe brick. Size depended on how important the occupant was in life (See Figure 2.23). Mastabas built during later periods sometimes had stone veneers. Inside, there was at least one chamber that served as a chapel in which perpetual rites for the deceased could be conducted. The interior might have stone floors and wall panels with relief carvings. A shaft (and sometimes stairs) led to the underground burial chamber, which was surrounded by rooms for statues, storage, and offerings. An effigy of the occupant was located in a room that had a false door used by the Ka. Mastabas continued to be used even after other tomb forms had become more popular.

Pyramid tombs were a product of the Old Kingdom. The oldest known pyramid is the

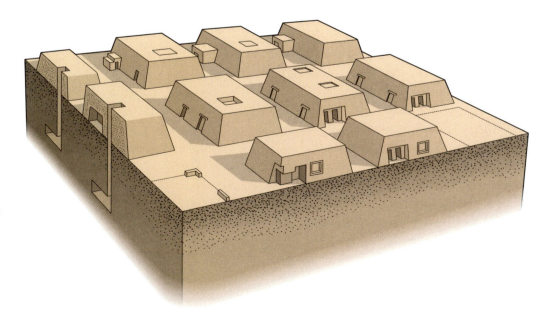

FIGURE 2.23 The mud brick walls of mastabas were battered at an angle of 75 degrees and reached 30 feet in height. Exterior surfaces were decorated with painted geometric forms.

FIGURE 2.24 The Step Pyramid was constructed of five steps of decreasing size, each with battered risers, which could be climbed by the spirit of the deceased to reach heaven.

Step Pyramid of Zoser (2750 BC) at Sakkara, the necropolis of Memphis. (See Figure 2.24.) The architect of record was Imhotep. The pyramid was rectangular in plan, more than 400 feet long and 204 feet high. The king was buried 90 feet below ground in a chamber decorated with blue green tiles that represented rolled mats much like modern bamboo shades and like the reed window coverings still used in the Middle East. From its position in the **serdab**—a small hidden room—a statue could watch rituals performed for the person it represented through small openings in the wall.

A limestone wall that ran more than a mile in perimeter surrounded the Step Pyramid; this wall had more than 200 alternating recesses and projections. A number of larger projections formed bastions, and there were 13 false doors, allowing the Ka access to every part of the kingdom. Only one actual door, however, cut through the walls. Other buildings inside the temenos included a pronaos with engaged columns. In the courtyards were façades of chapels with false doors that could be used only by spirits.

The true pyramids were constructed by Fourth Dynasty pharaohs. Several models were experimented with before the form was finalized at Giza. Fourth Dynasty pyramids are usually square in plan although there is at least one example that uses a rhomboid plan. The largest of the pyramids at Giza, that of Cheops (who ruled 3098–3275 BC), had a 756 feet square base and covered 13 acres. As with other pyramids of the time,

there were secret passageways and burial chambers within the pyramid but otherwise, it was a solid mass. There was no standardized plan for the pyramids; they all had different arrangements of passages and rooms. Egyptian builders made use of **corbelled** vaults over the corridors—vaults formed when succeeding layers of stone projected slightly beyond those below. In the Great Pyramid (2560 BC), a **relieving arch** was used over the King's Chamber. This triangular stone arch was designed to divert some of the weight of the stone above away from the chamber.

The pyramids were constructed of limestone. The apex of the pyramid—the **pyramidion**—was made separately of granite and plated with gold. Pyramids were part of a larger complex that included mortuary temples as well as tombs of high-ranking officials. Burial chambers were protected by misleading passageways and stone **portcullises**, or vertically movable gates or grills—in Egypt made of stone and designed to be used only once. All pyramids were eventually robbed, and the style of tomb was changed by the Middle Kingdom to those cut into rock cliffs. The pyramid, however, continued to be used for tombs of lesser nobility but only as an entry façade.

Rock cut tombs were hewn out of cliffs and, other than being underground, appeared much like temples of the period both on the interior and exterior. Columns left intact supported flat or vaulted roofs and formed a columnar hall within the earth. The size and number of rooms

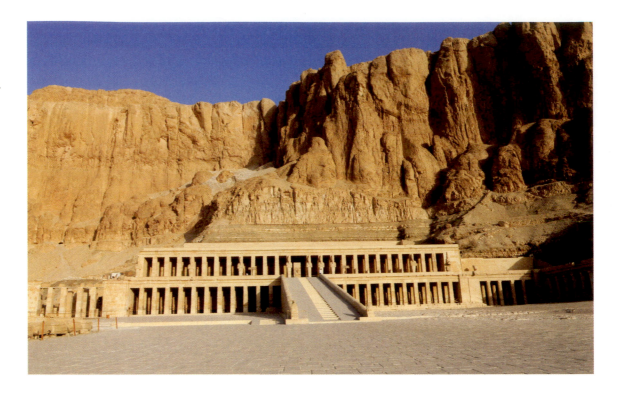

in the interior depended on the status of the individual and the location of the actual burial varied. Side chambers housed statues and often storage rooms were located beyond. The general plan consisted of a T-shaped quay, a dromos leading from the quay to the chapel fronting the tomb, and the tomb itself. There is evidence that the dromos was treated like a garden and lined with trees and other plants. The chapel fronting the tomb had replaced the valley and mortuary temples of older tombs and was an open covered structure supported by a few columns—usually two or four. A colonnaded portico or porch on the exterior housed a stele extolling the virtues of the deceased. The mummy rested on this porch before burial. The façade of the rock-cut tomb of Queen Hatshepsut (1550 BC) attributed to Senmut is shown in Figure 2.25. Later rock-cut tombs such as those at Abu Simbel featured colossal statues of the pharaoh on the exterior. See Box 2.5 for a summary of Egyptian architectural characteristics.

Box 2.5 SUMMARY OF EGYPTIAN ARCHITECTURAL CHARACTERISTICS

- Colossal statuary
- Monumental entrance statuary for temples and tomb complexes
- Relief sculptures including hieroglyphics on most surfaces
- Human- or ram-headed sphinxes with the bodies of lions
- Dromos lined with sphinxes leading to important buildings
- Post and lintel construction using columns or piers
- Colonnades
- Columns closely spaced
- Plant forms used for capitals
- Entrance pylons
- Obelisks and Hypostyle halls
- Pyramids
- Cavetto moldings over doors and at the tops of buildings
- Monumental stone blocks used for construction
- Temples and tombs made of stone; most other buildings of adobe brick
- Rock cut tombs during later periods

DOMESTIC ARCHITECTURE

Egyptian houses, whether for peasants or the pharaoh, were constructed much like temples, although they were much simpler in form. Like temples, some early Egyptian homes used bundled reeds to form a framework from which colorful mats woven in geometric patterns were suspended to form walls that rolled up. Openings, too, were frequently covered with such mats. Most houses had **wattle and daub** walls. Wattle was formed by weaving reeds and other vegetative matter between supports. This was then plastered over with mud, or daub.

The **serekh** was an early wooden house built by using leather strips to sew together vertical overlapping boards—much like board and batten structures today. (See Figure 2.26.) The first examples showed three symmetrical towers with two narrow doors. The walls of the towers rose above the flat roof forming a parapet. The bindings and cross members used at the top were obvious and later became horizontal designs. Although this type of house was replaced at an early date by others, the vertical projections and recesses formed by the boards remained a conventional feature of Egyptian architecture. Even the gateway between pylons of later Egyptian architecture may have been derived from the towers flanking the lower doorways in this type of house. The interior of the serekh house walls formed recesses where there were projections on the exterior. There is evidence that indicates the interior walls were "flattened" by stretching woven mats or textiles between the wood framing members.

The khekher house was a rectangular structure characterized by its distinctive parapet. Remains of the First Dynasty depict this type of house so it was an early form. The khekher house was a palatial form but was constructed not of wood but of wattle and daub or adobe brick. A two-storied house, it was crested with **khekhers**, which were formed when papyrus stalks were tied together at the top so they projected above the roof at the wall.

A prominent feature of Egyptian homes and palaces was the columnar porch that provided shade, a windbreak, and outdoor living space. A vestibule might be located behind the porch. Outside, a forecourt or walled enclosure provided additional living space.

Palaces The hieroglyphic sign for palace means "hut of the god," an indication of the status of the owner. Each pharaoh had a new palace constructed as it was considered undesirable to live in a previously occupied dwelling. The throne room was located at the rear of the palace in line with the main entry. Beginning with the Amarna period, the pharaoh's palace had a **window of appearance** on the external façade from which he could present himself to the public—a tradition still employed by the Pope, monarchs, and constitutional leaders. Typically, the window of appearance was over the main entry and faced the open courtyard beyond. A low balustrade protected the balcony, and a baldachin supported by four columns provided shade.

Palaces and houses of the wealthy had several stories, and archaeologists uncovered one that had 72 rooms. Such homes resembled temples in

their layout and construction. A covered portico supported by columns led to the entrance. Inside, whether located in the country or in the city, such homes always had large gardens. Only homes of the wealthy had bathing rooms—rooms in which a servant poured water over the bather's head. A drain led from the bathing room to the garden where the water was used for the plants. Toilet rooms were also located in many of these buildings—usually with a carved limestone stool with a slotted hole in the seat and a vessel beneath which could be emptied by the servants.

Homes Egyptian houses differed depending on whether they were located in an urban or rural area. As has been typical throughout history, land in cities is more expensive than is land in the country and urban houses use as little ground area as possible. The urban homes of Egypt had multiple stories—a basement, a first story, and an upper story with private living spaces. The basement contained storage rooms, workshops, and sometimes businesses. First story rooms were usually much taller than rooms in other areas, and it was in this space that guests were received and entertained. Exterior stairways led from one level to the next. Plants and trees were shown next to the houses in paintings although

FIGURE 2.26 The serekh was probably used first by the nobility, as its hieroglyphic sign came to mean palace and later, tomb. The exterior façade came to symbolize the power of the ruler.

FIGURE 2.27 The triangular projections on the roof are ventilating shafts, or **mulqafs**, that led from living areas in some homes and terminated in a vertical opening. The fronts of these shafts are depicted with square or arched openings.

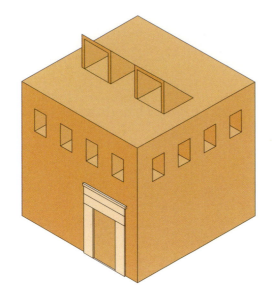

OPENINGS

Doorways—both interior and exterior—had wide moldings at the sides and often a cavetto molding at the top, making them similar in appearance to the gateways between pylons in temple complexes. It was always necessary to mount a few steps to reach the doorway. Windows were usually shown with grilles at least part of the way up. Windows, too, had large moldings around them and sometimes a cavetto molding over the header. (See Figure 2.29.)

EGYPTIAN INTERIORS

Interior rooms were relatively small because of the span of the materials composing the roof. One floor was painted to represent a pool of water with fish swimming in it and bordered by a band of painted plants. Walls were often divided vertically into two bands, each of which was painted with scenes.

EGYPTIAN FURNITURE

Wood was used in buildings, for furniture, and for some sculptures. Native woods were poor in quality, and the techniques used for sawing the timbers into planks produced only short boards. A log was tied to an upright post where it could be sawn vertically, so the length of the plank depended on the height of the post. It was thus necessary to join wood pieces together to manufacture most objects. In the Old Kingdom, joints might be lashed with leather or copper, but traditional wood joints appeared fairly early. During the Eighteenth Dynasty, a few bronze nails were used, although they were decorative and often gilded. While there is some evidence of turned objects, no depiction of a lathe has been found. The Egyptians also bent wood for furniture and chariots, probably using steaming techniques, although naturally curved pieces were also used. In fact, there is evidence from scene paintings of training plants to grow in shapes that could later be employed in furniture construction. Knots were cut out, and plaster was used to repair any gaps, to ensure a smooth surface over joints, and to create fine details in wood statuary. Wood was often decorated with inlays of ivory, faïence, or other materials. Some pieces were completely covered with gold or copper. Veneering was common with more exotic woods attached to native species.

there was not sufficient space for a garden. The flat roof supported a terrace with silos for grain and sometimes a garden. Paintings depict a parapet wall or one that extended beyond the roofline to form a low protective wall on the roof. (See Figure 2.27.)

Rural homes spread over a larger area and always had gardens and usually a pool of water. With the exception of the pool, the entire complex was surrounded by a wall with a formal entrance. The enclosure formed a courtyard in front of the house and included the gardens, shrines, and outbuildings. Rooms, including a reception hall, a living area, and bedrooms, opened off the courtyard. While the country home might have multiple stories, it was not as common as in the city.

Egypt's dry climate preserved numerous examples of furnishings although most of the extant

FIGURE 2.28 Floor plan of an upper class home at Amarna.

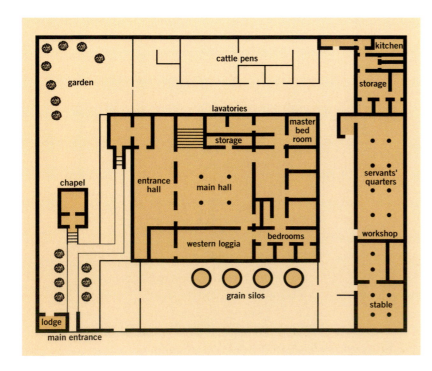

furniture is from the New Kingdom. Egyptian furniture consisted of stools, chairs, beds, chests, and small tables—all the basic forms used today. Most pieces were constructed of wood using joints still used today, but there are examples of metal or stone pieces. Furniture of the wealthy was inlaid with faïence, mother-of-pearl, ivory, and precious metals or were painted, gilded, or veneered. Geometric band patterns and floral patterns were common and paintings employed strong colors. Stools inlaid or painted with leopard-skin motifs were reserved for priests. Furniture for the majority of people was either undecorated or painted to imitate more ornate pieces.

The decorative portion of furniture legs began above a drum, which might be covered with copper or bronze. Furniture legs were square or rounded but the most delightful examples were carved representations of the fore or hind parts of various animals: bulls, goats, gazelles, or lions. A characteristic feature of furniture that employed these animal parts is that fore limbs were used on the front (and in the case of beds, the head) and hind limbs on the back of the furniture piece.

CHESTS

Chests provided storage and ranged in size from cosmetic boxes to large ones with interior partitions mounted on poles so they could be carried by numerous individuals. Most households, however, had few possessions they did not use on a daily basis and therefore needed few storage containers. Small chests were used for jewelry and were made of ivory or ebony. Medium-sized chests were often partitioned to enclose cosmetics. Large chests were used for storage of linens and other objects.

Lids were designed either to slide or to be lifted off. Dowels or other protrusions from the lid might fit into openings in the walls of the chest to secure the lid. It was only very late that copper hinges were used on a few examples. Some small chests had a single drawer in them but never multiple drawers. Game tables might also have a drawer. (See Figure 2.30.)

STOOLS

Stools of all periods were painted white or gilded. During the New Kingdom, the most common stools had **box stretchers** with vertical and diagonal struts between the stretchers and the seat. Box stretchers connect all four legs. Stools had

either three or four legs. Three-legged stools and sometimes chairs have been common throughout history and have the advantage of being more stable on uneven surfaces. In addition to the typical types of furniture legs, stool legs sometimes terminated in ducks' heads. (See Figure 2.31.)

Folding stools with a metal bolt and leather or skin seats were probably derived from stools used by military commanders in the field. For this reason, they may have been seen as a status symbol.

FIGURE 2.29 Doorways had shouldered architraves and splayed sides. The cavetto molding above this doorway is obvious.

FIGURE 2.30 Chest lids were flat or vaulted until the New Kingdom, when lids shaped like gable roofs were constructed. Short feet held the chest off the floor surface.

FIGURE 2.31 Stools have been found dating to the predynastic period. The first stools were framed with wood and had rush or leather seats. This type of seat continued to be used both on stools and chairs throughout the dynastic period. Although flat seats continued to be made, later stools often had saddled seats (seats with a curvature to fit the body), in this case saddled in both directions. This example is from the nineteenth-century Egyptian Revival.

FIGURE 2.32 This chair has a low back. The cushion on the seat continues up and over the back to provide greater comfort. Later chair backs were higher.

CHAIRS

There were fewer chairs than stools and in representations, chairs are seen more frequently in formal settings; stools in scenes of everyday activities—even for the wealthy. In fact, the hieroglyphic for "dignitary" was a person sitting in a chair—an indication that they were not only used mostly for formal occasions but by individuals with some status. In addition, the height of chair seats varies considerably, apparently as an indication of status. Some are a standard cubit from the floor; others a royal cubit. When arms were first used on chairs in the Old Kingdom, they were higher than would be comfortable but over time were lowered to a more natural position. Chair backs were curved to fit the body but at first were fairly low (see Figure 2.32) and sometimes had open work designs such as a bundle of papyrus, open slats, or decorated panels. Seats were like those of stools except that some were much more decorative. (See Figure 2.33.)

Palanquins, or carrying chairs, were used in Egypt and have been found in several tombs. These chairs were mounted on poles so they could be carried.

TABLES

Tables were like stools with longer legs, although they were relatively small and may have been used much like trays. Three or four legs supported the top, which was usually rectangular, although round examples have been found. Pedestal tables were also used. Stretchers increased stability. Like other furniture, tables were elaborately decorated. Some tables were used to support jars and other objects, but they are usually depicted laden with food in funerary scenes. Scribes sat on the floor and wrote on their laps and kitchen chores were carried out by crouching on the floor. For individ-

FIGURE 2.33 Some chairs had an angle larger than 90 degrees between the seat and the back, although often the back legs extended straight upwards. The increased angle was achieved by angling the back inward from the top of the upright supports.

FIGURE 2.34 With few exceptions, beds were relatively low to the ground and employed either woven string or hide supports between framing members. This technique was especially suitable for the hot climate, allowing air to circulate beneath the sleeper.

uals seated in a chair—especially one with a high seat, it would have been necessary to use a table for food, but common people probably did not use one for dining. Some tables were designed for games with the board inlaid in the top and sometimes a small drawer to hold the pieces used.

BEDS

The legs of beds were the same as those for other pieces of furniture, but there are numerous examples of beds with longer legs at the head, resulting in a slope downward to the foot of the bed. Footboards, but not headboards, were sometimes used whether or not the bed sloped. At first the footboards were separate and did not help support the bed; later examples served as support. Some New Kingdom beds were very high and required a mounting block. Side rails sometimes curved downward at the center. (See Figure 2.34.)

An example of a folding bed was found in the tomb of King Tutankhamen. Bronze hinges divided the bed into three sections requiring additional legs at each joint for a total of eight. The head rested on a crescent-shaped headrest supported by a pedestal similar to the one illustrated in Figure 2.35. Common people probably slept on the floor or on built-in mud brick platforms raised above the floor. These provided sleeping room for the family. Similar platforms are still common in rural Asia.

> INFLUENCE 2.14
>
> *The folding camp beds used in military campaigns were derived from the folding beds of Egypt and are still used as cots for camping.*

Uncovering the Past

In 539 BC, the Persians conquered Babylon and the Mesopotamian empires ceased to exist. Persian ascendancy, however, was not to last. The Macedonian Alexander the Great (356–323 BC) conquered the Persian Empire, extended its borders, melded Greek and Macedonian culture with that of Persia, and spread that civilization as far as India.

A second Persian Empire under the Sassanian Dynasty established in 226 AD was a centralized state that regained much of the lost territory. Within a few years of the foundation of Islam in the seventh century AD, Persia fell to Moslem forces. Arabic became the new language and Islam replaced the old religion. The Persians, however, continued to expand their influence under a new administration partly because they became the administrators. Islamic Persia extended its influence once again into India. During the Middle Ages in the West, Persia was the center of scientific thought.

With the defeat of the Ptolemies and the reduction of Egypt to a Roman province, ancient Egyptian culture faded into the mists of time, and medieval Europeans had no knowledge of it. In the fifteenth century, travelers wrote about Egypt, but it was the results of the 1798 invasion of Egypt by Napoleon Bonaparte that enlightened the world about this culture. Two hundred scholars accompanied Napoleon and were charged with exploring the area and recording their findings. It was during this expedition that the Rosetta Stone was uncovered. The text of a decree from 196 BC was carved into this basalt stone in three languages: Greek, Coptic, and hieroglyphics. After two decades, the Frenchman Jean-François Champollion was able to decipher some of the hieroglyphics allowing scholars to subsequently decipher other texts unlocking the history of this ancient civilization.

FIGURE 2.35 This simple wooden headrest is less elaborate than those of ivory, faïence, and other materials but serves the same function. The user's neck fits into the curvature of the headrest. In some cases, the headrest is used to prevent the wig or coiffure from being disturbed.

3

African Design

As late as the nineteenth century, Africa was still thought of by many Western historians as the "Dark Continent." Historians concentrated instead on the remains of Egypt, Rome, Greece, and other civilizations concentrated along the Mediterranean coast. The nineteenth century, however, was marked by Western archaeological research in Africa. One of the first major nineteenth-century "discoveries," for example, was Great Zimbabwe, a fortress that was older than the arrival of Portuguese in the early fifteenth century.

As we have seen in Chapter 2, the civilization along the Nile River developed very early (3500 BC), and there are records of trade between Egypt and other African areas. About 1000 BC, Phoenicians, and later the Romans, established a presence in North Africa. Since the desertification of the Sahara (c. 3000 BC), North Africa, however, has been essentially cut off from sub-Saharan regions (essentially all of the continent south of Northern African). After that time, sub-Saharan Africa and the Mediterranean coast had divergent histories.

In sub-Saharan Africa, the eastern and central regions are dominated by a series of mountain ranges, through which a region of savannah and tropical grasslands south of the Sahara Desert has facilitated east-west travel. In the southern part of Africa, there are both tropical rain forests and the Kalahari Desert. Temperatures often vary widely between day and night, soils are poor, and rainfall is unpredictable. In many areas of Africa, there was little to support population concentrations beyond the village level until the twentieth century.

African History

By approximately 750 BC, the kingdom of Meroe had emerged in what was Nubia and iron working gave it important military and economic advantages. The royal court commissioned temples and funerary monuments that provide an insight to that civilization. By 200 AD, the kingdom of Axum in Ethiopia rivaled the power of Meroe because Axum controlled trade between the Nile River valley and the Red Sea. Tenth- to fifteenth-century rock-cut churches provide evidence of continuing development in Ethiopia. As iron-age cultures advanced, Stone Age cultures were pushed into marginal areas and into southern Africa, where they remained until the twentieth century. About 500 AD, gold mining and fabrication became important industries and resulted in increasing trade and contacts with other African nations. Trade routes were established across the Sahara, and small kingdoms began to appear in West Africa. For a millennium, the trade routes affected developments in Africa and a number of political units (kingdoms and city-states) arose in West Africa: Ghana, Mali, and Songhai were the most dominant.

ISLAMIC INFLUENCE

During the period of greatest expansion of the Islamic religion, beginning in the seventh century, Moslems controlled most of North Africa, much of which was former Roman territory. In traditional West African cities where Moslems came to live, there were separate and unequal areas inhabited by each group. Native Africans continued to live in round wattle and daub structures while Moslem traders and immigrants from northern areas built with stone. Mosques were built in Moslem areas and they, too, were of stone construction. West Africa became more urbanized during the succeeding centuries, many of the small African states converted to the Islamic religion, and mosques became a common feature.

THE GOLD TRADE

Mali became the center of the gold trade in the thirteenth century. The power of Mali was concentrated in great cities such as Timbuktu and Jenne. By 1340, Songhai, a militaristic state in East Africa, took over control of the gold trade. It was not to last long. In 1591, the Berbers invaded and trade routes shifted. Yoruba, a kingdom on the Nigerian coast became the intermediary in the slave trade with Europe but it too was replaced by Ashanti.

Arab traders began to establish a series of trading posts in East Africa beginning in the tenth century. Beginning in the thirteenth century, Great Zimbabwe was the center of the Shona kingdom (also called the Empire of Great Zimbabwe). Gold mined in Zimbabwe was marketed through Arab coastal cities. Large numbers of foreign artifacts were found in Great Zimbabwe including those from Persia and China.

EUROPEAN INFLUENCE

Europeans became interested in Africa when Prince Henry the Navigator (1394–1460) sent Portuguese expeditions down the coast of West Africa in 1419. Prince Henry had earlier (1415) captured the North African city of Ceuta, which remained in Portuguese control until it was lost to Spain, with which the city is still associated. The purposes of Prince Henry's expeditions were

to create maps, to establish trade routes, and to spread Christianity. Prior to these explorations, no European sailors had returned from sailing around Cape Bojador, where frequent storms and strong currents imperiled them. Beyond that point, the Europeans called the ocean the "Sea of Darkness." In 1434, the Portuguese explorer Gil Eannes sailed beyond Cape Bojador and returned successfully. On subsequent expeditions, Portuguese sailors brought back commercial cargo, including slaves. In part, the success of that voyage must be attributed to the caravel, a smaller, more maneuverable ship than the carrack that had been used before. The caravel was capable of sailing in strong winds and ocean currents while also being small enough to sail up rivers. Bartolomeu Dias (c. 1450–1500), another Portuguese sailor, rounded the Cape of Good Hope at the southern tip of Africa in 1488.

In 1647, the wreck of a Dutch ship at the southern tip of Africa resulted in a small fort for the sailors. After a year, they were rescued but in 1652, the Dutch returned and established Cape Colony, now Cape Town, South Africa. The fort was designed as a way station for Dutch ships traveling farther East. In 1806, the English acquired the Dutch holdings in southern Africa. Diamond deposits were discovered in 1865 and gold in 1886. European nations scrambled for control of Africa, and by 1912 only Liberia and Ethiopia remained free of European control. During the mid-twentieth century, African nations began to assert their independence and currently, there are over 50 African nations free of outside control. Even during the rise and fall of outside powers, average Africans continued their cultural and artistic traditions.

AFRICAN ARCHITECTURE

Most structures in precolonial Africa were relatively temporary, although with regular maintenance, some lasted for centuries. Many societies moved frequently in search of pastures for their cattle, and others retained their hunter-gatherer traditions. Neither of these types of cultures required permanent structures. Agricultural societies constructed more permanent villages, but even these often moved after a few years as the soil wore out.

Climate and available materials affected the types of indigenous dwellings. Clay, adobe, and fired brick were common in the arid regions of

Africa and, in some instances, buildings were dug into the earth.

Sun-dried brick was the most typical building material in sub-Saharan Africa. In forest areas, mud (without forming it into bricks) was used without a binder. Fired brick was used in the Sudan and a few other places. Stone was used mostly in mountain areas. Many of the roofs in Africa were made of reeds, grass, bamboo, and palm fronds. Coral was used in some coastal areas as a building material. The Great Mosque at Kilwa, for example, originally had octagonal columns, each of which was carved from a single piece of coral.

Buildings for chiefs and rulers were often constructed with stone rather than mud brick and applied decoration was more elaborate. Decoration of early African buildings included life-size sculptures and reliefs, carved house posts, and elaborate doors. Thresholds were a particular location for decoration. On the interiors, women's rooms, shrines, and granaries were most frequently decorated.

Until mosques began to be built for the observance of Islamic rituals, there were few monumental buildings built by indigenous people. Monumental funerary architecture occurred mostly in Meroe and Axum, where pyramids similar to those built in Egypt were constructed. Megalithic burial sites have also been found.

In traditional African societies, the arrangement of buildings, the layout of individual structures, the material used for construction, and the decoration were indicative of status or gender. The forms of palaces, religious buildings, and funerary monuments were related to culture or climate rather than building type. Most houses were designed for extended families with more than one generation sharing a residence. The greatest privacy is offered to the older generation with less privacy for those who are younger. Often, the families live in compounds with numerous buildings while sharing a courtyard and kitchen. Polygamy is practiced in some cultures and typically, a house is provided for each wife within the compound.

Religious Structures

Adobe or fired brick was the most common material used for early temples in Africa. Some early temples were approached along avenues that were flanked by sculptures of animals, as they had been in ancient Egypt. Pylons and columns were used for these buildings arranged around a courtyard. Each area led to another, culminating in the sanctuary. Colonnades and ramps connected the different buildings within the complex.

Christian churches built by the Copts beginning in the sixth century were not built but were usually hewn from rock. As the carvers worked, they insured that pilasters, window and door frames, moldings, and bases were identifiable. These structures were begun at the top and were dug downward into tufa to a depth of up to 50 feet. The churches have Greek cross plans and have the outline of the cross on their roof tops. (See Figure 3.1.)

The Great Mosque of Djenné is one of the largest adobe structures in the world. The original mosque was constructed in the thirteenth century, but the current building was built in 1907. The structure is built on a platform raising it above the flood plain of the nearby river. The adobe brick is covered with mud plaster, giving the building its sculptural appearance,

FIGURE 3.1 The exteriors of the Ethiopian rock-cut churches were finished first, and then the interiors were carved beginning with the windows and doors. The interiors of these churches had arches, domes, pillars, lunettes, and other architectural features. Once the carving was finished, the interior walls were painted with religious pictures.

FIGURE 3.2 Palm wood bundles were incorporated during construction of the Great Mosque of Djenné to reduce cracking caused by the extreme temperature and humidity changes of the area. The wood projections also support scaffolding during frequent repairs.

FIGURE 3.3 The sides of Nubian pyramids were steeper than those of Egypt.

and buttresses project from the walls creating a strong rhythm. Three towering stepped minarets are incorporated in the structure and because of their square shape, echo the projecting buttresses. The conical spires originally represented ancestral spirits. Inside, 99 wooden columns support the log roof of the men's prayer hall. (See Figure 3.2.)

Nubia, or Kush, was situated immediately south of Egypt. During the eighth century BC when Egypt was relatively weak, a Kushite ruler took control of Egypt as far north as Thebes and his son ruled all of Egypt. The latter ruler, Piye, founded the Nubian Dynasty in Egypt. On his death, he was buried in a pyramid in Nubia—the first Egyptian king to be so interred in 800 years. In all, approximately 223 pyramids were eventually constructed in Nubia, although they were much smaller than Egyptian examples. Piye's pyramid was 26 feet on each side, while the Great Pyramid in Giza was approximately 700 feet on each side. (See Figure 3.3.) Other structures were subterranean but were sometimes connected to surface temples. Monolithic stellae were used to mark burial areas in Axum, some of which had carved representations of multistoried structures. One stele in Axum was 110 feet high. Pillar tombs were often constructed in coastal areas out of coral or stone.

Palaces

Great Zimbabwe (*dzimbawhe*) means house of stone and refers to an area spanning over 100 miles in which there are many such structures. Buildings of stone were constructed in Zimbabwe between the eleventh and fifteenth centuries, and their remains are some of the largest in southern Africa. There are no defensive features in the enclosing walls; they may have been constructed to proclaim the power and prestige of those who lived within. Monoliths mounted on the walls commemorated the owner's ancestors. The largest of the structures of Great Zimbabwe is the Great Enclosure, although there are at least 300 known complexes. The Elliptical Building, called by a number of names including the Temple, was probably the most important building in the complex. Individual houses within the enclosure were circular and built of wattle and daub (*daga*) with conical-shaped thatched roofs. Stone buildings were used for royal residences. Zimbabwes were built until the late twentieth century. (See Figure 3.4.)

FIGURE 3.4 Granite was used in the mortarless construction of the walls of the Great Enclosure of Great Zimbabwe; these walls reach as high as 36 feet. The walls extend approximately 820 feet, and it is estimated that as many as 300 people lived within the enclosure.

Earth as a Building Material

In Tunisia and areas of the Sahara, dwellings are sometimes dug out of hillsides or into the ground to take advantage of the temperature-moderating effects of the earth remaining cooler than surface structures. Other buildings were carved out of the rock. A light well was first carved into the earth, sometimes as much as thirty feet or more in depth. Individual dwelling units were then carved out of the rock or soil around this open courtyard. In Matmata, Tunisia, large courtyards were dug into the ground with individual rooms or dwelling units dug into the vertical sides. When the government of Tunisia decided to provide above-grade housing for the people living in these villages, residents lived only a few months above ground before retreating to their more thermally comfortable below-grade structures.

Ghorfa or barrel-vaulted storage chambers were also built in Tunisia. Partly below grade and partly above grade, these large units were also built around a courtyard with individual rooms opening on to it. Each unit then received light from the courtyard. The ghorfa were built either of stone or fired adobe brick.

In northern Africa, wealthy Islamic Berbers constructed dwellings ten or more stories high known as **kasbahs** out of clay and sun-dried brick copying indigenous structures. The Berbers, however, added the arch, vault, and dome to the indigenous architectural repertoire. Originally, kasbahs were located on hilltops or near harbor entrances and served defensive purposes. The expense involved in their construction and maintenance made them a sign of status as well. The tower blocks may have been extended upward as families grew or they may have housed separate families. The thick, unadorned adobe walls had only a few small openings except at the top where there might be larger windows. In the hot, dry climate, the walls themselves gathered heat during the day, keeping the interior cool. At night when even desert temperatures plummeted, the heat stored in the adobe dissipated into the cooler interior air, heating the spaces within. Kasbahs continue to be built in the Atlas Mountains today.

In parts of Sudan, adobe rooms are built around an interior courtyard. A single doorway leads into the courtyard onto which all the rooms open and no windows penetrate the exterior wall. Decoration includes white painted band patterns around the tops of walls and a relatively elaborate decoration around the entry door. Motifs used for door surrounds are Islamic in origin and include the crescent, star, and geometric forms.

In central Sudan, dome-shaped adobe huts (not adobe brick) are constructed around a walled enclosure. The walls do not surround the units but the units project through the walls partially

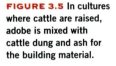

FIGURE 3.5 In cultures where cattle are raised, adobe is mixed with cattle dung and ash for the building material.

in the front. Separate huts are provided for storage, cattle, and sleeping.

In arid areas where cattle are herded, villages are laid out around a large **kraal**, or corral. The circular enclosure is made of vertical logs, thorn brush, or adobe. Sometimes, the kraals have storage pits for food reserves. Individual dwelling units are arranged around the kraal, often in a semicircle. Status is often associated with the location of individual houses. The headman, in Botswana, for example, constructs his house on the east side of the kraal. A semicircle of logs set vertically is erected facing the center of the kraal and a hearth is placed in the semicircle. Even large towns are laid out in the same way with numerous kraals. Towns are usually laid out around the chief's kraal in order of status. Resulting towns are often horseshoe shaped.

In rural areas of southern Africa, round houses of adobe, ash, and cow dung with thatched roofs are the most common. Larger villages may have mud houses called **rondavels** with thatched roofs that have metal caps to prevent leakage. In larger towns and cities, concrete plastered brick houses have almost replaced traditional buildings and glass windows and corrugated metal roofs predominate. The layout, however, continues as it has for centuries with chain link fences replacing adobe enclosures. Traditional houses and their molded designs and surface textures are painted in earth colors with the color depending on the minerals in the soil.

In French Morocco, some concrete Western-style apartment units were tried. Kitchens were located on the second story of each unit and had access to the flat roof. There was no internal courtyard and most of the Moslem families rejected the idea of living in units such as these.

In areas where there are trees, palm trunks are often used for support with bundles of reeds forming intermediate supports running both horizontally and vertically. The spaces are filled with woven palm fronds, or other light-weight material. The roofs are usually thatch. Again, the posts that flank the doorway are highly decorated, as is the lintel.

African Design Influences

The harsh climate, poor soil, and conflicts of Africa helped to retard the development of the continent by indigenous people except in a few isolated places. The Land of Punt (Ethiopia) and Egypt had well-known ancient cultures in part because of their locations and in part because of trade with other cultures, especially those centered around the Mediterranean Sea. The great civilizations of ancient Africa were little known outside the continent until the coming of the Europeans. Even then, the newcomers took advantage of the indigenous population and often remained isolated in their own conclaves. European design has affected that of Africa far more than African design has affected areas that are more technologically advanced. In fact, modern African cities have much the same appearance as those in the industrialized world. Indigenous African design, however, has begun to be more highly regarded and examples, especially of decorative techniques and designs, are becoming part of urban landscapes in some areas.

skin and men with a ruddy reddish brown complexion. In fact, the Greeks later called Minoan men *Phoinikes,* meaning "purple ones." (See Figures 4.4 and 4.5.)

Light wells ensured that light was available in interior living areas, although not for storage rooms. Because they penetrated all stories vertically, the light wells also served a ventilating function dissipating summer heat. Rooms were open to the light well where one or more columns elevated on low wall bases supported the ceiling. Other walls were mostly open with a number of closely spaced doorways or alternating columns and piers, the spaces of which were filled with screens.

MINOAN FURNITURE

Very little Minoan furniture has survived. At Knossos, there were stone benches and a gypsum chair that Evans called a throne. Details of the throne reveal its wood origins: four carved legs that form a pointed arch beneath the seat, a stretcher below the legs to connect them, and an inverted curve between the two front legs. The base of the throne extends to form a platform used as a footstool. Originally, it was covered with a baldachin. (See Figure 4.6.)

FIGURE 4.6 This wooden model was copied from the gypsum chair at Knossos. Like its predecessor, it has a high shaped back with undulating curves, a 90-degree seat-back angle, and a slightly saddled seat.

FIGURE 4.4 Like Egyptian figures, people were depicted with their faces in profile but with one eye shown frontally. In some of the illustrations, both shoulders of individuals were depicted, although the torsos were not turned frontally. The waists of both men and women were extremely small.

FIGURE 4.5 Unique to Minoan design were wavy sections of color or band patterns that ran behind the figures turning corners to continue on adjacent walls. A griffin and lilies can be seen in this example. The benches are made of gypsum.

The rectangular stone benches at Knossos were similar to clay models found in other Minoan buildings. A few depictions of beds showed four short legs supporting a framework that employed interlaced leather strips or cords to support a cushion or mattress. Some of the beds had raised head and foot rests. One built-in example at Knossos was a smoothly plastered oblong stone platform.

Mycenae (c. 1600–1104 BC)

From the sixteenth century BC on, a contemporary of the Minoan civilization was Mycenae on the Greek mainland. Major Mycenaean cities included Troy, Argos, Tiryns, and Mycenae.[2] Athens was one of the few Mycenaean cities to survive into the Greek period. Rhodes, Cyprus, and other Aegean islands also had Mycenaean cities. Much of the art and architecture of Mycenae resembles so closely that of Crete that some archaeologists suggest that Mycenae was either conquered or colonized by the Minoans. On the other hand, the Mycenaeans spoke Greek, while the Minoans did not.

MYCENAEAN MOTIFS

Mycenaean ornament featured many motifs from Minoan Crete and had traces of Egyptian influence. The spiral, zigzag (also called a chevron), spirals formed into heart-shaped motifs, rosettes, and an adaptation of the guilloche were all used. The cuttlefish, squid, and dolphin were recognizable marine animals. Remains of the Minoan stilted double rosette ornament can be seen along the base of a wall in one palace. (See Box 4.3.)

MYCENAEAN ARCHITECTURE

While there are similarities, there are also major differences between Mycenaean and Minoan architecture. Prior to 1350 BC, the citadel on which the Mycenaean palace was constructed had no encircling walls. Unlike Minoan cities, however, Mycenae was not protected by its location, and for the succeeding 150 years, surrounding walls were built and rebuilt. The walls of Mycenae were constructed of stones, some of which were extremely large; this caused the Greeks to name this type of construction **cyclopean** because they believed that only giants such as the one-eyed Cyclops could lift such heavy weights. At their narrowest width, these walls were over 16 feet thick. Rubble was used between interior and exterior surfaces, which were constructed of carefully laid stone.

INFLUENCE 4.4

Later, the Romans also used rubble between parallel walls constructed of stone.

The presence of walls required a city gate. The Lion Gate at Mycenae was ingeniously devised so that it forced enemies to come through a long, narrow walled passageway before arriving at the gate itself. Defenders could stand on the walls and cause serious damage to any attackers before they reached the gate. The gateway itself was constructed of stone posts and a lintel. (See Figure 4.7.) Above the gate were two angled stones that formed a relieving arch. Passages through the walls were roofed with corbelled arches. The corbelled arch is not a true arch but makes use of stones laid in courses, each of which extends beyond the stones below it.

BOX 4.3 MYCENAEAN MOTIFS

Mycenaean motifs included most of those used by the Minoans.

A frequently used band pattern was composed of a pair of stilted half circular rosettes separated by a vertical rectangle with its own circle motif.

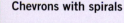
Chevrons with spirals

FIGURE 4.7 The space between the corbelled stones of the Lion Gate was filled with a 10-feet-high relief depicting an inverted Minoan column and entablature that was flanked by two lions whose faces were probably turned forward.

Like Minoan examples, the palace at Mycenae was constructed of plastered rubble with timber supports that resulted in alternating horizontal bands on the façade with the circular motifs of Crete prominent. The flat-roofed buildings had parapet walls that may have been surmounted by multiple horns of consecration. Elevation views of the Mycenaean palace appeared strikingly similar to those of Crete, although Mycenaean palaces were much smaller and had fewer rooms. The Mycenaean palaces were built around a courtyard, had entrance porches with inverted Minoan columns, and used stone piers below grade. The Mycenaean megaron, however, surpassed the palace courtyard in importance and became more private. By this time, the megaron was fully developed and consisted of three parts: a porch formed by an extension of the side walls of the building (**antae**) with columns between the antae (**in antis**), a **prodomos**, or vestibule, and a **domos** (comparable to the cella)—a large room with a hearth enclosed by four columns and an opening in the roof above the hearth.

It was at Mycenea that separate quarters for women, here called the **gynaeceum**, began in

FIGURE 4.8 The roof over the hearth, supported by columns, may have projected upward to form a "room" with openings in the sides for light to enter and smoke to escape. One Mycenaean megaron hearth uncovered by archaeologists was 11 feet in diameter.

Europe. The megara of the gynaeceum did not interconnect with those of men. Wall frescoes were similar to those of Crete, although with the addition of frescoes with a military theme. See Figure 4.8 for a reconstruction of a Mycenaean interior.

Some Mycenaean tombs were round structures called **tholoi** and were roofed with corbelled domes, which were then covered with earth.[3] An open dromos led downward to the entrance. Engaged columns of green stone with spiral and chevron motifs flanked the entrance to the Mycenaean Treasury of Atreus and the spiral motif was repeated on the relieving arch. (See Figure 4.9.)

MYCENAEAN FURNITURE

Mycenaean furniture was similar to that of Crete and more examples are known. Mycenaean texts alluded to the opulence of some of the pieces when they described the use of gold and inlaid ivory in designs that included pomegranates, griffins, and lion's heads.

One bronze throne had two vertical posts at the back forming the legs as well as the supports for an animal skin that would have been attached at shoulder height. A footstool was soldered to the throne.

Stools were depicted either with three or four legs, and some with X-shaped legs appear to have folded. Ivory legs and feet found in ruins were assumed to have been parts of ancient furniture that has since disappeared. Miniature terracotta footstools had four low feet, two looped ends, and a counterchange pattern on the top. (See Figure 4.10.)

Round-topped tables with either a single pedestal or with three legs were also depicted. Lion's paw feet, carved designs on the edges of table tops, and decorative top surfaces were known to have been used. There was at least one example of

FIGURE 4.10 Numerous terracotta sarcophagi like this Minoan example exhibited the form of chests that had either gabled or flat lids. Corner posts extended to form feet that raised the chests above the floor. Heinrich Schliemann[2] uncovered a chest with bas-relief animals on its sides.

FIGURE 4.9 The dromos leading to the Treasury of Atreus is 20 feet wide at the beginning and lined with dressed stone. The doorway itself is 9 feet wide. The interior is 43 feet high, and the stones of the corbelled dome were curved on the inside edges.

a rectangular table with four legs that appeared to have been turned, although it is doubtful the lathe was available during this time period.

Mycenaean culture spread throughout the Mediterranean world until the thirteenth century BC. What happened to the Mycenaeans is subject to debate, but its civilization lingered only in the poetry of Homer and in its influence on the design of subsequent cultures. That influence was felt most in the Greek culture that was to develop around the Mycenaean ruins.

Greece (776–146 BC)

Greece was a land of mountains, small plains, and peninsulas with 500 islands—a topography not conducive to the development of a strong unified nation. Ancient Greece called itself Hellas and its citizens Hellenes.

Greece exported wine, olive oil, honey, and dried fish, and imported grain, ivory, faïence, glass, and purple dye. During its history, Greece established cities in Asia Minor, Spain, France, Sicily, and Egypt and around the Black Sea. Southern Italy became Magna Grecia. The Greek city of Masillia (Marseilles) controlled trade throughout the Rhone valley. The colonies around the Black Sea became the granary of Greece and Athenian warships often accompanied grain shipments to preclude piracy by other cities.

GREEK HISTORY

After the fall of the Mycenaean culture, the art of writing was lost, art forms returned to more primitive models, and Greece entered a Dark Age that lasted until c. 1100 BC. About 1000 BC, two groups invaded Greece: the Dorians and the Ionians. The Dorians settled in mainland Greece and on some nearby islands; the Ionians settled first in central Greece and later on the coast of Asia Minor. These groups used iron, but they were not as culturally sophisticated as the Mycenaeans. While they brought new ideas with them, they also adopted much from the cultures of the people they displaced.

The history of classical Greece begins with the development of the **polis**, or Greek city, in the eighth century BC. Greece poleis fought among themselves, sometimes forming small kingdoms but never establishing a unified country. Each city had its own laws, and citizens were closely tied to their urban center. Greek cities protected their own citizens. Merchants from one city could not trade in another and strangers came at their own risk. By 750 BC, Greece was ruled by its people and each land-owning male citizen could not only vote but was expected to participate in the operation of the city-state.

A single city was usually ascendant. Sparta controlled much of the Peloponnesian Peninsula and by c. 800 BC most of Greece. A few centuries later, Athens was in control. Under Pericles (c. 495–429 BC), Athenian culture, art, and political stability achieved their highest levels.

Unique to Greece was the policy of establishing a new city when an old one had reached a certain population level. Two advantages were obvious: Satellite cities created new markets for trade, and the land available for growing food would not be overtaxed.

Athletics were a form of preparation for war and both the gods and heroes could be honored through athletic contests. In 776 BC, the initial Olympic Games were held signifying the first real unity of the Greeks as a people and even in ancient times, the Greeks dated their culture from those games. Athletes from all over Greece participated in these quadrennial games as well as in the Pythian Games in honor of Apollo at Delphi and the annual Panhellenic games.

GREEK ART PERIODS (1000 BC TO 31 BC)

Long before the historic period of Greece, pottery, sculpture, and architecture were being produced that culminated in their later perfection eventually becoming the foundation of Roman and later European forms for centuries. Both the pre-historic and historic periods are each divided into three eras.

- The Geometric period (c. 1000–700 BC) followed the Dark Age of Greece. Motifs were typically geometric in form with a few human figures and animals used. During the late Geometric period, Greek navigators explored the Mediterranean and established colonies in Italy and Sicily.

- During the Orientalizing period (700–610 BC), the trading port of Naucratis was established on the Nile Delta, the Corinthians traded with the Phoenicians and others from the coasts of Asia Minor, and Eastern influences became prevalent. The Orientalizing style featured bands of figures although scenes from everyday life—hunting, processions of soldiers, and battle scenes were also used. Human figures became much more lifelike and a variety of animals were incorporated including mythological creatures and some animals obviously from Africa. Oriental influences also included curvilinear and floral designs.

- During the Archaic period (c. 610–490 BC), the basic temple form was developed with stone walls, a unique exterior surrounding colonnade, and human scale. Both painting and architecture of the time revealed a knowledge of foreshortening and perspective.

- The Early Classical period (490–450 BC) was the first of the historic periods. It began with the first defeat of the Persians and saw its full flowering after their final defeat in 480/79 BC. Persians were identified with centaurs (half horse, half human), and female warriors (Amazons). Both were used in design to taunt the Persian love of luxury. The frieze of the most perfect temple of all, the Parthenon, was decorated with the battle of the centaurs, an allusion to the defeat of the Persians. All Greek art of the period strove for the ideal and the cities of mainland Greece and Magna Grecia competed to make their temples more splendid.

- The Classical period (450–323 BC) encompassed the Age of Pericles which has been called the Golden Age of Greece. Pericles sponsored the repair and construction of the Acropolis including the building of the Parthenon. It was during this time period that Greek styles were perfected. The Greek cities of Asia Minor became more prominent with Priene in Western Turkey one of the leaders. The theater became an important part of the urban landscape, ornate round structures appeared, and black marble was used to highlight architectural elements.

- The Hellenistic period (323–31 BC) followed the conquest of Greece by Alexander and encompassed the coming of the Romans. During this period, art in all its forms became more exuberant and ornamented. It was also during this period that Greek culture was spread over much of the then-known world first by Alexander's armies and later by the Romans. Hellenistic art depicted humans more realistically than did Classical art and it was during this period that the female nude sculpture was introduced. New to the Greeks were the sculptures of post-Alexandrian kings that provided visual images

of royalty to emphasize their power. Hellenistic design merged with that of the Romans in the first century BC when architectural emphasis changed from simple buildings with fine details to monumentality. Almost all the building types except the temple were added during the Hellenistic period. Numerous colonnades were constructed and pedestals were used for both sculpture and buildings.

GREEK ADVANCEMENTS IN KNOWLEDGE AND TECHNOLOGY

While the Doric Spartans were warriors, the Ionians, including those in Athens, were philosophers. Some of the philosophers were advanced in their thinking and the public was not yet ready for their ideas. The Greek philosopher Anaxagoras (c. 500–428 BC) insisted that the world was a sphere and revolved around the sun, but he was condemned to death for his heresy. Most philosophers, however, analyzed human beliefs and moral character and introduced tragedy and comedy as devices to teach morality and good citizenship. These plays became an integral part of Dionysian religious ceremonies.

The methods of observation developed by the philosophers, the interest of Alexander in science, and contact with Egypt and Babylon through the Alexandrian conquests gave impetus to the development of science during the Hellenistic period. Archimedes (c. 287–212 BC) demonstrated that small engines such as the pulley could be used to move large weights. Hero devised a steam-powered system that seemingly magically opened the temple door when a fire was lit on the altar outside. Eratosthenes of Cyrene (c. 275–195 BC) calculated the circumference of the earth to within 200 miles.

GREEK RELIGION

Tenets of Greek religion were dramatically different from those of Egypt and Mesopotamia. Individuals in those cultures considered themselves a minor part of the natural universe and their gods were given animal forms. Although Greek religion also had many gods, the gods were not only human in form but took on human characteristics. The Greeks essentially created the gods in their own images to represent the forces of nature. In Egyptian art, it had been necessary to show all essential parts of a figure depicting an actual person; this was because the Egyptians believed that such an image could be magically

Box 4.4 Greek Motifs

In the figure above, three band patterns are shown. On the top is the **water leaf**, in which leaves have a prominent midrib. The center band consists of the egg and dart motif. Ovals alternated with one of several dart forms, which gave their names to the stylistic variation on band patterns: egg and dart; egg and anchor; and egg and tongue. Beneath the egg and dart band is an anthemion band. Anthemia are connected by S-scrolls and alternated with a lotus form. These patterns were used on Ionic columns, over doorways, and painted in a variety of locations including the panels of coffered ceilings and on cyma recta moldings. Sometimes, anthemion bands were doubled forming mirror images; sometimes they were oblique or angled at 45 degrees.

Greek and Roman sphinxes were female rather than male.

The guilloche of the Egyptians and Mesopotamians was further developed by the Greeks to form more complicated patterns and double or triple rows.

The griffin, with an eagle's head and wings on a lion's body, was a popular motif with several of the early cultures, including the Greeks.

The branching scroll or vine represented the laurel crown of victory in athletic contests or the grapevine that was sacred to Dionysus. The branching vine, which had leaves that filled the open spaces between curves, became an essential detail in the Alexandrian rinceau motif. The rinceau combined the S-curve, the vine, the spiral, and the acanthus leaf and became one of the most important motifs of the later Renaissance.

The swag was used with several devices including representations of human heads such as shown here and with bucrania or bovine heads or skulls.

GREEK ARCHITECTURE

Greece's richest treasure was fine-grained marble, which was widely available both in mainland Greece and on some of the Aegean islands. Parian marble from Mt. Parpessa, on the island of Paros, and Pentelic marble, from Mt. Pentelicus about seven miles outside of Athens, were favored for buildings and sculpture because they allowed for crisp edges and minutely carved details. The Parthenon was constructed of Pentelic marble, and even the roof tiles were made of this material. Pentelic marble ranged in color from white to gray. Where marble was not available, as in Magna Grecia (Greek colonies in southern Italy), coarser stone was used and covered with stucco. Even then, however, marble might be imported for the decorative sculptures.

CITY PLANNING

Greek cities were walled with adobe brick, although by the Hellenistic period, the walls were more substantial and given rusticated stone facings. Rather than the crenels and merlons used in other areas, Greek city walls had continuous parapets. With few exceptions, cities grew haphazardly following contours of the hilly terrain before the time of Alexander. When rebuilding Miletus in Asia Minor after the Persian invasion, the Greeks used a grid iron plan for their streets, which became the model for new cities under Alexander. No provisions were made for rainwater runoff and the disposal of sewage. Fountains, often enclosed in ornamented structures, supplied water.

> INFLUENCE 4.6
>
> *The grid iron plan for cities was used by the Romans and almost every subsequent civilization.*

Each Greek city had an **acropolis**, or high city, located on a hill that served as a defensive refuge when it was attacked or besieged. It was on the acropolis that the most important religious structures were built. The cultural center of the city was the **agora**, which served as the marketplace, public square, and entertainment center.

GREEK STRUCTURES

The first structures were probably wattle and daub, and remains show that they had curved ends. Adobe bricks were first used during the

BOX 4.7 TERMS USED TO DESCRIBE FEATURES OF GREEK BUILDINGS WITH TYPICAL PLANS

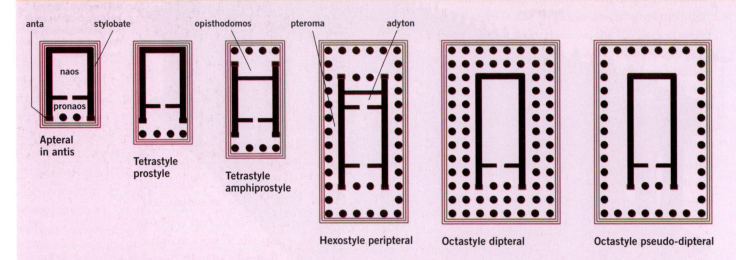

There are a number of terms used to describe the distribution of columns in Greek architecture. Several terms may be required to describe a particular building. For example, the Parthenon is a peripteral amphiprostyle octastyle temple.

The space between the external columns and the wall is the **pteroma**.

Number of Columns across the Façade

- Tetrastyle—4
- Hexastyle—6
- Heptastyle—7
- Octastyle—8
- Enneastyle—9
- Decastyle—10
- Dodecastyle—12

Column Location

- **Apteral**—Indicates the absence of columns at the sides of the building
- **Peristyle**—Columns around the entire building

- **Pseudo-peripteral**—A single row of columns surrounding the temple with the columns spaced two intercolumniations from the wall of naos.
- **Dipteral**—From *di* meaning *two*—indicates a double row of freestanding columns on all sides
- **Pseudo-dipteral**—A row of engaged columns or pilasters with an additional row of freestanding columns on the sides.

Presence or Absence of Porches or Porticoes

- **In antis**—Columns located between the antae.
- **Prostyle**—The presence of a porch across the front of the building with a full row of columns located beyond the antae. (The difference between the prostyle porch and the pronaos was its location. The pronaos was located between the antae, the prostyle porch beyond the antae.)
- **Amphiprostyle**—The presence of two porches or porticoes—one in front and one in back
- **Monoprostyle**—A porch with a single row of columns
- **Diprostyle**—A porch with a double row of columns.

building was **hypaethral,** or open to the sky. The **hippodrome** was similar but had a larger track for horse and chariot racing.

Theaters The Greek theater was an elongated semicircle or horseshoe shape, with a circular **orchestra** at the lowest level, seating in the **koilon,** or auditorium, a **skene,** or a building that served as a backdrop for the scenery. Unlike later Roman theaters, Greek examples were built into the side of an existing hill making use of the natural topography. Sacred choral competitions were held in the theaters and musicians and actors

used the orchestra for singing and dancing. (See Figure 4.19.)

A small moat surrounded the orchestra and when filled with water, enhanced the acoustics. In fact, the acoustics of Greek theaters are unrivaled even today. The best-preserved Greek theater is at Epidaurus, where it is claimed that a match struck on the stage can be heard from each of the 14,000 seats. In addition to the backless seats provided for most viewers, there were a number of marble chairs in the front rows for the priests of Dionysus and city officials. Seats, like those in modern theaters, were divided into sections by

FIGURE 4.18 The Stoa of Attalos in Athens had two stories, two rows of columns ranked in front of a wall, and a row of shops behind the wall.

walkways. A small roofed theater, known as the **odeion**, was used for poetry readings and musical performances. See Box 4.8 for a summary of characteristics of Greek architecture.

DOMESTIC ARCHITECTURE

Social life in Greece revolved around public spaces, not individual homes. If one were to spend large amounts of money for a building, it was more desirable to put that structure in a public space where everyone could admire it than to build a private space few could appreciate. As a consequence,

there were few large homes and no palaces in historic Greece before the Hellenistic period.

Greek homes were small and unpretentious and often shared walls with neighboring houses. Residential districts were crowded, and the democratic ideals of the Greeks caused individual citizens to shun ostentatious display. The home of a wealthy merchant might be beside that of a poor citizen. The Mycenaean megaron style was prevalent until the fifth century BC and remained popular in northern Greece long afterward. In other areas during the fifth century, the megaron

FIGURE 4.19 Because the theater was used for religious festivals, especially those honoring Dionysus, theaters were always a part of sanctuaries and there was an altar in the orchestra. As the style of Greek plays evolved, the size of the orchestra changed and the stage became more or less elaborate, but the form remained basically the same.

ported by arches continuously produces outward thrust on both sides. Early underground arches were stable because the ground provided sufficient counterthrust. It was the Romans who developed methods of counteracting the outward thrust not only with large masses but with other arches. This led to the extensive use of arcades where only the arches at the ends required additional support or to circular structures with continuous perimeter arcades. The Romans also placed arches in a series behind one another, which resulted in **barrel** or **tunnel vaults**. In this case, massive walls were necessary to counteract the thrust of the vault. By the first century BC, **arcuated** construction, that which depended on the arch for support, was most pervasive in Roman structures. (See Figure 5.5.)

Because the arch consisted of a number of small voussoirs, it could be made to span considerable distances—longer than could a timber or stone lintel. Roman arches commonly spanned 60 feet. When combined with concrete in the first century AD Pantheon dome, the span exceeded 140 feet. Such spans were what made possible the monumental open interiors of Roman buildings as well as larger openings in walls than had been seen before. Because the arch was not self-supporting until the last stone was in place, construction required the use of **centering**, or temporary wooden supports. Once the arch was stable, the centering was removed and reused to form another arch. Not only was the arch self-

supporting, but it could also carry loads placed on it. It was a simple matter, then, to stack arcades to create multiple stories.

By the end of the Republican period, the Romans had expanded their arch repertory to include the **cross** or **groin vault**, where two vaults meet at right angles, and the **dome**, which was a series of arches radiating from a central point. The Roman dome required support around its entire perimeter limiting its use to circular spaces. (See also Figure 5.6.)

FIGURE 5.5 The Romans usually used the semicircular arch (i.e., half a circle), making the change of direction between the wall or pier and the arch a smooth, continuous line without a visible break. Later, they used a few segmental arches (i.e., less than half a circle), which resulted in a distinctive break between the vertical support and the arch.

CONCRETE

Mortar, a mixture of burnt and powdered lime, sand, and water, had been used by other civilizations, but the Romans introduced two innovations. First, they added pozzolana, a readily available volcanic ash, to the mortar mixture which resulted not only in waterproof cement but one that hardened underwater. The second innovation, which had far-reaching results, was concrete, made by layering available rock with generous portions of pozzolana mortar. The pozzolana mixture dried quickly, so it was necessary to lay the concrete in **courses**, or rows. The Romans built two walls of undressed stones parallel to one another and spaced some distance apart and then filled the intervening spaces with additional rubble layered with mortar.

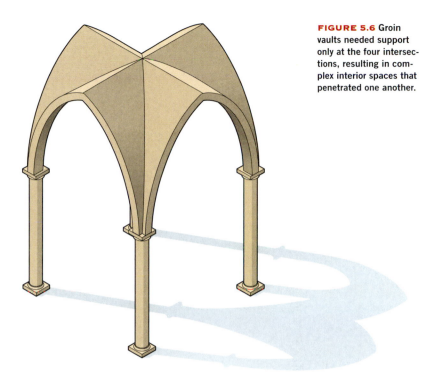

FIGURE 5.6 Groin vaults needed support only at the four intersections, resulting in complex interior spaces that penetrated one another.

INFLUENCE 5.3

Modern concrete is a direct descendant of Roman concrete, differing mostly in method. Modern concrete is a mixture of mortar, water, cement, and aggregates (e.g., sand, gravel, and or lighter-weight materials such as pumice or perlite), which are basically the same materials as Roman concrete. The aggregates in modern concrete, however, are mixed together with more water to create a mixture that can be poured. The Romans used mortar to cement together rubble, which was larger than most aggregates used today, within a wall, but they did not mix the two prior to construction.

Concrete made huge vaults and domes possible. Because concrete was laid in courses around domes, courses were typically stepped on the exterior. Regularly shaped facing stones as small as two inches were added on both the interior and exterior and the wall was identified by the pattern of those stones.

Brick, mosaics, tufa, cut stone (including marble), and stucco were all used as wall facings over concrete, and each had a different name. (See Figure 5.7.)

CONNECTING THE EMPIRE

As the Roman Empire expanded, it was necessary to construct roads and bridges to provide a dependable means of communicating with all parts of the Empire. Roman roads were unparalleled in the ancient world and remained the best road system in Europe until the eigh-

teenth century. Although it was necessary to go around some obstacles, Roman roads were relatively straight. Paths were carved along mountains, and viaducts and bridges spanned valleys and rivers. The center of the road was raised so water would run off, embankments or curbs on both sides might further define the path, and in some places, roadside seats were installed. In urban areas such as Pompeii, raised footpaths, or sidewalks, were constructed on both sides of the road. Mounting blocks at intervals made getting on horses easier, and at intersections, raised blocks facilitated pedestrian crossing.

While Roman bridges incorporating stone arcades had wider spans between supports than did earlier Babylonian and Greek examples, those

FIGURE 5.7 On this structure in Pompeii, Roman methods of building in concrete are exposed. The internal section is rubble layered with mortar between walls of regularly shaped stones alternated with courses of brick. The diagonally laid stone on the exterior is the reticulated facing that appears on all sides.

FIGURE 5.8 The ancient Pons Aelius, now the Sant' Angelo Bridge, was typical of Roman bridges. On the upstream side, the piers supporting the arches were reinforced and wedge-shaped to deflect debris. The present statues were installed in 1669.

spans were still relatively narrow by modern standards. The length of the bridge was unlimited because the arches could be repeated indefinitely. Bridges often had architectural features including facades with the appearance of triumphal arches, niches, pediments, and engaged columns. (See Figure 5.8.)

WATER SUPPLY AND DRAINAGE SYSTEMS

The Assyrians, Greeks, and Etruscans had all channeled water into some of their cities through **aqueducts** or artificial rivers, and it was from these antecedents that the Romans derived their basic knowledge of transporting water. The Romans not only improved the system but also devised ways to carry water long distances and over rough terrain, lavishly supplying cities throughout the Empire. Arcades maintained the level of aqueducts across low-lying areas, and to ensure sufficient water pressure for use, aqueducts usually ran above ground some distance before reaching a city. Raising the height of the aqueduct was often a challenge. The Pont du Gard in southern France was 161 feet high, the highest of all ancient Roman aqueduct bridges. To ensure stability in the presence of strong

winds, arches were limited in height and stacked to achieve needed height.

INFLUENCE 5.4

Beginning in the seventeenth century, the English built aqueducts to several major cities. Modern aqueducts include those in New York and California. Much of the water for New York City comes from the Catskill Aqueduct. The Colorado River Aqueduct carries water almost 250 miles to Los Angeles, and the California Aqueduct runs 444 miles.

Drainage systems had been used by the Etruscans for draining water from marshy areas, but it was Roman engineers who expanded the use of sewers and drainage systems[1] providing their cities with sanitation methods not seen again until the nineteenth century.

HEATING

Romans heated some buildings, especially baths, by means of the **hypocaust**, a type of radiant heating system. Masonry floors were raised on brick or stone piers, leaving a space beneath them for slaves to keep charcoal braziers burning. The heat rose, warming the floors and subsequently the spaces above. The system was later improved by the addition of vertical flues in walls which channeled heat upward around the rooms.

FIGURE 5.9 The piers that raised the floor for this hypocaust can still be seen. This heating system was not only used in baths but in other buildings, especially in the colder northern areas of the Empire.

---INFLUENCE 5.5

Modern radiant heating systems are derived from the hypocaust, although the heat is usually derived from electrical coils or heated water running through pipes in floors, walls, or ceilings. A type of hypocaust is still used in rural homes in Korea. Their ondal system is annually responsible for several deaths due to carbon monoxide poisoning caused by gases rising from the burner and filtering through the cracks between flooring members.

RELIGION

The Romans were polytheistic. Like the Greeks, they worshipped gods who presided over various aspects of nature or the human condition. In fact, many Roman gods were Greek or Etruscan gods with new names. Later, gods of conquered peoples were added to the Roman panoply; this was in part because of a belief that it was better not to offend even gods they had not previously recognized. Also, by recognizing these gods, the Romans could demonstrate respect for the beliefs of the conquered and thus perhaps win loyalty as well as obedience. Individuals worshipped gods whom they believed were most associated with them personally: Vesta, the goddess of the hearth; the Penates, or spirits of the pantry; and the Lares, or good spirits associated with the ancestors who protected the home. Most homes had a shrine, or **lararium**, in a niche or room off the atrium or peristyle, or a private chapel elsewhere at which the family regularly sacrificed.

Major temples were supported by public funds and the priests were state officials. The head of the state religion was the Pontifex Maximus, a title assumed by Emperor Augustus and subsequent leaders including the Pope.

ARTS AND DESIGN

Roman painting and sculpture began with Greek forms. In fact, the Romans imported and copied numerous examples although the style eventually became uniquely their own. A major difference between Roman and Greek designs was the Roman emphasis on historic subjects rather than mythological ones. Roman developments in glasswork, too, went far beyond anything known

before. Many examples of glasswork were not rediscovered until the modern era.

The Romans more frequently left objects in their natural colors than did the Greeks, although they did paint some surfaces. Subjects included still lifes, scenes from everyday life, and portraiture. Portraits were important due to Roman emphasis on genealogy and often had painted or sculpted round frames known as **tondi**.

During Imperial times, portrait sculptures were so realistic that even moles and warts were reproduced. Wax death masks were displayed to ensure that ancestors would be accurately remembered. Especially on sarcophagi, the features of an individual might be substituted on the head of a recognized hero.

A bust merging from a tapered pillar was a **term**, and sometimes feet were carved under the pillar. A head and bust alone was a **herm**. Bacchus, accompanied by grapes and vines, was a favored motif. The Romans also used human forms for support. The Roman **telamon** was similar to the Greek atlas except that the telamon was not bowed with its arms over its head.

The most important human figures used, however, were the **genius** for men and the **juno** for women; each represented an individual, a group, or a place. Personal genii began as protective ancestors and later evolved into guardian spirits. Genii representing senators were clothed in togas and had veiled heads; those representing ordinary individuals took two forms, a bust of a mature bearded man or a full-length semi-nude, clean-shaven youth. Genii often carried a shallow bowl used for offerings to the gods along with a cornucopia, a box for incense, or a rolled scroll. In addition, the Romans were fond of figures of naked winged babies known as **amorini**.

INFLUENCE 5.6

During the Renaissance, amorini—then called putti—were revived as decorative motifs.

GLASS

The Romans worked extensively with glass and used two techniques for forming it into vessels: blowing and molding. Free-blown glass was embellished with surface effects—pinching, indenting, ribbing, or adding threads of dark blue molten glass in coils to the vessel. Early in the first century AD, the Romans developed a method of blowing glass into a pottery or metal mold to create complex designs, a form of mass production. Lion heads, theater masks, and other designs were often molded and added to the surfaces of free-blown vessels. The most famous example of Roman glassware was the Portland Vase—a vase of dark blue glass (due to cobalt) that was dipped into molten white glass (containing antimony) to form a layer on the outside of the original vase. This technique is known as **flashed glass**. The white glass was then engraved with figures much like a cameo.

FIGURE 5.10
Uniquely, the Lycurgus cup shows two colors—green in daylight and red when light comes from inside the cup.

INFLUENCE 5.7

Josiah Wedgewood was inspired by the Portland Vase and reproduced the technique in pottery. Jasper ware and Wedgewood china continue to use the cameo technique today.

INFLUENCE 5.8

The success of two nineteenth-century glass workers in recreating the technique used for the Portland vase in glass resulted in a demand for cameo glass that lasted until the twentieth century.

The fourth century AD Roman Lycurgus Cup, housed in the British Museum had a solid cup on the outside of which were carved glass figures attached to the surface only by small shanks. This technique was known as **diatreta**, commonly known as **cage cup**, where figures form a cage surrounding the cup itself. (See Figure 5.10.)

INFLUENCE 5.9

Another glassmaking technique used by the Romans was millefiori (1,000 flowers) work. To create millefiori designs, small colored glass rods or strips were fused together to form a pattern and then cut into slices that could be used as inlay. This technique is still used today, especially in Venice.

The Romans also developed a technique for adding gold leaf to glass by sandwiching gold bands or designs between two layers of clear glass. Frequently, the designs were portraits, probably of the owners. Enameling on glass developed by the Romans required that the enamel be fired to fuse it to the glass. Glass was also engraved and cut into facets. Most of these techniques were lost and only rediscovered centuries later.

INFLUENCE 5.10

In the eighteenth century, the Germans rediscovered the technique for sandwiching gold between layers of glass, which became popular as zwischengoldglas.

The Romans were also excellent workers in precious metals and bronze. Their artisans created silver, gold, and copper vessels in abundance. The lost wax technique was used for casting bronze and other metals. In addition, bronze pieces were decorated with a technique known as **champlevé**. In this technique, glass was put into small compartments on the surface of an object and heated to fuse it to the bronze. Large numbers of bronze statues were produced but few survived the Renaissance when they were melted down for cannons.

ROMAN MOTIFS

The Romans used many of the motifs of Greece and Etruria, including the fret, swastika, egg-and-dart, patera, water leaf, and dentil. Roman motifs, however, were bolder, more elaborate, and more exuberant than Greek and Etruscan examples. Forms were often arranged into continuous spirals that were interwoven with floral and animal forms.

The acanthus leaf was the most pervasive Roman ornament and was used in numerous locations, often as a scrolling pattern that included floral motifs. The laurel wreath and the anthemion were carried over from Greece and used throughout the Roman periods. Animal forms were common: swans, lions, ram's heads, birds, horses, mules, and bovine forms were typical. Mythological animals such as the griffin, chimera, and female sphinx were also used. During the Imperial period, niches with shell semi domes, spiral column shafts, and small colonnettes mounted on brackets became popular. See Box 5.2.

ROMAN ARCHITECTURE

The Romans were familiar with the columnar architecture of the Greeks in southern Italy and the Etruscans in their immediate surroundings. It was this form they adapted for their specific needs. More importantly, they expanded their architectural vocabulary with the arch, vault, and dome. When combined with their developments in concrete, the resulting buildings became not supporting masses but volumes of enclosed space.

Overall construction of Greek buildings had been in the hands of a single individual who made major decisions but left details to the many skilled artisans hired to complete the work. The Romans, however, organized construction differently. Members of guilds who specialized in one aspect of building were in charge of a portion of the job and were aided by numerous slaves and unskilled workers. Decisions were made by the architect in charge rather than by the artisans.

INFLUENCE 5.11
Roman guilds were the precursors of medieval guilds and modern unions.

Like Greek examples, Roman buildings were axial and bilaterally symmetrical. In contrast to the Greeks, however, buildings were axially and symmetrically arranged on a site and processional pathways became superfluous as the importance of a structure was reflected in its position. Roman buildings, often even domestic examples, were raised in the Etruscan manner on a podium several feet high and accessible only from a stairway in the front.

Although buildings were often surrounded by columns, they were usually pseudo-peripteral with the columns on the sides reduced to engaged examples or pilasters. Roofs were flat, mansard, vaulted, or domed and pitched roofs were steeper than Greek examples. Building exteriors were highly decorated with tiers of columns, niches, and arcades often resulting in the appearance of the stage sets.

To the entablatures, moldings, architectural orders, and pediments of the Greeks, the Romans added the **apse**, or curved exterior projection of a building; the arch and vault; the **attic**, or façade above the entablature; the niche; and two new architectural orders. (See Orders of Architecture on page 113.) While the Romans used the semicircular exedra of the Greeks, they also added the **crytostyle** portico, a projecting curved colonnade. Balconies frequently graced Roman buildings. The Romans used more moldings than did the Greeks but less sculpture and by the first century AD had introduced the **broken pediment** and **open pediment**. (See Figure 5.11.)

FIGURE 5.11 In a broken pediment, the sides do not meet at the top and a decorative form may break into the opening. The open pediment features a full or partial pediment, but the entablature below is broken, usually to include an opening. This Baroque niche has both a broken and open pediment.

Box 5.2 ROMAN MOTIFS

The ox skull, or **bucranium**, was draped with a garland and favored for metopes. Swags composed of fruits and leaves, ribbons, and urns, were used alone or in combination with other motifs, such as with the bucranium in this figure.

Nilotic scenes (those featuring the Nile or Egypt) were common during the Imperial periods. As with other scenes, architectural motifs frame the picture.

The thunderbolt of Jupiter—a spiral pointed at both ends—was depicted held in the talons of an eagle, with wings, or as lightning.

The Imperial eagle of Rome had semi-folded wings and a turned head.

The rods of the fasces symbolized the power of an individual to beat a condemned person and the ax symbolized the power to inflict the death penalty.

Romans used vast quantities of fired brick, especially in areas where suitable stone was not available for building. Imperial buildings constructed of concrete were frequently faced with brick. The stone used for buildings was usually **travertine**, a type of readily available limestone; **tufa**, a lightweight volcanic stone in red, white, or black; or granite. Travertine could bear heavy loads and was not affected by environmental factors. Tufa was easily worked, although it readily deteriorated in exposed areas in freezing climates or near the sea. Like the Greeks, the Romans used copious amounts of marble; however, the Romans frequently applied it in thin sheets as a façade. (See Figure 5.12.)

ORDERS OF ARCHITECTURE

The Romans adapted the Greek Orders of Architecture but gave them Roman forms. They also added both the Tuscan and Composite orders. Columns were used in different ways. Roman columns were monolithic rather than constructed of separate drums put together on site. Shafts were often left unfluted, especially when polished marble was used, and engaged columns and pilasters were used decoratively although they had no structural purpose. (See Figure 5.13.) Some Roman columns were supported by a square pedestal with its own base and cornice that could be as much as a third the height of the column. The

FIGURE 5.12 This brick column was once covered with stucco and probably painted to give it the appearance of marble. The zigzag configuration enabled the finisher to easily flute the column.

Romans also continued the Hellenistic tendency to increase the distance between columns.

The **pilastrade**, or a row of pilasters to give the appearance of a colonnade, was a Roman innovation. Pilasters or engaged columns added to arch supports resulted in **arch orders**. Entablatures often surmounted engaged columns, pilasters, and arcades. All of these served not only

FIGURE 5.13 The Roman Maison Carrée in Nimes, France, built in 16 BC, was a pseudo-peripteral temple that employed engaged Corinthian columns on the sides. This structure served as the model for the Virginia State Capitol building.

a decorative function but to emphasize interior structural divisions on the exterior.

On multiple-story buildings, columns were often stacked. Each story used a separate order and had its own entablature, increasing apparent weight and complexity as the building rose. This arrangement of superimposed orders was used at the Flavian Amphitheater (70–83 AD), where there were four stories: Roman Doric engaged columns were used on the first story, Ionic on the second, Corinthian on the third, and Corinthian pilasters on the fourth. The orders used by the Romans included the Tuscan, Doric, Ionic, Corinthian, and Composite—three Greek Orders adapted to Roman tastes and two additional orders:

• The Tuscan Order has often been typified as simplified Doric, giving the impression that it had only Greek precedents. Like the Etruscan Tuscan Order, however, it had a base, an unfluted shaft, a small capital, and a height of seven diameters. The base consisted of a square plinth on top of which rested a single torus molding separated from the shaft by a fillet. Moldings were used only at the top and between sections on Tuscan entablatures that had a plain undecorated frieze. (See Figure 5.14.)

• The Romans adapted the Greek Doric Order by adding a base, increasing its height in relation to its diameter (from five-and-a-half

to seven diameters), and making the capital more decorative. Following the Hellenistic style, Roman Doric columns often had fluting only on the upper two thirds of the shaft and 18 flutes might be used rather than 20. The lower third of the shaft was frequently polygonal with the sides corresponding to the flutes above. In the Greek Doric Order, the entablature had a triglyph at each end of the frieze that met at the corner. In the Roman version, triglyphs were centered over all the columns including those at the end, leaving a **demimetope**, or half metope, at the external angle. Intercolumniations were larger than in the Greek Doric and often required two or more triglyphs. By the early Imperial period, the Roman Doric had become more ornate. The echinus had an egg-and-dart band, the neck was an ornamented band, and additional moldings were used.

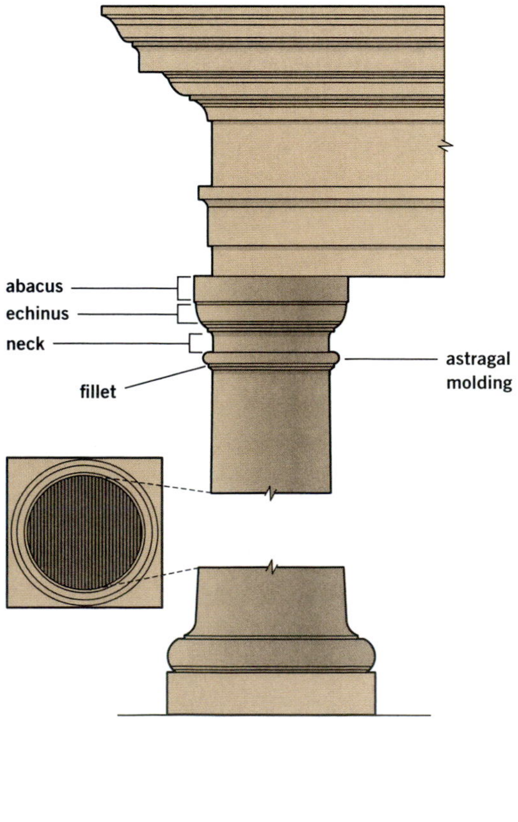

INFLUENCE 5.12

The demi-metope was again used during the Renaissance as well as in the eighteenth century.

• The neck of the Roman Ionic Order had a decorated band as in the Roman Doric Order. Like the Roman Doric, the Roman Ionic column was more slender than Greek examples—nine diameters in height rather than the typical Greek eight diameters. The most significant change, however, was in the capital. Whereas Greek Ionic capitals presented a flat face on the front and back and used angled volutes only at the corners of buildings, Roman Ionic capitals employed angular volutes at all four corners regardless of their position in the building.

INFLUENCE 5.13

The angular capital was favored during the Italian Renaissance when it was known as the Scamozzi Order.

• The Greeks used the Corinthian Order only for interiors but the Romans favored it and used it extensively both inside and outside. The abacus of the Roman Corinthian order was molded and 16 small volutes sprang from 8 caulicoli located between the eight acanthus leaves on the upper row.

FIGURE 5.14 The Tuscan capital was separated into three parts of equal height: neck, echinus, and abacus. A fillet and an astragal molding separated the shaft from the plain neck, which was itself separated from the echinus and abacus by additional fillets.

abacus
echinus
neck
fillet
astragal molding

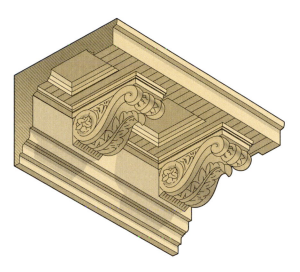

FIGURE 5.15 In the Roman Corinthian order, brackets known as **modillions** projected outward to support a wide overhanging cornice.

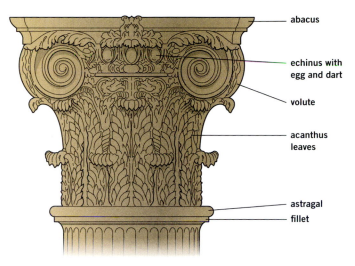

abacus

echinus with egg and dart

volute

acanthus leaves

astragal
fillet

FIGURE 5.16 The Composite capital was distinguished from the Corinthian capital in that the volutes were separated by a prominent echinus with one or more bands of molding. As in other Roman orders with volutes, those of the Composite order were angled at the corners.

• The Composite Order combined the volutes of the angular Ionic with the acanthus leaf decoration of the Corinthian. The Composite was the most slender of all Roman columns with a height of 10 diameters. (See Figure 5.16.)

CITY PLANNING

Like the Greeks and the Etruscans, the Romans had an urban culture with cities dominating political and social life. Hellenistic cities, such as Poseidonia (Paestum) in Italy, had been laid out by the Greeks in a gridiron plan such as that developed at Miletus. The Etruscans followed Greek examples and laid out the city of Capua in the same manner. As the Romans became stronger and established army camps throughout the empire, they too followed the gridiron examples around them. Although Rome was an old unplanned city, as the Romans established colonies, they used the gridiron plan even when the terrain was not conducive to such an arrangement.

Like most ancient civilizations, the Romans built defensive walls around cities that ignored all but the most difficult terrain and ran straight, although a few cities had distinctive topographical features that precluded this configuration. Even then, inside the walls, cities featured regular planning. Early cities had numerous gateways, or **porta**,[2] but the Romans reduced the number of monumental gates to one per side and highly embellished them. Additional small, unobtrusive **postern** gates were sometimes added.

Gateways frequently had two openings, one for carriages entering the city and one for those leaving. Because carriage gates were large, a small pedestrian gate, a **portula**, might be cut into the larger gate or side passages. Smaller openings usually used the post and lintel for support but wider ones required an arch.

Inside the walls, two main streets led from the gates. The east-west street was the **decumanus maximus** and the north-south street the **cardo maximus**. Smaller streets ran at right angles to main streets and divided the city into square blocks known as insulae, a term that was also used for the apartment buildings that covered some of them. In highly urbanized areas, especially in Asia Minor and North Africa, colonnaded streets were punctuated with fountains and statues, and triumphal arches were strategically placed. **Tetrapylons**, or four-sided gateways with intersecting vaults, were set up at major intersections and in some European cities, served as the location of the market.

Where the decumanus and the cardo intersected, the Romans followed Etruscan customs and established their major city center with the forum, basilica, temples, theaters, baths, libraries, and other public structures. Residential zones surrounded the civic area. The Romans built extensive public works, religious structures, civic buildings, **macella** (or markets), and entertainment venues. They also provided **insulae**,[3] or apartment blocks, for dwellings. Public buildings were designed to intimidate and to express political supremacy, while domestic structures were designed for comfort.

FIGURE 5.17 Porta had both an inner and outer gate with a space between them over which rooms were built, as in the Porta Nigra in Trier, Germany. Typically gates were protected with a **portcullis**, or a descending gate made of heavy wooden or iron bars. In Eastern parts of the Empire, it was traditional to conduct business at city gates, and it was there that judges sat ready to mete out justice. The Romans adapted these traditions and used rooms above the gateway for civil and commercial purposes. For this reason, these upper-story rooms often had windows. Flanking the gateway on one or both sides was a chamber, often used as a living space by the guard or porter.

THE FORUM

Roman life centered around the **forum**. Not only was the forum conveniently located at the major crossroads in a city, but it was where civic, religious, and public life took place. Early fora were axially and symmetrically arranged: as later monuments and buildings were added, the axial arrangement was maintained although symmetry was often sacrificed. By the first century BC, a monumental gateway led into the forum, and the major temple to Jupiter, Juno, and Minerva was located opposite the gateway.

Like the Greek agora, the forum itself was an open space where public assemblies and voting took place. A **rostrum**, a platform for speeches, was located in front of the Curia, or senate, building. The rostrum was a circular structure supported on an arcade with a platform at the top and accessed by two separate flights of stairs.

INFLUENCE 5.14

The Roman rostrum form was used for the pulpits known as ambones in ancient and medieval churches. The circular platform was raised above the level of the congregation with stairs on the east side for ascending and on the west for descending.

The forum was completely surrounded with buildings and porticoes. Like the Greek stoa, Roman porticoes were covered walkways supported by columns on at least one side and usually a building on the other side. They were frequently built in front of or around temples, along streets, and even around interior courtyards in private **villae**. Spaces between columns were filled with statues or shrubbery and exedrae projected on the perimeter. (Greek exedrae were benches sometimes located in a curved niche. By the time of the Romans, the term exedra was applied to the curved niche itself.)

INFLUENCE 5.15

During the Baroque period, the approach to spatial design was similar to that of Greece and Rome. It was the design of the space as a whole that was important, not individual buildings. The Greek approach to space as sculpture and the Roman idea of the open courtyard as a part of the design of an interconnected whole were further developed during the Baroque period.

Triumphal arches and columns in the fora reminded citizens of the deeds of their emperors. During the Empire period, **basilicas** not only provided additional **tabernae**, or shops, but an inside space for legal proceedings which had previously taken place outdoors. The **tabularium** in the forum housed the tablets of the law.

Macella One of the major early functions of the forum was to serve as a market. At first, stalls were set up on market days; later, some permanent tabernae were located in the buildings behind the porticoes. Although the forum continued to serve as a market for some goods, the Romans eventually moved most meat and produce to macella established near the forum in an effort to separate the functions of the two entities.

This first enclosed building designed specifically to serve as a permanent market was a Roman innovation. Macella were built around a courtyard in which there was a fountain or water supply available. Individual shops opened onto the courtyard, although larger macella had double rows of shops, with the outer row opening onto the street. Some macella had a central hall with a vaulted roof flanked by shops with additional vaulted roofs.

INFLUENCE 5.16

Roman macella were the first completely enclosed shopping malls similar to modern examples.

Triumphal Arches and Columns When highly placed government officials returned from successful conquests, the senate might allow them to participate in a triumphus or a solemn procession in which the leader, usually the emperor or a consul, entered the city with his army, prisoners, and important spoils of war. On entering the city, the procession passed beneath a temporary **triumphal arch** believed to draw off aggression and prepare the soldiers for life at home. Later, a more permanent arch was erected to commemorate the event. The earliest recorded triumphal arch was erected in 196 BC, but most were constructed during the Imperial periods. Usually the Corinthian Order was used for engaged columns or pilasters, the attic area above the entablature was filled with bas-reliefs, and a **quadriga**, or chariot pulled by four horses, often surmounted the structure. Two types of triumphal arches were constructed: those

pilaster

plinth

attic

ressaut

FIGURE 5.18 When columns were located in front of pilasters and the entablature projected outward over the column then back to the building between columns, the entablature was "broken," producing what is called a **ressaut**.

with one large arched opening and those with three, a large central arched opening flanked by a pair of smaller ones. (See Figure 5.18.)

INFLUENCE 5.17

The ressaut was again used during the Baroque period as the plane of moldings shifted in and out.

The Romans also erected two types of free-standing columns to honor distinguished individuals or to commemorate special events: the **columna cochlis** and the **columna rostrata**, or rostral column. Both were based on the Tuscan column and were supported by pedestals. The columna cochlis, named for its spiral reliefs, was a commemorative column that supported a statue at the top and that had a single spiral band of relief carvings winding from bottom to top. The diameter was sufficiently large to permit an internal spiral staircase, and at the top, there was a balustraded balcony. Trajan's Column in Rome is an example. The rostral column commemorated a naval victory. Rostra, or the prows, of captured vessels were attached to the column shaft.

INFLUENCE 5.18

The concept of the triumphal arch was revived during the Renaissance in Italy and again in the nineteenth century. The largest triumphal arches in the world are the Arch of Triumph in Pyong-yang, North Korea (195 feet high, 162.5 feet wide), erected in 1982 to glorify President Kim II Sung, and the Grand Arch of the Defense in Paris, completed in 1989 (325 feet high, 325 feet wide). The Grand Arch of the Defense is overtly modern while the Pyongyang arch is obviously a variation of the Roman triumphal arch.

FIGURE 5.19 While most basilicas had only two aisles, one on each side of the nave, larger examples had two aisles on each side separated by additional colonnades.

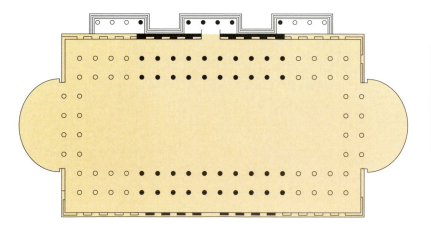

INFLUENCE 5.19

The Vendome column in Paris supported a statue of Napoleon and the spiral bas relief was made from the bronze of cannon captured at the Battle of Austerliz in 1805. The Nelson Column (1840–1843) in London's Trafalgar Square has a plain shaft but there is a staircase on the inside. The Berlin Triumphal Column was constructed in 1864. The rostral column was revived in the seventeenth and eighteenth centuries. The pair in St. Petersburg (1805–1816) had gaslights on the top and served as lighthouses.

The Basilica The basilica was a rectangular building wide enough to require intermediate support for its pitched tile roof. This support was provided by colonnades, or sometimes piers, that separated the interior space into a larger central area called a **nave** flanked by smaller side **aisles**. Often, there was a gallery level above the aisles but even then the walls of the nave rose beyond the aisle roofs to form a **clerestory** level, in which windows were placed to allow light into the central section. The gallery roof was supported by a second smaller colonnade above the entablature of a lower colonnade. For protection, a **pluteus**, or short wall or balustrade, ran between the columns of the gallery. Exterior stairways provided access to the galleries, some of which ran completely around the interior of the building. Originally, trussed timber roofs were employed although in later basilicas, vaults were used. (See Figure 5.19.)

Judicial proceedings took place opposite the entrance in a **tribunal**, which might need to seat as many as 180 judges and advocates. In later basilicas, the tribunal was located in a semicircular **apse** that projected outward from the structure, helping to decrease noise that might interrupt judicial proceedings.

INFLUENCE 5.20

In the fourth century AD, Constantine declared the basilica more appropriate for Christian worship than the pagan temple form, and so the basilica became the model for churches in the middle ages and later.

The basilica also housed shops on both the ground and gallery levels. While the exterior might be relatively plain, it was usually at least faced with marble, and it was not uncommon for shops and porticoes to be added on the exterior of one or more sides.

ROMAN BATHS

Quite possibly, hot air or steam baths were known in Greece by the fifth century BC and in Etruria by the third century BC, but it was the Romans who developed the bath into a social experience. There were two types of Roman baths: small **balnea**[4] and the great public baths known as **thermae** of the late Republican and Imperial periods. Early public balnea were used mostly by the lower classes because those who could afford them had rooms for bathing in their homes.

Thermae combined most of the features of Greek gymnasia with facilities for bathing, socialization, and recreation: gardens, libraries, fountains, tabernae, exercise facilities, barbershops, and even cultural venues such as museums and public lecture spaces were provided. Emphasis, however, was not on exercise as in Greek gymnasia, but on socialization.

Vast vaulted and domed rooms provided the necessary space for a multitude of bathers, some of whom bathed as many as eight times a day. Special chambers were provided for changing and massage. Separate baths were sometimes provided for women, but they lacked spaces for exercise and a cold-water pool.

Bathers could relax in the **laconicum**, or room with hot, dry air; bathe in warm water, usually from a vase, or sit in the moist heat of the **tepidarium**; use the hottest room, the **caldarium**, which contained a basin of hot water for bathing; and sit in cold water in the **frigidarium**.

INFLUENCE 5.21

Roman baths included the first public swimming pools. Modern spas reflect influences of the Roman baths.

A peristyle court provided an outdoor space for socialization and often included exedrae. Inside, coffered ceilings, marble walls and floors, and polychrome mosaics ensured luxurious surroundings; sculptures added to the artistic experience, and natural light poured through arched openings. As thermae became larger and more luxurious, so did bathing rooms in homes. Private baths eventually required several sumptuous rooms.

ENTERTAINMENT VENUES

With 180 holidays a year, it was necessary to provide entertainment for the Roman populace. Plays were enacted in theaters, music and poetry performed in the odeum, chariot races in circuses, and gladiatorial combats and other violent activities in amphitheaters. Some of these events had their origins in funeral rites, including those of the Greeks and Etruscans. All, however, were modified to suit the tastes of the more militaristic Romans. At first, entertainment venues were held in temporary wooden buildings erected for a major event and then removed. Later, permanent theaters, circuses, and amphitheaters were constructed throughout the Empire.

Theaters Both written plays and the theater itself were Greek ideas adopted by the Romans. Few plays were written by Romans, but by the third century BC, Greek plays were translated into Latin for Roman audiences, although plays were often read rather than performed. The Roman **odeum**, a small version of the theater but with a complete roof, was little used partially because the similar odeion in Greece was used for poetry reading and musical performances, neither of which was of significant importance among the Romans.

Roman theaters differed from Greek examples in that they were built from the ground up on arcades rather than into a hillside, the orchestra was semicircular in form and was used for seating for distinguished individuals, and the altar was omitted. The **scaena frons** had five doors (equivalent to the Greek skene, which had three doors) and was arranged with columns, niches, pediments, and statuary much as the facade of any monumental Roman structure.

The Circus The Roman equivalent of the Greek hippodrome was the circus. Like the hippodrome, the circus was a roofless narrow track with one rounded end. The opposite end was angled to even the distance covered by lanes around the track. Circuses were designed for chariot racing, but sometimes artistic equestrianism such as leaping from one horse to another was included. Running lengthwise down the center of the track was a short raised wall, or **spina**, on which there were a number of decorative and functional objects, including Egyptian obelisks, small temples, statues, and altars.

Amphitheaters Amphitheaters were used for "hunting" games in which exotic animals were killed, for gladiatorial combats that pitted men against one another in a fight usually to death, and for mock naval battles played out on a shallow lake that could be made to cover the arena. The first known amphitheater built entirely of stone was the Flavian Amphitheater, dedicated in 80 AD and now known as the Colosseum in Rome. Provincial amphitheaters were smaller than the Flavian Amphitheater, usually reaching only two stories in height.

Amphitheaters were elliptical in shape, making it possible to seat large numbers of spectators, all of whom had a good view of the proceedings. Like Roman theaters, the amphitheater was usually constructed on a flat site, which required that the seats were supported by a massive structure. The Romans employed the arch to good advantage for this purpose. (See Figure 5.20.) The **arena** was the open space in the center of the amphitheater on which the action took place. The arena could be transformed into a forest, a garden, or a lake, and no expense was spared for decoration. A large awning, or **velarium**, angled downward over the seats to provide shade without obstructing the view. The velarium was fixed to wooden masts held in place by openings in stones around the building.

INFLUENCE 5.22

The stadiums of the modern world are directly derived from Roman amphitheaters. Designed as they were two millennia ago are today's seating arrangements, aisles, accommodations for large numbers, the shape of the field, and even in some cases, a covering over the seating areas. Locker rooms, offices, and food venues have replaced the cells used by exotic animals beneath the amphitheater.

TEMPLES

The Roman equivalent of the Greek temenos was the **templum**, a space consecrated by the augers for a religious purpose and entered through a gateway, or **propylum**. Worship took place outside the temple where the courtyard was often colonnaded.

Like Greek temples, Roman examples needed no large gathering spaces, although cellae were

FIGURE 5.21 The front of the Pantheon originally faced a colonnaded courtyard. Inside, granite, marble, and porphyry covered the surfaces, and the half-spherical interior dome was coffered. Interior niches supported sculptures of emperors, gods, and heroes. The 142-feet-diameter dome was the largest in the world until the dome of Florence Cathedral (beginning in 1420) was constructed.

stepped concrete rings that become thinner toward the top   oculus

larger than those of Greek temples because in addition to the cult statue, trophies of war were housed within them. The Roman temple combined features of Etruscan and Greek temples. Following Etruscan models, the temple was set on a **podium**, or platform several feet above grade level, with the entrance via stairs at the front. Early temples followed the almost square plan of the Etruscans (with a 6:5 ratio), although later examples were more rectangular. Following the Greek preference for peripteral temples, the external colonnade often surrounded at least three sides and sometimes four, although typically the resulting building was pseudo-peripteral. Between the antae, intercolumniations were often closed with a railing or pluteus in which there were one or more gates.

A deep Etruscan-style colonnaded porch on the front led to the cella. Like the Etruscan temple, the porch took up half the space, the three cellae the other half. Later rectangular temples exhibited Greek influence when only one cella was used or when a **posticum**, equivalent to the Greek opisthodomus, was added. Inside, vaulted coffered ceilings were favored. Like Greek temples, some were hypaethral. Temples that were entirely roofed had a large cove molding between the wall and ceiling, forming a **testudo** ceiling. (Testudo referred to the shape of the back of a tortoise with its curved edges.)

Three types of circular temples were constructed by the Romans. Monopteral temples (without cellae) were more common in Rome than in Greece with a single circular colonnade covered with a dome or a nearly flat conical roof on top of which was an ornament. The **peripteros** was similar to the monopteral temple except that it had a cella and was usually domed. The third type of circular temple had a circular domed cella, a projecting hexastyle or octastyle porch, and lacked a surrounding colonnade. The Pantheon is the most famous example of this type of temple (Figure 5.21). The Pantheon, like many circular buildings, had a large circular **oculus**, or opening in the apex of the roof, that provided the only light for the interior. (See Box 5.3.)

Box 5.3 SUMMARY OF ROMAN ARCHITECTURAL CHARACTERISTICS

- Emphasis on exceptionally large public buildings
- Engineering projects such as roads, bridges, aqueducts
- Widespread use of concrete
- Interior spaces more important than exteriors
- Much public and commemorative architecture
- Copying of Greek forms
- Use of façades and stucco to imitate more expensive materials
- Five orders of architecture
- Stacked orders featuring lower orders at the bottom and subsequent layers with higher orders
- Freestanding columns
- Pilastrades
- Extensive use of decorative Orders including engaged columns and pilasters
- Stacked arcades
- Arch orders
- Domes
- Circular structures

DOMESTIC ARCHITECTURE

Roman domestic buildings consisted of insulae, **domus**,[5] palaces, and villae. The percentage of Romans who owned a domus or single-family detached dwelling was exceedingly low. In fact, in the fourth century AD, only 1 in 25 residences in Rome was a domus, although it was very common in provincial cities for even the poor to live in detached dwellings. Villae were larger dwellings located in the suburbs and in rural areas.

Insulae The high cost of land within the city walls of Rome made it necessary for most people to live in insulae, which were much like modern apartments with shared walls. Shops were often located on the ground floor, which was frequently arcaded. Identical adobe brick or wood units were stacked up to six stories high around a central courtyard. After a disastrous fire in 64 AD, regulations limited the height of insulae to 60 Roman feet (58 feet) or 5 stories, and brick or concrete were required for at least part of the structure.

Domus Most of the information about the Roman domus has been provided by extant writings of Vitruvius and from excavated portions of Pompeii and Herculaneum, both of which were buried by an eruption of Mt. Vesuvius in 79 AD. From the street, the Roman domus was usually unobtrusive and sometimes not visible at all. A one- or two-story blank wall usually faced the street, although tabernae or smaller houses might be located at ground level with the domus behind. Roofs were hipped, angled on all sides, rather than having gables. Sometimes, there was a terrace or **solarium** on the roof where there was a garden, space for basking in the sun, or pools of water.

Large homes had a **vestibulum** or raised area outside the entrance. Often, it was surrounded on three sides by the house or was simply a passage between shops. In the mornings, visitors assembled there to await entrance. Elaborate vestibules were adorned with colonnades, flower gardens, statues, and spoils of war. Inside the entrance was a passageway, or **ostium**, that led to the atrium where visitors were received. Behind the impluvium was the lararium dedicated to the household gods and at one side was the kitchen. (See Figures 5.22 and 5.23.)

The nuptial bed, or **lectus adversus**, was located opposite the entry to the atrium, although during later periods, it was moved elsewhere. In all likelihood, this arrangement continued to be used by all but the wealthiest families. Over time, the atrium in wealthy homes evolved into the main reception area where visitors were received and family activities were moved to the peristylium. Because it was the most important room, the atrium was splendidly decorated with paintings and sculpture and mosaics covered the floor. (See Figure 5.24.)

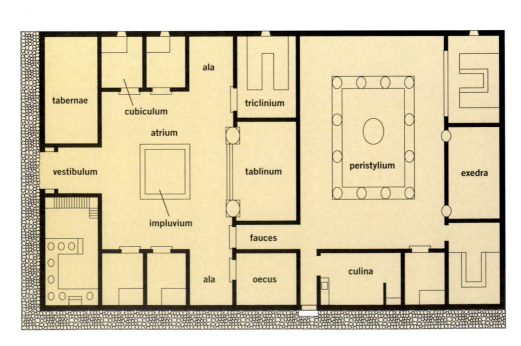

FIGURE 5.22 The arrangement of some rooms was fairly standard, although room size and opulence depended on wealth. The vestibulum, atrium, alae, tablinum, fauces, and peristylium were almost always the same in relation to one another and to the entrance. Other rooms were arranged in a less formal fashion and might be omitted. Rooms used in the winter were generally arranged where they would get the most direct sun.

FIGURE 5.23 In early Roman houses, the atrium served as the main living area where work such as spinning and weaving was done; here, guests were received, and the dead were laid out before burial. The atrium was usually open to the sky, with the roofs of surrounding rooms sloping toward a compluvium and associated impluvium.

According to Vitruvius, five kinds of atria were used in Roman houses.

- In the atrium tuscanicum, which was adopted from the Etruscans, the roof was supported by two beams with two shorter beams at right angles to form the compluvium in the middle. Due to the length of available timbers, this type of atrium was only found in smaller domus.

- The **atrium tetrastylum** was similar but columns supported the beams at the corners of the compluvium.
- The **atrium corinthium** had more than four columns around the impluvium.
- A house with an **atrium displuviatum** had the roof sloping away from the atrium so that rain water drained toward the exterior where it was carried away by gutters.

FIGURE 5.24 A centrally located marble table, the curtibulum eventually replaced and represented the hearth in the atrium. Here, the curtibulum is located adjacent to the impluvium as would have been typical.

• The **atrium testudinatum** was completely roofed with a testudo ceiling or vault.

Rooms were arranged around the atrium as far back as the hearth, although the back of the atrium was left open on both sides for the alae, which might be reduced to niches that housed the death masks and busts of ancestors. The doorways of rooms around the atrium opened onto it and provided the only natural light.

The dining room for formal occasions was the **triclinium**. Winter triclinia were inside the house, while those used during the summer might be located on upper stories, where breezes could be better caught or in an outside area. Couches were arranged around three sides of a large square, circular, or oval table, leaving the fourth side free for serving. Three people reclined on each rectangular couch or **lectus triclinaris** with their heads toward the table for a total of nine diners on the three couches around the table. Strict rules of etiquette dictated each person's place. When round or oval tables were used, a crescent-shaped or semicircular couch called a **sigma** might be used although it accommodated fewer than nine guests. Some triclinia were sufficiently large to have several dining tables.

Often considered part of the atrium was the **tablinum** located at the end of the atrium opposite the entry. The tablinum contained family records, served as a home office, and housed the portraits of the ancestors. The early Roman domus ended at the tablinum, so extra rooms around the atrium served as **cubicula**, or bedrooms. (See Figure 5.25.)

As the domus became larger, private rooms were moved to a second courtyard, surrounded by a colonnade or **peristylium**, behind the tablinum. The passageway leading from the back of the atrium beside the tablinum was the **fauces** and led to the peristylium. When the atrium became a reception room for visitors, the kitchen or **culina** was moved to the peristyle court opposite the tablinum. Because cooking utensils and food were under the protection of the Lares, the culina was decorated with paintings of those domestic gods.

Other rooms in the Roman domus might include exedrae, oeci, pinacotheca, bibliotheca, and cenacula. Walled gardens, balnea, latrines, and stables were part of the house although there was no established pattern for the arrangement of these areas.

FIGURE 5.25 The small cubicula were also moved to the peristyle court for privacy, and separate rooms were assigned for use during the day (located in the coolest area of the peristylium) and night (situated to receive morning sun).

• Exedrae with permanent seats, like those of the Greeks, were usually curved niches or projecting rooms that opened onto the courtyard.

• **Oeci** were reception rooms that sometimes served as triclinia and that were designed in a manner similar to atria but without a compluvium or impluvium. Columns supported the roof or upper stories, allowing oeci to be very large in size. Like the atrium, there were several types. The **oecus tetrastylos** had only four columns supporting the roof. The **oecus Corinthius** had a vaulted roof supported by a colonnade. The **oecus Aegyptus** or Egyptian hall had an internal peristyle which supported a second story walkway around which were windows through which light could enter. The side of the walkway had a shorter peristyle—about three-quarters the height of the peristyle below. An **oecus Cyzicenus** was a room that opened onto a garden or particularly nice view of the countryside and usually faced north for summer use. Folding doors closed the room when it was cold or not in use.

- The **pinacotheca** was used by the wealthy beginning in the Republican period for the display of pictures and sculptures.
- A **bibliotheca** or library was an indication of the education of the owner. Large numbers of books (scrolls) were kept in cylindrical boxes and cabinets. Statues of the Muses and Minerva ornamented the room.
- The informal family dining room or **cenaculum** was frequently located in a second-story room when there were two stories. Later, that term was used for all rooms above the ground floor.

Heights of ground floor rooms varied. Some ceilings reached the roof, and others might have a room above them with windows opening onto the internal courtyard or sometimes on exterior walls. Because ceiling height varied, second-story rooms were often disconnected, requiring separate stairways.

Palaces Palaces differed from the domus in size, shape, and ornamentation. Nero's Golden House, Domus Aureus, had an octagonal triclinium with a domed ceiling, beginning the trend for room shapes other than rectangular. Up to four stories in height, the palace was more complicated than the domus. Public and private spaces were separated on different levels, and even individual living quarters or apartments might have rooms on different levels.

Villae Villae were common throughout the Roman provinces with two major types: the villa rustica and the villa urbana. In the provinces, villae were often owned by members of the local population, although the layout was typically Roman. Both types of villae were surrounded by walls, were entered through a gateway, and had a water supply in a courtyard. The **villa rustica** was a rural villa designed for farming and included farm-related storage rooms, granaries, and stalls for animals.

The **villa urbana** was a residence for the owner located either in the suburbs or in the country and could be combined with the villa rustica. When this was the case, the domestic buildings were usually arranged in a different part of the complex. The villa urbana differed from an urban domus in that in the country, the peristyle court was closest to the door, while the

atrium was either behind the peristyle court or omitted altogether.

Unlike the urban domus, the villa looked outward, taking advantage of the surroundings. Rooms were variously shaped and often protruded from the structure. The triclinium had external windows or doors that looked out onto the surrounding countryside. The main bedroom often projected from the rest of the structure in either an elliptical or semicircular curve, with windows to catch light throughout the day. Colonnades on the outside of the villa connected living areas to a garden or **xystus**, which might also be surrounded by porticoes. The balneum associated with the villa urbana was often as luxurious as private baths in town. Libraries, collections of art and sculpture, fish ponds, aviaries, and other features were found in the most luxurious villae during the Imperial periods.

OPENINGS

Openings were treated architecturally, often with pilasters or carved marble bands at the sides surmounted by an architrave or complete entablature with or without a pediment above it. When columns or pilasters were used, the term **aedicule** applies to the treatment. When the entablature extends beyond the pilasters or columns framing the opening, the extensions are known as **ears**.

INFLUENCE 5.24

Renaissance and Neoclassic buildings often incorporated aediculated openings including those with ears.

The main entrance to a Roman building was through a door that swung on pivots with sockets located in the stone lintel and threshold. Only a few interior doors were used, as most Romans preferred draperies to close rooms. Doors were wooden, although those on public buildings were frequently made of bronze and sometimes gilded. Interior doorways were often aligned framing an extensive view within the structure. Such an alignment was known as **enfilade**.

INFLUENCE 5.25

During the Renaissance, doors were aligned enfilades, allowing an interior view from one end of a building to another.

CHINESE STRUCTURAL FORMS

In 1103, the publication *Yingzao fashi* (Building Method) established the correct methods of building construction and codified Chinese standards for structure and decoration. One principle stated that buildings had to be constructed of mortise-and-tenon joints so that they would move rather than collapse during an earthquake.

Traditional Chinese buildings are composed of distinct elements. There was no elaborate or deep foundation needed for the lightweight wooden buildings of the Chinese, but they were constructed on a raised podium, or base, composed of packed earth for humble structures and for grander buildings, faced with brick or stone. Height of the podium varied according to the importance of the building. In northern areas, raising the house above the ground not only provided a better view but prevented snow from building up next to the wooden framing members or adobe walls and causing deterioration.

Circular timber columns were placed on top of the podium on stone or bronze bases known as **chih**. It was these columns that supported the weight of the structure, making it unnecessary for wall filler to be load-bearing. Columns were sometimes straight but were often given entasis on the upper third of the shaft resulting in a shuttle-shaped form. Height of columns gradually increased from the center to the corners of the building creating a slight downward curve in the center. The differences in height were so slight as to be almost imperceptible. Chinese builders also inclined the columns slightly inward approximately one percent to improve the apparent stability of the structure. Notches in the tops of the columns provided a base for beams that ran the length of the building and connected columns at the top. On each of the columns, a board or capital, known as **lu-tou**, was placed over the beam in the notch. Across the width of the building, columns were held in place by beams of diminishing length. This type of roof can easily be expanded in both length and width. In addition, because mortise-and-tenon joints hold the beams together, the roof can move when stressed as during an earthquake.

Exterior walls were often curtain walls, or walls that bore no weight but their own. Support for the roof was provided by embedded posts. In some cases, curtain walls did not reach the roof so that the decorative brackets would be visible.

Roofs have low pitches but often curve toward the ridge as they rise to become slightly steeper. The quintessential curved Chinese roof, is known as the **chü-che**. Purlins, or the boards running horizontally between the rafters, were gradually "depressed." To accomplish this, a line was drawn from the ridge to the purlin at the eave, and then the first purlin up from the eave was lowered one-tenth the total rise of the roof. A line was then drawn from the first purlin to the ridge and the position of the second purlin was lowered one-twentieth of the rise. Each time the process was repeated, the depression of the next purlin was decreased by half. A tile ridge outlines not only the ridge, but the edges of the roof. A feature of most Chinese roofs was the large overhang. Some of the overhangs were cantilevered beyond the eave line, but most used a series of brackets to carry the rafters beyond the columns. There is at least one example—the temple of Fo-kuang (857)—where the eaves projected 14 feet beyond the columns. The cluster of brackets known as **dougong** or **tou-kung** appeared during the Chou Dynasty and forms a space between the top of supporting columns and cross beams that

FIGURE 6.8 Brackets were set on the lu-tou. Four sets of brackets at right angles to one another were typical although more or fewer were not unknown. Brackets were also used to support the middle of the span and were used beneath purlins.

support the roof. (See Figure 6.8.) The bracket sets were used to transfer the load across to the column and then to the ground. Tou-kung were located at the tops of columns and could also be placed at corners and between columns. There are several kinds of tou, or blocks, and kung, or arms. The type used was determined by their location and their purpose. The **lu-tou** was the block located at the bottom of the bracket set and bore the major load. **Hua-kung** were extensions at right angles to the wall that formed cantilevers both in front of and behind the block. Up to five successive tiers of hua-kung, known as **t'iao** or "jumps," could be used. Transverse kung may intersect the hua-kung.

Roofing boards were fixed (sometimes tied) to the rafters and covered with clay for insulation. Tiles finished the roof. In the northern areas, tiles were typically left in their natural gray color. In the south, blue, green, yellow, or purple glaze was fired on the tiles. In some areas parapet walls were finished with tiles at the ends. Roof ridges often had an odd number of mythical creatures arranged along them or at their ends, with the number indicating status. (Nine was for royalty.) The **chiwen** was a mythical bird that was supposed to be able to douse flames with water and was frequently used to protect buildings against fire.

CHINESE PLANS: THE FOUR BASIC ELEMENTS

Four basic elements were used in planning everything from humble individual homes to vast cities. Even temples, tombs, and palaces were laid out in the same manner. The four elements were the courtyard, walled enclosures, north-south orientation, and axiality.

Buildings were constructed on one or more sides of a courtyard, which was an important component of a home. The wall surrounding the courtyard separated the individual dwelling from the hustle and bustle outside it and provided a place for contemplation and peace. Courtyards often housed a garden with water, rocks, bridges, crooked paths, pavilions, and gates—all of which was lit by hanging lanterns. Unlike buildings, which were typically symmetrical and formal, gardens were curvilinear, asymmetrical, and symbolic. The opening leading to a garden was often shaped to frame a view. (See Figure 6.10.)

The shape of buildings within the compound was somewhat limited by the roof structure to a

FIGURE 6.9 Upturned roofs were more typical in southern areas than in the north, where heavier timbers had to be used to support the weight of snow.

FIGURE 6.10 Elaborate gardens were part of the courtyards in elaborate structures. Footbridges, pavilions, and gates were important components of even the small garden.

AFTER THE FALL OF ROME

North Sea

Ba

• Durham

YORKSHIRE REGION

■ Hardwick Hall

ENGLAND

■ Windsor Castle

Salisbury
Pevensey

THE NETHERLANDS

GERMANY

FLANDERS
• Ypres

• Cologne
Aachen

• Fulda

BELGIUM

• Mainz

• Trier

*Atlantic
Ocean*

■ Mont St. Michele   • Paris

ANJOU REGION

FRANCE

St. Gall •

SWITZERLAND

• Munich

■ Neuschwanstein Castle

Ottoma

LOMBARDY

• Milan

• Venice

• Santiago de Compostela

GALICIA

ASTURIA

• Ravenna

Puente la Reina •

Pisa •

TUSCANY

Siena •

• Assisi

*Adriatic
Sea*

SPAIN

PORTUGAL

• Belém

• Madrid

• Rome

ITALY

• Seville

• Granada

*Tyrrhenian
Sea*

Mediterranean Sea

SICILY

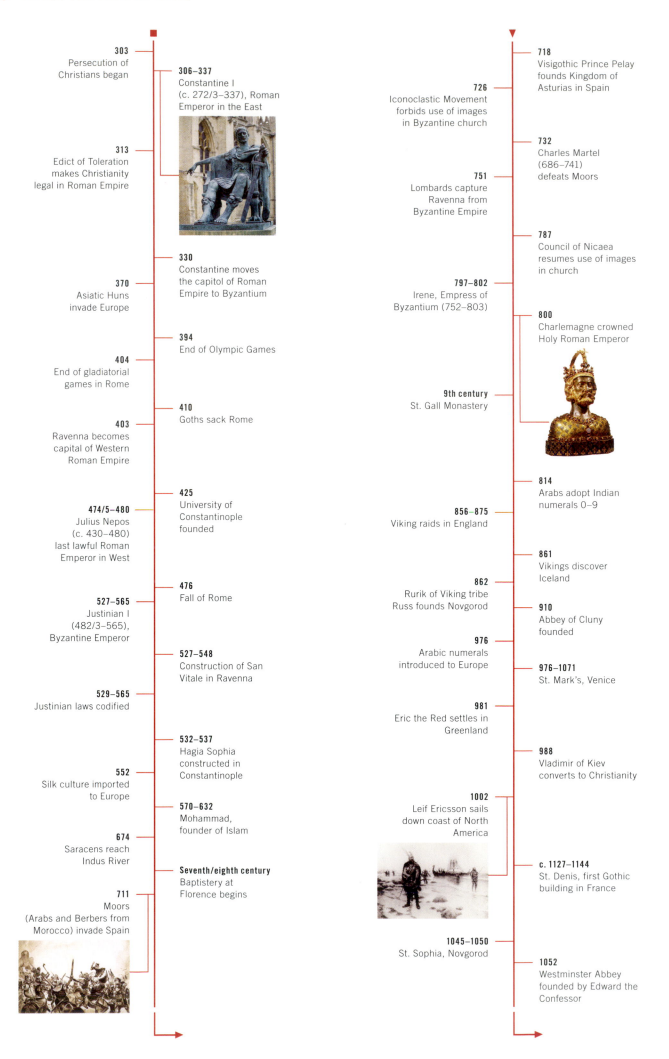

303
Persecution of
Christians began

306–337
Constantine I
(c. 272/3–337), Roman
Emperor in the East

313
Edict of Toleration
makes Christianity
legal in Roman Empire

330
Constantine moves
the capitol of Roman
Empire to Byzantium

370
Asiatic Huns
invade Europe

394
End of Olympic Games

404
End of gladiatorial
games in Rome

410
Goths sack Rome

403
Ravenna becomes
capital of Western
Roman Empire

425
University of
Constantinople
founded

474/5–480
Julius Nepos
(c. 430–480)
last lawful Roman
Emperor in West

476
Fall of Rome

527–565
Justinian I
(482/3–565),
Byzantine Emperor

527–548
Construction of San
Vitale in Ravenna

529–565
Justinian laws codified

532–537
Hagia Sophia
constructed in
Constantinople

552
Silk culture imported
to Europe

570–632
Mohammad,
founder of Islam

674
Saracens reach
Indus River

Seventh/eighth century
Baptistery at
Florence begins

711
Moors
(Arabs and Berbers from
Morocco) invade Spain

718
Visigothic Prince Pelay
founds Kingdom of
Asturias in Spain

726
Iconoclastic Movement
forbids use of images
in Byzantine church

732
Charles Martel
(686–741)
defeats Moors

751
Lombards capture
Ravenna from
Byzantine Empire

787
Council of Nicaea
resumes use of images
in church

797–802
Irene, Empress of
Byzantium (752–803)

800
Charlemagne crowned
Holy Roman Emperor

9th century
St. Gall Monastery

814
Arabs adopt Indian
numerals 0–9

856–875
Viking raids in England

861
Vikings discover
Iceland

862
Rurik of Viking tribe
Russ founds Novgorod

910
Abbey of Cluny
founded

976
Arabic numerals
introduced to Europe

976–1071
St. Mark's, Venice

981
Eric the Red settles in
Greenland

988
Vladimir of Kiev
converts to Christianity

1002
Leif Ericsson sails
down coast of North
America

c. 1127–1144
St. Denis, first Gothic
building in France

1045–1050
St. Sophia, Novgorod

1052
Westminster Abbey
founded by Edward the
Confessor

1063
Abbaye-aux-Dames,
Caen, France begun

1064
St. Etienne (Abbaye-
Aux-Hommes), Caen,
France begun

1066
Norman Conquest of
England

1066–1200
Norman architecture
in England

1093–1175
Durham Cathedral

1096
First Crusade

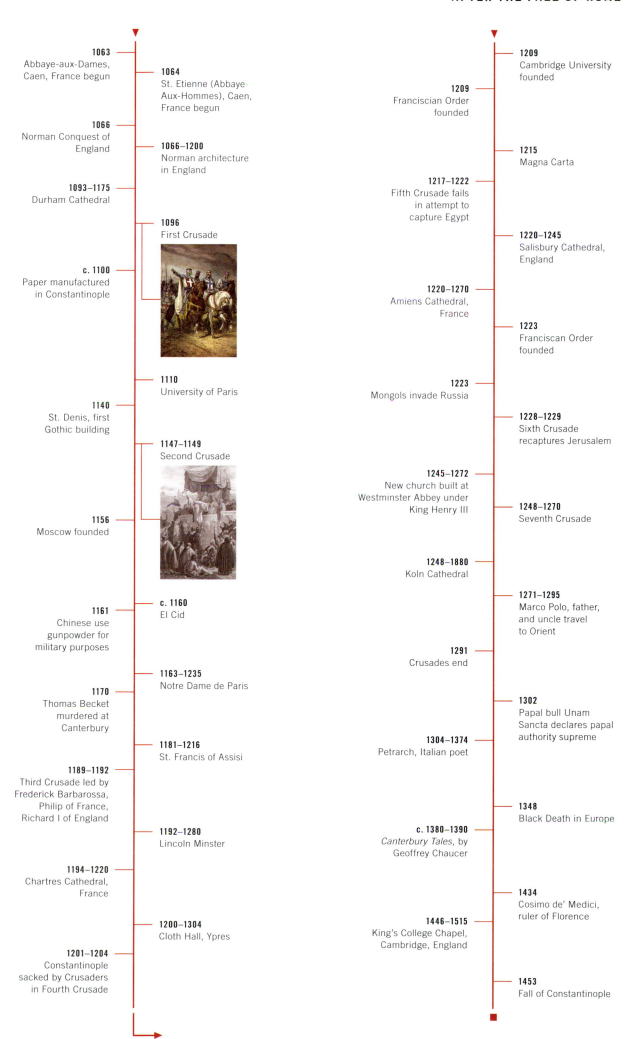

c. 1100
Paper manufactured
in Constantinople

1110
University of Paris

1140
St. Denis, first
Gothic building

1147–1149
Second Crusade

1156
Moscow founded

1161
Chinese use
gunpowder for
military purposes

c. 1160
El Cid

1163–1235
Notre Dame de Paris

1170
Thomas Becket
murdered at
Canterbury

1181–1216
St. Francis of Assisi

1189–1192
Third Crusade led by
Frederick Barbarossa,
Philip of France,
Richard I of England

1192–1280
Lincoln Minster

1194–1220
Chartres Cathedral,
France

1200–1304
Cloth Hall, Ypres

1201–1204
Constantinople
sacked by Crusaders
in Fourth Crusade

1209
Cambridge University
founded

1209
Franciscian Order
founded

1215
Magna Carta

1217–1222
Fifth Crusade fails
in attempt to
capture Egypt

1220–1245
Salisbury Cathedral,
England

1220–1270
Amiens Cathedral,
France

1223
Franciscan Order
founded

1223
Mongols invade Russia

1228–1229
Sixth Crusade
recaptures Jerusalem

1245–1272
New church built at
Westminster Abbey under
King Henry III

1248–1270
Seventh Crusade

1248–1880
Koln Cathedral

1271–1295
Marco Polo, father,
and uncle travel
to Orient

1291
Crusades end

1302
Papal bull Unam
Sancta declares papal
authority supreme

1304–1374
Petrarch, Italian poet

1348
Black Death in Europe

c. 1380–1390
Canterbury Tales, by
Geoffrey Chaucer

1434
Cosimo de' Medici,
ruler of Florence

1446–1515
King's College Chapel,
Cambridge, England

1453
Fall of Constantinople

of a governor. In 395 when Emperor Theodosius I died, the empire was permanently divided with one ruler in the West, usually in Rome, and the other in Constantinople. Germanic tribes finally took Rome itself in 476.

The fall of Rome began the Dark Ages in Western Europe during which religion was the primary focus. The invaders were evidently awed by the Christian religion and usually refrained from destroying buildings associated with it. The realization that treasures would be safe resulted in the transfer of valuables to church coffers, helping to establish the wealth of the Church.

Early Christian Architecture

At first, there was little perceived need for new buildings in which members of the new Christian religion could meet. They continued to meet in existing synagogues or in rooms in members' homes, some of which were decorated with painted motifs. Early Christians believed in the imminent return of Christ; as that expectation receded, as larger numbers of converts joined in worship services, and as the differences between Judaism and Christianity made the synagogue an unsuitable gathering space, it became apparent that suitable buildings were needed. The greatest requirement was for a worship space sizeable enough for large numbers of people. By the third century, existing buildings were being adapted and a few new churches were constructed. This was being done discreetly as the sporadic persecution had not yet ceased. After the Edict of Milan legalized Christianity and Constantine espoused its tenets, buildings became more sumptuous. Eventually additional structures were built for baptism, while others were set up to serve as memorials of events or people. Clearly, Christian architecture did not

begin suddenly after the Edict of Milan, nor did Christian forms replace older Roman building types. Large-scale secular buildings continued to be constructed on Roman models.

BASILICAN CHURCHES

Roman temples were unsuitable for reuse or even as models for Christian churches. Besides the fact that Roman temples had pagan connotations, they were not designed to house worshippers. Christian ritual required not only a space for group worship but for participation in the Eucharist, a ceremony reserved for initiates.

The Roman basilica served as an audience chamber in imperial palaces as well as a public meeting place and had no pagan associations. Only a few changes were necessary to the basilica for it to be suitable for Christian worship. Original examples were long rectangular halls, often with aisles flanking the central **nave** and separated from it by colonnades. The Roman model typically had the entrance on the long side with the tribunal facing it. When adapted for a Christian church, the entrance was moved to one end with the tribunal and its rounded **apse** opposite it. In Roman basilicas, a raised dais served as the platform for the throne or the seat of the magistrate; in the Christian church, this became the location of the bishop's throne. The tiered seats arrayed around the semicircle of the apse used by the Romans for participants in the judicial process were now used for the clergy. In Early Christian churches, the apse was often at the west end. The church nave was usually visually terminated by a triumphal arch or screen, known as a **templon**, located in front of the apse to separate it from the sanctuary reserved for the clergy. A large central opening was flanked by two smaller ones and led to the sanctuary. The highly decorated altar was located within the sanctuary and studded with jewels, gilded, and covered with a **ciborium**, or baldachin. (See Figure 7.2.)

As in Roman basilicas, galleries were often incorporated above the side aisles, and it was to this area that women were often relegated. As in Roman examples, nave walls were higher than the aisles, and clerestory windows allowed light into the building. Christian church builders often substituted an arcade for the Roman colonnade that separated the nave from the aisles. Because the new structures regularly reused components of older Roman buildings, the entablature was

FIGURE 7.2 Plan of a Christian Basilica

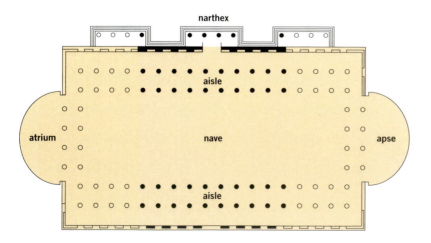

often omitted above the columns, and the columns themselves did not necessarily match. Most typically, the timber roof of the Roman basilica was retained, although there is evidence that some Christian basilicas had coffered ceilings.

A **narthex**, or vestibule, was added across the entry end of the basilica for the Catechumens, or individuals who were interested in the religion but had not yet been baptized and who were not allowed to enter the church itself to participate in the services. Sometimes an **exonarthex** was added on the exterior of the narthex. This open Roman portico spanned the width of the building and was sometimes flanked by towers. Beyond the exonarthex was the atrium that frequently included a fountain that was surrounded by porticoes. It was to the atrium or exonarthex that Catechumens retired while members participated in the Eucharist.

INFLUENCE 7.1

During the Romanesque and Gothic periods, towers often flanked the narthex itself, an obvious evolution of the towers beside the exonarthex.

The basilica plan was used for the first major Christian churches in Rome. Of those, St. Peter's, begun by Constantine in 330 and built over the tomb of Peter, was the most important. Two fifth-century basilican churches remain in Rome: Santa Sabina and Santa Maria Maggiore.

INFLUENCE 7.2

The basilican form continued to evolve and formed the basis for the Romanesque and Gothic churches that were to follow in Western Europe.

A development that was to have a strong influence on subsequent Western churches was the addition of a **transept**, or crossing between the apse and the nave that extended from both sides. This gave the plan itself a cross form—of great significance to the Christian religion.

The Roman basilica form was also used for covered cemeteries. Freestanding mausolea were built along the sides, and burial beneath the floor was also common. The aisles in these separate centrally-planned buildings became an **ambulatory**, or continuous walkway, around the sides of the building.

INFLUENCE 7.3

Medieval and Renaissance churches provided burial for some individuals beneath the floors, and crypts became common in churches' undercrofts for this purpose. During the Italian Renaissance, although most burials were moved to cemeteries, covered porticoes often surrounded these with additional burials beneath their floors.

CENTRALLY PLANNED BUILDINGS

In addition to the basilica, three new centrally planned building types emerged: the mausoleum, the **martyrium**, and the baptistery. Martyria and mausolea were both memorial structures. The baptistery was designed specifically for the ritual of baptism practiced by Christians. Centrally planned buildings could be circular, polygonal, or in the form of a Greek cross, having four short equal-length arms radiating from a central space. Such centrally planned buildings lent themselves to domed ceilings, although this was more typical in the Eastern Roman Empire. Typically, the interior dome was covered on the exterior with a square projecting second story with a hip roof.

Christians continued the practices of the common Roman people and were buried in catacombs. Land was expensive, but the soft rock beneath the surface was easy to tunnel through. Roman cemeteries already had buildings at which people met for commemorative meals, a practice Christians continued to follow. A few early Christians, however, followed the practice of wealthy Romans and were buried in mausolea. Typically the only difference between pagan Roman and Christian mausolea was in the subject matter of the decoration used. Santa Costanza in Rome (350), the mausoleum constructed by Constantine for his daughter, was a circular domed structure with a large ambulatory. There, the interior was covered with mosaics culminating in the dome of heaven. (See Figure 7.3.)

An extensive cult of martyrs developed early in Church history. Martyria, often as separate buildings, were constructed to commemorate an event such as the birth of Christ, as in the Church of the Nativity in Bethlehem, or to memorialize the dead. Often, the difference between a mausoleum and a martyrium was the number of people who could be expected to visit. Martyria became hallowed pilgrimage sites, and depending on the popularity of the martyr, it was sometimes neces-

FIGURE 7.3 Theodoric's mausoleum was a sixth-century decagon. The dome is made of a single stone from which 12 projections sculptured around the perimeter provided a means of sliding the massive stone into place. On the front of each projection is the name of an evangelist or an apostle. Inside, the building is in the form of a Greek cross.

sary to provide an ambulatory around the point of central focus to accommodate the devout.

The baptism practiced in the Church was looked upon as the death of an old sinful life and the beginning of a new one. The rite required a sufficiently large pool of water for immersion around which was sufficient space for clergy and onlookers. At first, the ceremony was carried out in Roman baths, but gradually, separate buildings were designed specifically for the rite. Most examples were centrally planned structures. The octagonal form was most common, reminding participants that the world began on the eighth day of creation just as initiates were regenerated and began anew. Here also, an ambulatory frequently surrounded the central area. When there was a dome above the central area, it was usually decorated with a fresco or mosaic representing Christ's baptism. (See Box 7.1.)

Christianity continued to grow in the West with a pope elected to oversee it. In eastern parts

of the empire, centered in Constantinople, the church also developed but somewhat differently. The differences between the western and eastern churches were to eventually become so great that the two entities separated.

The Byzantine Empire

In the seventh century BC when cities were overcrowded and food was not available in sufficient quantities to feed the population, some Greeks searched for new homes in more fertile lands and immigrated to areas around the Black Sea. Access to the Black Sea was through the Bosporus strait. Greeks from Megara, under the leadership of Byzas, consulted the oracle at Delphi in 657 BC for advice about where to seek lands. The words of the oracle indicated they should find a new home opposite the city of the blind. As there was no "city of the blind," the colonists set out toward the Black Sea. As they navigated through the Bosporus strait, they realized that a city located on its shores could control trade between the Black and the Aegean Sea and become wealthy in the process. At the southern tip of the Bosporus on the Asia Minor side, there was a city along the shore, Chalcedon, with good harbor facilities. Across from Chalcedon, the river broadened forming a large excellent harbor that could be easily defended. Near the potential harbor was a promontory of land surrounded on three sides by water. The colonists realized Chalcedon was the city of the blind, for who else would have selected the less defensible position of their city rather than the almost impregnable site just a few miles away. The new

BOX 7.1 CHARACTERISTICS OF EARLY CHRISTIAN ARCHITECTURE

- Centrally planned buildings
- Separate baptisteries
- Adaptation of Roman basilica form for churches
- Separation of interior of churches into nave and flanking aisles
- Clerestory
- Entrance of church opposite apse
- Towers flanking exonarthex
- Internal domes over crossing covered on exterior with square tower
- Ambulatory around some buildings

city established by the colonists was Byzantium. This Greek city prospered, although it did not become exceptionally large.

When Constantine became emperor, Rome was still largely a pagan city and was in constant danger of attack. Rome's most dangerous enemies were in the East, and when Constantine decided to move the capital of the Roman Empire, he also saw the potential of Byzantium and selected it. Within 100 years, the population of the city surpassed that of Athens.

In 330, after four years of building, Constantine dedicated the city as the capital of the Roman Empire. Although Constantine called the city New Rome, it later became known as Constantine's city—Constantinople (now Istanbul). The Eastern Roman Empire, later known as the Byzantine Empire, not only remained intact after the fall of the Western Roman Empire but thrived, held off eastern invaders for another 1,000 years, and retained the culture of classical civilizations while Western Europe was seeped in the Dark Ages.

BYZANTINE HISTORY

Some historians date the beginning of the Byzantine Empire to the reign of Justinian (482/483–565; reign from 527), some to Heraclius (610–641). Justinian had previously been a civil servant, rather than a soldier as other emperors had been, and was not only Emperor but also the head of the Orthodox Church. It was under Justinian that Roman laws were codified, laws that still continue to influence the West. Thanks to the military genius of his general, Belisarius, Justinian regained parts of Italy, North Africa, and Spain and established frontier posts as far as the Danube, expanding the empire to its greatest size. Much of the regained territory, however, was lost less than a century after the death of Mohammed (632) when Islamic armies composed of Arabs (Saracens) controlled Syria, Egypt, and North Africa, parts of Spain, and Persia and had reached the outskirts of Constantinople twice.

During the reign of Heraclius, Greek replaced Latin as the official language, and there was great social restructuring, including an attempt at a semi-feudal system, as the emperor reversed the ruined financial situation of the empire. Heraclius allowed Huns to settle in parts of the Balkans to protect that border while he concentrated on the Persian threat. Concerns about the West-

ern Empire faded as Byzantine emperors became increasingly apprehensive about holding on to the territory nearest to their capital city. The Italian cities of Venice and Ravenna retained close ties with the Byzantine Empire and it was through these cities that much of the trade from the Eastern Empire flowed into Western Europe.

Saracen forces raided Byzantine territories beginning in the eighth century, and in 1095, the Byzantine Emperor Alexius I Comnenus sought help from fellow Christians in the West. As a result, Crusaders trekked through the Byzantine Empire in an effort to save Christian sites in the Holy Land from the infidels. Unfortunately, the Venetians jealously looked to Constantinople as a rival for the lucrative trade with the East, and in 1204, during the Fourth Crusade, they were able to convince Crusaders to attack the Byzantine city with the promise that it would be turned over to Venice. The Crusaders kept only half the bargain—they took and looted the city but established the Latin Empire rather than give the city to the Venetians. In 1261, the Byzantine Emperor retook the city although there was little of the Empire left; only Greece, the Aegean islands, and the city of Constantinople remained.

As the power of the Saracens declined, the Byzantine Empire was threatened by another group. Asiatic Seljuk Turks had subdued the Saracens but in the process embraced the Islamic religion. By the fourteenth century, the Turks had won control of the lands around Constantinople, encircling the city they were unable to conquer. The city's defenses had included doubled stone walls with many defensive towers and Greek fire that reportedly burned on water, making it dangerous to approach the city by sea. In 1453, however, Sultan Mohammed II employed the Chinese technology of gunpowder in cannons and captured Constantinople, made it the capital of the Ottoman Empire, and renamed the city Istanbul. Churches became mosques or were destroyed, trade between the Orient and the West was cut off, and Turkish culture dominated.

Byzantine culture did not cease with the Empire. During its long history, Byzantine traders, envoys, and emigrants had exported classical culture to Slavic areas including Russia. These areas not only adopted the culture but the religion, some social organization, and writing. Russian leaders even claimed they had inherited the fallen empire. Byzantine culture, however, was not only influential in those groups around the Black Sea but with their conquerors. Neither the Saracens nor the Turks had an architectural heritage, and they adapted forms from those they conquered, resulting in a mixture of Persian and Byzantine design. In addition, the Turks had little administrative skill and retained Greek administrators who carried on as before.

Having saved classical culture, writings, philosophies, and ideas for a thousand years, when Turkish armies began to surround their capital city, some Byzantine citizens fled to the West, passing on art and architecture, the Oriental idea of absolute monarchy, culture and manners, and conveniences such as the fork. Theophanu (960–991), the Greek wife of the Byzantine Emperor Otto II (955–983), introduced the fork in Byzantium before 1000. In the eleventh century, a Greek princess introduced forks to the West when she used them at her wedding to the Venetian Doge, Domenico Selvo. Unfortunately, she died soon afterward, and her death was seen as a punishment for using such an instrument. It was used in Italy thereafter, however; from there it appeared in France in the fourteenth century, and was introduced to the English in 1611 by Thomas Coryat (c. 1577–1617) through his book *Coryat's Curdities*. Forks of the period had two straight tines and were often called split spoons. At first the fork was seen as effeminate and the Church disapproved of its use, considering it an insult to God, who had provided fingers for eating.

SOCIAL CLIMATE OF THE BYZANTINE EMPIRE

From the beginning, Constantinople was populated with members of diverse races and cultures, resulting in a mixture of social influences. Roman laws were retained as was their organization, but many of the artisans were Oriental, so Roman forms were fused with the opulent decoration of the Orient.

The diversity of the Byzantine Empire required a strong leader who could demand loyalty to both the church and the state. By the time of Justinian, emperors were crowned in a religious ceremony by the Patriarch of Constantinople, the head of the Eastern Church and the second most powerful individual in the empire. The fact that the patriarch participated in the coronation was a declaration that the emperor was chosen by God, essentially launching the divine right of kings. Following Oriental customs, the Byzantine state was authoritarian with the emperor ruling absolutely, but the people always retained certain freedoms. Although there were at times female rulers, women, for the most part, stayed in the home.

Many Byzantine citizens were intellectuals. Education included examination of the classical writings of Plato, Aristotle, and Homer, which at the time were unknown in the West. Even women were educated by tutors, although at home.

The hippodrome, the Greek equivalent of the Roman circus, was the center of social life and housed horse and chariot races, provided a place for the execution of martyrs or crowning of emperors, and served as a venue for triumphal processions. Like the Romans, Byzantines continued to bathe at public baths, although bathing more than twice a day was frowned upon. Aqueducts brought water to the city, where it was stored in large cisterns, distributed through numerous fountains, and drainage systems carried sewage to the sea. (See Figure 7.4.) Medical care was provided either by the church or the government.

RELIGION

In 325, Constantine called the Council at Nicaea to discuss differences in doctrine between the Roman and Byzantine churches, which had continued to develop dissimilarly. The prominent role Constantine played in this council later led to the advantageous position of the emperor of the Eastern Empire over the Orthodox Church. At the Council, the Eastern and Western Churches were unable to resolve their differences concerning the nature of Christ, the first in a long line of arguments that resulted in the separation of the Church into the western Roman Catholic Church and the Eastern Orthodox Church.

During the seventh and eighth centuries, Islamic forces laid siege to Constantinople. Although they were driven away by the Byzantine navy, influences of their religion lingered. In the eighth century, the Byzantine Empire lost much of its territory and there was a major volcanic eruption on Thera. Influenced by Islamic prohibitions against images, Emperor Leo III the Isaurian, without consulting the church, determined that these events were a sign of God's wrath because the Orthodox Church was encouraging idolatry through the use of sacred images. The ensuing Iconoclastic Controversy (730–787

FIGURE 7.4 This cistern supplied by an aqueduct in Istanbul is known as the Cistern of 1001 Columns although there are actually only 336 of them. The columns were reused Roman examples.

and again 813–842) forbade the use of figural representations of Christ, the Virgin Mary, and the saints. Many mosaics and paintings were destroyed and replaced with geometric forms, crosses, and foliage.

Although little is known for certain about the Orthodox liturgy of the period, the centrally planned church has retained its usefulness and the current liturgy and the structures mesh. Worship services in the Orthodox religion differ significantly from those of the Roman Catholic Church. The central space is reserved for use by the clergy, who enter along the main passageway in a procession, a practice known to be part of the original Orthodox ritual. Only the clergy participate in the Eucharist while hidden from view of the worshippers. This practice helped to retain the mystery associated with the Orthodox religion. It is known that after the Mass, the patriarch exchanged the Kiss of Peace with the Emperor in public view. The worshippers viewed the proceedings most likely from the aisles. Seating was not provided, nor was instrumental music allowed.

In Western Europe, cities vied one another for the highest or largest cathedral; this was unnecessary in Byzantine because the Orthodox Church believed the purpose of the building and its decoration was to glorify the divine being rather than to impress mere mortals.

The monastery is a Byzantine innovation based on the idea of the monk cell that was first developed in Egypt. The name indicates that the first examples were for those living alone. Over a period of centuries, however, monks formed communities although their purpose was the same—to live shut away from the world seeking spiritual communion with God. By 529 Benedict of Norcia had formulated rules of monastic life at Monte Cassino in Italy. Days were filled with prayer and work with meal times and rest periods dictated. These rules were later adopted by a number of monasteries.

It was from the Byzantine church that missionaries were sent to Christianize pagan lands and establish additional monasteries. The system spread into Western Europe and was adopted by the Roman Catholic Church. Although much of the work of the monastery involved the production of food, an important component of many monasteries was copying and illuminating manuscripts. It was in the monasteries that many of the ancient manuscripts were preserved through the Dark Ages.

Byzantine Arts and Design

Byzantine emperors were patrons of the arts. Artisans were well trained in classical traditions and produced brilliantly colored enamels, ivory carvings, cloisonné, and champlevé wares. Illuminated manuscripts created in monasteries were unrivaled. Silk and other textiles were embroidered, often with strands of gold.

Most art was in the service of the church with little secular application, although imperial personages were sometimes shown in religious settings. The subject matter reflected the interests of those who could afford to commission the artists. Ostentation was expected, and ornamentation was elaborate. A strict hierarchy was established. Except during the Iconoclastic Controversy in the East, beginning at the top, usually in a dome, Christ was depicted as Pantocrator, or ruler of the universe. The apostles were second in the hierarchy. The Virgin Mary was depicted most frequently in the apse. Still lower were others in descending order of importance. Saints with halos, or **nimbi**, were shown in the lowest register. In almost a thousand years, there was little change in artistic style. No attempt at perspective was made, and figures were characterized by their two-dimensional qualities.

Carving was limited to low relief. Although Constantine adorned public areas in his city with classic sculptures and even had a sculpture of himself erected on a porphyry column in the forum, following Oriental preferences, Byzantine sculpture was almost nonexistent.

REPRESENTATIONAL ART

Although mosaics dominated Early Byzantine design, the expense and labor involved caused mosaics to be replaced with frescoes by the late Byzantine period. Frescoes covered walls, ceilings, domes, and vaults. **Icons** were representations of saints, the Virgin Mary, or Christ and might have a single panel or be paired as a **diptych** or in threes as a **triptych**. The effectiveness of these devotional panels depended on how close the image was to established criteria. Depicted individuals usually held a symbol that identified them or were posed with ritualistic gestures. While faces were individualized, they were not lifelike. During the sixth and seventh centuries, most icons were painted using the encaustic technique, but tempera (pigment mixed with egg yolk), which was used at the same time, later completely replaced encaustic painting.

With the exception of the period of the Iconoclastic Controversy, humans were a favored motif. During the early period, individuals depicted were considered to be present in the room if both eyes were visible, even if they had died centuries before. Frontal poses were preferred, although when the scene required that two people face each other, such as the Annunciation, half profiles were permitted although both eyes were still visible. Because it was unnecessary for Judas Iscariot to be present, he was shown in profile with one eye.

Painting was also employed in manuscript illumination; this was usually done in monasteries where scribes wrote the text and artists painted pictures and decorated headings and capital letters. By the fifth century, a cursive script had been developed for use in documents and manuscripts. The work was done on parchment and consisted mostly of the Bible, the Psalms, lives of the saints, and devotional texts. The illuminator sketched the subject in a space left during the writing of the text. The drawing was then painted. Sometimes the painting was actually done on a separate parchment and added to the book later. Portraits of the writers of the gospels were typical, each depicted in his study. Secular manuscripts including poetry, philosophy, and even tomes on military tactics were also illuminated, although the illumination was typically simplified. Gold was considered symbolic of truth and incorruptibility and was used in manuscript illumination as well as on painted icons and in mosaics.

MOSAICS

Roman mosaics were the precursors of Byzantine examples. Roman mosaics, however, were used almost entirely for floors while Byzantine mosaics decorated walls and ceilings. Because of their location, Byzantine mosaics could be made of less durable materials, particularly glass and precious metals. Mosaics were, however, an expensive decorative form.

Byzantine tesserae differed from the small Roman cubes, mostly as a result of the materials used. Multicolored stones including marble and semiprecious stones, brick, terracotta, and glass were employed. **Smalti** were tesserae made of thick glass in which air bubbles were trapped, resulting in a rough surface texture. Like other glass tesserae, smalti were often backed with gold or silver leaf to reflect light. Gold was sandwiched between two layers of glass in some tesserae.

The tesserae were laid on the surface at an angle and left ungrouted to maximize light reflection. The surface on which the mosaics were to be laid was prepared first with a layer of plaster and then a layer of stucco that contained crushed pottery, called a setting bed, into which the tesserae were pressed. Some icons were made with miniature mosaics with individual tesserae the size of the head of a pin. (See Figure 7.5.)

INFLUENCE 7.4

Byzantine mosaics were used extensively in Italian cities that maintained close ties to the Empire as well as in Russia. During the nineteenth-century Byzantine Revival, mosaics were revived. London's Westminster Cathedral had extensive surfaces covered with brilliant Byzantine-influenced mosaics. In the eighth century, the Moors took mosaics and related tile art to Spain, where it remains popular. During the Art Nouveau period, Antonio Gaudi and others used broken pottery and found objects in their mosaics to cover building surfaces.

The predominant colors used in mosaics included gold, red, blue, and green. Figures were set against a solid color ground, usually lapis lazuli or gold, or against stylized landscapes. Narrative scenes taken from ceremonies or the Bible were common on larger surfaces, as were depictions of saints, apostles, and members of the royal family.

Representations of Christ, whether symbolic as a lamb, or as a person, were located in the dome. The Virgin Mary was depicted in a half dome of the apse. In small areas, crosses, monograms (usually the monogram of Christ consisting of the Greek letter chi and rho), and stylized motifs were used.

After the Byzantine Empire was overtaken by the Ottoman Turks, Islamic influence predominated and many of the churches were converted to mosques. Due to the prohibition against naturalistic images in the Islamic faith, the Byzantine mosaics in mosques were covered with stucco or whitewash or destroyed.

BYZANTINE CRAFTS

By the tenth century, cloisonné enamel was used for **reliquaries**, or containers for sacred relics; it was also used for book covers, vessels used in the church, and crowns, and pieces were sewn onto royal and ecclesiastical garments. Stone vessels were frequently set in a base of precious metals decorated with pearls, jewels, or cloisonné. Lapis lazuli, serpentine, obsidian, porphyry, and steatite were used for a variety of purposes, often for carved plaques. Silver was used for repoussé, jewelry, and frames for icons. Tiny beads of silver were soldered on a background to form filigree, and engraved silver depressions were filled with **niello**, a black substance made of silver and other materials to bring out the design. (See Figure 7.6.)

Silk was a luxury item imported from China and sold by weight. In the sixth century, silk moth

FIGURE 7.5 The mosaics at Sant' Apollinare in Classe (near Ravenna) depicted a procession along the wall above the arcade. On the north side, there were 22 female saints led by 3 magi heading toward a Madonna and child; on the south, 27 male martyrs were leaving Theodoric's palace (seen here) and proceeding toward the mosaic of Christ with 4 angels.

eggs were smuggled into the Byzantine Empire by monks who had learned the techniques of producing silk during their travels in the Far East. The Byzantine silk industry was housed in imperial factories where the state retained a monopoly on its production. Motifs on the twill weave fabric included animals arranged in rows or circles, representations of emperors, and scenes. Fabrics for draping or hanging on walls, for the making of altar cloths, and for ceremonial clothing were used by the imperial family and by the Church. Gifts of silk were sometimes made for visiting dignitaries.

During the fourth century, elephant ivory was carved into icons, panels for small chests, and book covers. Availability of ivory, however, depended on open trade routes to India and Africa. Those routes were cut off during parts of the sixth and seventh centuries by Saracen invasions, and it was not until the ninth century when ivory was readily available again that there was a revival of the art of carving the material. Later, during the twelfth century as the supply of ivory disappeared again, Byzantine artisans used bone, walrus ivory, and other materials or substituted frescoes or icons for decoration. Ivory diptychs and triptychs were used as gifts, panels were attached to furniture, and boxes were made of the material.

Censers used in the Orthodox Church, and crosses, lamps, and icons, were made of bronze or copper. A precursor of the chandelier, a **corona**, or **rowell**, was a hoop of metal with holders for oil on its rim. Byzantine artisans also learned how to cut glass to create designs and to enamel glass. **Fondo d'oro** employed gold leaf figures or designs sandwiched between two layers of glass.

BYZANTINE MOTIFS

As was typical of all art forms, religious subjects predominated. Depictions of the writers of the gospels with their associated symbols were common: Matthew with wings, Mark with a winged lion, Luke with a winged ox, and John with an eagle. Christ was sometimes represented as a lamb on a blue ground. (See also Figure 7.8.)

More complex pictures included Biblical illustrations such as Samson killing the lion; Nilotic scenes, which usually included crocodiles, gardens and landscapes; and mythological events, hunting scenes, and depictions of events

FIGURE 7.7 This fifth-century Byzantine ivory panel symbolizes the triumph of good over evil as Bellerophon kills the chimera—a fire-breathing monster with features of a lion, a snake, and a goat.

at the hippodrome. The four seasons represented Paradise, as did baskets of fruit. Interlaced linear motifs, often including animals, later recurred in Celtic art. The endless knot represented eternity.

Griffins copied from Persia, elephants, lions, and mythological creatures were used on textiles,

FIGURE 7.6 This bronze reliquary in the form of a cross hinged to open. It was probably made to hold a fragment of the True Cross. This example depicts the Virgin Mary.

FIGURE 7.8 Typical of Byzantine art, this gold pendant features a representation of the adoration of the Magi.

FIGURE 7.9 The Roman eagle was adopted as a Byzantine symbol but in the fourteenth century was changed to a double-headed eagle.

in relief carving, and in paintings. Doves represented the Holy Spirit, peacocks suggested immortality and the Resurrection, and the snake depicted evil. Signs of the zodiac included the typical animal forms. (See also Figure 7.9.)

Trees, flowers, and foliage were common. Geometric designs were especially popular during the Iconoclastic controversy.

FIGURE 7.10 Wind-blown capitals were those with carved acanthus leaves similar to those on Corinthian capitals, but the leaves were flat, had pointed lobes, and leaned to one side as if blown by the wind.

BYZANTINE ARCHITECTURE

The architecture of Byzantium followed Roman designs for most public buildings until Justinian's reign. Then, religious differences within the Orthodox Church resulted in five days of riots that caused extensive damage to the city. Justinian, encouraged by his wife Theodora, sent out the guards to restore order, which resulted in a massacre. It fell to Justinian, who had already been responsible for the construction of San Vitale in Ravenna and Saints Sergius and Bacchus in Constantinople to direct the rebuilding of the city. The massive building program he initiated resulted in a distinctively Byzantine architectural style. The architecture focused on ecclesiastical structures and was characterized by innovation, vaults rather than flat ceilings, and domes that covered central spaces. Most buildings were centrally planned, but even those differed from examples in the West, with greater complexity in the plan, interconnecting spaces that flowed together smoothly, and an increased focus on the central space. Strong walls and gates for defense, new aqueducts, cisterns for water storage, fora, baths, and hippodromes were needed. Partially due to the more religious nature of the Empire, there was little use for theaters and amphitheaters.

After the death of Justinian, church building almost ceased and palace architecture predominated. Domestic buildings have disappeared and there is little evidence remaining, although most used Roman designs and construction methods. Later Byzantine structures were usually smaller. Byzantine architecture changed little over a thousand years, and variations tended to be geo-

FIGURE 7.11 While there was a seventh-century prohibition of using the cross form on floors, crosses were depicted in every other location.

graphical rather than chronological. Regional variations included Armenian, Greek, Russian, and Venetian.

The materials used for Byzantine buildings depended on the geology of the area or on the number of Roman ruins that could be plundered. In much of the Byzantine Empire, there was no suitable building stone and brick was the material of choice. During the Late Byzantine period, alternating brick and stone resulted in stripes that became characteristic.

Buildings were opulent, brilliantly colored, and often monumental and reflected the wealth of the empire. When the Crusaders arrived, they were astonished at the richness and luxury seemingly everywhere. When they returned home, they carried with them luxury goods unlike any known in Europe. To ensure a constant supply of silks, spices, and other desirable commodities, European nations established and maintained trade with the Eastern Empire until the fall of Constantinople, when it became imperative to find other routes to the Orient.

PENDENTIVES AND SQUINCHES

Although Roman architects used the dome, it was limited to buildings with curved walls. The **squinch** had been used to fit a dome onto a square building in the East as early as the Persians. Squinches were used to reduce the area of a square building to be roofed to an octagon by placing arches or beams diagonally across the corners. One or more layers could be used to accomplish the transition. When multiple layers were employed, upper ones projected slightly over those below, gradually decreasing the size of the space.

Byzantine builders devised another way to put a dome on a square building. The **pendentive** was a triangular portion of a quarter of a sphere that rested on a single point and curved fanlike upward and inward to form a circular base on which a dome could be constructed. The sides naturally formed arches. An advantage of the pendentive was that it could be used not only with squares and polygons but with rectangles. (See Box 7.2.)

INFLUENCE 7.5
The pendentive has been in continuous use since its inception, although the form varies considerably.

COLUMNS

Classical columns were reused for many purposes, and early Byzantine examples followed classic models. During the early Byzantine period, the Roman Composite capital was favored, but newly designed capitals replaced this type relatively quickly. Byzantine columns disregarded classical proportions, and, although fluted columns con-

FIGURE 7.12 Brick was a favored material for Byzantine structures such as Sant' Apollinare in Classe. Here, the exonarthex is a roofed area with arched openings, although some are completely enclosed. The bell tower was constructed in the tenth century.

Box 7.2 Squinches and Pendentives

Squinch

Pendentive

tinued to be used, **solominic**, or twisted, columns became more common. **Doubled** columns, or those with separate paired shafts but with joined **capitals**, were common.

Because Byzantine columns typically supported arches rather than an entablature, a second squared block, called an **impost block**, or **dosseret**, was set on top of the circular capital of the column. The impost block rose to form a larger square to conform to the size and shape at the springpoint of the arch or vault. (See Figure 7.13.)

Many capitals had flat overall lace-like carvings, usually in the form of stylized foliage. The undercutting was so deep that the background appeared dark.

Protomai capitals featured animal forms; typically, these appeared only on the fronts, although high relief might release much of the animal form from the capital. Horses, griffins, lions, and eagles were all used for these capitals. Byzantine capitals were often ordered for buildings in the West, especially in Venice and Ravenna, where close ties were maintained.

CHURCHES

Early churches in the Eastern Empire were constructed on basilican plans, as were those in the West. Centrally planned buildings were preferred, as they focused attention on a single area, but such structures lacked sufficient space for processions, ceremonies, and participants. For

FIGURE 7.13 Impost blocks were often undecorated, although those that received ornament were often similar to the capitals of the columns and had monograms or low-relief overall designs carved into them. The designs were typically flat flowers, foliage, and sometimes animals, and did not project from the face plane. Here, a cross and a pair of animals form ornaments on the impost block.

FIGURE 7.14 At the top, folded capitals had four curved lobes that widened toward the top and were separated by deep depressions or smaller folds. Folded capitals usually had flat overall lacelike foliage carving. The undercutting was so deep that the background appeared dark.

FIGURE 7.15 Notably, the first great Byzantine structure, Hagia Sophia, was also its finest achievement. The minarets were a later addition. When originally completed, the interior of Hagia Sophia was filled with colorful mosaics. These had been replaced to be more suitable for the Islamic religion, which was practiced here until 1935, when the Hagia Sophia was converted into a museum. The interior is a vast open space with widely spaced columns for support. The lace-like capitals typical of Byzantium, the geometric designs characteristic of Moslem architecture, and the multi-colored marble and porphyry facings over the brick structure enliven the interior.

this reason, Byzantine builders experimented with a number of cross forms. Roofing a cross form was a simple matter when wood was used, but the vault was preferred in Byzantine design. Happily, the builders of Hagia Sophia, Isidore of Miletus (c. 532 to 537) and Anthemius of Tralles (c. 474 to 534), were able to combine a centralized focus with a cross form by using vaults over the projecting arms and a dome over the crossing. It was here that the two builders first used pendentives as transitions between a square base and a dome, each 60 feet high and projecting forward 25 feet. Quite possibly the unique approach to design by these scientists and mathematicians was due to their lack of experience in building.

The dome of Hagia Sophia appeared to float. Forty windows pierced the base of the dome, allowing light to penetrate to the interior, and exterior buttresses separated the windows while providing the necessary counterthrust for the arch of the dome. Previous arches had been supported by heavy masses: the dome of the Pantheon in Rome rested on 20-feet-thick walls. The Byzantine buttress was an innovative technique that was carried into every subsequent style that employed arches. These low buttresses had the appearance of a **drum**, or cylinder that raised the dome, but that was a development that was to come later. Although the first dome was demolished during an earthquake 20 years later, a new one was constructed in 563 and remains to this day. Hagia Sophia was constructed in just five years beginning in 532 on the site of a previous building with the same name.

── **INFLUENCE 7.6**

Hagia Sophia significantly influenced the design of mosques, particularly those built by Sinan in the sixteenth century.

Heavy ashlar stone was used in the piers that supported the arches beneath the dome of Hagia Sophia, but brick was used for both the structure and the dome. Brick vaults and domes were lighter in weight than Roman concrete, allowing builders to span large distances as demonstrated by the 107-foot-diameter dome. The brick was thin and laid in thick mortar beds. No centering was required, as Assyrian construction techniques were used. Two half domes of the same diameter as the dome helped to counteract the thrust on two sides, while heavy buttresses were used on the other two sides. The domes were roofed with lead rather than hidden by external timber roofing. Hagia Sophia had arcaded aisles and galleries, although at the ends, the arcades curved inward.

Inside, Hagia Sophia was covered with green, red, white, yellow, blue, and black marble. Five **bays**, or divisions, separated by columns, piers, or vaults were surmounted by seven in the gallery. Seven clerestory windows crowned each side. At each end, three lower-level bays were topped with seven above. A mosaic with a gold ground was laid in the dome and foliage, crosses, and other patterns were used for the half domes, vaults, pendentives, and soffits. When he dedicated the church in 537, Justinian declared, "Solomon, I have vanquished thee," meaning his church was more magnificent than Solomon's Temple, which had been razed in 70. (See Figure 7.15.)

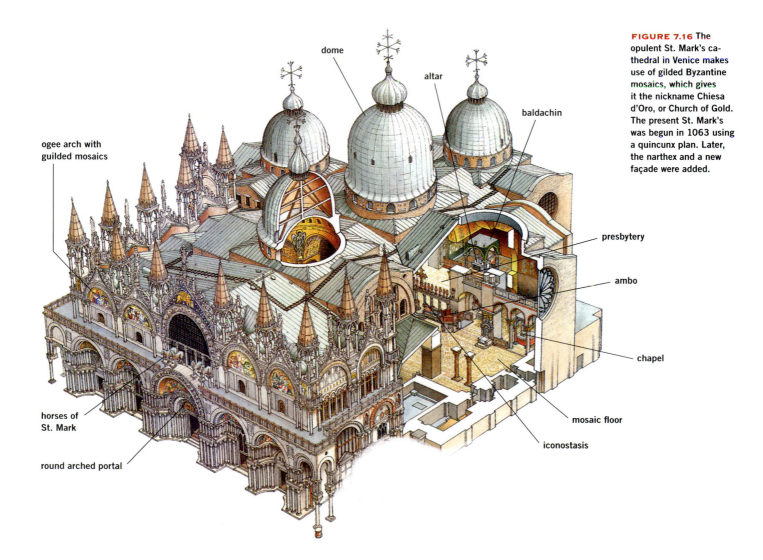

FIGURE 7.16 The opulent St. Mark's cathedral in Venice makes use of gilded Byzantine mosaics, which gives it the nickname Chiesa d'Oro, or Church of Gold. The present St. Mark's was begun in 1063 using a quincunx plan. Later, the narthex and a new façade were added.

dome

altar

baldachin

ogee arch with guilded mosaics

presbytery

ambo

chapel

horses of St. Mark

mosaic floor

iconostasis

round arched portal

FIGURE 7.17 In Greece, the drum was pierced by blind arches in which windows were located. The arcades often penetrated through the roof line, resulting in a sinuous circular roof form.

Early Byzantine churches focused solely on the central area. Whether aisles or an ambulatory were used was irrelevant, whether the cross was enclosed in an octagon or a square did not matter; and most of all, the external appearance was least important.

The **tetraconch** church had four semicircular lobes, or **conchs**, roofed with semi-domes that surrounded a central one. Often, a double shell design was used and the conchs projected into a surrounding ambulatory. Beginning in the fifth century, the tetraconch plan was used in Greece.

Another Byzantine innovation was the **quincunx**, or cross in square plan. Four vaulted arms of equal length formed a Greek cross, and a dome surmounted the crossing. An additional shorter dome was added to each of the arms. Some quincunx churches had projecting porticoes on three or four sides.

Few buildings in central areas of the Empire, however, changed their form, but late in the Byzantine period in outlying areas including Armenia, Greece, and Slavic areas, there was an increased emphasis on vertical lines and height, and domes were elevated on drums. In Russia, the drums became increasingly narrower, while the domes took on a steep bulbous shape to prevent snow from remaining on the roof. Drums were either round or polygonal but the latter was more common. (See Figure 7.17.)

In all types, compartments or rooms might be added on either side of the sanctuary. The **diaconicon** was located on the south side and was used to store the vessels, vestments, and books required during services. The **prothesis** on the north side housed the Eucharist and was where it was prepared and blessed.

Apses were typical not only at the sanctuary end of the church but at the ends of aisles or projecting from the side rooms. The smaller apses used on subsidiary aisles or spaces were known as **apsidoles**.

Beginning with Early Christian churches and developing in the Byzantine church was the screen that separated the nave from the sanctuary. In Early Christian buildings, the templon took the form of a triumphal arch. In Byzantine architecture, this screen, known as the **iconostasis**, was used to display icons. At first, it consisted of columns that supported an entablature. Often, curtains were used between the columns to obscure the view of the altar. As the liturgy of the Eastern Church developed, the iconostasis became taller and more opaque, so that it completely concealed the altar with its cimborio as well as the rituals taking place behind it. Beneath the dome was the ambo, or pulpit, which was raised above the **bema**, or platform, of the sanctuary.

At first, the exteriors of Byzantine buildings were plain and of little importance. Tenth-century changes resulted in alternation of stone and brick to create more striped façades. By the twelfth century bricks were carved with designs imitating writing or patterns such as frets or chevrons. (See Box 7.3.)

BOX 7.3 CHARACTERISTICS OF BYZANTINE ARCHITECTURE

- Multiple domes
- Central planning including Greek cross plan
- Round arches and arcades
- Mosaics, many with gold or lapis lazuli backgrounds
- Alternating stone colors or stone and brick
- Predominantly brick
- Pendentives
- Impost blocks on columns
- Extensive use of domes including half domes
- Vaults
- Conchs
- Quincunx plans
- Polygonal apses
- Cross in square plan
- Interiors divided into bays
- Separation of church interiors into sanctuary and nave

FIGURE 7.18 Interior of Sant'Apollinare in Classe, Ravenna, Italy.

BYZANTINE INTERIORS

The vast majority of Byzantine interiors that remain are ecclesiastical buildings that typically receive the most ornate and expensive interiors. On the other hand, Byzantine architecture was mostly ecclesiastical, and these models may not be more ostentatious than palaces or other public buildings.

Floors were tiled with colored marble, often in geometric designs framed by bands of color; Roundels inlaid with eagles, zodiac signs, hares, and scenes were created in opus sectile; and mosaics of a more durable nature than those used for walls and ceilings.

Every surface on walls and ceilings was ornamented. Frescoes, mosaics, alabaster, and marble incrustation were used most frequently. Marble was preferred on the interior, but it had to be imported or plundered. Mirror image marble slabs were often laid side by side to resemble the skin of an animal and a variety of colors were used. Jasper, alabaster, and onyx were used for wall incrustation, columns, or vessels. Windows sometimes employed translucent slabs of alabaster or marble rather than glass to soften and color the light. (See Figure 7.18.)

The phrase "born in the purple" meant that a son or daughter of the Byzantine imperial family was born in the Porphyra, a room in the palace lined with porphyry, a purple-colored stone and the title Porphyrogenitus was added to the child's name. Children born in the purple were immediately recognized as potential heirs to the throne. Purple dye from the murex was the most expensive color and was reserved for use by royalty.

BYZANTINE FURNITURE

Byzantine furniture was Roman furniture with greater ornamentation. Carving, animal forms, and inlays of gold, stone, and glass used for various parts made Byzantine furniture more ornate. In fact, it was probably the ornamentation of gold, ivory, and precious stones that hastened the destruction of many of the examples. Most furniture, including that made of bronze, had turned components. Byzantine artisans used the lathe and were able to create sharp edges and deep grooves while turning pieces.

Only very small chests, usually made with ivory panels, remain. Storage chests were probably simple and portable and raised on short legs or feet. Illuminated manuscripts show large cupboards with painted designs, some of which were gabled at the top. Freestanding cupboards were first used in churches and monasteries, and only later in homes.

The **lectern** was a stand designed to support a book and was often used in combination with a table or desk for writing. Its sloping top supported the codex, which was a folded manuscript or a scroll. Frequently, a cabinet was located beneath the lectern for storing books.

INFLUENCE 7.7

The lectern was the prototype for the Bible box of the seventeenth century, for pulpits through the centuries, and for secular reading stands.

Folding chairs were also depicted, some with arms. It was, however, thrones that were portrayed most frequently. Typically, the throne was placed under a baldachin draped with fabric. The most famous example is the sixth-century throne of the Archbishop Maximian of Ravenna. (See Figure 7.19.) Thrones might have architectural features, animal legs, turned legs, or, like the throne of Maximian, be covered with precious materials. Backs were high and either gabled or curved.

The emperor's throne was a wide chair on which two could sit. The right side of the throne was reserved for the Gospels, which represented Christ. When the emperor was acting in Christ's stead, he sat on the right side; otherwise, the emperor sat on the left.

From Byzantine depictions of the Last Supper, it is apparent that large tables had been substituted for the small individual tables used by the Romans for dining. Circular, semicircular, and rectangular forms were shown in manuscript illuminations, mosaics, and other visual media.

One Byzantine ivory carving depicted a bed with a canopy overhead. Another Byzantine bed shown on a carving is a simple frame with short turned legs, which appeared to be attached to the frame by tying the pieces together. A network of ropes formed the bottom of the bed. The ropes ran around an additional round pole across the width of the bed, probably to increase the tension as the ropes were tied.

INFLUENCE 7.8

The canopied bed was used in Europe from the medieval through the Renaissance periods.

Byzantine Influence in Russia

During the ninth century, the Viking Rus tribe had extended its influence south into the area now called Russia. The Rus carried on extended trade in furs with Constantinople and other Eastern regions including those controlled by the Moslims. These armed merchants established fortified posts and eventually, even as a minority, ruled both the commercial and political aspects of the area.

While Saracen forces gained control of parts of their territory in the seventh century, Byzantine influence continued to spread northward into areas untouched by the Romans. In 988, Grand Prince Vladimir of Kiev (c. 958–1015) married Anna, the sister of the Byzantine Emperor Basil II (963–1011), bringing the two nations closer together. A condition of that marriage was that Vladimir embrace Christianity, which he did, not only for himself but for his nation.

When Crusaders sacked Constantinople in the early thirteenth century, the lucrative Russian trade with the Byzantine Empire and beyond was ruined. Mongol invasions followed swiftly and completed the destruction of trade. Because the peasantry had never been armed, the Russians had little defense. In addition, the invaders came with firearms unknown to the Russians.

Russia essentially became a dependency of the Mongol Empire. Rulers were required to travel to Asia to pay tribute to the Great Khan and were cut off from Europe. The invaders made peace with the Russian church, exempting it from taxes

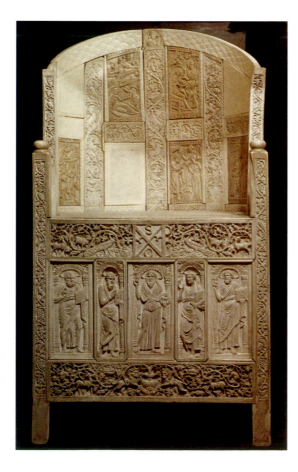

FIGURE 7.19 The wooden throne of Maximian was covered with ivory panels and was a gift to the archbishop from the Byzantine Emperor Justinian. Designed for ceremonial use, the throne lacks comfort.

and protecting its property and personnel in exchange for their recommendation that the Russians submit to the Mongols. The church, then, provided security unavailable through political leadership and, as in Medieval Europe, many individuals became monks. Others left their valuables in the hands of the church, increasing the wealth of the organization.

The Mongol invasion caused a two-century delay in the introduction of reforms and innovations to most of Russia from the West. In the twelfth century, the Vladimir-Suzdal region came under the influence of Western Europe; this resulted in some architectural innovations in which Romanesque features were combined with Byzantine elements.

The Romanesque influences of Europe in the Vladimir-Suzdal region resulted in square plans with semicircular apses and domes supported on four columns. Rather than the typical Russian brick, stone was used for construction and carved stone decoration replaced the frescoed ornamentation of walls. The splayed openings on these buildings were also a Romanesque influence.

From its beginnings, the Russian church was under the control of Constantinople with major centers in Novgorod, Pskov, and Kiev, along the trade route of the Rus. After the fall of Constantinople, Moscow claimed to be the third Rome and took control of religious, artistic, and political affairs.

RUSSIAN PAINTING

After contact with the Byzantine Empire, Russian painters were typically Greek or trained in Greek traditions and followed the iconography of the Byzantine church. The Russians added a number of saints of their own. Even in the fourteenth and fifteenth centuries when Russian icon painting was at its height, the painters were either Greek, such as Theophanes (c. 1330–c.1410) or painted in the Greek style, as did the Russian Andrei Rublev (c. 1360–c. 1430).

RUSSIAN ARCHITECTURE

Russian architecture was significantly influenced by Byzantine design. Prior to the tenth century, Russian buildings were constructed of wood and exhibited Nordic influences. That Nordic influence was combined with Byzantine features to create a distinctive Russian architectural style. Modifications of Byzantine forms to accom-

BOX 7.4 CHARACTERISTICS OF RUSSIAN ARCHITECTURE

- Central planning with octagonal plans common
- Early timber construction
- Steep roofs
- Tent roofs
- Multiple domes
- Onion domes
- Semicircular apses
- Tall narrow polygonal drums
- Pendentives or kokoshniki
- Bochka
- Begunki
- Brick
- High walls
- Exterior walled galleries and porches
- Extensive use of frescoes

modate the severe climate and heavy snows of Russia included steeper roofs and the raising of the flattened dome into a bulbous form. There was a proliferation of domes, steeply pitched roofs, and high walls, at first in wood. Windows were narrow. Later, interiors were separated into many small spaces. (See Figure 7.20.)

The first important stone church in Russia was St. Sophia in Kiev (1018–1037), although the domes were brick. When St. Sophia was rebuilt in the mid-twelfth century, the onion dome was used and became typical of the Russian style. The number of domes on Russian churches was often significant. Five represented Christ and the 4 Evangelists; 13 denoted Christ and the 12 apostles; and 25 the apocalyptic vision with God on the throne and 24 seats for the apostles and prophets. Other numbers also had religious significance.

Narrow cylindrical drums raise domes in tiers. A narrow decorative band near the top of drums that support domes was first used at Pskov and later throughout Russia. The bands, or **begunki**, employ arches, triangles, squares, or even lines. The specific decoration of this band depended on the area in which it was used.

Typically, octagonal plans were used in Russia. On the interior following Byzantine custom, the main dome is decorated with Christ Pantocrator, with prophets in the mid range, and angels lower on the drum. The Virgin Mary is depicted in the main apse behind the iconostasis beyond. Walls are decorated with scenes from the

FIGURE 7.20 Built in 1714 in the traditional wood architectural style of Russia that combined Nordic and Byzantine influences, the Church of the Transfiguration on Kizhi Island is a wood church with 22 onion domes. The double-curved bochka roofs beneath the domes, shaped much like pointed horseshoes, are typical.

FIGURE 7.21 The Cathedral of St. Basil was built in the Russian Byzantine style still popular in the late 16th century. When constructed, St. Basil's was painted white. In the seventeenth century when colored tiles became common, they were used to replace the original iron roofs.

Gospels, saints, and church festivals and councils. Russian churches often have royal doors used only by priests and deacons. (See Box 7.4.)

Most domes were supported on pendentives, but some churches were too small to house interior columns required for pendentives, so they were supported by **kokoshniki**, or recessed corbelled arches, often in successive ascending tiers. Kokoshniki became a favored Russian decorative element. Exterior walled galleries, porches, and arcaded bell towers became typical of Russian architecture after their introduction in Pskov.

St. Basil's Cathedral (1555–1561) in Moscow combined nine chapels. Surrounding a small central church are eight others. The four chapels on the chief axes are octagonal, two on the diagonals are square, and two are irregularly shaped. The central tower has a tent shape, a typical Russian innovation, surrounded by irregular steep domes in a variety of shapes. (See Figure 7.21.)

The Rise of Islam (632–1800)

Born in Mecca on the Arabian Peninsula, the prophet Mohammed (570–632 AD) established the new religion of Islam. He also conquered the people of the Arabian Peninsula and united its tribes into a single nation. Much like later Christian Crusaders, members of the religion began military conquests within a few years after the prophet's death, conquering territory in the name of their religion and eventually extending their influence throughout the Middle East, North Africa, Spain, India, and Central Asia. The Mongol leader Tamerlane (c. 1336–1405) and other leaders converted to Islam and the religion spread across India and further east, and as far as the Iberian Peninsula in the west. In the Islamic areas of India, the Mongols established the Moghul dynasty (beginning in 1526 until the mid-eighteenth century) with capitals at Delhi, Agra, Lahore, and Fatehpur Sikri. It is important, however, to understand that while the religion and its influences spread, the Moslems, or those who followed the religion of Islam, never formed a nation or empire. Like other religions, individuals of any nation could follow the practices of Islam. At first, most of the Islamic leaders in conquered territories were Moslem Arabs but power fell increasingly under the purview of indigenous leaders who converted to Islam.

The Moslems built great cities in the wake of their conquests. They established universities where sciences were taught. Many of these seats of learning preserved classical texts that were located in conquered territories, and when Europe came out of the Dark Ages these manuscripts were "rediscovered" by Christians. Moslem centers spread from Baghdad to Granada, Spain and to Delhi, India. One has only to look to see Islamic influences. The Taj Mahal (begun 1633) in Agra was constructed in the Moghul style that was derived from Islamic architecture. The cathedral in Granada, Spain is attached to an older Islamic minaret.

Because the religion developed in the hot, dry climate of the Middle East, the building types were designed for shade and coolness during the day and for the collection of heat by thick masonry walls that could be re-radiated at night. Regardless of the climate, Islamic structures continued to be built in the same manner. Some concessions were made in monsoon areas where improved air flow was essential to dissipate the heat and humidity. The forms, then, were related to ritual rather than function, although local influences were always felt.

The new religion had no artistic tradition. Partly for this reason, Moslem buildings employed indigenous architectural traditions of conquered territories. Because Persia was one of the first areas conquered, Sassanian designs significantly influenced those of Islam. From Persian buildings, Islam adopted the **ogee**, or **keel**, or double S-curved, arch, clustered columns, vaulted halls, the dome, and the squinch which was a method to attach a round dome to a square structure. It was also from the Persians that Moslem builders learned to construct country villas with **paradises**, or gardens that featured running water, rare flowers, shade and fruit trees, tiled pools, and open pavilions. As they continued their conquests, Moslems adopted other architectural features. From Syria came the pointed arch and **muqarnas** (Spanish **mocarbes**); from the Moors, the horseshoe arch which the Moors may have gotten from the Visigoths; and from the Egyptians, the use of geometric patterns. From the Byzantine Empire, the Moslems borrowed the arcade, intricate surface ornamentation, pendentives, and mosaics. Over time, these features became almost universal in Moslem-influenced architecture. A relatively late addition to Moslem buildings was the addition of a **pishtaq**, or tall façade with a high arch in a rectangular frame, that served as

FIGURE 7.22
Mukarnas were used for squinches, column capitals, the interior of domes and semidomes.

a monumental entryway. Often façades, arches, and the surrounds of openings featured contrasting colors of stone, sometimes alternated with brick. This **ablaq** technique may have been derived from Syria or from Byzantine buildings.

Homes were built like those of the Byzantines and had an interior courtyard, often of peristyle form, and sometimes two stories with a second story balcony. The courtyard featured a fountain or basin of water for ablutions and shade trees. Privacy was essential and the few windows and doors opened onto courtyards. Often there was a single window and it was covered with a wooden lattice or pierced wooden screen called a **mashrabiyyah**. The same treatment in stone resulted in the jali. The ornate pierced designs allowed occupants a view of their surroundings while they themselves remained hidden and reduced glare and dust. The main living area of affluent homes might be two stories and rise to a dome. Plaster walls were typically painted in multiple colors and hand-woven wool rugs introduced color to the floors. On three sides of the room, the floor was slightly raised forming a **diwan** covered with cushions on which occupants sat or reclined. Few articles of furniture or accessories were used.

The adopted architectural forms spread rapidly with the Islamic religion and drew inspiration also from Christian and Jewish buildings. Moslem buildings were different in spirit, however. Islam was spread through conquests and its buildings are substantial and masculine. Some are plain, looking much like military barracks although others are more graceful. Islamic buildings include mosques, palaces, citadels, and mausolea. (See Figure 7.23.)

The five pillars of Islam were a unifying theme: belief in one god with Mohammed as his prophet, prayer, alms giving, fasting during the month of Ramadân, and pilgrimage to Mecca. The Islamic religion rigidly interpreted the second of the Jewish Ten Commandments to mean that there could only be one god. To ensure that idolatry was not practiced, the Koran, the holy book of Islam, forbade the use of religious images including those of Mohammed, his relatives, other prophets including Jesus, and God. Often that prohibition has been interpreted to mean that images of any living beings are prohibited. Subjects that did not have the breath of life such as trees and vegetation were less risky to be used as ornament. Nevertheless, they were rarely used as such. Instead, intricate interlacing patterns using straight or curved lines and geometric forms were common. Mosques and other Islamic buildings were stripped of symbolism that might incline even slightly toward idolatry.

FIGURE 7.23 While the most important buildings were religious, the Moslems adopted the military architecture of the Byzantine Empire and built castles, forts, and walled cities wherever they conquered. Battlements were composed of complex pierced designs.

Mosques

The **mosque** is the most pervasive of all Islamic architectural forms. In the mosque, there is no focal point for adoration as is seen in Western examples. Windows that penetrate the space, if any, are high on the wall. The space, then, is removed from the world, its sights, sounds, and confusion. (See Figure 7.24.)

Mosques are always oriented on an axis in line with Mecca which terminates with the **mihrab**, or niche or chamber that indicates the direction of Mecca. Three types of mosques evolved. Because worshippers all had to face Mecca during prayers, the mihrab was located in the **qibla**, or the wall positioned in the direction of Mecca, on the long side of the prayer hall. Like ancient Persian structures, the early Arab mosque was constructed around a central courtyard with a fountain, or **sardivan**, for ablutions. The courtyard was often surrounded by a covered peristyle corridor or **riwaq**. The mosque itself was a colonnaded prayer hall, or **musalla**, located

FIGURE 7.24 The mosque was designed primarily for prayer rather than to inspire awe as is the case with most Western churches.

FIGURE 7.25 Over 850 columns support this prayer hall of the original mosque in Córdoba, Spain.

on the side of the courtyard that faced Mecca. This type of mosque is known as hypostyle due to the number of columns needed to support the flat roof of the hall. The construction method by which columns support a flat roof without intervening arches is known as **appadana**. Influenced by Byzantine architecture, the second type of mosque that originated in the fifteenth century, had a central dome over the musalla. The Moslems adopted the dome from the Byzantine Empire for use in their mosques. As their architecture developed, the single dome became a central dome surrounded by other domes and semi-domes. Smaller domes were often added throughout the mosque. The iwan mosque, almost exclusively used in Iran, has one or more open iwans that face a central courtyard.

On Fridays at noon, there are not only congregational prayers, but a sermon that may have political import. For this reason, Fridays are the most important days at the mosque. The sermon is preached from the monumental pulpit, or **minbar**, usually adjacent to the mihrab. The minbar is a raised platform accessed by a flight of stairs in the front and has a sounding board or canopy above it to enhance the acoustics. The imam, or prayer leader, stands on the top step rather than on the platform that is reserved for

the vacant throne in honor of the absent authority. In front of the prayer hall, there is frequently a peristyle court with running water, usually from a fountain, in the center. The faithful are required to perform ritual ablutions before entering the prayer hall and the fountain is provided for this purpose.

The primary purpose of the mosque may be prayer, but mosques are also gathering places where business may be transacted, education provided, and valuables stored. Early mosques had great libraries, guest quarters, and even baths, or **hammans**. Often attached to the mosque was the **madrasa**, or theological college.

Minarets, or towers known as **manaras**, may have been derived from the ziggurat through Syria, the bell tower of Christian churches, or from circular Persian forms borrowed from India. The faithful were called to prayer five times a day from the top of the minaret. Around the early minarets, there was a wall with towers at the corners. Moorish and North African minarets were square in plan. Minarets got their slender form, decorative arcades, balconies (or **serets**), and exterior tile surfaces during ensuing centuries. In fact, glazed tiles, both inside and outside, became one of the most characteristic features of Islamic buildings. (See Figure 7.26.)

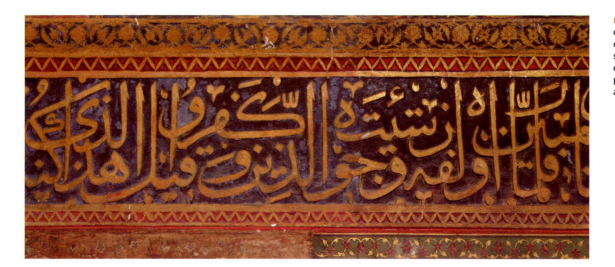

FIGURE 7.27 Bands of Arabic script using decorative characters surround mihrabs and openings, decorate pulpits and doors, and are used as friezes.

INTERIORS

In contrast with its exterior, the interior of the mosque was filled with brilliant color. Mosaics and tile designs covered floors and the interior surfaces of the mihrab and colored glass filled windows. The lower portion of walls might be faced with ablaq marble patterns and upper surfaces covered with an abundance of designs, some painted, some carved relief stucco or plaster known as **ataurique,** and some executed in glazed brick or tile. Any of these might be used for ceilings as well. Geometric designs, star patterns, floral forms, arabesques, and as prohibitions against their use relaxed, birds and animals, some real, some imaginary were included in the ornamentation. (See Figure 7.27.)

Out of Splendor into Darkness

The Byzantine Empire lasted for a millennium. Much of that time, the West was struggling to emerge from the decline that began when the Romans started pulling out their troops. The Byzantine Empire was a mixture of Oriental and Western culture and preserved the classical heritage, served as a point of trade between East and West, and spread arts and culture as far East as India and Russia. The Empire itself was affected by Islam as it spread, but in turn affected the arts of that religion. It was through the Byzantine Empire that the West learned of classical writings, Eastern and Islamic technology and science, and social customs such as the divine right of kings.

Romanesque Design in Western Europe

The period of time from the demise of the Roman Empire in 476 until about 1000 AD in Europe is known as the Dark Ages because there is little documented history. Roman advances such as roads and water supplies were no longer maintained and fell into ruin. During the seventh and eighth centuries, Germanic tribes including the Franks and Goths, Vikings (Norsemen or later, Normans), Slavs, and Magyars invaded and settled in parts of Europe, but governments were relatively unstable—a stark contrast to the organization of the Romans. Germanic Lombards invaded Italy, the Burgundians and Franks moved into Gaul, the Saxons established a presence in England, and the Visigoths and later the Moors, or Saracens, invaded Spain. In 732, Charles "the Hammer" Martel (688–741), ruler of the Franks, stopped the advance of the Moors north of the Pyrenees at the Battle of Tours, although they periodically threatened Western Europe afterwards. The Germanic tribes retained their social organization and customs throughout the Dark Ages, and it was these customs that were adopted by medieval knights.

After the fall of Rome in 476, the title Emperor in the West remained unclaimed. At the end of the eighth century, when Empress Irene (c. 751–803) was ruling the Byzantine Empire,

Pope Leo III saw an opportunity to regain ancient Roman territory in the East. In the West, women were considered incapable of ruling; therefore, in Leo's eyes, the throne of the Roman emperor was vacant. On Christmas day in the year 800, Leo crowned Charlemagne, King of the Franks, Roman Emperor in the West. By this act, the Pope insulted the Byzantine Empire, whose rulers believed themselves to be the only Roman emperors.

While Charlemagne is often considered the first Holy Roman Emperor, that title was not used until 962 after the coronation of Otto the Great. Although the position of Emperor of the West was an elected one, in practice, the title was generally inherited until there were no longer appropriate heirs. The emperor was ordained a subdeacon in the Church, effectively precluding a female from holding the office.

By crowning Charlemagne, Leo established a precedent of crowning the ruler, a practice that intimated the Pope's superiority over secular leaders—a power the Pope held until 1531 when the English King Henry VIII revolted against the Church, and even later in France, Spain, Germany, and other regions. A second result of the Pope's blessing on the ruler was that the rulers themselves could claim they ruled by divine right. Believing he had been chosen by God to rule, Charlemagne justified a number of his military campaigns as efforts to extirpate paganism. He not only wanted to unify the territory he controlled but to establish a Christian empire. In his effort to rid Saxons of paganism, he destroyed a tree trunk that Saxons believed to be a symbol of power for their gods. Charlemagne forced the Saxons to convert, an act the Saxons revolted against by burning monasteries, churches, and villages. By 814, however, the Saxons were subjugated, as were the Lombards in Northern Italy.

During the 150 years following the rule of Charlemagne, no Emperor in the West was able to create a strong government. Saracen pirates, Norse raiders, and Magyar horsemen raided periodically and internecine strife was rampant among those who owned vast estates. Cities were fortified and castles were constructed for defense. The difficulties were compounded by famine and plague.

Toward the end of the tenth century in northern France, the Christianized Normans established an orderly state and from there invaded and conquered England in 1066. Four decades later, the Normans increased their sphere of influence by conquering Sicily and parts of southern Italy. During the same time period, Hungary was Christianized and formed a buffer between the invaders from the East and Western Europe. By the year 1000 the modern nations were beginning to consolidate with France leading the way. As the economic situation improved, trade and travel, especially on Crusades or pilgrimages, fostered the interchange of ideas and goods.

Characteristics of Medieval Society

The most significant unifying factor in Europe during the Middle Ages was Christianity. The Church had continued to grow and prosper during the Dark Ages and slowly it emerged to claim divine power and invincibility.

Charlemagne, who was fluent in Latin, encouraged education and the provision of schools associated with the Church. Local churches and monasteries established schools where not only the basics (e.g., grammar, rhetoric, Latin, astronomy, and mathematics) but the classics could be learned. These schools continued to provide education even after the establishment of the first universities in Europe. Charlemagne also invited foreign scholars to educate monks and priests and to participate in civil service. Contact

with the Near East and with the Moors in Spain throughout the period provided other venues for classical learning to make its way into Europe.

MONASTERIES

The first European monasteries were established as early as the fourth century in Ireland, Britain, and Gaul. These early examples were primitive and consisted of hermits or recluses. Charlemagne imposed the Benedictine Rule, written c. 530, on monasteries in his Empire resulting in well-organized establishments with educated monks, many of whom were scholars or teachers. Monks traveled from one monastery to another often to copy manuscripts they could not otherwise obtain. As a result, ideas for building design and other artistic endeavors were carried from one place to another. Eventually, the buildings associated with monasteries took on the same characteristics although there were always some differences in style.

Monasteries thrived, multiplied, and grew rich while spreading Christianity. Their treasuries contained money, land, and other valuables bequeathed them by uneasy souls seeking absolution, and their brotherhoods grew as individuals sought peace and asylum in a period of chaos and war.

Through monasteries, Christianity was spread over ever-larger areas. The ninth century St. Gall in Switzerland was one of many that had libraries containing ancient manuscripts, both secular and sacred. While war raged around them, the monks were able to copy manuscripts in monastery scriptoria, or writing rooms, preserving them for future generations. The works of Aristotle, Cicero, Virgil, and numerous others may have perished without the efforts of these monks. Manuscripts were not only copied but, as in the Byzantine Empire, they were illuminated or ornamented with pictures and decorated letters. The various scripts in which the original manuscripts were written were sometimes difficult to read so during this period, a new script, known as Carolingian minuscule, was developed making copy work consistent. When this script was rediscovered during the Renaissance, scholars believed it to be classical and used it for lowercase letters in printed books. Monasteries required numerous buildings, including churches, cloisters, refectories (dining halls), scriptoria, hospitals, dormitories, and facilities for guests. As monasteries were relatively self-sufficient, space was also needed for gardens, granaries, brew houses, livestock, and workshops.

The **cloister** was an open courtyard that abutted the church. It was enclosed by a covered ambulatory around all sides off of which access could be gained to other buildings and parts of the monastery. Cloisters frequently had work or study carrels that opened onto them. Typically, there were two entrances to the church from the cloister. Other features usually located around the cloister included the **chapter house**, a room in which meetings were held and discipline was enforced. In England, the chapter house was most often polygonal and connected to the church itself. The abbot's lodging, lavatory, dormitory, guest rooms, and refectory generally opened onto the cloister as well. (See Figure 8.1.)

FEUDALISM

The Germanic tradition of an elected leader who controlled all land in the territory and could distribute it to others in return for services or loyalty was adapted as feudalism as early as the eighth century although its fullest development occurred in the tenth through the thirteenth centuries. Under feudalism, land was the chief form of wealth.

Kings granted land tenure, but not ownership, to nobles (who became the king's vassals) in exchange for military obligations. The vassals in turn became lords as they gave land tenure to their own vassals in exchange for the promise of military service when the need arose. Lords entered the relationship to ensure they could protect their property; vassals entered the relationship for the land itself. Major land holders—that is, the nobility—had full authority over their territory; they could coin money, tax their people, and build castles and fortifications for protection. Each noble desired to be self-sufficient, requiring no help from a distant sovereign who was often unwilling or unable to provide protection. This meant that landowners could build up considerable political influence as well as military supremacy.

Feudalism differed greatly depending on the area and the time period. In German areas, the vassals who worked the land became serfs and were tied to the land. In other areas, the relationship required only that peasants provide military service in time of need, give a portion of crops to the lord, and sometimes have grain ground at

the lord's mills. The obligation of the lords was to provide protection for vassals and to maintain the land. The Normans were responsible for introducing feudalism into England.

Nobles could not always be depended on to come to the aid of a distant king. Kings wanting to be independent of their nobles hired mercenaries to help fight wars and subsequently created standing armies. The Hundred Years' War (1337–1453) saw the demise of feudalism as soldiers began to be paid in gold rather than land. The result was that gold was widely distributed, undermining the land-based feudal system.

By the thirteenth century, land tenure began to shift from that for service to that for monetary rent. As the plagues of the thirteenth and fourteenth centuries receded, the population had been decimated and, as a result, there were fewer laborers and high demand. Peasant revolts throughout Europe dealt the final blow to tenure for service, and peasants became paid laborers.

COMMERCE

Some urban areas were major religious centers controlled by bishops, and it was here that the Roman model of government continued to exist. Other towns prospered through a continuation of trade with the Mediterranean. In Cologne, a

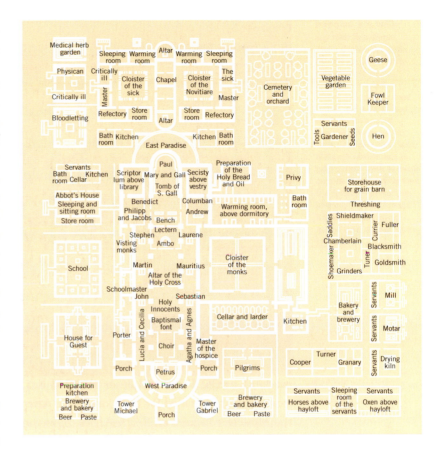

FIGURE 8.1 Founded in 613, the monastery of St. Gall in Switzerland houses one of the most extensive medieval libraries in the world. This plan represented the ideal medieval monastery, although it was never brought to fruition.

Latin monasteries, permanent Christian communities, and hospices that housed pilgrims continued to prosper. In 1009 a Moslem caliph ordered the destruction of the Church of the Holy Sepulcher in Jerusalem, breaking down relationships between Christians and Moslems. The caliph's successor allowed the Byzantine Emperor to rebuild the church and permitted pilgrims to once again visit holy sites. Reports of cruelty aimed at Christians, however, reached the West, fanning the flames of enmity.

In 1063, the Pope had granted his blessing to Christians who were killed fighting Islamic forces in Iberia. As the Moslem Seljuk Dynasty began to expand into the Byzantine Empire, the Byzantine Emperor Alexius I Comenus appealed to the Pope for help. In response, Pope Urban II launched the Crusades to regain control of the Holy Land and its spiritually important monuments from control of Islamic factions. The call went out from pulpits throughout Europe announcing that participants would be granted indulgences, although what that really meant is still questioned. These major religious conflicts lasted from 1095 to 1291. Even afterward, there continued to be minor crusades until the sixteenth century.

When Alexius asked for mercenaries to help regain not only the Holy Land but lost Byzantine territory, he expected control to be returned to him, but the emperor was to be disappointed. Pope Urban II saw the Crusades as an opportunity to increase the prestige of the Roman Church and possibly to regain control of Christianity in the East. The Crusaders themselves established several independent Latin kingdoms, including the Kingdom of Jerusalem. All of these factors widened the rift between the Eastern and Western churches.

Venice and Constantinople were rivals for the lucrative trade with the East. In 1204, during the Fourth Crusade, when Crusaders could not pay for the transportation and supplies they had requested, the Venetians demanded that in lieu of payment, the Crusaders sack the city of Constantinople. The successful attack resulted in a reduction of Byzantine territory and weakened the Empire, hastening its downfall.

The goals of the Crusades went unmet and the Islamic states continued to grow until all of the territory temporarily controlled by the Crusaders was eventually regained. The effects on Europe, however, were more lasting. The schism between the Eastern Orthodox Church and the Roman Catholic Church that had brewed for centuries became permanent. The Pope gained more control not only over religious matters but over political affairs in Europe. The way had been paved for the development of strong national governments as kings gained power through participation in the Crusades by themselves and their vassals.

In the East, the Crusaders were exposed to new cultures, luxuries unknown in the West, and novel ideas. From the Arabs, the Crusaders brought back algebra, engineering, and optics, and from the Byzantine Empire, political ideas such as the divine right of kings, luxurious living, and classical literature. Prior to the Crusades, Europeans had had some exposure to classical literature in their relationships with the Moslems in Iberia, who themselves had learned of that literature from the Byzantine Empire, from Christian Syria, and from the Moslem influence in Sicily. New foods including oranges and apples, spices, and gunpowder were brought back. Glass manufacturing techniques of the East were far beyond those of the West and the improved technology helped to make possible the large windows of the subsequent Gothic period.

European crusaders left a land where castles were wooden buildings on high ground. When they returned, they brought with them the concept of a strongly fortified stone castle. Both Moslems and Christians did share at least one change brought about by the Crusades: previously, the two had mutual respect for one another; the Crusades, however, fostered intolerance between them.

FEATURES OF MEDIEVAL EUROPE

Beginning in the ninth century, burghs (also called boroughs and buries) appeared across the landscape of Europe. These strongholds had surrounding walls with an external moat. Usually, they were circular, although it was sometimes necessary for walls to follow natural topographical features. A **keep**, or defensive tower, was located in the center along with a church or chapel, granaries and cellars for food storage, and small dwellings for the clergy and official visitors. Large supplies of food were stored within so that inhabitants could withstand a siege. Peasants provided necessary labor and tilled the soil. Merchants and artisans were often given permission

FIGURE 8.4 The city gate at Lubeck, Germany, with its two round towers is almost all that remains of the original city walls.

to settle near the outside of walls, forming the nucleus of a future town.

Many of the early medieval cities built up around the burghs or around monasteries. Additional walls enclosed the city and formed a clear line of demarcation between rural and urban areas. Like castle walls, town walls were crenellated, had projecting towers, a surrounding moat, and a gateway protected by one or more towers. These defensive measures were necessary not only to protect residents from attack by raiding tribes but by rival feudal lords. When cities outgrew their walls, they grew concentrically, forming another ring of walls outside the first to enclose more area. A number of European cities have ring roads that follow the lines of these medieval walls. (See Figure 8.4.)

A church and a city hall usually dominated the city center. A major market was located in the open space in front of the city hall and provided an outlet for the products and produce of surrounding rural areas. Narrow winding lanes broadened at intervals into other, irregular squares. As guilds developed, members gathered in close proximity, giving the name of their trades to streets or neighborhoods. Guilds were responsible for defense of specific sections of the wall or towers.

Although cities had high population densities for the time period, they were relatively small

(few cities exceeded 800 feet in diameter), and the countryside was only a short walk away. Many town dwellers pursued agriculture outside the walls, spending their days in rural environments. By the beginning of the tenth century, cities were located approximately a day's journey by foot, or about 15 miles, from one another.

Romanesque Arts and Design

Major artistic works of the Romanesque period were done under the aegis of the Church and rarely did artists select their own subjects. Because the local church served as the "poor man's Bible," it was necessary to follow the conventions established by the church when depicting religious subjects. Only God, Christ, and angels could be portrayed with bare feet, for example. Scenes might differ in detail, but stories had to adhere to accepted dogma. Typical narrative scenes included the Last Judgment, which might depict people naked, partially clothed, fully clothed, or distinguish between the saved and the dammed by clothing. A **nimbus**, or light-filled halo around the head of a figure, denoted sanctity, as it had from the earliest Christian period. When a cross was added to the nimbus, it was an indication that the figure was Divine. An **aureole** surrounded the entire body with the light of sanctity.

Romanesque art focused on the overall design and little thought was given to the minutiae of

FIGURE 8.5 By the middle of the period, Romanesque sculpture was organized with continuous narratives in deep relief. Figures were still stiff, and movements appeared jerky.

FIGURE 8.6 Ivory was a favored carving material. Elephant ivory was preferred because of its size and fine texture. Most ivory used in Western Europe, however, was walrus ivory or the bones or teeth of whales. The Lewis Chessmen were found on the Isle of Lewis in the Hebrides, which was ruled by Norway during the Medieval period, and may be Scandinavian in origin.

details. Art was two-dimensional, with no attempt at perspective and the choice of subject was dictated by location. Narratives or single images were used on interior vaults and walls of the nave, saints and prophets were depicted in the spandrels of arches, and Christ in Majesty was located in the apse. Large-scale murals were used again for the first time in Western Europe since the fall of Rome.

Although there was little room in churches for secular imagery, when artists did work with secular subjects, they had more freedom to express themselves. Zodiacal signs, seasonal activities, and personifications of the seven arts (grammar, rhetoric, logic, arithmetic, geometry, astronomy, and music) were common. Most statues were painted, as were wall surfaces, doors, and pulpits. Painting was relatively inexpensive when compared with Byzantine mosaics and later Gothic stained glass. Painting, however, could be easily damaged by the smoke of candles and the dampness associated with unheated buildings. Scenic murals were typically located on the upper parts of walls while the lower portions were painted with draperies or faux marble.

ROMANESQUE SCULPTURE

For several centuries, sculpture had been relegated to small pieces, but by the mid-eleventh century, Romanesque sculpture was bringing back larger sculptural works. Because of its durability, stone sculpture was often located on the exterior of buildings. Early examples were carved in relatively flat relief, loosely arranged, and not integrated with the architecture it adorned. (See Figure 8.5.)

Geometric forms were common and were easily incorporated into the multiple layers of moldings, or **orders**, around doorways. Jamb figures were carved on window or door jambs and could be Biblical characters, religious leaders, or secular leaders. Of necessity, the figures were elongated to adhere to the architectural background on which they were located. In Italy, few human forms were used but natural and stylized animals were employed in scenes, on capitals, and elsewhere. Gargoyles, **basilisks** (a type of lizard sometimes combined with a rooster), griffins, and lions were used individually or interlaced with vines and foliage.

Tympana provided the largest spaces for sculpture, and it was over the main doorway that the most important subjects were treated. In France, the tympanum of the central doorway was reserved for the Last Judgment, the right tympanum for the Virgin Mary, and the left for local saints.

Wood and ivory carvings featured the same subjects, but because they were not tied to architecture, could be figures in the round. Christ, the Virgin Mary, and crucifixes abounded. Many were painted and silver leaf was sometimes applied. (See Figure 8.6.)

ROMANESQUE METAL WORK

Translucent Byzantine cloisonné gave way to more easily worked opaque champlevé enamel. Enamel, gold, silver, gems, and ivory were used for reliquaries that were made in a variety of forms including images of small churches. Boxes were most typical for reliquaries, although many were shaped in the form of the part of the body held within.

ROMANESQUE MOTIFS

Celtic tribes had sacked Rome in 390 BC and Greek cities in 280 BC, and until near the end of the sixth century were dominant in Europe.

FIGURE 8.7 This German champlevé medallion is made of copper and displays the crucifixion.

FIGURE 8.8 Celtic ornament was used in Romanesque metalwork, carved in stone, and used for manuscript illumination.

The German tribes were probably either Celtic or greatly influenced by them. By the sixth century, Celtic tribes had been driven to Northern France and the British Isles, but their influence remained in Western Europe. By the eighth century, Celtic ornament was elaborate and made use of interlacing forms and the spiral. Snakes and dragon figures were characteristic, although these were Scandinavian in origin.

Religious motifs predominated in Romanesque ornament, although secular images were employed and even used in churches. Figures were often identified by an emblem or an attribute. John the Baptist was shown dressed in animal skins, St. Peter with the keys of heaven, and St. Francis of Assisi (1181–1226) with small animals. The dove, especially when bathed in light or with a nimbus, represented the Holy Spirit, the fish symbolized Christ as did the chi-rho monogram, and Christ as a shepherd indicated benevolence. Martyrs carried the instruments of their death: the beheaded St. Denis (died c. 250–270), for example, was shown carrying his own head. Signs of the zodiac, the labors for the different seasons of the years, and the days of creation graced paintings and later, Gothic windows. Figures representing human characteristics such as vices or virtues while serving as a warning or example had no obvious spiritual connotations. Griffins and unicorns were used to teach moral lessons.

Where classical influences remained strong, acanthus leaves, anthemia, and frets were used in abundance. The classic rinceau was modified: texture was added to the stem to give it the appearance of bark, branches sprang from the stem like grafts with a small ridge at their starting points, and leaves were simplified and their lobes rounded. The rinceau was sometimes doubled, forming ovals or heart shapes.

Diamonds, circles, and other geometric forms were often alternated in bands. Chip carved motifs were derived from those carved in stone on buildings, and furniture forms often took the shape of miniature buildings. This was especially true in France and after the Norman Conquest, in England, where arcades graced the fronts of chests and other case pieces. (See Box 8.1).

FIGURE 8.9 Zoomorphic forms including birds and animals were common through the fourteenth century but were probably derived from Lombardic or Byzantine sources.

BOX 8.1 ROMANESQUE MOTIFS

The **dog tooth** motif was a four-leaved ornament that radiated from a central point and that had a rib on each of the lobes.

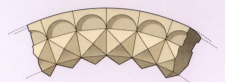

The **nailhead** was a three-dimensional square motif with the appearance of a pyramid. It was formed by four triangles meeting at an apex.

Zigzag or **chevron** designs were linear V-shaped band patterns, often used in multiples.

Lozenge patterns were four-sided diamond-shaped figures.

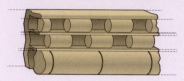

Billet molding consisted of multiple bands of alternating short cylindrical molding and equally sized open spaces. Rows alternated as well so that the billet in one row was flanked by spaces in other rows.

The **beak head molding** featured stylized heads of animals or humans carved into a concave molding. Heads had an elongated triangular beak that extended over a convex molding.

Moorish

The Moors were Arabs and Berbers from Morocco who adhered to the Islamic religion. They entered Spain in 711 AD occupying much of the southern part of the Iberian Peninsula where the hot, arid climate was familiar. Although they dominated the cultural life of the conquered territory, seventh-century Moors were tolerant of the Spanish religion and customs and allowed some inhabitants to keep both in exchange for a tax. Christians living in Moorish areas were known as Mozarabs. By the ninth century, the Moors had become intolerant of the Christians and made it difficult for the Catholics to remain in their homes in Moorish-held territory. As a result, many of the Christians moved north into parts of Spain that were not under Moorish control. As they went, they carried with them the Moorish architectural traditions with which they were familiar. Gradually, the Spanish began to drive the Moors out of the country with their final expulsion in 1492. The term Mudejar was applied to Muslims who remained in Christian Spain after this reconquest. Mudejar art was a combination of Moorish and Christian design characterized by an excess of ornament.

MOORISH ARCHITECTURE

Building exteriors were often plain but interiors were ornate. This combination may have stemmed from the tent used by Arab nomads as well as from their desire for privacy and seclusion. Like structures in other hot climates, Moorish buildings turned inward and were constructed around one or more courtyards. Iron gates and grilles provided security without deterring the flow of breezes. Most windows and doors opened onto the courtyard with only a few windows on upper levels in exterior walls. Shutters or pierced stone lattice work **mesherabijeh** (equivalent to Arabic mashrabiyyah) allowed breezes to flow freely but provided privacy especially for women, who were secluded. In Mudejar homes, ventilated shutters were either made with turned spindles or pierced holes in their panels—or with **Persiana**—or slatted blinds that opened and closed. Windows that looked out on a view were known as **miradors**.

Buildings had low-pitched or flat terra-cotta tile roofs with wide eaves. The **horseshoe arch**, with an opening greater than 180 degrees, was used extensively. Frequently, the arches had multiple small cusps or partial circles known as **foils**, but both the ogee arch and Roman semicircular arch were also used. Arches typically were framed in a rectangle and the spandrels filled with minutely scaled all over carved relief designs known as **yesería**. Moorish columns were slender with straight shafts and often had square capitals covered with pierced carved designs.

Ordinary Moorish houses were very small and built close together. Entry doors were made of wood and, in African style, were covered with wood or metal studs. Christian houses, known as **carmenes**, were several times larger than those of the Moorish neighbors. Mudejar homes had bathrooms, a feature copied from the Moors, while Christian homes lacked this amenity.

Tiles, or **azulejos**, were used for surrounds of openings and sometimes for the jambs. Walls often had a dado of colored tiles that protected the lower portion from damage. A section of a dado might be tiled with a particular pattern and color and an adjacent section even on the same wall with a different pattern and color. Between the dado and the frieze located near the ceiling, the plaster wall was covered with yesería—typically abstract foliage designs. Walls might also be covered with rugs or tapestries or by **guadamacileria**, or decorated leather that was punched, quilted, or embossed. A frieze of Arabic script or geometric forms finished the wall at the top.

Proto-Romanesque Architecture

The Romanesque and Gothic artistic movements produced the major widespread styles in Europe between the fall of Rome and the Renaissance. Other, more local, movements, however, preceded the Romanesque: Carolingian in Germany and France, Moorish and Asturian in Spain, and Anglo-Saxon in England. Of these, the Carolingian made the most significant impact on the Romanesque.

ASTURIAN DESIGN (EIGHTH–TENTH CENTURY)

While Southern Spain was under the influence of the Moors, Asturian territory in Northern Spain's Galicia region was Christian. Tradition indicated that St. James had preached in Galicia, and during the eighth century, his bones were miraculously found buried in a field. James was declared the patron saint of Spain, a shrine was constructed on the site where the bones were found, and his tomb was recognized by the Church in 813. When Charlemagne was crowned Roman Emperor in the West, there was a renewed interest in pilgrimages. Churches that had important relics were able to raise funds from pilgrims, especially when miracles were associated with them. The remains of St. James were significant and Santiago de Compostela, the church built to house the remains, became one of the four major medieval pilgrimage sites. This church had a cruciform plan with aisles and an ambulatory.

Asturian architecture was similar to that of Western Europe. The Asturians used barrel vaulted roofs over crudely built high stone walls with buttresses. Both Greek cross and basilican plans were used. Although a formal transept was not used, there were frequently chapels projecting from the sides of the church. The horseshoe arch was a part of Asturian Visigothic heritage and was typical, although semicircular arches were also used. Windows had carved stone grillwork, a concession to the climate. From the Romans, the Asturians borrowed the triumphal arch for use between the nave and the apse. Walls were covered with architectural frescoes similar to those of Pompeii, and vaults were painted to give them the appearance of Roman coffered ceilings. Byzantine columns and capitals were used. From their Visigothic forebears came round medallions, circumscribed stars, and cable moldings.

ANGLO-SAXON DESIGN (SIXTH–ELEVENTH CENTURIES)

Early Anglo-Saxon buildings of Britain were constructed first of timber and later of rubble stone. The churches had a broad nave without aisles. The squared projecting **chancel**, or sanctuary, had two chambers beside it; these were called **pastophoria**, and they served the same function as the Byzantine prothesis and diaconicon. Porticoes on the sides were used for burials, and the entry was through the narthex. Sometimes, the entry end was apsidal with a rounded projecting space. A triple-arched iconostasis based on the Roman triumphal arch separated the nave and the apse. Later Anglo-Saxon churches

FIGURE 8.11 The groin vault was an efficient vault because the thrust could be concentrated at four points supported by massive piers with all four vertical planes open for fenestration.

divide walls into panels. These narrow strips of stone without bases or capitals ran vertically and horizontally, forming panels that were plastered. Additional decorative strips might be used to form geometric outlines. As if to emphasize the strength of square corners and arch jambs, long and short quoins alternated. Quoins were usually made of a different material than the rest of the structure. They were precisely cut and laid so that they projected slightly from the wall surface. Towers were stepped back slightly in stages. In central Europe and the Low Countries, brick was a common building material, but most other Romanesque buildings were constructed of stone. The exterior of previous buildings had been unadorned, but Romanesque buildings began to reflect the interior organization into bays by the use of external buttresses, although the buttresses did not need to project very far due to the massiveness of the walls. **Lombard bands** derived from Northern Italy were small arcades often located just beneath the roof. (See Figure 8.12.) A blind arch was simply an arch in shallow relief on a façade and blind arcading was a feature of English Romanesque architecture. In Norman design, arcades were sometimes interlaced. Tiered external open arcades were typical of Pisa and other Northern Italian areas.

Ambulatories, when present, were located behind the choir. Beyond that, there might be multiple chapels, including a Lady Chapel dedicated to the Virgin Mary.

Romanesque columns were not tapered, often had incised decorations on the shaft, and employed a variety of capitals. Where Roman remains were influential, capitals were simplified Corinthian types. Pierced lace-like capitals, similar to those of the Byzantine era, were used where that influence was felt. Norman columns often had spur leaves connecting the base to the shaft; a thick, heavy ornamented abacus; and, especially in Northern France and Britain, a simple cushion capital. Some were cube-shaped with the lower corners rounded off so that the block would fit on a circular shaft. The four faces, then, were reduced to upside down semi-circular lunettes. The scalloped capital was similar, but the rounded lower corners were formed into trumpet-like shapes. (See Box 8.2.)

Historiated capitals were ornamented with animals, birds, or humans either alone or in combination with foliage and usually illustrated Biblical stories or moral lessons. By the mid-eleventh century, monsters were added to the repertoire.

FIGURE 8.12 The Lombard band is an example of a corbel table, which is a projecting course supported in this case by a small arcade. The Lombard band was often used to define varying levels of the building.

BOX 8.2 NORMAN COLUMNS

A variety of shaft styles were used on Norman columns. Most cushion capitals were very simple.

Corner figures resting on acanthus leaves graced some capitals. (See Box 8.3.)

ROMANESQUE CASTLES

During the centuries of chaos and war, defense was a priority. The first European castles of the Medieval period were of the **motte and bailey** form. The motte was a hill, usually artificial, and made by digging a ditch and using the earth to form the mound. There were examples of castles constructed on natural hilltops. The **keep** or, defensive tower, was constructed on top of a motte surrounded by a wide ditch called a moat. In France, the keep was called a **donjon**. The **bailey** was a courtyard, also called a ward, that was surrounded by a **palisade** fence or wall located below the motte. A palisade wall was constructed using side-by-side vertical timbers or posts. If a stone wall replaced the timber palisade, a **shell keep** resulted. Most motte and bailey castles, however, never had stone walls. At Windsor Castle in England, multiple baileys flank the motte. Other castles had concentric baileys, positioned one inside the other with inner and outer wards. A moat might be constructed around the entire castle although it was not always filled with water. Curtain walls were those that surrounded the entire complex. When there were concentric walls, the inner curtain wall enclosed the inner ward. Only a single opening protected by a drawbridge that could be raised or lowered

pierced the outer wall. Motte and bailey castles could be erected quickly: William the Conqueror had Pevensey castle constructed on this model in eight days. (See Figure 8.13.)

In 987, the Count of Anjou built the first recorded stone keep, but it was not until Crusaders returning from the East brought descriptions of Saracen defensive architecture that stone defenses became common. Several features of Saracen castles were adopted for use in the West. Between the moat and the wall was a flat area known as a **berm** that attackers would need to cross under fire to reach the walls. The stone walls were angled outward at the bottom to make them more difficult

FIGURE 8.13 William the Conqueror constructed a wooden keep on the motte that is now topped by the Round Tower of Windsor Castle. The motte itself is made of the chalk excavated from the ditch. The ditch was allowed to fill with water and became a moat. The windows were a later alteration.

Box 8.3 Characteristics of Romanesque Architecture

General Characteristics
- Semicircular arches
- Arcades
- Alternating column and pier supports
- Ambulatory connected to aisles
- Groin vaults
- Quadrant vaults over aisles
- Bays
- Cushion capitals
- Historiated capitals
- Decorated or plain column shafts
- Fortified appearance
- Westwerk on churches
- Nave, triforium, and clerestory levels in churches
- Plate tracery
- Openings with stepped architraves following arch
- Quire on raised platform
- Wheel windows

German Romanesque
- Cable moldings on openings
- Lombard bands
- Dominant stair towers at both the east and west ends with steep pointed polygonal or conical roofs
- Helm roofs on some towers
- Lower rounded apse projecting from a higher squared end
- Multiple towers—often octagonal
- Square bays
- Westwerk

Italian Romanesque
- Separate circular or square campanile near the west front except in Lombardy
- Arched niches in bands divide campanile into stages
- Separate baptistery often with eight sides
- Mosaics in Rome, Venice, and southern Italy used on floors and columns
- West front in Lombardy has a pair of towers
- Pisan Romanesque features tiers of freestanding arcades
- Colored marble on façades
- Dome over some crossings
- Modified cruciform plans—some with double aisles
- Projecting semicircular arched baldachin porches supported by

two columns at the outside corners, each of which rests on the back of a recumbent animal form in North Italy
- Screen façades surmounted by a single gable in North Italy
- Columns classical and decorated with foliage
- Solominic column shafts, fluted shafts, and shafts inlaid with mosaics
- Pisan Romanesque uses alternating light and dark marble
- Tuscan Romanesque features inlaid marble patterns
- Cupolas on domes
- Drums beneath domes
- Both basilican and cruciform plans used
- Apse end projects below the main roofline and has its own roof
- West front highly decorated but east end conservative. No westwerk
- Rib vaults especially in Lombardy
- Lombard bands

French Romanesque
- Radiating chapels extending from the apse forming a chevet
- The apse can be circular or polygonal
- An ambulatory separates the external chapels from the quire of the church in the apse end
- Simple barrel vaulting over the nave with half vaults over the aisles
- Blind arcading on the exterior
- Paired columns
- French grotesque masks, fantastical beasts, figures
- More bold sculptural forms used to decorate façades than other regions use
- Square towers in westwerk
- Towers at crossing and sometimes at the ends of the transepts
- Triforium is arcaded
- Compound piers composed of numerous shafts
- Full-height shafts rise through all levels to support the vaults

Features of Norman Architecture in England and Northern France
- Square or apsidal east ends
- Monastic churches may have two transepts

- Projecting chapels but not developed into a chevet
- Rood screen divides the nave from choir
- Paired towers at entry
- Tower or fleche (small spire) over crossing
- Cylindrical or clustered piers—sometimes alternating
- Incised geometric designs on column shafts and capitals
- Groin or rib vaults
- Galilee or lady chapel
- Square tower at center of west end
- Buttresses projecting on exterior
- Parish churches often battlemented
- Sculptural ornament around windows
- Interlacing arches
- Spur leaves at corners on column bases
- Cushion and scalloped cushion capitals
- Celtic ornament

Arab Norman style
- Pointed arches
- Inlaid marble wainscot with serrated cresting
- Mosaics on upper walls
- Solominic columns
- Open timber ceilings
- Cufic inscriptions

Spanish
- Mixture of Moorish Christian and French elements
- Protruding mass of masonry at doors
- Ribbed vaults with quadripartite or four compartments
- Covered arcades raised on pedestal
- Wall faces broken by vertical lines
- Lantern or cimborio over crossing
- Abstract ornament mixed with figural forms
- Moorish fish scale slate roofing
- Horseshoe arch
- Use of very large stone blocks.

Italian Romanesque

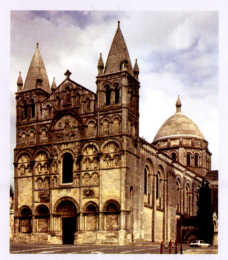

French Romanesque

Norman

Arab Norman

Spanish

to sabotage or to climb. Along the top of the thick walls where soldiers patrolled were crenellation, as well as on the keep. Frequently, the battlement projected outward as a corbel table beyond the walls on brackets to form a **machicolation**. Openings in the floor of this gallery permitted the defenders to pour molten lead or boiling oil on attackers, drop rocks on them, or shoot at them.

Outwardly projecting towers were located an arrow's flight apart on the walls. At first, towers had angled corners, but these were easily undermined by building a fire beneath a corner that could cause the structure to collapse. Round tower bases were more resistant to undermining because there were no corners to collapse, and they offered more angles for shooting.

The most vulnerable point in any castle was its gate. Two types of defense were used at that point. The approach to the gate incorporated right-angle turns, creating a bent entry that forced attackers to follow a winding path under enemy fire—a Saracen innovation used as far away as India. This type of entrance slowed riders on horseback as well. Because the turns angled to the right, it was necessary for attackers to expose their unshielded side to defensive fire. The bent entry also precluded the use of the battering ram.

The second line of defense at the gate consisted of towers constructed on both sides to allow shooting at enemies from multiple angles. The **barbican** consisted of the gateway and towers from which the drawbridge could be defended. The drawbridge was a platform designed to span the moat in front of the gatehouse and could be raised to block entry at night and in times of danger. The gate was protected by a heavy timber or iron **portcullis** that could be raised or lowered. Portcullises were often paired with one at the inner and one at the outer limit of the gate. Attackers could be caught between the gates and the murder holes above used to discourage the invaders. Usually there was at least one **postern gate**, a less important entrance that was sometimes secret to allow occupants to escape. The defenses of the castle made it possible for a small band of defenders to defend against a force many times its size. At times, defenders even propped dummies on the battlements to give the illusion of greater force. (See Figures 8.14, 8.15 and 8.16.)

Castles were erected on ever more elaborate plans until the mid-fourteenth century when gunpowder and cannons made the castle obso-

FIGURE 8.14 Malahide Castle near Dublin was begun in 1185. Later changes added windows to the towers and above the gate. Battlements and machicolations were retained.

lete. Manor houses of the wealthy, however, continued to be constructed as pseudo castles until the eighteenth century and beyond.

INFLUENCE 8.2

Pseudo castles were constructed even into the nineteenth century. Neuschwanstein Castle in Germany (begun 1869 and never finished), Coch Castle in Wales (1870s on the site of a ruined thirteenth-century castle), and Lynd-hurst in Tarrytown, New York (designed in 1838), are examples.

ROMANESQUE CATHEDRALS AND CHURCHES

Abbey churches and cathedrals were usually among the largest edifices in a region, although some remained small. While an abbey church was associated with a monastery or convent, a cathedral

FIGURE 8.15 Narrow vertical slits forming arrow loops through the walls were accessed through splayed recesses. The length of the slit allowed defenders to raise or lower their bows for better aim.

FIGURE 8.16 Stairways within the castle were spiral and wound upwards clockwise so attackers coming up the stairs would be hindered in their sword swing by the center post while defenders could freely use their swords.

FIGURE 8.17 Medieval churches and monasteries, like their civic counterparts, required defensive measures. Mont St. Michele in Normandy, France, was constructed on a small island that was cut off from the mainland at high tide, surrounded by gated walls, and the monastery itself was located at the very top of a granite rock that was about 273 feet in height. A village grew up around the abbey.

was a church that housed the cathedra, or the chair of a bishop. The two were not mutually exclusive, and a number of cathedrals had their beginnings as a monastery where numerous members of the Order said mass at multiple altars. Minster (English) and münster (German) are designations used to identify churches that have monastic origins. By the Medieval period, the cathedra was located behind the altar and in the quire when there was one. Cathedrals were necessarily large in order that certain liturgical rites, such as ordination, could be held in the presence of large numbers of clergy and lay people. As these churches were created to glorify God, it was appropriate that they should be constructed of the finest materials and artisanship available.

Most churches were on an east-west axis with the altar at the east end. It was there that the greatest diversity of form occurred. In England, for example, the east end was most often squared; in France, the east end was a complex curvilinear structure with projecting chapels radiating from it. On the exterior, the west front was the most ornate because that was the direction from which processions originated.

Inside, the basic form was that of a basilica, often with transepts added to form a Latin cross. Like the ancient basilica, the nave was separated from side aisles, which could be multiple, by a colonnade or arcade formed with alternating piers and columns or in some cases, slender and thicker piers. These supports extended to the spring of the vault. Piers at the intersection of large arches at right angles were typically cruciform in shape to provide support for each of the arches. In Germany, the aisles were frequently as high as the nave, resulting in a **hallenkirche**, or hall church. In other areas, a second story gallery, or **triforium**, overlooked the nave and had windows on its exterior walls. Windows on the third level were located in walls that extended the nave upward beyond the level of the aisle roofs and lit the center of the structure. (See Figure 8.19.)

FIGURE 8.18 Massive circular forms were known as drum piers. Others were square, rectangular, or formed of a group of components.

armless folding stools were derived from the sella curulis through the faldstool. (See Figure 8.26.)

CHAIR OF ESTATE

The **chair of estate**, accompanied by a footstool, was reserved for the highest-ranking individual present. In less affluent homes, the chair of estate might be the only chair and be of crude construction. The chair of estate often took the form of the faldstool with its curving X-frame. Late in the Romanesque period after the Crusades had begun, an influence from the Byzantine Empire led to the use of a canopy over the chair. The canopy served to emphasize the owner's position within the social hierarchy. The chair of estate was often raised on a dais as another symbol of the occupant's elevated status. On some occasions when high-ranking individuals met together, there were multiple chairs of estate, with each individual bringing his own.

TABLES

The **trestle table** was the most common Medieval table form, and it remained common until the eighteenth century. Two or more trestles or supports were used beneath a large board or several boards to create the flat surface needed for dining. When not in use, the boards and the trestles could simply be placed against a wall out of the way. Typically, guests were seated only along one side, while the other side was left open for serving. When a second table was needed, it was placed at right angles to the first table.

Guests washed their hands at both the beginning and end of the meal because they used their fingers to get food from a common container and to eat with. Guests brought their own knives; forks did not become popular until later. Food was placed on a piece of bread called a trencher rather than on a plate.

Tables were most frequently made of wood, although Charlemagne was said to have had a golden table. Other tables were made of precious metals, but this use was later discontinued and tables were covered with tapestries, rich textiles, and tissues of gold. The covering cloth was known as a **tablier**, or apron. Usually tables were long and rectangular, but there were instances of curved tables. King Arthur of Britain was said to have had a round table. Others were horseshoe shaped. The semicircular table designed to be placed against a wall and undecorated on the back began to be used during this period.

The enclosed cupboard was usually found in monasteries where it was used for storage of books and materials needed for copying and illuminating manuscripts. Small rooms might even be included, especially in monasteries where shelving for books was built in. The lectern continued to be used during the Medieval period mostly in churches and in monasteries.

BEDS

Beds are often mentioned in inventories and tax records of the period, but not all houses had them. People slept on pallets on the floor of the great hall and removed them in the morning, as do several Oriental cultures today. When there were beds, it was rare indeed that the bed was not shared. When traveling, sleeping at an inn often meant sharing a bed with strangers, and even royalty shared a bed with servants when spouses were not in residence.

The simplest bed was the **couchette**, which was used by individuals with little social status, sometimes as a day bed. Some beds were on wheels to simplify moving them, and frequently these beds folded for travel. In England, folding beds were called **trussing beds** because once folded or dismantled, they were trussed with rope or straps. Trussing beds were used through the Renaissance.

It was during the Romanesque period that the **bed of estate** with a separate canopy was developed. Only the highest-ranking member of the household used the canopy, which consisted of a tester and the hangings. The **tester** was a framework from which curtains could be suspended and was not part of the bed but suspended from the ceiling above. Later, it was attached to a vertical board or **celure**, on the wall behind the bed or supported by bedposts. Contemporary inventories sometimes use the terms celure and tester synonymously. A half tester, or **demicelure**, was one that did not extend to the foot of the bed and was used by individuals of slightly lower social rank. In northern Europe, the hangings around the bed were designed to shut out drafts. Sometimes, the area enclosed by the curtains was large enough to include not only the bed, but the chest containing valuables and a chair. A lamp was almost always located within the confines of the enclosed bed. In warmer areas, fewer curtains were used, often only covering the posts. (See Figure 8.24.) Later, royalty used the bed of estate only when receiving visitors whom they wanted to impress. Even kings and queens slept on less elaborate forms.

Out of Darkness into the Light

The Dark Ages, including the Romanesque period, were a time of cultural reorganization. Life was difficult for most people, and religion was their only hope. The rise of the middle class and the demise of feudalism led to a different social climate, and the fact that the world did not end as expected during this period led to a renewal of faith and hope. Exposure to the cultures of the East during the Crusades resulted in new technologies, increased comfort, and luxuries beyond imagination.

The stage was set for the Gothic period when buildings reached for the sky as a symbol of hope, building technology allowed light to pour into structures in unprecedented concentrations, and life became less difficult and more comfortable.

BOX 9.2 RIB VAULTING DESIGNS

Quadripartite vaults were divided by diagonal ribs into four compartments. **Sexpartite vaults** had an additional rib that divided the vault into six compartments.

Fan vaulted ribs spread outwardly from the top of a support and usually meet at the center of the vault.

In **stellar vaulting**, a star pattern is formed at the apex of the vault by the use of additional ribs.

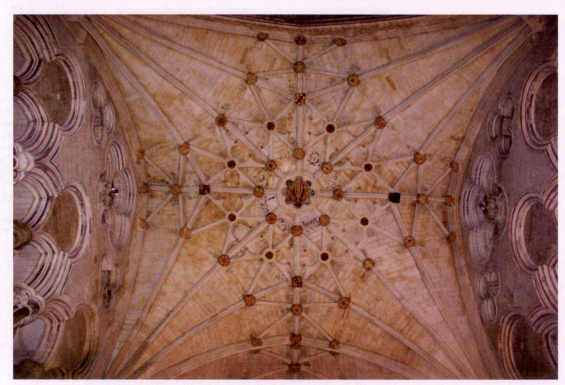

sides were of equal length; therefore, the semicircular arches were the same size. Two semicircular arches could meet at right angles without structural difficulties. Once the bay was changed to a rectangle, however, the arches were of different widths and therefore different heights. Semicircular arches are by definition half as high as they are wide. To ensure that when semicircular arches met at right angles they terminated at the same height, the narrower arches had to be stilted or raised above their supports. This resulted in both an awkward appearance and unsafe design. The solution lay in the pointed arch. Unlike the round arch, pointed arches used at least two centers, making it possible to fit their profile to any needed elevation. When the pointed arch was taller than its radius, the resulting thrust was more vertical, making it more stable than a semicircular arch. Unlike semicircular arches, pointed arches used a joint rather than a keystone at the apex. In England, late Gothic buildings employed a flattened pointed arch known as a **four-centered** or **depressed** arch. (See Figure 9.7.)

The pointed arch was first used in Europe (c. 1100), although it had been used in Assyria in the eighth century BC, in Persian architecture from the seventh century AD, and in Syria by the eighth century. It quickly became a feature of Islamic buildings and was known in Sicily and Spain through these structures.

FIGURE 9.7 The four-centered arch became characteristic of the Early Renaissance in England and has been termed the Tudor arch in honor of the ruling family. All Tudor arches, however, are not constructed on four centers but retain the low profile and point at the apex.

FLYING BUTTRESSES

Flying buttresses transferred the thrust of the arches diagonally to a buttress at the end, from whence the weight was carried downward to the earth. As walls rose higher, it was necessary for the flying buttresses to continue farther outward from the structure. In England, where extreme

FIGURE 9.8 Flying buttresses became a major design feature on the exterior of French cathedrals.

heights were not used, flying buttresses could be small. The nave at Salisbury Cathedral reaches 84 feet in height. At Beauvais in France, the nave soared to over 157 feet. (See Figure 9.8.)

Flying buttresses were connected through the wall to the weakest portions of the arch, the haunch and the springpoint. An arch or half arch carried the thrust of the vaults diagonally over the aisle roof to a heavy abutment away from the structure. Often there were two stacked arches. A pinnacle was added on top of the final abutment with a spire or other vertical element to pinion the arch to the mass vertically. In England, **gab-lets** or small gabled structures, served this function. Early examples were relatively plain but gablets were later ornamented with crockets.

The combination of these three elements decreased the load on external walls, freeing space for fenestration and making possible the soaring building heights achieved throughout Europe. As rivalries between towns for the highest, largest, and widest buildings increased, the technology was pushed to its limits. While the technical problems had been solved by the mid-thirteenth century, the engineering principles were not necessarily understood. Many structures fell before they were completed. In 1284, the choir of Beauvais Cathedral collapsed because the foundation was inadequate for the weight of the structure. Having learned from their errors, Gothic builders often rebuilt fallen structures, giving them greater strength and stability, and gradually improving building technology.

ROOFS

Gable roofs were constructed of timber over interior vaults and were covered with lead. To stabilize timber framing, Gothic carpenters introduced the **tie beam**, a horizontal member that crosses between pairs of rafters to tie them together and help counteract the diagonal thrust. The steepness of the roof often required several tie beams spaced along the rise to ensure stability. Tie beams, however, were not used on every pair of rafters. At Notre Dame in Paris, they occur only on every fifth pair. Carpenters added vertical timbers to the timber framework to connect the bottom joist with the various tie beams, forming a series of triangles increasing the stability of the roof structure.

The English **hammer-beam** roof employed the same principle of triangulation to help counteract rafter thrust. The hammer beam is a beam that protrudes from the wall a short distance and is supported by a diagonal or arched bracket. Several layers may be used to finally connect at the top. Each triangle transfers weight lower until it ultimately reaches a bracket on the wall. Few of these timber roofs have survived. (See Figure 9.9.)

PIERS

As in Romanesque architecture, piers were compounded by attaching engaged columns to their faces, usually four, whether piers were round, square, or octagonal. At Canterbury, contrasting stone was used for the piers and slender colonnettes to set them off. By the mid-fourteenth century, use of the bay was discontinued, capitals disappeared, the shafts on the piers reached from the floor to the vault in an uninterrupted line, and vaults became more complex. (See Figure 9.10.)

TRACERY

Tracery followed a similar development to that of piers. Windows were often 20 feet wide and 30 feet high, requiring intermediate supports, or **mullions**, for the glass. Gothic windows employed **bar tracery**, a type that was more delicate than the plate tracery of the Romanesque period. Rather than being pierced openings in stone, bar tracery was made of individual stone units shaped and fit together, filling little of the window space. The first known use of bar tracery was at the cathedral at Trier, Germany (c. 1227). Tracery began as decorative support sub-

dividing windows, or as simple vertical mullions surmounted by pointed arches. Later, curved or leaf-shaped divisions called **foils** formed circular patterns. Both plate and bar tracery formed **trefoils**, **quatrefoils**, and **cinquefoils**—three, four, and five foils, respectively. **Multifoil** designs featured more than five foils. Sometimes the center foil was pointed. **Cusps** were points formed at each intersection of two curved lines and could be decorative. Late Gothic tracery featured **ogive**, or S-curved, arches that the French called Flamboyant because the resulting designs were flamelike in appearance. While Flamboyant arches worked well as tracery, the arch itself was structurally weak, limiting it to relatively small openings unless under another arch and precluding its use in vaulting. Again, it was the English who experimented with tracery designs and created increasingly complex elaborations.

ROSE WINDOWS

The **rose window** had begun to be used during the Romanesque period but became characteristic of Gothic cathedrals. Rose windows were centered in the west front and often on the ends of transepts of churches. These windows were divided into segments by stone mullions, or separations, and filled with stained glass supported by bar tracery. Although the two terms denote slightly different versions of the same type of window, **wheel** and rose are both used to describe these circular windows. The first rose window appeared at St. Denis north of Paris, although it was filled with clear, not stained, glass. When stained glass became common, rose windows on the west front usually depicted the Last Judgment. Others featured signs of the zodiac to represent God's dominion over the heavens, and the labors of the months to indicate His control over the earth. Rose windows in transept façades often featured the Virgin Mary. In Moorish areas of influence, geometric and floral designs were more typical. (See Figure 9.11.)

BOX 9.3 CHARACTERISTICS OF GOTHIC ARCHITECTURE

- Ribbed vault
- Pointed arch
- Flying buttress
- Skeleton construction
- Large window areas
- Tie beams
- Half timbering
- Stone castles and town walls
- Great hall central living area
- Jetties
- Houses combined with shops
- Round, square, or octagonal piers
- Bar tracery
- Cusped designs
- Rose or wheel windows
- Soaring heights
- Slender column shafts
- No use of classical orders
- Pinnacles added for height
- Spires, sometimes of open work designs
- Towers
- Radiating chapels
- Most surfaces decorated
- Gargoyles

CATHEDRALS AND CHURCHES

The building of a Gothic cathedral was as much a cultural as a religious undertaking. Even members of the nobility might help to pull a cart loaded with stone or provide some other physical labor as a religious exercise. Most of the major French Gothic cathedrals were constructed in the twelfth and thirteenth centuries. By the fourteenth century, these enormous building projects were simply not economically feasible after the sweeping societal changes brought on by famine, plague, and the change in the role of the church from domination to succor.

Gothic buildings emphasized vertical lines not only through the use of precipitous towers,

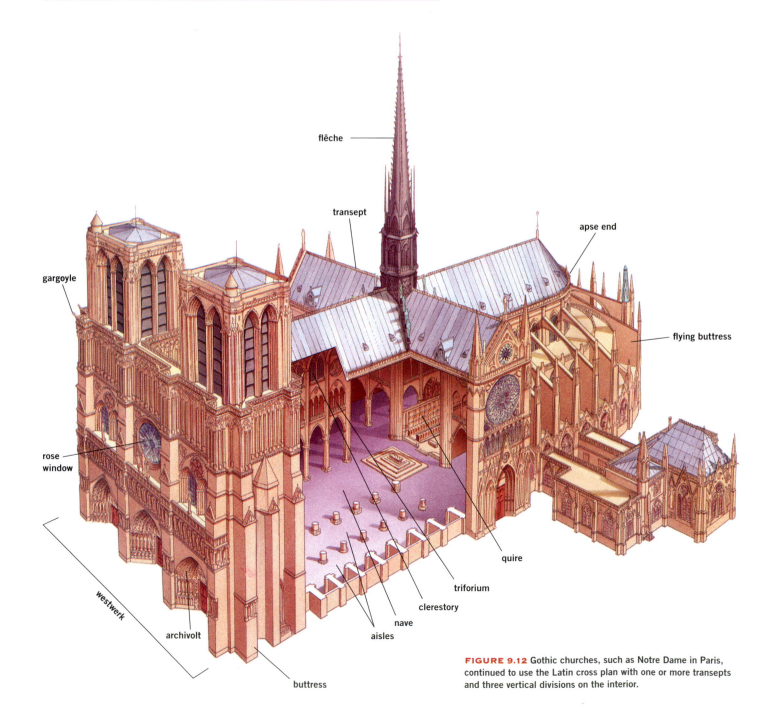

FIGURE 9.12 Gothic churches, such as Notre Dame in Paris, continued to use the Latin cross plan with one or more transepts and three vertical divisions on the interior.

slender shafts without capitals, and steeply pitched roofs, but by eliminating many of the horizontal moldings and details typical of pagan classical designs. Buttresses were surmounted by pinnacles made taller by the addition of weather vanes, and a slender tapering flèche crowned the crossing. (See Figure 9.13.)

Late in the period, the triforium was reduced in size to make room for longer clerestory windows and infrequently was eliminated altogether. The chevet continued to be used in France, where the radiating chapels were linked more closely than in Romanesque structures. Ambulatories and chapels were typical almost everywhere. Walls were reduced to minimal strips between buttresses. Beginning in the fifteenth century, **chantry chapels** were added to churches. Each was a miniature building that served as a burial chamber and had space for a sarcophagus, an effigy of the deceased, and an altar.

When possible, the high altar was located above the burial place of a saint to whom the church was dedicated. Once consecrated, the altar was not moved even during subsequent changes in the church because the spot on which the altar sat became sacred through consecration.

FIGURE 9.13 The flèche of Notre Dame in Paris is a delicate structure with crockets projecting on each of the vertical surfaces and figures of the apostles rising to its base.

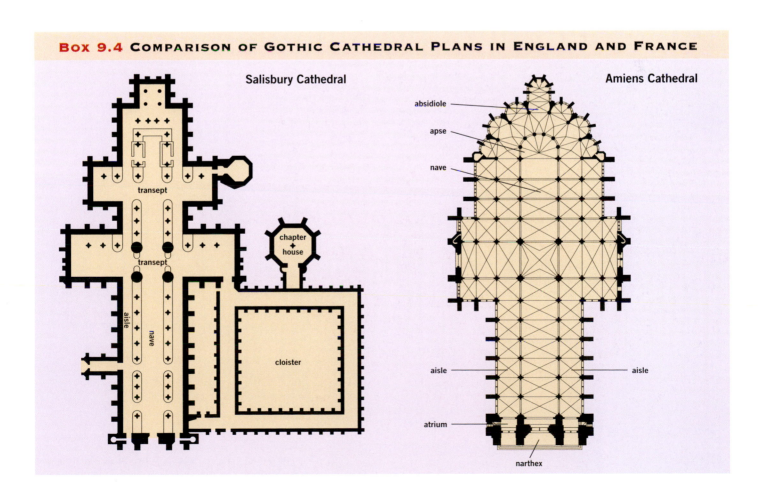

BOX 9.4 COMPARISON OF GOTHIC CATHEDRAL PLANS IN ENGLAND AND FRANCE

Salisbury Cathedral

transept

transept

chapter house

aisle

nave

cloister

Amiens Cathedral

absidiole

apse

nave

aisle

aisle

atrium

narthex

FIGURE 9.14 In the choir, the stalls typically had folding seats because prayers for the daily offices were said while standing. Beneath the folding seat was often a small shelf, or **misericord**, meaning act of mercy. This shelf provided a small projection against which an individual could lean while standing. Misericords, though almost hidden beneath the seats, were carved with great care and skill.

In England, the **retrochoir** behind the high altar became increasingly important.

Towers dominated the landscape as they stretched higher and higher. Open work spires were typical in much of Europe. Rather than having solid surfaces, these spires were almost lacelike in appearance. In Italy, polychrome, or multicolored, towers were usually separate from the buildings they served.

Although structural features of Gothic architecture were inherently decorative, the style employed numerous sculpted figures of kings, saints,

FIGURE 9.15 Figures were placed in horizontal rows, beneath small hooded **chaplets**, and occasionally in scenes. Sculptural groupings, however, were usually limited to the tympana.

and Biblical personages. Animals, dwarfs, and laborers with the tools of their trade were depicted as well. Textures and patterns infused almost every surface with ornament. (See Figure 9.15.)

Of the many figures depicted on Gothic buildings, gargoyles were often used as waterspouts. Many sculptured pieces were far out of range of human vision yet they were carved with extreme care and attention to detail. Often, gargoyles were **grotesques**, or mythical beasts with fangs or wings designed to scare away evil spirits. Heraldic animals such as the unicorn, lion, and griffin were also employed. (See Figure 9.16.)

EUROPEAN VARIATIONS

The Gothic style began in the Ile-de-France c. 1130, and the Early Gothic period in that country lasted until c. 1190. Rib vaults and pointed arches were characteristic. By the thirteenth century, French High Gothic (1190–fifteenth century) buildings made use of the flying buttress, and clerestory windows were elongated. During the fifteenth century, French Flamboyant Gothic was characterized by the ogee arch in tracery patterns reminiscent of flames. French Rayonnant architecture was not a specific period or style, but included features that were incorporated in French buildings after 1250 regardless of the specific period. The style was named for characteristic wheel patterns that radiated from a central point and is characterized by buttresses

FIGURE 9.16 Some gargoyles represented real animals such as this pelican on Notre Dame in Paris. The pelican was symbolic of Christ's love for the Church because it was believed that the bird would peck at its own breast to draw blood to feed its young when necessary.

that had delicate tracery masking their bulk. Pinnacles and gablets were added to the ends of buttresses. The spaces over openings were often pierced with tracery as well.

In England the Gothic style began half a century later. Early Gothic (c. 1180–1275) buildings were lower and longer than those on the continent. For this reason, there was little use for the flying buttress. As during the Romanesque period, English cathedrals continued to employ squared east ends and prominent, often doubled, transepts. Rather than the flèche of continental examples, English cathedrals had a tower over the crossing. Rose windows were used only on English transepts, not on the west end, and portals were relatively plain. Early English Gothic featured lancet windows without tracery, pointed arches, rib vaults, and profuse ornatmentation, especially on column shafts. Decorated English Gothic (c. 1250–c. 1380) made abundant use of tracery and toward the end, the ogee arch. It is characterized by sculptured ornament and vertical mullions parallel to the level of the springpoint which branched to form elaborate tracery patterns. Perpendicular Gothic (c. 1380–1520) was the last of the English periods. It was during this period that the English experimented most with multi-ribbed vaulting including fan vaulting and used four-centered arches. Ogee windows were large and were characterized by linear tracery and clerestory windows were elongated as the triforium began to disappear.

The style was known as Sondergotik (1350–1550) in Germany. At first, German churches continued to use apses on both ends and employed massive Romanesque-style buttresses. Later German Gothic churches featured almost continuous glass walls, ribs, soaring heights, and often flying buttresses, all French influences. West towers were typically taller than their French counterparts and topped by openwork spires. The hall church remained the most common form in German areas although internal piers became thinner. Helm roofs were often used on German towers with four short pinnacles at the corners.

In Italy, most of the few Gothic structures were unlike those in the rest of Europe. Frequently, Italian Gothic buildings have polychrome marble veneer on a brick façade, painted columns, and frescoed walls. Typically, Italian Gothic churches also have only a shallow apsidal chapel beyond the transept. (See Figure 9.17.)

FIGURE 9.17 Siena Cathedral is typical of Italian Gothic structures and follows French examples in the use of triple portals with sculpted figures, and a wheel window. A dome, rather than a tower, however, surmounts the crossing; interior and exterior striped marble emphasizes horizontal lines; and mosaics in the gable and interior apse end replace sculptural forms.

Early Spanish Gothic (twelfth century) and High Spanish Gothic (thirteenth century) were similar to French styles. During the Mudejar Gothic period (thirteenth to fifteenth centuries), however, the true Spanish character was evident as Spanish and Moorish features were combined. The period was followed by Isabelline Gothic (1474–1505), which was a transitional style from Gothic to Renaissance. Basket handle (semi-elliptical) arches, shields, and written text used decoratively were characteristic. Inside, a larger area was reserved for the clergy, often up to half the nave as well as the choir. The space was separated by a carved **reredos**, or screen behind the altar, that dominated the interior. **Rejas**, or decorative iron grills, separated the choir from the nave. The last stage of Spanish Gothic was known as Isabelline (1474–1505) and was a transitional

FIGURE 9.30 Cupboard was a term first used during the Gothic period to describe a board or shelf on which cups were placed. Later, a compartment closed with doors was added beneath the shelf to ensure safekeeping of cups, often made of silver.

FIGURE 9.31 The term credere meant *to believe,* and it was from this word that the name of the *crédence* was derived. Food was served from this unit, but a servant had to try each dish before it could be served. The wealthy had become paranoid about being poisoned, and it was in this way that they could believe the food was edible.

open shelves that held the necessary utensils and vessels for food preparation.

The **buffet** was a French piece used in the dining room and could be partly or completely enclosed. It was used to display and store glassware, silver, and other expensive objects. Typically shelves were arranged on the top in tiers in a pyramid form with each tier slightly recessed inward from the sides of the tier below. The number of shelves might depend on the social status of the owner. Six or more shelves were indicative of royal status although this number varied according to geographic location. It was often crudely constructed but was draped in fine fabrics and, late in the period, might have a canopy. Less pretentious buffets might be located in the same room and were used for serving food.

The **livery cupboard** was a ventilated unit in which food was stored. The door panels might be carved with pierced designs or filled with turned spindles. The first livery cupboards had a single door; later examples had two doors. Livery cupboards were sometimes small enough to be carried as food and other needed commodities were delivered (French *livré*) each evening to individuals within the household.

The **press cupboard** was enclosed by solid doors and used to store clothing, linens, and other items. Only the wealthy needed or could afford these cupboards. This form evolved into the more specialized clothes press, armoire, and wardrobe by the seventeenth century.

The **armoire** was the largest type of cupboard and was designed for storage of armorial equipment. Typically, it closed with a pair of doors. Only some armoires were movable. Frequently, they were so large that they were built into the wall. Some were even small rooms. In England, such a room was called the **garderobe** and was used for storing clothing. Typically, the garderobe was located adjacent to the room in which toilets were placed. It was believed that the odors would keep insects from attacking the clothing. The English furniture piece that was equivalent to the free-standing armoire was the ambry.

The **sideboard** was a shelf or table on which food could be placed prior to serving. This form was often decorated with carved designs or wrought iron work. The **crédence** was originally a small table that served the same purpose in France. In Italy, this piece of furniture was known as the **credenza**. By the fourteenth century, the crédence evolved into a table surmounted by a number of shelves such as the buffet. By the Renaissance, the piece became massive, enclosed, and richly decorated. (See Figure 9.31.)

TABLES

Although there were a few small tables, the board continued to be used for dining and had to seat numerous people in the great hall. Illustrations of the period depict tables placed in a U around the sides of the room—reminiscent of the Roman triclinium, although for a larger number of guests. Circular tables with a serving area in the center are also shown.

In addition to the trestle table, the fixed table, or **table dormant**, was developed during the Gothic period. The top of the table dormant was permanently attached, making it unwieldy to move from one residence to another, so it remained in one place. Crudely made, it was covered with rich textiles when the owner was present.

The **draw top** table was developed in the fifteenth century. Leaves were stored beneath the table top and when needed could be extended at both ends. The table required less space when it was not in use and when extended could seat larger numbers of people.

The **prie-dieu** (Italian *inginocchiatoio*), used in the bed chamber, was a prayer stand that combined a box for a kneeling bench with uprights that supported a small ledge. The lectern continued to be used as a reading stand in monasteries and by the late fifteenth century had begun to be used in homes, even those of the illiterate.

BEDS

While most people still slept on a pallet made of straw, the beds of the wealthy became more elaborate. Most sophisticated beds required the use of a step or a stool because the mattress was high off the floor. The bed of estate continued to be used by the highest ranking member of the household. (See Figure 9.32.)

Later beds, derived from the tent, had four posts to support the tester and hangings. The bed was often elevated on a platform and sometimes, a hinged surface provided access so that the platform could be used for storage. Italian beds were often paneled from the sleeping surface to the floor and more decorative than examples in colder areas. In part, this was because fewer curtains were used around the bed, often only covering the posts.

This practice was typical of the warmer climates of Spain and Southern France as well.

Enlightenment

Even while most of Europe was in the throes of the Medieval period, there were the beginnings of change in Italy where the glory that was Rome had never fully receded. Ancient manuscripts were brought to light, old philosophies were appraised, and the vagaries of the Church questioned. The technological advances of the Gothic period were examined and further developed as scientific processes led to ever-increasing knowledge and a new period of enlightenment based on classical Rome blossomed.

The Renaissance was not only a rebirth of classical culture but a synthesis of a millennium of experience, wisdom, and technology that resulted in a vibrant, flourishing, sophisticated society. Taste was refined, manners were polished, comfort was demanded, and luxuries heretofore unknown were accessible.

FIGURE 9.32 Especially in northern Europe where winters were cold, beds were often either in wall recesses that could be enclosed with curtains or doors or were separate cupboards that could be closed off with doors.

Enlightenment

Part Three

ENLIGHTENMENT

North Sea

Atlantic Ocean

N

0   300 Miles
0   300 KM

• Wollaton Hall

ENGLAND

Hatfield House
London •

NETHERLANDS
Amsterdam • • Zutphen

FLANDERS

Wittenbe

GERMANY

• San Quentin

Versailles • Paris
Fontainebleau •

Loire River

• Chambord

Cher River

Salzb

St. Gall •

BURGUNDY

SWITZERLAND

AUS

FRANCE

• Milan

Venice

Genoa •

Bologna •
Ravenna •

• Floren

• Pisa

ITA

ARAGON

SPAIN

PORTUGAL

• Madrid

Toledo •

CASTILE

*Tyrrher
Sea*

• Seville

ANDALUSIA

Mediterranean Sea

St. Petersburg

Moscow

RUSSIA

*Baltic
Sea*

*driatic
Sea*

es

HUNGARY

Black Sea

Constantinople

GREECE

*Aegean
Sea*

TURKEY

*Ionian
Sea*

1265–1321
Dante Alighieri, author
of *The Divine Comedy*

c. 1267–1336/37
Giotto di Bondone,
Florentine artist whose
work some credit with
the beginning of the
Renaissance

1304–1374
Francesco Petrarca
(Petrarch) who began
to collect ancient
manuscripts

1337–1453
Hundred Years' War
between England
and France

1380–1390
Geoffrey Chaucer
(c. 1343–1400)
begins writing
Canterbury Tales,
the first great literary
work in English

1400
Renaissance in Italy

1402
Work started on Gothic
cathedral of Seville

1412–1431
Jeanne d'Arc

c. 1416
Portugal's Prince
Henry the Navigator
(1394–1460)
establishes naval
station at Sagres for
the purpose of finding
a sea route to Asia

c. 1421
Hospital of the
Innocents constructed
in Florence

1444–1514
Donato Bramante,
High Renaissance
architect in Rome

1469
Ferdinand of Aragon
(1452–1516) and
Isabella of Castile
(1451–1504) marry

1473–1481
Sistine Chapel
constructed
(Giovanni de Dolci)

1478
Spanish Inquisition
began

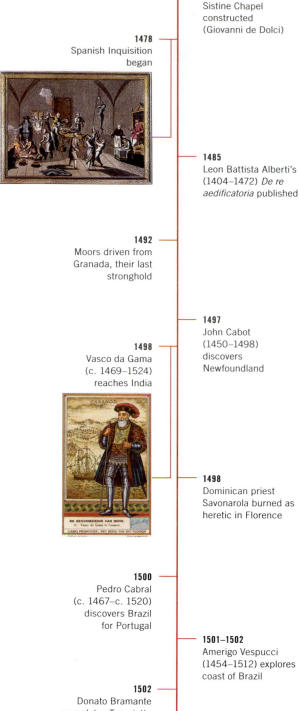

1485
Leon Battista Alberti's
(1404–1472) *De re
aedificatoria* published

1492
Moors driven from
Granada, their last
stronghold

1497
John Cabot
(1450–1498)
discovers
Newfoundland

1498
Vasco da Gama
(c. 1469–1524)
reaches India

1498
Dominican priest
Savonarola burned as
heretic in Florence

1500
Pedro Cabral
(c. 1467–c. 1520)
discovers Brazil
for Portugal

1501–1502
Amerigo Vespucci
(1454–1512) explores
coast of Brazil

1502
Donato Bramante
completes Tempietto
at San Pietro in
Montorio setting
the standard for
Renaissance buildings

**Sixteenth–mid-
seventeenth century**
Renaissance in Spain

1509–1547
Henry VIII
(1491–1547),
King of England

1510
Portugal takes
control of the city
of Goa in India

1513
Portuguese ships
reach China by sailing
around Africa

1558–1603
Elizabeth I
(1533–1603),
Queen of England

1563
Council of Trent,
which led to the ounter
Reformation, ends

1517
Portuguese
established a trading
post in Macao

1517
Protestant Reformation
begins

1567
Rio de Janeiro settled
by Portuguese

1582
Introduction of
Gregorian calendar

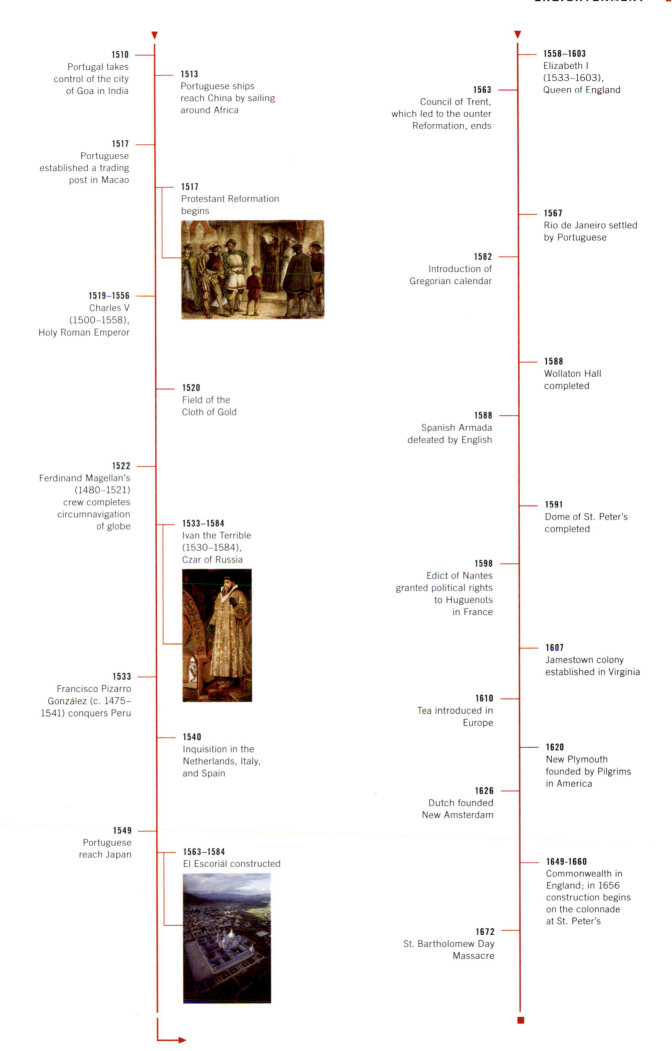

1519–1556
Charles V
(1500–1558),
Holy Roman Emperor

1520
Field of the
Cloth of Gold

1588
Wollaton Hall
completed

1588
Spanish Armada
defeated by English

1522
Ferdinand Magellan's
(1480–1521)
crew completes
circumnavigation
of globe

1533–1584
Ivan the Terrible
(1530–1584),
Czar of Russia

1591
Dome of St. Peter's
completed

1598
Edict of Nantes
granted political rights
to Huguenots
in France

1533
Francisco Pizarro
González (c. 1475–
1541) conquers Peru

1607
Jamestown colony
established in Virginia

1610
Tea introduced in
Europe

1540
Inquisition in the
Netherlands, Italy,
and Spain

1620
New Plymouth
founded by Pilgrims
in America

1626
Dutch founded
New Amsterdam

1549
Portuguese
reach Japan

1563–1584
El Escoriál constructed

1649-1660
Commonwealth in
England; in 1656
construction begins
on the colonnade
at St. Peter's

1672
St. Bartholomew Day
Massacre

part of it. Many of the works of Luca della Robbia (1397–1482) were used on buildings in tympana and in decorative panels attached to the building itself or used on pulpits and other associated objects. Although he worked in bronze at first, it was his terra-cotta forms for which he became most famous. Some of the work was done in white, with later works in blue and white.

Sculpture and painting were both under the patronage of the popes and nobility of Italy during the Cinquecento (1500–1520). Churches and public buildings had numerous sculptures, often lining roof balustrades. Later, Mannerist sculpture became more two-dimensional with elongated figures and stiff poses.

CRAFTS

Gilding, an old technique, continued to be used, although Venetian and Florentine artisans obtained a finer finish than ever before by applying gold leaf to a red background and burnishing it.

Pastiglia either used gesso, a gypsum compound, or white lead mixed with egg for a binder to form low-relief surface patterns that could be painted or gilded. Colored gesso could also be used. The surface was covered with canvas that was coated first with a layer of gesso or with plaster, and then additional gesso was painted on with a brush to form the designs. Sometimes the designs were applied after having been formed in carved molds. Gilding usually occurred while the pastiglia was still wet. Pastiglia was especially popular on small boxes but was used extensively on larger chests.

The **intarsia** technique employed a variety of materials ranging from exotic woods to metals such as silver and ivory or bone to form pictorial representations on the surfaces of walls or furniture. Intarsia pieces were fitted into gouged-out spaces in the wood to be decorated. Marquetry was conceived slightly later as the techniques for slicing materials into thin sheets was developed. Similar to intarsia in design, marquetry differed in that the thin pieces were applied to a surface rather than recessed into a surface. **Certosina** was a refinement of inlay work used from the fourteenth to the sixteenth centuries. Pieces of varying light-colored materials were used to form complex geometric patterns, such as circles, triangles, and rectangles as well as elaborate pictorial representations, especially on the flat surfaces of dark furniture pieces. This technique was especially popular in Venice and Lombardy.

Scagliola could imitate the more expensive pietre dure designs. An ancient technique, this mixture of powdered stone and plaster was used by the Romans especially on interiors to create architectural features, usually faux marble. It was in the sixteenth-century Italian Renaissance that scagliola was first used for furniture, usually for the tops of tables.

Scraffito was first used on the Gondi Palace in Florence. Scraffito work required at least two layers of variously colored plaster, stucco, or paint. Once dry, the design was scratched through the top surface(s) until the desired color was exposed.

FIGURE 10.5 Pietre dure, or Florentine mosaic, employed marble, pebbles, semi-precious stones such as agate, lapis lazuli, and jasper to create designs on tabletops, in the panels of case furniture, and sometimes on walls or floors. Few artisans had the necessary skills to create pietre dure pieces, and most were made either in Florence or Milan from where they were exported.

Glasswork reached its pinnacle in Venice, where glass was painted with colored enamels, and gilded. It was the secret of making completely clear glass, or **cristallo**, however, that was vigorously protected. In fact, in 1454 the Venetian government decreed that any glass artisan who left the city without returning would be secretly killed no matter where they were found. Cristallo glass cools very quickly, making it possible to create exceedingly thin intricate designs. **Lattimo** glass was an opaque milk glass that was often combined with cristallo to form lacy patterns.

The art of carving cameos and intaglios was revived and rock crystal, a colorless, transparent variety of quartz, was carved into decorative objects. Artisans also fired enamels on metal, and after 1620 created miniature paintings using transparent glass tinted with metal oxides. After being painted, the piece was fired to a relatively low heat (up to 1200°) when the enamel melted and bonded to the metal.

Motifs

Motifs included many derived from classical models: the anthemion, arabesque, and certain imaginary creatures. Many scenes were used, including religious subjects, astrology, the seasons, the hunt, mythological events, and the ages of man. Often these scenes were painted on panels or as murals on walls or ceilings. Natural fruits, flowers, and foliage were connected with flowing ribbons in both painting and sculpture. Other motifs are listed below.

- Common animals such as birds and squirrels were introduced during the Trecento period. The use of these creatures was a result of the impact of St. Francis of Assisi, who extolled the qualities of the natural world.
- Blackamoors were exotically clad figures of Africans used as table legs, bedposts, and candle stands.
- The chimera, an imaginary animal with the head, body, and front legs of a lion or a goat, wings, and a serpent's tail, was used especially on Mannerist furniture.
- The **candelabrum** was a symmetrical design used as a border. Here, a variety of objects, usually vegetative, flowed from a central stem to create a long, narrow design.

- The **colonnette** was a miniature column or pilaster carved on or applied to Renaissance and later furniture as a decorative device.
- Stylized dolphins, also derived from classical forms, were especially popular on Venetian furniture.
- Garlands and swags of fruits, including the pomegranate and the eggplant, flowers, and foliage, were used in architecture, interiors, and furnishings.
- The griffin, another classical mythological creature revived during the Renaissance, featured a lion's body with both the head and wings of an eagle.
- **Grotesques** were similar to arabesques and used flowing vines, flowers, and foliage to connect objects. Unlike arabesques, however, grotesques made use of depictions of animals, both real and imaginary, and humans. Grotesques were most popular during the Mannerist period.
- **Putti** were the amorini, or winged naked human babies, of ancient Rome that were used decoratively.
- The **cartouche** was derived from Roman prototypes but differed from ancient models in that Renaissance examples had the appearance of a piece of paper with scrolled ends or a shield or other device with curled edges. Used as early as the fifteenth century, the cartouche was most popular on Italian furniture during and after the seventeenth century.

Italian Renaissance Architecture

Renaissance architecture was considered more an art form than a method of building. The human body was considered the perfect form, and architects established ratios based on that form, as had the Egyptians and the Greeks. The **Golden Mean** of the Renaissance was the same as the Egyptian seqt and the Golden Rectangle of the Greeks—a ratio of 1:1.618. (See Figure 10.6.) When divided horizontally at the navel, the ideal human form has a ratio of 1 (the upper body) to 1.6 (the lower body). Man was independent and could shape the world through the arts. For this reason, the individual became more important, and it is from this time that the names of artists and architects are known. Renaissance architects also used a ratio of 1:2. Architects established mathematical relationships based on the Golden

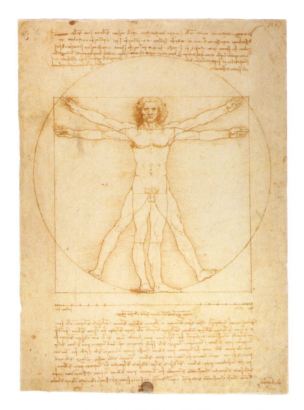

FIGURE 10.6 Leonardo da Vinci drew the Vitruvian man (c. 1490) according to the descriptions of the ideal human body by Vitruvius. These proportions were used in architecture, humanizing design. Buildings based on human proportions were considered harmonious with nature. Man was created in the image of God; therefore, the Creator could be represented in a structure when correct proportions were followed.

FIGURE 10.7 The major distinguishing characteristic of the Florentine arch was that the intrados and extrados were not concentric.

Mean between building components. Semicircular domes were exactly half the height of their width; cube-shaped rooms were visually divided horizontally by a prominent entablature.

Beauty was given priority and buildings were often treated as works of art. Symmetry was important. Rhythm was accomplished through the use of repetitive forms, such as columns, pilasters, windows, or even niches.

Roman public structures were used as models for early Renaissance buildings. Only later were classical temple forms employed. While they used classical forms such as the semicircular arch which dominated architecture, Renaissance architects used Gothic construction techniques and no innovative building techniques were introduced. The technology for making Roman concrete had been lost and most buildings were constructed of stone. The five Roman orders were employed, although Renaissance architects often adapted the forms to create unique columns that were only loosely based on classical models. It was, however, the Scamozzi Order that became the standard. This order was based on the Roman Ionic with the volutes at all four corners angled but altered by Vincenzo Scamozzi (1548–1616) to have more ornamental detail. The egg and dart band between the volutes had an emphasized central motif on each side. The Scamozzi order continued to be used during the Baroque period.

Sometimes columns were simply painted on a structural component to give the illusion of a colonnade. Like the Romans, Renaissance builders superimposed orders with lower orders, Tuscan or Doric, on lower stories and higher orders, Ionic or Corinthian, on upper stories. Column shafts were frequently left unfluted.

Arches supported by classic columns might have a small section of entablature between the capital and the springpoint of the arch. The new **Florentine arch** consisted of an arch that might have an emphasized keystone and added moldings. It often sprang from the capital of supporting columns or pilasters. (See Figure 10.7.)

Quoins were used to emphasize corners and were textured when the wall surfaces were smooth and vice versa. During the Early Renaissance, **rusticated** stone was used on walls, although during the High Renaissance very heavy rustication was juxtaposed against smooth surfaces—heavy rustication being used on the ground floor, lighter rustication on the second, and smoother surfaces above. (See Figure 10.8.)

The first great Early Renaissance effort was the dome added to the unfinished, Gothic-style Santa Maria del Fiore Cathedral in Florence. From the time of the ancient Romans when the dome of the Pantheon was considered representative of the celestial vault, the dome had maintained that significance. In keeping with its earlier style, the architect Filippo Brunelleschi gave the dome a slightly pointed profile. (See Figure 10.9.)

In 1481, a competition was announced that was won by Brunelleschi. He used a double brick dome that was self-supporting during its construction by employing a technique derived from Islamic sources. The technique was similar to Roman construction of the Pantheon in that brick was laid in courses around the dome and required no centering. (See Figure 10.10.) Hidden chains were wrapped between the inner and outer domes to help counteract the thrust of the arches. The dome itself was completed in

FIGURE 10.8 Rustication indicates masonry that is roughly shaped and that has emphasized joints as on this column.

FIGURE 10.9 Santa Maria del Fiore in Florence is the fourth largest church in Europe and dominates the skyline of the city. It was the dome on this Gothic building (1296–1418) that was the first major Renaissance effort in Italy. Without external buttressing on the drum that had already been completed, it was necessary for Brunelleschi to wrap chains between the two domes to ensure support. The octagonal dome spans 136 feet and is constructed of courses of brick that required no temporary centering.

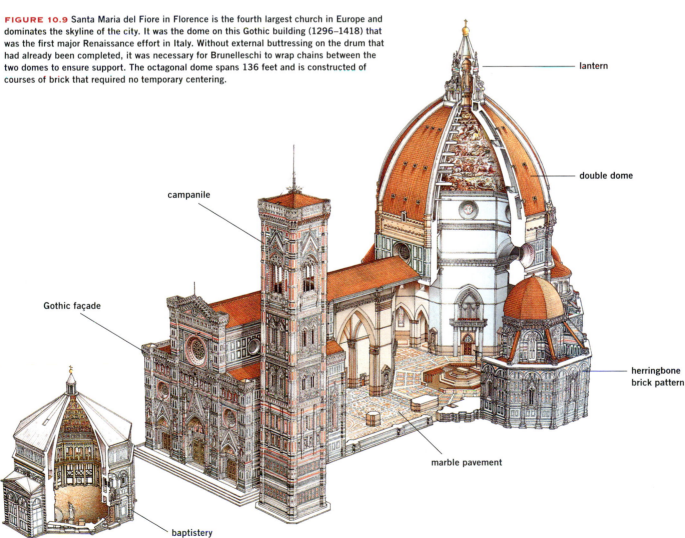

FIGURE 10.10 Another Renaissance innovation was the use of exposed metal tie rods or chains connecting the sides of arches to help counteract outward thrust.

1436, although its decoration remained unfinished for another 12 years.

As opposed to the verticality of Gothic architecture, Renaissance architecture was earthbound and horizontal. Cornices projected as much as 10 feet and were emphasized by heavy supporting corbels or brackets. **String courses**, or horizontal bands of masonry of a different color or material or on a different plane, marked the various levels of Italian Renaissance palazzi and drew the eye horizontally. **Loggias** were supported by colonnades or arcades and further tied the structure to the earth. Loggias differed from classical Roman porticoes that continued to be used in that the loggia was recessed between structural members, while porticoes were unimpeded by the structure itself.

The Florentine Ospedale degli Innocenti, or Hospital of the Innocents (c. 1419–1451), was an orphanage built around two cloisters and supported by the Silk Weavers Guild. In 1377, during the Trecento period (1300–1400), Brunelleschi designed this horizontally oriented building with an external arcaded loggia supported by Corinthian columns. Terra-cotta medallions were used in the spandrels and became a common feature

of Renaissance buildings. The succeeding Early Renaissance, or Quattrocento (1400–1500), was a period of experimentation when mostly classical forms were used.

It was during the High Renaissance, or Cinquecento (1500–1520), that most of the great artists worked. The High Renaissance began in Rome when Bramante began to reinterpret ancient Roman architectural forms. Less emphasis was placed on horizontal lines, domes were placed on drums, and circular buildings, such as the martyrium Tempietto de San Pietro in Montorio (1502) became fashionable.

The style of the Late Renaissance (1520–1600) was often termed Mannerism, a term applicable to painting. In architecture, Mannerism was expressed by consciously adapting classical forms for use in new ways or to create a different appearance to make buildings more appealing. In fact, Mannerism sought instability. Rhythm was broken by varying the width of bays, spacing columns differently, or placing windows irregularly. At the Palazzo del Te (1525–1535) near Mantua, every third triglyph was lowered. The figures carved by Michelangelo for the Medici tombs were placed diagonally and appeared to be sliding downward.

Mannerists were not concerned with whether their work was related to what others were doing, nor was it necessary for them to retain the same style over a period of years.

Typical Mannerist features included coupled columns that sometimes supported nothing, **blind windows**, or framed areas in walls that were filled in; and **giant order** columns that rose multiple stories. Michelangelo was credited with the first use of giant order columns on the Campidoglio and St. Peter's, both in Rome. While semicircular arches had been used during the High Renaissance, Mannerist buildings often employed segmental arches.

Architectural innovations of the Italian Renaissance included the tall **drum**, or a cylinder added beneath a dome to raise it above the roof. This served two purposes: to provide a vertical surface in which windows could be added to provide light beneath the dome, and to raise the dome sufficiently high so that it could be better seen when approaching the building. There are numerous examples of drums that have encircling peristyles, another Renaissance innovation. Later, a **lantern** or **cupola** superstructure was added to the dome. Lanterns had windows to provide light beneath, while cupolas did not.

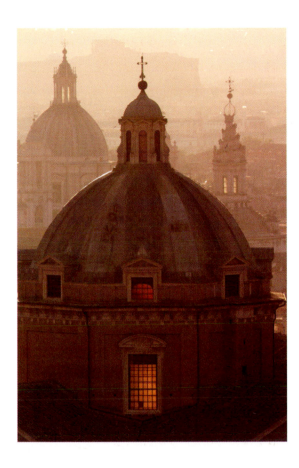

FIGURE 10.11 Domes with lanterns and cupolas, typical of Renaissance churches, began to dominate the skylines of cities across Europe, once the structural problems had been solved.

INFLUENCE 10.1

The nineteenth-century Renaissance Revival style was derived from the Italian Renaissance. The Early Renaissance style was used for secular buildings that had to appear dignified such as banks. The Mannerist style was emulated for nineteenth-century buildings that needed to be impressive, such as opera houses.

City planning worked with architecture to create focus on monuments and fountains. Wide streets were laid out in grid iron, radial, and star-shaped plans. Ideally, public spaces were planned as complete entities that included the buildings around them. Michelangelo accomplished this at Campodiglio, but there were more instances when the ideal form was not reached. See Box 10.3 for a summary of Italian Renaissance architectural characteristics.

MONUMENTAL ARCHITECTURE

Unlike other artistic periods, monumental architecture in the Italian Renaissance included not only churches and public buildings but the pala-zzi of the wealthy. The wealth of merchants and bankers in the fifteenth century rivaled that of royalty and the Church, freeing monumental architecture from their service. Each city-state competed with its rivals, seeking to build ever more splendid public spaces and architectural wonders. It was an age of great civic buildings that included the palazzo, which were both civic and private buildings. Living quarters for the owner were located on the second floor, or **piano nobile**; civic activities might occupy the lower story; and multiple apartments might be rented out.

Box 10.3 CHARACTERISTICS OF ITALIAN RENAISSANCE ARCHITECTURE

- Semicircular arches
- Florentine arches
- Fountains
- Rusticated stonework
- Superimposed pediments (one on top of the other)
- Classical orders of architecture
- Statuary decorating building façades
- Dome on a fenestrated drum
- Classical façades with columns, engaged columns, pilasters, and pediments
- Arcades
- Aediculated openings

FIGURE 10.12 The Tempietto was constructed in the cloister of the Church of San Pietro in Montorio in Rome and was loosely based on the Roman Temple of Vesta. Designed as a memorial to St. Peter, it was built over the supposed site of his martyrdom.

CHURCHES AND MEMORIALS

The central plan was successful in small memorial buildings and chapels. The Tempietto di San Pietro in Montorio (c. 1506) is an example. (See Figure 10.12.) Donato Bramante (1444–1514) was the architect of this slightly raised circular building that featured a surrounding colonnade with a classical entablature, and was topped by a drum surmounted by a dome.

> **INFLUENCE 10.2**
>
> *The Tempietto served as the inspiration for Michelangelo's dome on St. Peter's, for the Capitol building in Washington, D.C., and for the Pantheon in Paris among other structures.*

Although central planning was tried in some churches, the liturgy of the Church favored the Latin cross plan, which continued to dominate. By the second half of the sixteenth century, however, aisles were being replaced with cha-

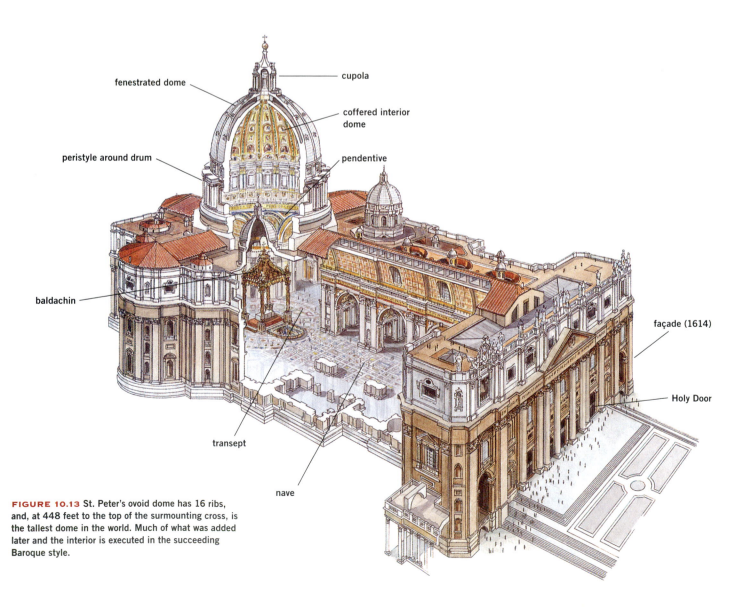

FIGURE 10.13 St. Peter's ovoid dome has 16 ribs, and, at 448 feet to the top of the surmounting cross, is the tallest dome in the world. Much of what was added later and the interior is executed in the succeeding Baroque style.

pels. Church façades resembled those of ancient temples and featured triangular pediments. The façade itself was broken into regular bays by arches, pilasters, or engaged columns. Triumphal arch façades were also popular. At San Giorgio Maggiore in Venice (begun 1566), Palladio used a screen façade that incorporated giant order columns. When the nave and aisles were of different heights, this fact was masked on the outside. Some architects used scrolls at the sides of the nave façade for this purpose.

Pope Julius II (1443–1513) decided to rebuild Old St. Peter's and the portions begun in the mid-fifteenth century by Pope Nicholas V (1347–1455). The chosen design was largely that of Bramante. Bramante's first plan for St. Peter's was a Greek cross within a square with five domes—essentially a quincunx plan—with towers terminating each arm. The central plan, however, was unsuitable for Catholic worship services, and ultimately elongated, resulting in a Latin cross plan. Bramante's planned dome was a stepped hemisphere similar to that on the Pantheon. During the course of construction, a number of architects were employed, including some who altered the plans. Raphael

(Raffaello Sanzio) was chief architect from 1514–1520, and Michelangelo redesigned the dome, although it was not completed until after his demise. The external ribs on the 138-feet-diameter double brick dome connected the paired columns around the drum with the columns around the lantern. (See Figures 10.13 and 10.14.)

PALAZZI AND DOMESTIC BUILDINGS

Although the cannon and gunpowder had made medieval fortresses obsolete, Italian Renaissance palaces continued to be constructed with formidable façades. They were often constructed with warehouses or shops and very little fenestration on lower floors. These palazzi were exceedingly large—so large in fact that Cosimo de' Medici was expelled from Florence because his palace was considered too large for an individual in a republic. Inside, the rooms were built on a grand scale. With the exception of dining rooms, which were not introduced into Italian homes until the nineteenth century, the rooms in Italian domestic buildings served the same functions as those today. For dining, tables were set up where they were needed.

FIGURE 10.14 The piazza in front of St. Peter's was designed by Gian Lorenzo Bernini and constructed between 1656 and 1667. The lines in the piazza that radiate from the central Egyptian obelisk are made of travertine.

FIGURE 10.15 The elliptical piazza of St. Peter's is bounded by Tuscan colonnades. The Baroque colonnades mask buildings crowded near the church and end with classical temple façades.

FIGURE 10.16 Like their Roman predecessors, Italian Renaissance Palazzi were constructed around a large courtyard onto which rooms opened.

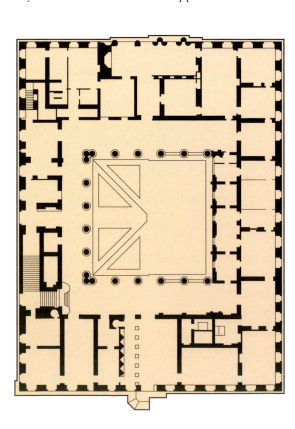

The most impressive room in a palace was the **studiolo**, or study, used by the master. It was here that artworks and books were kept. Even here, there were few pieces of furniture, aside from a table, a chair, and possibly a bookcase. The piano nobile served as the main living area, and the important bedrooms were located there. On the exterior, rustication decreased in intensity from the lower to the upper stories. Later

palazzi had classical features such as colonnades, arcades, pediments, entablatures, and pilasters. (See Figure 10.16.)

INFLUENCE 10.3

Factories and department stores of the nineteenth and early twentieth centuries used the Renaissance palazzo as a model.

The villas constructed for wealthy clients were designed to allow them to escape from the city into suburban areas, but unlike Roman villas, these were kept for entertaining or relaxing, not for living. In fact, there were usually no sleeping rooms. Users were expected to go for an entertainment or an evening and return to the city to sleep. Andrea Palladio (1508–1580), who designed La Rotonda, followed Vitruvian principles and based the building on mathematical principles (See Figure 10.17). Room proportions, for example, were designed with ratios such as 3:4 or 4:5 in width and length. Even façades followed such mathematical principles. Like many palazzi and villas, those designed by Palladio usually had three stories. The ground floor housed minor and service rooms, the piano nobile served as the main public space and was accessed by a monumental flight of stairs, and the third story housed bedrooms. Low wings were sometimes detached and connected to the main building by colonnades.

FIGURE 10.17 The Villa Capra, known as La Rotonda (1566–1571), was a centrally planned building with identical temple façades on all four sides. A dome crowned the central hall.

INFLUENCE 10.4

The Palladian style became popular in eighteenth-century America with Thomas Jefferson one of its foremost proponents. The Villa Capra itself served as a model for Federal period architects in America. Palladian colonnades that connected Palladian structures with wings that were not part of the main structure were employed in Southern plantation homes of the nineteenth century to connect outbuildings such as the summer kitchen with the house.

For those without excessive wealth, the town house had to suffice. Built as row houses with shared walls and a façade that gave the appearance of a palace, these units provided residents with an appearance of greater wealth.

Even the homes of the middle classes became more comfortable and convenient. Cities passed regulations concerning the distance of upper stories' overhangs that darkened the streets. The **domus de statio**, or residence, often served as both house and shop or office. Living spaces, as in palaces, were divided into rooms. Porticoes or loggias ran along the front of the building or along the inner wall, and each apartment opened onto them. Some of these houses had external stairs, and each floor was independent of its neighbors.

OPENINGS

Early Renaissance openings had no trim and were simply openings in a wall, but by the six-teenth century, openings were treated architecturally. Important openings on both the exterior and interior were trimmed with **aediculae**. (See Figure 10.18.) Sometimes the pediment was broken. Sometimes alternating aediculae were used—those with triangular pediments flanked by others with curved pediments. Both wood and marble surrounds were used.

By the Renaissance, it was common for windows to be glazed with small panes of glass joined by lead cames or frames. First-story windows usually had both interior and exterior shutters or exterior metal grilles. Walls were thick, giving openings deep reveals and resulting in a reduction of glare from even large openings.

FIGURE 10.18 Pilasters or engaged columns flanked aediculated openings and were surmounted by a pediment—triangular or curved—which might project sufficiently to support added decorative objects.

Medieval **bifore** windows continued to be used, especially in Florence. These windows had a slender colonnette dividing them into two arched lights. Semicircular windows were widespread. Later, **Guelph windows**, named for a powerful group that favored the pope, were common. (See Figure 10.19.) Casement windows, however, remained the most common, opened inward, and were generally square-headed. During the Mannerist period, the Palladian window was also employed. This was a three-part opening with a semicircular-headed center section flanked by shorter square-headed openings or windows.

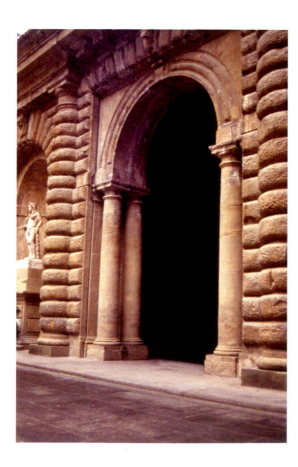

Doorways without doors were usually arched and featured a prominent keystone. Doors themselves were square-headed even though they often were set into a blind arch, or an arch that was outlined but filled in with wall material, or were surmounted by a pediment. (See Figure 10.20.) The central doorway on a façade was often accentuated with a cartouche mounted over it. Most Italian Renaissance doors were carved or paneled in which case the panels might be filled with marquetry or left plain with the decorative effects achieved by moldings around the door. On public structures, doors were much more ornate. Ghiberti's bronze doors on the east side of the baptistery of the cathedral in Florence had 10 panels that featured scenes from the Old Testament. Michelangelo considered the gates worthy of gracing paradise; thus, they are generally known as the *Gates of Paradise.*

Arched or square-headed niches, too, were sometimes aediculated, especially when they housed a sculpture or important decorative piece. Providing relief from flat wall expanses, they often established rhythms of their own. Inlaid marble designs decorated the interior of some niches; others were designed for storage and closed with pairs of doors or shutters.

Italian Renaissance Interiors

The ancient Greeks were concerned with the structure itself and interior space was unimportant; the Romans thought it unnecessary to coordinate the interior and exterior of a structure as each had its own character. During the Middle Ages, space was ill-defined, but during the Renaissance, interiors became as important as exteriors to which they generally related. Renaissance builders were familiar only with Roman ruins and did not realize that ancient Roman buildings were different on the inside than they were outside. They made the assumption that columns, pediments, and other architectural features would have been used on interiors and, in presumably following classical models, used those forms.

Shape of the interior spaces was usually rectangular, although later, circular components appeared that included apses, exedrae, and domes.

Space was organized around positive details such as doors, windows, pilasters, columns, or pediments. Like civic buildings, domestic structures also employed centralized planning with rooms arranged around a courtyard. Each room also opened into the next. In the late Renaissance, Palladio introduced a hallway that terminated at another hall or in a room to simplify circulation, precluding the need for passing through one room to get to another or for going outside to get to another room. Occasionally, suites of rooms were arranged. During the High Renaissance, houses became smaller in accordance with human scale and an increasing concern for cost. (See Figure 10.21.)

FLOORS

Floors were laid in patterns that often reflected ceiling designs. Both terra-cotta and **majolica** tiles were used. Both materials were made of clay, but majolica tiles were more decorative. While the clay was still wet, designs were outlined in the tile, creating raised and recessed areas. The raised areas allowed variously colored glazes to be used without running together when the tiles were fired. The square, rectangular, and hexagonal terra-cotta tiles were used to form a variety of geometric patterns such as herringbone, the most popular pattern.

Terrazzo, made by mixing marble chips with cement, was used on the floor and often was laid in repeated patterns. Marble, porphyry, granite, and other stones were usually laid in counterchange patterns like those of ancient Rome. Stone was sometimes cut to fit into large mosaic patterns to create opus sectile, pietre dure, or **Cosmati** designs on floors. Opus sectile means cut stone and indeed, unlike the tiny, relatively uniform pieces used in mosaics, opus sectile uses larger pieces of stone or glass shaped appropriately for the part of the design each fills. An entire flower petal, for example, might be a single piece of cut stone in opus sectile work. Opus sectile is sometimes known as Florentine mosaic. Pietre dure is a type of opus sectile that also employs glass and polished stone pieces, often precious or semiprecious, to create a design or even a picture. Unlike mosaics in which grout lines can be seen, pietre dure pieces are so closely set that joints are almost invisible, essentially creating a picture in stone. The pieces are instead glued to a substrate and the under-sides of

FIGURE 10.21 During the Early Renaissance, following architectural design, interiors were symmetrical and horizontally oriented. Later, there was an equal interest in vertical as well as horizontal organization of space.

pieces are often grooved to fit closely. Typically, pietre dure is framed and is often portable. Cosmati work, too, is a type of cut stonework sometimes known as opus alexandrinum. A marble or other stone background is used and intricate mosaics made of triangular and square stone or glass pieces are cemented into the background to create designs. The major difference between Cosmati and pietre dure design is that the mosaics of Cosmati work are separated by large plain stone areas in simple geometric shapes or bands, including guilloches, of contrasting color. When used on pulpits, choir screens, columns, or other more intricate surfaces, the mosaics may be separated by molding or carvings. Stone flooring was heavy and required substantial support so it was usually used only on the ground floor. Although stone was used in homes of the wealthy, it was more typical of public structures.

INFLUENCE 10.6

Because much of the pietre dure work was portable, examples were exported and many found their way to India and other eastern areas. The Taj Majal has some of the finest existing examples of pietre dure as it was interpreted by the Moghals.

Brick, sometimes glazed, was used for floors especially in less palatial surroundings. Variations in texture and shape resulted in interesting patterns. Lighter weight wide oak or walnut planks were used for upper stories and later, parquet patterns employing exotic woods were fashioned. Typical patterns for flooring included repeated circular designs within square frames, triangles, and squares. In the summer, fiber mats were sometimes laid on the floors, but rugs were typically used to cover furniture and as wall decorations rather than for floors.

WALLS

A number of decorative techniques were used for Italian Renaissance walls—often within the same room. Typically because of their protected location and because furnishings would not interfere, the upper sections of walls were more highly ornamented than lower ones. Until the sixteenth century, it was common to separate the wall from the ceiling with a strong cornice that was sometimes deep enough to use as a shelf.

FIGURE 10.22
Renaissance designers employed trompe l'oeil, adding apparent architectural elements—stairways, columns and pilasters, doors and windows, niches, and even entire rooms.

Renaissance walls were typically separated into three horizontal divisions, as had been Roman interiors. A dado at the bottom of the wall was painted or paneled, the major band above the dado was decorated with hangings or paintings, and the frieze near the ceiling was usually painted. Above the frieze was either a classical entablature or a cornice that was often carved with classical band designs. Later, walls were divided into compartments or panels separated by pilasters or columns or surrounded by moldings.

Most walls were plastered and then finished either with whitewash, a colored paint, or a fresco. Fresco designs included diaper patterns, faux fabrics, and stripes. Once the principles of perspective had been mastered, **trompe l'oeil**, or "fool the eye," murals were painted on walls to extend apparent space. This technique was also used to ensure symmetry within a room; a door might be painted on the wall, for example, to mirror another and create a symmetrical effect. Some of these doors were even painted as if they were open, with elements of the room behind painted in or with people painted in the doorways. (See Figure 10.22.) At San Satiro in Milan, Bramante painted a trompe l'oeil choir behind the altar, although there was not enough space to actually build a choir. Trompe l'oeil might be painted in a compartmental division on the wall or ceiling or over an entire wall. The trompe l'oeil technique was also used in intarsia and marquetry work.

Oil paint had been used for detail work before, but it was Jan van Eyck (c. 1410), a Flemish painter, who achieved better effects with oils. Once the technique had been developed and spread to Italy, paintings on canvas were also used on walls. The major advantage of oil painting was that paintings could be moved from one location to another. Both Florentine and Venetian buildings made extensive use of oil on canvas for decoration.

Colored marble incrustation was used on some walls. Stripes or borders of one color marble might surround panels of another color. The exterior walls of the largely Gothic Santa Maria del Fiore in Florence employed pink, green, and white marble.

Grotesques were a popular subject for wall paintings near the end of the fifteenth century. They were executed in fresco, majolica, and stucco and were painted on textiles. Most frequently, grotesques were framed in a wall compartment, although full-wall grotesques were sometimes used.

Wood paneling was also used on walls, often with marquetry designs or painted with oil. In most instances, the paneled wall was separated into compartments by moldings with a variety of profiles. Tondi, often with portrait busts, were also common. Glazed terra-cotta plaques featuring human figures, putti, or fruits, foliage, and vegetables were sometimes built into the wall. This type of plaque was an innovation of Luca della Robbia and typically employed a light blue background with white figures. Some examples had small areas of other colors. Busts were made of marble, terra-cotta, or molded stucco.

Textiles were also hung on the walls. During the summer, linens and silks were used and in winter months, heavier velvets, tapestries, or leather replaced them. Usually imported from Belgium, tapestries were expensive; scenes painted on linen were just as colorful and less costly. Majolica plates with elaborately painted scenes or arabesques were prized and hung on walls as decoration. Colors used on majolica ware were limited due to the necessity of using colors that would not fade when fired.

CEILINGS

The high ceilings of Renaissance rooms were greatly ornamented. The beamed ceiling was flat and composed of heavy, widely spaced beams that rested on corbels or projecting brackets at both ends. Perpendicular to and above the supporting beams were smaller, more closely spaced beams. The large beams were decorated with vividly colored stripes or other painted designs, and a coat of arms or cartouche might be introduced at the center of the room. Semicircular and segmental barrel vaulted ceilings were used especially in ground story rooms. Renaissance vaults were typically based on a square plan and lacked the ribs of Gothic examples.

A **cove** or concave curve between the ceiling and wall might segue to a flat ceiling. Like walls, ceilings, including coves, were often compartmentalized into coffers reminiscent of Roman ceilings. Before the mid-fifteenth century, most coffers were rectangular; later, squares, octagons, circles, and other shapes were used. Octagonal coffers were favored with straight sides of adjacent octagons joined. This configuration resulted

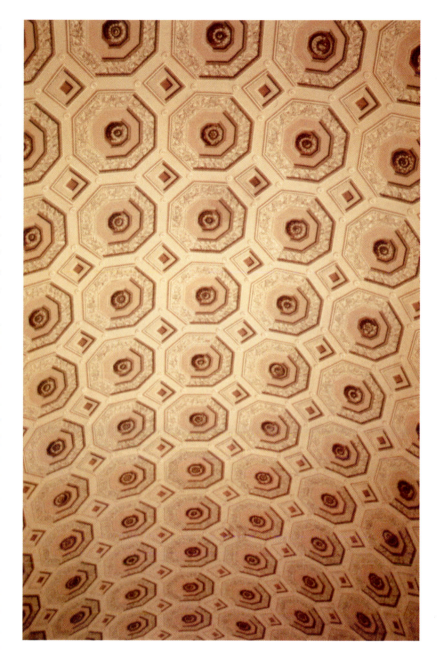

in a square coffer placed diagonally at the joining of four octagonal coffers. (See Figure 10.23.)

In the sixteenth century, the shape of the coffers became less regulated, irregular shapes were employed, and larger compartments were used.

Before the sixteenth century, walls and ceilings had been demarcated by use of a cornice, which could be carved with classical band patterns. During that century, this changed and the wall and ceiling were not differentiated by strong elements but rather, together through the use of a large cove. Decorative techniques used on the ceiling might be carried down the wall.

STAIRS AND FIREPLACES

Before the Renaissance, interior stairways were most frequently within the thickness of walls or

FIGURE 10.23 Coffers significantly decreased the weight of the roof and were especially important in monumental structures.

FIGURE 10.24 It also became more common to use paintings on the ceiling, filling the larger spaces either with oil paintings on canvas stretched across the panel and framed with stucco or wood or with fresco paintings, which were also sometimes framed.

in other places where support could be provided on both sides. Palladio, for example, considered that while stairs should be accessible, they should not be intrusive. Later, stairways ranged from small, private spiral staircases leading from an apartment to monumental stairways, an Italian innovation, leading from a public area to the piano nobile or to the main apartments. Individual flights were typically straight, although doubled flights were common.

Fireplaces were of a large scale with openings as high as 8 feet or more. At first, the Gothic hooded fireplace was used, but gradually fireplaces were trimmed with classical architectural features. Recessed fireplaces were trimmed with **bolection moldings**, which were actually a series of moldings that projected some distance from the opening. More elaborate fireplace surrounds included an entablature with a carved frieze that formed a shelf supported by brackets, columns, caryatids, atlantes, or pilasters—sometimes all of marble.

Italian Renaissance Furniture

The monumental furniture of the Italian Renaissance was suited to the large-scaled rooms where pieces remained as part of the wall composition; this was unlike medieval furniture that was designed to be moved from one dwelling to another. Renaissance examples were difficult to scale down successfully so they could be used in smaller rooms. For this reason, most existing furniture represents that of the upper classes, not that of peasants. Even then, although they lived in lavish surroundings, the Italians used fewer pieces of furniture than would be found in modern homes.

Continuing the procedure followed by medieval guilds, some Italian cities, such as Florence, established quality control measures so that customers could be assured of consistency and value in furnishings they purchased. These regulations stipulated the type of wood to be used for specific pieces and the types of joints required. Although the external surfaces of Italian Renaissance furnishings were magnificently finished, there was often relatively crude workmanship in parts that did not show.

Overall, furniture became more comfortable. While most pieces were rectilinear in outline and straight lines predominated, furniture pieces were often highly decorative and curves were used within the decoration and for a few structural components, such as shaped stretchers. It was the richness of the decoration that gave Italian Renaissance furnishings their luxurious character and the size of individual components that gave them their massive forms.

Walnut was the most favored wood. Sharper details could be obtained in the carving of finely grained walnut than could be obtained with more coarsely grained oak, resulting in carved forms such as foliage or fruit that were realistic in appearance. When furniture was to be painted or covered with pastiglia work, less expensive woods were used: chestnut, oak, pine, cypress, beech, and poplar were available. Monastery furniture was frequently made of oak or chestnut; softer poplar and beech were used mostly for peasant furniture.

During the Renaissance, a few new pieces of furniture were added. Chests, for example, developed into the chest of drawers and multiple seating units, serving pieces, and writing cabinets appeared. Bookcases became more common, and a larger variety of chairs was used. Medium-sized tables were introduced (larger than the side tables used in classical civilizations but smaller than those used for dining), and some beds became more architectural in nature.

CHESTS

The Italian chest, or **cassone**, was the most important article of furniture in the home until the Late Renaissance. The cassone had a hinged lid in one of a variety of shapes. Flat lids were larger than the chest and projected beyond the sides. Shaped lids had a raised center portion often created with moldings. Shallow arched lids were sometimes used. Rectangular cassoni with flat lids were designed low enough to be used as seating or sufficiently high to serve as a table.

In the fifteenth century, cassoni were typically rectangular and the front panel was treated as a single unit, usually with painted scenes from literature, classical mythology, the Bible, lives of the saints, life events such as triumphal processions and tournaments, and allegorical subjects. Often, classical backgrounds were part of the scenes. Cassoni were so important for display that many were painted by great artists including Uccello, Donatello, and Botticelli. Heavy moldings, including gadrooning, were used along the edges at both the

top and bottom. By the sixteenth century, pastiglia decoration was more common and the front might be divided into panels. Sixteenth century cassoni were more often carved and gilded than those of the fifteenth century. (See Figure 10.25.)

The **cassone nuziale** was a dower chest decorated with scenes from wedding celebrations and held the bride's trousseau and other valuable items of the dowry. These cassoni were carried from the bride's house to that of the groom in grand style so they were designed to impress. Usually made in pairs, these cassoni featured the coats of arms of the two families on the fronts, the bride's coat of arms on one and the groom's coat of arms on the other.

The **cassonetta** was a smaller chest similar in form to the cassone and highly decorated, often with pastiglia. The **coffer fort**, a type of chest with a complicated lock beneath the lid, served as a strong box.

Usually, cupboards were built into walls, but there were a few freestanding examples. A larger chest that evolved from the cassone was

FIGURE 10.25 During the fifteenth century, cassoni were also shaped like classical sarcophagi and rested on bases or on lion-shaped feet. A few examples rested directly on the floor.

FIGURE 10.26 This small fifteenth-century Italian chest is made of wood covered with carved bone panels inlaid with ebony and other exotic woods.

the **armadio**. At first, the armadio was a cassone that had doors on the front rather than a lid. Later, the armadio had an additional section placed on top, making it larger, although it remained a single piece. Decorated with massive architectural features, decorative pilasters often appeared to support the overhanging cornice.

The monumentally scaled **credenza** was a serving table on which food was placed before serving and was wider than it was high. The credenza had a lower cupboard accessed through two or three doors where linens and dishes were stored. Drawers might be hidden behind the door of one of the sections. Frieze drawers often locked so that expensive silver utensils could be secured. Pilasters decorated the corners and often separated the doors. In the sixteenth century, a slightly recessed upper section was added. The **credenzina** was a smaller version of the credenza, usually having only one or two doors while re-

taining monumental features, decoration, and the lion paw feet of the credenza.

The chest of drawers was introduced toward the end of the sixteenth century. A pair of smaller side-by-side drawers at the top usually surmounted three full-width drawers. The stiles were decorated with carving, often high relief, and the entire unit set on a decorative base with lion paw feet.

Bookcases were rare, but as the availability of books increased, more homes of the wealthy had them. Usually, bookcases were made in two sections: an upper cabinet and a lower cabinet, each enclosed with doors that were surmounted on a base made of heavy decorative moldings. There were sometimes drawers located above the doors of the base unit. The upper component was slightly set back from the base and, at the top, had a heavy overhanging cornice. Stiles in the form of pilasters often divided the shelves of the top into sections.

As more people became literate, furniture designed for writing was needed. The **bancone** was a fifteenth-century writing table with a rectangular top and a frieze, in which drawers were located. The top extended beyond the two end sections, which were recessed beneath the frieze and had drawers that opened to the ends.

The drop-front desk had a base supported on bracket feet with an upper section that closed with a bottom-hinged door. Inside the upper unit was a variety of small compartments and drawers. The base either had exposed drawers or closed with doors over either shelves or hidden drawers.

SEATING UNITS

The small **sgabello** was a portable chair with an elaborate, often pierced back with an overall triangular form. (See Figure 10.28.) The **panchetto** was similar to the sgabello, although it had three or four splayed legs rather than slab ends. Stools resembled either the sgabello or the panchetto but had no backs.

The chair of estate was heavy and rectangular with a high carved or inlaid back and was common only in homes of the wealthy. As in medieval Europe, the chair of estate was set on a raised dais and often had a cloth canopy over it.

The **Dante**, **Savonarola**, and **monastery** chairs were general-purpose X-shaped folding chairs: the amount of decoration depended on the wealth

FIGURE 10.28 A form of the Gothic slab-ended stool, the sgabello was supported by a trestle with shaped or carved front and back panels connected by a single stretcher. The small seat was sometimes boxlike, sometimes octagonal, and sometimes both.

FIGURE 10.29
The Savonarola and monastery chairs were similar; both had a series of crossed legs, often seven. The legs were arranged from front to back on Savonarola chairs and from side to side on monastery chairs. The legs of the Savonarola chair were curved, and that chair had arms while the monastery chair did not.

version of the sedia featured a prominent carved front stretcher located below the seat. Three other stretchers were plain and variously located but above the floor. Arms might be omitted. The backs of these chairs might also have carved crest rails. (See Figure 10.30.)

In the fifteenth century, arms and a back were added to the cassone resulting in a seating unit for more than one individual known as a **cassapanca**. The seat hinged to provide access to the chest, and a loose cushion made the seat comfortable. Both the arms and back were of the same height and featured decorative carving. Later, a similar bench was made without arms. Backless, armless benches continued to be used.

FIGURE 10.30 The sedia was the most common chair in wealthy homes by the sixteenth century.

of the family, but typically these chairs were either carved or had inlaid designs on them. The Dante chair was similar to the Roman sella curlius and had a pair of curved legs that crossed in an X-shape in both the front and back. Usually, the seat and back panels were made of leather or fabric (typically velvet). Cushions were frequently used on both the Dante and Savonarola chairs. (See Figure 10.29.)

The **sedia** was an armchair with a tall back and a relatively high upholstered seat. Both the back and arms were supported by extensions of the chair legs. Back legs were typically square, while front legs might be square or turned. Stretchers or runners on the floor connected the front and back legs, and a stretcher might connect the back legs about halfway between the floor and the seat. The back legs often terminated with a finial and the runners with simplified lion paws on the front. The upholstery of the seat often extended downward, covering parts of the legs and fringe was often used below the stay rail and around the bottom of the seat. A later

INFLUENCE 10.7

The cassapanca was the forerunner of the modern sofa.

Tables

The **refectory table** was so named because this type of table was originally used in the refectory of monasteries. The long, narrow table was similar to the Roman concrete or stone garden table. What the French later called the **table a l'Italienne** was a Mannerist refectory table on which the stretcher had become highly decorative. The stretcher might support an arcade or colonnade beneath the top. Although early examples had plain edges, later ones had heavy carved moldings along the tabletop edges as well as on the apron or frieze of the table. A drawer might be added in the frieze.

Less monumental tables were developed in the sixteenth century. These had four legs connected by a box stretcher near the floor. An innovation of the Renaissance was the draw-leaf table, which could be doubled in length by pulling outward on the ends and exposing the self-stored leaves beneath. This table had the advantage of requiring less space when it was not in use.

The Florentine table was a small table with a pedestal support designed to be seen from all sides. Carved scrolls sometimes stemmed from the central support, rising diagonally beneath the table top. Drawers were sometimes located in the frieze. Heavy moldings around the edges often gave even these small tables a monumental appearance. Marble tops were common. (See Figure 10.32.) In the sixteenth century, simple four-legged tables with box stretchers became prevalent. Legs were either square or turned.

Beds

Unlike the heavily curtained beds of northern Europe, Italian beds, or **letti**, had little, if any, drapery. Early Renaissance beds often rested on a **predella**, or platform, and had a low headboard and footboard, low sides, and only a small amount of decoration. The bed was often closed in to the floor.

The Tuscan bed was more elaborate and featured a highly decorative headboard without a footboard. Four solominic columns supported the bed at the corners and each typically terminated in a classic urn-shaped finial.

In Vittore Carpaccio's painting *Dream of St. Ursula* (1495), a bed with four very slender posts that support a short valance was depicted. The bed was raised on a predella and had an elaborate headboard.

FIGURE 10.31 Early Renaissance refectory tables had a single slab leg at each end connected by a perpendicular floor stretcher. Later, the table became more elaborate and shaped, carved slabs were used for the end supports. The stretcher and apron also became more decorative.

FIGURE 10.32 The tops of Florentine tables were often octagonal, although hexagonal, square, and round forms were also used.

Tester beds were architectural in nature and featured four columns, usually stop-fluted, with a heavy carved wood entablature. The entablature, however, was sometimes supported from the ceiling rather than by the columns.

MIRRORS

During the Medieval period, mirrors had been small, handheld polished metal plates encased in frames. Early Renaissance mirrors were larger sheets of polished metal surrounded by elaborate frames and covered with sliding doors and later, curtains, when not in use. These were the first mirrors designed to be hung on a wall. In the mid-sixteenth century, Venetian glassmakers developed a method of silvering glass to create mirrors that provided much better reflection. These modern mirrors quickly replaced the less desirable metal examples.

Sharing the Beauty

The Renaissance began in Italy in part because the Gothic style was never really accepted there, but also because so much that surrounded the Italians was ancient Rome. Italy's proximity to Byzantium, from where educated artisans and intellectuals emigrated, contributed as well.

The Renaissance was not to remain in Italy, however. Visitors from other European areas experienced firsthand the comfort, luxury, and freedom of Renaissance Italy and went home with the desire to emulate them. The Renaissance spread first to France and Spain. In subsequent centuries, artistic leadership waned in Italy and passed to Spain, France, England, and the Netherlands until all of Europe shared the vigorous artistic and intellectual spirit.

the Gothic style was very popular, Renaissance forms were used only for superficial ornamentation. It was only later that Renaissance structural forms were blended with those of any given area. The one exception was Spain, where pure Renaissance forms were introduced very early, although alongside Gothic forms that employed Renaissance ornament.

MECHANISM OF CHANGE

The printing press helped spread artistic ideas as well as knowledge. Books were published in vernacular tongues rather than in classical Greek or Latin, reaching an audience beyond the clergy and well-educated laypeople. The Bible was one of the first books published which allowed people to read for themselves what was written within. In 1517, Martin Luther tacked his 95 theses to the door of the Wittenberg Church, culminating a movement questioning the practices of the Church. Among other factors, the increase in literacy and individual knowledge coupled with the freedom to question contemporary practices led to the Protestant Reformation, although Italy and Spain remained staunchly Catholic. In Protestant areas, art was still reflective of religious ideas, while the art of Italy focused on classical forms.

AN EMIGRATION OF CULTURE

As other countries became more politically and economically advanced, they imported Italian Renaissance forms as an indicator of their improved positions. In addition, Italian artisans were invited to other countries, where they found new patrons to support their artistic pursuits. Often, however, these artisans were allowed less than complete design freedom, making it necessary for them to merge Renaissance and indigenous designs. Eventually, in each of the nations of Europe there were native artisans who studied Italian designs and successfully translated them into indigenous art—especially architecture.

In Spain, Juan Bautista de Toledo (d. 1567) espoused the pure Renaissance style, Inigo Jones (1573–1652) modified the style to fit English tastes, and Philibert de l'Orme (1510–1570) translated the style into the French idiom. The result was diversified forms in the varying regions of Europe and eventually national styles that were less dependent on Italian designs. By the time most of the European nations had formulated their own styles, the Baroque period had begun

in Italy, although the Gothic style remained strong especially in Northern Europe.

The Renaissance reached France and Spain first and later, through a royal marriage, Poland. Over time, Renaissance artistic forms reached the Low Countries, the Holy Roman Empire, and Scandinavia, and by the late sixteenth century, England.

The Renaissance in France

In the early fifteenth century, Jeanne d'Arc (c. 1412–1431), the Maid of Orleans, had focused French awareness on its heritage by helping to expel the English from their Continental territories and had helped to establish Charles VII (1403–1461) as King of France. It was, however, Louis XI (1423–1483) who transformed a collection of feudal fiefs and church lands and forged what became the most powerful nation in Christendom in the fifteenth century. He improved harbors and shipping, invited Italian silk weavers to France, and allied the government with the merchants who controlled the financial resources of France.

By the end of the century, French kings sought political gains by invading Italy. Charles VIII (1470–1498), Louis XII (1462–1515), and François I (1494–1547) each led troops into Italy with disastrous results. While they made no long-term territorial gains, they had invaded when the impact of the Renaissance was strong. There they glimpsed the luxurious lifestyles enjoyed by the Italian nobility. While the French court was wealthy, it was still medieval and without the grand costumes, elegant manners, and comfortable furniture of the Italians.

Most historians attribute the beginning of the Renaissance in France to François I. In 1525, he was captured and held captive in Pavia, Italy where he experienced firsthand the glories of Italian Renaissance artistic endeavors. When he returned to France, François was determined to encourage and patronize the arts to the glory of France. In addition to Leonardo da Vinci (in France, 1452–1519), who had been invited to France by Louis XII, father of François I (although he did not arrive until the year of Louis' death), François invited other Italian artists to France where they were successful in stimulating interest in Renaissance forms. François also encouraged native artisans, many of whom went to Italy to study their crafts.

François' successor, Henri II (1519–1559; King from 1547) married Catherine de' Medici, a Florentine, who brought with her sophisticated Italian social customs and who encouraged Italian art forms. After the death of her husband, Catherine continued to control the social and political climate of France as her three sons reigned successively. Henri IV (1553–1610; King of France from 1589) gained the throne after the death of Catherine's sons and he too married a Florentine—Maria de' Medici (1573–1642).

A Protestant, Henri IV converted to Catholicism in order to gain the throne of France, but it was during his reign that the Edict of Nantes was enacted. This law gave religious freedom to the Huguenots (Protestants) of France, and as a result, many of the Huguenots of the Netherlands relocated to France due to persecution under their Spanish overlords.[1] Many of the immigrants were artisans who brought with them not only Flemish influences on design but Spanish influences as interpreted in the Low Countries.

Designs of Italian provenance affected jewelry, textile design, and pottery first. It was only later that Italian designs executed by artisans from that country, French artisans who studied in Italy, and the numerous pattern books available at that time influenced architectural ornament. Italian designs typically made use of marble veneers but this was little used in French buildings largely due to the lack of indigenous sources. The Frenchman Philibert de l'Orme (c. 1510–1570) studied in Italy, worked for the pope, and was later put in charge of the design of Fontainebleau. He published two books on architecture, *Nouvelles Inventions pour Bien Bastir et à Petits Frais (New Inventions for Building Well and at Little Expense)* (1561) and *Premier Livre de l'Architecture (The First Book of Architecture)* in 1567. The first tome incorporated classical orders and even went so far as to propose a new more ornate French order.

Gothic forms continued to dominate French art during the Early Renaissance, or François I style, although Italian ornamentation was applied. By the Middle Renaissance or Henri II style, Italian influence was pronounced with Italian structural forms and decoration employed in architecture and furniture. After the Edict of Nantes (1598), during the Late Renaissance or Louis XIII style (1589–1643), Flemish and Spanish influences were mixed with Italian forms and Gothic forms had disappeared. So from the Gothic period until the Baroque, French art was under the influences of the Spanish, Italian, and Flemish. It was under Louis XIV (1638–1715), grandson of Henri IV, that a truly French artistic style was developed, but by this time, the Renaissance was over and the Baroque had begun.

FIGURE 11.1 Of note is St. Etienne du Mont, a French Renaissance church that was a mixture of Gothic towers, flying buttresses, and steep roofs with Italian pilasters, pediments, columns, and balustrades. The rood screen connected on either side to spiral stairs was probably designed by Philibert de l'Orme c. 1545.

Box 11.1 FRENCH RENAISSANCE MOTIFS

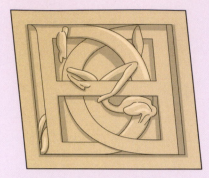

Monograms, such as the letter F for François I, were used decoratively. Henri II, whose courtesan was Diane de Poitiers (1499–1566), had the letters H and D ingeniously intertwined and used decoratively, and the wing he built to Chenoceau was ornamented with the mythological Diana.

The mascaron was a human face used in an unexpected place.

François I adopted the salamander as a personal emblem because legend said it could withstand fire.

Half figures were human forms that merged into scrolls, foliage, or a support below the waist. They were commonly used for brackets.

Fleurs-de-lys were symbolic of French royalty beginning as early as the tenth century and represented a lily.

Strapwork was ornamentation in bands, usually including curves, that was originally designed to represent leather or ribbons. It was often used in combination with creatures that it surrounded.

FRENCH RENAISSANCE ARCHITECTURE

When Charles VIII had returned ignominiously from Naples in 1495, he took with him back to France a number of Italian artisans including painters, architects, wood workers, and landscape architects. He commissioned them to transform the medieval castle at Amboise into a lodge worthy of royalty and in the Italian style. The quintessential European palace was the result. Fifteenth-century wars resulted in little building except for châteaux for royalty and nobility.

As the Gothic style had been mainly ecclesiastical, French Renaissance architecture was characterized by châteaux. Churches continued to be constructed, although the number of Gothic churches constructed left little need for additional centers of worship. The churches built during the Early Renaissance in France were still constructed in the favored Flamboyant Gothic style that had not yet run its course. Some existing churches were given new façades or ornamentation in the Italian style, however. French kings had asserted their divine right to rule and had subjected the weakened Church to the State. As a result, construction patronage was in the hands of the laity.

FRENCH CHÂTEAUX

The cannon coupled with increased security provided by a strong national government made châteaux forts, or fortified castles, obsolete and the term chateau was widened to incorporate the con-

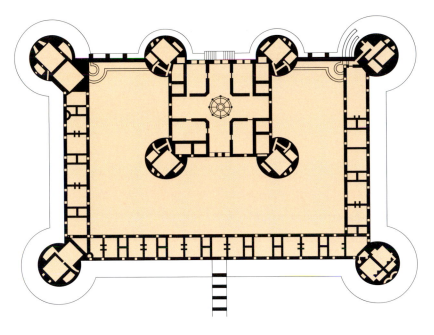

FIGURE 11.2 Like Gothic castles before it, the plan of Chambord château began by François I, has a donjor with four towers enclosed inside surrounding walls. The double helix staircase is crowned with a lantern.

cept of a comfortable home, the *châteaux de plaisance,* which dominated early sixteenth-century architecture. Typically, French architects familiar with Gothic structures were employed, while foreign artists executed sculptures and paintings.

Unlike their Italian counterparts, the French nobility preferred life in the country rather than in crowded cities. Accordingly, most of the châteaux were constructed along the Loire and Cher Rivers south of Paris. Buildings of French Renaissance châteaux were arranged around a

FIGURE 11.3 The roofline of Chambord (1519–1536) was purely French. Dominated by numerous towers, pinnacles, dormers, turrets, decorated chimneys, and steeply pitched roofs, the skyline was complex. Dormer windows pierced the roofline and each was emphasized by elaborately carved frameworks.

profitable. Portugal, spurred on by Prince Henry the Navigator (1394–1460), was the first to find a sea route to Asia by sailing around Africa. Spain, then, had to find another route and sent explorers west across the Atlantic. It was the voyages of discovery by the Portuguese and Spanish that brought the New World to the attention of Europe. Spanish navigators sailed west and brought back large amounts of gold and silver; this made Spain the richest, most powerful European country during the sixteenth century. But by the time Philip II (1527–1598) died, the Spanish armada had been defeated and Spain was nearly bankrupt.

In 1478, the Inquisition was restored under the monarchy of Ferdinand and Isabella and lasted well into the seventeenth century. Unlike the earlier Inquisition, sovereigns could now nominate the priests who would seek out and punish those who had been baptized but who continued to secretly practice Judaism or Islam. In gaining this concession from the papacy, the Spanish monarchs subjected religion to the will of the state. In 1492, the Inquisition was expanded to include nonbelievers. Most were allowed to leave the country, but without their property. While they could take portable goods with them, they were not allowed to remove gold, silver, or any form of currency. In this way, Christians obtained much of the property of those who left at a small fraction of its value. Some of those who left migrated to Portugal, although there they were allowed to stay only a few months. Italy accepted the immigrants and gained a rich treasure: artisans, merchants, scholars, scientists, and physicians who were expelled from Spain enriched Italian arts and sciences. As a result, Spain remained staunchly rooted in the Middle Ages.

In 1492, the Spaniard Roderigo Borgia (1431–1503) was elevated to the papacy, bringing Italy and Spain closer together. In 1522, the Kingdom of Naples came under the control of Charles V (1500–1558). By that time, the great wealth of Spain had begun to rival that of Italy and Spanish families desired to emulate Italian architecture with its luxurious appointments.

SPANISH ARTISTIC PERIODS

The Gothic style was deeply rooted in Spanish design and suited the emotional temperament of the people. Spanish Gothic, however, was directly derived from southern France. Seville Cathedral, constructed in the fifteenth century is the largest Gothic building in the world. The Moors had invaded Spain in the seventh century and until 1492 still lived in parts of Spain. Moorish art was extremely ornamental with great delicacy in its execution. Moorish leather work, wrought iron screens, and wood carving provided much of the decoration throughout Spain. It was the Italian influence that was new to Spain, but typically, Spanish artisans were able to adapt Renaissance designs to suit their tastes.

The Plateresque period (1500–1556) in Spain was characterized by small-scale ornament applied to almost every surface. The term platero meant silversmith, and it was from this source that Plateresque ornament got its style. From the Moors and the Visigoths, the Spanish gained consummate metal-working skills, and the influx of silver from the New World made it one of the most widely used metals in decoration. This style of ornament, however, was unique to Spain. Plateresque ornament combined Flamboyant Gothic, Moorish influences, and Italian designs. As Italian candelabra motifs and classical orders were interpreted, they became much more decorative than in their place of origin. It was the ornate Plateresque style that was first carried across the Atlantic to Spanish territories in the Americas.

The Desornamentado period (1556–1600) was based on the desires of Philip II, who was passionately religious. The style was based on pure Italian Renaissance forms, resulting in plain, severe structures. In fact, the term Desornamentado means "without ornament." As it was used in Spain, the classical style was so ordered and precise that it left little room for creative adaptations. The two most influential architects of the style were Juan Bautista de Toledo and Juan de Herrara (1530–1593). Within a very short period of time, the Desornamentado was followed by the Baroque style, which was more suited to the Spanish temperament. The greatest artist of the Desornamentado period was El Greco (the Greek), Domenikos Theocopoulos (1541–1614), indeed a Greek, who worked in Spain. His figures were passionate and had elongated limbs.

SPANISH MOTIFS AND DECORATIVE TECHNIQUES

Spanish motifs always reflected some Moorish influence including the use of vivid colors. In addition to geometric motifs, stylized foliage, floral forms, interlacing band patterns, lozenges, and wheel medallions were typical. To the motifs used by the rest of Europe, Spanish artisans added the scallop shell of Santiago and made greater use of the eagle that represented St. John. A Portuguese carving technique employed by the Spanish was the use of wavy parallel grooves, or **tremido**, on stiles, rails, and furniture legs.

Using Moorish techniques, Spanish metal workers produced exceptional wrought iron grilles for use in windows and doorways. Often, the lace-like grille was the only closure openings had in the hot climate of the Iberian Peninsula. Wrought iron was also used for railings, hinges, and locks. Metal workers formed rosettes, stars, and scallop shells to be applied to furniture and were also adept at creating pierced metal sheets with geometric designs used for furniture pieces that required ventilation. **Santas**, or religious statues, graced most Spanish homes and were frequently made of gold or silver.

Spanish artisans were skilled in the use of inlay using ivory, bone, ebony, silver, tortoiseshell, and bronze. So skilled were these artisans that they inlaid pieces of bone the size of a grain of wheat in walnut, a technique known as **pinyonet**, or pine seed. Marquetry vases, flowers, and leaves were popular designs on cabinets. Ivory was often painted in brilliant colors, but when it was left its natural color, it was etched with designs emphasized in black.

The **estofado** technique was a Spanish method of creating a design in gold. Gold leaf was used to cover an object that was burnished and painted. Much like scraffito, the design was then scratched through the paint to reveal the gold.

Spanish cordovan leather was the finest quality in Europe, and there was a strong demand for this product. Embossed leather, or **guadamicil**, was typical of Moorish work and continued to be used by Spanish artisans who also quilted, punched, painted, and gilded leather.

A device used by Spanish carvers to offset the effects of distance in objects high on a surface was to increase the depth of the carving from nearly flat in lower areas to bold cuts near the top.

Azujelos, or earthenware tiles, originated in the Near East in the ninth century, and were imported to Spain by the Moors. By the Renaissance, the tin-glazed Majolica technique was used on these tiles to cover them with decoration. Often the decoration was executed in blue on a white ground, but many tiles were covered with geometric de-

FIGURE 11.8 The process used for keeping various colored glazes from merging on azujelos differed over the years, but typically resulted in lines that were visible once the tile was fired.

signs, and by the Renaissance, groups of tiles were painted as a single scene. Not only were tiles used on walls but around doors, windows, and niches, on the interior surfaces of niches, on window seats, and on stair risers. (See Figure 11.8.)

Spanish Renaissance Architecture

Because Spain was still tied to the Middle Ages, the Gothic style continued to be used. Renaissance buildings appeared relatively early, but because there were few classical models in Spain, architecture that followed Italian designs lacked the proportions of the classical period.

While most new churches remained Gothic in style, Renaissance features included the use of classic orders on the piers that supported vaults. Spanish Renaissance cathedrals were given a **capilla mayor**, a domed sanctuary that was circular in plan and that housed the high altar.

Domestic Buildings

Once the religious conflicts of the fifteenth century had ended, the Spanish nobility moved from their fortified feudal castles into palaces in urban areas such as Madrid, Barcelona, and Seville. Most of their domestic buildings had a single story because Spanish law required owners to entertain the king and his retinue in second story rooms. Homes of the more affluent sometimes had two stories. In that event, public rooms, including a grand reception room, bedrooms, and a winter dining room, were located on the upper level with the kitchen and summer dining room on ground level. The **estrado** was the main public room and can be compared with the great hall. At one end, there was a raised platform with two elaborate chairs of honor, a table, and a cabinet.

FIGURE 11.9 The House of Pilate in Seville employed superimposed orders that supported two tiers of arcades—semicircular arches on the ground floor with segmental arches above. The walls behind the first-story arcade had a dado of azujelos in a variety of patterns. Following Moorish influences, the House of Pilate also has a fountain in the courtyard. The star-shaped design also has Moorish origins.

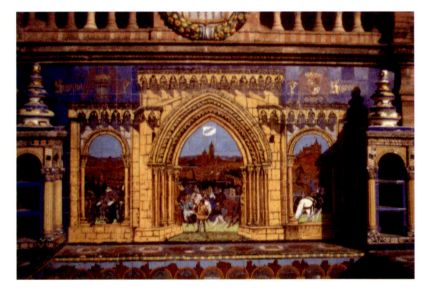

FIGURE 11.10 Poly-chrome tile decoration became common in the Iberian Peninsula, with detailed scenes covering numerous tiles.

The remainder of the room was more formally arranged than northern examples with seating, cabinets, and tables. Typically, a small room or a recessed alcove was located behind the dais and separated from it by columns. It was in this small area that the bed was located.

Domestic buildings were arranged around a **patio**, or courtyard derived from Moorish examples. The patio was surrounded by a colonnade or arcade that was often ornamented in the Plateresque style behind which was a covered walk-

FIGURE 11.11 Coffered ceilings in Plateresque buildings such as the House of Pilate were highly decorative.

way, or **corredor**. Rooms were arranged around the patio. It was the patio that was the main living area for the family, and it was lavishly decorated. In contrast, the exterior of Spanish Renaissance buildings followed Moorish practices and were extremely plain. Only a few windows pierced the exterior, and those were high above the street.

Especially in the south where Moorish influence lasted into the sixteenth century, carved plaster decoration known as *yesería* was used around openings, as friezes, and on any flat surface, although walls were sometimes relatively plain. Most of the motifs used continued to be Moorish, but some Italian Renaissance motifs were incorporated. (See Figure 11.9.)

The Andalusian house of the Pilato family was typical of most Spanish residences, although it was larger than most. The patio was reached through a long wide hall called a **zaguán**, which had storerooms, servants' quarters, and stables off its sides. A wrought iron gate from the zaguán led to the patio. Individual rooms were long and narrow, and the only room that might feature a fireplace was the salon. In the region of Aragon, houses often had small towers at the corners and

balconies although rooms were arranged as in Andalusian homes. Brick was typically used for construction and often featured sculpted decoration.

During the Desornamentado period when strict classicism was employed, few domestic buildings were constructed and those for the very wealthy. The style simply was not suited to the tastes of the public, and their houses continued to be built as before. (See Figure 11.12.)

The most austere of the Spanish Renaissance buildings was El Escoriál (1562–1584), built by

> **BOX 11.3 CHARACTERISTICS OF SPANISH RENAISSANCE ARCHITECTURE**
>
> - Capilla mayor
> - Classic orders on Gothic-style buildings
> - Estrado with raised dais
> - Patios with surrounding corredors
> - Moorish designs including yesería
> - Reception and living rooms on second story
> - Classical orders

FIGURE 11.12 The Renaissance Palace of Charles V in Granada begun in 1527 had a circular courtyard almost 100 feet in diameter surrounded by a two-tiered colonnade that employed superimposed Tuscan and Ionic orders.

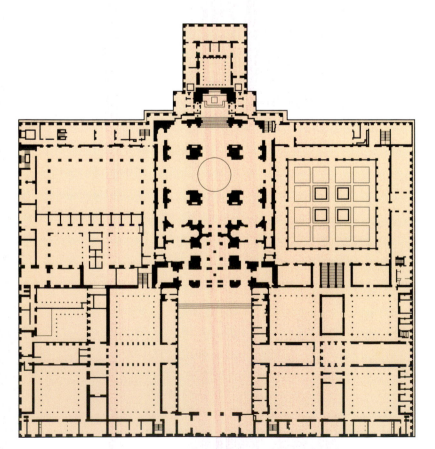

FIGURE 11.13 El Escoriál has plain, rectilinear walls with only three entrances: the main entrance and separate ones for the palace and the monastery.

Philip II outside of Madrid. Philip's palace was combined with a monastery and a cathedral. Juan Bautista de Toledo began the structure and Juan de Herrara completed it. The plan of El Escoriál was based on the gridiron—an instrument of torture on which St. Lawrence was martyred. Philip dedicated the palace to this martyr because it was on that saint's day that he got news of a Spanish victory over the French at the Battle of San Quentin, where artillery fire had destroyed a monastery dedicated to the saint. (See Figure 11.13.). See Box 11.3 for a summary of characteristics of Spanish Renaissance architecture.

INTERIORS

Spanish interiors differed significantly from those in other parts of Europe because they reflected their Moorish heritage. Floors were made of masonry on the ground floor, with brick, stone, or subdued tile units often laid in a basket weave pattern. Other stories had wood floors and, unlike the rest of Europe, carpets, or leather rugs, were also used on floors for warmth.

The upper portion of interior walls of Spanish buildings was often plastered or paneled with wood. Following Moorish precedents, the lower part of interior walls was covered with azujelos laid in panels while the upper portion was plastered or paneled with wood. Cordovan leather or Flemish tapestries with red fringe were sometimes hung on walls. Heraldic designs were embroidered or appliquéd on velvet and damask wall hangings and trimmed with fringe and braid. Majolica ware plates were also hung on walls. Wall niches were lined with azujelos and the openings surrounded by them. Some housed a small fountain or water container with a spigot at the bottom with a lavabo or wash basin beneath it.

In the northern parts of the Iberian Peninsula, ceilings were plastered but in the south, coffered ceilings employing Moorish intricate geometric shapes were used. Some ceilings were paneled with oiled pine without added ornament. (See Figure 11.14.)

Spanish Renaissance Furniture

Spanish furniture was relatively simple in structure, rectilinear in line, and bold in design although Spanish artisanship was not as fine as was found in Italy and France. Only a few chairs employed curved designs until later periods. Few moldings were used, and architectural details were absent. Spanish homes had fewer pieces and types of furniture than did homes in other European areas, and most of it remained against the walls even as others were moving pieces to the centers of rooms.

Furniture was ornamented with turned pieces including those with spiral designs, artesonado patterns, inlay, carving, painting, and gilding. Provincial pieces were typically decorated with chip or incised carving. As in other countries, the Spanish used decorative nailheads to attach upholstery, but they also used them decoratively on furniture surfaces. The Spanish raised the use of these **chatônes** to their highest art. Walnut was the most popular furniture wood in the Iberian Peninsula, although oak, pine, and chestnut were sometimes used and fruit woods were prized for inlaid designs. Mahogany was imported from the West Indies after 1550, and because of the enormous width of the logs, larger panels could be incorporated in furniture and on walls.

SEATING UNITS

The low stool, or **banqueta**, was similar to those in other regions, although many Spanish exam-

ples had leather or velvet upholstery. Turned or carved legs and trestle supports were common. Women often sat on cushions on the floor, even in church.

Most Spanish benches, or **bancos**, seated three people and were similar to those elsewhere in Europe with a box seat for storage and a back approximately the same height as the depth of the seat. Sometimes the back was shaped or folded down onto the seat. Other benches had paneled, arched, or spindled backs and, by the fifteenth century, arms. When used in more formal settings, bancos were upholstered with leather or velvet applied with chatônes. Benches were supported by trestle ends and sometimes **fiadores**, or wrought iron supports, angled beneath the seat.

FIGURE 11.14 The artesonado work in coffered ceilings was exquisite and usually incorporated much smaller coffers than were used in other parts of Europe. Each panel field was painted, gilded, or carved.

FIGURE 11.15 The sillon de cadera was a medieval X-shaped folding chair that was usually decorated with marquetry or carved, although metal examples were also made. Leather or another textile product—often embroidered—was used for the seat and back, and a loose cushion provided additional comfort.

A **sillon de cajon** was a medieval chair with a **gondola back** that continues to be used. The gondola back and arms curved around into one another and were solid to the floor. The back was typically carved.

The **Majorca chair**, also called a **cadeira de sola**, was a **ladder-back chair**, meaning that it had several horizontal rails that connected the back supports. Turned or striated legs were typical, with the back legs extending upward to form the supports for the high back. Finials terminated the back supports. Both the front stretcher and **crest rail**, or top rail along the back, of the Majorca chair were shaped with curves and carved. The crest rail ornament was almost a full circle.

The **silla** was an armless chair with a low upholstered back and seat. Sometimes the seat was made of rush or corded in an intricate design. The **frailero**, or monk's chair, was similar to the Italian sedia. It was a simple rectangular armchair with a relatively low leather seat and back panel attached with chatônes. The front stretcher was wider than the others which became its distinguishing feature. Square legs supported the chair, and the arms were straight. Early examples folded, but later ones did not. When used in more formal rooms, the leather was covered with embroidered velvet and fringe was added. Later examples were more elaborately decorated with carved or turned legs and arm posts or arcades along the back. When a frailero was designed for women, it was made without arms to accommodate full skirts.

INFLUENCE 11.2
The frailero was the predecessor of the mission chair popular in twentieth-century America. That chair, however, was copied from fraileros used in California missions, which were themselves poor reproductions of the originals.

STORAGE PIECES

The Spanish chest, or **arca**, was used for storage but was also a seat, a table, or a desk. Arcas came in all sizes and unlike the rest of Europe were not supplanted by cupboards and cabinets. Most arca lids were flat, but smaller arcas might have arched tops. Italian influence was seen in arcas that were painted on the inside with a second interior lid to cover the contents so the decorative one could be opened against the wall. The **arqueta** was a miniature chest designed as a jewelry box or a container for small objects. Most homes had a number of these boxes that sat on tables—a Moorish holdover. Some arcas had collapsible fronts that revealed a second inner front of drawers. This type of arca was a precursor to the vargueño, the most typical Spanish Renaissance furniture piece.

The term **encorado** was used to signify that a chest was lined or covered with leather that was attached with decorative chatônes. Oiled leather was used for traveling chests to waterproof them. Tooled leather was decorative and used on chests designed to remain indoors. **Ensayalada** chests were covered with velvet or brocade edged with braid. In northern areas, chests were raised on feet to keep them off the floors, which might gather moisture.

Spanish cupboards were recessed into the wall, and, like niches, both the interior and opening surround were lined with azulejos. Shelves provided organized storage space in these functional Spanish cupboards that are still used. Some freestanding cupboards were enclosed with two doors at the top and had a row of drawers beneath them. This type of cupboard was relatively low and was frequently used to serve food. The **fresquera** was a small cupboard that hung on the wall and was used for storing food. It was ventilated through the spindles or pierced panels that filled the doors.

The most typical Spanish **armario** was a double-bodied cupboard with two doors in the upper and lower sections. Each door was further divided into two sections. Lower doors were paneled, upper doors had one or both sections filled with spindles. The Moorish influenced version of the armario was decorated with artesonado. The armario was little used during the Renaissance in Spain but became very common in the succeeding Baroque period.

THE VARGUEÑO

The **vargueño** was the quintessential Spanish furniture piece. Unique to Spain, the vargueño was a writing cabinet with a vertical fall front as well as a hinged lid for the top. It had handles for carrying on both ends and was designed to be transported easily. The interior was divided into numerous drawers and compartments including secret ones. Like the French cabinet, vargueños were highly ornamented furniture pieces although most of the decoration was on the interior. The interiors of examples made after Italian influences came into Spain included architectural colonnettes and pilasters. Because the abuse of travel could easily spoil other types of designs, the exterior was often decorated only with iron bands, although these were sometimes gilded. The abuse of travel could easily spoil other types of exposed designs.

A variety of stands were made especially to support the vargueño. Each type had two slides that pulled out to support the drop front when it was in use. Often the ends of the slides, or **lopers**, were carved with a shell or animal mask. The **taquillón** stand was a chest with drawers, compartments closed with doors, or a combination of the two. Four feet supported the taquillón.

The **papelera** was a smaller cabinet similar to the vargueño that held documents and writing materials but did not have a drop front. The papelera was highly decorated, but because there was no front to conceal the decoration, its ornamentation was evident. It had ball feet and was placed on a stand or table.

TABLES

Mesas were Spanish tables and most were similar to other European examples. Splayed legs were typical and fiadores were used for support. Turned or carved table legs were often connected

FIGURE 11.16 This vargueño is supported on a trestle stand, or puente, a term derived from the word bridge. Each end had three small columns attached to a runner on the floor, with an arcaded stretcher connecting the trestle ends.

with a box or H-shaped arcaded stretcher. Unlike other European examples, the edges of Spanish tables were square and not carved or molded, and refectory tables tops extended farther beyond the frieze. A Moorish-influenced circular table, the **ratona**, had an iron or brass brazier surrounded by a wood platform supported on short legs and

FIGURE 11.17 The ratona is a Moorish-influenced circular table with an iron or brass brazier surrounded by a wood platform and supported on short legs.

designed to be used while sitting on cushions on the floor.

BEDS

Spanish beds, or **camas**, were similar to those of the rest of Europe. Voluminous hangings were usually omitted due to the climate.

Portuguese Furniture

Portugal and Spain share the Iberian Peninsula, and the cultures of the two countries have similar characteristics. Portuguese Renaissance furniture and other objects exhibited only slight differences from Spanish examples and this was mostly due to influences derived from trade with India and the Far East. Portuguese turnings were exaggerated in size and often included bulbous shapes. These bulbous forms influenced English Renaissance furniture and became characteristic of the Elizabethan style.

Portuguese chair backs and seats were sometimes **caned**, an influence from their trade with the East Caning originated in Malaysia and was made of woven strips of rattan, a type of palm. Caned seats and backs were cooler because they allowed air to circulate around users. Another Oriental influence on Portuguese furniture was the double-curved **cabriole leg**. Each leg curved outward at the top, called the **knee**, and inward near the bottom, called the **ankle**, and terminated in a foot that varied according to the period.

INFLUENCE 11.3

Cabriole legs became popular throughout Europe in the eighteenth century.

Portuguese trading vessels brought furniture back from Goa, India made specifically for the European market. The forms were European, the materials and patterns Indian. This furniture employed East Indian ivory inlay and veneer, pierced metal patterns, and exotic woods such as teak, ebony, and amboyna. Figures were used for supports or as decorative pilasters but most had the appearance of savages with large ivory eyes.

Central European and German Renaissance Design

Much of the Holy Roman Empire had little chance to develop Renaissance forms. Charles

FIGURE 11.18 Begun in 1614, Salzburg Cathedral was one of the first truly Renaissance buildings in German-speaking areas of Central Europe. Its dome and Latin cross plan would have been familiar in Italy, although the paired towers were typically German.

V's campaign to crush Protestant nobles created social instability that almost precluded the construction of new buildings. In 1555 the Peace of Augsburg established relative security, but that lasted only until 1618 when the Thirty Years' War broke out. This war was predominantly a religious war between Protestants and Catholics, and although most of the major nations of Europe were involved, it was Germany that was most affected. In the years between the fighting, German painting and sculpture were somewhat affected by Italian Renaissance forms but the deeply rooted Gothic architectural style was changed little.

German sculpture was mostly accomplished in wood. The man whom the historian Durant called the "greatest wood carver in history"[2] was the German Veit Stoss (c. 1445–1533) who worked both in Cracow and in Nuremburg just before and after the turn of the sixteenth century. Like most European sculptors, his subjects were religious.

Central Europe got its first taste of Italian Renaissance architecture when the Hungarian king Matthias Corvinus (1443–1490; reign from 1458) married Beatrix of Naples in 1476. With the new queen came Italian artisans. From that point, Italian designs dominated aristocratic buildings in Central Europe with domes on pendentives, castles built around courtyards with arcades composed of superimposed orders, and the use of four corner towers. Blended with these Italian features were the vernacular steeply pitched gables with multiple stories identified by tiers of dormers. Renaissance architecture remained a court style, however, until the seventeenth century.

German areas preserved much of the Gothic with its asymmetry, octagonal towers and turrets, steeply pitched roofs, and oriel windows. Figures known as **gaînes** were favored by German architects as decoration. These figures employed human torsos mounted on a pedestal, much as did the herms of ancient Rome. By the seventeenth century, German designs copied those in Flemish pattern books and became stiff and formal.

While court buildings followed Italian Renaissance designs closely, guild halls, town halls, and domestic buildings retained much that was Gothic and included features indigenous to native populations. In the large forested areas, timber was used for construction as well as for decorative detailing, with painted carvings typi-cal. Where stone was available, it was often covered with stucco and its surfaces painted. In the north, where there was an absence of both stone and timber, brick was the material of choice.

By comparison with other European nations, German areas had better sanitation. Public bath houses provided extensive services, as had Roman examples. Most domestic buildings had bathrooms, even those in rural areas. In fact, German homes provided more comforts than homes in other parts of Europe, although from the exterior, the buildings were quite similar. Lower stories of masonry construction were surmounted by timber upper stories that had overhanging jetties. German buildings also made use of terra-cotta tile for roofs and upper-story balconies. Large roof overhangs protected windows from the elements. In areas influenced by Flemish design, crow-stepped parapet gables were embellished with gaînes, statues, and curved scrolls.

FIGURE 11.19 German artisanship was high and even the Italians imported goods from German areas. German architects went to Italy, Spain, and other areas, especially to construct Gothic buildings.

A few domestic buildings were constructed similar to Italian models, with an arcaded ground floor and regularly ordered pilasters alternating with typically German corbels on upper floors, but even then above the cornice, there was German ornamentation. See Box 11.4 for a summary of characteristics of Germany Renaissance architecture.

Russian Renaissance Design

In 1485, Ivan III, Duke of Moscow, invited the Italian engineer Aristotele Fioravanti or Fieraventi (c. 1415 or 1420–c. 1486) to Moscow to rebuild the Dormition Cathedral (1475–1479) that had been damaged during an earthquake. The Czar, however, required Fioravanti to study traditional Russian buildings and re-create much of what was medieval in the cathedral. Five onion domes on typically tall slender Russian drums and semicircular arches, including those of the **zakomary**, or semicircular gables with shell-like detailing, dominated the structure. Triangular, ogee, pointed, and semicircular arched kokoshniki became decorative during this period rather than structural. It was also during this period (1530) that the first of the tent, or **shatyor**, churches were constructed in Russia. The shatyor roof became normal for bell towers that were usually detached. (See Figure 11.20.)

FIGURE 11.20 The Russian shatyor at Kolomenskoye is constructed of brick, although numerous other examples were also constructed of wood. The tent-roofed octagonal drum of this centrally planned structure is only slightly rounded at the top. Three tiers of Kokoshniki ornament the shatyor.

FIGURE 11.21 The Cathedral of the Archangel Michael, constructed by Italians at the beginning of the sixteenth century, used a mixture of Italianate forms and traditional Russian architectural design.

On Both Sides of the English Channel

The Renaissance reached the Low Countries of northern Europe and the British Isles later than other areas, in part because of the political and religious turmoil taking place in those areas. Additionally, the people in both areas were artistically conservative, and few of the excesses of other European courts were adopted. Both areas participated in voyages of exploration, seeking water routes to the East, although only the Dutch succeeded. Like other European nations, the Netherlands and England had successful colonial ventures, but neither became exceedingly wealthy as Spain had done.

FIGURE 11.22 Italian architects constructed a palace for Ivan III in the Renaissance style. The Palace of Facets, named for the way the faces of the stones were cut, is the only remaining portion of that structure.

Renaissance Design in the Low Countries and England

The Low Countries of Europe, now Belgium and the Netherlands, and England are separated only by the narrow English Channel. In general, the people of both areas are conservative and independent. The Renaissance reached each of these more northern areas later than much of Europe and, although Renaissance forms lingered, did not reach stylistic extremes. Relationships between the Low Countries and England were extensive. During much of the period, England controlled parts of France, there were close commercial ties especially through the wool industry, and many Flemish, German, and Dutch artisans immigrated to England, especially after the St. Bartholomew's Day massacre in 1572.

The Low Countries

As the Reformation spread, the northern portions of the Low Countries (Holland, as the Netherlands was then called) embraced Protestant faiths, while the southern areas (now Belgium, but at that time Flanders) remained primarily Catholic. Both areas were under the Spanish yoke from 1555 until 1581 when Holland declared its independence. The religious wars between Spain and the Low Countries ended with a separation of Belgium and the Netherlands into two distinct regions. Dutch independence was finally recog-

nized by Spain in 1648, but Belgium remained under the control of Spain until 1713. The religious differences of the two areas affected artistic tastes. During the seventeenth century, Flanders followed the rest of Europe in adopting the Baroque style. (See Chapter 16.) The Netherlands, with its Protestant leanings, never fully accepted the excesses of the Baroque, which the Dutch believed was associated with the splendor of the Catholic Church.

The feudal system was not well established in this area, where land had to be gained from the sea and required a communal effort. Life was more free and the people more equal than in other areas of Europe. Flemish towns throughout the Medieval period had been more economically developed than anywhere else in Europe with the exception of northern Italy. The textile industry dominated the economy, and the population was largely made up of merchants and farmers, both typically more influenced by pragmatism than by religion. Traders came from areas as far away as Russia and the Near East, and Italian bankers centered in Bruges provided the financial services required for extensive trade.

The Burgundian nobility who controlled most of the area during much of the sixteenth century were extremely wealthy and had a taste for luxurious objects such as tapestries, majolica, decorative glassware, and plate made of precious metals. The constant demand for these luxury goods nurtured the guilds of weavers, wood carvers, and lace makers who produced high-quality goods that were in demand all over Europe.

ADVANCES IN PAINTING

The fourteenth-century Dutch painter Jan van Eyck (c. 1385–1441) is credited with new painting techniques using oil colors. Oil paints were known even in classic times, but the materials needed were difficult to obtain and their use required great skill. Van Eyck produced the first stable oil painting mixture with a drying medium. At first, oil paints were used as glazes over a tempera base. As the technique developed, a number of artists including Michelangelo experimented with the ingredients, and by the seventeenth century, oil painting without a tempera base had become common. By then, the rich colors and hard-finished surface typical of modern oil painting had developed and light appeared to glow from within the paintings. Flemish artists adopted oil painting techniques and materials for their paintings to achieve hard-edged details and emphasize surfaces. By contrast, Italian paintings emphasized form and composition.

RENAISSANCE ARCHITECTURE OF THE LOW COUNTRIES

The wars with Spain had reduced the aristocratic class so much that merchants and officials dominated the political scene. There was little need for palaces nor for ostentatious display. Civic and domestic architecture predominated, and there was less emphasis on the construction of churches even during the highly religious Middle Ages. Tall, narrow multistoried medieval houses with steeply pitched stepped gables were retained. The ground floor was typically a shop and the attic space a warehouse. A large bracket projected from the front of the gable to support furniture and merchandise as it was hoisted to upper stories. Little architectural change was needed to incorporate Renaissance details on the façades. Classical moldings, columns, and pilasters were added to the exterior but were used little as interior treatments.

Homes were relatively small and human in scale. As window glass became less expensive and was readily available, the number and size of windows increased; this marked a boon in northern areas where letting sunlight into buildings was advantageous. Brick was the predominant building material and roofs were tiled. Like German Renaissance buildings, those in the Low Countries employed strapwork, gaînes, and stepped gables. Spanish influence was seen in the use of vaulted arcades. As the Baroque style reached Flanders, stepped gables were changed to those with multiple curves.

INFLUENCE 12.1

Because Flanders embraced the Baroque style relatively early and influenced English design, the curved gables became part of the English Renaissance landscape.

Pure Renaissance forms were used especially in Flemish architecture during the latter part of the sixteenth century. Although similar to French Renaissance examples, Flemish buildings frequently employed more elaborate ornamentation. The Renaissance style was relatively short-lived in Flanders because the ensuing Baroque style was readily adopted by the Flemish. The High Renaissance Antwerp city hall constructed in 1565 had a rusticated ground-story arcade, pilasters and entablatures that separated windows on the second and third stories, and a Spanish-influenced loggia on the fourth story. The central section projected from the remainder of the building, giving it emphasis.

The Netherlands, on the other hand, did not adopt High Renaissance forms until the last quarter of the sixteenth century, at least two decades later than had Flanders, but the style lasted longer. There the style was restrained and buildings were relatively plain. Classical orders, usually well proportioned, were especially common on guild houses and city halls. Doric and Ionic orders were most frequently used in keeping with the practical character of the people. Typically, buildings were symmetrical with the center section elongated vertically. Stone details were used on the brick façades.

TOWERS

Medieval bells were used as alarms, to define the hours of work, and to call people together. Although the **carillon** originated in the twelfth century, it was not until five centuries later that techniques for tuning bells were perfected by the brothers François (c. 1609–1667) and Pieter

Hemony (1619–1680), making the carillon a musical instrument. By definition, a carillon must have a minimum of 23 bells and the first tuned example was installed in 1644 in Zutphen, Netherlands. Carillons weighed as much as 200 tons, which required strong structural support in the towers in which they were mounted, usually in city halls or churches.

Hendrik de Keyser (1565–1621) was the most famous of the Dutch Renaissance architects and mainly constructed churches. Keyser's towers were relatively simple with a square base rising to approximately the height of the building and, above that, a series of stepped back square or octagonal stages emphasized by corner urns or other decoration. At the very top, a slender metal-covered wood spire rose high above the rooftops of the surrounding buildings. (See Figure 12.1.)

FIGURE 12.1 The Zuiderkerk, the first church in Amsterdam constructed for Protestant services, was designed by Hendrik de Keyser and built during the first two decades of the seventeenth century. The tower housed a carillon with bells cast by the Hemony brothers. Note the gable end of the structure with its curved parapet wall concealing a steeply gabled roof.

INFLUENCE 12.2

Church towers, as designed by Hendrik de Keyser, were to have the greatest impact on English design of the later Baroque period. Christopher Wren, one of England's most famous Baroque architects, was particularly influenced by Keyser's towers, and similar examples rose above English urban rooftops.

DUTCH TILES

The Netherlands became a seafaring nation, and as Dutch ships plied trade routes to the East, imported Oriental goods found their way into Dutch homes. In the early seventeenth century, tiles began to be imported from China. In emulating these tiles, Dutch potters in Delft and, later, other cities were able to create a superior ceramic product, although Dutch tiles still lacked the fine quality of Chinese porcelain. By the early seventeenth century, white tiles were produced with designs painted in blue. Typical designs were European rather than Oriental and included flowers, ships, scenes, and figures. Each tile had a decorative border as part of its design. These tiles were used for wall dadoes or baseboards, where they provided some protection against water seepage in these low-lying areas. Their fireproof qualities made tiles especially advantageous for fireplace surrounds. (See Figure 12.2.) The tiles were retained as an important design feature during the Baroque period in the Low Countries, and by that time Dutch tiles were used elsewhere in Europe.

FIGURE 12.2 While Chinese patterned tiles typically had a complete design within each tile, the Dutch also made tile pictures that covered multiple tiles, often in polychrome. These Dutch products were exported to the Iberian Peninsula, England, Germany, France, and later to America.

In addition to tiles, framed paintings, Oriental carpets, furniture finished with Chinese lacquer, and majolica plates and platters enhanced the plain white walls. Floors were tiled or laid with square stones. Ceiling beams were exposed as they had been during the Gothic period. See Box 12.1 for a summary of characteristics of the architecture of the Low Countries.

Renaissance Furniture of the Low Countries

Like their architecture, Flemish furniture was similar to that of France and at first simply added Renaissance details to Gothic forms. Walnut began to be used more frequently, and ebony was used especially in cabinets. Flemish wood carvers were among the best in Europe, and Flemish cabinetmakers were exceptionally skilled in the use of decorative techniques such as marquetry, gilding, veneering, carving, and elaborately painted designs. Their stile, rail, and panel cabinets were in demand throughout Europe. Carved bulbous supports were part of the Baroque period in Flanders but were taken to England, where they predominated during the Elizabethan period. Other supports used in the Low Countries included columns, figural forms (both animal and human), and classically inspired vase forms. Pilasters, scrollwork, strapwork, and pierced **crestings** characterized later Flemish furniture. In 1565, Jan de Vries (Hans Vredeman de Vries; 1527–c. 1607) published a book of drawings of ornaments that was used extensively not only in the Low Countries but in Elizabethan and Jacobean England.

Gothic furniture forms continued to be used and the cupboard bed remained popular, probably due to the warmth the enclosure provided on cold nights. Massive tester beds with architectural detailing were common, although legs were often replaced with paneling around the base. The tester was supported by columns or figural forms, and surmounting the tester at each corner was a finial that was usually designed as a plume of feathers.

Chairs were typically influenced by Italian forms with X-shaped chairs predominating. Side chairs and armchairs were both ornately carved. Tables were supported either on trestle ends, pedestals, or legs. It is the Flemish who are credited with the development of the draw table used throughout Europe and later in America. Chests remained common and were either carved or influenced by Spanish styles and covered with gilded, painted, or embossed leather. The cabinet was the most lavish piece of furniture, and it was on these pieces that the skilled artisans concentrated their efforts. As with the Spanish vargueño, separate stands were frequently used to support cabinets. Figural supports, numerous interior compartments and drawers, and carved doors were characteristic.

Renaissance England

Fifteenth-century England saw major struggles between various factions for control. The Wars of the Roses between two families, the Houses of Lancaster and York, caused political upheaval for 30 years. Due to the frequent intermarriages between royal families, English kings not only controlled some portions of France but had some claim to the French throne, an issue that also occupied the English during the same century. It was not until Henry VII (1457–1509) became King of England in 1485 and established the Tudor Dynasty that the major conflicts were concluded and even then peace was tenuous.

The Continental humanist movement affected England to some extent during this period. Manuel Chrysoloras, who had introduced the Italians to the classics, visited England in 1408 and introduced the principles of humanism to that island nation. Even amidst the turmoil of the fifteenth century, some of the English people embraced the new philosophy. English humanism, however, differed from that of Italy in that it continued to embrace, rather than reject, Christian principles. By the time Erasmus visited England in 1499, humanism was at its height.

THE TUDOR ERA

The beginnings of the Renaissance reached England c. 1500, although the first half of the sixteenth century was as tumultuous as the fifteenth century had been. Henry VIII (1491–1547) acceded to the throne of England in 1509. The second son of Henry VII, he had been raised to enter the church rather than to succeed to the throne. As part of a political arrangement typical of the period, it was arranged that 16-year-old Catherine of Aragon (1485–1536), daughter of Ferdinand and Isabella of Spain, would marry Arthur (1487–1502), the eldest son and heir apparent of the English king Henry VII. When Arthur died only a few months later, Catherine denied that the marriage had been consummated and wanted to return home with her dowry. Unwilling to release the Spanish dowry, Henry VII arranged for Catherine to marry his second son, Henry, who was six years younger than the Spanish girl. The marriage took place in 1509 shortly before Henry was crowned king. At the time of their marriage, both were Catholics.

Catherine bore several children, but her daughter Mary was the only one to survive. By the age of two, Mary was betrothed to the dauphine, or heir, to the French throne. This meant that if Henry had no male heirs, a French king would sit on England's throne, making England a province of France. This was unacceptable. Henry wanted and needed a son to continue the Tudor line. To that end, Henry sought to divorce Catherine, to whom he had been married over 20 years, so he could marry again. Henry's second marriage to Anne Boleyn (1501–1536) produced Elizabeth (1533–1603), but the question of an heir was answered in the person of Prince Edward (1537–1553), borne by Henry's third wife, Jane Seymour (1507/08–1537).

Thomas Cardinal Wolsey (c. 1471–1475 to 1530) was made Lord Chancellor for the young king. Henry left much of the governing to Wolsey—especially financial aspects—since he had had little training for his role. Later, Thomas Cromwell (c. 1485–1540) served as Henry's chief minister. It was Cromwell who suggested, and had the power in Parliament to push through, the Act of Supremacy that made Henry head of the Church in England, repudiating the pope's authority. This action on Cromwell's part endeared him to Henry because it considerably decreased

FIGURE 12.3 Having become extremely powerful and wealthy, Wolsey constructed Hampton Court Palace with some Renaissance details; when he realized his royal mentor had become dissatisfied with him, he presented the palace to Henry.

the power of the pope in England. The refusal of the Church to grant Henry a divorce from Catherine was the proximate cause of the rise of Protestantism in England. The underlying clash of the English Reformation was not doctrinal but rather a struggle between the monarchy and the pope for power.

By 1535, Henry was bankrupt, and as the new head of the Church, he looked enviously on the wealth of the numerous monasteries. He determined to investigate and to close monasteries with low incomes or that were found to be morally lax. Eventually, this Dissolution of the Monasteries resulted in the closure of all but six of the monasteries, and their lands and wealth reverted to the crown. Some of the confiscated property was sold to finance a navy, improve harbor facilities, and construct palaces. The purchasers of the property were typically minor nobles or wealthy merchants, all of whom had supported Henry and now had even more reason to further the cause of the king. The result was a new aristocracy with roots in commerce that grew to rival the old aristocracy dependent on heritage. Conservatism was replaced with forward thinking, and the monarch became absolute.

Even after Henry was named head of the Church of England, the religious conflicts did not end, especially in Ireland, where relationships between the two peoples had always been strained. Irish law forbade marriage between the Irish and English, precluded Irish entertainers from performing in English homes, and required that no English resident use the Gaelic language or Irish dress. The change in the English church exacerbated the problems between the two peoples. Although the Irish remained Catholic, all government officials were required to take the Oath of Supremacy that acknowledged Henry as head of the Church. Many of the Irish chieftains took the oath, giving up only a distant pope. The religious conflict resulted in a more intense struggle on the part of the Irish for freedom from the English yoke, a resistance that was to slow the interest of the English in colonization during the sixteenth century.

ENGLISH RELATIONSHIPS WITH CONTINENTAL ENTITIES

England was but a minor player in the political theater of Europe, but both the Holy Roman Emperor Charles V and the French king François I sought England as an ally against the other. The meeting between the French and English kings was held near Calais, and each side put on the best display possible to impress the other. Wine flowed in fountains, and the English constructed a temporary palace that covered about 12,000 square yards, with brick up to a height of 8 feet and, above that, fabric painted to give it the appearance of stone. The meeting was designed as a tournament, but the name—the Field of the Cloth of Gold—was derived from the extensive use of silk textiles woven with gold threads. Although the results of the event were politically unsatisfactory, the meeting was a signal event in English history as medieval English nobles came away from the tournament with a desire for the Renaissance refinements and luxuries of the French to which they had been exposed.

ECONOMICS

During the reign of Henry VIII, the feudal system was still in place in England. As farmers turned to raising sheep and began fencing what had previously been common property, landlords raised tenant rents or turned tenants out of their homes. Wool became the major export, and Flemish weavers made exorbitant profits using English wool. Later, Flemish weavers immigrated to England and the weaving industry began to dominate the economic scene. With an abundance of cheap labor, these industrial pursuits were highly profitable creating a new wealthy class.

While some of the tenants turned out of their homes found work in the textile industry, there was also a significant increase in the number of homeless and indigent. This was later to prove so worrisome that it stimulated English interest in colonization. Eventually, many impoverished English citizens were shipped off to foreign lands, providing a partial solution to the problem.

In the 11 years between the death of Henry VIII and the ascension of Elizabeth I, England was ruled first by the Protestant Edward VI (1536/37–1554), who was only nine when he became king; Lady Jane Grey for nine days; and then by Edward's devoutly Catholic half-sister Mary (1516–1558), who was half Spanish. She married Philip II of Spain, and their combined goal was to restore Catholicism to England. Finally, the throne passed to Elizabeth (reign from 1558), daughter of Henry VIII and Anne Boleyn.

THE ELIZABETHAN ERA

England had been relatively isolated in its island position on the edge of Europe, but the Elizabethan period marked the beginning of maritime exploits that brought England wealth and power and to war with Spain. Elizabeth's navy defeated the invincible Spanish Armada, her privateers looted Spanish treasure ships, and explorers established a colony in the New World. Textile manufacturing received further impetus by an influx of Flemish weavers fleeing the Spanish Inquisition. There was relative peace, the likes of Ben Jonson and William Shakespeare made literary advances, and the middle class became wealthier.

The splendor of the English court was well established by the time Elizabeth attained the throne. The Medieval period had been left behind, and a spirit of patriotism pervaded the land. Given the English love of pageantry, it is no surprise that the arts of literature and drama predominated. The theater, musical recitals, and masques were important components of the Elizabethan social scene. (See Figure 12.4.)

THE JACOBEAN ERA

The reign of Elizabeth was followed by that of James I (1566–1625; reign from 1603), the first Stuart king of England. James' reign was relatively peaceful and prosperous, although the religious conflicts continued. The Jacobean period of the seventeenth century saw England establish more colonies across the world than any other country of the period. A number of trading companies, including the East India Company, were established during this period, resulting in trade with North America, Russia, India, and the Levant. It was a prosperous, peaceful period, and the wealthy built stately homes in the countryside emulating royalty. In fact, it was during this time that the largest number of great houses of England were constructed.

As king of Scotland, James had enjoyed close relationships with France and married Henrietta Marie (1609–1669), the sister of Louis XIII. These connections resulted in an increase in French Renaissance influence in early seventeenth-century England. James was a devotee of Renaissance culture and patronized the arts. By the time of James' successor Charles I (1600–1649; reign from 1625), foreign travel had become common in wealthy families. When these travelers returned, they brought with them an increased understanding and appreciation for classical forms as interpreted in the Italian Renaissance. Collections became popular, especially paintings and imported Oriental objects such as porcelain.

Charles I was embroiled in conflicts of a different kind, although religion played a major role. It was during his reign that the English civil wars began in 1642, bringing an abrupt halt to artistic progress. The civil wars were basically a power struggle between the monarchy and Parliament led by Oliver Cromwell (1599–1658). Among the issues was a Puritan reaction to efforts to reestablish Catholicism, the religion of the majority.

When Charles was beheaded in 1649, the Commonwealth, or Protectorate, was established with Cromwell heading the government. Under the puritanical rule of Oliver, and later Richard (1626–1712), Cromwell, artistic pursuits, including most of the pageantry, masques, and theater performances, were stifled and little building was accomplished. Beauty and art, associated with corruption and immorality, were rejected. Persecution was widespread and many English citizens emigrated to other lands. It was only when the monarchy was restored in 1660 that English life became more settled.

ENGLISH ARTISTIC PERIODS

During the Early English Renaissance, decorative details were employed on Gothic structures as they had been in France. The English Renaissance is typically divided into four artistic periods. During the Tudor period (1500–1558), structural forms remained Gothic but Italian Renaissance forms were introduced and some symmetry was used in buildings. The Elizabethan

FIGURE 12.4 A love of pageantry and ceremony is still part of English life. The monarch's birthday is celebrated with great ceremony, pageantry surrounds the opening of Parliament each year, and the daily ceremonial changing of the guards at royal palaces speak of the pomp of bygone days.

As in the Gothic period, panels were carved and the linenfold motif remained popular. Diamond-shaped patterns or lozenges were frequently incorporated in panels. Pilasters were often regularly spaced with two or more panels between them. Jacobean panels were larger and fashioned into geometric forms rather than the rectangular panels of both the Tudor and Elizabethan periods. The carved linenfold design was sometimes altered during the sixteenth century to form a **parcheman** or parchment design.

Panels were painted throughout the English Renaissance. Strapwork was typically painted blue on a yellow ground, and the panel frames were painted red. White was used for cartouches, and gilding was used to emphasize some of the details. By the time of the Restoration, painted panels were no longer fashionable. Plaster walls were also used and were painted in solid colors, stenciled in diaper patterns, or decorated with arabesques or scenes. During the Jacobean period, wallpapers were imported and increasingly used. Tudor ceilings retained their Gothic forms with exposed beams, hammer beams, trusses, or coffering.

During the Elizabethan period, plaster ceilings became more common with small molded and bas-relief geometric designs incorporated. By the end of the sixteenth century, this **pargework** or **pargetry** was increasingly complex.

Pargework was also used on the exterior of some half-timbered houses. Often, the pargework was partially painted or gilded. Pargetry was used to imitate wood beams, coffers, and elaborate diaper patterns. (See Figure 12.16.)

Fireplaces were large and dominated rooms. Tudor fireplace openings were headed by a Tudor arch and surrounded by wood paneling. Later fireplace openings employed classical entablatures with a square-headed opening. By the Elizabethan period, stone, marble, or carved wood overmantles were highly decorated and served as a focal point in the room, and classical columns or pilasters flanked the fireplace opening. Often, heraldic devices, elaborate carving, or portraits were used for this purpose.

The monumental staircase of the Italian Renaissance reached England by the Elizabethan period. Stairways were located in the two-story hall that divided the upper part of the house into two sections. By the Jacobean period, elaborate open well staircases were emphasized by making them large in scale and using carved newels, pierced balustrades, and carved or painted designs on stringers and railings. Side walls along the staircases were lined with oak panels. Rather than the earlier straight run stairways, turns and landings were common.

ENGLISH RENAISSANCE FURNITURE

Life in Tudor and Elizabethan England was boisterous and furniture saw hard use. Furniture forms were massive and designed for utility and durability rather than for comfort. Jacobean furniture was rectilinear but smaller in scale than Elizabethan examples. Beginning about 1540, Flemish furniture was imported to England in large quantities. As a result, Flemish influences were incorporated in more English-made pieces.

Most Tudor and Elizabethan furniture was made of oak, which stood up well to the hard usage it was exposed to in great halls. In fact, regardless of style, the term "the Age of Oak" is often used to describe English Renaissance furniture. Even after the Elizabethan style had ceased to be popular, it continued to be used for oak furniture pieces. Some later Elizabethan pieces were constructed of walnut, which allowed for sharper and more minute carved detailing. Because walnut was less durable than oak, most of these pieces were located in the long galleries where they would be more protected.

FIGURE 12.16 Jacobean ceilings continued the use of pargetry, but in geometrically shaped compartments. This fireplace is typical with carved arabesques and birds symmetrically arranged on stone surround. The chimney breast has niches that flank a central heraldic motif with baluster turnings.

Advanced furniture construction techniques from Flanders were also introduced to England. Oak planks had a tendency to split as they dried, and much of the English furniture prior to the sixteenth century employed simple planks joined by pegs or nails. The Flemish brought stile, rail, and panel construction into England using mortise-and-tenon and tongue-and-groove joints. Stiles and rails supported panels that were only loosely held within their bounds. This allowed panels to move slightly so that in the process of drying they did not split. Construction, of course, required great skill on the part of furniture makers.

At the end of the seventeenth century, wood was no longer abundant in England. For this reason, the joiner became less important and the cabinet maker constructed more and more furniture. Turners who specialized in making pieces on a lathe could form a large variety of shapes that could be used on furniture pieces as well as bowls and other utilitarian objects.

Tudor furniture was still Gothic in form, and until 1530 there was little evidence of the new Renaissance style. After that time, Renaissance details were mingled with the older Gothic motifs. Elizabethan furniture was still fairly simply constructed, massive, and rectilinear in form, and elaborate carving ornamented many of the surfaces.

The heavy bulbous legs common on Flemish pieces were used as supports during the Elizabethan period. (See Figure 12.17.) English bulbous turnings, however, expanded in girth far beyond those of their Flemish counterparts. During the seventeenth century, their girth decreased. Bulbous forms typically had gadrooning carved around them. During the Jacobean period, bulbous supports were replaced with dwarf columns often twisted or solominic in form. Later, the supports were more simply turned and appeared more like balusters.

During the Tudor and Elizabethan periods, box stretchers connected furniture legs on or near the floor, although during the Jacobean period, they began to be replaced with those approximately midway between the floor and the seat of chairs. By the end of the period front stretchers were spirally turned.

Designs in Flemish pattern books affected those on English furniture. Strapwork, classic acanthus leaves, vases, swags, caryatids and other figural supports, scrolls, and masks were all Renaissance motifs used on English furniture but derived from Flemish pattern books. Arcading was also used as a design in furniture panels. The split spindle was used late in the Elizabethan period for decoration on furniture but was more popular during the subsequent Jacobean period.

The most common decorative techniques used for furniture of the Tudor period were painting and gilding, but by the Elizabethan period and through the subsequent Jacobean period, carving had become dominant. Designs were taken from pattern books imported from Germany and the Low Countries. While these designs were based on Italian Renaissance forms, they had already been adapted to include indigenous influences. As the designs were used in England, further adaptations were often made. Caryatids, masks, grotesque figures, lozenges, festoons, scrolls, and swags composed of fruits or flowers were frequently used. Architectural motifs included columns and pilasters and, later, arches. English carving was bolder and less refined than Flemish work. That there were excellent joiners is obvious from the superlative hall screens, staircases, and chimney pieces found in English homes, but the finest carvings were probably done by foreign artisans. Jacobean carving was more refined, and while there was less use of figural representations including masks and caryatids, there was greater use of carved strapwork. By the time of Charles I, classic band patterns such as the guilloche had supplanted strapwork.

Inlay was sometimes coarse, but finer-quality work was found on imported pieces. English inlay typically employed conventionalized floral motifs

FIGURE 12.17
Elizabethan supports featured a single melon or cup and cover design with gadrooning on its top and acanthus leaves carved in the bottom section. A crude classical Doric or Ionic capital finished the support at the top.

and geometric designs. During the Elizabethan and Jacobean periods, inlay was often combined with carved designs on the same piece. Holly, which is almost white, was used for light-colored areas and bog oak, which is very dark, was used for contrast. Cherry added a reddish color.

X-shaped chairs were sometimes upholstered during the Tudor and Elizabethan periods. The framework was often completely covered with upholstery and attached with decorative nailheads. Fringe was typical of Spanish furniture before Catherine of Aragon went to England, and it became more popular in England after she arrived. Upholstery became increasingly common during the Jacobean period partly as a result of French influences.

Throughout the Tudor, Elizabethan, and Jacobean periods, furniture types were relatively limited except in royal residences. Forms that had been used for centuries continued to be used: chairs, stools, benches, tables, chests, beds, and cupboards. There were few if any pieces that were not utilitarian in most homes.

Jacobean furniture was often architectural in character with overhanging top sections and arcading. Jacobean low relief carving included geometric designs, floral motifs, and strapwork. Tulips, the Tudor rose, sunflowers, and acanthus leaves graced some of the pieces. Chip-carved pieces usually employed geometric detailing: crosses, lozenges (sometimes enclosing a wheel), octagons, triglyphs, and motifs based on a square. Scrolls and leaves were also chip carved.

Jacobean furniture was rectangular and boxy with right angles and a solid appearance. Usually, back legs extended upward to form the backs of seating units, resulting in a 90-degree seat-back angle. Turned legs often had bulbous feet. Loose cushions improved comfort and were made of varying materials.

CHESTS

The chest remained an important piece of furniture until the seventeenth century, when it was replaced by more specialized pieces. Early Tudor chests were made of oak planks, as they had been since the thirteenth century. Six boards were joined with nails or dowels to form the six sides of the chest. The solid end pieces were elongated to form legs that raised the chest off the floor to prevent dampness from ruining the contents. These simple chests were carved, usually in simple geometric designs. Iron bands were sometimes used to strengthen the chest. Later Tudor chests were made of stile, rail, and panel construction, and the squared stiles were lengthened to form short legs.

Geometric patterns and linenfold designs were combined with Renaissance motifs that included Romayne work, which was usually painted. Other chests were marked for games such as tric trac or chess. Often the playing board was separate and fit inside the chest when not in use. Elizabethan chests more frequently employed arcades as decorative features on the fronts of chests. Stiles and rails were inlaid, carved, or left plain. By the end of the Tudor period, chests were ornamented with architectural detailing often with inlaid buildings on the front. The Tudor **Nonsuch chest** was an example of this chest type, and the term used to describe it was the inlaid building depicted on the front. Many chests were imported from Flanders beginning during the Elizabethan period.

FIGURE 12.18
Carving, inlay, and architectural motifs ornament this English Renaissance cupboard.

FIGURE 12.20 This early chest of drawers has doors covering the drawers at the bottom—a convention typical on the first examples. Dark bog oak, ebony, ivory, brass, mother-of-pearl, and snakewood were used on this piece of Jacobean furniture, dated 1653. Split spindles flank the doors.

FIGURE 12.19 Jacobean chests were often decorated with geometric patterns of inlaid bone, which was an Islamic influence derived from India. Mother-of-pearl was sometimes used instead. This japanned jewel chest featured geometric designs and vases of flowers.

The **Bible box** was a small portable box, usually elaborately decorated, designed to hold not only the family Bible with its genealogical information but important papers and writing materials. In the event of emergency, it could be quickly retrieved. All of these boxes locked. Early examples had a flat hinged top, but later ones had a sloped lid with a stop at the bottom to prevent a book or papers from sliding off. Such boxes were called **slopes** in England. The interior had small drawers and compartments called tills, which gave it its French designation of writing till.

INFLUENCE 12.11

The Bible box was the precursor of the slant-fronted writing desk.

The **mule chest**, introduced in the mid-sixteenth century, became increasingly popular during the seventeenth century. This type of chest featured one or two drawers called drawing boxes, or tills, beneath the large storage compartment. (See Figure 12.19.)

The chest of drawers was introduced during the Jacobean period from continental Europe, where it originated. Typically, cupboard doors closed to conceal the drawers. It was only during the Restoration period that the drawers were exposed. (See Figure 12.20.)

OTHER STORAGE FURNITURE

The **almoner's cupboard** was a large, coarsely constructed cupboard kept in the great hall of the Tudor period. It was named for the cupboard found in churches that held bread to be distributed to the needy. The hall and parlor cupboard was a descendent of the almoner's cupboard.

The **court cupboard** was introduced during the Elizabethan period and was derived from French models. This two-tiered open cupboard featured three shelves separated by turned, inlaid, or figural supports. Front supports were more elaborate than those on the rear. The top and center shelves had carved friezes, which often housed drawers. The carving itself was finely executed and intended to equal in richness the silver displayed on the cupboard shelves. This type of cupboard was in use until the Restoration.

The hall and parlor cupboard, also introduced during the sixteenth century was similar

FIGURE 12.21 The rectangular court cupboard was relatively short—rarely more than 4 feet in height. ("Court" means short in French.)

to the court cupboard, but doors enclosed the upper section. The enclosed portion was stepped back slightly from the front of the frieze. The shelf near the floor remained and front supports were more decorative than those on the back. A cornice finished the cupboard at the top. These cupboards were designed for use in living areas, such as the hall or the parlor, rather than for use in private rooms, such as bedrooms. Like the friezes on court cupboards, those on the hall and parlor cupboard also featured drawers. On a second type of hall and parlor cupboard, the enclosed section was canted backward on both sides of the center section. A third variety of the hall and parlor cupboard that remained popular until the Restoration had both the upper and lower sections enclosed with doors.

During the Elizabethan period, a small wall-mounted **livery cupboard** was placed in bedrooms. These two-to-three-feet-high wall hutches had spindles rather than piercings on the doors for ventilation. By the Jacobean period, the large livery cupboard was used only in large houses with numerous retainers. By the time of Charles I, the livery cupboard disappeared.

Jacobean dining tables, court cupboards, hall and parlor cupboards, and livery cupboards were only slightly changed from Elizabethan forms. The Jacobean press cupboard was a massive piece of furniture designed to store clothing. Because it was designed to be used in private areas of the home, its construction and decoration were less refined than more public pieces. The press cupboard was supported on short legs formed by extensions of the stiles. The number of doors varied and frequently, a row of drawers was located in the base. (See Figure 12.22.)

STOOLS AND BENCHES

Stools remained the most common seating unit throughout the Elizabethan period with the Gothic trestle form dominating. The truss ends were splayed, and the stretcher between the two ends was either shaped or pierced with carving. The three-legged stool of the Medieval period was used in ordinary homes as was the joint stool, which had four legs that were often shaped like columns. The joint stool had a box stretcher near the floor, and a flat top on which a cushion was used for comfort. These stools were used well into the eighteenth century.

The Elizabethan **tabouret,** a drum-shaped upholstered stool, was modeled after those in France. Used at court, custom dictated who was sufficiently privileged to use the tabouret, especially in the presence of the monarch. Typically, only nobles or lesser royals had a high enough social standing to sit on this armless, backless stool.

Gothic benches and settles continued to be used through the seventeenth century. The Elizabethan trestle bench had solid splayed truss ends. By the seventeenth century, the truss end support had been supplanted by splayed legs connected by a box stretcher near the floor and looked like an elongated joint stool.

A high back with partial sides and arms attached to a bench form identified the **settle,** which could be built in or movable. As in the Gothic period, a storage chest was usually accessed through the hinged seat. The Elizabethan **monk's table** was a settle with a back that folded down to form a table with a bench. Popular with members of the Puritan sect during the Jacobean period, it was known as the settle table. Jacobean settles were less massive than their Elizabethan

FIGURE 12.22 This mid-seventeenth century cabinet was constructed around inlaid floral panels purchased in Florence and featured solominic supports, bronze plaques, and a japanned finish.

counterparts. (See Figure 15.12.) By the mid-seventeenth century, settles had open arms, and the chest seat was sometimes replaced by turned legs connected with box stretchers.

CHAIRS

Until the Jacobean period, chairs were still somewhat rare and stools were the more usual seat. The wainscot chair continued to be used as did X-shaped folding chairs. The Gothic straight back armchair with a paneled back also continued in use into the sixteenth century. It was the **thrown** chair that became most common during the period. With the development of the lathe and guilds specializing in turning, there were numerous chairs made with turned or thrown spindles. Early examples had a triangular wood seat and a low back. The Harvard chair—so called because the president of Harvard University has used such a chair since the eighteenth century when granting degrees—is such a chair that has turned spindles that join the seat to the back rail. The number of spindles varies on different examples of the chair. (See Figure 12.23.)

The Elizabethan wainscot chair retained the paneled back but often added a more decorative crest rail. Sometimes scrolled finials were added to the top of the back supports. Rather than the closed arms of the earlier wainscot chair, this type had open arms that turned slightly downward

at the ends and legs joined by a box stretcher near the floor. This chair was lighter in weight and appearance than the Gothic wainscot chair had been. Later in the Elizabethan period, the chair became lighter still with a narrowed seat, fluting on the front legs and arm posts, and more elaborate carving. Infrequently, an open arcaded back was substituted for the carved panel. (See Figure 12.24.) A type of X-shaped Tudor chair was the Glastonbury chair. Introduced in the Elizabethan period, it was an ecclesiastical chair that differed from most folding chairs in that the X-shaped legs were at the sides rather than at the front and back. The back was often carved with a pair of arches.

The Elizabethan **monk's chair** was a chair table with a circular or rectangular back that pivoted downward to form a table.

The **farthingale chair** was an early Jacobean innovation designed so that women could comfortably sit while wearing farthingales, or voluminous whale-boned petticoats. The chair was small and armless with a high wide seat, an inherent cushion, and a low back. Both the seat and back were upholstered, and often the upholstery continued over the frame. When the frame was exposed, it was typically painted or gilded. This side chair had columnar supports on the front and plain squared ones on the back. A backless form was made as well.

The settee was introduced during the Jacobean period, but very few were made until the Restoration. The settee featured a high back, open arms, and an upholstered seat and back. The four to eight supports were painted or gilded and connected by a box stretcher.

TABLES

Throughout the Tudor and into the Elizabethan period, the Gothic trestle table continued to be used. As the great hall declined in importance and families dined more privately, dining rooms were added to homes. A permanent table could then be placed in the center of the room, and diners could be seated on all four sides. By the beginning of Elizabeth's reign, long, narrow refectory tables were also used. These, of course, did not disassemble when not in use. The top

FIGURE 12.23 The use of the Harvard chair by that university's president helped to establish a link between Harvard College and its prototypes in England—Oxford and Cambridge Universities.

FIGURE 12.24 This Jacobean wainscot chair has a panel back and down-curved arms typical of the period. It was used with a seat cushion to improve comfort.

FIGURE 12.25 This type of Palladian chair was copied from Italian sgabelli and used just prior to the English civil wars.

FIGURE 12.26 Turned supports were more typical on Jacobean tables than the carved cup and cover legs of the Elizabethan period. Note that the table apron is shaped.

time, a second leg and leaf were added to the other side, allowing more people to be seated around the table when it was open. Legs were turned except at the tops and bottoms where they were left square to facilitate connections to stretchers and aprons, a technique called **block and turning**. Often the apron was shaped with a semicircular arch and sometimes included a drawer.

Jacobean tables included a number of small examples, some of which were imported from Italy, France, and the Low Countries. Tea drinking and games required more small tables than had been used in previous periods. Examples varied considerably, and tops, sometimes folding, included octagonal, rectangular, and oval shapes. Underframes featured arcades, columnar legs, fluted legs, and, later, turned legs all connected with stretchers. Game tables had chess or backgammon boards inlaid in the tops.

BEDS

In the fourteenth century, the feather bed was introduced, making beds more comfortable. By the Tudor period, beds had four posts and a carved paneled headboard with a tester. At first the tester was supported by the four posts; later, the headboard became more massive and supported the tester at one end. This type of bed required only two posts at the foot to support the tester. These posts were not attached to the bed itself and stood beyond the end of the bed, thus their contemporary name: **standing bed**. Bulbous carvings were typical on the posts. Often, the posts themselves were supported by a carved plinth. The tester was made of wood and had the appearance of a classic entablature and the interior ceiling of the tester was richly carved or inlaid. Draperies were supported by the tester and allowed the bed to be enclosed to retain warmth. The headboard was typically divided by pilasters or carved figures into compartments and decorated with carved arcading. (See Figure 12.27.)

Jacobean beds were lighter in appearance than Elizabethan examples and featured tall, slender posts that supported a fabric-covered tester. Vase-shaped finials filled with ostrich plumes were used on the tester above each of the four corners.

The poor, of course, had no elaborate beds. They slept on the floor or in a shallow box, using straw for a mattress. **Stump beds** were used in peasant homes. These beds had posts, but they were usually short. Even when taller posts were

was heavy and the apron elaborately carved. The Flemish draw top table was also used in Elizabethan dining rooms. Box stretchers connected the legs near the floor and were often inlaid in a counterchange pattern. With the exception of the trestle table, each of these table types continued to be used into the eighteenth century, although details changed according to the period. Turkey work or carpets were used to cover tables.

The **counter table** was a table designed specifically for counting money. Until the sixteenth century, this type of table was crudely constructed, but when it gained popularity during that century, greater care was taken in its construction. Early examples had a hinged section at one end that could be raised to access the shallow cupboard built into the framework beneath the widely extended top. Later, the separate top section moved on sliders and users could access the contents of the cupboard without disturbing the coins on the top. A shelf or box stretcher connected the four supports.

Space-saving **gate leg** or **falling tables** were introduced during the Elizabethan period. These early examples had a single leaf and gate leg that swung outward to support the leaf. About 1620, the hinges of gate leg tables gave way to pivots facilitating the movement of the leg. About the same

FIGURE 12.27 The Great Bed of Ware is a surviving example of an Elizabethan bed. It is 10 feet, 8 inches square and 8 feet, 9 inches high. In the Canterbury Tales, Chaucer described it as capable of sleeping 15 people side by side. Originally, the bed was painted in bright colors. The inlaid panels feature imaginary buildings and were probably executed by German immigrants.

used, they did not support a tester or enclosing curtains.

Late in the Tudor period, the Italian daybed was introduced to England. At first, only one end had a chair back. Some seventeenth-century daybeds had two canted ends, but this fashion lasted only a short period. A box stretcher joined the legs. Daybeds became more common during the Jacobean period.

Most cradles were mounted on rockers throughout the Renaissance in England, although a few were like French models and swung between a pair of uprights. Either type could have a hood. Cradles of estate were more ornamental, but royal children used them only during special occasions and had a plainer cradle for everyday use.

CROMWELLIAN FURNITURE

Cromwellian furniture used Jacobean forms but little ornamentation. Turnings were used, but the elaborate carving of the Jacobean style was omitted. The bobbin turning with a series of knobs was most common, and some split spindles continued to be used. Cromwellian furniture was angular, heavy, and utilitarian. Dual-purpose and utilitarian pieces were common. This style was carried to America by the Pilgrims, where it is often called Pilgrim furniture.

The Cromwell chair often employed bobbin turnings for stretchers as well as for front legs. Front legs extended through the seat to support arms when they were used. Side and rear stretchers were squared rather than turned. Settles were made in the same manner, although panel backs and base were typical. Some were covered with leather.

Widening Horizons

During the time Renaissance ideas and art were spreading through Europe, a New World had been discovered. The nations of Europe had been seeking a route to the Orient and riches, and the discovery of an unknown continent was a boon for some, including the Spanish, who were able to extract great wealth from the new land. Others, who at first found no valuable commodities, such as England, almost ignored the New World and concentrated their efforts on affairs at home.

America became a melting pot with explorers, traders, or colonists from many European nations, but it was be the English who, after a century of disinterest, were most successful in their efforts at colonization. Each of the European nations involved made contributions to American design.

FIGURE 12.28 The Cromwell chair was upholstered with leather attached with nail-heads although padding was not used.

New Horizons

Part Four

NEW HORIZONS

Pacific Ocean

Atlantic Ocean

VERMONT

NEW HAMPSHIRE

Connecticut River

Exeter

Ipswich

NEW YORK

Fort Orange
Albany

MASSACHUSETTS

Topsfield
Salem

Hadley

Cambridge

Hingham

Hudson River

Plymouth

CONNECTICUT

Rhode
Island

Delaware River

Wethersfield

Guilford

PENNSYLVANIA

NEW JERSEY

Long Island

Manhattan Island
New Amsterdam

Wilmington

MARYLAND

WEST
VIRGINIA

DELAWARE

Potomac River

James River

Roanoke

VIRGINIA

Williamsburg

Surry County

Princess Anne County, Virginia

NORTH CAROLINA

MA

GREENLAND

ICELAND

Hudson Bay

CANADA

Newfoundland

Great
Lakes

St Lawrence River

Gulf of
St. Lawrence

Quebec
Montreal

Cape Breton Island

Wisconsin

NOVA SCOTIA

UNITED STATES

ornia

AMERICAN
SOUTHWEST

Ste. Genevieve, Missouri

Santa Fe

San Xavier del Bac,
Tucson

Mississippi River

Texas

Rio Grande River

New Orleans

St. Augustine

Florida

Atlantic
Ocean

Baja California

MEXICO

Yucatan
Peninsula

Tenochtitlan
Mexico City

Sayil
Labna

Chichen Itza

Caribbean
Sea

Oaxaca Valley

GUATEMALA

HONDURAS

EL SALVADOR

NICARAGUA

COSTA RICA

COLOMBIA

SOUTH AMERICA

PERU

Machu Picchu

Brasilia

BOLIVIA

CHILE

ARGENTINA

N

0   1000 Miles

0   1000 KM

All dates AD unless otherwise noted

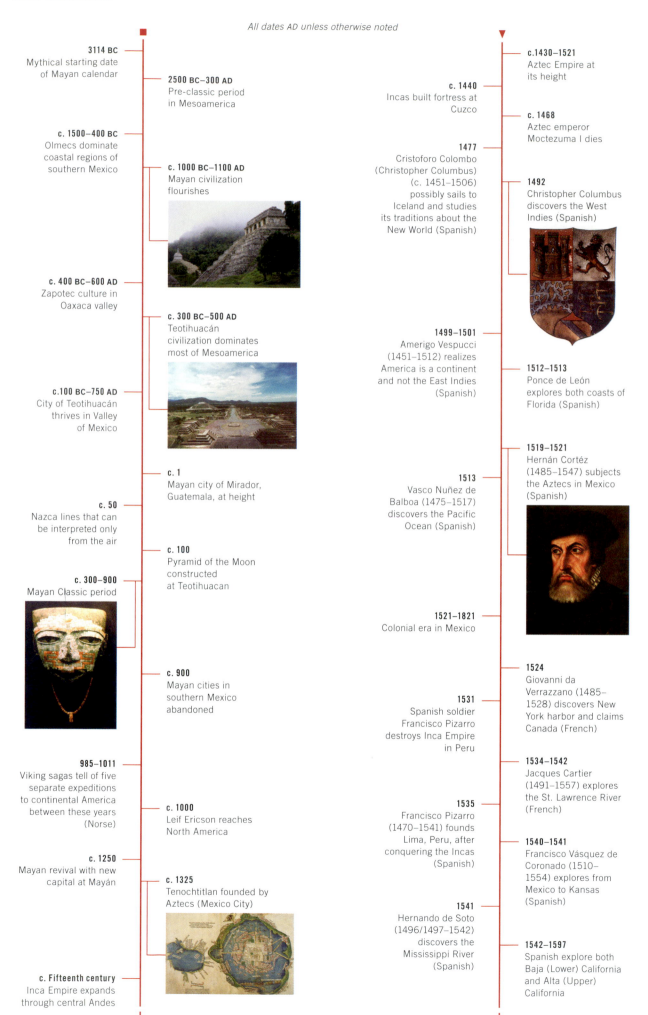

3114 BC
Mythical starting date
of Mayan calendar

2500 BC–300 AD
Pre-classic period
in Mesoamerica

c. 1500–400 BC
Olmecs dominate
coastal regions of
southern Mexico

c. 1000 BC–1100 AD
Mayan civilization
flourishes

c. 400 BC–600 AD
Zapotec culture in
Oaxaca valley

c. 300 BC–500 AD
Teotihuacán
civilization dominates
most of Mesoamerica

c.100 BC–750 AD
City of Teotihuacán
thrives in Valley
of Mexico

c. 1
Mayan city of Mirador,
Guatemala, at height

c. 50
Nazca lines that can
be interpreted only
from the air

c. 100
Pyramid of the Moon
constructed
at Teotihuacan

c. 300–900
Mayan Classic period

c. 900
Mayan cities in
southern Mexico
abandoned

985–1011
Viking sagas tell of five
separate expeditions
to continental America
between these years
(Norse)

c. 1000
Leif Ericson reaches
North America

c. 1250
Mayan revival with new
capital at Mayán

c. 1325
Tenochtitlan founded by
Aztecs (Mexico City)

c. Fifteenth century
Inca Empire expands
through central Andes

c.1430–1521
Aztec Empire at
its height

c. 1440
Incas built fortress at
Cuzco

c. 1468
Aztec emperor
Moctezuma I dies

1477
Cristoforo Colombo
(Christopher Columbus)
(c. 1451–1506)
possibly sails to
Iceland and studies
its traditions about the
New World (Spanish)

1492
Christopher Columbus
discovers the West
Indies (Spanish)

1499–1501
Amerigo Vespucci
(1451–1512) realizes
America is a continent
and not the East Indies
(Spanish)

1512–1513
Ponce de León
explores both coasts of
Florida (Spanish)

1519–1521
Hernán Cortéz
(1485–1547) subjects
the Aztecs in Mexico
(Spanish)

1513
Vasco Nuñez de
Balboa (1475–1517)
discovers the Pacific
Ocean (Spanish)

1521–1821
Colonial era in Mexico

1524
Giovanni da
Verrazzano (1485–
1528) discovers New
York harbor and claims
Canada (French)

1531
Spanish soldier
Francisco Pizarro
destroys Inca Empire
in Peru

1534–1542
Jacques Cartier
(1491–1557) explores
the St. Lawrence River
(French)

1535
Francisco Pizarro
(1470–1541) founds
Lima, Peru, after
conquering the Incas
(Spanish)

1540–1541
Francisco Vásquez de
Coronado (1510–
1554) explores from
Mexico to Kansas
(Spanish)

1541
Hernando de Soto
(1496/1497–1542)
discovers the
Mississippi River
(Spanish)

1542–1597
Spanish explore both
Baja (Lower) California
and Alta (Upper)
California

All dates AD unless otherwise noted

1551
University of Mexico
(Real Universidad de
la Nueva España) and
Universidad Nacional
Mayor de San Marcos
established in Peru
(Spanish)

1585
Ill-fated Roanoke
colony established
(English)

1590
Little trace of the
Roanoke colony could
be found

1598
Santa Fe founded
(Spanish)

c. 1600
First art school
in North America
established (French)

1607
Jamestown established
(English)

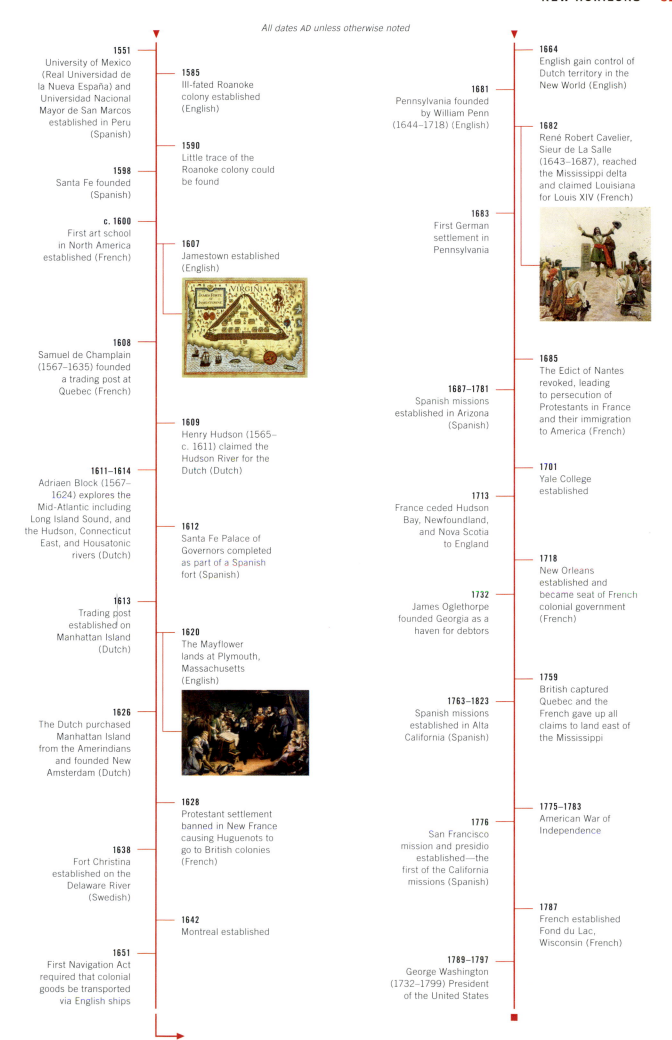

1608
Samuel de Champlain
(1567–1635) founded
a trading post at
Quebec (French)

1609
Henry Hudson (1565–
c. 1611) claimed the
Hudson River for the
Dutch (Dutch)

1611–1614
Adriaen Block (1567–
1624) explores the
Mid-Atlantic including
Long Island Sound, and
the Hudson, Connecticut
East, and Housatonic
rivers (Dutch)

1612
Santa Fe Palace of
Governors completed
as part of a Spanish
fort (Spanish)

1613
Trading post
established on
Manhattan Island
(Dutch)

1620
The Mayflower
lands at Plymouth,
Massachusetts
(English)

1626
The Dutch purchased
Manhattan Island
from the Amerindians
and founded New
Amsterdam (Dutch)

1628
Protestant settlement
banned in New France
causing Huguenots to
go to British colonies
(French)

1638
Fort Christina
established on the
Delaware River
(Swedish)

1642
Montreal established

1651
First Navigation Act
required that colonial
goods be transported
via English ships

1664
English gain control of
Dutch territory in the
New World (English)

1681
Pennsylvania founded
by William Penn
(1644–1718) (English)

1682
René Robert Cavelier,
Sieur de La Salle
(1643–1687), reached
the Mississippi delta
and claimed Louisiana
for Louis XIV (French)

1683
First German
settlement in
Pennsylvania

1685
The Edict of Nantes
revoked, leading
to persecution of
Protestants in France
and their immigration
to America (French)

1687–1781
Spanish missions
established in Arizona
(Spanish)

1701
Yale College
established

1713
France ceded Hudson
Bay, Newfoundland,
and Nova Scotia
to England

1718
New Orleans
established and
became seat of French
colonial government
(French)

1732
James Oglethorpe
founded Georgia as a
haven for debtors

1759
British captured
Quebec and the
French gave up all
claims to land east of
the Mississippi

1763–1823
Spanish missions
established in Alta
California (Spanish)

1775–1783
American War of
Independence

1776
San Francisco
mission and presidio
established—the
first of the California
missions (Spanish)

1787
French established
Fond du Lac,
Wisconsin (French)

1789–1797
George Washington
(1732–1799) President
of the United States

FIGURE 13.1 Here, an eagle is shown clutching a human heart.

highest celestial deity in the Aztec religion. The lower pyramid represented the earth, which was organized in nine layers, represented the female element, and was associated with dampness and darkness. Deities associated with the lower world were represented by the jaguar or the spotted coat of the jaguar and fangs.

Urban centers were sometimes constructed as cosmic models where residents such as the governors could become receptacles of the sacred and influence the all-important fertility cycles.

Religious festivals were based on a complex ritual calendar. Human sacrifice was practiced by all Mesoamerican cultures, although it was the Aztecs who made it a cornerstone in their ideology based on military expansion. Self-sacrifice was also practiced whereby spines of a fish or agave plant or obsidian blades were used to pierce parts of the body usually in an effort to induce visions or to contact the deities.

MESOAMERICAN RELIGIONS

Many religious traditions coexisted and each had numerous deities with varying manifestations. A unifying concept of Mesoamerican religions was the perception of the universe as two 4-sided pyramids joined at their bases with the earth between them. The upper pyramid, or cosmic mountain, represented the heavens and had 13 layers that housed the gods. The creator god lived at the top of the mountain. The heavenly pyramid represented the male element and was associated with light and warmth. Celestial deities were manifested as birds or other feathered creatures. The hummingbird represented the

THE BALL GAME

The ball game was a ritual game popular throughout Mesoamerica, although it was especially prevalent in areas around the Gulf of Mexico. The game is thought most likely to be symbolic of the battle between the sun and Venus at night. Wearing leather belts, knee pads, and gloves, players hit a rubber ball with their hips, buttocks, and shoulders. When played for religious reasons, the courts were considered a gateway to the underworld and the game participants were the victors of a battle who played against the losers. From the beginning, it was known who were to be the sacrificial victims at the end

FIGURE 13.2 Ball courts were shaped like a capital "I" and decorated by low-relief carvings on the court side. In rare events when a player managed to get the ball through the ring, it was an automatic win.

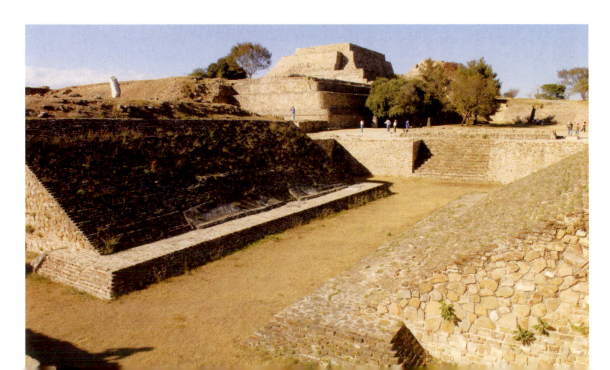

of the game. Games were also played for prizes of gold, slaves, fields, houses, and other valuable commodities. Late in the Mayan Classic period, vertical stone rings were installed at each side of the court. (See Figure 13.2.)

THE OLMECS

The Olmecs established the first major civilization in the area beginning c. 1500 BC. They devised a form of hieroglyphic writing and developed the first calendar in the Western Hemisphere. Olmec objects were spread throughout most of Mesoamerica, although their civilization was limited to the coastal areas of Southern Mexico. (See Figure 13.3.) Olmec objects were considered luxury goods by the emerging civilizations in the rest of Mesoamerica and were acquired to attest contact by certain individuals with the more prestigious Olmec culture, thereby confirming or giving them prestige and power.

As the Olmec culture began to wane, a number of cultures began to dominate the various regions. The Teotihuacan and later, the Aztecs occupied the area north of present-day Mexico City, the Zapotecs dominated the Oaxaca valley, and the Mayans became the strongest of the Mexican cultures spreading through the Yucatán peninsula, southern Mexico, and Guatemala. The period was marked by advances in agriculture, substantial increases in population in urban areas, and expanding trade networks.

THE TEOTIHUACAN

The city of Teotihuacan, named for the dominant culture of an area that stretched as far as Guatemala, was massive and had a monumental center surrounded by numerous residential areas. Some of these areas were occupied by Zapotecs and other groups who were possibly merchants, traders, or even ambassadors. The city's wealth was based on its almost complete monopoly of the obsidian market as well as by its advantageous location, enabling it to control trade routes. Teotihuacan was abandoned c. 1000 AD and remained empty until the Aztecs settled there.

THE MAYANS

The Mayan culture was influenced by Teotihuacan at this time, although it was during this period that most of their artistic forms, including the use of the corbelled vault, took shape. Around 600 AD, Teotihuacan influence in Mayan art ceased.

FIGURE 13.3 The Olmecs constructed earthen buildings including pyramids, but their large sculptures of governors and deities were carved in basalt.

Although there were numerous Mayan cities, there was not a single overall ruler. Each city administered its own affairs and might be ruled by a council or a king. The Mayans had two types of calendars, one based on the solar year that had 365 days and the other a 260-day ritual calendar. Mayan priests were excellent astronomers and could predict events such as solar and lunar eclipses—helping them to control the people. Their mathematical skills were among the best in the world at the time. Mayan agriculture was aided by irrigation networks and planting on raised terraces, although it may have been the depletion of the soil that eventually resulted in the downfall of Mayan cities. As Mayan cities were abandoned, the people established villages where the culture continued until the arrival of the Spanish.

THE AZTECS

The Aztecs immigrated from the north into central Mexico in the thirteenth century and dominated the area until the arrival of the Spanish. There was actually no group of people named Aztec but rather an alliance of peoples who spoke a common language. They are sometimes known as Mixtecs.

In 1323, the Aztecs received a vision of an eagle perched on a cactus clutching a snake. The place where they found this sign was to be the location of their new city. That city, Tenochtitlan, became the capital of their empire, and when the Spanish conquered it, they made it their own capital, now Mexico City. The Spanish destroyed the pagan Aztec structures and built on top of them, so there is little that remains. Like other Mesoamerican cultures, the Aztecs were a group of city-states, each ruled locally. In 1428, these groups emerged into the more strongly organized Aztec Empire, ruled by a single leader. The major contribution of the Aztecs was the system of roads that connected the cities. Rest areas were provided at regular intervals, every six to nine miles), and the roads were patrolled. The Spanish were amazed to find that women could safely travel alone on Aztec roads.

INFLUENCE 13.1

The symbol associated with the Aztec vision in 1323 is now emblazoned on the flag of Mexico.

Aztec society was stratified with a nobility that was not necessarily hereditary, as well as a peasant class that consisted of farmers, artisans, merchants, and warriors; and slaves. The merchants and traders traveled the roads and often served as spies for Aztec leaders. Slavery was used as a punishment for certain crimes, and captives from war who were skilled artisans might become slaves rather than sacrifices.

FIGURE 13.4 The aprons, or faces, of the terraces are finished with a vertical face outlined by an outset frame, known as a tablero, and an angled face beneath it, known as the talud. This type of building construction was characteristic of Teotihuacan architecture, although neither the Pyramid of the Sun nor the Pyramid of the Moon feature this type of terrace. This is probably because these two pyramids were constructed earlier than the tablero-talud was developed. Note also that the corners were finished with coursed rubble.

Aztec children received mandatory education at the age of 15. Boys were either taught a craft (which might include preparing to be a warrior) or mathematics, astronomy, and writing to prepare them for leadership positions. Girls were taught home crafts.

MESOAMERICAN ARCHITECTURE

Mesoamerican architecture focused on temples and palaces. Temples were typically of pyramidal form with square plans and had little, if any, interior space. Palaces enclosed significant interior areas usually arranged in linear fashion.

MATERIALS USED FOR BUILDING CONSTRUCTION

Stone and clay were the major building materials in Mesoamerica, although timber was frequently used. The Mayans developed very hard plasters from lime that sealed building surfaces and protected them from tropical rains, insects, and vegetation. Stone-cutting tools were used to cut the soft limestone of the area that hardened when it was exposed to air. In the Andes, mortar was necessarily composed of clay because lime was not available in massive quantities. Copper tools were used in the Andes, enabling the people to cut the harder stone indigenous to the region. In both Meso- and South America, highly structured social systems provided the human resources necessary to build monumental structures. Mesoamerican cultures developed pigments—usually red but sometimes blue for painting buildings, and polychrome for murals and sculptures.

The Mayan Vault The vault used by the Mayans was the most sophisticated structural device used among indigenous Americans. Some of these vaults were corbelled with succeeding layers overhanging layers below and finally coming together at the top. Others depended instead on mortar for support and were, in fact, built in two halves that were self-supporting. True corbels supported floors and roofs in Andean buildings, however.

MONUMENTAL ARCHITECTURE

The monumental architecture of Mesoamerica was similar in form regardless of the civilization that produced it. While there were variations in detail, structures were typically built on a raised platform. The monumental buildings were arranged around one or more large plazas or on

FIGURE 13.5 Typically, steep stairs were outset and rose to the top in a single flight as on this Mayan temple.

both sides of a wide avenue although not symmetrical. The buildings themselves were usually terraced with steep stairs providing access. Rubble stone in mortar was sometimes used to face the exterior surfaces. (See Figure 13.4.)

The monumental pyramidal structures prevalent in pre-Columbian cultures in Latin America were made of adobe (not brick) that was mixed with volcanic rock or rubble stone and then faced with stone set in mortar. The shape echoed that of the nearby mountains. At the very top, there was a large platform on which a temple was constructed. Red-painted plaster sometimes covered the surfaces of the pyramid, burnished white stone might serve as the finish, and carved designs provided ornamentation. (See Figure 13.5.)

At El Tajín, many of the buildings featured niches, sometimes with a design similar to the Greek key. Archaeologists believe that these symbols represent slices of shells that link them to Venus and the Feathered Serpent. (See Figure 13.6.)

FIGURE 13.6 The Pyramid of the Niches at El Tajín has 365 niches, one for each day of the Mesoamerican calendar year. This pyramid may have been a mausoleum for 13 Rabbit, the most famous ruler of the city.

FIGURE 13.7 The designs on the palace walls at Mitla are formed using cut stone mosaics. A single frieze may contain as many as 100,000 pieces.

TEOTIHUACAN ARCHITECTURE

Zapotecan architecture had little decoration. While Mitla was a Zapotec city, most of the design belongs to the Mixtec culture. The buildings use tablero façades with different geometric stone designs in each section. Some designs are carved from a single stone slab, and some are built up similar to mosaics. (See Figure 13.7.)

FIGURE 13.8 Chenes style architecture uses open jaws of the Earth Monster as the entry to this structure. One must walk on the monster's tongue to enter.

MAYAN ARCHITECTURE

Mayan art was used to glorify rulers and their ancestors. Their architecture is best exemplified at Palenque, one of the oldest and most important of the Mayan cities. This city was distinguished by the importance of its architectural decoration. In other Mayan cities, decoration was used on the altar and stelae, but most other structures were plain. At Palenque, there are low-relief carvings in stone and stucco on walls, pillars, and roofs. The palace was the most important structure, and the buildings of the palace are arranged around a courtyard and surrounded by a terraced base. Rooms were arranged in a linear fashion with two parallel suites separated by a wall along the long axis. (See Box 13.1.)

The Mayans occupied the Yucatán peninsula during their earliest history, and their architecture in that area is distinctive from other sites largely because they were influenced by the Toltecs living in the same area. Two Mayan groups, the Rio Bec and Chenes, each developed architectural styles of their own. (See Figure 13.8.) Rio Bec buildings had façades that made them appear to be pyramidal in form, although they were simply vertical walls. (See Figures 13.8 and 13.9.)

Like temples, palaces were also raised on a terraced base. Some had pillars that were carved in low relief. At Quetzalpapálotl Palace in Teotihuacan, the pillars feature birds of prey with rows of eyes and volutes that represent water. The crenellations on the roof were in the shape of the symbols of the year. (See Figure 13.10.) Other palaces, such as the Palace of the Gov-

FIGURE 13.9 Both the Rio Bec and Chenes styles made use of representations of the long-nosed mask of the rain god Chac.

Box 13.1 Mayan Palace Features

The Palace in Palenque has a tower that was probably used as an observatory.

Mayan architecture also used T-shaped windows.

Palenque architecture also featured combs or crests. Here, the Temple of the Sun stands on an unexcavated pyramidal base. Most of the crest is still intact.

False vaults or those made of two halves that would stand alone or corbelled vaults were used to support the roof. This type of arch does not span a large area, and Mayan rooms remained relatively narrow.

The Temple of the Inscriptions in Palenque was a mausoleum for the ruler, Pacal II, and was constructed around his sarcophagus. It has nine levels, the number of levels of the underworld according to Mayan tradition.

BOX 13.2 CHARACTERISTICS OF MESOAMERICAN ARCHITECTURE

- Stone masks
- Large doorways serve as windows
- Geometric spiral decorations
- Colonnaded halls
- Stepped pyramids
- Serpent decorations
- Structural insets and outsets
- Steep stairs

FIGURE 13.10 Quetzalpapálotl Palace has rooms around an open courtyard. The pillars have low-relief carvings over their entire surfaces.

ernors at Uxmal, were linear rather than constructed around a courtyard and lacked pillars and the shaded walkway behind them. The Palace of the Governors features a tablero façade above the openings that is highly decorated with stone mosaics. At Uxmal, Sayil, and Labna, there is yet another variation of Puuc structures that makes use of columns. At Chichén Itzá, there is a Patio of a Thousand Columns (although the number is much smaller), a Toltec influence.

The columns originally supported a roof and may have been a market.

AZTEC ARCHITECTURE

Aztec structures were similar to those of the Mayans, although some variations occurred. The Temple Mayor in Tenochtitlan had a double staircase and two summit temples, each of which was dedicated to a different god. Among other things, the god Quetzalcoatl was associated with the wind. Rounded pyramids have less resistance to wind and would thus not hinder the god from entering and a number of rounded pyramids were dedicated to Quetzalcoatl. Typically, these pyramids were elongated with only the ends curved.

FIGURE 13.11 At the Palace at Sayil, two types of columns are employed. One type is similar to Greek Doric examples and even shows entasis. The square block at the top serves as the capital. The second type of columns are placed side by side and feature banding.

South America

The Incan Empire stretched 2,500 miles from Colombia to Chile in South America. Most of its territory was mountainous. Without the wheel and with only the domesticated llama for a pack animal, the Incas hauled building materials to unprecedented heights. Cities up to 15,000 feet in altitude and sacrificial sites of more than 22,000 feet were constructed.

In pre-Columbian times, the Inca Empire was the largest civilization in the Western Hemisphere. Although Manchu Picchu is the best surviving example of an Incan city, the capital of the empire was at Cuzco. The empire was established in the thirteenth century in Peru and spread into Ecuador, Bolivia, Argentina, Chile, and Colombia. It was divided into four areas, each with a strong leader who reported to the emperor at Cuzco.

INCAN ARCHITECTURE

The Incas were excellent engineers and constructed roads and suspension bridges. In low-lying areas along the coast, Incan roads were unsurfaced. Roads in the mountains were not only paved with stones, but walls were constructed to prevent falling from precipitous heights. More than 8,700 miles of roads linked the empire, and some are still in good condition. In some places, roadways had to be cut through rock. Rest areas were provided along the way, as were temples. Narrow bridges were made from ropes and tunnels were built through hillsides. Manchu Picchu even had an aqueduct to supply water.

Because they built in mountainous areas, the Incas constructed numerous stairways. Most were wide and made of stones laid side by side. Other stairways were hewn from the rock, such as those leading to the House of Ñusta at Manchu Picchu.

INCAN CITIES

Incan cities were laid out in a regular plan—often a gridiron, or a close proximity of one. In some Incan cities, doorways were aligned in rows perpendicular to the major thoroughfares. The most important urban system, however, was the division of the city into upper (*hanan*) and lower (*hurin*) sections. The hanan section includes buildings for those with greater prestige. This system continues to be used in many Andean villages.

INCAN BUILDINGS

For buildings, the Incas made use of stone blocks weighing several tons. (See Figure 13.12.) In buildings, rectangular stones were laid in regular courses. In all likelihood, the stones were cut with tools made of stone, although bronze or copper tools may have been available. Much of the rock used by the Incas was hard igneous stone. In addition to stone, the Incas used adobe, which was often combined with stone. Stone walls would be laid up to a height of 6 feet or more with adobe finishing the top.

Plans were typically rectangular, and buildings had a single room. When additional rooms were needed, another was built beside the first one. There was no internal communication between rooms so to get from one room to the other, occupants had to go outside. Small buildings had a single opening, and as the length increased, so did the number of openings. As many as 14 entrances are known to have been used in a single long side of one room. Dividing walls between rooms were on the long axis so that a structure might be entered from both sides. Storehouses and funerary structures might be round but not dwellings. Most circular structures, however, were pre-Incan.

FIGURE 13.12
Although the stones are not regularly shaped, the Incas cut and worked them together using sand until each piece fit into the shape of the stones beneath it.

Battered walls were used for temples, with walls becoming thinner as they rose. Incan stonework has survived centuries of frequent earthquakes. Like other Latin American cultures, the Incas constructed their buildings around courtyards. There was little, if any, ornamentation on structures. Openings were trapezoidal in shape—smaller at the top than at the bottom. It is this trapezoid shape that identifies Incan structures throughout the former empire. Some examples have a stepped lintel and some have an inner lip that may have allowed a door to close against it. Stone loops on some doorways suggest that doors were tied into place.

Incan buildings were a single story, including temples and palaces, although these were sometimes constructed on platforms. There were no monumental buildings that projected above those around them. Thatched roofs were used possibly because in the event of an earthquake (a frequent occurrence), little harm would come to occupants if the roof caved in.

Arrival of the Spanish

In approximately 1511, two shipwrecked Spaniards arrived in Mexico: Jerónimo de Aguilar (1489–c. 1531) and Gonzalo Guerrero. Guerrero married a Mayan woman, was tattooed in the native tradition, and wore ear ornaments like those of the Mayans. Neither Aguilar nor Guerrero, however, made any significant impact on Mesoamerica or Spain. Two later Spanish arrivals by Francisco Hernández de Cordoba and Juan de Grijalva (1489–1527) also made little impact on Mesoamerica, with the exception of stories that were carried to the Aztec emperor Motecuhzoma II (Montezuma) concerning "mountains that sailed" and white men who exchanged glass beads for native gifts.

Aztec legend included a story about Quetzalcoatl, an ancient god associated with cultures that preceded them. The name Quetzalcoatl was also given to a great warrior king who lived c. 950–1000 and conquered many of the surrounding people. Over time, the god and the warrior became associated with one another. The Aztecs believed that Quetzalcoatl became the Morning Star (Venus) after his death and would return to reclaim his kingdom. The Amerindians associated the legend with the Spanish, who fostered the story as they traveled, easing the way for the

newcomers to conquer and almost destroy the indigenous populations.

SPANISH CONQUEST AND COLONIALIZATION

The aim of the expedition (1519) led by Hernando Cortéz (1485–1547) was to search for vast treasures that the explorers had heard rumors about; this was to prove tragic for the indigenous people. When the Spanish arrived, the Aztec capital of Tenochtitlan was larger than any city in the world with the exception of Constantinople. The city fell to Cortéz on August 13, 1521, the day on which modern Mexico is said to have been established.

The Spanish brought with them ships, firearms, armor, and the horse, and conquered the Aztec and Inca civilizations. But the devastation was even greater as diseases, brought by the Europeans and unknown in Latin America, waged another kind of war.

The colonial era lasted for three centuries, ending in 1821 when Mexico received its independence. The era was marred by the encomienda system that reduced the indigenous people to a form of slavery. Even when independence was attained, the system changed little with power in the hands of whites born in Mexico. Even in modern Mexico, the native populations form the poorest group.

In South America, the Incas were conquered by Francisco Pizarro in 1532. Prior to the invasion of the Spanish, European diseases had spread from Mesoamerica into the Andes region, weakening the Incan empire. In addition, the Spanish reached Peru while a civil war was in progress. With their superior arms and a great deal of deception, the Spanish captured the Incan leader and agreed to a ransom that was met. The Spanish, however, put the Incan leader to death rather than honor their commitment. The Spanish did not complete the conquest of the Incas until 1572.

SPANISH COLONIAL ARCHITECTURE

The Spanish conquerors destroyed much of the art and architecture of pre-Colombian cultures. Cities were razed and new ones constructed on the same sites. Valuable artifacts were melted down to make coins, and priests burned the Mayan and Aztec codices in which their history was recorded, considering them to be pagan influences. Cathedrals were constructed on the sites of former temples.

During the sixteenth century, most of the new building took place in Mexico. In the seventeenth century, the Spanish concentrated their efforts in Peru and Ecuador and the former Incan territory. The eighteenth century saw the Portuguese import Baroque art and architecture into Brazil.

The construction activity that took place in sixteenth-century Mexico was spurred on by religious leaders who established monasteries and churches using the free labor provided by the encomienda system. Since local artisans were used for the manual labor, the resulting buildings were a mixture of what the Spanish remembered from their homeland and Amerindian designs. Much of the Spanish influence was a mix of Romanesque, Gothic, Renaissance, and Mudejar elements.

By the seventeenth century, the efforts to convert the natives slowed somewhat, as most had at least paid lip service to the new faith. Churches and cathedrals were still required, but the authorities also needed civic buildings and palaces.

As the Baroque began to be used in Latin America, it first appeared in the severe style of Juan de Herrera. In the Andes, Baroque was mixed with Mudejar influences, such as geometric designs that were used especially for ceilings and polychrome tiles for wall surfaces. Wooden balconies were enclosed with **muxarabi**, or wood latticed grilles in geometric designs. By the middle of the eighteenth century, the Baroque Churrigueresque style had been brought to the Americas and, when combined with the Latin American temperament, became even more decorative than its Spanish prototype. Volutes, solominic columns, clusters of vegetation and produce, medallions, and human figures were used as decoration but were not part of the structure itself. The Baroque style was most exuberant in Mexico. (See Figure 13.13.)

Farther south, the Mestizo style resulted when Spanish Baroque was interpreted by Indian artisans, who also introduced native decorative elements. Parrots, monkeys, hummingbirds, chinchillas, jaguars, and other Indian designs were used alongside cherubs and the Virgin Mary.

Most of the European immigrants to Brazil were Portuguese workers. They constructed the same type of buildings familiar to them at home using stone and stucco. Churches were only a little more ornate than homes. Typically, it was the entry that received the most lavish decoration as it did in the Iberian Peninsula. The carved stone of the door surround contrasted with the plain white stucco of the building. Even when the Rococo style arrived in Brazil, the stucco was retained. Designs

FIGURE 13.13 The Churrigueresque façade of the cathedral in Mexico City is typical of Spanish colonial architecture and is relatively plain except for the entry surround.

FIGURE 13.14 The Catedral Metropolitana Nossa Senhora Aparecida in Brasilia (1958–1970) was designed by Brazilian architect Oscar Niemeyer. Sixteen hyperboloid concrete columns represent hands reaching toward heaven. Three angels are suspended from the ceiling.

became more curvilinear, but relatively little else changed. Most of the decorative sculpture prior to the nineteenth century was applied to the main façade. Inside, the decoration was used around altars and eventually for the reredos.

The nineteenth century marked the beginning of independence movements in Latin America. As a part of their moves toward independence, Latin American countries rejected colonial architectural styles and consciously applied French influences to design.

MODERN ARCHITECTURE IN LATIN AMERICA

In the early part of the twentieth century, improving Latin American economies, social changes, industrialization, and urbanization resulted in a building boom. Until the mid-twentieth century, however, traditional building designs continued to be used. The lack of building codes and clients who desired the avant-garde led to experimentation. There was little influence from North America, and Latin America turned instead to France and especially to Charles-Edouard Jean-

neret, known as Le Corbusier (1887–1965). The architect made several trips to South America and lectured in Brazil and Argentina. In each of the Latin American countries, there were one or two young architects who were either trained in Paris or in local schools and who taught Parisian methods. These architects followed Le Corbusier and the French Academy and passed that influence on to younger architects by teaching in Latin American schools of architecture. Eventually, however, the influence of the École des Beaux Arts in Paris waned in Latin America and influences from North America began to filter into the country.

Glass and steel construction has resulted in high-rise buildings in old colonial cities. Unfortunately, steel grilles must be installed in front of glass walls for protection against illegal entry. Often, American-style skyscrapers were built, but without the air conditioning they receive in American cities. In the hot, humid climates of Latin America such buildings can be uncomfortable, and shading devices are almost always necessary.

FIGURE 13.15 Most surfaces are finished with stucco, although ceramic mosaics are sometimes used to provide color and ornament.

OPEN PLANNING
FOR TROPICAL CLIMATES

The most successful Latin American buildings are those with open planning designed for living both inside and outside. Light colors, thin walls, and areas enclosed only by grilles suit the building to the climate. Le Corbusier's **brise soleil**, or "sun breaker," has been adapted for use all over Latin America. **Pilotis** are also standard on buildings, especially in Brazil. Pilotis are supporting columns inset from the wall plane that raise the structure off the ground. Roof gardens are common features of Latin American buildings.

Because of the climate, masonry and reinforced concrete are the most used materials. Wood is widely available, but there is little traditional building in wood, so it is rarely used. The use of masonry enables architects to incorporate curved walls, vaults, and free-form structures. Felix Candela (1910–1997) has constructed a number of hyperbolic parabolic concrete shells.

Derivative Design

Latin American design falls into three categories: indigenous design, European-influenced design, and modern design derived from twentieth-century technologies used in North America and Western Europe. Latin American native buildings exhibit environmentally suitable designs although these are only infrequently merged with other influences. Beginning with the Spanish and Portuguese conquests during the sixteenth century and later, urban design was similar to that in Europe. As South American countries gained independence, they looked to other sources for inspiration. Latin American design has had little influence on that of the rest of the world.

that what Columbus found was not the East Indies but an entirely unknown continent, there was disappointment in Europe. For another century, Europeans continued their quest for a sea route to the Orient, and settlement of the new continent was not a high priority.

The Spanish in North America (1492–1850)

The Spanish were the first Europeans after the Vikings to explore the New World, and during the sixteenth century they established footholds in the Caribbean, Mexico, Peru, Florida, and the American Southwest. Spain's stated purposes were twofold: to exploit the wealth to be found and to Christianize the natives. Spain's subsequent actions made it obvious that its most important mission was to enrich Spain's coffers, and indeed the riches from the New World helped make Spain the most powerful nation in Europe. Other nations, seeing the possibility of limitless wealth, sent more explorers in search of a route to Asia; this resulted in footholds on the North American continent by a number of nations.

The most damaging result of the early explorations was the introduction of European diseases to the New World. These included smallpox, measles, and typhus. In addition, the Spanish forced the Amerindians into intensive labor. These factors resulted in decimation of the native population. The estimated population of Mexico in 1519, for example, was as high as 25 million; by 1605, only 1 million natives remained—a reduction of up to 96 percent of the population.[3]

Most Spanish occupation and exploration remained south of the Rio Grande River. In Central and South America, the Spanish had encountered three complex civilizations: the Mayas, the Incas, and the Aztecs. These natives lived in concentrated urban areas, built monumental structures, and had agricultural economies, political systems, and standing armies.

Explorations by Francisco Vasquez de Coronado (1510–1554), Hernando de Soto (1496/1497–1542), Juan Ponce de León (c. 1460–1521), and Esteban Gomez (1478–1530) into North America revealed no advanced civilizations, no large cities, and neither gold nor silver. The indigenous population of North America was spread over a large sparsely populated area and had no domesticated animals, no written language, and, for the most part, no metal tools. It is estimated that only about 1 million natives lived in North America at the time of the Spanish conquest—fewer by far than the number of inhabitants south of the Rio Grande River. Spanish settlements in North America were limited to Florida, the Southwest, and the coast of California.

Three generations of Spanish settlers had occupied New Spain before other nations established permanent settlements in the Americas.[4] Universities had been founded, the cathedral in Mexico City had been begun, and the first printing press had been brought to the Americas. Political decisions of Spanish colonial outposts in North America were made by the Spanish monarchy or by their representatives on-site and local citizens had little voice. Land ownership was limited, and a semi-feudal system was introduced whereby Amerindians often served Spanish masters.

MATERIALS USED BY THE SPANISH

In the Americas, it was necessary for the Spanish to make use of the building materials at hand. These varied according to climate. In coastal Florida, the Spanish used seashells as building materials in two ways. **Tabby**, or **tapia**, was a combination of ground or loose shells, lime mortar, sand, and water. As such, it was a primitive form of concrete. Tabby required the use of forms made of planks into which the tabby was laid in layers. Each layer had to dry before additional tabby could be added. It was a time-consuming process that limited its uses at first to floors, foundations, and roofs. By the time the British gained control of Spanish Florida in 1763, however, more than a third of the houses had tabby walls. **Coquina** was a natural material that consisted of multiple layers of shells from small marine crustaceans that hardened together when exposed to air. Some coquina was mostly sand, some mostly shells. While coquina had been found by 1581, it was not used in structures for another three quarters of a century. Quite possibly the delay was due to the lack of skilled masons. The most readily available source of coquina was on nearby Anastasia Island. Considered a type of limestone, coquina was so porous that when the British shot cannon balls into it, the shock was absorbed by the rock and the cannon balls either bounced off or penetrated only a few inches. Both tabby and coquina were coated with whitewash to finish them. (See Figure 14.1.)

FIGURE 14.1 Coquina could be cut into blocks and its use resulted in structures that were more durable than those constructed of tabby. Individual shells of which coquina consisted can be seen in the inset as can the differences in consistency of the blocks.

When the Spanish arrived in the North American Southwest, the Amerindians were using two types of construction: rubble stone and adobe puddle construction. Puddled adobe was simply mud daubed on in layers. In their rubble stone construction, the Amerindians employed mud for mortar. When the Spanish later used this type of stone construction, they plastered the finished wall with adobe. In all likelihood, the Spanish introduced the Amerindians to the Moorish technique of making regular blocks out of adobe with straw as a binder. This technique was suitable to the skills of the Amerindians and quickly replaced puddled adobe construction. When an adobe brick wall was finished, it was plastered over with more adobe on both the exterior and the interior resulting in a smooth surface. Over time, the final coating of adobe had to be replaced, resulting in rounded edges and corners. Adobe remained in common use in the Southwest until the coming of the railroads in the 1880s. After that time, the lumber transported by the railroad was used for most structures except in remote areas.

Although adobe was sometimes reinforced with rubble stones, the Spanish did not teach the Amerindian laborers the techniques of quarrying and cutting stone. However, a small number of masons from Spain came to North America to construct churches with vaulted ceilings in Texas.

As in East Texas, wood was used where it was available. There, **jacales**, or small rectangular houses with thatched roofs, were built. Four forked posts formed the corners and supported the roof, while wattle and daub or any material at hand formed the walls. Wood was also used in Florida, especially where it was not in contact with the ground; there, the climate precluded most wood structures from enduring. A significant difference between Amerindian and Spanish structures made with wood was the size of the logs. Without metal tools it was difficult for the Amerindians to cut large timbers. The size of their harvested logs usually limited the width of their rooms to 8 to 10 feet. With their metal tools, the Spanish could cut larger timbers that resulted in rooms commonly about 15 feet in width and up to 35 feet in some larger buildings.

SPANISH ARCHITECTURE IN NORTH AMERICA

At the time of the great explorations, the Baroque style was in favor in Spain. In South and Central America and in Mexico, the Spanish erected structures that were recognizably Baroque. In North America, however, life was much more harsh and the natives less experienced with complex construction; therefore, buildings usually had only a few Baroque details. Later, Neoclassic forms were used, and most Spanish buildings in California emulated that style.

In North America, the Spanish built royal forts, or **presidios**; towns, or **pueblos**; and missions, or **misiones**.

FIGURE 14.2 The star-shaped Castillo de San Marcos was begun by the Spanish in St. Augustine, Florida, in 1672. The projecting corners allowed defenders to protect the walls.

FIGURE 14.3 Bastions projected outward from the main wall and were sometimes pointed rather than rounded.

PRESIDIOS

The presidio was a Spanish settlement accompanied by a garrison of soldiers and situated to protect trade routes and secure Spanish claims to the land. The presidio was a walled enclosure usually with a square, rectangular, or polygonal shape, although this depended on the terrain. (See Figure 14.2.) Generally, walls enclosed an area 200 to 650 feet long on all sides. A gate with guardhouses on both sides provided some protection. Buildings were constructed against the interior of the fortified walls and one or more stone **bastions,** or defensive towers, might be constructed at the corners to raise cannons above the walls. (See Figure 14.3.)

Inside the wall was a well, an arsenal, quarters for soldiers, often a church, and the captain's quarters that were located opposite the main gate. Buildings surrounded a large **cuadrángulo,** or open area, and had a single entrance. In times of danger, the civilian population sought refuge within the walls much as they had in medieval castles. Presidio walls often had **tronecas,** or loopholes, that served the same purpose as a battlement. Tronecas were also used on missiones and houses, especially those located some distance from a presidio.

Prior to the construction of the Castillo de San Marcos in St. Augustine, masonry construction for presidios had been limited to ports that protected the fleets of galleons carrying silver to Spain and to Acapulco, where Spanish ships brought treasures from Asia for transshipment to Spain. Most presidios had surrounding wooden palisade walls instead. Some presidios were never completely enclosed, and of those that were, later Spanish visitors reported their deterioration and commented that the only real defense was the garrison itself.

PUEBLOS

A pueblo was laid out according to royal ordinances that resulted in a classical organization. By decree, pueblos were to be constructed near a waterway or road, on elevated fertile land, and near Amerindian settlements. Like the presidio's cuadrángulo, the central area of the pueblo, or **plaza**, was a large open space around which the most important structures were located. In a port, the plaza was constructed near the water rather than in a central location. Principal streets led from the plaza to the gates, and straight streets divided the remaining area within the surrounding walls into square blocks.

The church was supposed to be erected on one side of the main plaza, although when the Spanish settled in existing Amerindian communities, it was often located a short distance away. Other buildings around the plaza included government buildings, an arsenal, and sometimes an infirmary. (See Figure 14.4.) The remaining central spaces were assigned to merchants who conducted business on the first story of their homes. Defensive towers, or **torreones**, were sometimes incorporated at the corners of the plazas. Usually two stories, these towers featured a single strong door, either high windows or peepholes, and a trap door leading to the roof.

MISIONES

Jesuit or Franciscan friars accompanied Spanish explorers. These friars established the familiar chain of missions in the American Southwest and, beginning in 1769, up the California coast as far as San Francisco.[5] While a misión housed a church, it was more than solely a place of worship, including everything necessary for a settle-

ment. Because of the distances and remote locations of Spanish misiones, it was imperative that they become self-sufficient relatively quickly. In fact, in many cases, it was the responsibility of the misión not only to meet the needs of its own people but to supply the presidio, of which they were often a part, with food and other products. The most important requirement for a misión was the availability of a dependable water supply. Water to some California misiones was supplied by stone **zanjas**, or aqueducts with fired clay tile channels. In order to produce sufficient food, it was necessary for the misiones to have associated land for growing crops and for grazing animals. With the help of the Amerindians, whom they conscripted as laborers, and depending on the climate in the area, the misión fields produced not only grain (e.g., barley, maize, and wheat) but fruits for which the Spanish had imported seeds and that were not indigenous to North America (e.g., figs, grapes, oranges, apples, peaches, and pears). In addition, olives were grown where the climate allowed furnishing the necessary oil for cooking. Grapes were converted into wine for sacramental purposes as well as for trade.

Some misiones had forges for blacksmiths, although iron ore had to be imported. The iron was fashioned into crosses to top the misiones, screens and gates, strap hinges, and, of course, cannons.

Over a period of years, the misiones also constructed kilns in which to fire brick and roofing tiles, or **tejas**. Fired bricks, or **ladrillos**, were used

FIGURE 14.4 Structures with colonnaded portales (also known as corredors), or covered porches, surrounded the plaza to provide shade and protection against inclement weather. The Palace of the Governors in Santa Fe had a typical portal.

for the decorative projections on adobe structures, for arches including vaults, around openings, and for supporting pillars.

Arrangement of a Misión Complex The misión complex was similar to the presidio in that buildings often surrounded a cuadrángulo used for festivals and religious purposes. Around the enclosure were the church, usually at the northeast corner; reception rooms, or **salas**; sometimes a library; possibly a chapel; and guest quarters. The buildings surrounding this public area, especially in California, often had covered arcaded walkways, or **soportales**, that faced the open space. Structures in less public areas of the complex, usually found in regions other than California, typically had portales of post-and-lintel construction if any shade or protection was provided. When the required structures did not completely surround the courtyard, adobe walls were constructed to complete the enclosure. Once tejas became available in an area, they were often used to cap enclosure walls to protect them from damage by rainwater.

While a few North American misiones had more, most had only two priests, minimizing the need for living areas. Regardless of size, the convento, or monastery (living quarters for the padres), was located adjacent to the church. Infrequently, a private patio was provided for the convento.

An additional patio behind the convento was more public and was surrounded by workshops, storerooms, kitchens, shops, laundries, and monjeria, or quarters for unmarried native women and children. Living quarters for married Amerindians might be located in a village nearby or within a palisade wall that surrounded early misiones. Village locations followed pueblo planning principles.

North of the church and connected to it by a doorway from the nave was the cemetery, or **campo santo**. This open area was enclosed by a wall. Burial places for the Spanish and the Amerindians were usually separated either within the campo santo or by providing a cemetery for Amerindians a short distance away.

Misión Church Design The mission church was not always oriented with the façade facing west, as would have been the case in Spain. In fact, the rationale for this orientation had been forgotten over the years in the Spanish colonies, and churches faced in any direction for practical reasons. In New Mexico, they typically faced the east to provide light on the altar through a transverse clerestory window made possible by constructing the sanctuary walls 2 to 3 feet higher than those of the nave. California examples had larger windows in the nave and a single window in the sanctuary but lacked clerestory windows.

FIGURE 14.5 A low wall separated the courtyard, or atrio, in front of the church itself from the surrounding area. It was in this area that outdoor services were conducted. Sometimes, it was also used as a cemetery if there was not another place for burial.

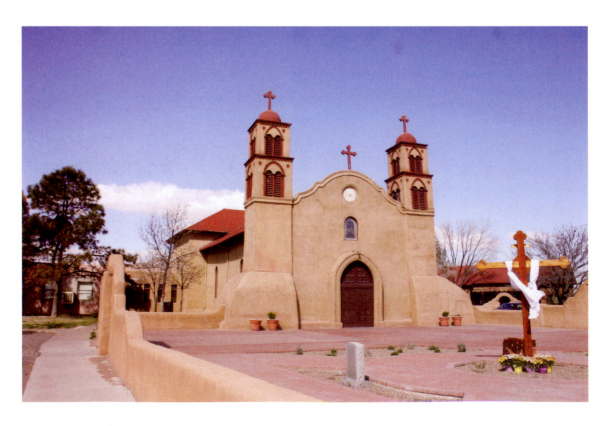

Most of the churches had a single story and were constructed of adobe, although fired brick was used for some structural components that included arches, pillars, and areas around openings and on parapet walls above the roofline. In adobe structures, solid parapets, some of which had tronecas, often surrounded flat roofs; other parapets were constructed of ladrillos laid in an openwork pattern.

Square pillars provided support when arcades were employed. Most pillars had an ornamental projection just below the springpoint of the arch and the corners might be chamfered and/or painted dark red. Arches were generally semicircular, although widths within a single arcade varied. In post and lintel construction, **zapatas**, or doubled sawn wooden corbels, flanked posts at the top to help support the structural members above. (See Figure 14.6.) On both the façade and in the interior, elaborate Baroque **estipites** were sometimes used. These columns or pilasters consisted of stacked sections, resulting in a broken profile. (See Figure 14.7.)

The style of Spanish misión churches varied from crude adobe structures to elaborate Baroque examples, although most were relatively simple. Inside, elaborate European-styled carved altars and reredos were placed alongside vividly colored native motifs and native interpretations of Spanish motifs. The misión of San Xavier del Bac in Arizona was one of the most elaborate of the Spanish missions in North America, although the present structure was not begun until 1783. Inside, the vaults were constructed of fired brick, and almost every surface including the vaults was painted with brilliantly colored designs.

Corner towers and certain types of belfries sometimes served as buttresses, but additional ones were often necessary. On the interior, decorated pilasters corresponded to exterior buttresses. Misión churches often had a projecting balcony over the main entry that might extend the full width between buttresses or towers. Although the balcony provided some ornamentation, its function was to provide a platform for the priests when outdoor services were conducted.

Most misión churches had a single aisle that was limited in width by the length of available timbers. In a few stone-walled examples, there was some attempt at creating a cruciform plan that usually resulted instead in large recessed areas on either side of the nave at a point where

FIGURE 14.6 Some zapatas were chip carved or painted.

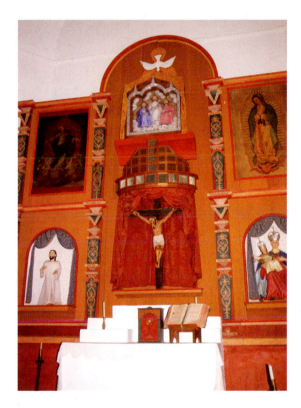

FIGURE 14.7 The reredos behind the altar in this Spanish mission church has painted estipites that divide it vertically into sections.

FIGURE 14.8 Church façades were relatively plain, often due to their adobe construction, although some later examples had curved parapet walls and, in towns, flanking towers. Both adobe and rubble stone construction required thick walls and, especially when the walls were high, buttresses to offset the outward thrust of pitched roofs. Note the angle of the walls in this church that reveal the change in wall thickness necessary in adobe construction.

FIGURE 14.9 The sanctuary was raised above the nave to elevate the celebrants above the congregation, and separated from the nave by a railing.

FIGURE 14.10 Typically, the campanile was two or three stories in height with the usually windowless first story at least as high as the façade of the church it adjoined. The second and third stories were slightly stepped back and a projecting fired brick molding topped each story. In Mexico, the dome is typically tiled.

the crossing would have been. With few exceptions, North American Spanish misiones did not employ transept entrances and these recesses were dead ends.

Inside, the church had a **sanctuary**, or sacred area around the altar, and a room for a sacristy either to one side at the rear of the church or behind the sanctuary. The sanctuary terminated either in a rectangle, a trapezoid, or sometimes a curve reminiscent of a European apse. Altars were often constructed of adobe brick, and some had a wooden baldachin supported by solominic columns. Painted bands of floral decoration or Amerindian designs adorned the altars. Unlike churches in Spain, the choir was located in a balcony above the main entry and was accessed by interior or exterior stairs. Although in a few misión churches, the baptismal font was located in a separate room either inside the nave or in a separate building, most were located just inside the entry to the church or in a corner near the entry.

Wooden statues, or **bultos**, usually of Christ or the Virgin, executed by the Amerindians, were carved and painted and sometimes gilded. The statues were often set in a **nicho**, or niche, that was formed into the sanctuary wall above the altar. Frequently, the nicho was rounded and had a shell-shaped top, a Mudejar influence.

Belfries Four types of supports for bells were used in Spanish misiones. The simplest was a beam supported by two vertical posts and from which the bell was suspended. The **campanile** was a tower that housed the bells much as in European architecture. Usually, the campanile was a solid structure filled in with rubble, although there were some examples of campaniles that housed a baptistery in the base and a few with an internal staircase. Corners were sometimes chamfered, and ornamental finials were often used at the corners of the upper stories. The second story of the tower had arched openings, usually one on each of the four sides, although some examples had paired openings. The towers terminated with a dome to which a lantern or cross was sometimes added.

The **españada** was a parapet wall at the gable end of the building that was roughly triangular and that often exhibited Baroque influence by incorporating a variety of curves. This type of façade was introduced only in the seventeenth century after immigrants from other areas of

North America had penetrated the Southwest and was similar to the curved Dutch gable. Españadas were pierced with arched openings and housed bells; when there were no openings for bells, the crowning portion of the curvilinear façade was a **remate**, a device later used on houses.

The last of the belfry types to appear was introduced in Alta California. The **campanario** was a separate, thick multistoried wall in which there were openings for the bells. Like the decorative brick cornices of the campaniles, brick was also used for projecting decoration on the españada and the campanario. (See Figure 14.11.)

> ┌ **INFLUENCE 14.1**
> *The Mission style became popular for residences during the late nineteenth century borrowing the españada of Spanish missions and combining it with soportales.*

SPANISH DOMESTIC ARCHITECTURE

The first Spanish houses in Florida were wattle and daub and later of wood planks. The climate, however, caused both types of structures to deteriorate, and the settlers sought other alternatives. Cedar and cypress wood could be used because they did not rot, but the preference was for masonry walls on the first floor with timber roof framing. Parapet gable-end walls and steeply pitched roofs were common in the rainy climate of the Southeast, but buildings in Florida differed significantly from those in other Spanish settlements. In the hot, humid climate, houses were oriented to catch as much breeze as possible, entrances led to patios, and separate kitchens were constructed to prevent heating the interiors when cooking. (See Figure 14.12.)

In the Southwest, adobe or stone was used for walls and adobe for roofs. In California, adobe buildings usually had thatched or bitumen roofs. Once tejas were available, they were widely used and became characteristic of Spanish colonial buildings in California as well as in other areas where pitched roofs were used.

Although Amerindian adobe structures had multiple stories, each stepped back from the next, Spanish structures had only a single story and, in fact, began as a single room. Up to ten additional rooms were joined end to end, making the buildings linear in form with a **placita**, or small courtyard, behind. In smaller homes the placita

was enclosed with adobe or palisade walls; in larger homes, by rooms arranged in an L, a U, or quadrangle. Low-pitched (California) or flat (Southwest) roofs were used on these one-room deep structures. A Moorish-influenced beehive-shaped outdoor adobe oven was used for cooking in drier areas. Three distinct styles of Spanish colonial houses were constructed: Spanish Colonial, Territorial, and California styles.

> ┌ **INFLUENCE 14.2**
> *Amerindians in their native pueblos later used the outdoor ovens introduced by the Spanish.*

FIGURE 14.11 The campanario could be attached to the side or the façade of the church, free standing, or added to the top of the building, sometimes at a corner. Like the españada and the campanile, the campanario was pierced with arched openings for the bells.

FIGURE 14.12 Two-story houses in St. Augustine were often constructed of tabby as in this example. The second story was sometimes wood. A projecting second story balcony on one side was common.

Spanish Colonial Style[6] *(1598–1821)* Buildings in the Spanish Colonial style were similar to indigenous adobe structures and to the Moorish buildings of Spain. These structures had parapet walls that surrounded flat roofs and supported large timbers called **vigas**. Vigas spanned the shortest distance across the building and projected on both ends. It was necessary to travel long distances to obtain these timbers, so they were used sparingly. In indigenous structures, vigas were often of uneven lengths due to the difficulty of cutting them without metal tools. In Spanish structures, vigas were typically cut evenly to desired lengths. Vigas in some residences were even cut off so they did not extend past the wall, and their ends were plastered over with adobe. **Latillas**, or small peeled poles, were laid across the vigas and covered with moss or straw before being plastered with adobe on the top. (See Figures 14.13.)

Canales, or hollow spouts, led from the flat roof to the outside of the adobe walls to drain water. Originally, canales were hollowed from wood, although later examples were made of fired clay. Canales projected some distance from the walls to minimize water damage.

Corredors were attached to buildings on the courtyard side of some Spanish Colonial homes, although this was not a universal characteristic.

This was a major difference between the Colonial and later Territorial buildings, which had corredors on the external façade. Roofs of the corredors were sloped and intersected the walls at a point slightly below the top. Round columns consisting of peeled logs supported the portal roof.

INFLUENCE 14.3

When New Mexico became a state in 1912, the Santa Fe railroad promoted tourism by stressing the origins of the Spanish Colonial Style. With some changes, the Spanish Colonial Style returned as the Pueblo Revival Style. Unlike the Spanish Colonial Style, Pueblo Revival examples featured central planning, multiple stories, and stepped back rooflines to make them more suitable for contemporary families.

Territorial Style (1846–1890) Like Spanish Colonial style buildings, Territorial style structures were constructed of adobe and had a roof of vigas and latillas. Due to improved technology, corners were more square in Territorial style buildings than in previous examples. Porch supports were often squared and some had sawn shaped designs. Zapatas served as capitals distributing the weight of the porch roof over a wider area. Influences from the contemporary Greek Revival style were evident in the location of the portal on the main façade, the treatment of the top of the walls, and the use of trim around openings. Sometimes, the portal was recessed so that porch roof supports rested on the side walls. Ladrillos might be laid to resemble an entablature with dentil molding at the top of the adobe wall. After the coming of the railroad c. 1880, Territorial style buildings began to assimilate the central planning typical of the East while retaining familiar exterior features. Sizeable glazed windows were added to exposed façades, boards were used for door and window trim, and the new corrugated metal was sometimes used on roofs. Although milled lumber brought by the railroad changed much of the building in the Southwest, the Territorial style lingered in more remote regions. The Palace of the Governors in Santa Fe is an example of a Territorial style building. (See Figure 14.4.)

Spanish California Style (1769–1850) Spanish settlement in California began later than that in the Southwest, and houses reflected contemporary trends, including features of the Greek

FIGURE 14.14 A covered passageway, or *zaguan*, led to a large double door, or *portón*, through which carriages and livestock could be driven. A smaller pedestrian door, the *postigo*, was set within or beside the portón.

FIGURE 14.15 Spanish doors were generally shorter than those of other colonial styles. Openings might be shell-shaped at the top as is this doorway at Misión Nuestra Senora del Espiritu Santo de Zuniga near Goliad, Texas. The three cherub faces appear to have Amerindian features but are typical of the Baroque style in Europe.

Revival style popular in the rest of the country. Spanish colonial California homes were constructed in much the same manner as those in New Mexico—that is, adobe wall construction in a linear form with corredors facing a placita. The amount of rainfall in California made sloping roofs more practical, although some flat-roofed structures were built. It was on these low-pitched side-gabled or shed roofs that locally made terra-cotta tejas were first used. Eaves extended past the walls to provide shade and to protect the adobe from weather. (See Box 14.1.)

INFLUENCE 14.4

The Spanish California Style was combined with traditional architecture of the East Coast to create the two-story Monterey Style in the nineteenth century. Later, the Spanish California Style became the inspiration for the ubiquitous ranch style house so familiar in modern America.

OPENINGS IN SPANISH COLONIAL BUILDINGS

In the Southwest, pre-Spanish indigenous structures had an opening in the roof through which the structure was entered via a ladder, and window openings were limited in both size and number. With their metal tools, the Spanish could more easily cut timber and hew boards to frame and trim openings and to make shutters and doors to close them. Spanish colonial buildings had a single doorway on the façade, a doorway from each room that led to a courtyard, and, sometimes, a few small window openings on the courtyard side.

Early Spanish colonial doorways were covered with reed mats, blankets, or skins. A **pintle** was a wooden pin that fit into a socket in the door frame and allowed the door to pivot. Doors swung on pintles, not hinges. Wooden **puncheon** doors required boards, a scarce commodity because it was necessary to hew them by hand, a time-consuming process. Puncheon doors, then, were a sign of status. **Batten** doors, which required milled lumber, became more popular after the coming of the railroad. Eventually, these doors, made of boards nailed to other boards, evolved into **Penasco** doors, which emulated the more elaborate artesonado of Spain. Penasco doors were

BOX 14.1 CHARACTERISTICS OF SPANISH COLONIAL BUILDINGS

- Low-pitched or flat roof
- Parapet walls, or little overhang on sloped roofs
- Use of indigenous materials including coquina, tabby, and adobe
- Adobe brick construction in dry climates
- Fired clay roofing tiles in California
- Arches used in arcades and over openings
- Covered walkways or porches
- Buildings planned around a courtyard
- Elaborate wooden doors
- Niches in walls
- Adobe fireplaces
- Shaped columns and zapatas
- Blending of Amerindian, Moorish, and Spanish designs and motifs

FIGURE 14.16 Patterns in Penasco doors were usually geometric with crosses, stars, and lozenges most popular.

In early colonial homes, windows were located only on the courtyard side of the structure. Some windows, especially in public buildings, were glazed with mica or selenite, a form of gypsum that is colorless, transparent, and has a pearl-like luster, set into divided light wood frames. Important windows were sometimes foliated. After the arrival of the railroad, clear glass, prefabricated windows, and milled lumber became readily available, and windows were glazed with glass and jigsawn boards were added to shutters and window and door trim.

INTERIORS OF
SPANISH COLONIAL BUILDINGS

Interiors of all the Spanish colonial styles and of churches were similar. In homes, typically, a main reception room received the most lavish decoration because this was where guests were greeted and entertained. In addition to the reception room, the typical home had a bedchamber, a dining area, a kitchen, and a chapel.

Floors were usually packed earth on which **jergas**, or coarsely woven rugs, were laid. There were few stone floors, and after the coming of the railroad, wood floors became widespread. Later, the tiles common south of the Rio Grande also appeared as flooring.

formed by applying handmade moldings and jigsawn patterned boards to the door. Moldings separated the door into individual panels, where floral motifs were sometimes carved. Boards laid diagonally within panels were common. (See Figure 14.16.)

Interior walls were painted after the final coating of adobe had dried. The adobe walls were at first whitewashed on the interior with **tierra blanca**, a type of gypsum that included mica. The mica chips glittered in the light so this finish continued to be used in churches. **Tierra amarillo**, made from yellowish clay that contained flakes of mica, was sometimes used to finish walls. Later colors included blue, buff, pink, green, ochre, red, brown, and purple. Colors were used especially to highlight openings, including niches, and for stencil designs painted around openings or used as borders. The reredos in churches was often painted to give it the appearance of stone. Small mirrors, or **espejos**, were frequently used on surfaces inside misiones to reflect light, an influence derived from the Moors.

FIGURE 14.17 Early Spanish windows were simple openings protected by interior shutters, or **ventanas**, or by projecting grilles, or **rejas**, made of turned wood spindles, metal, or cactus ribs. It was only in the late nineteenth and twentieth centuries that wrought iron grilles were used on Spanish-influenced structures.

Niches were typically recessed into wall thicknesses, providing places for statues of saints, or **santos**, which were the only nonutilitarian objects in most homes. A string of chili peppers, a ristra, hung on the wall ready for use in cooking. Vigas and latillas were exposed on the inside, allowing dust and mud to filter into the structure. Vigas

FIGURE 14.18 Because the whitewash rubbed off onto clothing easily, walls often had a dado of a darker color or of cloth. A dado of solid-colored or faux-marble painted panels was set below murals, stylized floral designs, geometric motifs, or a plain-colored wall.

FIGURE 14.19 This original Spanish kitchen in St. Augustine features a trestle table with fiadores as well as an imported varqueño. The exposed beam ceiling can still be seen.

were often supported at both ends with corbels or zapatas. At first, a **manta de techo**, or ceiling cloth, might be stretched beneath the ceiling to prevent the infiltration of dust. Sometimes, this cloth was covered with a flour and water mixture to give it the appearance of plaster. With the coming of the railroad, **tablas**, or boards, were sometimes used for ceilings instead.

An adobe fireplace with a chimney was used for cooking and for warmth. Most had nichos. A **fogón de campaña**, or bell-shaped fireplace, was located in a corner and might adjoin a **padercita**, or stepped adobe wall, that often featured a built-in bench. Later fireplaces located along a wall had sloped hoods and sometimes a shelf supported by wood posts on which a person could sleep.

SPANISH COLONIAL FURNITURE

Wooden furniture had simple lines, straight legs, and little decoration, although chip carving or painting were sometimes employed. Furnishings were relatively heavy in appearance. **Bancos**, or benches, were built of adobe against walls, frequently flanking the fireplace; and these were used for sleeping and seating. Only a few chairs were used, and these resembled the Spanish frai-

lero, although shaped components were often substituted for turned ones. Cupboards might be built into the wall (**alacenas**) or freestanding (**trasteros**). Either type was closed with doors, usually doubled, that were made of spindles or sawn wood designs. Other furniture pieces were either imported from Spain or modeled on Spanish examples. As in Spain, leather was used on chairs and chests and attached with châtones. Chests or hollowed logs were used for grain storage, or **graneros**. When hollowed logs were used for this purpose, only a small opening was cut so that it could be easily covered to keep out vermin.

The French in North America (1534–1763)

France, too, sent explorers searching for riches in the New World and to find a passage to the Orient. Giovanni Verrazzano (1485–1528) claimed Canada for France (1524), explored the east coast of North America from the Carolinas to Nova Scotia, and discovered New York Harbor. Between 1534 and 1542, Jacques Cartier sailed up the St. Lawrence River as far as present-day Montreal and Quebec, but it was not until 1608 that the first permanent French colony was established at Quebec.

FIGURE 14.20 This simple-back stool, common in homes, has three legs and a shaped seat.

During the seventeenth and eighteenth centuries, French settlements were established along major waterways, including the Great Lakes, the Gulf of St. Lawrence, Hudson Bay, and the St. Lawrence and Mississippi rivers. Forts and trading posts were established by fishermen or fur traders, but there was little real colonization by the French on the vast area they had claimed until 1699. Even then, few French settlements other than in the St. Lawrence valley developed into prosperous communities. Although numerous French Huguenots immigrated, there was a ban on settlement by Protestants in New France and the Huguenots settled in British areas.

New France was controlled from Europe, and no local government institutions were established. Support from the government was minimal, and the few settlers spread over a large area. There were three separate areas of French influence: northern areas from Newfoundland to Lake Superior, Louisiana, and the Territory of Illinois, which loosely connected the other two.

By 1763, the British had gained control of most of the Northeast, although Quebec and a few other pockets of French influence continued. French influence, however, remained strong in parts of the Mississippi valley including New Orleans until Napoleon sold the Louisiana territory to the fledgling United States in 1803. Regardless of political control, French building traditions remained viable in New Orleans and in parts of Canada until the middle of the nineteenth century.

French Construction Methods

In Northern France, some buildings were constructed with grooved upright framing members into which planks were fit. This plankwall construction served as a model for the **poteaux et pièce coulissante**, or "posts and sliding piece," construction used for large buildings in the area of Quebec. There, however, rather than employing sawn planks, which were laborious to make, squared timbers were used for the fill. Post and sliding piece construction could easily be used for multistoried structures. In Quebec, stone foundations were used and the roof was completed with trusses. In outlying areas, poteaux et pièce coulissante construction was simplified: no foundation was used, the roof framing employed a ridgepole and rafters rather than complex trusses, and pins were used only where necessary for stability. Without the pins, the fill timbers

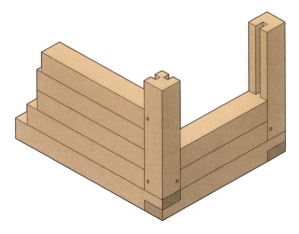

FIGURE 14.21 In *poteaux et pièce coulissante* construction, tenons on each end of a log fit into the grooves on the uprights, and pins were used to hold the timbers in place.

could slide downward as shrinking occurred due to drying minimizing the need for re-chinking. (See Figure 14.21.)

Smaller structures, usually single-storied, sometimes employed **piéce-sur-piéce** construction, a variation of the log cabin technique used where the ground was relatively dry. French examples differed from Swedish models in that timbers were squared rather than round, the overlapping corner joints were angled downward so water would drain away quickly, and timbers were cut so they did not extend beyond the corners.

In the Illinois territory, French settlers used two other types of construction: **poteaux-sur-sole** and **poteaux-en-terre**. In poteaux-en-terre construction, vertical wall posts were placed several feet in the ground in a trench. Hewn timbers, flat on two or four sides, were then set vertically on the sills usually less than a foot apart. Spaces between the uprights, or **interstices**, were filled with one of two types of material. **Bousillage** was a mixture of clay and grass, Spanish moss, or hair; **pierrotage** was a mixture of clay and rubble stone.[7] (See Figure 14.22.)

The French also constructed some stone and brick houses. Stone was used especially in the St. Lawrence River Valley. Brick was used in southern areas of French influence and rarely north of New Madrid, Missouri.

French Architecture in Colonial America

French settlers lived in towns and commuted to fields outside the community. Unlike those in other groups, few secluded dwellings were constructed. In northern areas, houses followed

French designs more closely than did those in warmer areas. In Quebec, homes of the wealthy resembled French models with stone walls, hip roofs, and round towers. Concessions made to the hot, humid climate in parts of the Louisiana territory probably came from the West Indies and included dormer windows, full-length casement windows, and **galerie**, or external covered porches. Where water tables were high, such as in the swampy land in the Mississippi delta, the structure was raised off the ground, often on brick pillars. Most of these structures had a single story, although some, especially later, were two stories.

INFLUENCE 14.5

The galeries of French colonial houses were combined with Greek Revival homes in the antebellum south on numerous examples of plantation homes.

Raising the structure off the ground served two purposes: it prevented damage from high water tables and it elevated the structure sufficiently to catch more breezes than were present at ground level. When homes were of two stories, the bottom story was often of masonry and housed the kitchen and sometimes servants' quarters. Sometimes, the kitchen was located in an outbuilding to keep the heat from cooking from rising into second-story living areas for the family. The second story was constructed of wood, and since houses were a single room deep, large window areas could be located on both sides of a room, allowing for ventilation. These French doors provided access to the galerie, which ran at first along one side of the house and later around all sides. Exterior stairways led to the second-floor galeries. Galerie roofs were extensions of the main roof, although often there was a more shallow pitch over the galerie. The galerie roofs were supported by columns and shaded the walls, keeping the rooms cooler than would otherwise have been possible. Galeries also offered access to other rooms, provided outdoor living areas, and protected exterior wall finishes.

Steeply pitched roofs were necessary to provide runoff for rain water. Both hip and gable forms were also employed. Side-gabled roofs were found mostly in urban areas, where they reduced the amount of roof drainage into the narrow passageways between houses. When galeries extended around all sides, a hip roof extension with a gentler pitch beginning at the wall line formed the roof. Later, hip roofs with uniform slopes on all sides were more common. Roof eaves were often flared to overhang the front façade in urban areas, even though galeries were rare in cities. (See Figure 14.23.)

Early roofs were finished with thatch or bark. Some roofs were protected with slate, a roofing material that was expensive and only available in France. In the American South, the climate was too warm for these dark-colored roofs, but settlers often used them because of their associated status. Later, shingles were used for roofs. The later New Orleans style house was a mixture of

FIGURE 14.22 Pote-aux-sur-sole buildings employed a horizontal sill laid either on the ground or on a stone foundation high enough to protect the structure from flooding. This technique also served to minimize the damage to the floor from moisture and insects.

FIGURE 14.23 Palisade fences made of logs to protect inhabitants from attack surrounded French colonial houses, their gardens, and their orchards. The exterior walls of the houses were plastered and whitewashed, and chimneys were constructed of stone.

French, Creole, and Spanish influence popular in the eighteenth century. These houses employed elaborate lacy wrought iron detailing including balustrades for balconies and the use of wrought iron for pillars.

Openings were often placed asymmetrically. Doors were tall and narrow, were often paired, and frequently had lights, or individual panes of glass, separated by wood muntins. Full-length divided light casement windows became known as French doors. A transom above the door was a common feature, although a fanlight later superseded it. Doors swung inward, while the full-length shutters that protected glazed doors swung outward. The shutters covered both the doors and transoms but not the fanlights. Windows were inward swinging, divided light casements protected by wood shutters. (See Box 14.2.)

Interiors of French Colonial Buildings

Interior walls of French colonial houses were typically plastered and then whitewashed. In northern areas where continental French architectural features were used, some rooms had paneling on the walls. Ceiling beams were exposed on the underside, but flooring for sleeping areas above was laid across the beams at the top, resulting in a flat, closed-in ceiling for the rooms below.

The Dutch in America (1609–1664)

Dutch merchants, who had become wealthy during the Renaissance, relied heavily on trade, and by the early seventeenth century, began to seek a route for that trade to reach the Orient. Dutch exploration was different from that of the Spanish, however, in that it was not the central government that sent out explorers beginning in 1602 but the Dutch East India Company, a joint stock company established by merchants. The Dutch eventually established footholds in Africa, the East Indies, and North and South America. Dutch interests in the New World included parts of the Caribbean, a section of South American coast, and coastal areas and river valleys in the northeast section of what was to become the United States. In the Northeast, Dutch settlements extended from Henlopen (Lewes, Delaware) to Fort Nassau (Fort Orange, Albany, New York).

The Dutch followed the same route around Africa to India as did the Portuguese, who continually harried them. For this reason, the Dutch East India Company commissioned the Englishman Henry Hudson to find a northern route across Russia to the Orient. After an unsuccessful beginning, Hudson informed the company he would sail west instead, and he reached Newfoundland in 1609. While seeking passage across the northern areas of the continent, he discovered Delaware Bay, sailed up the Hudson River as far as present-day Albany, made friends with the Amerindians, and reported the prospects of excellent farming and fur trade. Two Dutch stock companies were successively established to trade in North America. Trinkets, weapons, and tools were traded for beaver, otter, and mink furs, making them less expensive than those obtained from Russia, the traditional supplier of furs.

The Dutch West India Company granted large tracts of land in North America to individuals who would establish semi-feudal estates with the stipulation that each land owner bring a minimum of 50 tenants to work the land. Tenants were required to work a specified number of years to pay for their passage and were required to give the landowner a portion of their crops and animals. The major problem with this type of land distribution was that by simply crossing a river, anyone could obtain land for themselves. By 1646, the Dutch West India Company opened up the areas under their control to all settlers with the promise of land ownership. Some of the settlers who immigrated were not Dutch, although Dutch customs were retained in most areas of Dutch influence. Dutch immigrants settled in lowlands in coastal areas or along rivers on land much like that with which they were familiar in the Netherlands. Waterways were used for transport of goods, and wheat and other products were easily delivered to ocean-going cargo vessels. Two areas of Dutch settlement predominated: that of New Amsterdam on Manhattan Island and those scattered along the Hudson River Valley. The area claimed by the Dutch virtually separated two British enclaves, New England and the Middle Atlantic area.

Although the Dutch purchased Manhattan Island for $24 worth of goods, from the beginning the island was inhabited by individuals from numerous countries, including England. In 1643, a French missionary reported that in New Amsterdam alone, 18 languages were spoken. It was the English, however, whose customs the wealthy Dutch on Manhattan and Long Island began to emulate, building Georgian mansions as fine as those of their British neighbors and adopting certain British customs. The Hudson River valley remained more a Dutch enclave.

Government was in the hands of a director-general appointed by the company and who was in complete control of the colony. The failure of the Dutch settlements was due in part to the tyrannical nature of the director-generals appointed. As director-general, Peter Stuyvesant (c. 1602–1672) insisted, for example, that colonists attend the Dutch Reformed Church and fined or banished those who held other religious services. The venture in North America was never profitable for the company, and it had to levy heavy taxes to support the colony. Furthermore, the company had a monopoly on trade and colonists were not permitted to trade with anyone else. Once complete independence was obtained in the Netherlands, where citizens enjoyed peace and liberty, owned their own property, and were free of religious persecution, there was little incentive to leave. In fact, some immigrants returned to the Netherlands, leaving the problems of North America behind. Those who preferred to remain became increasingly dissatisfied.

In 1664, Dutch and English controversy over trade culminated in an English fleet sailing to New Amsterdam and demanding its surrender. The citizens overruled Stuyvesant and accepted the British promises of equal rights with British citizens, trading rights, religious freedom, participation in government, and the permission to continue their own traditional inheritance customs. Without shots being fired, the Dutch surrendered and the English gained control of the area.

MATERIALS USED BY THE DUTCH

The Dutch constructed no public buildings other than churches. It was their homes that were of primary importance. The first Dutch Colonial houses, with steeply pitched thatched roofs, were constructed of timber. When more permanent structures were built, it was the H-shaped **anchor bent** framework that identified a Dutch Colonial house, not features on the exterior. Two vertical timbers were connected with a horizontal timber a few feet from the top. These anchor bents were arranged in a series from front to back and became the framework for walls and an upper garret or loft. Rooms were linearly arranged and during the initial construction, it was a simple matter to increase the length of the structure by adding anchor bents. Width was limited to the length of the timbers used for cross pieces in the anchor bents. (See Figure 14.24.)

In the seventeenth century, Holland did not have large forests nor was stone common, so brick was the typical building material. Because colonists were familiar with brick buildings in the Netherlands, brick was the most desirable building material in America even though wood was plentiful. Brick may have first been brought to the New World as ship's ballast, but the Dutch quickly set up kilns in the new country, making

FIGURE 14.24 In some areas, the spaces between anchor bents were filled with brick nogging and the walls were then covered with boards or brick veneer. In this Dutch barn, the anchor bent is visible.

anchor bent

it possible for them to manufacture brick. Brick veneer was most common in urban areas and was often laid in all-over patterns that included Dutch cross bond, diamond, and chevron patterns. A date or the initials of owners might be centered on a wall.

The veneer was held in place by decorative iron ties often shaped as a fleur-de-lis. In rural areas where sandstone or limestone were available, load-bearing walls of stone were common because they were less expensive than was brick veneer. Both fieldstone (rubble) and coursed stone construction were used, sometimes on the same house. Coursed stone was preferred, but when economics were important, it might be used only on the front. Often stone was used only up to the gable, which was finished with brick or with shingles over timber framing. Decorative **mouse tooth (muisetanden)**, or brick zigzag, edges were frequently used in gable ends.

Both brick and stone were considered more stylish and more durable than board walls, but they were difficult to alter. Typically, when more space was needed, the Dutch simply constructed a larger building next to the original structure either in a continuation of the linear arrangement or as an ell. Regional variations reflected the availability of materials and sometimes building practices of neighbors from other countries. In areas where there was close contact with English colonists, for example, Dutch houses were sometimes built using wood framing.

INFLUENCE 14.6

Dutch rafters were notched to provide a flat support that attached the rafters to the wall timbers. This notching is widely used in modern construction methods where the roof rafters attach to the wall.

Although the first roofs were thatched, locally made fired terra-cotta **pantiles** quickly re-

placed thatch as the preferred roofing material. Because pantiles required at least a 56-degree roof angle in order to keep water out, steep roofs continued to be built. Pantiles were S-shaped and overlapped at the side, creating a roof with vertical ridges and furrows. (See Figure 14.25.) Slate was infrequently used and also required a relatively steep pitch. Less steeply-pitched roofs required shingles.

DUTCH ARCHITECTURE IN COLONIAL AMERICA

Many of the Dutch immigrants were merchants with an industrious work ethic who enjoyed a relatively high standard of living. Few artisans and farmers emigrated. Dutch homes were comfortable, more sophisticated than those of their neighbors, and sometimes pretentious. The Dutch settlers enjoyed a variety of finished goods imported from Europe.

Although some in English-dominated areas constructed their houses like the English and some characteristics were associated with other neighboring groups, the majority of settlers continued to construct their homes similar to those in the Netherlands. Dutch Colonial buildings were more closely related to medieval European examples than to Renaissance models. Dutch building traditions continued long after the English gained control of Dutch territory: on the Hudson River, in Bergen County, New Jersey, and in Rockland County, New York.

DUTCH COLONIAL BUILDING FEATURES

All Dutch Colonial styles had similar characteristics and were similar to their Old World counterparts. The anchor bent construction resulted in most homes having one-and-a-half stories. Dutch houses in urban areas had steep gable roofs with concealing **corbie-** or **crow-stepped** gable ends. (See Figure 14.26.) In an effort to conserve valuable space within the city walls, houses were several stories high and often so close together that they shared side walls. The entrance was in the narrow end that was turned toward the street. As in the Netherlands, a heavy metal bracket near the roof facilitated moving furnishings into upper stories.

Houses in rural areas, where land was less expensive, usually had a side entry and were often

FIGURE 14.25 Parapet gable ends helped to seal the pantiles, which overlapped only a single row of the tiles below. Roof tiles were usually red or blue.

FIGURE 14.26 Typical of buildings in the Netherlands, corbie-stepped gables were parapet walls that terminated in squared or curved steps that projected above the roofline.

only one or one-and-a-half stories high. Gable roofs were common but without the stepped ends of urban houses. Frequently, a characteristic of homes of their Flemish neighbors was seen at the eaves where the roof flared outward, a feature known as a Dutch or Flemish kick. To allow for a gradual curve at the kick, these roofs had a relatively low pitch—too low for the use of tile as a finishing material, so these roofs were necessarily shingled. With the exception of roofs with a Dutch kick, roof overhangs were usually shallow, although in some areas, the roof extended beyond the eave line several feet, sometimes far enough to cover a porch. This feature was used most frequently in southern areas of Dutch influence, where snow did not accumulate as deeply as in more northern areas.

The hip roof borrowed from their British neighbors was sometimes used, but it was the gambrel roof, popular throughout the English and Dutch colonies after 1750, that later became associated with Dutch Colonial buildings. Although it was not a Dutch innovation, the gambrel roof facilitated an increase in roof span so it could be used on houses two rooms deep, which made the attic space more usable. Gambrel roofs were double-pitched, meaning that there were two slopes on each side of the ridge line. The upper slope had a pitch of about 30 degrees; the lower slope up to 45 degrees. Sometimes, lower-pitched gambrel roofs featured a Dutch kick. Dutch houses—especially in rural areas—featured a **stoep**, or covered entry porch, raised above the ground that often had a built-in bench on both sides. A pair of posts or columns supported the stoep roof. An alternative to the stoep was the **pentice**, an unsupported roof protecting the entry.

OPENINGS IN DUTCH COLONIAL BUILDINGS

Openings in Dutch houses were located where needed without regard to symmetry. Sometimes there was a single or double row of small lights across the top of the door opening, and late in the period, some openings were surmounted with curved relieving arches. Dutch houses were usually constructed with an exterior door from each room. The door itself was split horizontally, which allowed the upper section to be opened for light and air while the bottom section remained closed to keep children in and animals out. Often painted red, this style of door continued to be used even after the Dutch settlers began to build in the English style.

FIGURE 14.27 This Dutch kitchen has an enclosed cupboard beside the fireplace, possible because the fireplace did not project from the structure. The wood plank floor, wood dado, and exposed beams are typical.

Casement windows, or those that hinge from the side and open much like a door, were composed of small panes of glass held together in a frame by lead cames to form divided light windows. After 1715, sash windows that slide up and down were more common. Glass was the most frequently imported material for use in homes, and diamond-shaped lights were common. A type of window similar to the Dutch door was the **kloosterkozyn**, or a fixed window above a casement window. The lower portion of the window had a shutter, as did most windows to protect the glass when closed. **Shutter dogs** were decorative iron pieces that projected slightly and rotated to keep open shutters in place.

INTERIORS OF DUTCH COLONIAL BUILDINGS

Early Dutch houses had a single room, but three rooms arranged linearly quickly became common. The rooms were approximately equal in size and consisted of a kitchen, a bed chamber, and a **groote kamer**, or best room, used for reception of guests and entertaining. Early interior walls were whitewashed. Later, some board walls were painted bright blue. In addition to pictures and mirrors, everyday objects such as plates, bowls, and utensils hung on the walls serving as decoration when they were not in use. (See Figure 14.27.)

Fireplaces were constructed at one or both ends of the house. Unlike their English counterparts, fireplaces in Dutch homes had no sides or jambs and projected into the house rather than to

---

BOX 14.3 CHARACTERISTICS OF DUTCH COLONIAL BUILDINGS

- Extensive use of brick in a variety of patterns
- Owner's initials or date worked into brick pattern
- Coursed stone sometimes used up to eave with brick or wood gable
- Anchor bent construction
- Pantiles on roof
- Parapet wall at gable end with corbie-step finish
- Decorative iron ties on building exterior
- Roof overhang on side sometimes wide enough to cover a porch
- Stoep or pentice at entry
- Door divided horizontally
- Row of small windows over door opening
- Fireplace at end did not project from building

the exterior. Often there was no evidence of the position of a fireplace on the exterior of the house except where the chimney penetrated the roof. The fire was built on a hearth made of red terracotta tiles, and smoke ascended lazily to a chimney hood supported by the anchor bents above the ceiling. A valance hung from the anchor bent to keep smoke from entering the room. The wall behind the hearth was usually plastered and whitewashed, although in wealthier homes, imported Delft tiles in blue and white, or mulberry and white, covered it. (See Box 14.3.)

Dutch Colonial Furniture

Colonial furniture was either imported or patterned after furniture in the Netherlands and was typically Baroque in style. Few authentic Dutch Colonial furniture pieces survived. Dutch Colonial furniture was heavier than British models, with legs up to 4 inches wide. Gateleg tables had turned legs, and other tables had steeply splayed legs. Fiddleback and ladder-back chairs with woven rush seats were typical. Ball feet, club feet, and the bun foot were popular on Dutch furnishings.

The most important piece of furniture was the **kas**, a large upright chest with doors designed for storage of bedding and other textiles. The kas was often given to a bride before her wedding. Decoration was in the form of painting: a bride's kas was often ornamented with symbols associated with good fortune and fecundity. Door panels were frequently painted with flowers, fruit, and geometric forms, often in **grisaille**, or monochrome gray. Grisaille painting simulated the carving used on more elaborate European furniture. (See Figure 14.28.) The **wachseinlegen** technique was also used for decoration on Dutch furniture. In this seventeenth-century process, incised patterns were filled with a mixture of sulfur and wax or putty, resulting in yellow lines. The **Hackensack cupboard** was a two-piece cupboard consisting of a base with short legs or feet, a combination of drawers and doors with shelves behind, and a top section with shelves and glass doors. It was very similar to modern china cabinets.

INFLUENCE 14.7

The British later modified the interior of the kas, making it suitable for hanging clothing and called it the clothes press.

FIGURE 14.28 The kas was usually constructed in four sections. The entire piece was so large—up to 6 feet in width—that the kas was often sold rather than moved. Typically, there was a separate base raised on short brackets or ball feet. The second piece was a drawer unit that might have a single full-width drawer or a pair of side-by-side drawers. The main storage area was mounted on the drawer unit, closed with double doors, and had interior shelves or later, drawers. A separate cornice had a large overhang.

Cupboard beds, like those in the Netherlands, were often positioned permanently in a corner of a room and enclosed with doors or curtains for warmth and to keep out night air, which was thought to be harmful.

Wooden spoon boards, or **lepel borties**, hung on the wall and displayed spoons probably purchased or obtained as a gift when each child was born. Three ledges with cut slots held inserted spoon handles: 12 openings were typical. The back was usually formed with baroque curves. At the bottom, there were either shaped lobes or attached turnings. Spoon racks were decorated with chip carved geometric forms, birds, tulips and other stylized flowers, and wheels that represented the wheel of life or the wheel of fortune.

Spoon boards might be entirely painted or have only the carved design painted.

The Swedish in North America (1638–1655)

During the seventeenth century, Sweden was one of the major powers of Europe and included all of Finland and parts of Norway, Russia, and most of the countries surrounding the Baltic Sea. Sweden too was lured by the promise of obtaining fine furs inexpensively in North America, but the hoped-for wealth did not materialize because settlers had to compete with both the English and the Dutch for the furs.

Employing Peter Minuit, a former New Netherlands director-general, the New Sweden Company established Fort Christina (present-day Wilmington, Delaware) on the Delaware River in 1638 and subsequently other settlements along the river in Maryland, Pennsylvania, New Jersey, and Delaware. The colonists were mostly prisoners convicted of burn beating, a slash-and-burn technique for clearing forests, in Europe. By the end of these colonists' tenure in New Sweden, there were still fewer than 1,000 immigrants in New Sweden, and most of them were Finns. The Dutch West India Company considered the area settled by the Swedes its own, and in 1655, the Swedish lost their holdings to the Dutch.

Although New Sweden was short-lived, its influence lingered. The Scandinavians brought round, notched log construction techniques with them and built log cabins in their territory. The round logs were joined with interlocking notches, and the horizontal logs extended beyond the corners. Corner notching of the logs precluded the need for additional framework, and the use of logs was much less laborious than sawing planks for walls. An old tradition, log cabins had been constructed in Northern Russia, Germany, and Scandinavia since the Bronze Age. With large stands of timber, the materials were readily

available and could be easily worked with simple tools. However, log construction suffered from one significant problem. Green wood was necessarily used, and as the logs dried, they shrunk in width although little in length. This shrinkage resulted in gaps between logs and at the top of the walls, which had to be re-**chinked**, or filled with mud, periodically. Oiled paper covered the windows, allowing some light to penetrate, and a single door provided access.

The advantages of the log cabin building technique quickly became evident in North America: materials did not need to be carried long distances, and nails were unnecessary for construction. Until the nineteenth century, nails were made by hand and were so expensive that people moving from one area to another might burn down a house to obtain the nails. During the westward expansion in North America, the log cabin was quickly adopted for building in areas where timber was available. It was not until the railroad penetrated much of the west that logs were replaced by milled lumber.

INFLUENCE 14.8

During the nineteenth century, the president of the Adirondack Railroad, William Durant, suggested that urban dwellers escape the heat of the city during the summer by taking the train to camps in the Adirondack Mountains. Large, luxurious log cabins were constructed to serve as hotels. As the National Park system became established, many of the lodges associated with parks were also constructed using the log cabin technique.

It was also the Swedes who introduced the double-sloped gambrel roof to North America. The gambrel roof had a shallow upper slope and a steep lower slope. The shallow upper slope allowed sufficient head room beneath the roof for a living space. The Swedes' English neighbors adopted the gambrel roof and passed it on to the Dutch. (See Box 14.4.)

The Pennsylvania Germans in North America (1683–1800)

William Penn, who received the Penn's Woods land grant for Pennsylvania in 1681, was English but recruited colonists in the Palatinate region of Germany where Louis XIV's pillaging troops had forced many to flee their homes. Penn of-

---

BOX 14.4 CHARACTERISTICS OF SWEDISH COLONIAL BUILDINGS

- Round log cabin construction with log ends projecting at corners
- Corner notches on logs
- Some gambrel roofs

fered free land and religious freedom and members of a number of religious sects immigrated—Moravians, Mennonites, Amish, Quakers, and later, Lutherans. These German immigrants were less affluent than their English neighbors.

The people who settled parts of Pennsylvania west of Philadelphia were actually Germans, or *Deutsch,* not Dutch. The term Pennsylvania Dutch may be derived from the language they spoke or from a misinterpretation of the term Deutsch. By definition, the Pennsylvania Germans were those who came to Pennsylvania prior to 1800 and spoke a German language. Their first settlement in Pennsylvania was established in 1683, but most arrived between 1711 and 1750. Geographically, these German-speaking people settled in southeastern Pennsylvania but spread into neighboring areas of Maryland, West Virginia, Virginia, and North Carolina.

Pennsylvania Germans were similar to the Dutch. In Europe, Germany and the Netherlands adjoined one another and had many similarities. Other immigrants were from Alsace and Switzerland. Many of the Pennsylvania Germans were originally peasants in Europe and came to America as redemptioners, or people who had to work off the fare for their journey once they arrived. In America, they preferred to live on farms in rural areas rather than in cities and became self-reliant. Individuals were skilled in the practical arts,

making it unnecessary to depend on others for common products such as soap and textiles, or for specialized labor such as grinding grain or shoeing horses. Their consequent isolation resulted in little contact with the outside world.

PENNSYLVANIA GERMAN HOUSES

Some German immigrants constructed log cabins, but in contrast to those of the Swedes, German examples employed squared off logs; this required less chinking, or mud filling, between the logs. Other Pennsylvania German houses were constructed of fieldstone—freely available as they cleared fields for plowing. The German immigrants were skilled masons; even when using fieldstone construction, they used cut stone or brick for the perimeters of openings, and segmental brick or stone arches above them—distinctly German features. The owner's coat of arms or initials were carved into the stone lintels, worked into a brick pattern, or carved into a stone panel inset in the wall. Cut stone was used for construction, especially in urban areas—limestone in Eastern cities, green serpentine in Philadelphia, and soft "cotton" stone in the Midwest. As later additions were made, however, other materials such as clapboards might be used.

Unlike Dutch homes, Pennsylvania German homes were symmetrical, with a central entrance in the side-gabled structure. The chimney was

FIGURE 14.29 The German immigrants were skilled masons; even when using fieldstone construction, they used cut stone or brick for the perimeters of openings, and segmental brick or stone arches above them—distinctly German features.

usually centrally located, although when placed on an end wall, angled into a corner. Like Dutch doors, those of the Pennsylvania Germans were often divided horizontally. When made of a single piece, the door was visually divided by a horizontal shelf near the vertical center. (See Figure 14.29.)

The large families necessary to carry out agricultural activities required large homes. Most houses had two-and-a-half stories. The Germans

preferred sloping sites so the house appeared to be a single story and a half on the front. Often, the houses were built near or even over water sources. Streams channeled through the cellars made it easier to keep dairy products cool. Typically, there were three rooms on the first story: a kitchen (**kuche**); a stove room (**stube**), which housed a cast-iron heating stove and which was used for entertaining; and a room used as a bedroom or for other purposes. The second story housed bedrooms. The steeply pitched roofs often allowed two stories of attic space which might be pierced by shed-roofed or gabled dormers. (See Box 14.5.)

Motifs Used by Pennsylvania Germans

Pennsylvania German motifs were similar to those of the Dutch and were expressions of a simple, peaceful lifestyle. Birds, especially doves; pomegranates and other fruits; flowers, including tulips, often used in threes to symbolize the Trinity, lilies, and sunflowers; hearts that symbolized a welcoming, embracing heaven; and stars were favored. Geometric designs were also popular. Bright colors predominated such as red, yellow, pink, green, and blue. Painted or metal stars were frequently added to barns and were considered to bring good luck similar to that brought by hanging a horseshoe. It was the painted-star designs that were later viewed as hex signs that were rejected by some of the sects. Whether these designs actually had any symbolism has been debated for a number of years.

Pennsylvania German Furniture

Pennsylvania German furniture was utilitarian, provincial German furniture with straight lines, panel construction, simple turnings, and little ornamentation. Woods used included oak, pine, and black walnut—those native to the areas in which they lived. Some case furniture was painted, typically in a single color without additional decoration. Blue, red, yellow, green, and mottled brown were common. Important furniture pieces such as those that were used in the parlor might receive further decoration in the form of chip carving or stenciled or painted designs incorporating flowers, pomegranates and other fruits, birds, unicorns, or other motifs. Front panels of chests and other case furniture

FIGURE 14.30 The Moravian chair was a chair with a heart-shaped opening carved through the back.

frequently had split spindles and other moldings attached. The fronts of case furniture might be separated into panels during construction, or arched panels might be painted on later. Familiar Continental styling was retained for ordinary furniture, but the more formal English Chippendale style was adopted for desks, case clocks, and a few other pieces.

The chairs used were relatively simple models including the wainscot, the ladder back, and, later, the Windsor chair. Chair seats were sometimes upholstered, but leather and rush seats were common. Cabriole, straight, tapered, and turned legs were typical. The ball and bun feet were most often used. (See also Figure 14.30.)

Case furniture included the dower chest made by a bride's relative, which was more decorated than other furniture pieces. The **shonk**, called the shrank in Europe, was similar to the Dutch kas and was the most massive piece of furniture in most homes. It differed from the kas only in that it was made in three sections rather than four, with the feet attached to the drawer base. It was decorated with painted or wachseinlegen designs in the door panels. Like their Dutch neighbors, the Pennsylvania Germans had chip-carved spoon racks on their walls.

> **INFLUENCE 14.9**
> *The sawbuck table is the forerunner of the modern picnic table.*

Fraktur paintings were hung on walls and consisted of decorated documents such as birth or baptismal certificates or house blessings. Fraktur referred to broken or fractured writing similar to the illuminated manuscripts of the Medieval period. Brilliant colors were used to decorate these documents.

FIGURE 14.31 Sawbuck tables were typical, with X-shaped supports sometimes shaped into flat curves and connected with a center stretcher.

The British Are Coming

Life in colonial America was difficult, and immigrants needed a compelling reason to come and to stay. Many came, some not by choice, but many returned to Europe when conditions there became better. Those who came for riches were almost always disappointed. Those who came to Christianize the natives were destined to hardship and deprivation but sought their reward in a heavenly realm. It was those who came for religious freedom or to obtain land of their own and who expected and endured hardship that were most successful. The largest percentage of early immigrants did not come from Spain, France, the Netherlands, Scandinavia, or Germany, but from England, where overpopulation, lack of available land for ownership, and religious persecution combined to make immigration and long-term settlement desirable. As a consequence, by the eighteenth century, North America had become an essentially British enclave.

addition, England changed from an agricultural economy to one dependent on commerce, and as the wool industry began to dominant English commerce, farmers began to raise sheep rather than crops. The resultant rise in food prices and unemployment increased the number of debtors filling prisons and the number of beggars roaming the streets. The establishment of a colonial presence in America could help to alleviate some of the problems facing the English by creating new sources of raw materials, new markets for English products, and a home for the indigent and undesirable.

Yet another factor that furthered the desire to establish a colonial presence in the New World was the English law of primogeniture, which required that the eldest son inherit everything while younger sons received little, if anything. Land was equated with wealth and this practice prevented large land holdings from being subdivided and through generations reduced to the point that they could not support the owners' lifestyles.

EARLY ENGLISH SETTLEMENT

The early English attempts to plant American colonies for purposes of extracting wealth, for trade, or as a base for piracy against Spain were no more lasting than those of the Dutch and French, with few settlements becoming permanent. It was only when settlement became individually rather than politically inspired that more enduring colonies were established. The English government was often involved to the extent that it issued charters granting trading privileges and the right to settle and govern specific areas in the New World, but the funds came from private individuals, not the Crown. While the rights granted under English charters were extensive, there were some restrictions. Colonists must establish an Anglican Church, all goods for the first five years were to be kept in common, and certain portions of valuable commodities, such as gold, silver, and copper, were reserved for the English monarch. The restriction that was to cause the greatest dissatisfaction, however, was the dictate that the colonists could not trade with any nation other than England, and eventually even this was restricted to trade in English ships.

Had life in sixteenth-century England been peaceful and serene, the resulting colonization might have been much slower and less permanent, but unlike colonists from other nations many of the English colonists came with the express purpose of settling permanently.

The first English effort at settlement in the New World was instituted by Sir Walter Raleigh and his half-brother Sir Humphrey Gilbert, who sent colonists to what is now Roanoke, Virginia, in 1585 and again in 1587. In 1590, however, little trace of the colony could be found. In 1606, James I granted charters to the Virginia Company. In 1607, Jamestown, Virginia, was settled by the Virginia Company. That settlement remained the only successful English effort at colonization in America until 1620 when the Mayflower landed with 99 passengers,[1] but the accomplishments of these ventures and the troubles in England resulted in the establishment of other settlements relatively quickly. The location of natural harbors and navigable waterways was a significant factor in determining where settlements were to be established. The Hudson, Connecticut, Delaware, James, and Potomac Rivers provided access, either directly or indirectly, to the Atlantic and the immigrants first settled along these rivers and in coastal areas. Pennsylvania was the only one of the original colonies that had no seacoast. Philadelphia on the Delaware River, however, became a large port city.

EFFECTS OF RELIGION ON AMERICAN COLONIZATION

England remained in the throes of religious conflict for much of the seventeenth century affecting the rate of immigration. A third of those who came on the Mayflower were Puritans, and New Plymouth was established as a Puritan enclave. During the Protectorate (1649–1660) when the Puritans were in power, persecution of members of that group ceased and some who had already arrived in America returned to England. As political and religious differences in England reconciled during the Restoration, emigration from England slowed considerably. (See Figure 15.1.) In 1685 the Revocation of the Edict of Nantes stimulated emigration of French Protestants (Huguenots) to the Americas, most of whom settled in English colonies. Still, the larger immigration from England increased the percentage of English in the American colonies.

Although one of the major reasons for emigration from England during the early years of

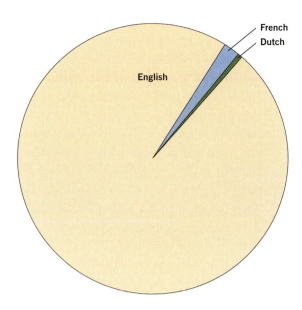

FIGURE 15.1 Shortly after the English began to establish colonies in North America (1625), they far outnumbered the French and Dutch; by 1650, less than 3 percent of the Europeans in North America were not English.[2]

settlement was to attain religious freedom, the colonies did not grant complete religious freedom to their members. In most of the colonies, all members had to pay taxes to help support the dominant church as had been the case in England. Most colonies had some anti-Catholic bias up until the Revolution, and there was often discrimination against radical Protestant sects such as Puritans and Quakers. Each of the religious groups represented, however, had at least one colony in which they could freely worship. William Penn advertised complete religious freedom to attract settlers and Mennonites and Lutherans, many from Germany, settled in Penn's Wood. By the middle of the eighteenth century, there were members of numerous religious groups in most of the colonies and the early biases were shifting to toleration.

DIFFERENCES IN THE COLONIES

Early settlers were from different social strata, religious backgrounds, and economic conditions. Because of where they settled, they encountered geographic and climatic conditions that further emphasized their lifestyle differences. In New England, settlers were largely from the literate middle class. The majority were farmers, yeomen, and artisans who immigrated along with their entire families. Some were motivated by religious intolerance, others by poor economic conditions in their homelands.

These immigrants sought sufficient land to cultivate crops, raise livestock, and build homes. In New England, the land was hilly and rocky, a topography conducive to the establishment of small land holdings, self-sufficient farms, and small villages. Neither was the short summer season conducive to large-scale agricultural pursuits.

Tall timbers suitable for ships' masts as well as other materials necessary for the construction of ships allowed some to pursue fishing or ship building, and fur trading remained a profitable venture. Mountains were close to the sea in the North, with rivers furnishing abundant waterpower for manufacturing; by the middle of the seventeenth century, urban areas began to build up in these locations.

In the colonial South,[3] numerous navigable rivers facilitated the movement of goods and materials. Large open areas of fertile land, longer growing seasons, relatively level ground, and plenty of rainfall were ideal for vast land grants for younger sons of English nobility to establish large plantations. Other immigrants to the South included gentlemen, farmers, and some artisans. Many of the immigrants in the South had no quarrel with the Anglican Church, remained loyal to the English monarchy, and retained as much culture and luxury as possible. Clothing, furniture, rugs, and other goods were imported from England, requiring that little be manufactured in that region.

By 1700, the wilderness conditions originally intimidating to settlers had been tamed and America was not just a land of opportunity for brave, robust individuals but for those with less hardy appetites. Cities had been created, an economic base that included manufacturing was well established, and jobs were plentiful. As the standard of living increased, expert artisans immigrated and colonists were able to obtain fashionable goods without the necessity and expense of importing them. During the early eighteenth century, numerous factories were established, especially in the North, expanding job opportunities and immigration.

From the beginning, English colonies were peopled by those from a number of nations as well as by those of varying religious and economic backgrounds. The melting pot that was America created a mixture of design for a century or more with each group influencing others in a variety of ways.

Architecture in English Colonial Areas in the Americas

Not surprisingly, early buildings in the North were adaptations of middle-class domestic structures common in England. Most were late Elizabethan and Jacobean half-timbered wattle and daub structures with thatched roofs. Houses were small and had few furnishings. Renaissance structures had just begun to appear in England in the early seventeenth century, and the yeoman farmers who settled in New England were unfamiliar with the classical forms employed. As a result, classicism was rare, especially in New England, until the end of the seventeenth century.

The Middle Colonies—now New York, New Jersey, Pennsylvania, and Delaware—were first settled by the Dutch and Swedish, but during the latter part of the seventeenth and into the eighteenth century, large numbers of immigrants from several other European nations settled in these areas. The resulting religious, ethnic, economic, and political diversity was reflected in their buildings. English immigrants employed timber frame construction. German and Welsh settlers generally ignored the large supplies of timber and constructed homes using cut stone, as they had in their homelands, and the Scots and Irish typically built log homes. It was, however, English fashions that predominated, although the English did adopt gambrel roofs and elaborate brickwork patterns from their neighbors.

Early homes in the South were also constructed of wood, although they were larger and more fashionable than typical homes in the North, reflecting the social stature of the more privileged class. The size of the land grants dictated that neighbors would be located at some distance, requiring large homes to house servants and, later, slaves, as well as visitors. Life centered around the plantation, and few urban centers developed until after the Revolution. It was in the South that classical forms first appeared in the colonies. In New England, civic, commercial, and ecclesiastical buildings were constructed in more fashionable styles earlier than were domestic buildings, but it was only in the last quarter of the seventeenth century that style became important. Even then, colonial buildings were modest in scale and lacked the time-consuming finishes and fine detailing found in European examples.

EFFECTS OF CLIMATE ON STRUCTURES

Unlike the mild climate of England, New England suffered from extremes of temperature, extensive snow and ice, thunderstorms, and high winds. Although large timbers, frequently 10 inches or more across, were used for the framework, the expansion and contraction of daub resulting from freezing and thawing required constant repair. A more adaptable building form was needed.

Unlike in England, wood was abundant in America and, in order for the land to be cleared for agriculture, had to be cut. The colonists began to protect the wattle and daub by covering it either with weatherboards or clapboard. **Weatherboards** were sawn, had the same thickness throughout, and were laborious and time-consuming to produce. The bottom edge of each board was rabbeted and fit over the board beneath it. Later, these joints became more pronounced and often featured bead moldings. The use of **clapboard** was more common. Made of riven timber, clapboards were wider at one side than the other and feathered out to a narrow edge, which was then overlapped by a succeeding row. (See Figure 15.2.) Later, wattle and daub was abandoned altogether and structures were built entirely of wood.

FIGURE 15.2 The exterior covering was usually left unpainted and weathered to a gray color, but some buildings were painted in earth tones. On this reproduction of an early colonial building at Plimouth Plantation, vertical weatherboards cover the walls and clapboards protect the gable.

┌ INFLUENCE 15.1

The clapboard used by the colonists was the forerunner of today's siding.

The torrential rains and heavy snows of New England made thatched roofs unsuitable for the American climate. Moreover, because of the danger of fire, early laws forbade the use of thatch roofs. Hand-hewn riven wood shingles (today called shakes) were substituted, but the steep roof pitched required by thatch remained.

> **INFLUENCE 15.2**
>
> *Wall shingles were not used in Europe and were a later American innovation derived from early riven roof shingles. Wall shingles have remained common to the present.*

The development of the chimney made it possible to close off the attic space, and the loft could be used for storage or sleeping. The addition of windows in the gable ends and sometimes fenestrated shed-roofed dormers on the sides provided light to the attic area. Common in colonial garrets was the lie-on-your-stomach window, so termed because it was located just above the attic floor. New England houses remained compact to retain heat, and when larger homes were needed, rather than spreading the plan out, a second story was constructed so that heat rising from the fireplace warmed the upper floor. Unlike their European counterparts, New England colonial homes often had a cellar beneath at least part of the building that was accessed from outside or later from under the stairs to a second story.

In the first single-room houses, the fireplace and chimney were necessarily placed on an exterior wall. In the North, where the extremely cold climate made it desirable, when houses were enlarged, a room was located on the opposite side of the fireplace so that heat ordinarily lost to the outside could be conserved. In the north, then, there was usually a single chimney located in the center of the house that might serve two or more fireplaces. In the South, fireplaces continued to be located on exterior walls so that the heat from cooking fires would dissipate outdoors. There, fireplaces were typically located at both ends of the building, and later when houses were two rooms deep, there were often double chimneys at each end.

Materials

Although wood was the most prevalent building material, other locally available materials were also used for construction. The scarceness of lime in New England, except along the seashore where shells could be ground for use in mortar, made brick and stone houses rare in New England. Foundations were made of mortarless fieldstone rather than cut stone to save labor and decrease cost. In Rhode Island, stone-enders were a regional variation that employed stone in association with a fireplace on an end wall. Stone houses predominated in Pennsylvania and along the Hudson River Valley, where stone was plentiful, lime was available, and colonists were often more familiar with this type of construction at home.

When the colonists first arrived in America, brick had only just begun to be used on unpretentious structures in England and was therefore not as familiar to the yeomanry as was timber construction. Although some handmade brick was used, the material was infrequently employed in English buildings of the North. In addition, the price of brick reflected the high cost of transporting it via land routes. Manufactured brick was more prevalent in the Middle Atlantic areas and in the South, where navigable rivers made transportation less expensive; where natural stone was scarce; where lime was available for mortar; where the clay was more suitable for making bricks, and where settlers were often of the upper classes and were more familiar with brick construction at home. (See Figure 15.3.)

Domestic Plans

The earliest colonial American **hall house**, sometimes called a "half house," had a single room with a fireplace and chimney at one end and sometimes a loft. Like the great hall of medieval buildings, this room housed all the activities of the family—cooking, eating, working, and sleeping. The loft might be used for storage or, because the number of occupants often reached ten or more, for extra sleeping space. As wilderness conditions began to be tamed and colonists could afford it, a parlor was added, resulting in the **hall and parlor** house. The hall remained the main living area. The parlor was the room in which guests were entertained, where funerals and weddings occurred, and where the head of the household slept. It was there that the best furnishings were kept. If the household had a cupboard, it was located in the parlor in order to more visibly display the accoutrements of wealth. In New England, the hall and parlor house had a small entry area that abutted the central chimney and sometimes steep

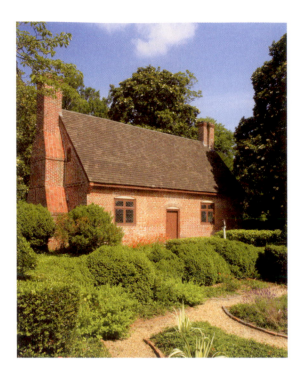

stairs leading to the loft. The hall and parlor plan was the most common by the middle of the seventeenth century. (See Box 15.1.)

In colonial buildings, the masonry of central fireplaces and chimneys helped to support the framework. One or more large beams, known as **summer beams**, rested on the chimney at one end with the other end supported by an exterior wall. Ceiling or floor joists ran perpendicular to the summer beam and were supported by it. Often a single masonry unit had fireplaces in as many as four rooms.

As the need arose and finances allowed, these early buildings were expanded. As in the common homes of England, added spaces resulted in irregular, asymmetrical plans and the changes were generally visible from the exterior. The additions were usually smaller in size than the original structure and might have lower rooflines and ceilings. (See Figures 15.4 and 15.5.)

By the eighteenth century, the typical home included a parlor, a hall, one or more bedrooms, and sometimes a separate kitchen with a pantry or buttery. In the North, rooms were massed around one or more interior chimneys, resulting in houses that were two rooms deep. When the house was one-and-a-half or two stories, sleeping areas were upstairs.

NEW ENGLAND COLONIAL HOUSES

The same artisans who constructed furniture and ships built early colonial homes and there was no difference in the style. It was only later that furniture and housing styles changed at different rates. By 1700, when the wilderness conditions had been somewhat tamed and the settlers became more economically secure, English architectural forms began to be introduced and the colonists were able to have luxuries and comforts required for polite living. New immigrants brought with them the knowledge of the new styles, governors appointed by the Crown wanted their residences to be of the latest style to reflect their importance and their position, and books on architecture were circulated. As book designs began to spread, there was increasing similarity in styles regardless of the cultural background of the area. The time lag between the develop-

ment of English styles and their use in America became approximately the same as for provincial areas in England.

Several structural forms of English colonial homes have developed into well-known individual styles of their own. These are widely recognized because of their distinctive characteristics and, in modified form, have been used for many homes built since the 1920s. These styles are familiarly known as the Cape Cod, the Saltbox, and the Garrison. All were side-facing structures, even in urban areas, because land was plentiful. Those sited near water, especially that which served as a transportation route, often had the rear or side facing a road while the front of the structure faced the water.

THE CAPE COD HOUSE (1690–1800)

The Cape Cod house was a small story-and-a-half dwelling that had a steeply pitched gable roof with a low central chimney. These symmetrical houses had a centered entry and one or two windows on either side of the door. Windows in the gable ends provided light for the attic and modern examples usually have dormers. There was little

FIGURE 15.5 As houses increased in size, wall gables, overhangs, dormers, and complex rooflines made later New England colonial homes visually complex. Door and window trim also increased in complexity as residents became more prosperous. The Turner House, better known as the House of Seven Gables, in Salem, Massachusetts, was originally a two-room, two-and-a-half story house. Notice the drops on the jetty above the door.

roof overhang or exterior decoration to resist coastal winds. Like other houses, the Cape Cod began as a hall house, became a hall and parlor house, and later became two rooms deep with a sleeping loft in the attic. In the southern colonies,

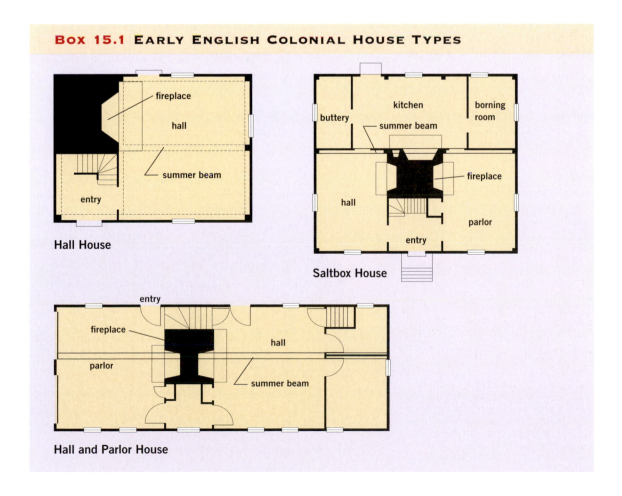

BOX 15.1 EARLY ENGLISH COLONIAL HOUSE TYPES

Hall House

Saltbox House

Hall and Parlor House

where masonry construction was common, the Cape Cod house was constructed of brick and the chimneys were placed on the ends.

The Cape Ann house was a variation of the Cape Cod style that originated in a specific area of Massachusetts. It had the same features as the Cape Cod house except for its gambrel roof, which provided more living space in the attic. Occasionally, a **rainbow roof** with a slight outward curve was built.

THE SALTBOX HOUSE (1620–1700)

The Saltbox house was common in England by the end of the sixteenth century and was named because its shape resembled that of the box used to store salt. Originally, the saltbox house was a hall and parlor house one room deep. Its distinctive feature was a lean-to addition on the back of the house over which the side-gabled roof extended. When possible, this addition was on the north side of the house to provide a buffer from the predominant winter winds. The addition housed a central kitchen flanked by a **borning room,** or nursery; buttery; and sometimes a staircase. The kitchen fireplace was located adjacent to the existing one forming a T-shaped chimney. (See Figure 15.6.)

Saltbox houses were symmetrical and had a central entry with an equal number of windows flanking the door on both sides. Often there were no windows in the rear of the house. Openings were simply trimmed using plain boards, and exterior corners were trimmed with vertical boards against which the siding abutted. Doors often had six panels or, on less pretentious houses, were board and batten. By 1720, other additions were constructed to house animals or extra bedrooms. Generally, these additions projected at the sides of the house and had shed roofs. The **outshot house** had additions that resulted in an L-shaped plan.

THE GARRISON HOUSE (1660–1700)

The Garrison colonial house was common in Connecticut and Massachusetts, where settlers had been familiar with the Elizabethan style in England. From the Elizabethan house, the Garrison derived the second-story overhang, or jetty, up to 2 feet in depth on the front that provided some protection for the entry and increased the living area on the second floor. Some Garrison houses had an additional jetty at the eave line. Occasionally, gables were also given jetties. In early Garrison homes, vertical structural members at the corners and along the width of the structure extended downward to form a **drop,** or decorative pendant, that was often carved in the form of a pineapple or acorn. Four drops were typical. In later Garrison examples, the structural members did not extend beneath the overhang and the drops were attachments.

FIGURE 15.6 Before 1680, the roof of the saltbox addition had a lower pitch than did the main roof to allow for headroom in the kitchen even though the ceiling height was lower in that room. This resulted in a change in the roof pitch that was obvious on the exterior as in the Scotch-Boardman House in Saugus, Massachusetts. Later, houses were initially constructed with the rear projection and the roof maintained a single slope, although one side of the roof remained longer than the other. In the south, this type of roof was known as a catslide roof. Note also the jetty on the front of the house.

The Garrison house sometimes used the same floor plan as the saltbox house, and indeed there are examples of Garrison houses with and without the saltbox roofline. Other examples were hall and parlor houses with two bedrooms on the second story—similar to the I-house. The symmetrical two or two-and-a-half story side-gabled buildings had a central entry with windows ranged on both sides. Second-story windows were located above those on the first floor but were typically smaller. Dormers might pierce the roof to provide light in the attic space.

DIFFERENCES BETWEEN EARLY NORTHERN AND SOUTHERN HOMES

Homes in the South and Middle Atlantic followed the same plans and styles as did those in the North. Differences were in the materials used in detailing and in adjustments for the climate. The soil in the Tidewater area, for example, was relatively damp, requiring that brick or stone be used where the building met the ground rather than the timber sills used in drier areas. Even early in the seventeenth century, Southern homes employed more fashionable segmental or flat brick arches over openings—a detail not feasible with the timber construction in the North. In addition to being located on the ends of houses, fireplaces in the South were constructed outside the building rather than projecting inside, as did those in the North, allowing more heat to dissipate outdoors. Brick chimneys were ornate and featured decorative brick work and medieval horizontal projections, or **necks**, near the top. Southern homes were more likely to employ dormers in the attic spaces because the garret was typically used for sleeping rather than storage.

By 1670 in the South, separate summer kitchens were often added with a walkway between the house and the kitchen, precluding the need for a cooking fire in the house. This structure was only a short distance away and typically connected by a covered passageway to the main house called a **curtain** if it was enclosed with walls and a **colonnade** if it was left open. Typically, Southern homes also had a separate exterior entrance to each bedroom on the first floor. By the mid-seventeenth century, Southern homes were also designed using the central plan with four rooms on the first story, two on each side of the central hallway where the stairs were located.

The **cross house** was the first version of what became the Southern manor house and was a combination of the central hall plan and the cruciform plan used for churches. Projecting wings or towers were centered on the front, rear, or both. On the front, the wing housed an entry (and infrequently a stairway) with a bedroom above.

Unless situated on a waterway, Southern homes faced the prevailing summer breeze and were located on top of a hill to maximize the exchange of air inside the house during hot weather. Near the end of the seventeenth century, Huguenots who had immigrated into Carolina began to construct homes that were a single room deep with floor to ceiling windows to encourage cross-ventilation. These homes had south-facing full-width covered porches—features copied from the West Indies that provided shade for the walls and cooling for air before it entered the building.

INFLUENCE 15.5

The West-Indian–inspired Southern building became the typical plantation home during the eighteenth century.

In the Middle Atlantic areas, homes of the wealthy might have a cross plan and curvilinear Flemish parapet walls at the gable ends.

NONRESIDENTIAL ARCHITECTURE

There were few nonresidential buildings in seventeenth-century America. Churches, meeting houses, and taverns resembled domestic buildings in scale and style. In New England, public buildings were arranged around a central green space with domestic structures close by.

In the Puritan enclave of Plymouth, the fort and meeting house were combined with a space on the flat roof for cannons and an assembly area in the lower section. There was no precedent for the Puritan meeting house. Because their form of worship differed significantly from that of the Church of England or the Catholic Church, traditional church structures were unsuitable for Puritan services. The major difference was the focal point around which services revolved. In traditional European churches, that point was the altar that was associated with the sometimes-mystical rituals of the high church such as communion. Puritan meeting houses placed importance on the sermon that took place from the pulpit. It was the pulpit, then, that supplanted the

FIGURE 15.7 The Old Ship Church in Hingham, Massachusetts, begun in 1681 served not only as a meetinghouse for religious services but for town meetings. Meetinghouses also served as schools. During the early part of the eighteenth century, the structure was enlarged in the then-current Georgian style.

altar in the important position opposite the door and that the benches faced. (See Figure 15.7.)

INFLUENCE 15.6

From the colonial period on, most American Protestant churches have been arranged as was the Puritan meetinghouse.

Anglican churches throughout the colonies were based on English models with a long nave, an entrance on the west end facing the altar lo-

cated near the east end, and a railing or step to separate worshippers from the more sacred area. (See Box 15.2 for a summary of characteristics of English colonial buildings in America.)

OPENINGS

Colonial windows were placed nearest the exterior wall surface, resulting in a deep interior reveal. They were generally centered on the interior walls of front-facing rooms; thus, when rooms were of unequal size, the windows were asymmetrical on the exterior. In later examples, windows followed English trends and were symmetrically sited on the exterior. In the South, windows were frequently located across from one another to maximize airflow through the structure.

At first, the few windows used were simple openings. Oiled paper, cloth, or sometimes horn filled the fixed or casement sashes and, later, glass or isinglass panels. Glass, however, had to be imported from England and was very expensive. The small lights were separated by lead cames into rectangular or diamond-shaped panes as was typical of English Jacobean architecture. By 1715, the double-hung sash window was introduced and quickly replaced earlier types. The first double-hung windows had either 9 over 9 or 12 over 12 lights. A technological innovation c. 1700 made it possible to make larger panes of glass, and 6 over 6 lights became more common by the middle of the eighteenth century.

As with windows, doors were located for convenience in the earliest homes but later, the centrally located door became more common. Early English colonial doors were board and batten and were hung on strap hinges. Panel doors became fashionable late in the period but were more expensive and were only employed in homes of the more affluent.

Interiors of English Colonial Buildings in the Americas

Before 1650, the earth served as a floor, although occasionally a stone floor was laid. Later, random-width wood planks, sometimes as wide as 36 inches were pegged to joists.

Although the timber framing members were covered on the exterior, they remained exposed on the interior and were typically chamfered or carved. Spaces between the timbers were plastered or covered with vertical boards, resulting in a palisade wall. Where lime for plaster was scarce,

---

Box 15.2 CHARACTERISTICS OF ENGLISH COLONIAL ARCHITECTURE IN AMERICA

- Adaptations of English Renaissance buildings
- Few civic or commercial structures during early part of period
- Diversity of forms reflecting varying ethnic groups who settled
- Typically timber construction, at first with wattle and daub
- Where lime available, stone or brick used
- Summer beams supported second-story floor
- Overhanging jetties on some buildings
- Weatherboard and clapboard finishes
- Compact with central fireplace in Northern homes
- Cellars under homes in North
- Homes more fashionable, larger, and with end fireplaces in South
- Homes developed from single rooms to more complex plans over time

FIGURE 15.8 Single board-and-batten casement shutters, designed to be functional rather than decorative, protected windows. Board-and-batten units were constructed of a layer of vertical boards attached to horizontal boards at the top and bottom—sometimes one or two additional horizontal boards spaced along the vertical axis, and usually a diagonal board resulting in a Z-shape.

often only the fireplace wall was plastered. Oak was the most common wood used for palisade walls until the eighteenth century, when pine became more common. Because green wood was used, shrinkage occurred as the wood dried, resulting in cracks between the planks. This problem was solved by the use of tongue-and-groove

joints. Like exterior surfaces, interior wood was allowed to age without additional finishes. Pine had a tendency to become slightly reddish in color as it aged, creating interiors with a relatively dark warm tone. In the South, where plaster was more common, most walls were plastered and then whitewashed. In Rhode Island, painted faux-marble designs were popular on paneling. More affluent homes might feature textiles and, later, wallpaper on walls.

Fireplaces were often sufficiently large enough to walk into them, and they dominated rooms. They were used not only for cooking and heat but for light. No mantels decorated early fireplaces, but there was frequently a lintel at the top of the opening. Mantels ornamented with bolection moldings began to appear late in the seventeenth century. Where the fireplace projected into a room, cupboards or closets were built into the niches beside them. (See Figure 15.9.)

Ceilings were low, about 7 feet in height, beams were exposed and sometimes painted, and the roof planks could be seen on the inside between the beams and rafters. In the South, plaster was sometimes used between the ceiling beams, and by the end of the seventeenth century, the beams themselves were plastered.

FIGURE 15.9 When the fashions of the Restoration period in England arrived in America, walls—especially fireplace walls—began to be paneled as they were in England using rectangular shapes framed by moldings. Typically, this paneling was also left unfinished, although Indian red was a popular color when it was painted. Here, the large summer beam can be seen along with the perpendicular joists it supports.

Highly saturated colors were used for textiles and on painted furniture, but little thought was given to matching or coordinating colors within individual spaces. The few carpets were so valuable that they covered cupboards or tables rather than floors adding additional color at various levels throughout the room.

American Jacobean Furniture

Homes were small and furniture was generally limited to essential pieces even in homes of the affluent. Few furnishings were brought by the original colonists, and it was not until about 1640 that furniture construction in America began. Early American-built furniture was based on English Elizabethan and Jacobean models, although the proportions were different, details were less refined, and the pieces were simplified. As with any provincial furniture, new designs were introduced in America several years after their appearance in England. Time lags of up to 20 years were typical in the North, where the colonists were conservative. In the South where the colonists were often more affluent, fashionable pieces were more quickly adopted. Jacobean furniture continued to be used in settled areas until the middle of the seventeenth century and, due to their simple forms, on the frontiers into the eighteenth century.

Most new furniture was either copied from the little furniture brought with the colonists or made from memory. Unlike England, America had no guild system to regulate crafts, although apprenticeships were common. Furniture varied according to the skill of the joiner and to regional preferences. In Puritan areas, sumptuary laws limited ornament on furniture to simple forms. In areas populated by Anglicans, more elaborate ornamentation was common. Jacobean forms were made with stile, rail, and panel construction and employed the mortise-and-tenon joint. It was not until c. 1680 that cabinetmaking techniques began to appear in America with more intricate joints, inlay, and veneering.

Much of the early furniture was painted or stained, a less time-consuming method of decoration, although even carved pieces were highlighted with paint. Painted designs were similar to carved ones with the addition of arabesques, diaper patterns, and simulation of the expensive marquetry of Europe. Painting also had the advantage of concealing the differences in the vari-

ous woods used for construction. Natural materials were used for stains, and paint pigments were imported from England. Black, verdigris (blue-green), Indian red, and Spanish brown were used during the early years, with verdigris most common. Later, yellow and green were added. Painting replaced carved decoration by 1700 and remained common until c. 1820.

Applied decoration became common after the mid-seventeenth century. This type of decoration was introduced to Europe by the Moors in Spain, carried to the Spanish Netherlands, and with the added influences of the Dutch and Flemish, finally arrived in England and America. Called **jewel work** in America, it consisted of turnings, applied split spindles, and round or oval turtle-back bosses mounted diagonally. Much of the applied decoration was **ebonized**, or treated to give it the appearance of ebony.

Loose cushions improved comfort and were made of varying materials. Imported silks covered cushions in Southern homes but most cushions were decorated with **stumpwork**, **turkey work**, or needlepoint. Stumpwork was a type of raised appliqué needlework that was most frequently used around mirrors and to decorate boxes. Turkey work was a relatively crude type of needlework that employed designs based on those of carpets imported from the Near East. Wool yarn formed a pile on a coarsely woven textile base. Turkey work, however, was less common in America than it was in England. When upholstery began to be used, the material of choice was Russian leather, which was tanned with birch oil rather than with tannin from oak. The upholstery was attached to furniture with exposed brass-headed nails, usually with four-angled sides forming a small pyramid.

The furniture used in the main hall included seating units, tables for eating, cupboards, shelves, chests, and small boxes. Once the parlor began to be used, it not only housed other seating units and cupboards but the best bed. Bedrooms generally included several beds for members of the large families. Because the rooms were small, furniture was frequently multifunctional. By 1700, even English court furniture was made in the colonies, furniture was lighter in weight and in appearance, turnings were more complex, chair backs were raked, flat carved stretchers replaced turned ones, and metal drawer pulls were used.

CHESTS

Jacobean furniture included a variety of chests, which was the most common furniture form. Their flat tops could be used for seating, as tables, and even for sleeping. The dower chest continued to be used and was identified by the initials of the couple. Typically, dower chests were decorated with flowers, and arabesques.

American chest frames differed from English examples in that American chests had chamfered edges and the edges of the lid were finished with a thumbnail molding. Chests were made with stile, rail, and panel construction. The lids were hinged at the back and made of a solid plank. Early chests were raised above the floor on extensions of the corner stiles. Later, ball feet were used.

The basic Jacobean chest form was the mule or blanket chest—a late sixteenth-century English type. A hinged lid provided access to the largest storage compartment under which was a single full-width drawer, two full-width drawers, a pair of side-by-side drawers, or a combination of these. By the late seventeenth century, other features differentiated among the types of mule chests in America.

The Connecticut sunflower chest (1675–1720), for example, had three vertical recessed panels across the front. The name was derived from the triple sunflower motif carved or painted on the center panel. (See Figure 15.10.)

The Hadley chest also featured three front panels with drawers beneath. It differed from the Connecticut chest only in its decoration. Simple flowers and foliage were carved in low relief and highlighted with paint or stain in an all-over pattern. Tulips were the most common flower used and typically had two petals. Unlike the Connecticut sunflower chest, carving was not limited to the panels but meandered over the entire front surface. No applied decorations were used on the Hadley chest.

The Ipswich chest also had three front panels and added two plain panels on each side. Although some chests had plain front panels, most featured carved arcades, lunettes, or bands of roses. Arcades usually enclosed either lozenge-shaped medallions or foliage palmettes. Two types were made: one featuring identical front panels and one with a central foliage-decorated panel that was flanked by panels decorated with tulips. Occasionally, the top of the Ipswich chest had four recessed panels more typical of English chests.

The chest on frame was a short-lived Jacobean furniture form that featured longer legs to raise the chest and make drawer use more convenient. Although rare examples appeared in New England by the middle of the seventeenth century, it was not until the dawn of the eighteenth century that the chest of drawers began to replace other chest forms, and even then the popularity of the William and Mary highboy retarded its development. Chests of drawers were taller than mule chests and the top was fixed, permitting small objects to be displayed on it.

FIGURE 15.10 Jewel work ornamentation on this Connecticut sunflower chest is evident. Ebonized split spindles ornamented the stiles between panels and handles for the one or two full-width drawers are diagonally placed wooden ovals.

INFLUENCE 15.7

The chest on frame later developed into the highboy of the William and Mary period.

FIGURE 15.11 The Guilford chest had no front panels, no carving, and no split spindles. Painted flowers and curvilinear designs reflected both Dutch and English antecedents with tulips, thistles, and roses predominating. The Taunton chest differed from the Guilford chest only in that it employed birds in the decoration.

OTHER STORAGE FURNITURE

The cupboard evolved from the medieval shelving unit used to display plate. American versions were a blend of English and Flemish designs. Cupboards were large in scale, making them less portable than other furnishings. Because it was used to display the trappings of wealth such as porcelain from the Orient, silver, and pewter, the cupboard was the most highly decorated piece of furniture in a home. It was usually ornately carved and bright textiles or cushions were used on top. Large bosses, spindles, and dark paint against light-colored woods gave these rectilinear forms interest and importance.

The English court cupboard was used in America during the last quarter of the seventeenth century. The early court cupboard used in America had three open shelves with separate turned supports for each layer. The design of the supports, however, might differ on each layer. The cupboard was raised slightly above the floor on short squared feet. Americans also used the aumbry with two tiers of open shelving at the bottom for storage or display and a top section that was closed by doors. The press cupboard, also known as the hall cupboard, was in vogue during the last quarter of the seventeenth century and was used for display as well as storage. Derived from the Dutch kast, it usually stored clothing. Two tiers included an upper enclosed section that was recessed slightly away from the front of the lower section, leaving a small shelf. The upper section was divided into three separate compartments closed by doors and often the flanking compartments were angled backward widening the shelf at the sides. The lower section consisted of either a set of drawers or a shelf. A decorative cornice at the top was supported by a pair of carved columns or colonnettes, which later evolved into drops. The press cupboard was elaborately carved and had applied decoration in the form of split spindles and bosses. Sometimes, the press cupboard housed a bed.

The Bible box, also called a desk box or writing box, continued to be used for important papers and books. Later, a framework was made to support the box, and it quickly evolved into a desk.

The wall cupboard was small, hung on a wall, and closed with a door. Sometimes there was a shelf beneath the cabinet and usually the top of the cupboard was ornamented with molding. The spice box or spice chest was a small cabinet designed to sit on a surface. A lockable door concealed numerous small drawers that stored spices and small items. The saltbox was a small box that hung on the wall, had a slanted hinged top, and was used to store salt.

STOOLS

As in England, the usual seat was the joint stool, which was used through the seventeenth century. While most chairs had a 16- to 18-inch seat height, stools were approximately 2 feet in height, making them suitable for use at the higher dining tables of the period. An oblong top with slightly rounded edges about 18 inches wide was attached above a four-sided apron supported by four turned legs. Legs, often splayed for greater stability, were connected with a box stretcher slightly above the feet and terminated either in ball feet or small knobs.

The medieval form, or bench, continued to be used especially for dining at trestle tables. Splayed legs were common. By the eighteenth century, the increasing number of chairs anticipated the demise of the joint stool and form.

CHAIRS

In the seventeenth century, chairs were less common than stools and armchairs, called great or elbow chairs, were rare. Jacobean chair types used in America included the back stool; the wainscot chair; the turned, or thrown, chair; and the Cromwell chair. The space-saving **chair table**, called a monk's chair in England, was also used. (See Box 15.3 for various chair types.)

The triangular back stool, used for a short period immediately after the middle of the seventeenth century (1650–1670), was a medieval furniture form found in most homes. It had a triangular wood seat supported by three legs connected with stretchers. One leg extended upward to make a crude back, there was usually a crosspiece at shoulder level, and some examples had shaped arms.

Like their English counterparts, colonial wainscot chairs were architectural in nature and were derived from the wainscot on walls featuring wood panels framed by stiles and rails. Like the wall treatment, the wainscot chair was expensive and relatively rare. As a consequence, it was always used as a seat of honor. The wood seat was rectangular, slightly overhung the sides and front, and had molded edges. A cushion was usually used to improve comfort. Later wainscot chairs retained the panel back but it usually had a seat-back angle greater than 90 degrees. Rather than being paneled to the floor on all sides, these chairs had separate arms and legs. The seat rail sometimes had a geometric low-relief carved design. The arms were shaped and curved downward at the ends and were supported by a continuation of the front legs. The front legs were turned, but the back legs, which extended upward to support the back were square. The crest rail at shoulder level was either straight and plain, shaped, or carved in low relief or with an arcade.

The height of the back of a wainscot chair was an indication of the status of the owner. Sometimes finials were added to the back supports to further increase height. The panel itself was elaborately carved, although American panels were less ornate than those in England. Geometric forms, strapwork, initials, and dates were common designs used on wainscot chairs. A few examples have plain panels.

There were several types of turned chairs, also called thrown chairs. These were the most common type of chair in America and retained their popularity even as furniture styles changed. Some were armchairs. Thrown chairs had turned uprights that were approximately twice the diameter of the turned stretchers. The back legs extended upward to support the back, resulting in a 90-degree seat-back angle. Both the Brewster and Carver chairs were of this type.

The Brewster chair was named for William Brewster the Elder (1567–1644), the religious leader of the Plymouth colony, who may have brought one with him on the Mayflower. The chair was relatively crude and heavy, and its front legs extended above the arms. All four of the supports ended in a finial shaped like a ball or an urn. The crest rail and arms were also turned. Vertical spindles were located in a number of places on the Brewster chair: between the arms and the seat and sometimes an additional row beneath the arm on each side that extended from beneath the seat to the stretcher, which was often doubled. On the back, there was a double row of spindles between the stay and crest rails. Some examples had a single or double row of spindles beneath the seat across the front as well. The seat was typically made of rush (called **flag** in America).

The Carver chair, named for John Carver (1571–1621), the first governor of Plymouth colony, was also probably imported from England. In New England, all four legs terminated in a finial

Box 15.3 English Colonial American Chair Types

Wainscot chair

Brewster chair

Carver chair

Ladder back chair

and the front legs extended above the. In the South the front legs of Carver chairs ended beneath the turned arms and had no finials. Later examples in both areas lacked arms. The back had a single row of vertical spindles—fewer than those on a Brewster chair—and, infrequently, a row of vertical spindles beneath the arms. A single stretcher joined the back legs but other stretchers were doubled. The seat was either a wooden plank or was made of rush.

The Cromwell chair (1660–1700) predated the reign of Oliver Cromwell. It was derived from the medieval English farthingale chair, but the seat was lower and wider. The low back was supported by the extended squared back legs. The open space between the seat and back was filled with a large cushion. The armless Cromwell chair was distinguished by its upholstered seat and back padded with grass or wool. The leather, turkey work, or other textiles used for upholstery covered the seat rails and was attached with brass-headed nails that were made by hand until late in the eighteenth century. Front legs were turned, occasionally in spiral forms, typically in New York and New Jersey. The box stretcher consisted of a turned piece at the front located halfway between the seat and the floor and plain squared members positioned near the floor on the other three sides. Sometimes there was an additional stretcher on each side located about midway between the floor and the seat. Cromwell chairs were often made in sets, and inventories of the period list 6, 12, or 15. A few Cromwell chairs were expanded horizontally, forming an early type of sofa.

The **ladder-back chair**, also called a **slat-back chair**, was popular in America from 1670. The framework of the ladder-back chair was composed of turned members, and as with other turned chairs, the back legs extended upward to support the back and ended with a finial. The three or more horizontal concave slats across the back of ladder-back chairs were derived from German and Dutch antecedents. Rush or cane seats were typical. When arms were present, they were either composed of a horizontal spindle or a flat, shaped board and were supported by arm posts that rose above them and terminated in flattened knobs. When there were no arms, front legs generally extended slightly above the seat. Ball feet were typical. Ladder-back chairs remained popular during the eighteenth century, when they became higher and narrower.

INFLUENCE 15.8

Ladder-back chairs were again popular during the 1920s when colonial houses and furniture were revived.

The medieval chair table was a piece of convertible furniture that served as both a table and a chair, conserving space in small colonial homes. The top was hinged and formed a back for a chair when not in use as a table. Supports were solid, or had four legs that were either turned or square. Sometimes, the support consisted of a box form in which there was a drawer. The seat had rounded edges and overhung the supports.

The medieval **settle** was a long bench with a back designed to protect users from drafts and was usually located in front of the hearth. Jacobean settles in America had solid sides up to the height of the armrest with a wing extending from that point upward. The high back was also solid and might have a horizontal board across the top to form a hood. The seat was often hinged to provide access to a box below. (See Figure 15.12.)

The Restoration chair, called the Charles II chair in England, was popular in America during the last quarter of the seventeenth century. It had a rake increasing the seat-back angle to make it more comfortable, and its tall back with spirally turned uprights terminated in finials. Flemish influence could be seen in the carved scrolls that served as a crest rail. The front legs had either a turned stretcher or a flat carved one. The arms were curved downward at the ends and supported by extensions of the front legs. Cane seats and back panels predominated in England, but Russian leather upholstery was more typical in America where upholstered chairs could be made to com-

FIGURE 15.12 The table was also combined with the settle as seen here. Wooden pins were used to attach the top as a chair back or as a table.

pete in price with imported cane chairs. The chair remained popular in America during the William and Mary period.

Restoration furniture also included the wing back, or "easie," chair that was fashionable in England during the late Restoration period but more popular in America during the succeeding William and Mary period. Usually located in front of the fireplace, the wings or upholstered panels at the top of the back curved down and forward to meet outwardly scrolling arms and provided some protection from drafts. A loose cushion or **squab** improved seat comfort. Sometimes, the seat apron concealed a chamber pot. (See Figure 15.13.)

TABLES

Pine was the most common wood used for tables because wide planks could be easily obtained for the overhanging tops. Many tables had turned legs, but sawbuck and trestle tables continued to be used. Some tables featured drawers in the apron. Stretchers were commonly molded or shaped rather than turned, and the apron was sometimes shaped as well, usually with one or more curves.

The trestle table was the earliest type used. Like the medieval board, it had a removable top supported on trestles and was probably set up only when being used. Most employed one or two planks for the top, which might extend as much as 12 feet in length. The trestles—two or three of them depending on length—were either turned or T-shaped and connected by a single flat stretcher that extended through a hole in the trestle and was held in place by wooden pins. Trestles were supported on a blocklike foot called a **shoe** because it angled upward to form a wedge.

The five-stretcher Cromwellian table had a small oblong top over a plain apron with a full-width drawer. Spiral turned legs often had square sections within them and terminated in knob or pear-shaped feet. Five stretchers were used—the front and back stretchers were located approximately half the distance from the floor to the top. Side stretchers were located slightly above the feet and were joined to one another by a central stretcher forming an H. Stretchers were turned in the same pattern as the legs.

Gate leg and swing leg tables had a hinged drop leaf on one or both sides. The leaves of the drop leaf table dropped to a vertical position at

FIGURE 15.13 Easie chairs were often used by the elderly or infirm who best appreciated the warmth.

the side when closed. Folded leaf tabletops folded back over the top when closed. Both were narrow when closed, making them popular as space-saving furniture. The tabletop was supported by "gates" that swung outward when in use. When the gate had a stretcher, it was a gate leg table; when the gate lacked a stretcher, it was called a swing leg table. The swing leg table was more popular by the eighteenth century. The number of gate legs depended on the length of the table. Some tables had a single gate. Two was most common, but there are examples of tables with as

FIGURE 15.14 The gateleg table itself was supported by four turned legs with a box stretcher. An apron beneath the table top supported the top of the gate and the bottom was attached to the stretcher.

FIGURE 15.16 It was the outer shape of the leg that gave the butterfly table its name. Splayed legs connected by a box stretcher gave the table a sense of movement.

FIGURE 15.15 The tuckaway table was a space-saving table with a top that tilted to vertical when not in use.

many as 12. Gate leg tabletops were shaped and could be round, oval, or oblong. By the end of the seventeenth century in America, this type of table was usually supplanted by other styles. (See Figure 15.14.)

The butterfly table was an American form of drop leaf table of the late Jacobean period that remained popular during the subsequent William and Mary period. Less formal than the gate leg table, it had two or four solid shaped legs that swung outward to support the raised leaves. When the butterfly table had a rectangular top, four legs were needed for support, two near each end. (See Figure 15.16.)

Other common tables included round, oval, and rectangular topped tables supported on four legs. In America, table legs were often splayed—a difference between American and English tables. Draw top tables were also used.

BEDS

Beds were frequently only a simple frame on which a mattress could be supported. Most were undecorated, although a low panel headboard was common. Four turned posts protruded at least slightly above the rails that formed a box. Rope was threaded through holes or drawn taut around knobs to form a support for the mattress usually filled with feathers or straw. A combination of woods was used for beds. There were a few elaborately carved bedsteads imported from England, but these were not made in the colonies until much later.

Under eave beds were designed to fit in the angled space beneath the roof in sleeping lofts. Head posts up to 36 inches in height were turned above the point where they attached to the rails and were connected by a low headboard that was sometimes slightly arched. Foot posts were shorter and extended only about 3 inches above the rails, and no footboard was used. All posts might terminate in a decorative finial.

The **slaw bed** was a folding bed used for guests and was located in the living room where it was hidden by curtains. The bed consisted of two tall posts at the head—up to 7 feet in height—which supported a short tester frame that in turn supported curtains. The tester was further supported by two diagonal braces from the posts. Side rails were hinged approximately 2 feet from the head posts to permit the bed to be raised and hidden behind the curtains. A third pair of legs at that point supported the bed when it was folded.

The **press bed** unfolded from a large cupboard known as a **press**. The cupboard door

FIGURE 15.17 A trundle bed was low enough to be stored beneath another bed where it rolled on wheels when not in use.

William and Mary Period in America (1690–1730)

During the William and Mary period in America, the economic conditions in the New World had become attractive and a new wave of immigration began. By this time, merchants in American seaboard cities and Philadelphia, the second largest city after Boston in 1720, and the wealthy planters in the South and Middle Atlantic areas desired and could afford the accoutrements of wealth and followed English fashions in clothing, architecture, and furniture.

WILLIAM AND MARY ARCHITECTURE

In keeping with the new affluence in America during the last decade of the seventeenth century, there were fashionable changes in architecture reflecting what was happening in England. More than 40 design books made their way to America, making it possible to exactly copy English styles. Built-in shelves were located in the niches beside fireplaces and plaster concealed the structural members that had formerly been exposed. Rooms became specialized, and activities that had previously taken place in one or two rooms now took place in rooms designed specifically for a single function. The parlor became a room for entertaining guests, and the bed was removed to a bedroom. The dining room appeared, and more bedrooms were added to homes. The library became an important room in homes of the more educated. Rooms became squarer in plan, and classical forms including pilasters and pediments adorned the previously plain doorways, windows, and fireplaces. Diamond-shaped panes in casement windows were replaced with rectangular panes in new sash windows.

hinged at the top and became a tester for the bed when open and supported by additional posts.

INFLUENCE 15.9

The nineteenth-century Murphy bed was a version of the press bed. By the time the Murphy bed made its appearance, the tester was no longer in style and the cupboard doors could swing sideways. Like the press bed, the Murphy bed hinged downward when needed and was enclosed in the cupboard when not in use.

The four-poster tester bed was similar to the slaw bed except that it did not fold out of the way and all four posts were full height to support the tester. The bed was based on French court models and was often called a French bed. The bedstead itself was relatively simple because it was designed to be hidden with curtains and valances, which were the most costly furnishings in the home. The draped bed was typically located in the parlor because of its importance and indication of status.

WILLIAM AND MARY FURNITURE

Toward the end of the seventeenth century, prosperous colonists imported fashionable furniture from the Old World. At the same time, among the immigrants were cabinetmakers skilled in creating new furniture forms and in making not only mortise-and-tenon joints, used almost exclusively in Jacobean furniture, but in more complicated joints, such as the dovetail. Cabinetmakers were also skilled in using the new decorative techniques that included japanning, veneers, inlay, and elaborate carving. Japanning was popular in Boston and other urban areas where the English technique of using raised designs formed with gesso was employed. The elaborate marquetry popular in England and on the Continent was not used in the colonies, and painting often substituted for more labor-intensive and expensive techniques. Upholstery became more popular and usually cost more than the furniture frame. During the William and Mary period, the upholstered armchair was introduced.

While oak had been the wood of choice for Jacobean furniture, it was gradually replaced with woods that were more highly figured, meaning they had more variations in their grains. Walnut and maple predominated, and mahogany was used in America before it was used in England because it came from the West Indies. The advantage of mahogany was that large planks could be cut from its logs. Mahogany, however, was expensive, and in New England, cherry was often substituted because the color was similar.

Baroque curves replaced the rectilinear lines of earlier furniture Lighter, more delicate framing members replaced the bulky Jacobean forms, and vertical lines predominated, with furniture increasing in height. A William and Mary chair, for example, was up to 10 inches higher than previous examples. Table aprons, seat rails, stretchers, and the bottom rails of case furniture were shaped with C scrolls replacing turning as the predominant decorative element. The complex Flemish scroll chair, popular in England during the William and Mary period, was also used in America and featured the same C-scrolls. Foliated carving in deep relief on arched crest rails and front stretchers replaced the shallow carving of Jacobean furniture, and trumpet and inverted cup legs replaced turned ones. The Flemish scroll foot with an inward-turning scroll carved at its base, single and double ball feet, and bun were also used.

SEATING UNITS

By 1700, the formal wainscot chair and the simple Cromwellian chair were both being replaced by more contemporary forms. The banister back chair was a late Jacobean form introduced during the Restoration period in England but became common in America later during the William and Mary period. The banister back chair incorporated split balusters, flat on the front and rounded in the back and made like split spindles. The Jacobean banister back chair had four banisters, but later versions had five,

FIGURE 15.18 Furniture feet also followed European examples and employed the Braganza foot—termed the paintbrush foot in America because the vertical grooves on its upper surface suggested the details of a paintbrush. The paintbrush foot was especially common on chair legs.

FIGURE 15.19 This early version of the banister-back chair has turned stretchers, four banisters, and a simple crest rail. Although the back supports are turned above the seat, they are left square beneath the seat joining where the greatest strength was necessary. This technique is known as block and turned.

FIGURE 15.20 The Boston chair was sometimes called a spoon-back chair and remained popular until the Revolution. The back sometimes had a single vase-shaped splat in the center that joined a stay rail above the seat rather than the seat itself. The seat and the back were both upholstered with Russian leather—a less expensive alternative to caning. The upholstery was attached with a double row of brass-headed nails—the only applied ornament.

that supported a crest rail. The seat was splayed and made of rush. When coarser **splint** was used, the seat was woven in a basket weave. The back legs rose beside the banisters forming a 90-degree seat-back angle and terminating in vase shapes, balls, or finials. The design of the crest rail differed according to region and furniture maker, but it was frequently carved and sometimes a drop was added at the center of the stay rail. A heart and crown were indicative of a chair made in Stratford, Connecticut, for example. In later versions of banister back chairs, front legs were often fashioned in the form of a Flemish scroll. Turned box stretchers were single or paired and the back stretcher was simpler than the others. When banister back chairs had arms, they ended in a downward curve with shaped handgrips. (See Figure 15.19.)

The **Boston** chair was an American innovation early in the eighteenth century that originated in Boston, from where it was exported to the remainder of the colonies. This inexpensive simplified version of the Flemish scroll chair was successfully copied all along the Atlantic coast. The back supports of the Boston chair introduced curves that at first curved slightly backward before changing direction to flow upward. A turned stretcher replaced the ornately carved William and Mary version and the crest rail was simplified, forming shoulders at both sides before merging into the crest itself. Turned front legs were used on early examples, although these were replaced with cabriole legs that terminated in cloven hooves called **pied de biche** feet in the succeeding Queen Anne period. Most of these chairs were stained either red or black. (See Figure 15.20.)

The daybed, intended for resting during the day, was simply an armless chair elongated to 60 inches or more. Because of its length, six or eight legs were required. Generally, these were turned, as were the stretchers. The backrest canted backward, most at a fixed angle, although some were hinged so they could be adjusted. Typically, daybeds were used in the bedroom rather than in the parlor.

The settee was essentially a double, triple, or quadruple chair with six or more legs that had appeared in the previous period but was more frequently used in the colonies during the William and Mary period. At first the back had the appearance of separate chairs, but later the high back was designed as for a single unit. Settees designed to seat two were sometimes known as the courting chairs. Box or serpentine X-shaped stretchers frequently joined the legs of William and Mary pieces. Serpentine stretchers usually had three centers with a finial at the crossings. The long bench, or form, was similar to the settee but without arms or back.

The stool was largely replaced by chairs during the William and Mary period but there were some examples. These rectangular or circular stools were usually upholstered and often had fringe.

TABLES

Tables were sold by length, with 3, 4, and 5 feet most common. Although oval-topped tables were most frequently listed in contemporary inventories, round, square, and rectangular examples occurred. The newly separated dining room could house a larger table than previously, although the typical arrangement was to seat guests at numerous small tables located around the room. Gate leg tables remained common, as did tuckaway and butterfly tables, but the legs were thinner and more delicate.

STORAGE FURNITURE

The chest of drawers, which had begun to appear during the late Jacobean period, became increasingly popular, and by the eighteenth century had replaced the mule chest. The first low chests of drawers were frequently used as dressing tables, but this function was removed to the lowboy as

FIGURE 15.21 While daybeds in England were typically upholstered or caned on the seat and back, in America loose cushions were used instead.

that piece began to appear. At the same time, chests of drawers became higher and had more drawers. Drawer construction became more refined, with dovetail joints used first in Boston and later throughout the colonies. Chests of drawers usually had three or four full-length drawers except in Pennsylvania, where two tiers of side-by-side drawers were situated over two full-length drawers. Drawers were frequently veneered, japanned, or infrequently inlaid. Like the mule chests before them, chests of drawers were raised slightly off the floor on extended stiles, or on ball, turned, or turnip-shaped feet. William and Mary drawer pulls were brass drop handles rather than the earlier wood pulls. A backplate located behind the pear-shaped drop handles with matching escutcheon plates protected keyholes.

As in Europe, American furniture included the highboy—called the **tallboy** in America—which was a chest mounted on another chest. The stand or lower portion of the tallboy had either three side-by-side drawers with a curvilinear apron and was mounted on tall legs or had three or more full-width drawers and was mounted on short feet similar to those used on chests of drawers. When tall legs were used, there were usually more legs across the front than in the back—four was typical. These legs were joined by stretchers, and the front stretcher followed the curvature of the bottom of the unit. In America, this type of stand was reproduced as a **lowboy** that served as a dressing or toilet table; this became the most important piece of furniture in the American bedroom.

The upper drawer unit of the tallboy typically had four tiers of drawers, most of which were full-width and graduated in height, with the tallest drawer located on the bottom. Occasionally, the top one or two tiers of drawers were divided into two or three side-by-side drawers.

Corner cupboards replaced the court cupboard for use in displaying expensive objects including imported ceramics. The flat-top surface of corner cupboards sometimes had an added stepped form used for further display of objects.

DESKS

The **slant-front desk** was a William and Mary innovation that evolved from the Jacobean Bible box placed on a frame. The first models were also supported by a frame—usually with gate legs to support the writing surface. By 1700, most slant-

FIGURE 15.22 While the top of the English highboy featured a complete entablature, American tallboys had only a simple molding at the top.

front desks were mounted on a drawer base, with three full-width drawers surmounted by a pair of side-by-side drawers. Like the lowboy, there were typically four legs in front and two in the rear. Sometimes, small drawers were pulled out to support the lid. Inside the top, the area was divided into small drawers and pigeonholes.

The secretary, too, was a new William and Mary furniture form and was designed in two sections. The lower section had a hinged slant front over a row of side-by-side drawers, which were themselves above three full-width drawers. Infrequently, the top row was a single false drawer front that could be pulled out, had a hinged front that could be used as a writing surface, and was fitted with pigeonholes or small drawers inside. The top section was a cabinet with two doors that rested on top of the base and inside of which were drawers and separate compartments. Mirror panels sometimes graced the

FIGURE 15.23 The top section of the slant-front desk was designed for writing and for storing writing materials and important papers. The front of the top was angled slightly backward, and a book ledge was frequently located at the base, providing a lectern for reading. The angled covering could be opened to form a flat writing surface supported on lopers, or slides at the sides.

FIGURE 15.24 Beds with four low posts were more common in warmer areas.

fronts of the doors. Typically, the secretary was either veneered or japanned. It sat on bracket feet or ball feet and had a double arched cornice. A variation of the secretary was the secretary bookcase, which featured adjustable shelves behind the doors of the top section.

The kneehole writing table was also a new furniture form during the William and Mary period. It had a long drawer in the apron, typically two side pedestals with drawers, and a shallow recess beneath the center section to accommodate the knees of the user.

INFLUENCE 15.10

The kneehole writing table of the William and Mary period became the standard desk form in America.

BEDS

Beds changed little from the Jacobean period and most of those early forms continued to be used. In homes of the more affluent, the four-poster bed became common. The posts themselves were not highly decorated because they were covered with voluminous curtains, making the bed hangings the most expensive item in many household inventories. Mattresses were stuffed with straw or—in some cases, as much as 60 pounds of feathers.

Living the Good Life

By the dawn of the eighteenth century, the standard of living and quality of life of American colonists had improved to a level of comfort some of them might never have experienced in England. The English Parliament was preoccupied with European affairs and until the mid-eighteenth century interfered little. As the colonies prospered, immigrants continued to pour into the land of opportunity and the population continued to increase. The socially elite in a number of cities considered themselves English, although many of them had never been to England. Colonists were increasingly able to produce necessary goods and to import luxury items from the mother country. Buildings and furnishings often followed European styling with little time lag. Life was good and filled with promise. There was little indication of the harbingers of change that were to lead to American independence less than a century later.

1503
Ambrogio Leone de Nola (d. 1525), archaeologist, marks ancient Herculaneum on a map near its actual site

1592
Domenico Fontana (1542–1607), Roman architect, digs up ancient stones in Pompeii but does not discover the city

1709
Marble statues discovered at Herculaneum as well is dug for a monastery

1715–1723
Philippe Charles (1674–1723), Duke of Orléans, regent for Louis XV

1725–1727
Catherine I (1684–1727), widow of Peter the Great, becomes empress of Russia

1738
Charles VII (1716–1788), King of Naples, orders excavations at Herculaneum but keeps it secret

1739
Account of excavations at Herculaneum reaches French Academy

1748
Permission granted to excavate at Pompeii

1750
Intact Villa dei Papiri discovered at Herculaneum along with almost 1,800 papyrus scrolls containing ancient philosophical works

1758
Publication of Julien–David Leroy's *Les Ruines des plus beaux Monuments de la Gréce* (The Ruins of the Most Beautiful Monuments of Greece)

1759
Josiah Wedgwood (1730–1795) founds a firm that produces ceramic products

1762
Publication of the *Antiquities of Athens* by James Stewart (1713–1788) and Nicholas Revett (1720–1804)

1762–1796
Catherine II (1729–1796), the Great, Empress of Russia

1764
James Hargreaves (1720–1778) invents spinning jenny

1765
Temple of Isis discovered at Pompeii

1767
Townshend Acts impose taxes on products imported to America

1769
Steam engine developed by James Watt (1736–1819)

1770
Boston Massacre

1770
Sir William Hamilton (1730–1803) publishes four books of illustrations of antiquities, some from Pompeii and Herculaneum

1770
Townshend Acts repealed

1773
Boston Tea Party

1774–1789
Louis XVI
(1754–1792),
King of France

1775–1783
American War of
Independence

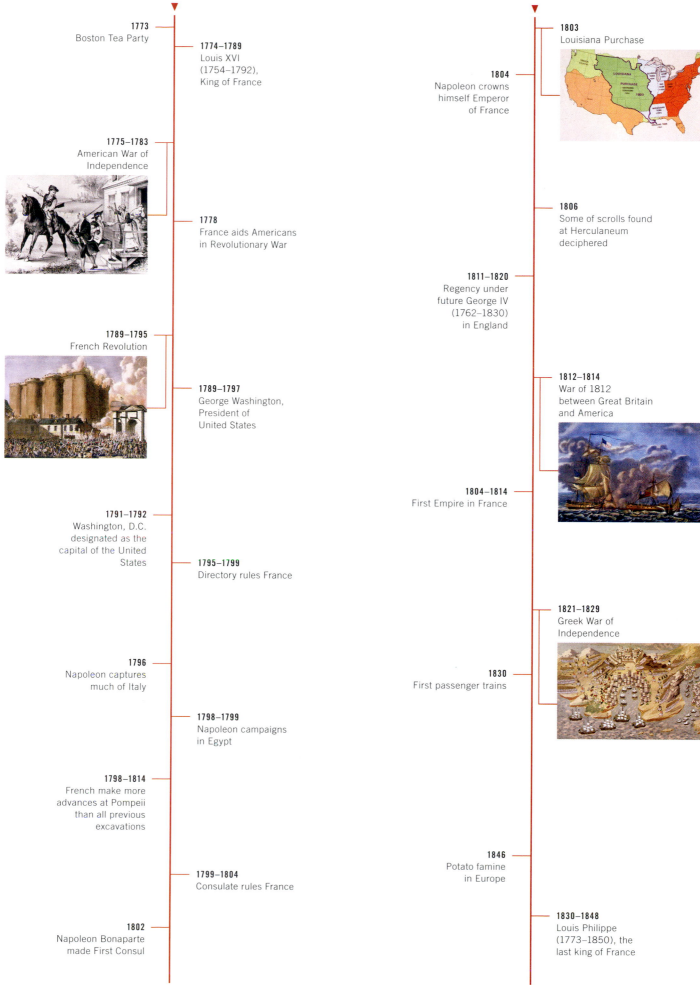

1778
France aids Americans
in Revolutionary War

1789–1795
French Revolution

1789–1797
George Washington,
President of
United States

1791–1792
Washington, D.C.
designated as the
capital of the United
States

1795–1799
Directory rules France

1796
Napoleon captures
much of Italy

1798–1799
Napoleon campaigns
in Egypt

1798–1814
French make more
advances at Pompeii
than all previous
excavations

1799–1804
Consulate rules France

1802
Napoleon Bonaparte
made First Consul

1803
Louisiana Purchase

1804
Napoleon crowns
himself Emperor
of France

1806
Some of scrolls found
at Herculaneum
deciphered

1811–1820
Regency under
future George IV
(1762–1830)
in England

1812–1814
War of 1812
between Great Britain
and America

1804–1814
First Empire in France

1821–1829
Greek War of
Independence

1830
First passenger trains

1846
Potato famine
in Europe

1830–1848
Louis Philippe
(1773–1850), the
last king of France

FIGURE 16.3 The façade of Chiesa San Marco is typically Baroque with ressaut projections, textured surfaces, and numerous decorative elements.

wood, and stone was carved so sumptuously that it lost its appearance of strength. It was effect that was most important.

Elaborate ornamentation was incorporated, and almost every surface had some decoration. Forms such as domes and moldings were multiplied and repeated on various planes.

By 1630, illusionism was an important part of Baroque art and architecture. This movement began with the painting in the dome of the church of *Sant' Andrea della Valle* in Rome by Giovanni Lanfranco in 1625–1627. After that time, illusionism in ceiling paintings became particularly important, although wall paintings in trompe l'oeil were also incorporated in Baroque buildings. Figures appeared to lean outward over balconies, people apparently strolled out of doorways, and groups seemed to be involved in social discourse. Some of the figures were so real looking that George Washington was said to have bowed to a figure descending a stairway before realizing he was acknowledging only a painting. Trompe l'oeil was also used on furniture, and tabletops might have a realistic-appearing deck of cards sitting in the center, or a piece of jewelry might appear to have been left behind. The Italian term **sotto in su** is used to describe trompe l'oeil ceiling paintings of the Baroque period. Meaning "up from under," the term describes how a painter was required to foreshorten figures for them to appear to be real. Favored sotto in su paintings in churches made the heavens appear to open for an ascension or assumption of a holy personage. (See Figure 16.4.) **Quadratura** described illusionistic paintings that appeared to extend architecture beyond the actual space of the building. All of these techniques required great skill and they were used mostly in religious structures and palaces.

Sculptural forms, usually putti or angels, were executed in high relief, colored to appear natural, and lit by hidden or exposed light sources. These **peinures-vivantes** often emerged from stucco clouds that might spread over architectural features or moldings often concealing parts of the structure. Other illusionistic ploys included the use of stucco that was painted with wood grain or a faux marble finish. Truth in materials was unimportant.

INFLUENCE 16.2

Since the 1960s, trompe l'oeil murals have been painted on building exteriors in American cities. Some feature people, often doing a job such as painting the side of a building. Other murals feature buildings, automobiles, and even animals that are part of the normal cityscape.

FIGURE 16.4 The earliest example of sotto in su painting was executed in 1474 by Andrea Mantegna, an Italian artist. Trompe l'oeil walls on the wedding chamber of the Ducal Palace in Mantua were scenes of the Gonzaga family's life. On the ceiling, it appeared as if there was an oculus or open area to the sky with a peacock and figures leaning over the balustrade to look below.

The interior experienced the most changes, and there was an overall lack of restraint in Baroque design that was recognized even during its height. Palladio's *Quattro libre* were written in an attempt to encourage a return to stricter classical forms. (See Box 16.1.)

CHURCHES

In churches, the aisles disappeared and chapels, some of which were domed, flanked the nave. Vertical and horizontal curves predominated on both the interior and exterior and often even the structure itself had curves rather than corners. The apse was still located behind the quire and frequently had a domed roof. Barrel vaults were interrupted by fenestration. Major churches made use of central domes at the crossing that were most frequently raised on a high fenestrated drum. Domes had external ribs as seen at St. Peter's in Rome, St. Paul's in London, and the Church of the Invalides in Paris. (See Figure 16.5.) In central European areas and in Russia, onion domes were more typical of Baroque buildings. Italian-influenced balustrades were used on rooftops, around domes, and in interiors. The focal point and artistic climax of the church was the high altar with secondary focus on other altars.

Work continued on St. Peter's in Rome, and the hemispherical dome planned by Michelangelo was changed by Giacoo della Porta to an

---

Box 16.1 SUMMARY OF BAROQUE ARCHITECTURAL CHARACTERISTICS

- Curves based on a circle
- Undulating walls with alternating concave and convex spaces
- Circular and oval-shaped spaces
- Conscious use of light in design
- Chiaroscuro (strong contrasts between light and shadow)
- Solominic columns
- Giant scrolls
- Serpentine and broken pediments
- Faux finishes
- Use of stucco for decorative forms
- Gilding
- Domes with external ribs
- Lanterns on domes
- Elaborate ornament
- Putti
- Illusionistic paintings including trompe l'oeil
- Central projections on building exteriors
- Elaborate exterior and interior staircases
- Extended use of balustrades on both the interior and exterior
- Blurring of boundaries between painting, architecture, and sculpture
- Pear-shaped domes in central European areas

FIGURE 16.5 The church associated with the Hotel des Invalides in Paris had a dome like those of Italy. The high drum was supported on four piers with arches leading to the chapels that filled the corners of this centrally planned Greek cross structure. The dome itself was tripled—a highly decorated exterior gilded dome, a middle dome on which paintings were executed on the under side, and an inner dome with a large oculus through which the paintings of the middle dome could be seen. The external ribs were characteristic of Baroque buildings, as was the lantern that surmounted the dome. The dome was gilded later.

FIGURE 16.6 Many churches featured **glories** composed of gilded rays emanating from a central point. Angels, doves, or holy personages were mounted in front of the rays.

FIGURE 16.7 The baldachin over the high altar in Baroque churches often featured twisted, or solominic, columns with gilded twining vines, putti, and often a crowning finial.

egg-shaped dome. The interior was executed in the Baroque style.

FRENCH BAROQUE

The Baroque period in France saw two results of the foresight of Henry IV (1553–1610; reign from 1589). After years of persecution of French Protestants, or Huguenots, it was Henry who had signed the Edict of Nantes in 1598 granting them equal political rights with other French citizens along with freedom of worship. Many of the Huguenot émigrés to the Netherlands, Germany, and England returned to France at this time. Since many of them were middle-class artisans, their return significantly affected the arts. In 1685, Louis XIV revoked the edict, which resulted not only in a mass exodus of over 200,000 Huguenots, including some who went to America, but in a more hostile attitude toward France by the largely Protestant countries bordering that nation. As French artisans emigrated, they enriched the arts of other countries and, at the same time, disseminated French ideas.

Henry IV had also invited hundreds of artisans to work in the Louvre Palace in Paris. For the succeeding two centuries, royal patronage of those artisans remained in place until Napoleon I finally disbanded the workshops. At the Louvre, artisans had an environment that fostered their efforts, apartments where they lived, and wages to enable them to pursue their arts. The director of the Louvre workshops was the most powerful artistic personage in France and controlled all work accomplished for the monarch. Spanish, Flemish, and Italian artisans took advantage of the opportunity and French artisans usually spent some time in the Low Countries or in Italy learning their crafts before returning to France. In addition, foreign queens, including Anne of Austria and Marie de' Medici, and ministers such as the Italian Jules Cardinal Mazarin served as regents before Louis XIII and XIV became old enough to rule. France was slow to develop a national style due to the overwhelming number of foreign influences.

Jean Baptiste Colbert (1619–1683) was the French Minister of Finance for Louis XIV. It was Colbert who reformed French manufacturing by regulating the guilds, brought Venetian glass makers and Flemish weavers to France to establish respective French industries, and established the tapestry works at Beauvais. He also obtained foreign markets for French goods and supported the French Compagnie des Indes,[2] as it imported goods such as coffee, sugar, spices, and fur. Even with Louis' excessive expenses for war, and his extensive building projects, Colbert was able to keep France solvent, although by the end of Louis XIV's reign, the country was almost bankrupt.

With their control over the arts, Cardinal Richelieu (1585–1642), who served as chief minister for Louis XIII, Jules Cardinal Mazarin, who served both Louis XIII and Louis XIV, and Louis XIV himself were able use the arts to glorify the monarchy and to help establish the king as an absolute monarch. As a result of the financial reforms of Colbert and wealth flowing in from the colonies, France was the richest country in seventeenth-century Europe.

Colbert continued subsidies for artisans at the Louvre and established academies, or groups of prominent artists who discussed aesthetic topics at regular meetings. In 1666, a branch of the French academy was established in Rome that assured that French artisans would be classically trained. These discussion groups resulted in a set of strict guidelines for artistic products, ensuring that French art and architecture would be clas-

sically oriented and more sober than Baroque in other areas. Artisans who did not comply lost their places in the workshops and their patronage. Essentially, artistic control was centralized, and there was little allowance for creative forays outside the rules. The Italian architect Bernini was invited to submit a design for a new façade for the Louvre, but his curved design was rejected because it strayed beyond acceptable parameters of classical architecture. The concentrated efforts of the French gave them European leadership in the arts, which it has retained for four centuries.

When Mazarin died in 1661, Louis XIV, at the age of 23, took charge of the government and determined to be his own prime minister. He held the reins of power tightly in order to retain absolute control and he established a rigid code of conduct with a strict caste system at his court. In order to ensure that nobles could not establish a rival power base, Louis demanded that those of a certain rank spend a significant amount of time at court each year. Because of this, the Palace of Versailles, in which the court was located, was necessarily large. Versailles, as built by Louis XIV, was designed to house as many as 10,000 people. Other monarchs envied not only the wealth of France but the position of absolutism held by Louis XIV, the Sun King, and sought to emulate his successes by using the arts to their own advantage. Named for the King, the French Baroque style is known as Louis *Quatorze*. Numerous other European rulers, including Peter the Great in Russia, used Versailles as a model for their own palaces in an attempt to validate their grandiose political ambitions.

FRENCH BAROQUE ARCHITECTURE

France was the leader in secular architecture in the Baroque style. The first example of a Baroque palace in that country was the Palais du Luxembourg, a sober classical structure with a projecting three-story central section known in architecture as the **corps de logis** that served as a frontispiece and replaced the tower of medieval castles. A separate roof crowned the corps de logis. Typical of French baroque palaces was an open symmetrical layout with three wings. The two side wings were smaller and treated as inferior to the central section. Lofty complex roofs were typical of French Renaissance palaces and this form was retained during the Baroque.

FIGURE 16.8 The corps de logis on the courtyard façade of the Palace of the Louvre was the most prominent feature before the glass pyramid was added in 1989.

It was François Mansart (1598–1666) who is credited with bringing the Baroque style to France in its fullest form. Mansart omitted many of the elaborate decorative effects of Italian Baroque, which are limited to ornament rather than structural forms. The mansard roof named for him was used by the major architects of the period and was not exclusive to buildings designed by Mansart. This type of roof has a double slope on all sides, the one on top very low and a second steeper slope below. The advantage of these double-pitched roofs was that an almost full living story could be usable beneath them. All that was required were dormer windows for light and ventilation.

The greatest of the French Baroque buildings, however, is Versailles. A small hunting lodge built for Louis XIII served as the core of the building, but Louis XIV had it greatly enlarged and it was here that he moved the French court. At Versailles, The architect Louis Le Vau (1612–1670), painter Charles Lebrun (1619–1690), and landscape designer André Le Nôtre (1613–1700) were responsible for the classical forms, sumptuous interiors, and formal gardens that were was frequently combined with Baroque architecture.

Like other French Baroque palaces, Versailles had a **cour d'honneur**, or a courtyard that was sometimes used for special occasions or honors, in front of the façade. This courtyard faced the town and was accessed through the main gate. Typically, the cour d'honneur was horseshoe-shaped. Giant, or colossal, orders were used on later façades to make them more impressive, and Italian balustrades were often used on the roof. Gardens were located in the back rather than in the front.

SPANISH AND PORTUGUESE BAROQUE

In Spain, the Baroque style was known as *Churrigueresque* (1664–1760), named for the family that promoted the style. José Churriguero (1665–1725) was the most prominent member of that family, although the style was well advanced by the time he began work. Spanish Baroque was a reaction to the severity of the Desornamentado style. Churrigueresque was wildly exuberant, and the Spanish people enthusiastically embraced it. Baroque forms were heroic in scale, and Spanish Baroque ornament was larger than that of the Plateresque.

Unfortunately, due to mismanagement of the vast wealth extracted from the New World during the sixteenth century, Spain was nearly bankrupt and only a few Baroque structures were built. Altars, retables, and church screens received Baroque decoration. In homes, Baroque styling was usually limited to furniture and accessories, although frescos were sometimes combined with plaster representations of structural forms, as they were in more prominent buildings. The Baroque style was used for façades, and even medieval cathedrals such as Santiago de Compostela were given new Baroque facelifts. Often, however, it was only the entry that was treated with exaggerated ornament. Niches continued to be used, and the interiors were either painted in bright colors or lined with azulejos. Bold curves, florid details, and innovative treatments of classical orders characterized Iberian Baroque.

INFLUENCE 16.3

The Churrigueresque style was again used for the buildings constructed for the 1915 Panama-California Exposition in San Diego.

INFLUENCE 16.4

Some Spanish Baroque buildings, such as the Hospicio de San Fernando in Madrid, had extravagantly curvilinear façades. This type of façade was again used during the Art Nouveau Period. The façade of Sagrada Familia and Casa Mila, both designed by the twentieth-century architect Antonio Gaudi, also reflect Churrigueresque design.

The Baroque style continued in Spain until Philip V (1683–1746; reign from 1700 with a short interruption during 1724.), grandson of Louis XIV of France, became king. Philip preferred the less ornate French Baroque style, and the indigenous Spanish version was replaced by more sober ornament that facilitated the transition to the Neoclassic style. It was, however, Spanish and Portuguese Baroque that was imported to their respective colonial entities and became fused with native American elements. Spanish Baroque was prominent in Mexico, Guatemala, and Peru, while Brazilian Baroque followed Portuguese examples. Franciscan and Dominican friars directed the construction of missions and administration buildings long before the Pilgrims landed at Plymouth. Neither architects nor designers, the friars built structures that were a mixture of Gothic, Plateresque, Moorish, and Baroque. Because the structures were built by Amerindians, European design was also mixed with native Incan, Mayan, Aztec, and Mexican forms. Elaborate gold leaf ornament covered many of the surfaces, especially altars and retables. Some buildings employed glazed tiles on façades and domes. Because the Baroque style was used on the façades of medieval cathedrals with paired towers in the Iberian Peninsula, many of the Baroque churches in the Americas were initially constructed with twin towers. This colonial style remained popular in the Americans long after the Neoclassic style had replaced it in Europe.

BAROQUE IN CENTRAL EUROPE

The Baroque style was limited to Catholic areas of the Holy Roman Empire, and although there were some indications, the style did not flourish in central Europe until the eighteenth century due to the Thirty Years' War and the Ottoman presence in Austria. As in Italy, curved walls and intersecting circular or oval spaces were employed. Like other Baroque churches, the hall church exchanged its aisles for a series of open chapels separated by pillars. These **wall-pillar** churches retained the barrel-vaulted nave and the style continued to be used until the nineteenth century. The subsequent Rococo style was even more popular especially in Southern Germany and Austria. The most prominent German Baroque and Rococo architect was Balthasar Neumann (1687–1753).

FIGURE 16.9 *Lüftmalerei* was a Baroque technique used in northern Italy and Southern Germany to decorate building façades—especially houses. Buon fresco was used to paint religious scenes, architectural detailing such as the trim around openings, and scenes from fairy tales on the stucco finish.

FIGURE 16.13 The elaborate Baroque door surround leading to the palace in Monaco has rusticated columns, a typical Baroque feature, a broken pediment, and the arms of the Grimaldi family.

FIGURE 16.14 Baroque architecture made use of the *oeil-de-boeuf* or bull's eye window. This type of window was round or oval in form and was often used on upper stories or in dormers on the roof.

niches, or decorative panels between the windows. Versailles saw the first use of double-valve floor-to-cornice windows, now called French windows or French doors. The practice of locating a large mirror directly opposite a window to increase light in the room was begun at Versailles as well, although because of the effectiveness of the technique, was widely emulated.

INTERIORS

Baroque interiors were sumptuous and designed as backdrops for the theater that was life. As such, they were formal, pretentious, and ornate. Public rooms were large in scale in order that vast assemblages might be entertained. Large-scale details composed of rich materials ornamented structural components so that an entire room became one artistic composition. Like Italian palazzi, French Baroque palaces were two rooms deep with the major apartments on the piano nobile, or second story At Versailles, the apartments of the king and the queen were the same size, an unusual arrangement for the time. Each suite had seven rooms, all of which were connected by doors located next to the window wall. This **enfilade** arrangement that allowed an uninterrupted view through all the rooms was typical of Baroque buildings. During the Renaissance, Palladio had used the same type of arrangement, although the doors were located in the center of the walls rather than at one side. Rooms were arranged in a hierarchical sequence that moved progressively from public to private areas. A secret passage led between the two royal apartments. Each room was decorated according to a heavenly body—the sun (the king's bedroom), the moon, and several of the planets with allegorical scenes featuring Roman gods associated with the heavenly bodies alluded to the heroic deeds of Louis XIV. The Galerie des Glaces, or Hall of Mirrors, is the most famous of the rooms at Versailles and was used for state functions.

Floors were often of elaborately patterned wood parquet, terrazzo, marble tile in counterchange patterns, brick, or stone. At Versailles, marble floors on the main level are inlaid with metal. Rugs were used on floors and their colors and patterns were in harmony with those of the rest of the room.

Walls had large panels that were often flanked by pilasters with true classical proportions. Far from classical capital design, Baroque pilasters often featured masks, grotesques, fleur-de-lis, a small sun emblem for Louis XIV, or palm leaves rather than acanthus leaves or volutes. In formal rooms, these components might be made of marble or other stone and walls might even be faced with it. In less public areas, wood panels were more typical. Pilasters might begin at the floor but more often, rose from a low dado that surrounded the

room to the architrave of the entablature. The entablature, however, was usually located some distance below ceiling level leaving an **attic** that might be divided into panels by additional pilasters superimposed on those below. Alternatively, a large cove was located above the entablature or above the attic and curved into the ceiling.

The panels between the pilasters were hung with framed paintings, tapestries, fabrics including damasks and velvets, and embossed leather. Wreaths, cornucopias, shells, and cartouches and large-scale carved wood or stucco compositions appeared on walls in isolated places. Hung paintings and areas painted with frescoes featured portraits, scenes from classical mythology or historic events, and floral arrangements.

Technological developments in glassmaking resulted in larger panes of glass and the extensive use of mirrors. By modern standards, these panes were still small, but they were fit together to form windows and mirrors that extended almost from floor to ceiling. Panels of mirrors were especially luxurious due to their high cost. Typically, they were located opposite windows to reflect natural light and candle stands, or **girandoles**, **flambeaux** that were figures holding candelabras, and crystal chandeliers were placed so that candlelight could also be reflected and multiplied. Convex mirrors that reflected light over a greater area were also used.

Rectangular wooden wall panels were typically framed with moldings that curved across the top, carved motifs were used at both the top and bottom of panels, and there was often an additional carving centered in the panel. The moldings and ornaments were typically gilded while the panel itself was painted, usually off-white. During the succeeding Rococo period, panels were sometimes painted in pastel colors. Some panels were waxed

FIGURE 16.15 French Baroque interiors were lavish, formal, and large in scale. Structural components received multiple decorative features and the room itself became an artistic composition.

FIGURE 16.16 The Galerie des Glaces at Versailles featured 17 large mirrors, each made of 21 individual panels, that reflected light from the arched windows across from them. The room was the largest in the palace with a length of over 239 feet, a width of more than 34 feet, and a height greater than 40 feet.

FIGURE 16.17 Even the wall frieze was divided into separate panels, each of which was highly ornamented. Here, gilded putti, classical urns, and musical instruments are located just below the cornice.

rather than painted with the natural grain of the wood serving as part of the ornament.

Ceilings were either flat or vaulted, and domes were used not only in churches but in palaces, especially in Italy. A strong cornice served as the boundary between the walls and ceiling. Quadratura and sotto in su paintings extended apparent space and were typical of ceilings that became the dominant focal point of rooms.

STAIRWAYS

Exterior stairways were monumental and often had a gradual ascent, meaning that the treads were deep, sometimes several feet. Stairways were often doubled with the two sides mirror images and frequently formed a horseshoe shape such as at Fontainebleau. Balustrades were bold and often separated by panels. Metal balustrades were common on the exterior and were often gilded.

Major interior stairways were moved from the center of the entry vestibule to the side. Like exterior stairs, the balustrade was often interrupted by panels above which were located sculptural forms. Sculpture was also mounted on newels. Some of these sculptures were contemporary; others were actually classic pieces that had been moved from their original locations. Statuary was also used on the flat balustrades surrounding the stairs on upper levels.

FIREPLACES

In Baroque rooms, the fireplace and chimney piece projected less prominently than those in Renaissance rooms. Fireplace surrounds, however, were ornate and often had sculptural figures including atlantes and caryatids or adaptations of classical columns supporting a mantel. Paintings or carved designs typically decorated the chimneypiece, although there were a few examples of small mirrors that forecast Rococo design. Mantels were usually made of marble, and the firebox opening was rectangular. A bolection molding was often used to transition from the firebox to the mantel.

Baroque Furniture

During the Renaissance, the aristocracy had begun to live in a single residence rather than moving from place to place. By the Baroque period, it was no longer necessary for furniture to be portable. In fact, massive pieces were often designed as part of the wall composition for a specific location, becoming part of the décor of the room itself. It remained necessary in rooms of state or large salons to leave space in the middle of the room for general activity, so much of the furniture in those rooms remained in place along walls. Furniture was often decorated only on the sides that were to show, and pieces designed to fit against a wall were often plain on the back side.

Lifestyles were formal and required lavish furnishings designed to impress and rooms were grandiose and required large-scale, ponderous furniture. The use of architectural forms in furniture continued, and sculptural elements were added. New materials were extensively used. Some of these, such as rosewood, ebony, and tortoiseshell, were imported from the Orient.

Status was still associated with furniture, and the largest chairs were reserved for those of substantial importance. The cabinet that was often supported by a separate stand became increasingly important and replaced the buffet as a display piece. Unlike the buffet, which was itself rather plain, the cabinet became a showpiece employing expensive materials and techniques. Veneers, lacquer panels, and marquetry were used on these pieces. Because lacquer work was imported from the Orient, it was expensive and European artisans developed imitations of the work. Oriental designs and scenes were often incorporated in European-made furniture—a fashion known as **chinoiserie**. Marquetry increased as exotic woods became available, and floral designs in that medium were common.

French **Boulle work** was expensive and consisted of tortoiseshell and metal marquetry panels. Two sheets were glued together, a sheet of silver, brass, or pewter, and a sheet made of tortoise shell. The design was sawn through both sheets at one, resulting in two sets of identical designs—one with a metal background and one with a tortoiseshell background. Because of this, furniture was often made in pairs with contrasting decorative components. The technique is known as Boulle work because it was extensively used by André Charles Boulle who was appointed the master cabinetmaker to Louis XIV. Boulle work was little used after the end of the Baroque period.

After the furniture piece was finished, **ormolu** mounts were added. In many cases, the mounts were located to protect the edges of the veneered pattern and to keep the corners of pieces from becoming damaged.

Pietre dure continued to be used, often in the form of pictures, but also with elaborate scrolling forms and cabochon shapes. Scagliola was less expensive than pietre dure and was employed for trompe l'oeil effects on table-tops and furniture panels. When used, scagliola was in liquid or clay-like form and could be poured or worked into molds or spaces hollowed in a background of stone. Veining to give scagliola the appearance of marble in addition to chips of colored stone made fine detailing possible.

Carving became a specialized skill during the seventeenth century, and in France, only members of that guild could execute most of the carvings on furniture. Native woods including oak, walnut, sycamore, and others were common but rarer woods such as ebony were in demand for court furniture and by others who could afford it. Low-relief designs were typical on hardwoods, and elaborate pierced designs were used on chair backs and front stretchers. Oval-shaped masks, grotesque masks, and fruits carved in swags were typical carved designs in central Europe, the Low Countries, and England. Grinling Gibbons (1648–1721) was the most famous of the English carvers of the period, and his realistic-looking swags of fruit and vegetation were in high demand. Gibbons carved the organ case and choir stalls at St. Paul's Cathedral in London. With the exception of religious carvings, Gibbons included a five-petaled flower such as a Tudor rose or a periwinkle in his carvings.

Painted furniture was common in northern Italy and central Europe as well as in peasant homes. The more luxurious examples had gesso forms that were painted with watercolors and then coated with varnish. Gilding was not used on painted furniture. Indo-Portuguese furniture was imported from Goa, where European-style furniture was made in indigenous ebony with spiral-turned supports and stretchers. Much of the furniture made in India also incorporated ivory, sometimes so much of it that the furniture appeared to be completely made of the material. Silver furniture was popular, especially in Germany.

European furniture legs were often square or columnar in keeping with the architectural character of many pieces. The **cabriole** leg, in all likelihood, derived from Oriental influences, became the most common. The cabriole leg was a stylized animal leg with a double curve—a convex curve near the top known as the **knee** and a concave curve near the bottom known as the **ankle**. Curvilinear stretchers were also introduced but the shape of the cabriole leg improved the balance of the furniture on which it was used, and in many cases, stretchers could be omitted.

SEATING UNITS

During the seventeenth century, chairs were still the purview of the wealthy and middle-class homes might have only one or two. The chair with a low back is often called a back stool and was typical of English designs. High-backed chairs were used typically in halls and along walls.

Chairs had high, angled rectangular backs that were often upholstered as were seats, but upholstery was limited to the very wealthy. Later in the period, the East Indian practice of caning was adopted and seats and backs of furniture were woven in this material because in Europe, it was less expensive than upholstery. Nailheads that attached the upholstery to the frame continued to be exposed. Late-period side chairs often had spoon backs or those with a compound curve shaped to the human form, elaborately carved crest rails, and a carved center splat that extended from the crest rail to the stay rail near the seat. Chair seats were typically wider at the front than at the back.

By the eighteenth century, some furniture was moved to the center of the room although it was usually decorative and not intended for use. The French **siège courant** was such a chair and could be moved from one location to another. The **siège meublant** was designed to remain against a wall.

FIGURE 16.18 The Restoration chair was an early English Baroque chair introduced just after Charles II (1630–1685) gained the throne in 1660. The curves were a Flemish influence.

The **fauteuil**, comparable to the sedia in Italy, was a French chair with an upholstered back, seat, and armrests. The arms themselves were open and a stay rail ended the back above the seat. The wood frame was exposed and the seat rails were shaped with Baroque curves and decorated with shells, foliage, or flowers.

The **bergère** was a French upholstered arm chair with a curved back and relatively wide seat. Its distinguishing feature was that the space beneath the arms was upholstered as well. One of the most innovative seats of the Baroque period was the **voyeuse**, an armless chair with a low seat that had a padded horizontal section across the top of the back. It was designed to be straddled with the occupant facing backwards and resting his arms on the padded back. As such, it was a man's chair. A similar lady's chair, the **voyeuse à genoux** was also made but was designed for women to kneel on rather than straddle. When these mid eighteenth century chairs were used in England, they were called **conversation chairs**. The English, however, did have a similar chair known as a **library chair**. Instead of the padded horizontal addition, this chair had a section that angled backward from the back of the chair to support a book. Padded horizontal extensions at the level of the top of the back allowed readers to rest their elbows.

The **wing chair** was first used in France. This high-backed chair had wings that extended to the sides to minimize drafts and to retain heat from the fireplace. It was only later that the wing chair was upholstered.

The armchair was extended in length to seat two or more people, resulting in the settee and later the sofa. In France, the upholstered version was the **canapé**. As the length of the unit increased, so did the number of legs. Six or eight legs were typical with X-shaped or crossed stretchers between each pair.

English Restoration furniture included the so-called Restoration, or Charles II, chair that was similar to the high-backed carved wood chairs on the Continent. The back, crest rail, and front stretcher were highly decorated. Two lighter wooden chairs, the Derbyshire and Yorkshire chairs, had arcaded crest rails beneath which there was a row of spindles. The front legs were turned, but back legs were squared. A box stretcher was supplemented by additional stretchers on the sides, sometimes paired and with spindles between them.

STORAGE UNITS

The chest continued to be used and inside, there was often a second lid to cover the contents, as the lid itself was frequently left open to display the highly decorative detailing on the underside. Because it was no longer necessary to move frequently, the chest was gradually supplanted by the **commode** that had two or more drawers or a pair of doors.

The cabinet, **stippone** in Italy, was the most important piece of furniture in any home. Numerous drawers and compartments were individually decorated and separated by architectural detailing including columns and niches complete with sculptured figures, often of mythological origin. Balustrades, also with figures, ran across the tops of cabinets. Birds, flowers, foliage, and scenes were executed in marquetry, or pietre dure, or painted and gilded. Supports included atlantes and caryatids. The vertical aprons beneath the tops of cabinet stands or below cabinets on high legs were sometimes composed of scrolls and shell motifs. Other stands employed turned legs with plain, straight aprons. (See Figures 16.19.)

Smaller cabinets were made for traveling or for use on a table and were often similar to the Spanish Renaissance vargueño with a fall front and interior drawers and compartments. The interiors of both types were highly decorated. In Spain, the vargueño became more common and the decoration changed from earlier geometric forms to architectural motifs and elaborate Baroque designs.

In Portugal, a new type of luxury cabinet known as the **contador** was made. A deeply carved apron and turned legs and stretchers were used on the separate stand made to match the cabinet it supported. Architectural motifs including columns flanked a series of drawers in the top section.

The four-door court cupboard continued to be used especially in the Low Countries and England, although its decoration changed to suit Baroque styling. By this period both the upper and lower sections had been enclosed. During the Baroque period, the upper portion was usually accessed through a pair of doors and the base had either doors or drawers. The cornice was elaborate and extended over the sides and front of the cupboard. Sometimes a writing slide was housed between the two sections. Ball feet were typical. The armoire was distinguished by full-length doors, although some had one or two drawers on the bottom. In the Low Countries, they were called kasten (kas in America) and in Germany, schrank.

As postal services began to be established, writing furniture became more important. The term **bureau** was used in France to designate writing furniture. It was only later that the English used the term for a chest of drawers. Bureau is derived from the French *bure,* which was a type of medieval linen cloth that covered surfaces on which clerks worked. The term secrétaire is often used synonymously with bureau but was used by the French to indicate

FIGURE 16.19 This Italian cabinet has painted glass panels with a central niche treated with architectural detailing. The solominic legs were typical.

that papers could be covered and locked up. The French bureau was a writing desk with a fall front that concealed drawers and compartments and that had drawers beneath the writing surface. A similar but smaller version with a single drawer was the **bureau en pente**. Some bureaus en pente are double and, like later English partner desks, were arranged back to back so that two people faced each other when using them. This double desk was the **secrétaire en dos d'âne**. The **bureau plat** was a writing table with three side-by-side drawers in the apron. Smaller versions were known as **tables à écrire**. Both versions had a leather-covered top. When the bureau plat had a set of drawers or pigeon holes in a cartonnier, the desk was a **bureau à gradin**. The fall front was usually angled backward, although there were examples of fall fronts on a vertical plane. The **bonheur du jour** was a small late eighteenth century writing table designed for women. Usually, it was in the form of a table with a cabinet at the back edge that closed with a tambour door. The cabinet had shelves, drawers, or pigeon holes for writing materials or might be fitted out as a toilet table with separations in the cabinet for cosmetics and grooming items in which case it was called a **bureau toilette**. Some had an additional shelf or enclosed space beneath the table top. In addition to the bureau à

cylindre (Figure 16.20), there was another large bureau. The **bureau Mazarin** was what today would be termed a kneehole desk although the kneehole had a small cupboard in the rear of the space between the drawer pedestals. A single drawer was located in the center of the apron and three drawers on each side. The desk was supported on short legs. The **bureau bookcase** had a drawer base, a central section with a fall front that served as a writing surface, and an upper section with doors to hold books. Often the pair of doors concealing the bookshelves and compartments in the upper section was arched.

TABLES

In European courts, many tables had pietre dure or scagliola tops. In the Low Countries, tiled tabletops set in a wood framework to protect them from breakage were more common. More informal tables often had a drawer in the shaped apron. Turned and stretchered legs were common on ordinary tables.

Console tables often had marble tops, sometimes with pietra dure inlays. Bases were extensively carved and employed foliage and figures, often mythological in character or were entirely gilded.

Florentine tables were supported by a pedestal on three or four carved slab legs with lion

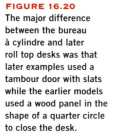

FIGURE 16.20
The major difference between the bureau à cylindre and later roll top desks was that later examples used a tambour door with slats while the earlier models used a wood panel in the shape of a quarter circle to close the desk.

paw feet and often had octagonal tops. **Pier tables** were designed to set beneath a tall mirror known as a **pier glass**. The two pieces were made as a set and the designs matched. Pier tables often had legs joined by serpentine stretchers with a knot, or **noeud**, at the crossing. During the succeeding Rococo period, the noeud was often asymmetrical.

During the seventeenth century, tea, coffee, and cocoa were introduced to Europe. Catherine of Braganza, wife of Charles II, was said to have introduced tea to England. From there, it spread to America. The drinking of these beverages became a social event, and new tea tables were designed specifically for serving them. Tea tables had a raised lip or gallery rail around them to prevent the dishes from sliding off the table as the table was carried in and out by servants.

Playing cards were introduced to Europe in the fifteenth century, but it was not until the end of the seventeenth century that special tables were constructed for playing. Card tables reveal the passion for gambling and card playing that was almost universal among the wealthy. Early examples had scooped out **guinea holes** in the corners. Card tables almost always had a folding top. Other game tables included those specialized for backgammon or chess, often with reversible boards or a second board that folded beneath the top in the compartment used to store game pieces.

Utilitarian tables for private rooms and for the less wealthy were similar to those previously used. Trestle tables remained common, as did tables with turned legs connected by low stretchers. (See Figure 16.22.) The large refectory table usually had six, eight, or even more legs, all connected by stretchers and was designed to remain in one place. Some had drawers in the aprons. The aprons themselves might be shaped with Baroque curves or have the appearance of a classical entablature. The William and Mary gate leg table retained its popularity well into the eighteenth century. Draw tables had a large overhanging top made in two layers. The bottom layer pulled out to extend the top when needed. Draw tables frequently had a relatively large apron in which drawers were located.

BEDS

Beds most often had completely upholstered headboards, footboards, and sometimes side panels. Some beds were painted, especially when the woods used were inferior. Testers were sometimes supported from the ceiling or wall behind, rather than by tall posts, and were draped in fabrics. Tall posts were still used on some beds, and the finest examples had a plume of feather, called a **panache**, above the tester on each post. Beds were often separated from the remainder of the room by a balustrade, especially in palaces, to separate visitors from occupants. Only individuals with a certain status were allowed beyond the balustrade. In addition, the bed might be raised on a dais. In hot climates such as Spain and sometimes Italy, beds often employed turned spindles in headboards, and curtains were often omitted. Some iron beds were made; these beds were more sanitary because small creatures did not burrow into their components.

FIGURE 16.21 Console tables were always very decorative because they served no practical function and were designed entirely for ostentatious display.

FIGURE 16.22 This English marquetry table has typical twist-turned legs with a cross stretcher. Note the drawer in the apron.

In England, where cabinetmakers were experienced with the techniques of veneering, Queen Anne furniture was made of oak and veneered with walnut. Some mahogany was used but the import duty made it prohibitively expensive until the succeeding Georgian period when, in 1733, the duty was removed. During the English Georgian period, mahogany imported from the Caribbean was so extensively used that the period is sometimes known as the Age of Mahogany.

While the grain was not as interestingly patterned as was that of walnut, mahogany was resistant to attack by worms, a significant problem with walnut. Because mahogany was easily carved and resulted in finely detailed ornament, the use of marquetry declined. Mahogany trees were exceedingly large and wide boards suitable for furniture tops were easily obtainable. Mahogany also had greater strength than walnut making it possible to use more slender, delicate supports that required no stretchers.

American Queen Anne differed from English examples in that solid walnut pieces were common partially because walnut was plentiful and partially because American cabinetmakers were less experienced with veneering. Other native American woods used for Queen Anne furniture included maple and cherry, which looked like the more expensive mahogany.

Régence in France (1700–1730)

When Charles LeBrun, head of the French academies under Louis XIV, died in 1690, the rules established by the academies were somewhat relaxed. Louis XIV, too, seemed to have changed, as he remarked that decoration should include playing children rather than classical heroes. A reaction set in to the severity of the Baroque. The revocation of the Edict of Nantes had resulted in the emigration of large numbers of artisans, the end of the wars of Louis XIV resulted in a change in the balance of power in Europe, and a rising middle class brought about changes in lifestyles that ushered in a demand for increased comfort and informality. As French people prospered, more were able to afford stylish furnishings. On the death of Louis XIV in 1715, Louis XV (1710–1774) at the age of five became king of France. The style of the Régence, which had already begun, was so named because Louis XV was too young to rule and a regent, Philippe II, Duc d'Orléans (1674–1723), ruled for him until he was

considered mature enough to take the reins of government at the age of 13. The style was transitional and introduced the free-form curve that was to become a dominating feature of the subsequent Rococo style. The reaction to the formality of social life resulted in an appreciation of simple pleasures, an appreciation of nature, and socialization with smaller groups. Homes, and even palaces became smaller, rooms more intimate and comfortable, and décor reflected the spirit of the times. Painters employed scenes of love, foreshadowing the romanticism of the Rococo style.

Rococo Design

Rococo design was a continuation of the reaction against the heaviness and formality of French Baroque art that had begun during the Régence period. The style name is derived from two French terms: *rocaille* which was used to describe artificial grottoes and rock formations and *coquille,* or cockleshell, both of which were used decoratively. Baroque pieces were heavy in appearance and as rigid as court life. As humanism continued to develop, people became more optimistic and Rococo design mirrored the predominant lifestyle of the aristocracy during the latter part of the eighteenth century. While lifestyles of the era were more casual and intimate, they were also more artificial with make-believe and game-playing taking on a prominent role. Self-indulgence and a lack of morality and self-discipline were typical. Rococo art spread throughout Europe, and although it was less formal than the Baroque had been, it was still essentially a style of the aristocracy and was often rejected by the common people whose lives were still relatively difficult.

Although called the Louis XV style in France, Rococo design began when Louis XIV's apartment at Versailles was redecorated in 1701 in a less formal and more graceful style than the Baroque. Philippe II, Duc d'Orléans, moved the court from Versailles to Paris, where it was to remain. As a result of this relocation, French artistic initiative was also transferred to the city. French ornamental forms were typically executed in wood, which allowed less freedom in design than stucco forms used elsewhere.

As with other styles, there were differences in Rococo design in the various European areas. Like the Baroque, Rococo design was most popular in strongly Catholic areas, and it was in Germany, Bohemia, and Austria that it found its most exuberant expression beginning in the second quarter of the eighteenth century. In these areas, Rococo design was a natural outgrowth of the more exuberant German Baroque style, which was itself less formal than French Baroque. Forms were exaggerated with bold lines and strong asymmetry, and fanciful shapes were possible because stucco was used as a design medium. German designers relied more on natural forms than did those in most other areas. It was also German artisans who were able to most closely imitate Chinese porcelain. Manufacturing of German porcelain began c. 1709 in Meissen, where it spread to other centers in Europe.

In Italy, only the papacy and the city of Venice retained their former power and prestige during the Rococo period and most of Italy retained Baroque forms rather than adopting the Rococo style. Italian Rococo forms are often identified as Venetian because it was in that city that most Italian Rococo design was incorporated. Italian Rococo churches frequently employed a centralized plan with four apses. Multiple vaults and domes were incorporated in these buildings.

In England, the Rococo style was concurrent with a revival of Gothic architecture, resulting in a mixture of influences—Rococo, Oriental, and Gothic. Although the Rococo style was deemed "in the French taste," it has since been named for Queen Anne (1665–1714; reign from 1702) and for Thomas Chippendale (1718–1779), a furniture designer who created pieces in all three contemporaneous styles. The style itself was employed mostly for textiles, porcelain, and silver, but some rooms in noble houses could have been found on the Continent.

A subdued version of the Rococo style as influenced by England was found in colonial America. There, however, the style did not begin until a decade after Queen Anne's death, and it was mostly limited to furniture.

> **INFLUENCE 16.5**
>
> *Rococo design was revived in Europe beginning c. 1820 and in America c. 1830. In England, the revival of the form was mislabeled as the Louis XIV style. In the first decade of the twenty-first century, major furniture companies also added Rococo designs to their catalogs.*

Rococo design was used mostly in interiors where ornament often overshadowed structural forms, for furniture, and in accessories. Rooms were planned as complete works of art; furniture, paintings, mirrors, tapestries, and other decorative accessories were important components of the overall design. There were, however, some changes in architecture, especially in domestic buildings. The architectural orders faded from interiors. Structures themselves were often plain on the exterior with little indication of the exuberance of forms used inside. Rococo design was characterized by purely ornamental forms, the use of numerous graceful free-form curves, soft pastel colors, delicacy, and sometimes mild asymmetry. Geometric curves and straight lines that do not appear in nature were avoided in favor of riotous, irregular free-form curves and details. Rococo forms were smaller in scale than Baroque forms, although the complex forms of that style were retained. Many forms were borrowed from nature, and others were adapted from books. Of the books, those published by *Juste Aurèle Meissonier* (1695–1750) were most significant and featured numerous engravings using shell designs, a feature employed in Rococo architecture, interiors, and furniture. Early Rococo designs were based on flowing ribbons, and later designs on elongated S- and C-curves. Scrollwork was used in abundance and often combined with foliage, shells, flickering flames, branches, clouds, birds, masks, and garlands of flowers or fruit. Instruments used in professions were included in design, with musical instruments especially fashionable. The varieties of love were common themes in Rococo design: the love of a mother as well as erotic and romantic love. By 1730, Oriental designs, mostly from China, were incorporated in Rococo design.

Rococo forms were used alongside those of the Baroque until both were superseded by the Neoclassical style. Rococo forms were discontinued in French urban areas by 1785, although they remained fashionable in the provinces until replaced by the Empire Style associated with Napoleon I. (See Box 16.2)

ROCOCO INTERIORS

In contrast to Baroque rooms, those of the Rococo were smaller, more human in scale, and designed to enhance feminine beauty. Comfort, convenience, and emotional appeal replaced heroic scale and the ponderous glorification of the monarchy of the Baroque. New rooms were added for specific functions including dressing, socializing with small groups, and listening to music. Some rooms remained for large gatherings, but smaller rooms and hideaways in gardens or on the grounds of an estate provided for an increased emphasis on privacy. Spaces for public and private functions were better defined. In keeping not only with privacy but with an interest in mechanical devices, the dining table in the Petit Trianon on the grounds of Versailles sat on a floor panel that could be lowered to the pantry below, reset for the next course, and raised into place again without disturbing the occupants of the room. **Cabinets particuliers** were hidden rooms accessed through secret panels and used for private rendezvous.

Wood parquet and marquetry floors were typical, although, as in the Baroque period, public and exterior spaces were often floored with more durable marble squares in a counterchange pattern. Carpets from the Middle East and the new French factories at Aubusson and Savonnerie covered portions of rooms.

Unlike the high-relief forms of Baroque design, Rococo designs were executed in very low relief. Sculptural architectural forms were eliminated, and smooth-surfaced panels and walls were interrupted only by openings and chimneypieces. Doors, windows, and panels frequently ran from floor to ceiling on walls and might cover ceilings as well. **Boiserie** panels were typical. These ornate verticle wood panels were intricately carved, but the designs were usually either centered, at the top, or at the bottom rather than all over. Although panel sides were generally straight, the tops and bottoms of panels were more often formed by curves. Small moldings outlined the panels, which might be used not only for rooms but on doors and furnishings. Often these moldings were strongly asymmetrical. Pictures were sometimes set into these boiserie panels, carved ornament might be substituted with painted compositions, or panels might be covered with textiles or tiles. (See Figure 16.24.) When dadoes were used, they were very low, al-

FIGURE 16.23 Rococo interiors were even more elaborate than their Baroque predecessors. In some cases, almost every surface was covered with ornamentation, often gilded. The ornament was smaller in scale than Baroque decoration had been.

FIGURE 16.24 Early boiserie panels were un-painted but after 1720, most were painted—usually in ivory but sometimes in pastel colors. Notice that the designs in the ceiling panels are mildly asymmetrical.

though they were often eliminated. Idyllic pastoral scenes, musical instruments, floral bouquets and garlands, and scenes from pursuits such as hunting, and, toward the end of the period, motifs associated with love including Cupids and hearts were typical.

As Chinese influence increased, wallpaper, called **domino**, was introduced. Chinese wallpaper was hand-painted but less expensive than European examples. Panels were sometimes painted or otherwise decorated with chinoiserie, or motifs influenced by Oriental designs. Not only did these include typical Chinese designs but an associated style of decoration termed à la Turque derived from Turkish designs. Panels in this style featured women of a harem, men in turbans, and other Middle Eastern or Islamic forms. These designs were often used in arabesques and grotesques.

Rococo Furniture

The Rococo had begun in France, and it was there that the most elaborate furniture was made in the style for the court of Louis XV. In fact, Rococo furniture is also known as Louis XV, or Louis Quinze. Rococo furniture was light in weight and appearance, had minute detailing, and made use of the new cabriole leg. This type of leg was used typically only on the front of furniture with straight legs used on the back.

Bun, scroll, and slipper feet were typical on cabriole legs, and it was the English who introduced the claw and ball foot, which they also used with this leg. The claw and ball foot was inspired by Chinese bronzes imported to Europe, although Chinese furniture of the period did not make use of this design.

Like interiors, Rococo furniture made extensive use of shells, S- and C-scrolls, acanthus leaves, and asymmetry. After porcelain manufacture had been established in Europe, painted plaques were sometimes incorporated in furniture. In some areas where furniture was taxed but art was not, the addition of a painted porcelain plaque gave furniture the status of art, in which case it was not taxed. Porcelain slabs were also incorporated as furniture tops.

INFLUENCE 16.6

During the Rococo period, those living in rural areas of France became sufficiently stable economically to create a demand for stylish furniture such as that of the nobility but with simpler, modified designs. This style became known as French Provincial and was revived during the twentieth century.

French cabinetmaking was dominated by guilds in Paris with strict rules concerning which artisans were allowed to work on specific por-

FIGURE 16.25 This English carved wood and marble Rococo chimneypiece and overmantle was originally located in Winchester House in London. It was typical of English design that the complete fireplace surround and overmantle were carved as a single unit.

was used only sparingly in English and American designs due to the conservative nature of the clientele and ormolu was rare.

Oriental designs began to influence European designs during the seventeenth century, but it was Rococo rooms, furniture, and accessories that were most affected. One result of trade with the Orient was the importation of Ming Dynasty furniture and porcelain. The furniture featured straight legs with slightly curved edges, open fretwork, and lacquer finishes—all imitated by European furniture makers. **Japanning**, a technique used in Europe to imitate lacquer, was

tions of furniture or to use specific techniques. A *menuisier,* or cabinetmaker, was responsible for creating wood furniture but, with the exception of simple designs, was not allowed to execute carvings. Only sculptors were allowed to create elaborate carving for furniture. Ebenists made seating furniture and some case pieces, but they also used veneers and marquetry and created ingenious mechanisms for secret compartments and fall fronts. Others made ormolu mounts, but menuisiers attached them.

French Rococo inlaid designs were the most elaborate in Europe with a combination of tortoiseshell, silver, pewter, and gilt bronze with ebony. Ormolu mounts were gilded bronze forms attached to furniture pieces—a technique used extensively by André Charles Boulle. Ormolu often framed inlaid patterns or veneers. In France, gilding was applied in profusion to furniture, sometimes to entire pieces. In England, the use of veneers emphasizing wood graining was common and inlay was rarely used. Gilding

FIGURE 16.26 Monkeys (called singerie) that echo those in the room's tapestries are featured on top of this door surround. Such animals were typical of the exotic forms in Rococo design.

known in France as **vernis martin**. A new technique of the period that originated in Venice was that of **lacca povera**, or poor man's lacquer, called **découpage** in France. As the Italian term indicates, this was a way in which high-gloss designs could be added to inexpensive furniture to imitate imported Oriental furniture. Designs were simply cut out, applied to furniture, and varnished. When dry, gilding was sometimes added to details in the designs.

Italian furniture was often based on French models. German furniture was heavier, and English and Dutch furniture was more somber in appearance. Italian furniture used more marquetry, lacquer, and painted scenes.

Jeanne-Antoinette Poisson, Marquise de Pompadour[3] (1721–1764) was the most famous of Louis XV's courtesans. She greatly influenced architecture and furniture design by her patronage of those arts. As a result, Rococo furniture was lighter in appearance than were Baroque pieces. The tops and fronts of case furniture often featured compound curves. **Serpentine** tops had horizontally oriented curves. **Bombé** fronts had vertical curves, usually on more than one plane. Ogee bracket feet and scrolled feet were used on case furniture and in England early in the period, bun feet. Marble tops were often incorporated on tables. Stretchers were usually unnecessary on seating furniture, although some X-shaped serpentine stretchers were used for chairs. When table legs were exceptionally curved inward, they might be connected with a stretcher, but most tables did not require connecting the legs. Table legs were also self-supporting and required no stretchers. Spanish furniture typically retained stretchers. Especially in France, furniture feet were often cambered and covered at the base with ormolu mounts known as **sabots** to help protect the foot from damage. The backs of seating furniture were often shaped to match the paneling in a room.

The changing lifestyles of individuals during the eighteenth century resulted in numerous new types of furniture including matching pieces, more extended use of mirrors, innovative tables, and new seating units.

SEATING UNITS

A number of new chair types appeared during the Rococo period. Most had lower backs than Baroque examples in order to accommodate

FIGURE 16.27 Once clocks had decreased in size sufficiently, they were used in homes. This tall case clock exhibits characteristics of the artistic period and features ormolu mounts and sabots.

the elaborate hair styles fashionable during the period. Comfort was improved as more upholstered furniture became available. During the third decade of the century, chair arms were reduced in length to accommodate the elaborate hoop skirts worn by chic women.

The French **duchesse brisée** was a two-piece upholstered chair and elongated footstool much like a two-piece chaise longue. The footstool was often sufficiently long for users to stretch the entire length of their legs and often required six legs for support. The chair itself had a rounded back, often extending around to the sides, and arms, all of which were upholstered. (See Figure 16.28.) The French **duchesse** was a one-piece chaise longue with a rounded back. When it was made in two or more pieces with a chair and a separate footstool, the term duchesse brisée was used. On the **duchesse en bateau**, the footstool might have a three-sided curved back or the back might be on a third piece.

The fauteuil continued to be used. Cabriole legs were added, arms were padded but open, and X-shaped cross stretchers were typical. The **fauteuil a la Reine** was designed to sit permanently

against a wall and had a high straight back. The *fauteuil en cabriolet* was smaller and easily moved anywhere in the room but it was also more comfortable than the fauteuil a la Reine because the back had a slight vertical concave curve to fit the human form better. Italian versions often had higher backs that widened toward the top in a fan shape.

A new piece of furniture during the Baroque period was the **divan**. Originally, the *diwan* was a government council in the Ottoman (Turkish) Empire. The council sat on long seats composed of mattresses laid on the floor or on a raised framework along the sides of the room. Loose cushions were placed against the wall to lean on. The English began to use the name of the council for a cushioned or upholstered seating unit. At first, these seats were used in bedrooms; only later were they moved to more formal areas. In France, this sofa was called a canapé. In Italy, the completely upholstered **pozzetto** was an elongated

bergère designed to sit against the wall and the **divani da portego** was a settee, an elongated seating unit that consisted of two or more chair backs placed side by side with a single bench seat.

STORAGE FURNITURE

Chests with drawers were stacked on top of other chests with drawers, usually with a small setback between the two pieces. Tall case pieces such as these **chests on chests** often featured a broken architectural pediment with a decorative center finial. Many eighteenth century chests had built-in writing surfaces as well.

The French armoire with two full-length doors replaced the four-door buffet during the period. In Spain, the armario continued to be used as a wardrobe although there were usually four doors rather than two. In England and America, the lowboy continued to be used, although it was given cabriole legs and Rococo detailing.

Early versions of the **commode** during the Baroque period had two drawers in the same height unit. Later examples feature three or more drawers. As a result, two drawer commodes had taller legs. An apron or skirt projected below the bottom drawer in a curvilinear shape that was frequently emphasized by ormolu mounts. The front of the unit was treated as a single surface rather than each drawer being separately decorated. During the Rococo period, legs of two drawer commodes were similar to cabriole legs and had a double curved form. Three drawer units had shorter legs, and the curvature of the apron was slight. Commodes were often made in pairs, each of which was placed beneath a pier glass, or tall, narrow mirror with an elaborate framework. Pier tables, or console tables, without drawers were also made to fit beneath pier glasses. The term encoignure indicates "corner," and a **commode a encoignure** was a commode on which the drawers were flanked by quarter circle shelves. The **commode en console** appeared relatively late and had a single drawer. The **commode a vantaux** was an innovation of the Rococo period but was most common in the succeeding Louis XVI style. The commode a vantaux had two doors behind which was located a pair of drawers. The Italian **cassettoncino** was a small version of the commode with squared ends and typically three drawers. Small Italian chests with a single door were **comodini**. These often had a single small drawer above the door.

The bureau cabinet was developed in England. Most had two mirrored doors. The similar china cabinet differed in that the doors were glazed and shelves for display were located behind them. The lower section might have a bombé front (especially in the Netherlands) and contained drawers. The bureau bookcase was similar, but the top was enclosed by wood doors behind which were shelves. Frequently, the bombé base and the bookcase at the top were separated by a fall front writing surface with compartments behind it.

Writing furniture included the **bureau plat**; the **secrétaire a abattant**, or fall-front desk; and the mechanical writing table. The secrétaire a abattant had a pair of doors at the bottom, but the upper portion was closed with a single door that dropped down to form a writing surface. The fall front concealed a number of drawers. The mechanical desk was similar in appearance

to the bureau plat, but when the center drawer was opened, an adjustable writing surface could be angled upward. Side drawers had hinged covers. A brass gallery rail, or a short raised lip around the top, prevented objects from rolling off the top.

TABLES

Console tables continued to be used and changed little. Many had only two legs, as the back was designed to be attached to the wall and some were gilded or painted.

Small tables were made for a multitude of purposes. In Italy, the **trespoli** was designed to support a mirror used for dressing. This piece was found only in bedrooms. **Guéridons** were small tables with a tripod base that supported a carved pedestal. Some had marble tops.

FIGURE 16.29 The extreme inward curve of the legs of the pier table require the use of a stretcher, in this case, a solid one. Swags of carved fruit and foliage, a lion mask, S-scrolls, and representations of Diana, Roman goddess of the hunt, decorate this marble-topped table.

FIGURE 16.30 This English Rococo console table employs foxes for supports, and the design is centered around a mask of the Roman goddess of the hunt, Diana. Built for Longford Castle in Wiltshire, it was probably used in a room with a hunting theme.

FIGURE 16.31 Four gilded winged dragons guard the pagoda-like canopy of the Badminton Bed made in the mid-eighteenth century in English Chinoiserie style. The bed was japanned in several colors—typical of the period and made for the fourth Duke and Duchess of Beaufort. It was originally located in Badminton House in southern Gloucestershire.

BEDS

Beds remained similar to those already in use although the decoration changed to suite the lighter Rococo style. (See Figure 16.31.) Three new types were introduced during the Rococo period in France: the **lit à la Polonaise** and the **lit à la Duchesse**. The lit à la Polonaise had a small oval or round canopy overhead that was supported by curved metal posts. Curtains emanating from the canopy were gathered to the posts below mid level and covered the framework. The lit à la Duchesse had an elaborate half tester from which elegant swags, garlands, and fringe were supported. The curtains themselves were limited to the space near the head of the bead. The English called this type of bed an **angel bed**. The lit à l'anglaise was a bed with equally sized head and footboards joined by a member of similar height along the back. The bed was designed to fit into an alcove.

QUEEN ANNE AND CHIPPENDALE FURNITURE

In 1754, Thomas Chippendale (1718–1779), an English furniture designer, published *The Gentleman and Cabinet Maker's Director,* which helped to popularize Oriental designs. His book categorized Rococo design as French, Chinese, or Gothic. In his furniture construction, Chippendale employed elaborate carving using French designs but omitted inlay and ormolu. English furniture of this period also included Queen Anne style pieces that were delicate and featured restrained Rococo forms. Almost every part of Queen Anne seating furniture employed S-curves. Crest rails on chair backs formed yokes—a pair of symmetrical S-curved sections that curved downward at each end. Colonial American examples were more graceful than their English counterparts.

American Queen Anne furniture had more delicate proportions, substituted carved ornament for inlay, sometimes retained stretchers even though they were structurally unnecessary, and used less gilding than did English examples. English Queen Anne furniture made extensive use of lion or satyr masks as decoration especially on the knees of cabriole legs. These forms were exceedingly rare in America. The graceful splat-backed Queen Anne chair was known as a **fiddle-back chair** in America because the splat resembled the shape of that instrument.

Queen Anne furniture made extensive use of bombé fronts and **bonnet tops** on case pieces. Bonnet tops were similar to pediments and were most frequently curved. Corkscrew finials were often used on both sides and in the center of these tops. Bonnet tops were also used on American Chippendale-style pieces.

It was in Newport that the Chippendale style saw a new development. **Blockfront** furniture was common in northern Europe during the eighteenth century but not in England. Brought to America, the finest examples were made in Newport, Rhode Island. With the exception of the block front, designs followed contemporary pieces. Block front pieces were always case furniture—chests of drawers, desks, secretaries, or chests on chests. In Newport, each section had an arched top and a carved shell. In the center section, the shell was recessed, and on the projecting outer sections, the shell was raised. Job Townsend (1699–1765) and John Goddard (1724–1785) were

FIGURE 16.32 This graceful Queen Anne-style game table has a folding top and cabriole legs with ball and claw feet and shells carved at the knees.

FIGURE 16.33 Blockfront furniture was divided into three vertical sections of equal width. The center section was recessed, while the sides ones projected. All three sections were curved—the two outer sections had convex curves and the center section had a concave curve.

FIGURE 16.34 This English chair made c. 1760 features a combination of clustered Gothic columns for the legs, a pagoda-shaped crest rail, and Chinese fretwork in the splat and on the chair rails and back supports.

FIGURE 16.35 Typically, different woods were used in the same Windsor chair, taking advantage of the characteristics of each type of wood.

the most prominent American block front furniture makers. (See Figure 16.33.)

Although various American cities established Chippendale styles with specific features, in general, American Chippendale pieces derived from pattern books, were more simple than English examples.

What has become known as the Queen Anne chair was first developed in the Netherlands. This chair has cabriole legs, a yoked back, and a solid vertical splat with shaped edges. Unlike William and Mary chairs, the splat was connected to the seat rail and not to a stay rail above the seat. Between the center splat and the back supports, the chair back was open. Chippendale chairs often featured pierced splats, claw and ball feet, and a serpentine crest rail. (See Figure 16.34.)

Windsor chairs were of English origin but were used in all English-influenced areas. In America, the early versions were known as Philadelphia chairs. Early Windsor chairs were relatively large; it wasn't until the mid-eighteenth century that smaller, more feminine forms were made. The seat was saddled to add comfort. On English examples, legs were not splayed and stretchers were used infrequently. The backs of English Windsor chairs might have a shaped splat similar to that of the Queen Anne chair. American Windsor chairs used spindles for the entire back rather than a splat, legs were splayed, and a variety of stretcher styles were used. Legs of American Windsor chairs were turned, while English examples often had cabriole legs. (See Figure 16.35.)

Rediscovering the Past—Again

The Baroque and Rococo styles lasted until there was an increased interest in classical forms stimulated by the rediscovery of the buried cities of Herculaneum and Pompeii. Madame du Pompadour in France was one of the leading exponents of classicism, and she encouraged further examination of classical forms and a return to the simplicity of the period.

Neoclassical, Empire, and Greek Revival Design

Neoclassism was in part a reaction against the excesses of the Baroque and Rococo; it also resulted from a renewed interest in classical forms. Part of the ancient Roman city of Herculaneum that had been buried by lava when Mount Vesuvius erupted in 79 AD had been uncovered in 1709, and statues had been taken from it. Excavations began at Herculaneum in 1738, and Pompeii, buried by ash in the same eruption, was rediscovered in 1748. The translations of the ancient manuscripts found in those excavations resulted in significant interest in classical cultures. In addition, archaeologists and scholars eulogized classical art and philosophy. Archaeology became fashionable, and people flocked to the ancient sites and enthusiastically embraced classical philosophy.

Development of the Neoclassical Style

The resultant reaction in Europe, led by Paris, was to idealize and romanticize Roman civilization. In accordance with what were presumed to be ancient ideals and values, Europeans reacted against the Rococo as frivolous and decadent. Simplicity and morality, romantically associated with classical cultures, became the focus of the arts, and the Neoclassical style was restrained and dignified.

Study of the ancient civilizations also resulted in a movement known as the Enlightenment that stressed the importance of reason and the existence of natural order. This intellectual and philosophical movement spread through eighteenth-century Europe and America. It rejected the authoritarianism of absolute monarchies and espoused instead reason as the basis for authority. Results of this widespread doctrine included increased rights for common people and a decrease in influences from traditional sources of power. It was believed that reason could be applied to actions of individuals, society, and government and from this intellectual framework stemmed a number of movements for independence—in the United States, France, Latin America, Greece, and the Balkans. The writers of the American Constitution established a government based on Roman models and even used the term Senate for one of its governing bodies.

Neoclassical Architecture (c. 1750–1850)

The revival of classical architecture beginning in the mid-eighteenth century looked back again to classical designs. Helsinki, St. Petersburg, and other cities were revitalized during the period employing Neoclassicism. While publications resulted in similar designs over a wide area, there were still variations.

FIGURE 17.1 Helsinki, Finland, was built in the Greek Revival style.

Neoclassical buildings were characterized by the use of ancient Roman and Greek designs. Building façades often had the appearance of ancient temple fronts with a colonnaded portico and sculptured tympanum. Other buildings incorporated long, severe colonnades without the pediment. Moldings, anthemia, and antefixae were used appropriately on these symmetrical structures. Latin inscriptions often replaced sculptural groups such as those on the frieze of the Maison Carrée. Renaissance domes raised on fenestrated drums featured surrounding colonnades.

Box 17.1 Summary of Characteristics of Neoclassical Architecture

- Classical style sculpture on buildings
- Colonnades and porticoes
- Triumphal arches
- Quadrigas (chariots drawn by four horses)
- Domes on drums
- Classical temple front façades
- Latin inscriptions on buildings
- Symmetry on exteriors
- Some Palladian influences
- Palladian windows used on upper stories
- Openings flanked by sidelights and surmounted by rectangular or fanlights
- Segmental and triangular pediments over openings
- Sculpted or carved swags and festoons on exterior surfaces
- Belt courses sometimes visually divide the exterior horizontally
- Brackets or dentil moldings beneath roof edge
- Giant order pilasters dividing façade vertically
- Projecting central portion of building with a front-facing gable

Triumphal arches were copied from ancient Rome and were used for celebrating the glory of an individual or nation. The Arc de Triomphe in Paris is the most familiar of these arches, although there are numerous others, some of which were constructed in the last 50 years. The Wellington Arch in London was erected as a ceremonial entrance to Buckingham Palace but was later moved to Hyde Park Corner (1882). In St. Petersburg, the Moscow Triumphal Gate (1834–1838) was designed to celebrate victory in the Russo-Turkish War (1828–1829). Quadrigas, or chariots drawn by four horses, were sometimes mounted on the roof of structures such as The Brandenburg Gate in Berlin (1784). Some of these groupings incorporated individuals in classical garments.

The Parthenon in Athens, the Roman Maison Carrée in Nimes, and the Pantheon in Rome served as the major models for public structures. Many Neoclassic buildings, however, add a dome on a drum to the classical form, never a feature of ancient buildings. Monumental domes rose behind classic temple front façades and featured Palladian fenestration, balustrades, lanterns, and surrounding colonnades. La Madeleine in Paris begun in 1806 was based on the Maison Carrée, although there are domed bays on the interior.

An offshoot of the Neoclassical style was the Greek Revival style, which was popular mainly in Northern Europe and the United States. Edinburgh is called the "Athens of the North" due to its numerous Greek Revival structures, and much of Helsinki's city center is in the Greek Revival style. In Germany, only the courts in Berlin and Munich made use of the style, and the Brandenburg Gate is an example of their structures. In London, the British Museum was designed in the style. Typically, Greek Revival buildings have a temple front complete with pediment and a colonnade, but it is sometimes difficult to distinguish between Greek and Roman influences. In most areas, there was no differentiation between Greek- and Roman-influenced buildings. (See Box 17.1.)

Rapid growth of European cities demanded good city planning. Wide avenues emanating from central squares or circles divided cities and linked important buildings. The grid iron plan was used for most cities, with streets oriented to the cardinal directions. In Washington, D.C., major diagonal avenues radiating from the Capitol and the White House cross the grid iron of streets. Squares became an important part of

Neoclassical cities and often served as a backdrop for a sculpture or monument. In 1829, following the Egyptian influences of the Empire style, the Obelisk of Luxor, a gift to France from Egypt, replaced the guillotine in the Place de la Concorde. Residential buildings were often arranged around less grandiose squares or circles, providing places for the aristocracy to get away from the pollution, noise, and bustle of urban centers.

Neoclassical domestic buildings were more comfortable and convenient than their predecessors, but their exteriors changed little. Lightness in appearance was characteristic. Life was less formal, and that lifestyle was reflected in dwellings with smaller rooms, greater privacy, and ease of service. Often a hallway was added to access rooms without moving through other rooms. Mezzanines were built above some rooms, which lowered the ceiling and made rooms easier to heat. The large drawing room was divided into a bedroom, a dressing room, and a parlor or dining room. Other rooms were included to make living more convenient—sometimes even a bathroom.

Neoclassical Interiors

Until the mid-eighteenth century, European architects had interpreted only the exteriors of existing Roman remains, the large majority of which were either temples or public buildings. There was no information about Roman interiors; therefore, Renaissance and Baroque architects had copied and adapted exterior Roman forms for interiors. The cities of Pompeii and Herculaneum were well preserved and revealed more about classical life than had ever been known. Roman interiors, even of residences, were revealed for the first time. As Neoclassism developed, a new understanding of classical forms resulted in interiors unlike those of the Renaissance as Neoclassical design reflected actual ancient examples. Ancient Greek monuments were discovered slightly later, and books published in 1758 and 1762 piqued interest in Greek designs and ultimately led to the Greek Revival style.

Louis XVI Style in France

Late eighteenth-century France was ruled by Louis XVI, whose name the Neoclassical style takes. French participation in the American War of Independence, its war with Austria, and the unbridled spending of French monarchs left France heavily in debt. It was the French peasants who were most heavily taxed to meet financial obligations. (See Figure 17.2.) Writers such as Jean Jacques Rousseau (1712–1778), Voltaire (1697–1778), and Denis Diderot (1713–1784) promulgated the importance of human reason and natural order. Social reforms failed to keep pace with philosophical developments, creating further dissatisfaction. In 1789, the French Revolution began. In 1792, the French monarchy was officially abolished, and eventually both Louis XVI and his wife, Marie Antoinette, were executed for treason. In 1794, the Directory replaced the unstable government. The Directoire lasted five years and was replaced by the Consulate, with Napoleon Bonaparte as First Consul. In 1804, Napoleon proclaimed himself Emperor of France (1804–1814), and the Empire period was born.

FIGURE 17.2 Louis XVI was weak and ineffective, and his Austrian wife, Marie Antoinette, immaturely followed Rococo precedents as she play-acted as a dairymaid in the hamlet built for her at Versailles. The monarchs had no conception of what was happening to the French people.

FIGURE 17.3 The Panthéon in Paris had a Greek cross plan, a Corinthian order temple front complete with classical sculptures in the tympanum like that of the Roman Pantheon, and barrel vaults which were taken from Palladian designs.

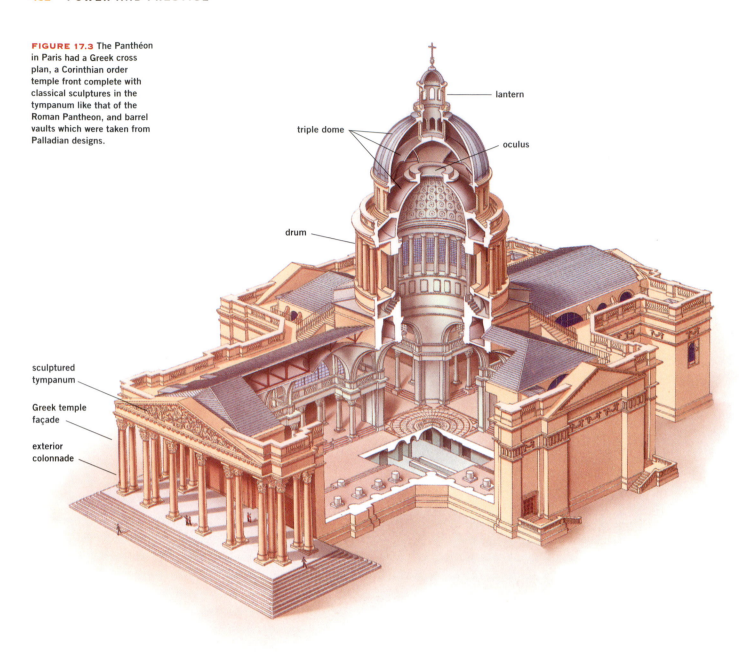

lantern

triple dome

oculus

drum

sculptured tympanum

Greek temple façade

exterior colonnade

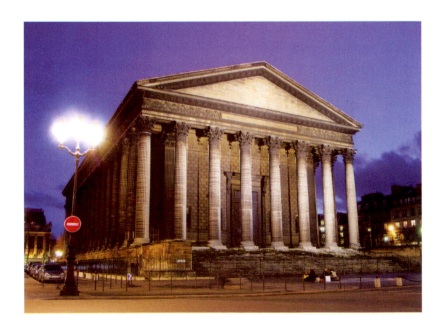

FIGURE 17.4 La Madeleine has 52 Corinthian columns surrounding the building, each of which is 65 feet in height. The sculpture in the tympanum represents the Last Judgment.

The Neoclassic period was cut short in France with the Revolution, but there are a number of examples of Neoclassical buildings. The Panthéon in Paris (1755–1781) had a Greek cross plan with a dome over the crossing. The dome was raised on a Renaissance drum with a Corinthian peristyle surrounding it. The structure was designed specifically as a protest against the excesses of the Baroque and Rococo and is an imitation of a Roman Corinthian temple complete with classical sculptures in the tympanum. (See Figure 17.3.)

La Madeleine (begun 1763) was based on the Maison Carrée, although it had three domed bays inside. Napoleon determined that this Corinthian building should be dedicated to his army, and it was not until 1842 that the structure was dedicated as a church.

FIGURE 17.5 On the grounds of Versailles, the Petit Trianon (1762–1768) was a Neoclassical structure with four pilasters across the façade. Inside, rooms are rectangular and the ceilings are flat.

Development of the Empire Style

In 1798, Napoleon Bonaparte led a military campaign in Egypt, hoping to seize control of the overland route to India and destroy British trade with that area. Napoleon was especially interested in classical civilizations, and on his campaigns in Egypt, he took with him biologists, linguists, archaeologists, and other scholars to record everything they found. The resultant *Description de l'Égypte* in 20 volumes was published in 1828. In 1799, Captain Pierre François Bouchard found the Rosetta Stone, on which a text was written in three scripts: Greek and two Egyptian scripts—demotic and hieroglyphic. The Frenchman Jean Francois Champollion translated the text by 1824. The key had been in translating the names of the Pharaohs from Greek. From that beginning, the numerous hieroglyphics in Egypt were translatable. Translations of the Rosetta stone were published and sold out quickly. Interest in Egyptology remained high during the first few decades of the nineteenth century, and the influence of Egyptology on Empire design was significant. Napoleon associated himself with the ancient civilizations and adopted motifs associated with them. Because Napoleon was a popular military leader, motifs associated with campaigns were added to the mixture of influences that resulted in the Empire style: French, Roman, Egyptian, Greek, and military influences. With a few exceptions, this style had little effect on architecture and was mainly one of interior design and furniture. In general, architecture continued to be Neoclassical in form.

FRENCH INTERIORS

French Neoclassical interiors retained much that was Rococo except that most curves were replaced with straight lines. Those that were not were changed to portions of a circle rather than the free-form curve of the Rococo.

FIGURE 17.6 In France, the triumphal arches of Rome were revived, enlarged, and employed as propaganda, to celebrate military victories, and to further associate the Empire of Napoleon with classical Rome. Here, the Arc de Triomphe in Paris stands at the center of a circle from which twelve avenues radiate and celebrates the victories of French soldiers in many battles beginning with those of Napoleon. It is beneath this arch that the French Tomb of the Unknown Soldier is located. The nineteenth century arch is in a direct line with the twentieth-century Grand Arch of the Defense.

FIGURE 17.7 The straight lines of the Neoclassical design are evident in both this room and its furnishings.

Walls were finished with painted plaster, faux marble designs, wallpaper scenes, wood paneling, or draped or stretched fabrics reminiscent of the interior of a military tent. Sometimes, fake tent poles appeared to hold up the textiles. Columns and pilasters were used on the interior as they had been in Pompeii and often flanked openings. Windows themselves were covered with voluminous draperies, valances, jabots, swags, and trims such as fringe.

Near the ceiling, there was either a cornice or a classical entablature, although ceilings themselves might be plain. Other ceilings were finished to give the appearance of the interior of a military tent.

Neoclassical Style in Italy

Rococo design continued in Italy until the time of Napoleon when French influences resulted in some Neoclassical designs. The Italians, who established a republic in 1802, had sought a leader and settled on the young Napoleon, who became king of Italy. A year after Napoleon declared himself emperor of France, Italy proclaimed itself an independent kingdom, but French design influence continued.

Georgian and Adam Styles in Great Britain

The British Empire continued to expand under George I (1660–1727), George II (1683–1760), and George III (1738–1820), for whom the early part of the Neoclassical period in England is named.

A revival of learning had begun during the Renaissance in England, and the interest in literature had continued. Educated people could still read Latin and Greek, but beginning in 1697, when John Dryden (1631–1700) translated and published Virgil's *Aeneid,* classical works were translated to the vernacular, making them available to the masses. A classical education became essential for a gentleman and included a Grand Tour of Europe with stops at major archaeological sites to experience classical architectural forms.

The Rococo style had never become universal in England, where taste was relatively conservative. Palladianism had continued to be fashionable, and as Neoclassical influences penetrated the country, there was little need for change. Both Palladianism and Neoclassicism built on the same Roman sources, although Palladianism was influenced by Renaissance interpretations of

Wood flooring was typical and parquet patterns common. Rugs were used to define specific areas of the room.

Rectangular wood wall panels predominated, less ornamentation was used, motifs were more classically oriented, and the asymmetry of the Rococo was replaced with formal symmetry. Walls often had a single large central panel with a centered motif flanked by smaller panels. Panels were often painted one color and the moldings around them another color. Wallpaper or fabrics were sometimes used in the panels rather than a central decorative motif. Walls opposite one another were treated similarly. Entablatures were used in rooms with high ceilings and coves or cornices in rooms with lower ceilings. Architectural orders were again used in interiors.

Mirrors continued to be used over fireplaces, although sometimes paintings were used instead. Grisaille paintings were often used over doorways in a lunette. Trim around openings was elaborate and in formal rooms might have a complete entablature. Ceilings were typically either plain or painted as a sky complete with clouds.

Empire interiors were masculine in keeping with the role of Napoleon. Square rooms were typical, although some had curved ends similar to those of ancient Rome. Pompeian and military decoration prevailed.

Floors often employed marble squares in counterchange patterns like those of ancient Rome or wood parquet. Carpets from French factories were often used to define areas within a room.

classical forms. Buildings and rooms of the two were very similar, although Greek elements were introduced in Neoclassical structures. George I was uninterested in artistic matters, and leadership in the arts fell to individuals who espoused the principles of Palladio and Inigo Jones (1573–1672).

New building laws in English urban areas sometimes forbade the use of projecting eaves, so a balustrade was usually substituted. English exterior design of the period was a mixture of Palladianism and Roman classicism, and on the interiors, Baroque and Rococo mixed with the more strict classical forms. Red brick was used for the exterior, with contrasting stone quoins at the corners. Wood trim around windows and doors often included pilasters or columns that supported a pediment, sometimes curved, over the doorway.

Late Georgian houses were large, formal structures much like Early Georgian examples, but with a projecting central gable on the front façade, a balustrade along the roof (on mansard roofs at the change in angle of the roof), and dormers projecting through the roof to provide light and ventilation to the attic. The doorway located in the central projection might be flanked by sidelights and surmounted by a semicircular fanlight. Often a pediment surmounted the first-story entry, with a second pediment in the gable of the projection. Columns supported the first-story projecting pediment. A tripartite Palladian window was featured over the central entry on the second story. Quoins often finished the corners, and a belt course visually divided the stories. Like Early Georgian buildings, Late Georgian examples also had a slightly overhanging roof with dentil moldings beneath. The symmetrically arranged windows were surmounted by flat arches of stone or brick.

INFLUENCE 17.1

Georgian designs greatly influenced those in the American colonies until the Revolutionary War, which occurred during the reign of George III.

Row houses, or townhouses, were constructed in urban areas so that people might have a sense of living in palatial surroundings without the expense associated with them. In England, these rows were known as **terraces**.

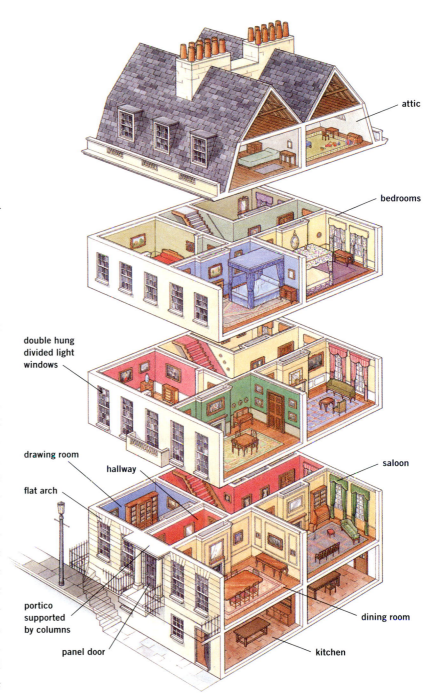

Typically, these row houses faced a park, square, or river. Usually the structures were four or more stories in height. Basements housed the service areas including the kitchen; on the ground floor were the reception rooms; the second floor was for large, formal rooms designed for entertaining; upper stories housed private family quarters including bedrooms. Smaller townhouses were designed for middle-class patrons and still smaller ones for artisans, laborers, and servants. (See Figure 17.8.)

Each terrace unit in Georgian town houses had a separate entry, although it was typically set at one side rather than centered in the façade.

FIGURE 17.8 The growth of urban areas during the eighteenth century resulted in the need to increase housing density. Georgian townhouses made it possible to build numerous small houses with fashionable façades. Thick walls between townhouses helped to preclude the spread of fire, and carried the weight of chimneys.

In England, detached Neoclassical structures were often designed to be set in large parks that incorporated English-style gardens such as those designed by the English landscape architect Lancelot "Capability" Brown (1716–1783) or by more formal gardens reminiscent of Renaissance examples. Brown's garden designs employed informal and natural features: serpentine lakes, large expanses of grass that extended to the house, and belts and clumps of trees were arranged so as to be "gardenless."

ADAM STYLE

Robert Adam (1728–1792), who became one of the most influential English designers, spent four years studying Greek and Italian buildings in those countries beginning in 1754. It was Adam and his brother James (1739–1794) who transformed Palladianism in England from the ponderous, formal style to Neoclassicism characterized by lightness and elegance. Using dramatic contrasts such as different room sizes and shapes, diverse decorative motifs, and a variety of forms within a single structure, their buildings exemplified what was termed the "principle of movement." Adam-style houses featured arches above openings, stucco finishes, and classical decoration such as urns, paterae, and wreaths on both the interior and exterior.

Kedleston Hall was designed by Robert Adam and constructed in Derbyshire, England, in the 1760s. The dome is similar to that of the Pantheon in Rome and surmounts the saloon, which houses a collection of classical sculptures. The first story is constructed of rusticated stone, while upper levels feature smoothly dressed stone. The front portico has six Corinthian columns on the projecting central section, giving the appearance of a classical temple. The south façade, designed by Adam, is based on the Arch of Constantine in Rome, although the arches are blind. The family wing is separate from the entertaining area. Curved **hyphens** connect the three larger buildings. (See Figure 17.9.)

INFLUENCE 17.2

The Adam style was to have a significant impact on the American Federal style.

GREEK INFLUENCES

James Stuart (1713–1788) and Nicholas Revett (1720–1804) met while taking the popular Grand Tour of Europe. They documented classical ruins in Athens and on returning to England published *The Antiquities of Athens* in 1761. This book served as a sourcebook for Greek designs on both sides of the Atlantic for two centuries and stimulated the development of the Greek

FIGURE 17.9
Kedleston Hall is a Georgian mansion constructed in the 1760s. The dome is similar to that on the Pantheon in Rome and surmounts the saloon which houses a collection of classical sculptures.

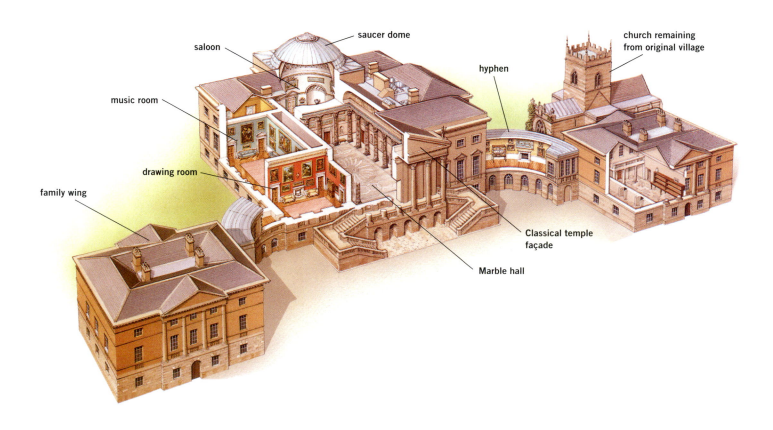

FIGURE 17.10 St. Pancras church in London employed numerous elements of Greek design. Added to the Greek temple form is a caryatid porch copied from the Erechtheion in Athens. In addition, the church tower was designed to emulate the Tower of the Winds in Athens.

Revival style of the nineteenth century. Stuart was, among other things, an architect, and after returning to England, designed several structures including Spencer House in London, one of the first Neoclassical buildings in that city.

Neoclassical designs influenced by Greek buildings typically had temple façades. It was difficult to design these façades with windows in them, since Greek temples did not have windows. The style was suited to banks, libraries, railroad stations, and museums but rarely to homes. For this reason, Greek-inspired buildings often have only a screen façade and the remainder of the building follows Greek designs less closely.

REGENCY IN ENGLAND

In his later years, George III suffered from a mental disorder, and his son, the future George IV (1762–1830), served as Regent for almost a decade beginning in 1811. By this time, English architectural styles had begun to change, and the ensuing style was named Regency. The Regency style was characterized by strict imitation of classical forms and was greatly influenced by concurrent French Empire designs.

Regency residences were similar to Georgian examples but typically had sidelights or tall, narrow stationary windows on both sides of the door. A blind segmental arch was usually used above the door itself. A small octagonal or round window might replace the window above the entry. Segmentally arched dormers might protrude through the Regency roof. Segmental arches are part of a circle but less than 180 degrees. Typically Regency houses were constructed of brick, sometimes painted white. Shutters flanked windows and the hip roof had little overhang.

English Interiors

Georgian walls and ceilings were ornamented with plaster moldings in a variety of shapes including swags, arabesques, and vegetative forms. Walls were treated with Chinese wallpaper with scenic designs, paneling until the middle of the century, framed paintings, some from China, and large mirrors to improve light reflection. Walls were further enhanced by the treatment of windows, which received elaborate draperies including valances and cornices.

Later Adam-style rooms employed forms that were more true to classic, especially Greek, examples. Numerous publications spread the style throughout Great Britain and America. Unique to the period was the conscious effort to ensure that every part of the interior conformed to the

FIGURE 17.11 This middle Georgian dining room relies on molding plaster decorations and richly carved trim around openings, on the fireplace surround and overmantle, and in the panels for its charm.

style. Robert and James Adam were leaders in the field of interior design and used columns with entablatures, plaster ceilings, semicircular arch-headed wall niches with classical sculptures, and formal arrangements. Domed ceilings were not uncommon, and end walls were often either curved or octagonal and treated with architectural orders similar to the treatment of Roman tribunals and exedrae. Walls were sometimes paneled with wood, but after the mid-eighteenth century, plaster became more common. These plaster walls were painted white or with a pale color, faux marble, or faux wood grain. White plaster moldings continued to be applied to wall surfaces and contrasted with the color or finish of the walls behind. Greek or Roman designs were used both for plaster ornament and painting.

Ceilings featured plaster designs except in small homes. These plaster casts were lighter and more delicate than previous examples had been. Garlands, paterae, rinceaux, arabesques honeysuckle, frets, husks, urns, and swags were all used as decorative motifs.

Fireplace mantels were architectural in nature, with an entablature beneath which there was a decorative frieze. In Adam examples, there is typically a center motif in the frieze flanked by varying colors of marble or flutes. The mantle

might be supported by columns, pilasters, caryatids, or a decorative molding.

Regency rooms employed Egyptian motifs, numerous curves, plain painted plaster walls in dark colors, Doric and Ionic orders, and simpler ornament such as the honeysuckle and fret. Segmental arches were common and might be used with a large cove beneath the ceiling. It was during this period, however, that past styles began to be used again, some of them exotic. Brighton Pavilion (1815–1823), built for the Prince Regent, incorporated a superimposed cast-iron framework over an existing dome to create an Indian-style structure. Chinese influence on the interior included gilded dragons and imitation bamboo. The ceiling of the kitchen is supported by cast-iron posts surmounted by palm leaves.

Neoclassical Styles in America

American design followed English designs relatively closely as the country grew more prosperous and self-sufficient, and the Georgian style popular in England was also common in America. Unreasonable taxation and laws designed to limit American trade with other nations were among the reasons for the Revolutionary War by which America gained its independence. Americans were also inspired by the ideas of the Enlightenment and used Neoclassicism as a symbolic link between pre-Augustan republican Rome, the democracy of Greece, and the new United States. During the Revolutionary period, design was stagnated. After the war, the Neoclassical influences that continued were termed Federal in honor of the new republic. Both Benjamin Franklin and Thomas Jefferson were ambassadors to France and were influenced by their visits to that country. In addition, the Louisiana Purchase in 1803 and the influences of France on English design resulted in a blending of French, English, Roman, and Greek influences in American design. (See Figure 17.13.) The Neoclassical period in America ended with the Greek Revival style. Americans who had just successfully obtained their independence were sympathetic to the Greek struggle against the occupying Ottoman Turks (1821–1829). In America, it was a period of great expansion, and the Greek influences felt during the period resulted in numerous American cities named for Greek ones: Sparta, Athens, Ithaca, and Syracuse, to name a few. Expansion required the construction of new buildings and many were built in the Greek temple style.

In America, libraries and public buildings were typically constructed in the Georgian style, the first phase of Neoclassicism in the United States. Independence Hall in Philadelphia was a modest Georgian building to which the steeple was later added.

A **belt (or string) course**, or projecting horizontal band, was used in masonry buildings to

FIGURE 17.13 Thomas Jefferson was particularly influenced by the Maison Carrée in Nîmes, which he later used as a model for the state house in Virginia. The Virginia Capitol, however, employed unfluted Ionic capitals rather than fluted Corinthian ones. The number of windows and doors was also increased to suit the needs of occupants. (Compare with Figure 4.13.)

define the extent of each story on the exterior. The entry was often treated with a single row of small rectangular windows in the header above the paneled door. Hip, gable, or mansard roofs were common and projected beyond the junction with the wall. The underside of the resulting cornice was decorated with dentil moldings reminiscent of classical forms. (See Figure 17.14.)

AMERICAN FEDERAL STYLE

In America, multistoried Federal-style buildings were used alongside Georgian examples. Federal-style buildings were also symmetrical and

FIGURE 17.14 Like Georgian buildings, the Federal Capitol building in Washington, D.C., has a main central area flanked by two buildings with classical temple façades that serve as chambers for the House of Representatives and the Senate. These buildings are separated from the central structure by hyphens, or smaller, lower buildings that connect larger structures.

FIGURE 17.15 The Early Georgian houses were plainer than those of later Georgian architecture. They had a simple boxlike shape, were typically two or three stories high, and had one or more large chimneys. Chimney location depended on the climate, but end chimneys were common in warm climates; central chimneys in cold climates. These houses used three, five, or seven "ranks" or vertical lines of openings across the front with the entry centered. Five-ranked buildings were most typical.

generally five-ranked. (See Figure 17.15.) The central doorway was surmounted by a fanlight that was typically semi-elliptical in shape. The roof balustrade at the edge of the roof almost hid the low-pitched hip roof. There was typically little roof overhang, although when there was it was treated with dentil moldings. A fenestrated **belvedere**, or enclosed projection through the

roof, might also feature a balustrade. Ornamentation was delicate and might include swags and festoons, ribbons, or bows.

JEFFERSONIAN STYLE

Jeffersonian Classicism was used for impressive structures. Monticello is an example. Symmetry was important, and the front entry was centered on the façade and covered with a projecting portico designed as a Greek temple front and supported by columns. A semicircular fanlight might be incorporated in the tympanum. The entry doorway was usually surmounted by a triangular pediment, and windows were arranged symmetrically. Pilasters were often used on walls. Like Late Georgian homes, Jeffersonian Classical buildings may feature a balustrade on the roof. (See Figure 17.16.)

GREEK REVIVAL STYLE (1820–1850)

European buildings typically employed masonry bearing-wall construction that required cutting and transportation of stone or manufacture of bricks. American settlers moving westward in the nineteenth century had neither the time nor skill to devote to such labor-intensive processes. Wood had been widely used in America during the colonial era and beyond for building construction but in the form of heavy timber-framed construction that required more than one worker to

FIGURE 17.16
Monticello had a central octagonal dome raised on a relatively short drum, which was fenestrated with circular and semicircular windows.

lift and place structural units. This method also required expertise in making joints that would ensure stability of the structure.

The **balloon frame** was an American innovation developed when Greek Revival was popular, what Walker Field calls "the first great impact of Americanism upon architecture" (Field, 1942). Making use of lightweight lumber put together with nails, balloon framing supports the weight of the structure. The wall infill bears no weight but its own and can be any material. The regularly spaced framing members distribute the load evenly. Field cites two reasons for the development of this type of framing in the nineteenth century: the lack of skilled labor and the dominance of wood construction. Balloon framing was first used in Chicago by Augustine Taylor in 1833 for St. Mary's Church. Called Chicago construction until the last quarter of the nineteenth century, the term balloon framing was a derisive one. Since the framework was constructed of relatively lightweight boards, critics assumed the structures would not be durable.

A major advantage of wood frame construction was the flexibility of the plan. No longer was it necessary to build boxlike structures. Light framing facilitated the construction of numerous corners and projections that would otherwise have been exceedingly expensive. This flexibility made possible the variety of building forms used after its introduction. Another advantage of wood frame construction was that buildings could be constructed by people with little training, especially when nails were used. Buildings could also be erected quickly: some of the early Chicago houses were built within a week. Above all, framed houses were much less expensive than timber framing.

The Greek Revival style was first used in America in public buildings in Philadelphia. Americans were disenchanted with the English after the War of 1812 and sympathetic to the Greeks, who began their own bid for independence in the third decade of the nineteenth century. Public structures were built of stone or brick and several stories in height. The Doric order was used most frequently with triglyphs and metopes in the entablature. The tympanum was usually plain and lacked the carvings of classical examples. Like their ancient predecessors, Greek Revival buildings might feature a peristyle, or colonnade around the entire building.

FIGURE 17.17 This small Greek Revival building is typical of such structures with the centered doorway, an even number of columns across the front, and pilasters at the corners of the main structure.

Public buildings were much more elaborate than domestic structures.

Until the development of the balloon frame, Greek Revival structures were restricted to public buildings and homes of the wealthy. When balloon framing was applied to these structures, all that was necessary was to add a pediment and a few columns to support a porch or portico roof. With this, the Greek temple returned to its original pre-Hellenistic wood form. These less ostentatious American Greek Revival buildings had front gables with a pediment framed by simple moldings, a plain frieze above a simple entablature, and typically columns or pilasters across the front. A covered, colonnaded porch might be present. Centered doorways in the symmetrical façades often featured sidelights. Most had white-painted clapboard on the exterior. Typically, smaller homes were a single story but when the style became popular in the South for large plantation homes, they were almost always two or three stories with a colonnaded porch across the front. The style lasted until the Civil War in America.

Neoclassical and Biedermeier Styles in Germany (1815–1848)

Neoclassical design did not reach Germany until late, around 1780, and was based on English and French examples. By the time Neoclassism had begun to spread through Germany, Napoleon had occupied part of the country, bringing with him the French Empire style. As a result of military conflicts, Germany was impoverished. After the defeat of Napoleon at the Battle of Waterloo in 1815, German urban areas grew as a result of increasing industrialization and workers moving into cities for job opportunities. At the same time, the political situation became oppressive, and it became unsafe to discuss politics or to criticize the government. Censorship of printed matter resulted in concentration on nonpolitical topics, and social discourse moved from public cafes to the domestic scene, where it was safe to discuss matters with close associates. Domestic life became more important, and because people spent more and more time at home, comfort became a priority.

The grand Empire furniture was too expensive for most people to afford. A simplified version, known as Biedermeier, however, became extremely popular especially with the middle class and lasted for much of the nineteenth century. The term Biedermeier was not applied until 1900 but was derived from the name of a humorous character, Papa Biedermaier, in satirical writings about the first half of the nineteenth-century political situation. The style was one of furniture and some interiors rather than architecture.

Biedermeier furniture symbolized the middle class and consisted of simplified interpretations of French Empire pieces. It was the first furniture style that was introduced by and for the middle classes, although it was used by all classes eventually. Pieces were simple in form, comfortable, and utilitarian. In contrast with Neoclassical fur-

niture, curving, rather than straight, lines dominated. Comfort and function were paramount. To that end, seating furniture, writing cabinets, display cabinets, and ladies' worktables were common. In the simple, plain interiors, there was little use for more decorative pieces. Biedermeier furniture, along with French and English examples, was adopted in Russia as well. Biedermeier furniture was revived during the last decade of the nineteenth century when it was also influenced by Victorian designs.

FIGURE 17.18 A significant principle underlying Biedermeier furniture was truth in materials. The furniture employed fruitwood, elm, or other woods indigenous to each area rather than expensive mahogany. Much of it used light-colored woods. Expensive finishes such as marquetry, ormolu mounts, and veneering were absent from most pieces.

INFLUENCE 17.3

The truth-in-materials principle was influential in later Bauhaus designs.

INFLUENCE 17.4

The elegant simplicity of Biedermeier furniture was influential in Jugendstil, Art Nouveau, and Bauhaus designs.

Due to the political turmoil, fewer Neoclassical buildings were constructed in central Europe than in other areas, and those were late in the period. Typically, they followed French forms. The Brandenburg Gate in Berlin was based on the propylaea, or gateway, on the Acropolis in Athens. (See Figure 17.19.) Several museums and art galleries were constructed in the style as well. However, neoclassicism did not suit the masses who were spending more of their time in homes. Their houses were now constructed back away from the street as an indication of the privacy they preferred as a result of the political climate.

Neoclassical Furniture

Neoclassical furniture was characterized by straight lines, a reaction to the multiple curves of Rococo. When curves were used, they were mechanical rather than free-form, so segmental and semicircular curves and ellipses predominated. Furniture legs were tapered and typically round in cross section with flutes or twisted turnings or square in section. These legs had a square block at the top that often had a decorative carving such as a rosette. When cabriole legs were used, the curves were shallow.

Case furniture was rectangular, although circular or oval tabletops were sometimes used. Tabletops had no moldings but, rather, squared edges. Marble was sometimes used for tops of small tables and case furniture. Leather was

FIGURE 17.19 The Brandenburg Gate in Berlin uses six pairs of Doric columns through which five roadways pass. The goddess Viktoria, driving the quadriga surmounting the gate, carried the olive wreath representing peace. Later, the quadriga was carried away to Paris by Napoleon. When it was returned, the wreath was replaced by an iron cross and the goddess changed to one of victory.

used as a surface for writing on desks and writing tables.

LOUIS XVI FURNITURE

French Louis XVI furniture was graceful and refined, with perfect proportions. Delicate ornament softened the severity of the straight lines of the symmetrical pieces. Marquetry continued to be a favored decorative treatment and was set off by carved moldings and ormolu mounts. Ormolu mounts were frequently cast from original molds and were difficult to distinguish from baroque examples. Floral designs and ribbons were used in profusion and, unlike other designs, were not necessarily strictly symmetrical. Other pieces, especially mahogany, were plain with veneered surfaces and panels framed by one or more parallel borders. Late in the period, the borders were inlaid brass strips or contrasting wood rather than narrow, sometimes bronze, moldings.

Like other Neoclassical designs, Louis XVI furniture made use of circles, ellipses, and ovals. Semicircular arches were used on crest rails, panels, and for the tops of tables and commodes. Sometimes, oval, elliptical, or circular insets were used within rectangular panels and might surround a marquetry floral design in a vase or basket. Marquetry in diaper patterns and band patterns was common and often featured diamond or lozenge shapes. The lozenge shapes of reticulated marque-

try might enclose realistic-appearing marquetry flowers. Chains of beads, husks, or leaves formed festoons and vertical drops.

Like ancient Roman architecture, Louis XVI furniture often featured multiple moldings separated by fillets, but the moldings were reduced in scale from Baroque designs. Ormolu mounts were also smaller and minutely detailed. The dark background of ebony and japanned pieces furnished a dramatic contrast to ormolu garlands, wreaths, or knots or to the porcelain plaques that were sometimes added to furniture.

FIGURE 17.20 Although Louis XVI furniture was typically rectangular, the corners were often treated with an inward curve or a squared-in cutout.

Although some **harlequin** furniture, or that which had complex mechanical devices, was used earlier, it reached its peak under Louis XVI. Often, when set in motion, the mechanical devices revealed secret compartments, but many of the devices transformed furniture pieces.

INFLUENCE 17.5

Harlequin furniture was a precursor to the patent furniture of the Victorian era when complex mechanical devices were again used. Some contemporary pieces, such as the sofa bed, have similar features.

Supports for Louis XVI furniture included tapered forms employing either a quadrangular or cylindrical form.

Louis XVI fauteuils were less comfortable than were Rococo examples and always had straight legs. Chair frames were gilded, **parcel gilt** (gilded only in some places), or left in their natural state. Some curving lines softened the rectilinear profile; bowed seat fronts and incurving arm supports were typical. The inward curve of the arms was designed to accommodate the panniers or extended sides of women's dresses. Once panniers were no longer fashionable, arm posts were baluster shaped and vertical. The back was usually slightly concave, or **cabriolet**, to better fit the human form. Two types were made: those with oval medallion backs and those with rectangular backs. Frequently, chairs with oval backs featured a carved bowknot in the crest rail. Rectangular backs were square or almost square, although some examples were slightly splayed outward at the top and had a slightly arched crest rail. The top of the back itself might be straight or match the curve of the crest rail. On this type of chair, the slanted back supports were often surmounted with finials. The open arms of all types of fauteuils had upholstered pads, or **manchettes**, that covered approximately three-quarters of the arm top, leaving wood exposed at both ends. The arms were joined to the back in a downward curve that might begin as high as the top of the back uprights. On the front, the arm posts were attached at the top of the legs rather than inset. The canapé was often designed en suite with the fauteuil and followed its design.

Another armchair was used at dressing tables or writing tables with a circular seat that often revolved. The low horseshoe-shaped back contin-

ued around the sides to form arms that rested on incurved supports. Typically, all four legs were tapered fluted cylinders. The back of this chair was often caned.

The side chair without arms was known as a **chaise**. Some were made of mahogany; others used inexpensive woods and were gilded. The seat might be caned or upholstered with leather. Pierced splats and solid splats with a **hoop back** or a single piece of wood curved around to form both the side supports and the crest rail. The most fashionable type of chaise, however, featured a lyre back in the shape of a musical instrument.

BEDS

All of the types of Rococo beds continued to be used, although the lit à la duchesse and the lit d' ange were most popular. The lit à la Turque continued to be used, and the lit à colonnes, or four poster bed, was reintroduced. In the colder regions of Europe such as northern France, the cupboard bed, or **lit clos** in France, continued to be used because it offered warmth. An upper berth was often included so that all family members could sleep comfortably in the warmth generated by their own bodies. Spindles, pierced ornament, or shutters provided ventilation. Typically, a chest was located in front of the opening to provide a step. The lit demi clos was closed off with curtains rather than with doors.

TABLES

Louis XVI tables were similar to those of the Rococo period, although serpentine tops were no longer fashionable. Pierced gallery rails that extended three-quarters around a table or desk or completely around a piece of furniture became common. The chiffonnière, tricoteuse, guéridon, and table à pupitre continued to be used. (See Figure 17.21.)

Some pieces were designed as part of a wall composition including commodes, entre-deux, or low cupboards, corner cabinets or encoignures, and marble-topped console tables. Semicircular tabletops were fashionable, and two could be placed back-to-back to form a larger table. The table à dèjeuner was a small portable table used for serving tea, coffee, or small meals. The surrounding metal gallery was designed to keep dishes from falling off when the table was transported.

The **athénienne** was a small tripod washstand or table based on Pompeiian forms. The

FIGURE 17.21 The bouillotte table was designed for playing the card game after which it was named. A metal gallery rail surrounded the round-topped table. The frieze or apron of the table was fitted with two drawers. Four legs supported the table.

three supports were typically surmounted by a figure, such as an Egyptian caryatid, ram's head, or swan, and often had an animal's foot at the base. The feet were sometimes joined by a solid stretcher at the bottom and might have an intermediate shelf of triangular shape to support a pitcher or ewer. The circular support at the top held a metal or stone lavabo or washbowl. When the athénienne was a table, it usually supported a vase. It could also serve as a support for a perfume burner. The stand was used in both the Louis XVI and Empire periods.

All of the writing furniture used during the Rococo period continued in use during the Louis XVI era, with the bureau à cylindre and harlequin tables most fashionable. Sometimes, the top of the bureau à cylindre had three small drawers added to it. A three-quarter gallery rail was common on this desk. Beneath the writing surface, there were five drawers: a long central drawer flanked by a pair of stacked drawers on either side. A **cartonnier** was a shelf that sat on the end of a writing table and that held papers. The **bureau à caissons latéreaux** was a writing table with compartments beneath the writing surface similar to the drawers of the bureau à cylindre. It looked much like modern kneehole desks. The back side of the bureau was fitted with faux drawer fronts. The secrétaire à abattant continued to be used and was often designed en suite with encoignures, commodes, or both.

CABINETS

Cabinets continued to be luxury pieces and featured secret compartments and numerous small drawers.

The **commode desserte** was a type of commode with drawers and shelves: the drawers occupied the center section, and shelves were fit into the corner between the drawer section and the end of the piece. The shelf section was rounded into a quarter circle. Frieze drawers included a single central drawer and side drawers that might swing out rather than slide out. Beneath the center drawer was an additional pair of drawers. Beneath the lateral drawers were two shelves. Infrequently, a semicircular, or **demi-lune**-shaped, top was employed. The commode desserte served the same function as the medieval buffet. The **desserte** had a semicircular top and shelves rather than center drawers.

The **vitrine** was a cupboard with glazed doors behind which were display shelves. Typically, the furniture piece itself was plain so as not to detract from the objects displayed within it.

The jardinière was introduced during the Louis XVI period. Also called the table a fleurs, it was designed to hold flowers and plants. A frieze hid the metal-lined interior that enabled the flowers to be watered. The jardinière was supported on four legs. The mid-eighteenth-century perfume burner, or brûlete parfum, was a classic urn made of stone or metal with a perforated top. A metal liner held charcoal on which perfumed substances were sprinkled. Their fragrance emanated as the charcoal burned. Typically, they were supported on a tripod base.

DIRECTOIRE FURNITURE

As the penchant for classical design increased, there was a desire for closer imitation of antique models, a characteristic of Directoire furniture. Ebony, mahogany, and even more exotic woods such as kingwood were used more than for previous styles. Caryatids, canephorae, and columns were employed for supports; classical band patterns such as dentils, guilloches, frets, and Vitruvian scrolls were used on friezes; and Roman rams, lions, dolphins, goats, and eagles decorated furniture and interiors. In fact, most of the decorative motifs of ancient Rome were incorporated in Directoire design. Greek designs had begun to be known, and Directoire design also incorporated Greek forms. French designs also continued to combine such classical motifs with floral arrangements in vases or tied with bowknots with ribbon streamers. Mythological subjects, musical instruments, and designs associated with agriculture, the sciences, hunting, and pastoral life were also common. The lyre form, star, and lozenge were especially suitable for furniture. Motifs used during the French Revolution were sometimes used on Directoire furniture, although by that time, most of the symbols had ceased to be used. The Phrygian bonnet, also known as the cap of liberty, symbolized the third estate, or common people; the Roman fasces, clasped hands that signified brotherhood, the cross representing the clergy, the sword representative of nobility, and the tricolor (red, white, and blue) cockade (a type of hat) symbolic of the new republic were used on furniture, textiles, and in paintings.

Tapered quadrangular or cylindrical supports continued to be used and often terminated with brass caps on the feet to which casters were attached. The **toupie**, or top-shaped leg and the quadrangular leg that curved outward were also used. Much of the furniture used was a continuation of pieces used in the previous period. Only the decorative elements had changed.

It was during the Directoire period that the Greek klismos was once again introduced. The broad crest rail was sometimes rolled over, and the back often had a larger angle than had classical examples. Like their ancient predecessors, the Directoire chair had slightly concave quadrangular back supports that splayed backward. Arms were often added to the chair and supported on vase shaped or baluster-turned supports. Front legs, too, flared outward in a curve. When the back was rolled over, the front of the seat was often bowed. Sometimes a classic urn was carved in a lozenge-shaped panel on the back rail. A number of designs were used incorporating a variety of splats and rail types. Many of the chairs were painted, usually with a light background with details painted in a darker color. Gondola bergeres continued to be used. Arm posts sometimes incorporated swans, the motif used by Josephine, or terms. Canapés followed the same designs.

During the Louis XVI period, the daybed became a common item of furniture and was derived from classical couches designed for dining. These daybeds continued in use, especially the Récamier bed (named for Madame Récamier whose portrait was painted while sitting on one). The sides of daybeds rolled outward and were either of equal height or unequal height. Toupie legs were typical.

FIGURE 17.22 Chair backs of Directoire furniture were often scrolled. Here, back legs of chairs reflect Greek antecedents while front legs are turned.

The Directoire bed had ends, or **dossiers**, of equal height either surmounted by pediments or scrolled outward. The vertical supports were baluster turned. During the Empire period, a sculptured figural support with two feet was most common.

Large oval or round dining tables were typically constructed of mahogany. Gate leg and drop-leaf tables were used for smaller meals. Center tables were designed to be permanently located in the center of a room and typically had round marble tops. These tables continued into the Empire period.

EMPIRE FURNITURE

During the Consulate, Napoleon began to reestablish the luxurious traditions of France. Although he had no new palaces constructed for himself, Napoleon ordered the redecoration of a number of existing buildings, including Malmaison, which was his wife Josephine's home. For all of his work, Napoleon called on the expertise of Pierre François Léonard Fontaine (1762–1853) and Charles Percier (1764–1838). It was their designs that began the Empire style. Furniture for Napoleon and the ruling class was made by trained cabinetmakers, but much other Empire furniture was not. The French Revolution had disrupted the guild system, and there were few new artisans being trained.

Napoleon desired to associate himself with the ancient Roman Empire and continued the practice of employing motifs from that era. Although Greek designs were used during the Directoire period, they were not adequate to express the power and majesty of the man from Corsica. The designs initiated during this period led to the French Empire period that officially began only when Napoleon crowned himself emperor in 1804. Empire design was pompous, heavy, formal, and more masculine than Neoclassical or Directoire design. Like Directoire design, Empire forms closely imitated Roman examples. Some changes were necessary largely because the ancient Greeks and Romans had very different lifestyles from the nineteenth-century French.

The imperial eagle of Rome was introduced as a motif symbolic of the French Empire under Napoleon, and the winged figure of Victory symbolized Napoleon's conquests. Greek and Roman deities and heroes, and also military emblems, were employed as motifs on Empire furnishings.

Although the Empire itself lasted only a decade, the style lasted two decades and influenced furniture design throughout the nineteenth century. German Biedermeier furniture was derived from Empire pieces and became popular with the middle class in that country.

Empire furniture was mostly rectilinear and angular, although curves were sometimes used in seating units. Corners remained sharp, and the overall appearance was blocklike. Large uninterrupted surfaces were decorated only with veneers and depended on graining for its aesthetic qualities. The difficult techniques used in previous periods such as marquetry and japanning were not employed for Empire furniture. Round columns with bronze bases and capitals were employed on furniture—sometimes engaged, sometimes freestanding. Bases were often massive. Empire pieces were severely symmetrical, and even small details had to conform. Even the arrangement of furniture was dictated by symmetry. Low-relief carving was occasionally used and might be gilded. Marble tops were used, as were a few inlaid metal bands. Ormolu mounts, however, continued to be used and became a dominant feature of much Empire furniture. (See Figure 17.23.)

Supports included winged sphinxes, lions, chimeras, eagles, monopodia, terminal figures, and swans.

Directoire pieces continued to be used, although decorative detailing was different and the forms were more massive. Supports on the backs

FIGURE 17.23 Unlike previous uses of mounts that protected corners and the edges of veneer from damage, Empire mounts were truly decorative and served no other function.

FIGURE 17.24 Like Directoire furniture, Empire chair backs were often scrolled backward. In this example, the chair legs are similar to those in ancient Egypt: the back legs of the chair are in the form of the rear legs of an animal and the front chair legs in the form of front legs of an animal. Ormolu sabots in the form of paw feet terminate the legs at the floor.

FIGURE 17.25 About 1814, the *lit à couronne* became fashionable. This bed had a round or oval canopy from which textiles draped to the ends of the bed.

of chairs were almost always quadrangular and of concave form. The major exception to this was the curule chair derived from the sella curulis of the Romans. Front supports included carved figures, and cylindrical or square pillars. **Saber** legs, or concave legs that have no separation between the leg and the foot, appeared late in the period.

The méridienne was a type of daybed with scrolled ends of unequal height and a back panel. Beds were designed so that one long side fit against the wall, often in an alcove. The most unusual Empire bed was the boat bed, lit en bateau, which had rolled ends of equal height that narrowed as they rose. A concave side gave an unbroken curved line to the bed. The bottom of the side rail was straight and low. Some of these beds were mounted on an additional platform. (See Figure 17.25.)

INFLUENCE 17.6

The American sleigh bed was derived from the lit en bateau

TABLES

Empire dining tables were round, heavy, and designed with figural or columnar supports. Marble-topped center tables were common. Supports were often connected by a heavy incurved base. Small tables such as guéridons were often supported on a central pillar that was then supported on three curved legs. Console tables were often supported by a pair of caryatids. Lyre-shaped supports were used on toilet tables, known as a coiffeuse. Two uprights supported a mirror above the tabletop so that it would swivel. During the Empire period, the **psyche** was introduced. Known today as a cheval mirror, the psyche was a long mirror supported on a frame on which it could pivot. Smaller versions were also made to stand on a table or fit into a drawer.

With the exception of the bureau en pente, all the writing furniture used in the previous periods was made in the Empire style.

English Furniture of the Neoclassic Period

The Georgian style began in England. Thomas Chippendale's work spanned from the Rococo period through both the Queen Anne and Georgian periods. His Rococo designs are discussed in Chapter 16. Early Georgian furniture was similar to Queen Anne furniture with the exception that Georgian pieces were more elaborately ornamented, including architectural forms, and more massive in structure. Fluted pilasters, Corinthian capitals, classic cornices, pediments, and ancient band patterns and moldings were used on Georgian pieces. Mahogany was first used in Georgian furniture, replacing the walnut used for Queen Anne pieces. The cabriole leg continued to be used on Georgian furniture but was more massive and less graceful. The claw and ball foot introduced during the Queen Anne period was used much more extensively. Occasionally, the dragon claw was replaced with eagle's claws.

Marquetry was replaced in the Georgian period with carving, and japanning was fashionable. The shell motif used during the Rococo period continued, although Georgian shells had more detailing.

Working in the new Georgian style, Chippendale included designs in Gothic Revival forms, which were also in vogue at the time. (This early revival of Gothic forms was short-lived and lasted only about a decade. The nineteenth-century Gothic Revival was more widespread.) Chippendale also incorporated Chinese designs in his pieces.

Robert Adam (1728–1792), too, designed furniture in the Georgian style, usually based on Greek and Roman examples. His brother,

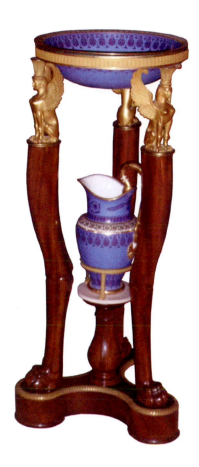

FIGURE 17.26
Elongated swans form the supports for this American version of an Empire table. The base is incurved and connects the three supports.

James, worked with him on many of his interior designs. The first half of the reign of George III was dominated by the Adam style. Adam maintained contacts in Italy and strictly followed Roman designs. Both Robert and James Adam published engravings of their designs that helped to popularize them. Adam furniture was curvilinear and often employed oval forms. It was graceful, refined, and never overpowered by ornament. Adam furniture and interiors, however, were only for the very wealthy.

George Hepplewhite (c. 1727–1786) was an English designer whose furniture was fashionable from about 1780–1795. Many of his designs were posthumously published in the *Cabinet Maker and Upholsterer's Guide,* making his name a household word and his furniture designs copied not only in England but in America. Hepplewhite furniture was light, elegantly proportioned, and had simple lines. Slender supports were generally quadrangular and tapered, although cylindrical legs were also used. His furniture legs were plain, reeded, or fluted. Hepplewhite made use of the spade foot, a rectangular form that tapers downward. Hepplewhite was known for five types of chair backs, although he used others as well. The camelback chair had a serpentine or triple-arched crest rail that continued as the uprights of the back. A pierced splat was typical on this chair. Shield, heart, oval, and wheel backs were also used by Hepplewhite. He used the three ostrich feathers representative of the Prince of Wales, vases, ribbons, and festoons in his designs. (See Figure 17.27.)

Thomas Sheraton (1751–1806) was the third of the great English furniture designers of the period along with Chippendale and Hepplewhite. He published furniture designs in *The Cabinet-Maker and Upholsterer's Drawing Book*. No piece has ever been assurredly attributed to him, and it is possible that he designed furniture but never actually made any. The straight line was dominant in Sheraton designs, although segmental curves were sometimes used. Sheraton made use of porcelain plaques to ornament furniture pieces. He used the same types of furniture legs as did Hepplewhite, although because the backs were rectilinear, the back legs could con-

FIGURE 17.28 While the Federal style was popular, and as a result of the War of 1812, which was mainly a naval war, both ships and the bald eagle became more commonly used as motifs. Ships were usually placed on mirrors or clocks. The eagle was frequently used as a finial or support. Here, the eagle is used as a marquetry design on a Federal sideboard.

tinue upward to form the back support. Sheraton included a stay rail, and vertical portions of the backs of furniture extended from the stay rail to the crest rail and not to the seat.

AMERICAN NEOCLASSIC FURNITURE

Georgian furniture was used in America prior to the Revolution because by the time the Georgian style had become popular, Americans were sufficiently prosperous enough to purchase stylish furniture pieces. Georgian furniture was copied from pattern books imported from England, and were actual examples of the pieces. During the Revolution, furniture making stopped and fewer items were imported.

Chippendale furniture had been made and used prior to the Revolution, and Adam influence was mostly limited to buildings, so it was the furniture of Hepplewhite and Sheraton that became popular during the Federal period (1790-1820). Because many of the artisans making furniture during this period were trained in England, there is little difference in American and English furniture with the exception of the type of wood that was used. French design was also influential during the Federal period but mostly among the wealthy in the South. (See Figure 17.28.)

One of the most influential furniture makers in America during the period was the Scottish immigrant Duncan Phyfe, who worked in New York City. Phyfe used Sheraton designs in his factory, where he employed about 100 men. Because there was no strict guild system in America, each artisan was typically capable of performing numerous jobs associated with furniture construc-

FIGURE 17.27 Hepplewhite designs such as this shield-back chair were copied both in England and in America. The curvature of the crest rail was also used on other Hepplewhite furniture often for a serpentine table or console top.

tion. As furniture manufacture in America expanded, specialization increased.

American cabinetmakers who worked near major waterways or port cities made more use of mahogany than did artisans who worked inland. There, walnut was more common and cherry was used to simulate the color of mahogany.

Phyfe also worked in the Empire style, and his designs are often called American Empire. French Empire furniture made by American artisans was heavier than French examples and simplified for American tastes. Ormolu mounts were omitted or replaced with gilded wrought iron. Phyfe favored reeding and used animal feet, the cornucopia leg, the lyre form, bowknots, and other contemporary motifs. American Empire furniture was used in Greek Revival houses. (See Figure 17.29.)

Another of the American furniture makers of the early nineteenth century was Lambert Hitchcock (1795–1852). Hitchcock made chairs based on Sheraton Empire designs for the masses. He established a factory in Connecticut, where a large number of the chairs could be made and sold at reasonable prices. Usually, rush seats were used and chairs were sometimes painted, the legs and stretchers were turned, and the crest rail was shaped in a gentle curve. (See Figure 17.30.)

Industrialization Takes the Lead

The nineteenth century was to see major changes in Europe with the Industrial Revolution. Classicism would continue in the form of the Greek Revival style but would be replaced by numerous revivals of other previous styles. It was Victorian England that was to take the lead in industry and to affect the arts for much of the century.

FIGURE 17.29 Duncan Phyfe used the concave curve in chair backs, legs, and pedestal supports for tables.

FIGURE 17.30 Hitchcock chairs were painted black and stenciled with stylized contemporary designs including the cornucopia, eagle, fruits and vegetables, and birds. Gilt decals were sometimes used instead.

The Modern World

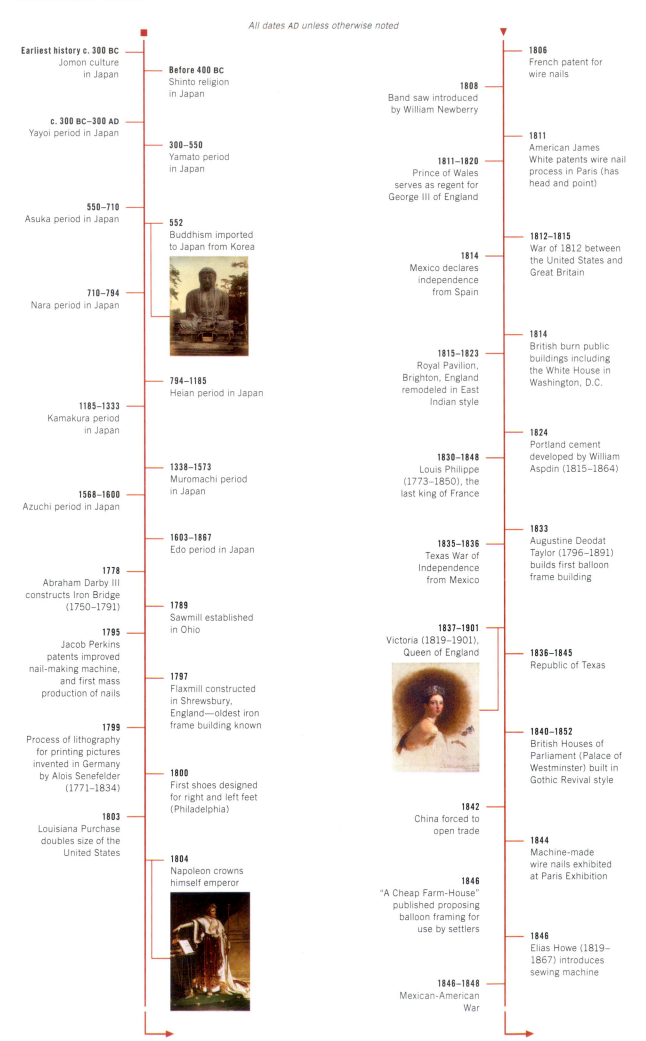

Part SIX

All dates AD unless otherwise noted

Earliest history c. 300 BC
Jomon culture
in Japan

Before 400 BC
Shinto religion
in Japan

c. 300 BC–300 AD
Yayoi period in Japan

300–550
Yamato period
in Japan

550–710
Asuka period in Japan

552
Buddhism imported
to Japan from Korea

710–794
Nara period in Japan

794–1185
Heian period in Japan

1185–1333
Kamakura period
in Japan

1338–1573
Muromachi period
in Japan

1568–1600
Azuchi period in Japan

1603–1867
Edo period in Japan

1778
Abraham Darby III
constructs Iron Bridge
(1750–1791)

1789
Sawmill established
in Ohio

1795
Jacob Perkins
patents improved
nail-making machine,
and first mass
production of nails

1797
Flaxmill constructed
in Shrewsbury,
England—oldest iron
frame building known

1799
Process of lithography
for printing pictures
invented in Germany
by Alois Senefelder
(1771–1834)

1800
First shoes designed
for right and left feet
(Philadelphia)

1803
Louisiana Purchase
doubles size of the
United States

1804
Napoleon crowns
himself emperor

1806
French patent for
wire nails

1808
Band saw introduced
by William Newberry

1811
American James
White patents wire nail
process in Paris (has
head and point)

1811–1820
Prince of Wales
serves as regent for
George III of England

1812–1815
War of 1812 between
the United States and
Great Britain

1814
Mexico declares
independence
from Spain

1814
British burn public
buildings including
the White House in
Washington, D.C.

1815–1823
Royal Pavilion,
Brighton, England
remodeled in East
Indian style

1824
Portland cement
developed by William
Aspdin (1815–1864)

1830–1848
Louis Philippe
(1773–1850), the
last king of France

1833
Augustine Deodat
Taylor (1796–1891)
builds first balloon
frame building

1835–1836
Texas War of
Independence
from Mexico

1837–1901
Victoria (1819–1901),
Queen of England

1836–1845
Republic of Texas

1840–1852
British Houses of
Parliament (Palace of
Westminster) built in
Gothic Revival style

1842
China forced to
open trade

1844
Machine-made
wire nails exhibited
at Paris Exhibition

1846
"A Cheap Farm-House"
published proposing
balloon framing for
use by settlers

1846
Elias Howe (1819–
1867) introduces
sewing machine

1846–1848
Mexican-American
War

All dates AD unless otherwise noted

1849
John Ruskin (1819–1900) publishes *Seven Lamps of Architecture*

1851
Isaac Singer (1811–1875) invents sewing machine

1851
First nails out of wire

1851
Crystal Palace houses Great Exhibition in London

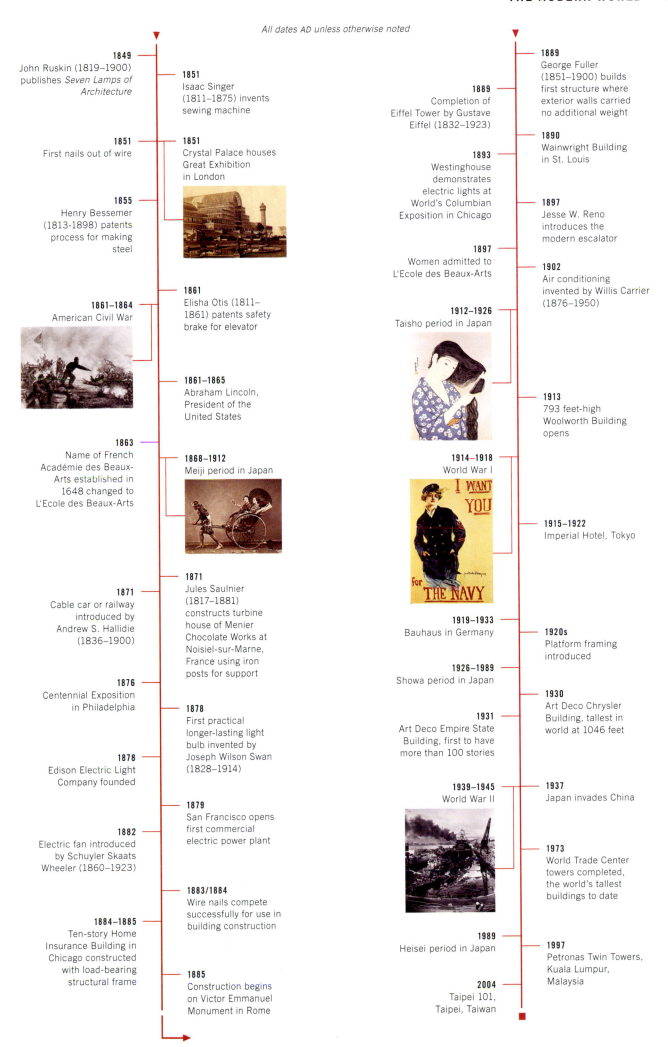

1855
Henry Bessemer (1813-1898) patents process for making steel

1861–1864
American Civil War

1861
Elisha Otis (1811–1861) patents safety brake for elevator

1861–1865
Abraham Lincoln, President of the United States

1863
Name of French Académie des Beaux-Arts established in 1648 changed to L'Ecole des Beaux-Arts

1868–1912
Meiji period in Japan

1871
Cable car or railway introduced by Andrew S. Hallidie (1836–1900)

1871
Jules Saulnier (1817–1881) constructs turbine house of Menier Chocolate Works at Noisiel-sur-Marne, France using iron posts for support

1876
Centennial Exposition in Philadelphia

1878
First practical longer-lasting light bulb invented by Joseph Wilson Swan (1828–1914)

1878
Edison Electric Light Company founded

1879
San Francisco opens first commercial electric power plant

1882
Electric fan introduced by Schuyler Skaats Wheeler (1860–1923)

1883/1884
Wire nails compete successfully for use in building construction

1884–1885
Ten-story Home Insurance Building in Chicago constructed with load-bearing structural frame

1885
Construction begins on Victor Emmanuel Monument in Rome

1889
George Fuller (1851–1900) builds first structure where exterior walls carried no additional weight

1889
Completion of Eiffel Tower by Gustave Eiffel (1832–1923)

1890
Wainwright Building in St. Louis

1893
Westinghouse demonstrates electric lights at World's Columbian Exposition in Chicago

1897
Jesse W. Reno introduces the modern escalator

1897
Women admitted to L'Ecole des Beaux-Arts

1902
Air conditioning invented by Willis Carrier (1876–1950)

1912–1926
Taisho period in Japan

1913
793 feet-high Woolworth Building opens

1914–1918
World War I

1915–1922
Imperial Hotel, Tokyo

1919–1933
Bauhaus in Germany

1920s
Platform framing introduced

1926–1989
Showa period in Japan

1930
Art Deco Chrysler Building, tallest in world at 1046 feet

1931
Art Deco Empire State Building, first to have more than 100 stories

1939–1945
World War II

1937
Japan invades China

1973
World Trade Center towers completed, the world's tallest buildings to date

1989
Heisei period in Japan

1997
Petronas Twin Towers, Kuala Lumpur, Malaysia

2004
Taipei 101, Taipei, Taiwan

rooms. In both England and America, the rising middle class had fewer, if any, servants, reducing the amount of space needed.

THE EXPOSITIONS

The steam-powered rotary printing press and mechanical typesetting made books and periodicals inexpensive, and ideas could be widespread in a short amount of time. Like the international fairs of medieval Europe, however, there was another venue for distributing information to large numbers of people. The great exhibitions of the nineteenth century were showcases of design that facilitated the widespread knowledge of technological innovations as well as design. The first of these exhibitions was held in London in 1851 in the specially constructed Crystal Palace. In 1889, the Exposition Universelle was held in Paris to mark the 100th anniversary of the storming of the Bastille, which began the French Revolution. The Eiffel Tower served as the entrance. The World's Columbian Exposition in Chicago in 1893 celebrated the 400th anniversary of the discovery of America by Columbus. Numerous other trade fairs were held in places as far-flung as Cape Town, South Africa; Kyoto, Japan; and Sydney, Australia.

FIGURE 18.1 The English portrait chair was an exhibition piece rather than one designed for use. Porcelain plaques such as this one with a portrait of Queen Victoria were surrounded by the best-quality carving of the period. This chair was designed especially for the 1851 Crystal Palace Exhibition.

At the international stage provided by the expositions, exhibitors brought their best items to show. Awards were given in various categories, and the exhibitions were seen as competitions. As a result, most of the pieces exhibited were technically complicated or flamboyant rather than items in general use. At the first exposition in London, it was the French who took away most of the prizes for furniture, not the English. (See Figure 18.1.)

Effects of Technology on Architecture

Several technological innovations of the nineteenth century changed architecture significantly. Some, such as the Bessemer process for making steel and the elevator brake, impacted public structures. Others, such as tools that made sawn lumber more readily available, the mass production of nails, and improvements in the cast-iron stove, made more of an impact on domestic buildings. An associated technological development, the mechanical lawn mower made lawns no longer the purview of the wealthy but enabled middle-class citizens to enjoy natural surroundings.

Faster, better, less expensive transportation methods such as the railroad made it possible to transport building materials such as brick or lumber to building sites far from the point of origin of the materials. The result was an increased similarity in buildings in locations far removed from one another.

New materials developed as a result of the Industrial Revolution opened architecture to new possibilities. The first of the new types of structures was the Iron Bridge built in Coalbrookdale, England, in 1779, which was made possible by new techniques in iron smelting. Iron bridges were lighter in weight and stronger than traditional stone bridges. The construction of bridges initiated the separation of architects from engineers, although for some time architects continued to build them. Like Roman bridges centuries earlier, many of the bridges of this new era followed contemporary architectural styles. The pylons supporting the cables of the Clifton Suspension Bridge (1806–1859) in England were reminiscent of Egyptian pylons, for example.

Other than utilitarian purposes, however, there was little vision as to what could be accomplished with iron until the Crystal Palace and the Eiffel Tower were constructed. (See Figure 18.2.) Joseph Paxton (1801–1865), the builder of the Crystal Palace, designed a number of other iron and glass buildings. The Crystal Palace was 1,851 feet in length and built of prefabricated components. The cast-iron framework was entirely enclosed with sheets of plate glass, another new technology of the period. The central section of the Crystal Palace was raised on arches to a height of 72 feet to enclose a stand of trees. Later, the iron frame was used for other structures, but generally only internally where it made large open spaces possible. Warehouses, markets, and prisons were among the first building types to take advantage of the qualities of iron frameworks.

BESSEMER PROCESS

A single innovation improved the strength of iron, making it even more desireable as a structural component. At the beginning of the nineteenth century, British steel was manufactured by adding carbon to imported Swedish wrought iron. The process took about a week and required up to three tons of high-quality coal to produce a single ton of steel. Other processes were experimented with, but it was the Bessemer process developed by Henry Bessemer (1813–1898) that made it possible to convert pig iron to steel by removing impurities rather than adding carbon. Less coal was required, and the process took less time. Even when the manufacturers added a significant amount for profit, Bessemer steel was less expensive than that produced by other methods. Steel framing was an American innovation and allowed buildings to rise as high as nine or ten stories. An additional innovation of the period was reinforced concrete that was to replace stone in load bearing walls of large buildings.

ELEVATOR BRAKE

For years, a hoisting system had been used to raise materials, but the platform was unsafe for passengers because when a cable broke, the platform would plummet to the ground. In the mid-nineteenth century, Elisha Graves Otis (1811–1861) invented a braking system for the platform that would prevent the cab from falling if the cables were severed. In a publicity stunt at the New York Crystal Palace[1] in 1853,[2] Otis demonstrated the safety of the device by cutting the cables while he was raised on the platform. After that, sales increased dramatically. The first passenger elevator using the device was opened in 1857. The same process is still used and elevators worldwide bear the name Otis Elevator Company. Without this device, buildings were limited to about six stories. Elevators made skyscrapers feasible.

TOOLS FOR WORKING WITH WOOD

The circular saw, band saw, and planer were all developed in the nineteenth century, facilitating the manufacture of lumber. The first steam-driven saw was patented in 1793, and its use in sawmills across the country increased lumber output dramatically. Previous sawmills had been located next to flowing water, which was their source of power. The steam-driven saw made it possible to locate sawmills near sources of timber where it could be cut up before delivery. It was much

FIGURE 18.2 The startling Eiffel Tower, on view at the Universal Exposition in 1889, introduced many people to the possibilities of iron construction. Four arches link the piers on which the tower is supported. At a height of 986 feet, it weighs 7,300 tons.

easier to transport boards than logs. Even as late as the 1830s, demand often exceeded supply. Chicago was a major center of the lumber industry, although most of its wood came from Canada. The use of steam-driven saws also factored into the beginning of standardization of lumber sizes.

NAILS

Until the nineteenth century, nails were made by hand. They were so expensive that settlers moving on might burn down their houses in order to retrieve the nails for reuse. After 1590 when a machine was introduced in England to cut flat sheets of iron or steel into uniform sizes, the maker had only to make a point and a head for the rectangular nails, or "square nails" but the work was still labor-intensive. In 1795, Jacob Perkins (1766–1849) patented a machine that made square nails with a head and point, and the price of nails began to decline. In 1851, round wire nails began to be manufactured in the United States, although several people are credited with it. The first wire nails were small, however, and intended for nothing larger than furniture. It was not until c. 1880 that wire nails were consistently used in house construction. The advantages of wire nails over cut nails were that they could be driven into thin boards without splitting the material and they could also be more successfully driven into hard woods.

CAST-IRON STOVES

The Franklin stove, based upon Benjamin Franklin's 1742 invention, was a significant improvement over the relatively inefficient fireplace. The cast-iron stove sat inside the room, where heat from its surfaces warmed the area around it rather than dissipating through masonry walls to the outside. Developments in the stove improved its efficiency, and by the mid-nineteenth century, stoves were sufficiently economical in terms of usable heat produced per unit of fuel to allow rooms to be larger.

CHICAGO STYLE

Chicago was one of the most important cities in the United States by the mid-nineteenth century. As a major railway hub, it served as a crossroads for trade for much of America. In fact, by the time of the Chicago fire in 1871, the city was the largest in the country. As the city began to rebuild after the fire, there was great demand for

commercial and office space far exceeding the availability of land within the area of the city. The solution was to use the iron and steel beam skeleton construction system and build upward, in essence creating more land. The world's tallest building that employs masonry bearing walls is Philadelphia's City Hall (1901) at 548 feet. Chicago's stone Monadnock Building, completed in 1893, was 17 stories (197 feet) high, but even before construction was completed, the building began to sink and steps had to be added to access the entrances.

A new type of construction was necessary. In 1854, James Bogardus (1800–1874) constructed the Harper and Brothers Building using a system of iron columns to support outer walls for a building with Renaissance details. Light flooded into the building through its large windows. The same type of system was used by William LeBaron Jenney (1832–1907) when he constructed what has been called the first skyscraper, the Home Life Insurance Building in Chicago, in 1885. The building was nine stories tall and included a basement. Another innovator of the skyscraper was George A. Fuller (1851–1900). Fuller constructed the Tacoma Building (1889) in Chicago using Bessemer steel beams. It was

FIGURE 18.3 Cast iron stoves could be made to suit any decorative style.

the first structure to use internal supports so that exterior walls would not carry extra weight.

Steel beams were used as a framework that was then filled in with brick and other materials including large expanses of glass. As in the Medieval period, retail outlets or sometimes offices typically occupied ground floor space.

Once reinforced concrete was perfected, the buildings could soar even higher into the sky. Although the techniques for constructing high-rise buildings were first developed in England with prefabrication and iron skeleton construction, by 1880, the United States had taken the lead in architectural innovation, and there it has remained since that time. Chicago served as a model for other cities and gave trade-oriented design its form but it was quickly overshadowed by architecture in New York City.

In the beginning, the skyscraper employed historical design references in its decoration although very quickly, it was determined that the multi-storied building did not need to be cloaked in historic references. Characteristic of Chicago skyscrapers was tripartite construction. The façade was divided into horizontal levels much like that of columns with a base, a shaft, and a capital. Each division was separated by projecting bands. The middle section was the most dominant part of the façade.

There were also height limitations in some cities; in London, for example, Queen Victoria disliked the modern designs that soared beyond the rooflines of traditional buildings, such as St. Paul's Cathedral, and until the mid-twentieth century, there were limitations on structure height in that city that prevented the building of exceedingly tall buildings.

In addition to a new type of structure, skyscrapers required an improved method of calculating loads and stresses, elevators, central heating, and plumbing systems. Although the beginnings of skyscraper construction occurred in the nineteenth century, they became commonplace in the twentieth century and even the Great Depression of the 1930s only briefly slowed the construction of new skyscrapers, and they continued to be built higher and higher Now major cities all over the world have a similar appearance.

Architectural Styles of the Nineteenth Century

In 1848, the art and social critic John Ruskin (1819–1900) published *Seven Lamps of Architecture* in which he espoused the idea that past architectural styles were sufficient and nothing new was needed. His book had great impact on English thinking, and revivals of past styles continued. Some of the previous styles lent themselves best to public structures, but it was houses that were most affected because there were more of them and because new ones were constantly being constructed.

FIGURE 18.4 The term skyscraper was used in the 1880s, but there is no precise definition. Many cities define a skyscraper as any building that projects beyond the roofs of other buildings and impacts the shape of the city's skyline. Others define a skyscraper as having a minimum height of 500 feet.

The nineteenth century was one of architectural revivals and a continuation of the Neoclassical idea of the appreciation of nature. Such ideas resulted in picturesque buildings that were designed to be constructed in open areas and that were a reaction to the formal symmetry of the Greek Revival style. A number of historic styles were revived, although nineteenth-century knowledge of previous styles lacked accuracy and usually there were only a few features of a structure that were reminiscent of earlier ones—and sometimes not the style they were purported to be. In England, for example, Tudor, Elizabethan, and Jacobean were all considered Gothic styles and features seen on Tudor buildings might appear on Gothic Revival structures. Styles, then, were eclectic, meaning that features from a variety of sources were combined to create a new style.

Although dependent on historic styles for influences, nineteenth-century styles were not replicas. Life was different than it had been in the past and called for changes in building design, especially in houses that went from formally arranged interiors to those more suited to family living. New types of buildings were necessary—factories, railway stations, department stores, and concert halls. Many of these buildings had to be larger even than the ancient monuments. For most buildings, the load-bearing wall continued to be used, so windows were located as they had been in the past—in vertical lines—although windows were larger. After the techniques were developed in the 1840s to make large sheets of glass, windows had fewer separations and the

FIGURE 18.5 When London's Palace of Westminster (better known as the House of Parliament) burned in 1834, Charles Barry won the competition for the design of the new structure. From the clock tower that houses Big Ben to the interior details, the building is purely Gothic Revival.

display windows in department stores that are so common today became possible.

The Greek Revival style continued to be used until c. 1830 and remained influential for an even longer period. In Northern Europe, there was a strong taste for Gothic styling, and as nineteenth-century knowledge of the period improved, the style began to dominate.

GOTHIC REVIVAL (1820–1870; IN AMERICA 1840–1860)

During the nineteenth century, England saw a great religious movement that called for people to return to the church and for the restoration of deteriorating cathedrals and churches. The church looked to the medieval Gothic period as a time when Christianity was dominant and values were supposedly high. The Gothic Revival was a result of this movement that called for a return to Christianity and conservative values. Augustus Welby Northmore Pugin (1812–1852), known by his initials A.W.N., was a leader of the Gothic Revival style. He believed Gothic architecture to be the only Christian architecture and that classical forms were irredeemably pagan. His writings were widely read and subsequently influenced the Gothic Revivals throughout Europe and America.

A singular event gave the movement impetus. In 1834, the Palace of Westminster that accommodated the British Houses of Parliament burned. There was debate in Great Britain concerning the style of the new Houses of Parliament. Although Neoclassical design was fashion-

able, it was too similar to what had been used in the United States for government office buildings and was thus associated with revolution and republic, an anathema to the monarchy. Authorities selected the Gothic style as most appropriate.

Ninety-seven designs were submitted but the Perpendicular Gothic design proposed by Charles Barry (1795–1860) was selected. Barry was more comfortable with classical design and relied on his friend A.W.N. Pugin to provide exterior detailing and to design the interiors. Begun in 1840, the structure was not completed until 1868. (See Figure 18.5.) In the United States, the architect Richard Upjohn (1802–1878) designed Trinity Church in New York City as a Gothic Revival structure based on English parish churches. In 1878, St. Patrick's Cathedral in New York City gave Americans their first impression of what a French Gothic structure looked like.

In both England and America, the style was most frequently used for homes. The style gained popularity in America partly through books published by Andrew Jackson Downing (1815–1852), an American landscape designer. The books featured houses designed by his friend and one of the most influential architects of the nineteenth century Andrew Jackson Davis (1803–1892) and significantly affected American designs. Downing promoted the style as part of the picturesque movement and encouraged people to build where they could experience nature. Some of the drawings were of large houses and had rooms for servants as did other large homes. Two very distinct types of Gothic Revival houses were constructed. Kingscote in Newport, Rhode Island, is a typical large Gothic Revival house completed in 1841. Other designs for large homes were castlelike. (See Figures 18.6 and 18.7.)

Both Downing and Davis also advocated the construction of picturesque cottages in the style small enough that there was no need for servants. Smaller domestic structures built in the Gothic revival style had steeply pitched side-gabled roofs and often a centered cross gable or a pair of cross gables on the front. Central gables were typically on the same wall plane as the wall they crossed, but paired gables might project forward to form wings. L-shaped plans with a single cross gable were also popular. The newly invented jigsaw and scroll saws made it possible to cut out fancy shaped boards that were used on diagonal gable edges; these are known as **vergeboards** or **barge-**

FIGURE 18.6 Kingscote was designed as a summer cottage for a southern planter but during the Civil War, was sold to the China trader William Henry King. Like most buildings designed in a revival style, Kingscote is not true to the original Gothic style. Gothic features include the steeply pitched complicated side-gabled roof and diamond pane glass in the windows.

boards. (See Figure 18.8.) When vergeboards were not used, a shaped and sometimes pierced board was used at the peak of the gable. Patterned wood boards in the shape of a pointed arch were also used above square-headed windows to create the illusion of a window in that shape. The cornice beneath the roof overhang of Gothic Revival

FIGURE 18.7 The mansion of Lyndhurst epitomized grand building in the Gothic Revival style in domestic structures. Its battlements, towers, and stone walls recall medieval defensive structures, its pointed windows are Gothic, and its bay and four-centered arches are Tudor. The façade was designed by Andrew Jackson Davis.

FIGURE 18.8 The band and jig saws made possible the characteristic exterior trim on Victorian building such as the bargeboards on this structure.

houses had no soffit and was either sheathed parallel to the roof or open so that the ends of the rafters were exposed. A single-story arcaded porch was common. vertical board and batten siding was typical on frame houses, drawing the eye upward, and a finial at the roof peak further increased apparent height.

There was usually at least one pointed window, often with tracery, located in the most visible and prominent gable on Gothic revival houses but other windows were often square-

headed. Windows were sometimes grouped together. Oriel or projecting bay windows were common and prominently located. Windows were typically protected from water runoff with a **drip mold** that projected at least over the lintel and sometimes down at least partway along window sides. Changes in color, texture, or both around windows and sometimes in horizontal bands on walls were characteristic of what is called High Victorian Gothic.

In combination with the new balloon framing, Gothic Revival houses had floor plans that varied considerably from one building to another and almost always outside the rectangular parameters of classical buildings. Although fewer buildings were constructed in the style immediately after the Civil War, it again became popular late in the century.

OCTAGON HOUSE (1850–1860)

In 1849, Orson Squire Fowler published *The Octagon House, a Home for All*. In it, he advocated a healthy interior environment that he suggested resulted from the octagon-shaped house. An octagon encloses more space per linear foot of exterior wall than a square or a rectangle. Therefore, heat loss could be reduced, building costs minimized, and light and ventilation through

FIGURE 18.9 The wood panels that compose the Grove walls in this Gothic Revival room run from floor to the cove. A variety of woods were inlaid to form the patterns. Pointed arches are the only identifiable Gothic feature.

window area increased. Fowler also advocated the use of two innovations of the period to improve environmental quality: central heating and indoor plumbing. Unfortunately, the resulting room shapes were difficult to work with and rooms could have windows on only one side. These houses had two or three stories and sometimes an octagonal belvedere for ventilation projecting through the roof. Most had encompassing single-story porches. (See Figure 18.10.)

VICTORIAN ARCHITECTURAL STYLES

A number of nineteenth-century building styles are termed Victorian only because they were popular during the long reign of England's Queen Victoria (1819–1901; reign from 1837). Some of these styles were adaptations of medieval buildings although only loosely based on the originals. In other cases, house designs were without precedent, such as the octagon house, or they were adaptations of contemporary European styles, such as Second Empire. Styles overlapped even into the twentieth century, and for that reason, details of one style were often found on homes of another style. Homes were more affordable for the masses as mass production of components made them less expensive, mail-order catalogs made prefabricated ornament readily available, and the newly laid railways transported materials across the country. In general, roofs were steeply pitched, buildings were asymmetrical, and multiple textures and colors were used for finishes.

ITALIAN VILLA (1830–1880) AND ITALIANATE (1845–1880)

Other styles began to overlap the Gothic Revival style in both England and America. Two styles inspired by Italian buildings were popular before and after the Civil War: the Italian villa and the Italianate house. The villa appeared first, but the later Italianate had many of the same features. The villa, however, was a distinct form, while the Italianate house simply involved decorative detailing.

The Italian villa was an asymmetrical, two-storied L- or T-shaped house designed for the countryside and inspired by Italian Renaissance villas. A three-story square tower, or campanile, was sometimes located either in the angle between the two sections of the structure or at one end. Tile or tin hip or gable roofs were low-pitched often on the same building, and had

FIGURE 18.10 Octagon houses were not a style but a plan. Trim varied according to the whim of the owner, but most employed Italianate or Gothic Revival details. Here, at Longwood in Natchez, Mississippi, the more exotic Moorish Revival inspires the trim and an onion dome replaces the belvedere. Begun in 1860, the house was never finished on the inside due to the Civil War. When finished, it would have had 32 major rooms.

wide overhanging eaves supported by paired or single brackets. Openings were three-, five-, or seven-ranked and major points of decorative interest. Tall, narrow windows were larger on the first story than on upper ones. Segmental arches or square-headed windows and doors dominated and were often emphasized with U-shaped trim or with surmounting pediments. Windows were often grouped in pairs or threes. Doors were also sometimes paired and contained large panes of glass. A single-story bay window projected from

FIGURE 18.11 The Italianate structure differed from the Italian villa in that it was usually symmetrical. These almost cube-shaped houses often had a central square cupola on the roof instead of a tower, and a gable projected slightly from the front. A small central or larger full-width porch was located on the front of the building and posts supported the porch roof.

FIGU
the 19
Neo-E
this wi
theate
cemeti

FIGURE 18.17 A rectangular or square tower might be located in the corner of the L or at the center front of a Second Empire house. The tower roof frequently matched that of the house, although ogee or convex tower roofs were not unusual. Roofs of the towers usually had additional dormer windows that could be round or shaped like the other windows in the house. A square cupola with its own roof might project through the center of the roof.

FIGURE 18.18 On Stick style houses, chimneys typically corbel outward toward the top to form a chimney pot. The Mark Twain house in Hartford, Connecticut is a rare brick version of the Stick style house.

be an additional decorative "truss." The decorative boards remain flat with square corners and serve as the only decoration. Large overhangs on steeply pitched complicated intersecting gable roofs leave rafter ends exposed. Where there are bays or angled corners on the first floor, there may be second floor projections at the corners to square off the bay area. Three-story examples are not uncommon. Porches are located beneath projecting jetties or added anywhere and are

supported by posts at the outer edge. Diagonal or curved braces spring from the posts to spread the weight. Most examples were constructed in the Northeast, and in the last decade of the nineteenth century the style was imported to San Francisco, where it became increasingly elaborate.

ROMANESQUE REVIVAL (1860s AND 1870s)

Although not all Romanesque revival buildings are known as Richardsonian Romanesque, it was the American architect Henry Hobson Richardson (1838–1886) who promoted the style. Richardson attended the École des Beaux-Arts in Paris and brought the style back to the United States. Romanesque Revival buildings were often used for courthouses, churches, and other public buildings where they were almost always constructed with ashlar stone. Homes, on the other hand, might be constructed of stone or another material, although masonry of some type was most common. Many consider the Queen Anne style to be Romanesque Revival in wood because many of the features are identical. Round or polygonal towers located on the front, for example, set these buildings off from their neighbors.

Like its predecessor, Romanesque Revival structures use semicircular arches over openings that have deep reveals. Frequently, porches have low parapet walls and the arch for the major entrance springs from the ground, not from the top of a pair of columns. (See Figure 18.19.)

QUEEN ANNE (1880–1910)

Queen Anne style houses have multiple stories and steeply pitched irregular complex roofs. Both hip and gable roofs may be used on the same structure, although there is usually a prominent gable in the front. Like the Stick style, Queen Anne houses have surface decoration, but in this case, it is usually of patterned shingles. Some examples have one or more surfaces (usually a gable end) patterned with flat boards like the Stick style. Variously patterned sections of wood shingles might also be used to create interest. In fact, each story might be treated differently. Even bands of differently patterned shingles are used, often to define an interior change in level. Gables are more elaborately treated and a prolific use of color is characteristic.

Porches, supported on turned posts, are balustered and might have a suspended frieze of spindles or beads. The latter is a characteristic seen in Eastlake furniture, and when Queen Anne houses make extensive use of spindles, they are sometimes called Eastlake. In some instances, classic columns are used rather than turned posts for porch supports, often raised on a pedestal support or grouped in pairs or threes. Windows might also be grouped, and Palladian windows on upper stories are not uncommon. Corner wall overhangs might be left as bays are cut away beneath them. A hallmark of Queen Anne style houses is the change in wall planes both vertically and horizontally. Although there was at least one American example prior to 1876, it was at the Centennial Exposition that the British exhibited two examples. Soon they were sold through mail order catalogs.

SHINGLE STYLE (1880–1900)

Shingle style houses were large, multistoried, irregular, and asymmetrical, with gable, hip, and gambrel roofs often all in the same structure. Bays were usually rounded, as were towers. Towers and their roofs often blended back into the structure behind them, becoming bulges on the surface rather than separate units. Jetties on upper stories were typical, a new one on each succeeding story. Semicircular arches were often used at porch entries, bands of windows were common, and chimneys were corbelled outward at the top to form a chimney pot. Extensive porches had short, shingle-covered walls in place of balustrades. Unusually, Shingle style houses were almost always designed by architects, and the style never made it into the vernacular vocabulary. The dominating characteristic of the Shingle style house was the use of shingles to cover all of its surfaces, often including porch supports.

COLONIAL REVIVAL (1880–1955)

The celebration of the American Centennial was a reminder of the country's colonial heritage and piqued interest in the varying colonial styles. The resulting houses were often almost identical to colonial examples, especially Georgian and Adam houses. Other styles that were revived included Dutch Colonial houses with gambrel roofs, Garrison style houses with second-floor overhanging jetties, and single-story Cape Cod houses. Most of the houses resembled their prototypes, but living conditions had changed dramatically and other than Georgian and Adam houses, there was often little resemblance except for symmetry,

FIGURE 18.19 Romanesque Revival buildings had multiple rooflines but usually the main roof was hipped. One or more cross gables were present, typically at least one on the front and another on one side. Romanesque Revival structures were asymmetrical. Dormers were often present and usually had parapet end walls. Windows were grouped.

FIGURE 18.20 The Queen Anne structure is asymmetrical and might have a corner tower on the façade, or less frequently, in the corner of an ell. Towers are round, polygonal, and sometimes square and either rise from the ground or are cantilevered from an upper story.

FIGURE 18.21 Although designed by Burges in the nineteenth century, the interior of Castel Coch was not completed for 100 years. Gilding, multiple interior domes, furniture with what was perceived to be a medieval appearance, wood carvings, and paintings with birds and small animals were combined to create an interior that was supposed to reflect those of the medieval period.

FIGURE 18.22 As part of the mania for monumental structures of the last quarter of the nineteenth century, the newly-unified Italy constructed a monument to its King Victor Emmanuel II (1820–1878) that is known in Italy as the typewriter or wedding cake. It houses the Altar of the Nation and an unknown soldier's tomb.

a treatment of a doorway, or a roof style. Often, stylistic features were mixed. Cape Cod cottages received pedimented entries and dormers, and Georgian houses received broken pediments over fanlights and got bay windows. Most Colonial Revival houses were less expensive to build than their Victorian counterparts because they were boxlike with simple detailing. The revival lasted well into the twentieth century.

FANTASY BUILDINGS

With the new materials and technologies, the wealthy were able to create romantic, eccentric buildings. Neuschwanstein, the fairy-tale castle in the Bavarian Alps that inspired Disney's Sleeping Beauty Castle, was built for Bavarian King Ludwig II (1845–1886), who was a great patron of theater and opera. The castle was never completed but briefly served as a stage set for the fantasy life of the king. Castel Coch (1870s) in Wales was built to look like what a nineteenth-century romanticist believed a medieval castle looked like. It was built on thirteenth-century ruins for the Third Marquess of Bute by the English architect William Burges (1827–1881). (See Figure 18.21.) After such extravagancies, the world was ready for the more down-to-earth realistic Arts and Crafts movement that followed.

OPENINGS

Developments in glass manufacturing made large panes of glass feasible and affordable. Sash windows were most common, although some casement windows were used. It was important that windows open because fresh air was considered healthful—even during the winter. The surrounds of openings related to the style of the building.

Pediments surmounted some doorways and the doors themselves were paneled. Glass was increasingly used in doors and was sometimes surrounded by a stained glass border.

Victorian Interiors

Unlike most previous styles, Victorian interiors were not necessarily associated with the style of the building, nor was any particular furniture style used in specific Victorian structures. Sometimes, specific styles of decoration were considered appropriate for individual rooms. In France, dining rooms were decorated in Henri II style while drawing rooms received Baroque, Rococo, or Neoclassic treatment. Libraries were considered a masculine domain and were decorated with dark, massive furniture.

In Victorian plans, hallways provided access to most rooms, although sometimes occupants had to go through one room to get to another. The dining room was typically the largest room in the house, as it was used not only for family meals but as a gathering place in the evenings. The parlor was a more formal room where the "best" furniture was located, and children were often forbidden its use. More and more people of the middle class throughout Europe and America were able to afford homes, but they typically had fewer, if any, servants. Thus, there was little need for additional space for servants to live and work.

The houses of the English upper classes were complex, with specific spaces for children, servants, men, and women. Stairways and halls, too, were often segregated. Part of the reason for this segregation was so that servants could be invisible to the family. The English drawing room was considered feminine and was used for afternoon tea, women's gatherings, visits, and even balls. French fashions were copied for interior decoration.

Floors were wood, sometimes parquet, and often rugs helped to define areas within spaces.

FIGURE 18.23 Victorian rooms were filled with an abundance of furniture and accessories. Everything that could be adorned was.

For example, in a large room, a rug might be used to define a sitting area and seating would be arranged around it. The rug was bordered by wood flooring, and if parquet was not affordable, designs were stenciled on the floor to imitate parquet. Floor cloths were printed canvas that could feature parquet, tile, or carpet designs.

Walls continued to be divided vertically into a dado, central section, and architrave that in-

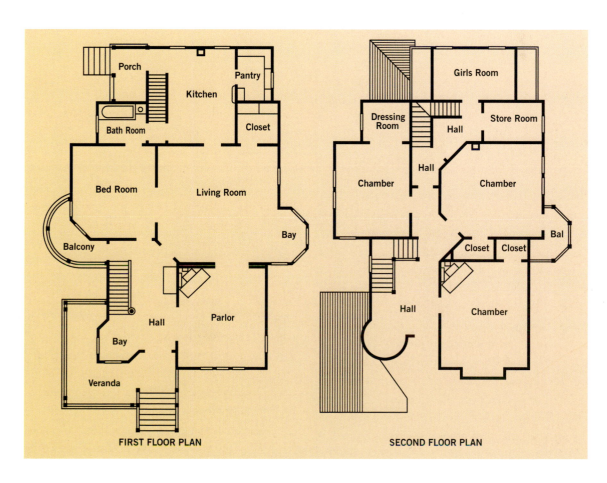

FIRST FLOOR PLAN

SECOND FLOOR PLAN

FIGURE 18.24 The balloon frame negated the need for boxy plans. There was no precedent for space planning once builders were freed to design plans to suit the purpose of the building rather than being limited by structural concerns.

cluded a frieze between two sets of horizontal moldings. Wallpaper, wood panels, faux marble finishes, stenciled decoration, and textiles were all used to finish wall surfaces.

Ceilings were high in large houses, although typically the ceilings of upper stories were lower than those below. They were commonly finished in the same period style as the room. Painted ceilings, some with frames, included trompe l'oeil paintings. Central rosettes of papier mâché or plaster were important components of the ceiling. If the rosette was the only thing a family could afford, that's what was used.

Voluminous draperies, often in several layers, covered and framed windows. Swags and jabots finished the top and fringe edged some of the pieces. Typically, heavy fabrics in dark, rich colors were used.

Victorian Furniture (1840–1900)

As the nineteenth century began, furniture was handmade. By the end of the Victorian era, mass production was the norm. It was during this century that furniture moved from expensive individually designed and made pieces to factory production that fashioned affordable furniture for an entirely new class of individuals. The idea of the furniture factory stemmed from the French academies and Royal Manufactories; this concept was employed elsewhere as machines, specialized tools, and a power supply for them were developed. Quality of construction was debased as a result of machine manufacture and eventually resulted in a call for a return to artisanship.

There was much trial and error as the industry adapted to factory production and machine processes. Furniture was reduced to its simplest shapes, to which historically influenced ornament was added. Whether ornament related to the shape or style of the piece was irrelevant. Increased mechanization resulted in the use of heretofore unused materials for furniture such as coal, glass, and cast iron. New processes involving steam bending and lamination were developed to produce completely new types of furniture.

Comfort became most important, and to that end, plush upholstered seats and backs were fashionable. By the middle of the Victorian era, upholstery often concealed the framework. This was possible only because of the improvements in the coil spring during the first part of the nineteenth century and the increased production of textiles possible because of power looms. The new upholstery was deep and often button tufted.

Overall, the period was eclectic, and a mixture of styles could often be seen in homes. Sometimes, the influences of two or more styles were seen on the same piece of furniture. Pattern, ornament, and accessories resulted in cluttered rooms. In American urban areas, trained artisans still designed furniture and set the standards, but furniture in areas away from those influences was often made by local artisans who copied what they liked, adapted designs to suit the capabilities of their new tools, and created pieces with great originality but with only a modicum of relationship to more stylish pieces. American Victorian furniture was truly a mixture.

Some of the furniture of the Victorian era had no historic antecedents. The 1851 exhibition had included a suite of German furniture made with stag horns, a style popular in Germany and Austria. Queen Victoria ordered a set for Balmoral Castle made from Prince Albert's hunting trophies. Antler and horn chairs were a result of the picturesque movement in which natural elements were emphasized. In the northern areas of the Unites States, members of the deer family shed their antlers annually. These were used for furniture legs, chair backs, and decorative objects such as chandeliers. Horn furniture was more typical of the American West, where cattle were raised. (See Figure 18.25.)

FIGURE 18.25 Western lodge furniture, particularly that made for dude ranches popular in the nineteenth century, was often made of cow horns and cow hide. Each piece of horn furniture was unique because the horns came from real cattle. Some of the furniture found its way to the Eastern United States where an interest in the "Wild West" was growing.

A papier-mâché compound was used for small articles of furniture (1845–1870). which were then japanned or lacquered. Boxes, trays, and table tops were common. Papier-mâché furniture with mother-of-pearl inlay was shown at the Crystal Palace Exhibition.

New Furniture Pieces

A few new pieces of furniture were made during the Victorian period. These included the following:

- The **borne**, an introduction of the French Second Empire period, was an oval-shaped island-seating unit with back-to-back seats in both directions. Usually the long sides could seat two people and at each of the ends, one additional person. The borne was completely upholstered with no exposed wood.
- The **ottoman** was a round or oval seating unit similar to the borne, although the backrest was a truncated cone on top of which was a flat surface for a piece of sculpture or vase of flowers. The units were entirely upholstered.
- The **pouf** was an upholstered bench, usually round, that appeared about 1845 during the French Second Empire period and continued to be used throughout the rest of the century. The wood legs were visible.
- The **show-frame chair** had a padded seat, back, and arms, but the framework was exposed. The front cabriole legs curved inward to form the fronts of the arms, and the crest rail curved around to frame the back down to the arms.
- The **slipper chair** had low legs, might or might not have arms, and was designed for use in a bedroom. Most were upholstered, although some examples of caned chairs were made.
- The **gentleman and lady chairs** were often made to match. The arms and back of the lady chair were lower than those of the gentleman chair.
- The **confidante** was another Second Empire piece with a straight-fronted central seating unit flanked by triangular seats and separated from them by arms that were an extension of the back. Sometimes the end seats could be removed.
- The **tête-à-tête** or **vis-à-vis** was an S-shaped double chair. The serpentine back separated the seats, and users half-faced one another.

A second type of tête-à-tête had a small table between two seats that were slightly angled toward one another at the ends of a long sofa. Sometimes the tête-à-tête was called a courting chair because two people could quietly converse while the serpentine back or table ensured modest behavior.

- The **whatnot** was an English and American version of the French étagère, a set of open shelves sometimes designed to fit into a corner.
- The **sleigh bed** was an adaptation of the French Empire lit en bateau, or boat bed. The bed was heavy and the headboard was paneled and rolled outward. The footboard curved upward and usually rolled outward, but there were examples of footboards that rolled inward instead. The bed was named for the horse-drawn sleigh it seemed to resemble.
- The Jenny Lind bed, as the low-post bed with an open-framed headboard and footboard was popularly known, had spoon- or ring-turned spindles. Jenny Lind (1820–1887), known as the Swedish Nightingale, was an opera singer who made a highly popular tour of the United States beginning in 1850. Later, other spool-turned furniture was named for this soprano who toured with P.T. Barnum during the time the furniture was introduced. Split spindles were often applied to flat panels on the furniture.

FIGURE 18.26 The **boudeuse** was a seating unit with a backrest in the center and a seat on each side.

FIGURE 18.27 The Victorian balloon back chair had an unfilled framed back.

FIGURE 18.28 Pillar and Scroll designs depended on single and double scrolls that could be cut with a band saw (the scrolls) and the pedestal base (pillar).

Styles of Victorian Furniture

As with architecture, furniture designs of the past were revisited, although not faithfully reproduced. Knowledge of past styles was mixed, and previous style names were often associated with characteristics far removed from the style. There was an overall quest for novelty, and previous styles were rarely slavishly copied but loosely adapted. Often carvings and other pieces were removed from older furniture and incorporated on new pieces.

Like the architectural styles, the various furniture styles overlapped and were mixed even within the same room. New trends emerged. During the 1870s in England, much of the furniture was an imitation of the Neoclassical style popular during the eighteenth century. Chippendale, Hepplewhite, Adam, and Sheraton pieces were reproduced; it can sometimes be difficult to determine whether these were made in the eighteenth or nineteenth century.

CONTINUATION OF THE EMPIRE STYLE (1830–1840)

Furniture of the Neoclassical and Empire periods in America was predicated on designs in French and English pattern books, and English designs themselves were often influenced by those of the French. Although much furniture design was simplified and coarsened toward the end of the Empire period as a result of industri-alized manufacturing, pieces remained massive; this resulted in the Pillar and Scroll style. The style was popularized through *The Cabinet Maker's Assistant,* published in 1840 by nineteenth-century architect and draftsman John Hall. Most of the pieces were veneered with mahogany. Neoclassical ornament was sometimes applied. (See Figure 18.28)

GOTHIC REVIVAL

The British purported to emulate Gothic designs, but in reality, it was only in the ornamentation that Gothic influences could be seen. In addition, English Gothic Revival pieces included idealized versions of Tudor and Elizabethan designs. German Gothic Revival style furniture was more elaborate than in other areas and employed polychrome marquetry. The France of Louis Philippe followed the historic styles popular in the rest of Europe, although its Gothic Revival style, termed **gothique troubadour,** frequently incorporated religious motifs and strong architectural forms. In these areas, Gothic Revival furniture was typically used in Gothic Revival houses. Although Gothic Revival architecture was popular in America, the same style of furniture was little used. (See Figure 18.29.)

FIGURE 18.29 The pointed arches beneath the arms of this English Gothic Revival chair are the only stylistic features from that era. The ormolu mounts, structural curves, and upholstery are all features of much later styles.

SECOND EMPIRE STYLE (1852–1870)

By 1830, aristocratic traditions in France had been reduced to unrestrained ornamentation, curved lines, and eclectic detailing. Much of the furniture was covered with upholstery and cushions with rich textiles, providing design emphasis. In France, Napoleon III and his wife Eugénie led the way to a return of elegance, although it was the upholsterer rather than the carver whose work was most visible. The resulting Second Empire style was a mixture of Louis XIV, Louis XV, and Louis XVI styles with a mixture of Baroque, Rococo, and Neoclassical forms. Ivory and mother-of-pearl inlay, intricate marquetry, and ormolu mounts were characteristic of this furniture. The Second Empire style also embraced Oriental designs with dragons and demons and Chinese fretwork. Upholstery became more prevalent, and chairs were upholstered with tapestry. The style was emulated in Spain and Portugal where French designs continued to dominate but were fused with details from their Moorish past and from Morocco, just across the Straits of Gibraltar. Isabellino furniture was the Spanish version of French Second Empire furniture although with greater detailing. Turned and twist-turned spindles, common on the Iberian Peninsula for centuries, continued to be used, as did the ogee arch. Arabic script was also carved in furniture pieces. In Portugal, British influence was stronger than that of France; this resulted in cabriole legs and paw feet.

In Latin America, where there had never been French influence, English pattern books were used to create furniture in Chippendale and Hepplewhite forms in a Neoclassical Revival.

Michael Thonet's Invention

Michael Thonet (1796–1871) was an innovative Prussian (Austrian) cabinetmaker. Thonet experimented with local beech wood and rejected traditional furniture construction methods that disguised joints with elaborate carvings. Thonet experimented with laminated, bent wood but settled on using a process that involved steaming a solid piece of wood and allowing it to dry in a jig. Some of his pieces designed in the Rococo Revival style had extravagant curls. Because it was stylish and low in cost, bentwood furniture was used on a large scale in restaurants and coffee houses. Much of the bentwood furniture was designed for seating. (See Figure 18.30.)

ROCOCO REVIVAL FURNITURE

The Rococo Revival began in France and is also known as the French Antique style. Rococo Revival furniture replaced Empire furniture in France, was copied in Italy, and was used along with Biedermeier furniture in Germany. This style of furniture became fashionable in London especially after the French won most of the awards for furniture design at the 1851 Crystal Palace exposition. Through pattern books, it quickly became popular in America, where it lasted until the twentieth century. Like its Rococo antecedent, revival furniture employed curved lines, extensive carving, and cabriole legs. Revival furniture, however, was heavier and less delicate. Marble tops were common.

The most famous American maker of Rococo Revival furniture was the German immigrant John Henry Belter (1804–1863). Like Thonet, Belter worked with bent wood. Belter developed a steam laminating process whereby he placed 3 to 16 thin layers of glued hardwood in molds with the grain of each layer perpendicular to the next, put them under great pressure in the presence of steam, and formed large panels with curves in the shape of the mold. The "solid" wood was then carved. When extra thickness was required, Belter applied additional solid pieces of wood to permit deep carving and three-dimensional effects. Belter used East Indian and Brazilian rosewood but also oak, mahogany, and other woods, which he usually ebonized. Dramatic curves are a hallmark of Belter furniture. Flowers, fruits,

FIGURE 18.30
Thonet's Model 14 bentwood chair that is still produced today has only six wood pieces, reducing the number of joints necessary and using screws rather than glue to hold the pieces together. For his innovative work, Thonet received a bronze medal in London's 1851 exhibition and a silver medal in Paris's exhibition in 1855. Thonet came home with a gold medal in 1867.

FIGURE 18.31 John Henry Belter's furniture was always expensive and ceased to be made when he died. The deep carving was done only by artisans from the Black Forest region of Germany whom Belter thought were more skilled than artisans from other areas.

and vines along with classical scrolls were the typical motifs. (See Figure 18.31.)

RENAISSANCE REVIVAL FURNITURE

The Renaissance Revival style employed features of Italian Renaissance, French Baroque, and Neoclassical forms. It spread as a result of London's 1851 Crystal Palace Exhibition; the style reached America by c.1870. Exaggerated curves, heavy carvings, and marble tops were characteristic of this furniture style. Usually, Renaissance Revival furniture can be distinguished by arched or broken arched pediments used on sideboards, tapered baluster legs with capitals for supports, and Baroque-style cross stretchers with a classical urn at the center. Commodes, cupboards, and shelves often featured quarter-circle shelves or cupboards at each end. (See Figure 18.32.)

In Germany, porcelain plaques painted with scenes were produced for use on Renaissance style forms. The background was ebonized, painted black, or infrequently veneered with ebony. In addition to the plaques, porcelain was often used for pillars, spindles, and furniture legs and feet.

Italian artisans produced exceptional Renaissance Revival pieces with classical forms and deep carving. They also used the **micro mosaic** technique to create detailed pictures on furniture. The technique began as a way to repair some of the famous paintings that were beginning to deteriorate. Like the Romans before them, nineteenth-century Italian artisans used tesserae, although in their case a single tessera was only about an eighth of an inch in length and only slightly wider than a human hair. Each thread was made of enamel or glass and was pushed into putty. Only the end showed. As many as 5,000 tesserae per square inch were used in these "eternal paintings." Boxes, jewelry, and even table tops in this style were carried throughout Europe by travelers, and demand was great.

After the American Civil War, the Renaissance Revival style became fashionable in that country. Many pieces were displayed at the 1876 Philadelphia Centennial Exhibition. At the same time, the Centennial celebration fostered a revival of American colonial buildings and furniture.

The last part of the nineteenth century saw another rise in interest in Egyptian features as exhibitions toured the country. Typically, Egyptian motifs such as the sphinx, lotus, or winged disk were applied to Renaissance Revival furniture.

THE INFLUENCE OF CHARLES LOCKE EASTLAKE

Charles Locke Eastlake (1836–1906) designed furniture adapted from the Gothic style and combined it with Japanese influences and pieces that could be made by machine—especially turnings. He called for a return to good artisanship and simplicity in his *Hints on Household Taste,* which he published in 1868. Incised lines, chip carving, and turnings were used on resulting pieces. Tiles with medieval designs were sometimes added to panels, as were Oriental-inspired designs. His philosophical approach to design was readily accepted in Germany, England, and the United States.

CAMPAIGN FURNITURE

In his 1803 *Cabinetmaker's Directory,* Sheraton appealed to the military gentleman to carry with him fashionable collapsible furniture. He even listed

FIGURE 18.32 This Renaissance Revival cabinet won the grand prize at the Paris Exhibition in 1878.

as "necessary" a dining table that would seat 20 people. Napoleon used campaign, or **knockdown**, furniture in his military campaigns. Merchants, military officers, and seamen made use of this transportable and collapsible furniture. Leather linings, upholstery, and secret compartments were as luxurious as the pieces made for homes. Pieces with drawers usually had a hinged rail to keep the drawers in a closed position during travel. Even upholstered sofas were made to collapse in order to ensure the comfort of the owner regardless of other circumstances. Brass mounts were located at points where furniture pieces might be damaged during transport. Handles were sunk into the furniture rather than protruding from it. Canvas and cane seats were common, as much of the furniture was used in tropical areas. Many of the pieces were made in the areas in which they were to be used. A military officer in India, for example, might have furniture made to order as it was needed.

PATENT FURNITURE

Victorian patent furniture was similar to the harlequin furniture of previous eras. Furniture was made to serve two or more functions—for example, a table-chest or a wardrobe-bed. Most of the mechanical devices used were designed to save space. Some were useful, but some were not. Among the pieces of patent furniture was the Wooton secretary, a large desk with three sections. It had a main central area and a pair of doors approximately the same depth as the desk that opened outward. Each section contained pigeon holes, shelves, or drawers. Like the secretaire à abattant, the central section had a fall front that folded down to become a writing surface. Another, less useful, piece of patent furniture was a chair with louvers that moved as the user rocked, in essence fanning the air to cool it. (See Figure 18.34.)

Miscellaneous Victorian Furniture

Cast-iron garden furniture, twisted wire furniture, and brass and cast- iron bedsteads were made. As advertised in contemporary periodicals, metal bedsteads had the advantage of not harboring insects.

The nascent trade with Japan resulted in the use of bamboo for furniture. The wood was durable and sturdy but less expensive than more exotic imported woods. The Americans also made rattan and wicker furniture.

Rediscovering Simplicity

Toward the end of the Victorian era, the Arts and Crafts movement began in England and called for a return of fine artisanship and a decrease in the excesses of the style. Another revival of classicism was concurrent with the movement as the 1893 World's Columbian Exposition in Chicago exposed visitors to classical structures—most of which were temporary.

FIGURE 18.33 Eastlake furniture was rectangular rather than curved, much simpler than contemporary Victorian pieces, and designed for comfort.

FIGURE 18.34 The user of the Wooten secretary could access everything easily while working, and in order to close the desk had to clean the work area to raise the writing surface and close the doors.

FIGURE 19.16 The Arts and Crafts Rossetti chair was based on early nineteenth-century French folk furniture and was made from about 1863 well into the twentieth century. Subtle painted red stripes accentuated major lines.

FIGURE 19.17 The adjustable-back chair was an improvement in comfort and was derived from the basic Sussex chair style. Typical of the period, the chair is ebonized. Philip Webb designed this example.

CRAFTSMAN-STYLE ARCHITECTURE

The style in furniture appeared first and only later, after the beginning of Stickley's publication, did it affect architecture. (See Figure 19.18.)

FIGURE 19.18 Better known as "Mission furniture," Craftsman furniture has straight, clean lines and was sturdily made. Most was made of varnished oak. Paint was never used, and joinery was typically exposed. Roycroft furniture was similar.

Craftsman architecture (1910–1925) dominated the design of domestic buildings, called bungalows,[1] but was not used for commercial or public spaces. In India where these houses originated, the living and dining rooms had exceptionally high ceilings with clerestory windows for ventilation. Shaded verandahs provided outdoor living areas. Craftsman bungalows were relatively small with a shaded porch across the front with a doorway that led directly into the living room without an intervening vestibule or hall. The roof pitch was low, chimneys protruded minimally, and wide eaves shaded the walls. These single-story (or sometimes story-and-a-half) structures had numerous windows. Asian influences were common. A brick or stone fireplace served as the focal point.

Craftsman style bungalows were sold through mail-order catalogs and were so popular that Sears, Roebuck even named its line of tools for the style. In California, high-style examples of the houses were known as Western Stick style. Typically, the ends of rafters were exposed beneath the wide overhangs of the roofs, and at the rake, three or more decorative beams were visible. Porches projected and porch roofs had an extra gable when the porch did not extend the full width of the structure. Porch posts or columns were supported on battered piers that continued to ground level. Houses might be front-gabled or side-gabled, with the porch roof serving as a cross gable.

The Gamble House in California embodied Craftsman principles. Designed by the Greene brothers, Charles Sumner (1868–1957) and Henry Mather (1894–1934), the bungalow-style house employed natural materials, exposed joints that became part of the design, and simple interior spaces. The shadows formed by the large overhangs helped to emphasize the horizontality of the structure. The third-story billiard room had windows on every side so that rising hot air could be ventilated outside. Sleeping porches were associated with bedrooms to provide comfort on hot nights. (See Figures 19.19 and 19.20.)

Most bungalows, however, were neither as large nor as sophisticated as the Gamble house. Although designed for middle-class families, bungalows were not inexpensive. Because they were spread out and usually one-and-a-half stories, both foundation and living space walls were extensive and the roof covered a large area. One advantage of the bungalow, however, was that the exterior could have features of almost any style.

INTERIORS OF BUNGALOWS

Interior walls had wood dadoes that were sometimes stenciled. Exposed ceiling beams appeared

to lower the ceiling, but plenty of light flowed through windows to the interiors. Floor plans were open, especially in the kitchen area. Built-in furniture was sometimes used, including cabinets, shelving, and often a breakfast nook.

Art Nouveau (1892–1910)

Art Nouveau was an aesthetic movement that began in 1892 in Belgium. It was inspired by the Arts and Crafts movement in England as well as by developments in wrought iron. The two styles were used concurrently and each affected the other. An important difference in the execution

FIGURE 19.19 This entry staircase of the Gamble House was elegantly constructed and based on Japanese furniture designs.

FIGURE 19.20 The Greene brothers, architects of the Gamble House in Pasadena, espoused the Arts and Crafts philosophy that an artisan should be involved in every aspect of design. They were also greatly influenced by Japanese design and carpentry and hired Japanese artisans to complete much of the work.

FIGURE 19.21 The modest size of the bungalow made it affordable to many Americans even when located in an urban area on a small plot of land.

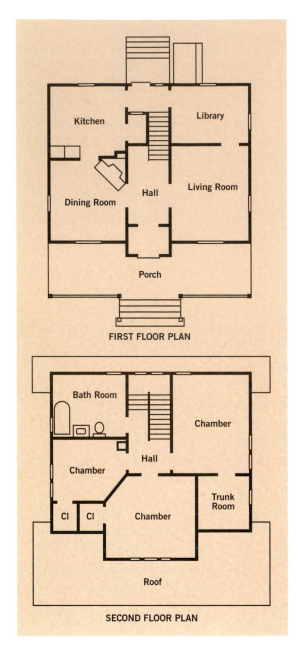

FIRST FLOOR PLAN

SECOND FLOOR PLAN

was derived from the lines of flamboyant Gothic and the capricious lines of the Rococo. Resulting works were airy, graceful, and light. The forms were most successful for architectural ornamentation and interiors. In Italy, the style was known as *Stile Liberty* after the English department store that sold many of the products, or *Stile Floreale;* in Germany, it was called *Jugendstil* (youth); in Spain, *modernismo;* and in Austria, *Sezessionsstil.*

The Arts and Crafts movement looked to the past, and practitioners selected traditional materials such as wood. French engineers and architects had debated the merits of iron since the middle of the century. A leading proponent for the use of iron in architecture was Eugène Emmanuel Viollet-le-Duc (1814–1879). Le Duc was an architectural restorer who worked on many of the medieval buildings that still draw crowds of tourists such as Mont St. Michele in Normandy

FIGURE 19.22 Columns in the Tassel House resembled vegetative stems rather than conventional columns. Instead of a capital, Horta attached twisting metal fronds that echoed the tendril decorations on walls, ceilings, and floors. Horta used curved lines and glass on façades and opened interiors with wide doorways and open stairwells.

of the two styles was that in France a tradition of artisanship still thrived, while in England such a tradition had almost been destroyed by the Industrial Revolution.

Art Nouveau was a conscious attempt to create a style that was completely free of classical connotations. In part, it was a reaction to the teachings of the École des Beaux Arts with its classical values. In addition to Gothic, Art Nouveau drew its inspiration from medieval art, from Japan, and, to a lesser degree, from Rococo. The style was the first truly new one since the Gothic period and was characterized by flowing asymmetrical plantlike forms with an almost complete rejection of straight lines and right angles. These flowing lines turned back on themselves to form what are known as **whiplash** lines. Inspiration

FIGURE 19.23 In 1900, Hector Guimard designed the enclosed entrances to the Paris Metro in the Art Nouveau style, although these were designed in cast iron rather than the more expensive wrought iron. Today, only one remains.

and Notre Dame in Paris. He, too, saw Gothic architecture as a vital influence. Le Duc's own designs were innovative. His contributions to architecture included exposing the supports of a structure, organizing the parts of a building by function rather than symmetry, and exploiting qualities inherent in materials. Le Duc was also innovative in suggesting that the malleability of iron be exploited to form decorative patterns as part of structural elements. Art Nouveau proponents looked to the future and selected materials that resulted from new technologies such as iron and large sheets of glass. Art Nouveau architecture depended on engineering. Iron was used for structural frameworks, especially for buildings that required large open spaces. In England where Arts and Crafts was strong, when iron was used, it was concealed. In Art Nouveau buildings as influenced by Le Duc, the iron was exposed.

As an architectural style, Art Nouveau emerged in Belgium. Victor Horta (1861–1947) began the Tassel House in 1892 and on the interior employed exposed iron columns that supported much of the structure. Curved lines continued on doors, banisters, and light fixtures. Horta also included skylights in his structures. Like Arts and Crafts designers, Horta controlled all parts of the design to the smallest detail. (See Figure 19.22.)

In France, the leading proponent of the style was Hector Guimard (1867–1942). An architect trained at the École des Beaux Arts, he was also greatly influenced by his visit to Horta's Tassel House in Brussels. Although Guimard designed a few buildings in Paris, his most lasting legacy is the entrances to the Paris Metro (subway). (See Figure 19.23.)

In Spain, Antonio Gaudi (1852–1926) led the movement in architecture. Gaudi used what he termed nature's organic shapes, the parabolic arch, or **catenary curve**. Gaudi admired Gothic architecture but called the buttresses architectural crutches. In his designs, he employed the parabolic arch that carries the weight of the structure directly to the ground, precluding the need for buttresses. The parabola is the shape a string or chain would take if attached at both ends and allowed to hang freely. So Gaudi often actually designed his structural components upside down, the easiest way to generate a parabolic arch. The arch can, of course, be mathematically calculated as well.

Gaudi is most famous for three structures: La Sagrada Família, Parc Guell, and Casa Mila, all of which are in the Art Nouveau style and employ undulating curved lines and warped surfaces. Sagrada Família was designed to have 18

FIGURE 19.24 Broken tiles were used to create the mosaic seen here in a technique known as trencadis.

FIGURE 19.25 Gaudí's buildings and interiors were organic in that they were influenced by natural shapes.

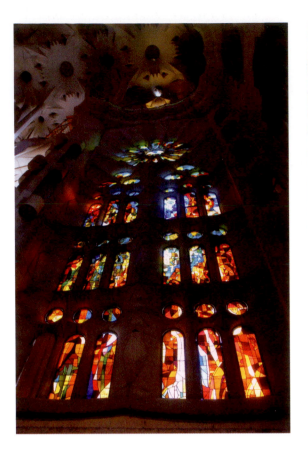

FIGURE 19.26 Gaudí's Casa Milà (1906–1910) was traditional in that it was designed around a central courtyard that serves as a light court but its sinuous curves and organic forms not only in the facade but in the design of grilles, chimneys, and structural components.

towers, one each for the 12 apostles, the 4 evangelists, Mary, and Christ. At Gaudí's death, the structure was unfinished. Gaudí did not use blueprints, and as construction continues, there are obvious differences in style. At Parc Guell, Gaudí used a technique known as **trencadis**, which creates mosaics from broken tiles. Most are used outside. (See Figure 19.24.)

Art Nouveau Interiors

Glass and iron were used imaginatively in Art Nouveau interiors. Light was an important component of Art Nouveau interiors, and hexagons or octagons might be used to avoid dark corners. Stained glass windows let in subdued light and might form a colorful skylight over a stairwell. A guiding principle of Art Nouveau interiors was that everything in the room should be designed as a unified whole. Although straight lines were used, sinuous curves predominated.

Curves of furniture doors, screens, and chairs complemented one another and the architectural components of their surroundings.

Art Nouveau Furniture

Art Nouveau, like Arts and Crafts, promoted handcrafted production and originality, and furniture was affordable only to the wealthy. Art Nouveau furniture was often strongly asymmetrical and employed flowing curves not only as decoration but as structural components such as arms, legs, doors, and backs. Emile Gallé (1846–1904) was the leading French maker of Art Nouveau furniture and instituted the use of inscriptions such as *Travail est Joie,* or "Work is joy" on furniture pieces.

or horizontal rows of squares, while Olbrich favored rows or clusters of circles.

The Times, They Were a Changing

World War I interrupted the development of design but as the world emerged from the conflict, people were eager to celebrate life. Art Deco with its streamlined forms pervaded the aesthetic world. Travel was streamlined, light reflecting materials were used, skyscrapers soared into the sky, and then the market crashed.

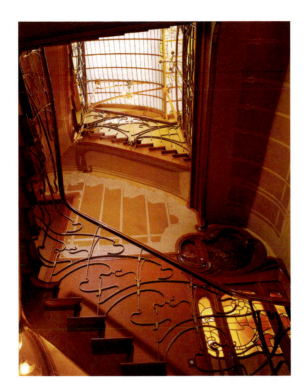

FIGURE 19.27 The staircase at Horta House employs iron railings in curvilinear organic forms.

FIGURE 19.28 The overriding characteristic of Art Nouveau furniture was its fluid lines and plastic forms with stylized decoration that sometimes approached the abstract.

FIGURE 19.29 Mackintosh chairs may have backs as high as six feet and typically have oval insets with simple pierced designs, such as crescents or squares.

While the Arts and Crafts movement in England almost precluded Art Nouveau designs, there was one Art Nouveau center in Great Britain. Furniture designer Charles Rennie Mackintosh (1868–1928) working in Glasgow, Scotland, was the guiding light of the English Art Nouveau style. Mackintosh designed each piece of furniture for a specific setting; therefore, when taken out of context these pieces often appear eccentric. (See Figure 19.29.) The Glasgow school melded influences from Arts and Crafts, Art Nouveau, Japan, and a Celtic revival that was associated with a new Scottish national spirit. Glasgow furniture was relatively simple and incorporated large plain surfaces. Overall, there was a tendency toward vertical lines.

In Austria, Art Nouveau arrived late and was strongly influenced by Arts and Crafts ideals. Called the Secession style, Austrian Art Nouveau was influential almost exclusively in Vienna. The leading proponents of the Secession movement were the architects Josef Hoffman (1870–1956) and Joseph Maria Olbrich (1867–1908). Rather than the flowing curves of other Art Nouveau expressions, Secession designs featured squares or circles with a preponderance of black and white. (See Figure 19.30.) Hoffman preferred vertical

FIGURE 19.30 The Stoclet Palace (1905–1911) in Brussels features rectilinear forms with contrasting edges that look forward to Modernism. Every detail including eating utensils was designed by the architect Josef Hoffmann (1870–1956).

Japanese Design

Japan consists of a chain of islands in the Pacific Ocean that stretches from northeast to southwest. Although there are more than 3,000 islands in the archipelago, four large islands account for 97 percent of the land. The narrow Korea Straits separate it from South Korea. The country is divided by two major faults, resulting in frequent moderate-to-severe earthquakes and volcanic eruptions. Most of Japan is covered by rugged mountainous terrain with deep gorges that run in a north-south direction, although there are a few areas of broad plains. Although most of the country is in the temperate zone, the northern part of the country is subarctic, and the southern portion subtropical. Its location between the Pacific Ocean and the Sea of Japan, its mountainous spine, and its warm current on the eastern side result in a climate with abundant rainfall, high winds, and plenty of humidity. Large quantities of timber grow readily in many parts of Japan. Japanese history has been characterized by long periods of isolation alternating with periods in which outside influences were welcomed.

Japanese History

Japan has a paucity of land for settlement. Crowded together in relatively small areas beside the mountains, its population must make the best use of available land. To provide privacy and a place for contemplation, most structures are set within at least a small garden.

PROTO-HISTORIC PERIOD

Until about 300 BC, Japan was populated by hunter-gatherers who lived in pit dwellings and evidently did not practice agriculture. Between 400 and 300 BC, immigrants of Mongoloid stock brought with them iron, bronze, and rice culture. This culture was dominant from c. 300 BC until c. 300 AD; this is known as the *Yayoi* period. Contacts with the Asian mainland increased during the subsequent proto-historic period that lasted until the mid-sixth century. During this period, the Japanese emperor was said to have descended from the sun goddess, who was the primary deity.

The Shinto religion dominated the area. This religion had no established moral code and stressed ancestor worship and the worship of nature. No temples were needed, nor were images or statues. As in Egypt, the Emperor served as the chief priest and society was theocratic. The deified emperors were buried in elaborate tombs, or tumuli, with grave goods that allow archaeologists to determine much about the culture.

Japan was to be influenced by a number of foreign cultures. Most often, the Japanese embraced the new ideas and copied many of the forms that

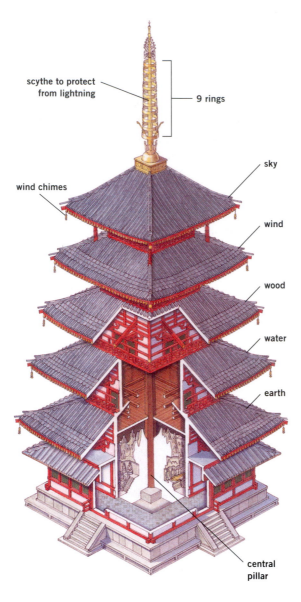

scythe to protect from lightning

9 rings

wind chimes

sky

wind

wood

water

earth

central pillar

were introduced. In each instance, however, the Japanese eventually discarded influences that were not suitable to their culture and assimilated those that made a positive contribution or that expressed Japanese ideas of beauty.

Historic Period

The historic period in Japan began late and is dated from the introduction of Buddhism in the mid-sixth century. The religion was brought through nearby Korea along with the Chinese language, a new form of government, and different construction techniques and building styles. Buddhism has never replaced the Shinto religion in Japan but established itself alongside the older religion. Buddhism brought with it from China the idea of grand-scale buildings.

The close proximity of China was to have significant effects on Japan over the centuries with periods of strong Chinese influence alternating

with those in which Chinese influence was rejected. In 645, reforms in government based on Chinese models were introduced. The Shinto religion taught that when an emperor died, the city in which he lived became defiled, and it was necessary to move the capital of the country to a new location. Even royal residences of the period were not considered permanent structures for this reason. The governmental reforms of the seventh century resulted in the construction of a new capital in Heijo early in the eighth century (710). This new city was laid out with a gridiron plan copied from the Chinese capital. The city, of course, included an imperial palace. The capital of Japan was to be moved a number of times during subsequent periods, not as the result of the death of an emperor but rather an indication in the shift of power from one location to another.

Historians consider the eighth century to be the classical period of Japanese architecture. The conflicts of the eighth century with the indigenous Ainu, the attempted Japanese invasion of Korea, and the increasing power of Buddhist priests caused the new capital to be moved twice more during that century. In 794, the capital was moved to Kyoto, beginning the Heian period (794–1185). This period was characterized by less contact with China and a process of selecting only the parts of Chinese culture that the Japanese found to their taste. The bureaucratic government was even replaced with an aristocratic government headed by an emperor, who often retired to a monastery at an early age. It was also during this period that the Japanese aesthetic ideas were formulated with beauty the primary concern. None of the wooden palaces remain, but descriptive passages in Japanese literature and depictions in contemporary paintings provide some information about their design. A few representations of humbler dwellings are also known.

In Kyoto, Buddhist monks acquired sufficient power to force the aristocracy to meet some of their demands. In areas away from the capital that were usually controlled by relatives of the Kyoto aristocracy, skirmishes not only with the Ainu continued, but rivalries built up between powerful families, resulting in some significant battles.

THE SAMURAI PERIOD

In 1185, Minamoto-no-Yoritomo (1147–1199), a provincial warrior, had acquired substantial power and set up a military government in the city of Kamakura that lasted until 1333. The emperor was forced to confer on Minamoto the title of shogun. This was the beginning of the feudal samurai period in Japan that lasted until 1868. The imperial system remained but controlled only some outlying regions.

During the Samurai period, interchanges between Japan and China became more extensive, and Zen Buddhism was introduced in the twelfth century from China. This Buddhist sect stressed contemplation and succeeded in Japan largely because it appealed to the samurai. Enlightenment could be achieved through archery, flower arrangement, and the tea ceremony. Both Shintoism and Buddhism concentrated worship on informal exercises rather than formal gatherings. Often these religious exercises were carried out in the home, although pilgrimages to holy shrines were encouraged. As the tea ceremony was important in Zen Buddhism, the product was imported for the first time into Japan from China, along with new Chinese building styles.

During the fifteenth and sixteenth centuries, Japan was in chaos with a civil war between varying factions dominating for a century. In the midst of the turbulence, however, there was great economic growth in the country with goods being produced by villagers to the point that local demand was exceeded and surplus either sold or bartered for other goods. New market centers developed, including port cities where a wealthy merchant class developed. Japanese ships began exporting goods, and the first contacts with Europeans occurred when Portuguese ships reached Kyushu. Christian missionaries, led by St. Francis Xavier (1506–1552), followed. Japanese envoys even visited Europe in 1582.

THE EDO PERIOD

In 1616, a new capital was established at Edo (Tokyo), beginning the Edo period (1603–1868). In organizing the government to give him absolute control, the new shogun Tokugawa Ieyasu (1543–1616), established a new social class system with rigid dress codes, standards of behavior for each class, rules concerning eligible marriage partners, and even regulations that dictated the type of dwelling in which members of each class could live. Separate areas of cities were established for different classes. The overseers of outlying areas—the daimyo—were controlled by requiring that each maintain a residence in the capital; this essentially made hostages of their families, who had to remain in the city.

Before the middle of the seventeenth century (1638), the new shogunate expelled foreigners, including the Spanish and Portuguese; closed Japan to foreign trade; and tried to eliminate Christianity and its influence by martyring most of the priests who had come to the country. The only contacts with outsiders were with the Dutch and Chinese on the man-made island of Dejima in the harbor at Nagasaki, where limited trade was allowed. Only prostitutes and merchants, who were considered of the lowest classes, were allowed contact with the foreigners on Dejima. The resulting two centuries of relative peace and lack of outside influence resulted in the development of distinctive cultural and economic conditions that Japan carried into the modern period. In 1853, Commodore Matthew Perry (1794–1858) sailed into Japanese waters and demanded that Japan open its doors to trade. The shogunate continued to desire isolation but lost the support of the daimyo, and in 1867 it surrendered all power to the emperor.

THE MEIJI PERIOD

During the Meiji Period (1868–1912), the seat of government was moved to Edo, which was renamed Tokyo at that time. The emperor established himself and his heirs as living gods by declaring Shintoism the state religion. He was also in favor of westernization and industrialization. Western styles were adopted, often to the detriment of traditional practices. The military was strengthened and Japan invaded China, Russia, and Korea between 1894 and 1910.

Japanese Architecture

Japanese traditional architecture exhibits a preference for blending buildings with their environments. When Zen Buddhism was introduced to Japan, the symmetrical Chinese layout of Buddhist temples changed as the new monks constructed their compounds in mountainous areas and related the buildings to the site rather than to a strict plan. The result was asymmetry, and much subsequent Japanese architecture used this format.

Japan has large quantities of stone, but generally it is fractured due to seismic activity; therefore, most of the stone is suitable only for veneers, foundations, and fortifications. Stone was used for plinths and column bases as well. Stone was used for support, including that for pillars and often to form a platform on which a building could be erected. Stones were also used in some instances to hold down the boards used for roofing. Even if Japan had plenty of suitable stone, buildings would not be constructed of the material because of the damage that would result during the frequent earthquakes.

What Japan does have is excellent timber. From an early period, Japanese artisans developed methods of working with wood and for building with the material. As in Europe, guilds were organized and membership was limited and often hereditary. Wood buildings were ideal for the Japanese climate, absorbing humidity in the wet season and releasing it during the dry season. Unlike their counterparts in other areas of Asia, Japanese wood buildings usually exploit the natural qualities of wood and framing members are not painted. Wood, however, is susceptible to fire, although some Japanese wood structures have lasted for a millennium with periodic repairs.

Buildings of the Jomon culture, the earliest in Japan, were pit dwellings, or **tateana**. Pit dwellings were either oval or rectangular in form with the floor excavated to a depth of two feet or slightly more. Four posts were set into the ground inside the pit and supported lintels. Each of the four lintels then supported posts that leaned against them at an angle and met some distance above the lintels to form a tent-like structure on which bark or thatch was laid. The ends of the ridges remained open to allow smoke to escape. The number and arrangement of poles sometimes varied, and there are examples that had a drainage ditch around the outside. Settlements had numerous dwellings.

A second group of early Japanese constructed raised huts similar to those in Southeast Asia and Oceania. These immigrants may well have arrived in Japan from one of these regions, although they most probably came through Korea first. These Yayoi people probably used bronze and dominated the Jomon culture. While Jomon groups built their settlements on hilltops for defense, the Yayoi settlements were located in low-lying areas close to fields suitable for cultivation. Their huts were raised on posts so that the floor was above grade level with steps or a ladder required for access. Some examples, which may be huts or shrines, show that the verges, or diagonals at the edge of the vertical section of the roof, projected beyond the gable end, which itself was left open for ventilation. A pillar supported the extended overhang. (See Figure 20.2.) Modern hall shrines, or **jinja**, make use of the same type of structural form. In late forms, the central post supporting the ridge was moved, the doorway was moved within the gable end, or the doorway was moved to the side of the building.

INFLUENCE 20.1

When designing his Prairie Style homes, Frank Lloyd Wright consciously incorporated the Japanese penchant for blending the building with the environment. The bungalow style that followed used the same principle. In addition, a number of the architects of both styles of buildings incorporated other Japanese details. Greene and Greene, in designing the Gamble House in Pasadena, used Japanese joinery throughout the house.

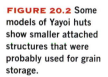

FIGURE 20.2 Some models of Yayoi huts show smaller attached structures that were probably used for grain storage.

FIGURE 20.3 Himeji Castle is made up of 83 wooden structures and is sometimes known as the White Heron Castle. The path from the main gate to the keep is complex and spirals around the major structure making it confusing for attackers. The current castle was erected in 1601.

From an early date, the Japanese made an effort to renew wood buildings to increase their life expectancy, recycle materials, and preserve and restore damaged materials. An early custom commonly associated with Shinto shrines was periodic rebuilding, a practice that also occurred in indigenous Central and South American cultures. In the case of Japanese building, a copy of a structure was built and then the original was torn down. Sometimes, during the process of rebuilding, structures were remodeled to conform to a new style or to make use of the building for another purpose. The Higashi Ch sh den, an eighth-century building designed for palace workers, was changed to a lecture hall when it was moved during the same century, and during the thirteenth century, was again remodeled.

The Japanese also recycled building materials. Unlike their Chinese counterparts who discarded tiles when buildings were torn down or destroyed by natural causes, the Japanese frequently salvaged not only durable fired clay tiles but also lumber, posts, and other materials. During the period when the capital was moved periodically, this practice provided ready materials for the new construction.

In addition, as buildings began to deteriorate, steps were taken to preserve what was possible. Rotted portions of wood were cut out of lumber or posts and replaced with plugs of the same material. In the modern era, new technologies such as the injection of carbon fibers are used to preserve damaged areas. Sometimes it is necessary to completely replace parts. The original Hi-gashi Ch sh den was again taken apart in 2000, made possible because it was held together like a jigsaw puzzle rather than with nails. Damaged pieces were replicated before the structure was re-erected.

Traditional Japanese architecture used only post-and-lintel construction with light infilling of the framework for protection from earthquakes. These buildings are more suited to the hot, humid climate of summer than to the rigorous cold of winter. Walls could often be opened to permit air circulation. In the countryside, wall infill may be of wattle and cob, or mud mixed with chopped straw. Steeply pitched roofs, originally thatch, allowed water from heavy rains to run off quickly, and the structures often had raised floors derived from early grain storage buildings, sometimes supported on stilts some distance above the ground to protect against standing water and heavy snowfalls. Roofs were often supported on bracketed and corbelled beams, a practice taken directly from Chinese building technology. The wide overhangs provided shade during the summer and carried rain runoff further from the structure.

Ceremonial buildings tended to be more colorful and complex than residential buildings that were designed to provide an atmosphere for relaxation. Large ceremonial buildings used strong color contrasts with white plastered walls and red posts. Such structures typically were symmetrical, were elaborately decorated, and employed curved lines. In fact, many Japanese buildings are deceptively simple when viewed from a distance. A closer inspection, however, reveals that even small details, some of which may be unseen when the building is completed, were elegantly designed. Joints in the buildings were made so that no nails were needed and so that building components could be easily replaced. As for Chinese structures, curvilinear interlocking brackets were repeated a number of times, creating a pleasing rhythm while supporting the large roof overhangs.

It was only in the Edo period that building proportions were standardized. Separate rules were made for temples, monasteries, and domestic buildings, leading to a similarity of design throughout the country. It was not until Japan was opened up to the Western world that building design changed again.

SHINTO ARCHITECTURE

When rice growing was introduced to Japan in the third century BC, permanent villages could be constructed. Festivals were instigated to implore the deities for good crops and sufficient rain and to express thanks for bountiful harvests. For these festivals, a sacred site was prepared and probably at first was only distinguished by a fence, or **tamagaki**, with a gate, or **torii**. Later, a post or column was erected in the middle of the sacred area to represent the deity. This column later assumed a more complex architectural form.

The torii was a freestanding sun gate located at the entrance to Shinto shrines. It had no doors and always remained open. The purpose of the torii, then, is not to keep people out but to serve only as a dividing line between the sacred and the profane. Torii are usually constructed of wood, but stone and metal examples are known. They are often painted red. Three types of torii were used for Japanese temples. The gate is usually indicative of the importance of the temple or shrine to which it leads. Large, complex gates were used for the most important buildings. The simplest type of torii has a single story and is supported by two posts. Four posts, two deep, indicate a step up in importance. Eight posts, four across and two deep, are sometimes used with single-story roofs. Two-story gates are usually supported on eight or more posts and may have a single or double roof.

The Shinto shrine developed early, has survived almost unchanged through a millennium and a half, and had the greatest influence on Japanese architecture until the twentieth century.

FIGURE 20.4
Typically, two posts were set into the ground and connected by a crosspiece below the top to form a torii. The lintel at the top extended past both posts and was often protected by a small gable roof that extended past the lintel.

Like Mesopotamian temples, the shrines were designed for use by the deities as they paused on their journeys. Unlike Mesopotamian temples, however, the shrine was used only once by the god. After the introduction of Buddhism, Shinto shrines became more important and received the status of monuments. The Ise Shrines, dating to 478, was the shrine of the Japanese imperial family beginning in the seventh century and continuing into the modern era. The Ise Shrines became the model for other shrines throughout Japan and featured thatched roofs, wide overhanging eaves, and light timber framing, all built on a platform. The shrines were surrounded by a tamagaki that enclosed several buildings including storehouses. In all likelihood, the layout was similar to that of imperial residences of the period.

Buildings at this shrine were constructed of columns buried in the ground; hence, there was a need for periodic reconstruction. Very early, the tradition of **shikinen-sengu**, or the rebuilding of shrines every 20 years, was established. Because during rebuilding, the new structure was completed before the old one was dismantled, adjacent sites of equal size and shape were needed. Today's Ise Shrine was last rebuilt in 1993 and is next scheduled for rebuilding in 2013.

The hall, or **do**, was the most important feature of the complex. Raised on a platform, or **kidan**, of stone slabs or on piles over a mound known as the turtle's back, the hall was constructed of wood columns or posts known as **hashira** with extremely light infilling. Above the walls is the **kumimono** or impost area formed by supporting blocks, or **masu** or **to**, and bolsters, **hijiki**, that projected outward to support the overhanging eaves. The roof may be finished with tile or shingles made of cypress. Four types of roofs are common: the gabled roof, or **kirizuma-zukuri**; the hipped roof, or **yosemune-zukuri**; what is known in the west as the Dutch hip, or **irimoya-zukuri**; and the tent roof, or **hôgyô-zukuri**. Each of these roof styles was imported from China. Inside the hall, the rafters, or **taruki**, are exposed or there is a coffered, or **tenjô**, ceiling.

The plan of the hall centers on the **moya**, or core, also known as naijin; it is the most sacred area and is outlined by the roof posts. The moya is the most sacred area, or **naijin**. The roof in this area usually consisted of three tiers of projecting supports, or **mitesaki**. Surrounding the moya, there are usually passages, or **hirsashi**, similar

to the aisles of medieval churches that serve as an outer sanctuary, **gejin**. This section has a less complex roof system than does the moya. Both of these roofs are quite similar to the Chinese T'ang roof. A second passage may also be included in the enclosed space, or **mokoshi**, although these generally have a separate lean-to roof, or **sashi-kake**. There were two early types of halls: the main hall or golden hall, or **kondô**, and the teaching hall, or **kôdô**, by the seventh century. Later, the functions of the two halls were combined into a single hall, **hondô**, which was square or almost so and divided into two sections—a smaller inner sanctuary and a larger outer sanctuary. The paradise hall (the hall for perpetual transformation), or **jôgyô-dô**, was constructed in a manner similar to palaces with a small inner sanctuary and an outer area wide enough for two columns.

Tombs of the period were tumuli and were based on Korean examples. Fired clay cylinders were used for the sides and the summit was decorated with human heads and figures.

BUDDHIST ARCHITECTURE

In the ninth century, a new form of Buddhism, Shingou, was introduced to Japan. In this religion, worship is centered around diagrams of the spiritual universe, or mandalas, which were influential in the design of temples. It was these temples that were located in mountainous areas away from the city, the court, and the social influences associated

FIGURE 20.5 The Ise Shrine consisted of numerous Shinto shrines although there are two main ones. Said to have been established by the daughter of an emperor approximately two millennia ago, the High Priest or Priestess of the shrine must be a member of the Japanese Imperial family.

FIGURE 20.6 The Todai-ji temple in Japan was completed in 751. The reproduction built in the seventeenth century and that exists today is approximately two-thirds the size of the original and remains one of the largest wooden structures in the world.with Shintoism, this roof type later became indicative of royal status.

with them. Buddhism required new structures for housing statues and chanting sutras, and for living and working quarters for priests and nuns. Korean and Chinese artisans, who had been invited to live in Japan, carried out much of the construction work required for the first Buddhist temples. The Buddhist temple was a world in miniature. Each of the buildings was oriented with its sides facing the four cardinal directions, because at the time, the earth was considered to be a square. Buildings, however, could be square, rectangular, or sometimes octagonal. Shrines, a hall for prayer and teaching, a sanctuary or main worship hall known as the **kando,** and a tope or **tô,** or sacred tower (pagoda) were arranged within the walled and gated complex. Stairs were centered on each of the sides of the halls. One seventeeth-century temple complex had 41 buildings.

By the seventh century, the tô was the most important building in the Japanese temple complex. Derived ultimately from the Indian stupa, this Buddhist form differed from Chinese pagodas in that Japanese examples were framed, while those in China were often almost solid. The upward-curving roofs finished with fired clay tiles and supported on brackets were Chinese in form. Typically, the Buddhist pagoda had three, five, or seven receding stories with a pinnacle on

the topmost section. Later examples had as many as thirteen stories. The pinnacle, copied from the Indian stupa, was in the form of small umbrella-like forms representing Buddha's many-tiered canopy. Sacred relics are buried beneath the stone base for the central pillar, or **shimashira**. Some pillars are actually suspended from the beams at the top of the building. During an earthquake, the post swings like a pendulum and helps to stabilize the structure. Only the first story of these square structures is usable.

Additional buildings within the temple complex include various gates, a bell tower, living quarters for monks, and sometimes a library.

By the thirteenth century, the brackets supporting the roof had changed to reflect the contemporary Chinese or Indian styles. Indian brackets often had 10 tiers and were the most complex.

Temple complexes constructed by Zen Buddhists in mountainous areas were slightly different not only in plan but in the use of materials. Bark roofs replaced those of clay tiles and wood planks were used for floors rather than beaten earth.

CASTLE ARCHITECTURE

The seventeenth century was one of insecurity and the defensive castle was introduced to Japan as a result. The castle was designed to house not only a feudal lord but his vassals or soldiers. Japanese castles were less complex than European or Chinese examples. Halls linked by covered passages, or **watadono**, were grouped around courtyards, and pavilions were located on small islands. On the interior, movable screens and sliding doors, **fusuma**, made it possible to open much of the structure to the natural surroundings or to gardens. There was no other decoration other than paintings on these screens. Neither was there any furniture on the tatami mats laid in geometric patterns. Palaces employed the same techniques as did temples with bracketed roofs and wide, overhanging eaves.

When the capital was moved to Kyoto, the city was laid out in a gridiron pattern like the Chinese T'ang capital Ch'ang-an. The Imperial Palace was located in an enclosure in the center of the city, which it dominated. Within the palace compound, there were administrative offices and ceremonial halls for official use. Temples, shrines, and mansions of the aristocrats were located around the imperial complex. Most new buildings were wooden structures covered with plaster to protect them from fire. The plaster was painted white, the pillars were red, and the roofs were finished with blue-glazed tiles. Although the more formal parts of the plan of the palace complex followed Chinese examples, the architecture was Japanese and beyond the formal buildings, symmetry was less important. Because Chinese plans were strictly symmetrical, the palace buildings were laid out accordingly, and the moya of the Front Hall of Audience was directly in line with the main gate. Before this was a courtyard enclosed by arcades with the gate at one end. Later, the moya located opposite the main gate served as the throne room for the emperors. A raised dais stood in the center of the moya to serve as the throne. The front of the building had inner and outer verandahs separated by rows of red-painted columns. The spaces between the columns of the outer row were filled with hanging vertical **shitomido**, or wood lattices covered with paper. It was these shitomido that were later used for exterior walls of Shinden mansions. The shitomido could be swung up to open the wall completely. **Sudare**, or roll-up bamboo shades, were hung outside the shitomido as well as between the inner columns.

The emperor's living quarters were similar in construction but were divided into receiving rooms and small apartments. The largest room in the building was used as the emperor's living room and for receiving guests. Within the room is the **Sekkaidan**, a polished plastered rectangle that was covered with dirt during inclement weather. Certain Shinto rituals required that the emperor stand on earth, and this enclosed patch of earth was more convenient than standing in the rain. A circular hearth was located within the rectangle and covered with a copper disk.

During the fourteenth century, palaces became more elaborate. Wall niches, or **tokonoma**, and shelves, or **chigai-dana**, were used for displays; walls might be gilded; and doors and screens were painted with bold colors.

Although castles had been constructed earlier, the fortified castle, or **shiro**, was introduced in Japan after European firearms were brought by the Portuguese in 1541. Japanese castles were sometimes constructed in the middle of towns and served both as fortresses and as centers of administration. Other castles, like those in Europe, were constructed to guard strategic sites such as river crossings or crossroads. The landscape itself was often incorporated as part of the defensive mechanisms of the castle. Streams were diverted to create moats. Castles were often raised on 45-degree, mortarless stone bases. A complex system of moats and baileys, or **maru**, was developed—some concentric, others arranged in a row. Gates were arranged with defense in mind. Those placed at corners resulted in a bottleneck effect and the location of others forced invaders to move beneath windows from which rocks and other missiles could be dropped in order to reach a gate. The keep, or **tenshukaku**, was located within the central bailey along with the main residence, living quarters for soldiers, and the storerooms. The keep was designed to be imposing and aesthetically pleasing at the same time. The structure was typically three to five stories in height, although the perception from the exterior of the number of stories rarely corresponded to the actual number.

Towers, or **yagura**, were located at corners and over gates and served the obvious defensive purposes, but most often they were used for other functions. Some were water towers; others designed for viewing the moon at night. Balconies were incorporated so that the scenery could be enjoyed.

There was a central main tower with multiple stories known as the **tenju**. Gun slits were incorporated in the plaster-covered wood walls.

The same complex roofing structure was used in castles as in temples and other buildings.

SHINDEN (NINTH–TWELFTH CENTURIES) AND SHOIN DWELLINGS (1336–1573)

During the Heian Period, the keep, or **tenshukaku**, of Nagoya Castle had a pair of kinshachi, or tiger-headed fish, on the upper roof because they were said to prevent fires. Burned, however, in 1945, the traditional wooden structure was rebuilt in concrete. Land around the palace enclosure was granted to court nobles where they built mansions around a central open courtyard. The main rooms were in the Shinden, which faced south onto the courtyard. **Tainoya**, or lesser living quarters, were symmetrically arranged on the east and west sides and connected to the Shinden by watadono, or wide corridors. Smaller corridors completed a U-shape around the courtyard. Later, corridors were shortened, and finally they disappeared. Associated buildings were then attached to the main structure.

The features of Shoin dwellings were derived from Zen Buddhist examples and included the **tokonoma** and **shoin** window. By the sixteenth century, the shoin dwelling had become the norm. In feudal Japan, the shoin dwelling served as a reception area for visitors and also as a private place for the lord, much like the great hall and its associated solar in Medieval Europe.

The tokonoma was originally the private altar in the dwelling of a priest that had a low wooden table, incense burner, votive candles, and floral arrangements beneath a Buddhist scroll hung on the wall. The shoin itself was an alcove with a window that projected onto the exterior verandah and overlooked a garden. Originally, it too was used by Zen priests but as it was translated into ordinary domestic buildings, became a status symbol in the main living area. The freestanding bookcase of the priests became a built-in area with shelving known as the **tana**. The floor of this room was sometimes raised on a **jodan**, or platform, in which case the room was then known as the **odanoma**. Houses with both the tokonoma and shoin were said to have been built in the Shoin style.

TEA HOUSES

Tea was brought to Japan by Zen monks who drank it to keep awake while they meditated. Later, a ritual was developed around drinking tea that honored the first Zen patriarch, Bodhidharma (fl. 526). Over the years, the tea ceremony became a time for friends to gather in an isolated location to drink tea and discuss the artistic merits of objects within their view. The tea room or tea house, known as a **chashitsu**, was reserved specifically for art appreciation and for practicing the art of "being in the world."

FIGURE 20.8
Japanese interiors are uncluttered and depend on the beauty of construction and materials for their appeal.

As tea was imported to Japan with Buddhism, the tea house was a simple structure that blended with the landscape and was typically two to four-and-a-half tatami mats in size. The structure was a hutlike form such as homes found in rural areas. The entry, or **nijiri-guchi**, known as the "kneeling in," was only about two-and-a-half feet square, requiring some measure of humility to enter. The house was small with gray walls and had a single tokonoma with only one object of art in it. There was no furniture in the tea house except for **shoji screens** to diffuse the light.

MODERN JAPANESE ARCHITECTURE

Japan was opened up during the Meiji Period in 1868, and in 1874 Josiah Conder, a student of the Arts and Crafts designer William Burges, established a College of Architecture at the University of Tokyo. Frank Lloyd Wright, who had made numerous trips to Japan and was influenced by Japanese design, constructed the Imperial Hotel in Tokyo (1916–1920), and other projects were completed by European and American architects, including St. Luke Hospital in 1928 and a chapel at the Christian Women's College in 1934. The first Japanese architect to construct a building in the contemporary International Style was Togo Murano (1891–1984). This building was the Sôgo Department Store in Ôsaka (1936).

Prior to World War II, monumental buildings were often influenced by European designs and employed classic details such as columns and pediments. Because of the devastation in many Japanese areas during World War II, the need for rebuilding on a large scale provided an impetus for making Japanese architecture more modern in appearance. Western building materials, technologies, and styles were introduced and the Jap-

anese cityscape was filled with structures made of steel, concrete, and glass. Western Modernism replaced European classicism as design inspiration. Much of the recent Japanese architecture has been constructed with the rough concrete of Brutalism, a twentieth-century construction method that employed unfinished or roughly-finished concrete. (See Chapter 22.)

By the 1950s, a number of Japanese architects had trained with Le Corbusier and later designed Japanese structures. Three of them—Kunio Maekawa (1905–1977), Junzo Sakakura (1904–1969), and Takamasa Yoshisaka (1917–1980)—constructed the Museum of Western Art in Tokyo (1955–1959) to Le Corbusier's design. Kenzo Tange (1913–2005) has been one of the most important Japanese architects since World War II. He is responsible for the Town Hall in Shimizu (1954) and in Tokyo (1956), both of which made use of glass walls. Tange was also responsible for the Olympic Sports Stadium

FIGURE 20.9 The traditional Japanese tea house, or chashitsu, is a separate structure designed for the tea ceremony. It is simply furnished so the emphasis can be on a single artistic piece or on the ceremony itself. The tea ceremony is derived from religious ceremonies associated with Taoism and Zen Buddhism.

FIGURE 20.10 The minka house was a private residence of farmers, artisans, and merchants. Samurai lived in other types of structures. Minka differ depending on climate but are usually either farm houses, houses in a fishing village, or town houses.

(1963–1964) whose roof was reminiscent of an ancient Japanese heraldic whorl-shaped device known as the **tomoe**.

JAPANESE DOMESTIC BUILDINGS

The traditional **minka**, or domicile of the middle class, served both as a dwelling and workplace. Many of these houses were as finely detailed as palaces but differed in that individuals practiced their occupations in the home. Ceiling height and location varied according to the economic status of the residents. Some houses had no ceilings, and the underside of the roof was visible from the living areas. Others had bamboo ceilings on which silkworms could be raised. Walls were usually made of bamboo lattice between supporting posts with daub plastered over it. A variety of other materials were used for these traditional walls including wood, thatch, and a combination of wood and daub. The **doma** had a beaten earth floor and served not only as the entry but as the kitchen and family work area. It was also used for drying grain. A plank floored **ima**, or sitting room, was raised 15 to 19 inches above the doma floor. On the back wall of the ima, there was a raised alcove or niche, or tokonoma, for art objects or floral arrangements.

By law, wooden Japanese houses may have a maximum of two stories, although buildings constructed of steel or concrete are permitted to have a greater number of stories. Lofts are permitted but only as storage spaces. Traditionally, Japanese children live with their parents even after marriage. A modern desire for separate units has led to the design of two-generation housing—a single unit with two separate living quarters, much like American duplexes.

There are only a few rooms in Japanese houses that are designed for specific functions: others are multifunctional. The entrance area, or **genkan**, is a small area at grade level and as people arrive, they remove their shoes in this space, careful to point the toes of their shoes toward the outside when they place them in the cabinet, or **getabako**, or on a shelf. In modern homes, the kitchen is separate and includes appliances similar to those of Western kitchens—a range, refrigerator, and a broiler for cooking fish. The toilet room is separate from the bathing room, or **ofuro**, and usually is very small. It houses only the toilet, which often appears to be a bench. A sink is in another room that is also used for dressing, and the same room may house a washing machine. The bathing room is located away from the toilet room and houses the bathtub—a teak or cedar unit designed for communal bathing. The room itself is usually waterproof and has a separate shower or washing space used prior to getting into the tub. In modern apartments, a single room known as a unit bath may house all three fixtures.

Japanese Interiors

Japanese interiors are simple and their arrangement is based on **ma**, or the balance between space and objects. Colors are muted, and accents are in red, black, yellow or gold, and sometimes green. There is little furniture, as traditionally, people sit on the floor. Most furniture is low to allow seated individuals to see over the pieces. The interior has flexible boundaries and is divided by sliding doors, or **fusuma**, and by sliding paper **shoji** screens, facilitating their use for different purposes. Both fusuma and shoji slide on wooden tracks. Fusuma are sometimes made of opaque materials such as wood slats, bamboo, or cane but they may also have paper panels that are translucent, reducing glare while allowing diffused light to enter the room. The papers on these movable partitions can be changed, although traditional examples had painted scenes. Often the entire exterior wall opens up, allowing individuals to commune with nature and to feel a part of the environment.

Natural materials are preferred with paper, wood, bamboo, and straw common. Floors are completely covered with formally arranged

tatami mats made of rice straw or rush and edged with fabric. The size of the room is measured by the number of tatami mats required to cover its floor surface. The tatami is used as a basis of measurement, and doors are one mat wide and two mats tall. There are a number of rules concerning the arrangement of tatami mats. Grid patterns and arrangements where corners of three or four mats intersect are thought to result in bad fortune. Shoes are removed before entering the room, keeping the tatami clean. In the hot, humid summer months, tatami absorb some of the moisture and heat and allow for some air to circulate beneath individuals seated on the floor.

Lighting is typically provided by paper lanterns. Although the lanterns are similar to Chinese examples, Japanese lanterns are plainer and lack the tassels and calligraphy of Chinese examples.

JAPANESE FURNITURE

The traditional Japanese house had movable partitions, and the little furniture used had to be portable. Screens and chests were the basic pieces used in most homes. Because they traditionally sat on the floor, the Japanese made no seating units. Tables were very low—less than 12 inches in height, and were supported either on four short legs or on two solid side panels. Japanese furniture has simple, clean lines and although decorative brass or copper mounts might be used at corners, little other decoration was used. Traditional and modern alike, furniture is minimalist.

Japanese furniture is made of solid wood and designed to stack. Wood grains are usually visible, although a variety of lacquering techniques are also used. Japanese lacquer was usually decorated with scenes painted in gold on a black background. **Maki-e** was a type of Japanese lacquer finish in which gold or silver dust was applied to the wet lacquer surface. **Raden** employed mother-of-pearl in either powdered form or in tiny pieces that were applied to wet lacquer, resulting in a finish with a shimmer. Europeans tried to copy lacquer finishes and had a modicum of success. The finish made in Europe was known as japanning.

> **INFLUENCE 20.2**
> *Arts and Crafts designers copied the straight simple lines of Japanese furniture.*

Japanese furniture was imported to Europe during the Renaissance and after the 1868 opening of Japan to foreign trade, Japanese forms were combined with Western examples so exports would suit Western tastes. The bracket foot was often used on these hybrid forms.

The **shibayama** was a nineteenth-century decorative device the Japanese used mostly on furniture to be exported to Europe and America. It was an ivory plaque or sometimes even an ivory covering that was inlaid with semiprecious stones and mother-of-pearl.

> **INFLUENCE 20.3**
> Japonisme *of the latter part of the nineteenth century in Europe and America made use of Japanese features in western products.*

SCREENS

The **byobu** was a folding screen with two to six wooden panels that were hinged together. Both sides were covered with paper. The wooden framework was lacquered and often had metal mounts at the corners. The joint between the paper and the frame was covered with a band of brocade. Most had paintings on the paper panels, either a single scene or separate scenes in each panel.

The **furosaki byobu** was a low screen used in conjunction with the tea ceremony, had two panels, and was sometimes made of woven rush. The two panels are rigidly attached at right angles and often have a small shelf for holding the utensils necessary for the tea ceremony. Typically, this type was used to screen the fire beneath the pot used for boiling water.

The **tsuitate** was a single-panel screen located between the entry of the house and the room beyond to protect against drafts. Low feet supported the wide panel.

CHESTS (TANSU)

The term **tansu** actually indicated wood cabinetry but was used for a variety of chests. (The term is altered to **dansu** when used in a compound word.) Few existed before the Edo period (1615–1868) when the wealthy merchant class emerged.

- The oldest and simplest of the tansu types is the **nagamochi**. It is a simple rectangular chest approximately three feet in height with a hinged lid. Sometimes, drawers or compartments were added and concealed by doors.

- The **katana-dansu** was a long rectangular chest designed for storing a sword. Traditionally, it was only owned by a samurai.
- The **isho-dansu** had a stack of four drawers, three of which were full-width. The bottom drawer was flanked by a small door on the right that concealed two smaller drawers. Sometimes the unit is divided into two, each with a pair of drawers. In this case, the bottom section retains the arrangement of the single unit.
- A small tansu, the **nomen-dansu**, has square drawers for storing masks used in Japanese drama. This type of chest was only owned by the aristocracy.
- The **kusuri-dansu** was a pharmacist's chest designed with a number of small drawers to hold drugs and herbs. Some have one or more larger drawers at the bottom.
- The largest Japanese tansu is the **kaidan-dansu**, or staircase chest. It has the appearance of a staircase and can be up to 10 feet in height. Numerous drawers and compartments provide access from one side. The form was developed late and only appeared near the end of the eighteenth century. It was originally used as a staircase to provide access to the lofts of single-story traditional buildings. The compartments were added later.

- The **kuruma-dansu** is a tansu on four wheels. It is a large cupboard with a frame beneath that has two axles for the wheels. Typically there were two bypass sliding doors that concealed an arrangement of shelves, drawers, and compartments. A seventeenth-century form, it was made for two centuries.
- The **mizuya-dansu** was a type of tansu used in the kitchen. This double cabinet had hinged or sliding doors in both the upper and lower sections. The doors sometimes had wire grilles in them to permit air circulation. Other doors had thin vertical slats. The upper section most often had a row of drawers beneath the doors. Doors on the lower compartment were slatted and covered the entire front. Behind them was a variety of compartments and shelves.
- The **funa-dansu** was used by Japanese sailors when at sea to hold their personal belongings.
- A small tansu with drawers designed to store an abacus and writing materials was the **suzuri-bako**. This piece of furniture was almost always found in Japanese shops.
- The **zeni-dansu**, named for an Edo period coin, was a small, thick-walled locking chest used to store valuables. The main compartment was enclosed by a hinged lid and there were often small drawers beneath that compartment. Secret drawers and compartments were common.

TRADITIONAL PIECES

The **kyosoku** was a wooden armrest used while sitting on the floor, most typically while eating. (See Figure 20.12.) The **makura** is a wood headrest consisting of a paneled rectangular box with a cylindrical pillow tied to the top. Makuras designed for travel have one or more drawers. The **butsudan** was a household shrine shaped like a cupboard. High open shelves supported a statue for either the Buddhist or Shinto religion and offerings in the form of food or drink.

The **hibachi** was a metal, earthenware, or porcelain vessel or, more commonly, a wooden box with a compartment in the top that was lined with clay, which was then covered with copper. The open compartment was designed to hold burning coals to heat a room. Beneath the box, there were often drawers and compartments for storing smoking pipes, tea, or incense. The hibachi was often used with a cubical **kotatsu** stand to

FIGURE 20.11
The kaidan dansu, or staircase chest, was typical in the homes of merchants and farmers because it was they who had two-story homes. Typically, these chests were relatively deep because they were used as stairs to carry merchandise or farm supplies.

raise it slightly above the floor during the winter. A table placed over the arrangement supported a **kotatsu kakebuton**, or quilt, that spread over the legs of those seated around the table. In homes of the more affluent, there might be a recessed area in the floor to accommodate people's legs and a second, deeper recess in the middle of the first one in which the kotatsu might rest. The family gathered around the unit for warmth.

A miniature form of the hibachi used by pipe smokers was the **tabako-bon**, or tobacco box, introduced after the Portuguese brought tobacco to Japan in the sixteenth century. Usually it was rectangular and had very small drawers and compartments. A circular receptacle lined with copper was incorporated in the top and held coals for lighting the pipe. A piece of bamboo was also incorporated in the top to hold ashes.

The **kimono rack** was a set of poles on which clothing could be hung. Two vertical poles, each with a wide foot, were connected by three horizontal poles. At the base, one of the poles connected the feet, the second horizontal member connected the vertical poles about midway in height, and the third horizontal member consisted of a pole that crossed the vertical posts and extended slightly beyond them.

In the traditional house, Japanese sleep on **futons**, or mattresses on the floor. The traditional Japanese futon consists of the **shikibuton**, or cushion similar to a mattress, on which the individual rests; the **kakebuton**, or comforter; and the **makura**, or pillow. The shikibuton is stuffed with cotton or down and wrapped in sheets (**shikifu**). The makura is filled with beans or buckwheat chaff. When not in use for sleeping, the futon is folded and put in a closet known as an **oshiire**, which has two shelves concealed by sliding doors.

FIGURE 20.12 One or two kyosoku, or armrests, were used by individuals seated on the floor. Cushions placed on kyosoku made them more comfortable.

FIGURE 20.13
Butsudan shrine from a Damio's palace at Kyoto, contains representation of a temple with graduated pagoda roof (gilded wood) by Japanese school.

OTHER FURNITURE FORMS

The **kyodai** was a miniature dressing table about six inches high with tiny drawers. A hand mirror was kept in the lidded compartment at the top of traditional kyodai. Modern examples often have a mirror supported by two uprights.

The **shodana** was a Japanese display cabinet with an asymmetrical arrangement of drawers, shelves, and compartments designed for the export market after 1868. Fretwork was often used, shibayama motifs were sometimes incorporated, and the pieces were usually lacquered.

Influencing the West

Japanese designs were entered in the nineteenth century European exhibitions exposing greater numbers of people to Japanese furniture and accessories, and, as trade opened up, the demand for Japanese products dramatically increased in Europe and America. The simple, elegant designs were appealing in a world filled with complexity and conspicuous consumption. Leaders of the Arts and Crafts movement were particularly impressed with the construction techniques and overall quality of Japanese products. Architects, including Frank Lloyd Wright, employed Japanese architectural features, especially along the West coast of America.

Twentieth-Century Design to Mid-Century

The technological developments of the nineteenth century resulted in the need for a number of new building types. All that was required of some of these structures, such as train sheds, was that they were simple and economical, although often it was the design and construction of these buildings that explored the possibilities of new materials first. Train sheds were supported on slender columns with iron trusses that spanned the tracks to create large open spaces. Architectural styling was unnecessary. Railway stations, on the other hand, required aesthetic qualities at first provided by following historic precedents. As better transportation became available, people moved from crowded, polluted cities to the suburbs in the United States. There homes could be spread over a larger area for less cost than in the cities. In Great Britain, they moved into "ribbon developments" that were located along major transportation arteries. The move out of urban areas made it possible for many to afford land and homes of their own.

Stronger Materials, New Possibilities

The new materials generated by the Industrial Revolution were at first used in traditional ways, and with few exceptions the characteristics inherent in the materials were rarely exploited until later. The Coalbrookdale Bridge constructed in England in 1779 was the first iron bridge, but it was constructed in a manner similar to stone bridges of the period. It was over a century later that the Brooklyn Bridge (1883) made use of the inherent qualities of steel, the stronger replacement for iron.

EXPANDING INTERIORS

When iron or steel was combined with the newly manufactured large sheets of glass, an entirely new building type became possible—a technique used at the Crystal Palace at the Great Exhibition of 1851 in London. The new space created by this marriage of metal and glass was indeterminate in size and had no real boundaries except the curtain walls on the exterior.

The Crystal Palace in London was the first of the impermanent exhibition spaces required for the numerous expositions of the latter part of the nineteenth century. Influenced by the popularity of the expositions, the interest in archaeological subjects, the advancements in science, and new methods of transportation that made travel more affordable, permanent museums began to be constructed. More schools, too, appeared, as it became evident that education should not be reserved for the wealthy but provided for the masses.

FIGURE 21.3 Simple lines, built-in components, and open spaces characterized the Prairie Style interior.

his chairs had an uncomfortable 90-degree seat-back angle.

ORGANIC DESIGN THEORY

Like other architects of the period, including his mentor Louis Sullivan, Wright employed what was termed "organic" design—relating interior spaces, the structure, and the natural environment. Nature, theorists purported, reflected divinity through its irregularity and the unique characteristics of a given location. In order to design well, an architect had to have empathy with the site. Therefore Wright sometimes stayed at a site many hours watching the play of light and shadow before designing a structure for it. Organic design principles were influenced by Andrew Jackson Downing's argument that building design is directly related to the

which were large and almost full-width. Concrete slabs were used for floors and might cantilever outward to form porches, as at Falling Water, the house Wright designed for the Kaufmanns on Bear Run, in Pennsylvania. Façades became geometric patterns of contrasting colors or materials. The Frederick G. Robie House in Chicago exemplified the mature Prairie style. There, the façade reflected the interior arrangement. At ground level there were children's play areas and a billiard room. Living rooms were on the upper level where they would be out of the line of sight from the street. The second level was offset from the first level, making the house strongly asymmetrical. The Prairie style was less popular with the American public than revival styles but was better received in Europe. (See Figure 21.2.)

PRAIRIE HOUSE INTERIORS

Screens and grilles with rectilinear designs separated large open spaces inside Prairie houses. The focal point of the interior was the fireplace, which, although it anchored the building, projected minimally through the roof so as not to disturb the horizontal lines. The fireplace was located in the largest room, and other rooms were small by comparison. Wright often built furniture in so that it blended with the architecture and so that he, alone, could determine where it should be placed to enhance the building itself. Wright even designed much of the movable furniture, including dining room chairs. Typically,

FIGURE 21.4 Falling Water, on Bear Run in Pennsylvania, was Wright's most organic design. Wright located the house itself above a waterfall and anchored it into the jagged stone hillside behind it.

land and vegetation of the site and that architecture should harmonize, not contrast, with its surroundings.

AMERICAN FOURSQUARE (1895–1930)

The American Foursquare was an adaptation of the Victorian house popular with the middle class. The Victorian house was basically a box with porches, turrets, bays, and wings. Usually, there was at least one wing for servants, often at the back of the house, with its own set of stairs. As the servantless middle-class family developed, the American Foursquare house took the place of the rambling Victorian house. It was sometimes called the Prairie box, as it shared many of the features of that style, including an open plan, or one in which there were some rooms without walls between them.

Foursquare houses were simple houses, square or rectangular in shape and two-and-a-half stories in height. There were four rooms on each of the first two stories. Most had low-pitched hip roofs with large overhangs and a dormer centrally located on the front. On the interior, the Foursquare had a family-friendly kitchen and built-in units or cabinets. While these are common in today's homes, early twentieth-century homes were usually not that well equipped.

MODERNISM (1910–1940)

Modernism was an outgrowth of social changes, many of which were a result of World War I and its aftermath. Much of Europe was in ruin, housing had been destroyed and there were millions of homeless, and cultural values were being questioned. Technological innovations changed society: the telephone, the increasing availability of electricity, air travel, mass production that resulted in average citizens working fewer hours a week, and increased leisure time affected lifestyles.

Modernism rejected all that had been associated with autocratic regimes, including historic associations in buildings and militarism. Modernism was also concerned with health, and buildings were intended to be filled with light and open up vistas to the environment. Modernism took different forms in Europe and the United States. European architects desired to change design completely. Both European and American modernists claimed that their architecture was based on rational forms and almost

FIGURE 21.5 The exteriors of Foursquare houses often borrowed features from other styles including towers from the Queen Anne style, stucco finishes and parapet walls from Spanish Colonial styles, pediments from Colonial Revival buildings, and very often exposed rafter ends reminiscent of Craftsman houses.

removed humans from the design equation, yet they believed they could create better living conditions for people by controlling their environments. Le Corbusier (1887–1965), one of the most influential architects of the twentieth century, stated this philosophical approach well: "A house is a machine for living in." The dream was to create a Utopia driven by machines but that never became a reality.

In America, the Modernism movement was not widespread until 1932, when the New York Museum of Modern Art opened its International style exhibition. Modernistic buildings had large amounts of glass, typically in horizontally oriented windows that allowed sunlight to pour into them. Brises-soleil (sun breaks) often designed as louvers were used to shade windows or serve as roofs to provide shade. (See Figure 21.6.) **Pilotis**, or supporting posts set back from the edge of the structure, were used to raise the structure above the ground, making the main living level on the second story in a manner similar to the Renaissance piano nobile.

The major architectural patrons in the late nineteenth and early twentieth centuries were the captains of industry—largely due to an increased need for factories to house production lines. The first factories were designed with flexible interior spaces and were basically utilitarian. References

Factory in Alfeld-an-der-Leine, Germany. (See Figure 21.8.)

Bauhaus (1919–1933)

The Bauhaus was a German organization that contributed to the acceptance of prewar factories as architecture. The Bauhaus was the creation of Walter Gropius, who had been the director of both the German Academy of Art and the School of Applied Arts. In 1919, Gropius combined both under the name Bauhaus to enable

FIGURE 21.6 The brise soleil, meaning sun breaker, is any type of shading device located on the sunny side of the exterior of a building. Louvers are typical as they allow some low-angle winter sun through them while blocking summer sun. A variety of techniques are used, however, and even patterned concrete is used to provide building shade.

to historic ornament were sometimes included but were unnecessary. These factories revealed their structural elements, components that had long been concealed. Early factories were not so much designed as simply constructed. Cast-iron motifs were sometimes applied for aesthetic effect, but this was the exception. Industrial buildings were monotonous, shapeless, and denuded of character. Even before World War I, some individuals had become concerned with the lack of attention to design that was spreading rapidly as more and more factories were built. Occasionally, a firm's leader consulted an architect, who would build a factory that would reflect the perceived status of the company while retaining its functional characteristics.

In 1909, the German Peter Behrens (1868–1940) designed a turbine assembly factory for AEG, a Berlin electrical company. His structure was to have far-reaching effects as he transformed the factory from a strictly utilitarian structure to one with pleasing aesthetic qualities. Behrens used concrete for the corners, but the rest of the wall structure was composed of glass, which supported no weight other than its own. The pediment at the end of the building bears the company's logo, serving as a focal point of the exterior design. (See Figure 21.7.) Two other German architects, Walter Gropius (1883–1969) and Adolf Meyer (1881–1929), followed Behrens' lead but carried their design a step further by eliminating the concrete corners and making the entire façade one of glass panels at the Fagus

FIGURE 21.7 Peter Behrens designed the AEG factory, which employed some historic references in the form of columns and the tympanum which featured the company logo (also designed by Behrens) rather than sculptures.

FIGURE 21.8 The Fagus Factory (1911–1913) was one of the first structures with floor to ceiling glass windows that helped to minimize the differentiation between the interior and exterior.

FIGURE 21.9 It was at the Bauhaus that Marcel Breuer (1902–1981) created chairs using bent tubular steel.

contact between artists and artisans. The aim was to find a common ground between technological innovations and art. Ludwig Mies van der Rohe (1886–1969) was one of the instructors and later became the director. Each student was trained by an artist and an artisan, so they each learned painting and how to work with hand tools but had little training in mathematics, structure, materials, or technology. Art history was specifically excluded.

Bauhaus precepts united technology with design. Building plans were logical, and their structural forms were adapted to the materials used. Linear forms including bands of windows, the colors of the Dutch De Stijl movement (white, gray, and primary colors), and completely functional design characterized Bauhaus buildings.

In 1933, the Bauhaus was closed by the Nazi government, but the style it espoused had already spread. As it was a style of commercial structures, it was never really appreciated by the common people. Gropius, van der Rohe, and Breuer all immigrated to the United States to practice their crafts. Van der Rohe became Dean of Architecture at the Illinois Institute of Technology, and Gropius and Breuer taught at Harvard. All were in a position to affect the Modern movement in the United States.

De Stijl (1917–1931)

During World War I, the Netherlands remained neutral and the Dutch people were not allowed to leave their country. The Dutch, then, were almost entirely cut off from artistic developments in the rest of the world during that time. The Dutch De Stijl, literally "the style," movement was founded by a group of artists, among them the Dutch painter living in Paris, **Piet Mondrian** (1872–1944), who had been visiting the Netherlands when travel privileges were rescinded. One of the influential writings that led to the De Stijl movement was that of Professor Otto Wagner of Vienna. In *Modern Architecture,* Wagner wrote that new materials must result in new forms and that artists should create what the public *should* like, not what it does like.

Frank Lloyd Wright's earlier works, especially his Prairie style, possibly influenced the group,

FIGURE 21.10 The building that housed the Bauhaus in Dessau was designed by Gropius and finished in 1926. Three-story glass walls were surmounted by a flat roof and the building was free of ornament.

FIGURE 21.11 Influenced by the De Stijl movement, Rietveld repainted his Red and Blue Chair in the palette of primary colors with black, gray, and white typical of that style.

which advocated a universal abstract design that would be suitable for all. Lines were constrained to vertical and horizontal. In three-dimensional objects, including architecture, lines were placed in planes that did not intersect, making each element independent. Black, white, gray, and primary colors were the only ones used.

One of the most influential members of the De Stijl movement was Gerrit Rietveld (1888–1964). Three of his works became internationally known: the Truus Schröeder House in Utrecht, the Netherlands (1924); the Red and Blue chair (1917); and the Zigzag chair (1934). The Schröeder house was one of few buildings that employed the principles of De Stijl. In addition to geometric shapes, De Stijl structures used modern materials: glass, concrete, and some metals including aluminum.

The Schröeder house has two stories, and the ground floor houses everything but bedrooms, which are located on the second story. Second-story interior space is divided only by sliding panels so that privacy can be had at night but children can play in a larger space during the day. It was Mrs. Schröeder who stipulated design criteria including access directly outside from each room, a water supply for each room, and in bedrooms, at least two positions suitable for the bed. It was the geometric forms, straight lines, and strong colors representative of De Stijl that set the house apart.

FIGURE 21.12
Reitveld had designed the Zigzag chair by 1934. The original used brass fittings and was constructed of oak. Made only of planes, the chair had no legs making it different from previous examples.

ART DECO (1920–1939)

Following the 1900 Universal Exposition in Paris, several French artists, including Hector Guimard, famed for his Art Nouveau entrances to the Paris metro, formed La Sociètè des Artistes Décorateurs, or the Society of Decorative Artists. Its purpose was to promote French design and leadership in the arts. It was this group who instigated and planned the 1925 Paris Exposition Internationale des Arts Decoratifs et Industriels Modernes, or the International Exposition of Modern Decorative and Industrial Arts. Promotional literature for the exposition stated that designs that imitated classical styles would not be accepted.

The name Art Deco was derived from the Paris society although it was not actually used until 1968, when the book *Art Deco of the 20s and 30s,* by Bevis Hillier, coined the term. Art Deco was used not only for architecture but for jewelry, clothing design, industrial design, interiors, and cinema. It was the first architectural style popular in America that broke from traditional forms. The style was purely decorative without the philosophical undertones of some nineteenth-century styles such as Arts and Crafts and Art Nouveau.

FIGURE 21.14 Art Deco buildings were futuristic for their time and employed geometric forms, streamlining, zigzags, and influences from ancient cultures. Egyptian features were often used in Art Deco buildings because Howard Carter (1874-1939) uncovered the tomb of King Tutankhamen (1922) while Art Deco was in style.

FIGURE 21.13 The planes of the Schröeder house are visually detached from one another, giving each component importance.

Art Deco was influenced by Art Nouveau, Cubism in art, Aztec structures, and the Machine Age. Machine Age influences included streamlining, electricity, skyscrapers, and ocean liners. Modern materials such as aluminum, shagreen (sharkskin), glass, and stainless steel were used with bold stepped forms reminiscent of Aztec (and Mesopotamian and Egyptian) design, chevrons, zigzags, and sunbursts, and sharp angles. (See Figure 21.14.) Curves, too, were bold and often turned through 90 degrees or a quarter circle. It was a lavish style—a reaction to the austerity of the war years.

Art Deco buildings were painted in a variety of colors, often with more than one color used. Smooth-surfaced materials including stone, concrete, and metal were typical for exteriors with terra-cotta and glass accents. The Art Deco style was frequently used for apartments, office buildings (including the Chrysler Building in New York), and theaters. Building setbacks, piers, and crowning decoration were characteristic especially of large buildings, and gave a sense of verticality to the structures. Art Deco began to decline in Western countries as it became mass-produced and less elegant products flooded the market. The end came with World War II. In other countries, such as India, however, the style continued to be used for another two decades.

ART DECO INTERIORS

The stepped forms continued on the interiors and light reflects from large mirrors and metals that cover much of the interior surfaces, although light sources are concealed. Tortoise-shell, leather, and exotic woods were used for details and accessories. Floors were often wood, a material avoided by members of the De Stijl movement, with rugs placed in geometric patterns. Black lacquer geometric forms were often outlined with contrasting materials to emphasize them. Walls, floors, and ceilings were often subdivided into visual strips of light, contrasting materials, or color. Few colors were actually used although blue was used to represent electricity and the inherent colors of the materials were allowed to show through. Murals and details in metal were prominent features.

FIGURE 21.15 The spire of New York's Chrysler Building features a sunburst design, a motif that was frequently incorporated in Art Deco buildings.

FIGURE 21.16 Stepped forms reminiscent of Mesopotamian ziggurats, sweeping curves derived from Art Nouveau influences, and metal surfaces were typical of Art Deco buildings.

FIGURE 21.17 The Art Deco style was a response to the technological developments in electricity and transportation and was incorporated mostly in interiors of the wealthy with natural motifs, high contrasts in materials, and geometric shapes.

FIGURE 21.18 Thousands of electric lights in a variety of Art Deco designs graced the interior of the Tuschinkski Theater in Amsterdam, built in 1921.

FIGURE 21.19 Like skyscrapers in New York City, skyscraper furniture was characterized by a number of set-backs or steps.

ART DECO FURNITURE

Rich materials were used in furniture and accessory design, with polished metals and other reflective materials common. Furniture forms employed the same lines and motifs as did buildings, with the addition of forms directly taken from modern paintings. Streamlining with curved corners and step backs were common. Art Deco interiors were expensive and limited to wealthy clientele. The style was sometimes used for ocean liners, theaters, and monumental building lobbies. Paul Frankl (1886–1958), a Viennese-born American designer worked from New York City and developed the skyscraper furniture designed to resemble the shapes of the New York City skyline. (See Figure 21.19.)

INTERNATIONAL STYLE (1930–PRESENT)

The International style was developed in Europe after the First World War and was associated with the Bauhaus. Building technologies that utilized concrete, glass, and steel were common. The style was especially suitable for commercial structures because it could be constructed in modules. Buildings in the International style were rectangular, asymmetrical boxes of one or two stories with flat roofs. Low-pitched shed roofs were sometimes used to shed water more readily. Frequently, the roof extended beyond the structure to provide shade.

Like Prairie style structures, International style houses were horizontally oriented. They often had the appearance of Art Deco buildings, with smooth white surfaces devoid of ornament. Bands, or ribbons, of windows and corner windows were characteristic. Windows were large and in some instances, such as the Farnsworth House in Plano, Illinois, formed the entire exterior wall except for widely spaced intermedi-

FIGURE 21.20 The original lipstick sofa designed by Salvador Dalí in 1936 was based on the lips of the actress Mae West.

ate supports. Glass block was occasionally used. Supporting columns were often exposed on the ground floor, and cantilevers were frequently employed. Plans were open, although some architects adapted the style to American tastes and used traditional floor plans and materials such as stone and wood siding that were less controversial than glass for residences.

Charles Edouard Jenneret (1887–1968), better known as Le Corbusier, was a Swiss-born French architect whose dogma was that "a house is a machine to live in." As such, his architecture in the International style features no ornament but relies instead on proportion and simple lines. Le Corbusier introduced pilotis, or supporting columns that were located some distance in from the exterior walls but that supported the entire weight of the structure. This design resulted in complete freedom in the location of both exterior and interior walls.

Le Corbusier's Villa Savoye (1930) was one of the most important International style houses. The main living area was raised on pilotis, leaving the ground story for servants' rooms, a garage, and turning spaces for vehicles. The structure therefore appears to float above the ground. Bands of windows surround the house. Le Corbusier's work influenced that of Oscar Niemeyer (1907–), who subsequently designed the buildings for the new Brazilian capital, Brazilia. (See Figure 21.22.)

Later International style houses included the glass boxes: the Farnsworth House designed by Mies van der Rohe and architect Philip Johnson's house in New Canaan, Connecticut. It is, however, difficult to live in a glass box, and the style appealed to few.

Art Moderne (1920–1950)

The Art Moderne style originated with the Bauhaus movement. It was similar to Art Deco and was more popular for residential buildings than that style. Art Moderne buildings were asym-

FIGURE 21.21 The Villa Savoye was an early example of the International Style. It is supported on pilotis, has an almost continuous band of windows, and features a flat roof. Inside, a spiral staircase leads to the upper level.

FIGURE 21.22 The new capital of Brazil, Brasilia, was planned in 1956. Lúcio Costa (1902–1998) planned the city itself and Oscar Niemeyer served as the principal architect. Glass, steel, and concrete structures predominated.

FIGURE 21.23 Art Moderne structures typically feature little, if any, ornament other than the horizontal bands. Door and window trim made use of modern materials such as aluminum or stainless steel.

metrical, one- or two-story houses with flat roofs without cornices or eaves and with rounded balconies, projections, and corners that were sometimes emphasized by wraparound windows. Shaped like a cube, exterior surfaces were smooth, usually white painted stucco. There remained a strong horizontal emphasis with bands of trim and ribbons of steel-framed windows. A circular window was sometimes incorporated along a wall. Large sections of glass block were incorporated, as were steel pipe railings and balustrades. Art Moderne followed the new streamlined shapes of aircraft. For this reason, Art Moderne structures were often used for railway stations, airports, and other industries associated with speed and streamlining. Floor plans were open. (See Figure 21.23.)

ART MODERNE INTERIORS

Within a single structure, Art Moderne and Art Deco features were often combined, but the styles remained different. Art Moderne interiors, like those of the Art Deco period, often featured streamlining with numerous curved surfaces including those on appliances and furnishings. Because of mass production and unlike many previous styles, Art Moderne was affordable to all. In fact, streamlining was popular in almost every product associated with the home or with transportation. Even kitchen utensils were modernized by streamlining.

Homes for the Masses

The population had increased rapidly, and especially after the First World War there was an increased demand for housing. Apartments in urban areas and houses in the suburbs were built on speculation. Individuals moving from rural areas found these residences more fashionable than what they had left, and the magazines and speculators convinced them that only a few touches would result in a style used by the wealthy.

At first, some developers used the same house plan for numerous houses in row after row resulting in what critics called cookie-cutter houses—all the same. Later, the same house plan was given a few Spanish details to become Mission style, iron railings to transform it into a New Orleans style house, or, most popular of all, any number of features of New England colonial styles (e.g., Cape Cod, Georgian, Dutch Colonial) to become colonial. The furnishings and interiors of these homes rarely had much in common with their predecessors, only with a romantic notion of the style. White or off-white walls, textured ceilings, and little trim made these houses affordable. There was little of design interest in interiors.

COMMON INTERIORS FOR EVERY STYLE

The architects of the late nineteenth century often designed not only skyscrapers but buildings in eclectic styles. Even skyscrapers sometimes had eclectic features of Renaissance Revival, Beaux Arts, or any other style popular during this period. Some of the architects created interiors and furniture for their buildings, but most did not. The interior decorator filled a void by being able to create rooms in appropriate styles to fit the building they were in. Typically, interior decorators had extensive knowledge of period styles—information still required of modern designers. In addition, the interior decorator could locate sources of antiques.

The Interior Designer

Before the early twentieth century, interior design was the purview of architects and, in some cases, artisans. The Adam brothers were among the first architects to design interiors with as much care as they did the exteriors, even going so far as to design the furniture. In the 1920s, department stores began to create vignettes to display furnishings and accessories, decorators' clubs were formed, and design education became more available during the latter part of that decade. The first formal organization, however, was the American Institute of Interior Decorators founded in 1936 in Chicago.

ELSIE DE WOLFE

Elsie de Wolfe (1865–1950) is considered the first successful decorator and among the first to be called an interior decorator. De Wolfe was a figure in high society with contacts in many areas. Her first project was to redecorate her own home from Victorian clutter to more modern, simple styling. To do so, she used white and cheery colors, as opposed to the dark colors of the Victorian era, and chintz fabrics with floral prints. As her guests admired her work, they also often asked for help. Stanford White, a principle in the architectural firm McKim, Meade, and White, asked for her help on some of his architectural projects.

De Wolfe also did work for the Duke and Duchess of Windsor and Anne Vanderbilt, among other famous early twentieth-century personalities. She received a great deal of publicity and published *The House in Good Taste* in 1913. As with earlier architectural publications, this one had far-reaching influence. Interior design became a popular subject in periodicals of the era. *House Beautiful, House and Garden, Good Housekeeping* and others showcased interiors of famous people and printed articles about eclectic decors; this kept interior design in the forefront until after World War I.

De Wolfe's personal tastes did not run to historic imitation, but in order to work with clientele who lived in eclectic buildings, she learned how to merge historic styles with good taste. She was not concerned with accurate reproduction of any given style. De Wolfe combined delicate wallpapers, simple forms, and antique French furniture and reproductions, resulting in simplified interiors that were light and airy.

RUBY ROSS WOOD

Ruby Ross Wood (1880–1950), a socialite and writer, worked with de Wolfe, eventually branched out to form her own design firm, and published a book of her own: *The Honest House* (1914). Wood made use of strong colors, flowery wallpapers, and antique English furniture. She became part of the decorating staff of the John Wanamaker store in New York City, and later opened her own design firm.

Wood worked with Billy Baldwin (1903–1984) for a number of years who was known for his theatrical interiors. After World War II, Baldwin established his own design firm. Baldwin believed that architecture always remained preeminent, with scale and proportion most important, and that designers had to work within the parameters of the structure.

ELEANOR MCMILLEN BROWN

Eleanor McMillen Brown (1890–1991) studied at the Parsons School of Design as well as in Paris. In 1924, she opened an interior decorating firm in New York. McMillen used French furnishings in eclectic style rooms and gave attention to scale and architectural detailing.

DOROTHY DRAPER

Dorothy Draper (1889–1969) established the first commercial interior design firm in the United States (1923). Draper was a modernist in that she avoided period rooms. She was one of the first to design the interiors of public spaces, including the "Dorotheum," a restaurant in the Metropolitan Museum of Art in New York City. Department stores, corporate offices, theaters, and vehicles were also designed by Draper, who used vibrant colors, cabbage roses, chintzes, bold stripes, and counterchange patterns on floors. She was well known for using elaborate plaster moldings on surfaces including ceilings, doors, and walls. She wrote a column for *Good Housekeeping Magazine,* giving decorating advice, and designed furniture and textiles.

INTERIOR-DESIGNED INTERIORS

During the late nineteenth and early twentieth centuries and until World War II, most structures had eclectic interiors. Those who could afford them hired decorators who had extended knowledge of period styles to ensure that interiors were suitable for structures, whether they were residential or commercial.

Until World War I, interiors associated with historic styles were often dark and ponderous in keeping with the colors used when soot from kerosene and gas lamps and from coal-burning furnaces or fireplaces settled on objects. By the time the war was over, designers had led the way in convincing the public that it was no longer necessary to accurately re-create a period style—only to give the impression of that recreation. Thus, lighter colors and more delicate designs could be combined with period furnishings. When Art Deco was a popular architectural style, interiors often combined streamlining and Art Deco motifs with classical forms. These interiors, however, were better suited to public, commercial, and government buildings than to houses. The general populace was introduced to eclecticism in museums, theaters, commercial establishments, and libraries and by the numerous popular publications that reported on the uses of styles. Mail-order houses provided catalogs with pictures of items people could order for their homes, often dictating features of interiors simply by availability. Department stores began to carry furniture and "decorators" were on hand to advise as well as sell furniture and accessories.

The interiors of middle-class homes were also affected by the cinema. Action took place in fabulous Hollywood sets that often at least alluded to historic styles or featured modern rooms of the very wealthy. In addition, the theaters themselves were richly decorated, usually in an exotic style—Persian, Chinese, or Middle Eastern.

Furniture for the Masses

The middle class living in their homes with some historic references usually preferred furniture that also had historic significance. Upper-class homes were filled with Mission-style furniture and accurate revivals of European and American historic furniture. Accuracy, however, was costly, and most Americans accepted modified versions. Happily, examples of simplified versions of historic pieces were available at affordable prices.

Manufacturers of revival furniture had another problem to solve as well. Many of the forms of furniture common in the early twentieth century, such as the coffee table, were unknown during the historic era they sought to emulate. Regardless of the problems, American furniture manufacturers provided an astounding array of choices that were affordable to middle-class citizens. In Europe, more accurate reproductions were available at modest prices. There, Gothic as well as Renaissance furniture reproductions were popular.

GOLDEN OAK FURNITURE

By the end of the nineteenth century, the supply of walnut had dwindled, so manufacturers switched to oak. Low-end furniture was made of less expensive woods and finished to have the appearance of oak. This furniture was made in a number of styles ranging from Chippendale chairs to Neoclassical Roman curule chairs. For most pieces, the historic references were inaccu-

FIGURE 21.24 Modern furniture designs often look back to past styles even though the pieces themselves may not have been available in the historic period.

rate or even nonexistent. Inexpensive furniture was often termed "borax" furniture because some of the manufacturers of borax soap included coupons that could be collected to obtain furniture.

FURNITURE IN MIDDLE-CLASS HOMES

In the entry hall rather than the modern closet, most homes had a massive chair with numerous hooks for hanging coats and hats, storage in a chest beneath the seat, and a mirror in the upper section of the back.

During the Victorian era, **parlor suites** had become popular. Most had at least seven pieces consisting of a number of seating units and small tables. The smaller homes before World War I did not have space for this many pieces or for the massive forms in which they were typically made. Smaller sets were made but still usually consisted of an armchair, rocker, sofa, and one or more parlor chairs. Some early twentieth-century seating furniture was overstuffed, but other pieces had exposed wood frames around upholstered sections with a lighter overall appearance.

The **davenport sofa** was designed in a number of styles, but all featured a back that folded down to form a double bed. Especially in apartments, concealed beds that were the successors of Victorian patent furniture were common.

The nineteenth-century center table was replaced by the square **parlor stand** designed to display bric-a-brac or perhaps a stereoscope, or to support a lamp. Four turned, splayed legs, sometimes with brass claw feet holding a glass ball, supported the table that had a single shelf beneath the top. Pillar and scroll parlor tables remained popular with their oval tops and scrolled legs. New varieties of tops also became available, such as heart and clover shapes.

Bookcases were common because reading was a pastime that could be enjoyed by all. Typically, modest homes had freestanding bookcases, some of which revolved or stacked.

Sideboards were used in most dining rooms, but the china cabinet or china buffet with curved glass doors began to replace it. Round dining tables replaced rectangular Victorian examples. Carving on the table pedestals was reminiscent of an historic style, often colonial. Because families were often large, these tables could extend some distance and often had six or more leaves. Most people purchased five chairs and an addi-

tional armchair for the hostess with dining room tables. Chair legs featured turned spindles, splats, or bent wood because cabriole legs were more expensive.

Bedroom furniture was elaborate. Leaf carving, scrolls, and serpentine curves were applied to bedsteads, and head and footboards might be painted with cupids included in the panels. The towering head and footboards of the Victorian era began to be replaced by lower examples. Metal beds of brass or iron remained popular until metal was rationed as a result of World War I. Their popularity stemmed from the experiments of Louis Pasteur (1822–1895) and Robert Koch (1843–1910), who proved that microscopic organisms could live in upholstery and wood frames. In fact, the Montgomery Ward catalog advertised metal beds as having no chance of supporting vermin.

In addition to the bed, bedroom furniture usually included a dresser with an attached mirror and washstand, which had a cupboard to conceal the chamber pot, a towel rack, and either a built-in washbowl, an opening for one, or a washbowl that sat on the stand's surface. Wardrobes were used to store clothing, since there were still no closets in homes.

After World War I, most furniture for middle-class homes was veneered, sometimes with printed paper, which lowered its price. This practice continues today, as particle board is covered with vinyl finished to give the appearance of wood. Paint covered lower-quality woods in furniture, and bright colors, such as yellow, red, blue, or green, were typical. Some pieces had additional hand-painted details or decals.

The Rise of Technology

World War II brought the focus on architectural and interior design to a halt. After the war, as if to make up for time lost, an increasing number of new buildings were needed not only for homes but for hospitals, corporations, and schools. New materials and technologies aided the process. The International style continued its development, and the glass-walled skyscraper became symbolic of corporate success. High-rise buildings were constructed without operable windows, as mechanical heating, ventilating, and air-conditioning systems made it possible to control interior air quality. Design itself became international as ideas spread through a variety of media.

shortage of housing. In order to construct housing units quickly, prefabricated roughly cast concrete was employed. The first examples were considered ugly and were unsuccessful as housing because they quickly became a haven for muggers.

Later examples, such as Trellick Tower (1966–1972) in London, have been more successful partly because their almost sculptured forms are more pleasing to the eye. The fashionable address of Trellick Tower, however, is probably of greater significance. This housing complex, like many skyscrapers, has a façade that is almost completely glass, providing great views. Only the ends of the building seem to anchor it to the ground. At one end is a detached elevator. London's new National Theater building (opened 1976) uses raw concrete forms as well. Its stacked forms and horizontal lines are reminiscent of ancient ziggurats. Such buildings nevertheless remain an anomaly. Concrete is inexpensive; therefore, Brutalism is more frequently used for less obvious structures, such as sewage treatment plants and parking garages.

SCULPTURAL ROOF FORMS

The sculptural roof form has been increasingly explored since the early days of Post Modernism. For the 1964 Tokyo Olympics, Kenzo Tange, a Japanese architect, designed an elongated curvilinear gymnasium structure where the roof is supported by steel cables suspended from a concrete tower. The Oriente railway station in Lisbon designed by Calatrava has a roof of steel with glass pyramids and an entrance canopy that projects outward like a wing to form a steel and glass awning. Also by Calatrava, the Lyon Satolas railway station has the appearance of a bird with raised wings that form giant arches of steel and glass and come together at ground level in a single point. Tent roofs appeared at the 1972 Munich Olympic stadium and were later copied and reinterpreted in a variety of ways.

INNOVATIVE FORMS

In exploring the possibilities of materials, architects have used a variety of new forms or old forms in different ways. Postmodern buildings make extensive use of technology to create new forms that range from the geodesic domes of Buckminster Fuller to external elevators.

GEODESIC DOMES

The geodesic dome was first designed by Walther Bauersfeld (1879–1959) to house a planetarium on the roof of the Zeiss plant in Germany. R. Buckminster Fuller (1895–1983) further developed the concept and received a U.S. patent on it.

The geodesic dome employs a series of triangles, the most stable of the geometric forms because if one angle changes, all must change. Therefore, if one angle remains stable, they all must remain stable. The geodesic dome is the only structural form that gets stronger as it gets larger. Geodesic domes make more efficient use of materials and are relatively light in weight. Be-

FIGURE 22.5 One of the most unusual of the twentieth-century buildings in London is 30 St. Mary Axe, better known as the Gherkin and colloquially as the Pickle because of its shape. Rising 590 feet, the building has a circular floor plan that has several five-story triangular atria. Each floor plan is rotated 5 degrees from the one below. The double-skinned building is designed for energy efficiency with operable windows in the external skin.

FIGURE 22.6 This beach house features a geodesic dome that helps to resist the forces of the winds coming off the Gulf of Mexico. The dome makes it possible to have a large open living space beneath it, as it needs no intermediate supporting walls.

FIGURE 22.7 Buildings like the Pompidou Center (1971–1977) emphasize technology and result in large uninterrupted interior spaces.

cause winds go around the structures, they can withstand high winds. A variety of forms are possible: the triangles can be flat or prismatic in shape as long. There is, however, a lack of complete understanding of the engineering principles involved. A stress on one side of the structure may, for example, cause damage on the other. Fuller used glass and steel, but any material can be used. Geodesic domes are often used for mountain and beach retreats. (See Figure 22.6.)

HIGH-TECH ARCHITECTURE

Brutalism exposed the origins of the materials and structural processes. For the design of the Pompidou Center in Paris, the philosophical approach was similar to Brutalism and exteriorized the structural form itself, including services such as pipes, ducts, and electrical conduits, making it obvious that the building is a machine. The major advantage of exteriorizing components is that it frees up interior space. At the Pompidou Center, the iron and steel structure is external, thereby freeing interior space of the necessity of dividing partitions. The Pompidou Center not only has exposed elements such as pipes, but calls attention to them by painting them in bright red, white, and blue. (See Figure 22.7.)

The first building in England to reveal its service components was the Lloyd's Building (1979–1984) designed by Richard Rogers (b. 1933). Pipes, cranes, ducts, staircases, and elevators are exposed on the exterior. Towers surround the

FIGURE 22.8 Because it fronts on Victoria Harbor, the Hong Kong and Shanghai Bank headquarters building is believed to have good feng shui and those associated with the building may prosper because of it.

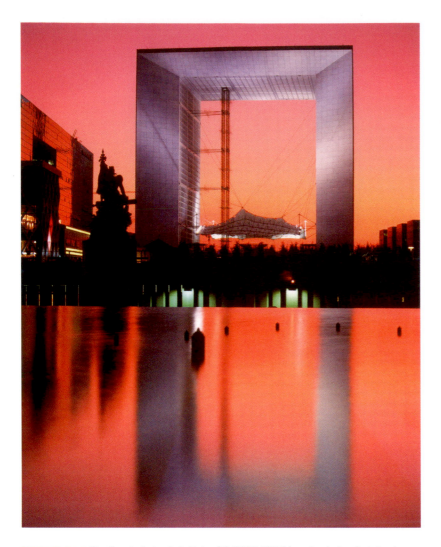

FIGURE 22.9 The Grande Arche de la Fraternité (1982–1987) is a classical revival structure reminiscent of the Arc de Triomphe, on the same axis through Paris. Rather than celebrating military victories, the Grande Arche is a monument to humanity.

large central atrium that is the main work area of the space. Escalators lead to most upper galleries that circle the 200-feet-high atrium, which is lit by a barrel-vaulted glass roof.

The Hong Kong and Shanghai Bank Head-quarters building in Hong Kong designed by British architect Norman Foster (b. 1935) also reveals its structural form on the exterior. In this building, which was constructed of prefabricated parts, giant mirrors were installed at the top of the central atrium to reflect sunlight into the building in order to conserve energy. (See Figure 22.8.)

EXTERNAL ELEVATORS

As part of the movement for expressing the interior workings of buildings on the exterior, external elevators are used on many types of buildings, including hotels, office buildings, and monuments. Usually constructed of almost all glass to take advantage of the views provided as users move vertically, these elevators have the added advantage of not taking up floor space in the main component of the building.

CLASSICAL REVIVAL

Once again, as part of the Postmodern movement, classicism returned, but this time in a very modest way. Philip Johnson's AT&T Building in New York City (opened 1984) featured a broken pediment at the top, a seemingly incongruent feature on a high-rise building. In Britain, new Georgian-style houses and shops were constructed (1979–1990). The Getty Foundation commissioned a new museum in Malibu, California, that resulted in a structure that was not only influenced by ancient Rome but was a relatively accurate replica of a classical Roman villa. In France, giant columns made of prefabricated concrete were used to decorate the corners of apartment buildings, and a modern version of a triumphal arch was raised in the courtyard of the Le Palais d'Abraxas housing complex. The National Museum of Roman art in Merida, Spain featured thin Roman brick arches in a series that have the appearance of the understructure of the Roman Colosseum. Glass in the ceiling allows light into the structure.

FIGURE 22.10 At the Portland Public Services building (opened 1982) the red columns evoke classical examples with projecting triangular sections serving as capitals.

Mies van der Rohe was famous for his "less is more" idiom, but the architect Robert Venturi (b. 1925) led a reaction against the international style, saying "less is a bore" in his book *Complexity and Contradiction in Architecture*. Venturi believed that architecture should enrich and delight. The resulting architecture was sometimes playful. Michael Graves' (b. 1934) Public Services Building in Portland, Oregon, exhibits characteristics that are a reaction against the International style. Small square windows peek out from boldly colored façades on which stylized versions of traditional designs can be seen. (See Figure 22.10.)

Deconstructivism

Deconstructivism, or **Deconstruction**, developed as a part of the Postmodern movement during the late 1980s. In this architectural movement, traditional building components are rearranged to form a new type of whole. During the design stage, fragments of buildings are moved around in unpredictable ways. The resulting buildings are complex, unconventional, and eschew the right angle. The addition to the Jewish Museum (1992–2001) in Berlin makes use of Deconstruction. Designed by Daniel Libeskind (b. 1946), the structure is an irregular zigzag entered underground through the museum's original Baroque building.

FIGURE 22.11 The focus of Deconstruction is on form rather than on function. A few avant-garde houses make use of Deconstruction, but it is generally a style of monuments and public buildings such as the Seattle Central Library (opened 2004).

FIGURE 22.12 Prize-winning architect Frank Gehry (b. 1929) designed the Deconstructionist style Guggenheim Museum (opened 1997) in Bilbao, Spain. The building is a sculptural form clad in titanium and, like most of Gehry's buildings, is composed of free-form curves.

FIGURE 22.13 At the Jean Marie Tjibaou Center (1995–1998) in New Caledonia, vertical wood slats made of iroko wood that does not rot and will withstand high winds filters the breeze into the complex. Glass louvers cover the exterior of the buildings and automatically open and close depending on wind speed.

FUTURISM

Computer-aided design has made a number of inroads in architecture. At first this technique helped architects design spaces quickly, but by the late 1980s CAD, as its commonly called, had become a design tool as well. The Bilbao Guggenheim Museum features complex curves in a variety of shapes all covered with titanium tiles. Ghery made use of CAD technology during the design process, but CAD does not take the place of the designer. (See Figure 22.12.)

The Jean-Marie Tjibaou Cultural Center in New Caledonia is designed in a format similar to Kanak tribal villages—a series of huts along an enclosed central alley designed to represent the ceremonial alley of traditional villages. In this case the "huts" include exhibition space, a cafeteria, library, and conference rooms. The center takes advantage of the breezes coming from the lagoon to provide natural ventilation. (See Figure 22.13.)

DOMESTIC BUILDINGS

Houses rarely have high-style features, nor do they necessarily conform to architectural styles of the period. The twentieth century was no exception. By mid-century, the ubiquitous ranch style had appeared, and variations on that theme

dominated the latter part of the century. More recently, historic traditions have begun to reenter the housing scene.

RANCH STYLE (1945–PRESENT)

The Ranch style house is a single-story house with a relatively large footprint. Low-pitched roofs are typical, with hip roofs favored because they are more economical to construct. Typically, they are rectangular, although L- and U-shaped designs are not unusual. Large windows are arranged in the asymmetrical façades and may include picture windows, operable windows, and sliding-glass doors. There may be some open areas in the house with rooms connecting visually to one another. Typically the family room, living room, kitchen, or dining room may be combined. On the exterior, the ranch may appear to be Mission style, Colonial Revival, Elizabethan Revival, or any number of other historic styles. In some subdivisions, the same house is constructed with varying façades to give the appearance of individuality.

From the Ranch came a number of variations:

- The **split-level** home has a single-story section beside a two-story section with two short sets of stairs that connect the parts. The entry is usually in the single-story section. An additional short set of stairs may be added when both sides of the structure have two levels.
- The **split-entry** home also has two short sets of stairs, but there is no living space on the entry level. One level may be partly below ground.
- The **raised ranch** is located on a hillside and on the front appears to be a single-story structure. At the back, the presence of two stories is revealed.

NEOECLECTIC (1965–PRESENT)

The Neoeclectic home combines a number of stylistic features in the same structure, drawing from historic references and freely adapting their features. Roof shape, window type, posts or columns, projections, and materials may reflect different styles. Modern materials are used, sometimes purposely to imitate more expensive ones. Stone or brick tiles may be used to give the appearance of a masonry structure. Vinyl siding replaces wood clapboards. The term McMansion is frequently used by critics to describe pretentious versions of Neoeclectic homes.

FIGURE 22.14 The Hardoy chair was originally designed by three Argentinean architects in the late 1930s but only became common after World War II.

FIGURE 22.15 The Barwa chair, designed by Jack Waldheim and Edgar Bartolucci in 1946, was made of aluminum tubing and sold throughout America.

Furniture of the Mid-Twentieth Century

World War II was a turning point in American furniture design for the mass market. The world had changed and with it the attitude of the American public. Simplified furniture was not only less expensive than traditional examples but more in keeping with the new lifestyle. As American soldiers went to Europe to fight in a war, factories were filled with women who were working outside the home for the first time on a large scale. The tradition of the extended family that had been part of American culture became obsolete when soldiers returned from the war. Neither the men nor the women wanted to return to the homes of their parents, and there was not only an increased demand for housing but for furnishings.

By the early 1950s, many had left the cities and migrated to the suburbs. As they started new families, their needs changed and for the first time, Americans moved on the average every three or four years. These moves required that furniture be light and portable. There was a similar trend toward informality in entertaining and in lifestyles in general. This relaxation of domestic behavior occurred in part because the care and maintenance of a home is not an easy task, but rather a time-consuming occupation.

Beds with bookcase headboards held the paraphernalia that had previously accumulated on traditional night tables. Dining rooms were an infrequent feature in homes, and eating was often relegated to the kitchen. Open plans were easier to clean and made it possible to rearrange space for alternate uses.

Furniture was modernized and acquired curvilinear forms and amorphous shapes often known as biomorphic. Plywood and plastic were easily shaped to conform to these designs. Parabolic curves were sometimes featured, as in the Hardoy chair, better known as the Butterfly or Sling chair. (See Figure 22.14.)

CONTEMPORARY FURNITURE

Furniture that was called Contemporary was actually based on Scandinavian furniture with plain wood frames and upholstered cushions. Real Scandinavian furniture was dominated by the use of teak and was handcrafted. Because of their simple lines, however, Scandinavian were easy to reproduce. The term Danish Modern was used to describe variations of this furniture.

GEOMETRIC FURNITURE

The geometric appearance of Bauhaus designs began to be more common in the late 1950s. Geometric furniture ranged from the individual pieces designed by Frank Lloyd Wright for his homes to inexpensive forms sold through Sears catalogs. Most of this furniture was based on squares, triangles, circles, and hexagons. Wright designed a number of pieces for Heritage-Henredon Furniture Company, but the manufacturer produced only the most conservative.

Tubular steel or aluminum furniture often combined with Formica tops, especially dining tables and chairs, became common and even moved into the living room. (See Figure 22.15.)

FIGURE 22.16 It was the Eames lounge chair with ottoman, produced by Herman Miller, Inc. in 1956, that was perhaps the most comfortable chair ever made. The original models were made of rosewood, but walnut has been substituted in recent years due to the fast-disappearing rain forests in South America.

Late in the 1950s, plastic laminates were silk-screened to suggest Art Deco materials.

Mid-Twentieth-Century Chairs

Innovative chairs of the 1960s included biomorphic chairs that were supported on cone-shaped plastic bases. The Tulip chair, made by Knoll International, was molded white fiberglass. Other chairs included the daffodil, lily, jonquil, and buttercup chairs.

FIGURE 22.17 Eero Saarinen designed the womb chair in 1948 and it is still produced by Knoll. The chair is constructed with a molded fiberglass base, upholstered and supported on tubular steel legs.

EAMES CHAIRS

Charles and Ray Eames were not only architects but designed furniture. One of the most famous chairs of the period was the Eames plywood chair, which debuted in 1946. The chair was made of laminated and molded wood and had gently curved shapes. It was designed to be mass-produced quickly. The design of the chair was changed as the Eames realized that the seat-back intersection could not withstand the stresses placed on it. Later versions were made with a separate back and seat. The Eames also made other furniture using the same material including storage systems and tables. The Eames fiberglass shell chair is ubiquitous. (See Figure 22.16.)

BARCELONA CHAIR

Another of the famous chairs of the mid-twentieth century was the Barcelona chair designed by Mies van der Rohe. It was later manufactured by Knoll Associates. Stainless steel quadrangular continuous curving legs formed an X-shape at each side. (See Figure 22.2.)

WOMB CHAIR

The womb chair designed by Eero Saarinen had a molded fiberglass shell covered first with a layer of foam rubber, then with upholstery. Seat and

FIGURE 22.19
Although this Venturi chair references the Queen Anne style, it is modern in conception and materials.

FIGURE 22.18 Cardboard furniture symbolized disposability. Frank Gehry used cardboard in 1970 for inexpensive furniture, although it was not designed to be disposable.

back cushions were added for comfort. Chrome-plated rods were used for supports.

In the decade of the 1960s, Knoll International and Herman Miller continued to produce modern designs. (See Figure 22.17.)

VARIETIES OF THE SIXTIES AND SEVENTIES

The decades of the 1960s and 1970s produced a wide variety of colorful plastic furniture, often in geometric forms. Plastic, however, lent itself well to organic forms, many of which were made by Italian firms. In the 70s, even inflatable furniture appeared on the scene, although the pieces were relatively uncomfortable. The same technology, however, made waterbeds possible and they became widespread during the '70s. In addition, campaign furniture was revived during the '70s partly because it used geometric forms.

After the Americans landed on the moon in 1969, silver became the most popular color and chrome furniture, usually with tubular legs, found its way into a large number of American homes. (See also Figure 22.18.)

SEVENTIES NEOCLASSICISM

The 1970s were a period of inflation, political scandals, and a loss of faith in American institu-

tions. It was comfortable, then to return to historic forms, including Art Deco and Art Nouveau, and combinations of past forms and pop icons. In the 1980s, High Tech designs were characterized by the use of materials and forms taken out of context. Tractor seats, for example, were used as stools. Furniture was designed to have the appearance of beams or girders used for structural support in buildings. Furniture edges were hard.

By comparison, the Neo Modern movement of the '80s had softer lines and subtle details. Geometric forms and the backs of chairs were softened with rounded corners.

Much of the American public, however, retreated into historic furniture styles. Robert Venturi called for more complexity in furniture design, with ornament from historic and contemporary styles used freely. In contrast to past styles, however, this furniture made use of modern materials—plastics, fiberglass, and plywood. (See Figure 22.19.)

THE MEMPHIS STYLE

The Memphis style began in Italy, and although not rejecting function, it placed its importance behind that of form. Tables sometimes had narrow tops and massive bases, making it difficult to sit at them. Ornament of Memphis style furniture was derived from pop art and Italian culture. Plastic laminates with brightly colored printed patterns, including leopard skin, were combined with marble, inlays, neon tubes, and glass. Memphis style furniture was avant-garde, elitist, and not affordable to the masses.

Glossary

abacus *pl. abaci* The square block at the top of a column capital. Can be obvious or almost invisible depending on the order. Also refers to a small rectangular Roman table with a raised rim.

ablaq The use of alternating colors of stone, brick, or a combination of the materials on a surface.

acerra A Roman lidded incense box with short legs. The lid often features projections, or "horns."

acropolis The high part of an ancient Greek city on which the major temples were constructed. Acro, meaning "high," and polis, meaning "city."

acroterium *pl. acroteria* Literally a plinth at the angles of a roof façade on which sculptures are placed. In common usage, includes both the plinth and the sculpture.

addorsed Objects placed back-to-back.

adobe Mud reinforced with straw, animal hair, or moss and used in building construction.

aedicule *pl. aediculae* A building opening ornamented with a pediment and usually flanked by engaged columns or pilasters.

aegicrane Greek ram or goat head.

agora Greek marketplace.

aisle The passageway in a building located beyond a colonnade or arcade on one side of a nave.

ala *pl. alae* Rooms or recesses behind the hearth on both sides of the atrium in a Roman home. Literally "wings."

alacena A Spanish cupboard built into a wall and enclosed by doors.

alignment Prehistoric grouping of standing stones in rows.

almoner's cupboard Large, crudely constructed English Renaissance cupboard.

alto relief See *high relief.*

ambo *pl. ambones* A raised place for a single individual. Used for reading scriptures and speaking to congregations. Typically, one is located on each side of the nave near the altar.

ambulatory Walkway. In churches, located between the apse end and the interior space usually occupied by the altar.

amorino *pl. amorini* Unclothed winged figures of babies. Also called putto.

amphiprostyle A building with a porch or portico on both the front and back in classical architecture.

amphithalomos A bedroom in a Greek house typically used by unmarried daughters.

anchor bent A type of framework used by the Dutch in which three structural members are formed into an H-shape. The vertical posts become the wall frame, and the horizontal member located several feet from the top becomes the ceiling framework. Because the vertical framing members rise beyond the ceiling, additional headroom is created in the attic area.

ancon *pl. ancones* Scroll-shaped bracket that supports a cornice in classical architecture. Often used over doorways.

andron Dining room in a Greek house. Used by men.

andronitis The men's section of a Greek house.

androsphinx A sculptural form that uses a lion's body with a human head.

ankh The Egyptian decorative motif symbolizing life. A variation of the cross form with the top arm formed into an oval.

ankle Narrowing of a furniture leg near the bottom before spreading out again at the foot.

annulet A fillet around a column located near the top of the shaft and beneath the capital. Used especially in the Doric Order.

anta *pl. antae* The extended side walls of a Preclassical or Classical structure between which columns may be located.

antefix *pl. antefixae* The decorative terra-cotta forms used at the ends of curved tiles on classical roofs to cover the openings.

anthemion *pl. anthemia* Honeysuckle ornament used in ancient Greece. Composed of a number of "petals" radiating from a central point that springs from a pair of volutes.

fiadores Curved wrought-iron stretchers placed diagonally on Spanish furniture.

fiddle-back chair American Queen Anne chair with a wide splat in the back whose shape was reminiscent of that of the instrument for which it was named.

fillet A small flat molding often used to separate other moldings. Also used between flutes in Ionic and Corinthian columns.

flag American colonial term for rush.

flashed glass Glass that has been dipped into molten glass of a different color. The outside glass layer is then carved through to show both colors.

flat arch A flat header for an opening formed by individual wedge-shaped units.

flèche Slender, tapering spire over the crossing in a Gothic building. Often of openwork design.

Flemish bond Brick pattern that employs alternating headers and stretchers in each row, with headers centered over stretchers in the row beneath.

fleur-de-lis *pl. fleurs-de-lis* A stylized lily motif.

fleuron A stylized flower used in the center of each side of an abacus of a Corinthian capital.

Florentine arch An arch with a semicircular intrados but whose extrados is not concentric. The keystone was often emphasized as it was larger than other voussoirs.

Florentine table An octagonal, or, rarely, hexagonal, table supported with carved slab legs.

flute A vertical concave curve.

flying buttress An innovation of the Gothic period, flying buttresses transferred thrust of building arches to the ground by carrying it outward beyond the walls on diagonal open arched structures that terminated in a vertical buttress.

fogón de campaña Bell-shaped fireplace usually made of adobe.

foil Curved or leaf-shaped divisions within a pattern.

folded capital A column capital with four curved lobes separated by deep depressions and widening toward the top. Byzantine.

fondo d'oro Gold-leaf figures or designs sandwiched between two layers of glass.

forum Ancient Roman meeting place with temples, markets, and other buildings.

four-centered arch An elliptical or pointed arch with a low profile that is typically drawn using four centers—two below and two on the springline. Also called a depressed arch or Tudor arch.

frailero A Spanish armchair upholstered with leather and characterized by a broad-front stretcher.

fraktur A decorated document such as a birth or baptismal certificate or a house blessing.

fresco secco Painting on a dry surface.

fresquera Small, wall-hung, ventilated Spanish food storage cupboard.

fret A pattern that employs straight lines with 90-degree angles that turn in on themselves. Simple frets are also known as keys. May be oblique.

frieze A horizontal decorative band.

frigidarium The room in a Roman bath in which there was a either a pool or basin of cold water for pouring over bather's heads, or in which bathers could sit to close their pores after the hot bath.

frontispiece Highly decorative projection at the center front of an English Renaissance structure that was usually, but not always, taller than the rest of the building. Same as French corps de logis.

fulcrum *pl. fulcra* The angled support at the end of a Roman bed against which a semi-reclining individual could rest.

funa-dansu Type of Japanese chest used on ships where a single-hinged door on the front conceals the drawers. Corners and door are usually reinforced with decorative ironwork.

furosaki byobu A two-panel Japanese screen used as a backdrop for tea ceremonies.

fusuma A lightweight Japanese sliding door.

gablet Small structure with a gabled roof or a gable-shaped canopy over a niche or sculpture used on Gothic buildings.

gadroon A short convex flute carved on turned pieces or flat areas.

gaîne A sculpture of a human torso mounted on a pedestal. German.

galerie French covered porch.

gallery grave Prehistoric grave with a chamber that may be divided.

garderobe Small room in English Medieval houses for storing clothing.

gate-leg table Type of table with hinged leaves supported by "gates" or legs that pivoted from stretchers.

gejin Outer area in a Japanese temple used by those who are uninitiated.

genius *pl. genii* The ancestral spirits that protected males in Roman society. See also *juno*.

genkan The entry hall in a traditional Japanese home.

gentleman and lady chairs Matching chairs designed for a man and a woman during the Victorian period.

geodesic dome A part-spherical structure made of triangular sections. The edges of the triangles create a network of geodesics, or great circles, on the surface.

ger Type of circular tent used by Mongolians with vertical sidewalls. Also called a *yurt*.

getabako Cabinet for shoes placed at the entrance of a building.

ghorfa Barrel-vaulted storage chambers built in North Africa. Individual rooms open off of a central courtyard and are often partly below grade level.

giant order Columns that rise more than one story.

gilding The application of thin sheets of gold to a surface.

girandole Candlestand.

glory Gilded rays emanating from a central point, usually behind a figure.

glyph In Greek architecture, a groove used in the frieze. Usually a combination of two hemiglyphs and two glyphs formed a triglyph.

Golden Mean See *Golden Section*.

Golden Rectangle See *Golden Section*.

Golden Section A ratio of 1:1.618. Same as Egyptian seqt, Golden Rectangle, and Golden Mean. Determined by ancient architects to be the most pleasing proportions.

gondola back Back of a seating unit that curves around to form arms.

gothique troubadour Nineteenth-century French-Gothic Revival style.

gouge carving A type of carving in which a scoop-shaped tool is used to create the design.

graneros A Spanish furniture unit used for storing grain. Some were simply hollowed logs, others were chests.

Greek cross A cross form with four relatively equal length arms.

griffin A mythological creature that is part lion, part eagle, and part snake.

grisaille Decoration painted in monochrome gray to simulate more expensive carving.

groin vault See *cross vault*.

groote kamer Dutch "best room" used for entertaining.

grotesque A type of arabesque that includes animals, birds, or human figures.

guadamicil Spanish embossed leather. Also guadamacilería.

guanmaovi Chinese armchair with a curved crest rail that resembled an official's hat. A similar chair, the *deng'gua yi*, differed in that it had no arms.

Guelph window Italian window type named for a prominent Renaissance family. Two perpendicular wood pieces form a cross on the exterior of the opening, and boss is sometimes added at the crossing.

guéridon Small French table supported on a tripod base.

guilloche A band pattern that uses interlacing curved forms.

guinea holes Depression in the corners of a game table to hold coins.

gutta *pl. guttae* Small conical sections that project beneath regulae and mutules in Classical architecture.

gynaeceum The women's section of a Greek house.

gyronny A counterchange pattern that employs triangles in alternating colors or textures.

Hackensack cupboard A two-piece Dutch cupboard. The lower portion consists of a combination of drawers and doors enclosing shelves and resting on short feet, while the upper portion has shelving enclosed with glass doors.

half timbering A type of construction in which timbers are used as a framework and the spaces between filled with brick or wattle and daub. Framing timbers are exposed on the surfaces.

hall and parlor house Two-room house with one or more fireplaces and sometimes a central entry with or without a passageway.

hall house House with a single room in which all activities took place.

hallenkirche German hall church with aisles the same height as the nave.

hamman In Islamic architecture, a public bath.

hammer beam A short timber beam supported by a diagonal or arched member. Used in series to transfer the weight of the roof to the walls in English Gothic buildings.

hari-bako A small Japanese chest with multiple drawers to hold small objects.

hashira Japanese posts or columns that supported the roof of a hall.

Hathor column A column with a capital with the head of the cow-headed goddess Hathor. A sistrum surmounts the head.

hawksbeak A molding with a convex curve on the exterior but that has a concave curve beneath it.

helix A design that curves around a center point remaining at a fixed distance from the center.

hemiglyph Half of a glyph or groove.

henge See *cromlech.*

heptastyle A building façade with seven columns across the front. Rare.

herm *pl. hermes* Originally a head or bust of the Greek god Mercury; later, any sculptural bust.

hermetic columns Column in which the capital is composed of a human head.

hexastyle A building façade with six columns across the front.

hibachi Japanese fireproof vessel for burning coals.

high relief A type of relief carving in which the design is undercut to release the back from the background.

hijiki Japanese bracket arm used for support.

hippodrome A Greek racecourse similar to the Roman circus. Also used in Byzantium.

hirsashi Posts or columns used to support a Japanese hall.

hôgyô-zukuri Square Japanese building with sloped roof.

hondô Main hall in a Buddhist temple.

hoop back Back of a seating unit formed with a single piece of wood bent to attach to the seat at both ends and to enclose spindles, splats, or other ornament beneath it for a backrest.

horns of consecration A pair of bull's horns used decoratively in Crete and Mycenae.

horseshoe arch An arch that forms approximately five-eighths of a circle.

hortulus Enclosed garden in Roman house.

hu chuang Chinese seating unit raised above the floor.

hua zhuo Square-topped Chinese table used as a surface for writing or painting.

hua-kung Member of Chinese bracket set that runs at right angles to the wall forming extensions both in front and in back of the wall to help support subsequent brackets and eventually, the roof.

huche French term for hutch.

hutch Crude English medieval chest sometimes made of a hollowed-out log.

hypaethral A building or portion of a building that is open to the sky.

hyphen A smaller building flanking a larger center one. Usually connected to additional larger buildings at both sides.

hypocaust An under-floor heating system designed by the Romans. A type of radiant heat in which the heat from a brazier beneath heats the masonry floor above, radiating heat into the room. Later, tile flues were used to carry the heat through the walls as well.

hypostyle hall An Egyptian hall supported by many closely spaced columns.

hypotrachelion One or three horizontal grooves encircling a column a short distance beneath the capital. The flutes continue through the hypotrachelion.

icon Byzantine and later paintings of saints, Christ, and the Virgin Mary.

iconostasis In a Byzantine or Russian church, a screen that separates the altar from more public spaces and that was used to display icons.

Ictinus Flourished c. fifth century BC. Greek architect who, with Callicrates, designed the Parthenon in Athens.

ima Living area in a Japanese home, usually with wood floors. Shoes are removed before entering.

imbrication Ornament composed of overlapping scale-like units.

imitation An attempt to create an object such as a flower that has the actual appearance of a real one.

impluvium A cistern or pool into which water from the roof ran in both ancient Greece and ancient Rome.

impost A second block mounted between the capital of a column and the entablature or arch it supports. It may be decorated or plain. Also called a *dosseret.*

in antis Columns located between antae.

incised carving A type of carving in which the pattern is cut below the surface.

inginocchiatoio Italian term for prie-dieu.

inlay A technique that requires a shaped space that is then filled with a piece of any material of the same shape.

insula *pl. insulae* Originally a Roman block. Later the stacked apartments with shared walls that filled the block.

intaglio A designed carved beneath a background surface. Used especially in jewelry.

intarsia Italian Renaissance term for marquetry.

intercolumniation Space between columns at the bottom of the shaft.

interior design Design of interiors that enhances the quality of the space and improves function or aesthetics.

interstice Space between vertical uprights in a building.

intrados The inner curve of an arch.

irimoya-zukuri A type of Japanese house with a roof that has long eaves, is disproportionately large for the structure, and has a decorative ridge pole supported by crossed bamboo poles. The roof itself is the irimoya.

isho-dansu Japanese chest with drawers used to store folded clothing.

iwan Persian open-fronted semi-domed hall, usually faced with glazed tiles.

jali Pierced screens common in Islamic architecture.

japanning A type of imitation lacquering using shellac as a base.

jardinière A small table designed to hold plants or flowers. A metal-lined container concealed by an external frieze ensured that the plants could be watered.

jerga Coarsely woven Spanish rugs.

jetty An overhanging second story or eave.

jewel work Applied ornament such as turnings, split spindles, or bosses on Jacobean and Colonial American furniture.

jeweled strapwork Strapwork with intricate banding decorated with lozenges or studs.

ji Chinese armrest for use while reclining or sitting.

ji tai shi an Tall, narrow Chinese table for religious functions. Ends of the top turned up and some had drawers in the apron. Placed in an important location in a Chinese home—often in the entry hall.

jia zi chuang Chinese four-poster bed.

jodan Raised area in a Japanese Shoin-style room.

jôgyô-dô Twin halls linked by a passageway used in shrines and temples. Covered by a single roof.

joint stool English Medieval stool.

juansha Convex-shaped wood blocks at the ends of brackets in Chinese architecture.

juno *pl. junones* The ancestral spirits that protected females in Roman society. See also *genius.*

kachelöfen Ceramic tile stove.

kaidan-dansu Japanese chest with drawers and/or storage compartments arranged in steps. The chest may be used in traditional homes to access a loft.

kakebuton Traditional Japanese comforter that is part of a futon set that also includes the makura, or pillow, and the shikibuton, or mat.

kando Hall for worship in a Japanese Buddhist temple.

k'ang Platform bed in a Chinese house.

kas Also known as kast. *pl. kasten.* A traditional Dutch furniture piece made in four pieces—a base with feet, a drawer base, a large storage cabinet closed by doors, and an overhanging cornice. See also *shonk.*

kasbah Multistory dwellings constructed by Berber tribes from clay and adobe brick.

katana-dansu Long, low Japanese chest for storing swords.

katsuogi Poles that are laid perpendicular to the ridgeline of traditional Japanese shrines.

ke hui Also known as Coromandel lacquer. Paintings on a plain-colored background.

keel arch See *ogee arch.*

keep A medieval defensive tower constructed at first of wood and later of stone.

key A simple type of fret.

keystone The wedge-shaped unit at the apex of an arch.

khekher Egyptian ornament that resembled the tuft created when bundles of supporting reeds were tied together at the top of a structure.

kibotos *pl. kibotoi* A Greek chest. Lid can be flat or angled.

kidan Platform of stone on which a Japanese hall is constructed.

kimono rack Set of poles for hanging clothing in Japan. Constructed with a stretcher at the bottom, one near the midpoint and one at the top.

kirizuma-zukuri Japanese gabled roof.

kline *pl. klini* A Greek bed.

klismos *pl. klismoi* The ancient Greek chair with shaped curved splayed legs with a seat-back angle greater than 90 degrees and with a curve in the crest rail on the back.

kloosterkozyn A fixed window located over a casement window on a Dutch house. Only the casement window was protected with a shutter allowing light into the room even when the shutter was closed.

knee The bulging, often carved upper portion of a cabriole leg.

knockdown Furniture that can be easily taken apart and reassembled.

knot garden Square Jacobean gardens with plants forming intricate knots.

kôdô Hall used in Japanese Buddhist monasteries for studying.

koilon The seating area in a Greek theater.

kokoshniki Ascending tiers of recessed corbelled arches resulting in pointed gables that project from the wall. Used in Russian architecture first to counteract the thrust of domes and later as a decorative element.

kondô Great hall in Japanese Buddhist temple.

kore *pl. kore* Archaic Greek sculpture of a young female.

kotatsu A low Japanese table under which a heating device can be located. A comforter is placed over the table to encompass the legs of those who sit around the table.

kouros *pl. kouroi* Archaic Greek sculpture of a young male.

kraal Open space in the center of an African village surrounded by individual homes and an enclosing wall.

kuche Pennsylvania German kitchen.

kumimono A complex set of brackets that support wide overhanging eaves in Japanese buildings.

kuruma-dansu Japanese chest with two horizontal sections enclosed by sliding doors.

kusuri-dansu Japanese chest with numerous small drawers used to store traditional medicines such as tree bark, herbs, or powders.

kylikeia A classical Greek cupboard that had shelving hidden by doors.

kyodai Very short Japanese dressing table with tiny drawers.

kyosoku Japanese armrest.

labrys A double ax used as a motif by the Minoan civilization.

lacca povera Italian term for découpage.

laconicum *pl. laconica* A room with hot, dry air in a Roman bath. Usually circular to allow air to circulate into every part of the room.

lacquering A method of coloring a material using a medium made from the sap of a tree. Finish is very hard and can be carved and is resistant to the effects of water, heat, acids, and alkalis.

ladder-back chair A chair with several horizontal rails across the back. Also called a *slat-back chair*.

ladrillos Fired brick. Spanish.

Lamassu A sculpture with human head and wings in the form of a bull that shows two legs from the front and four from the side, giving a total of five legs. Mesopotamian.

lancet window Type of tall, narrow English Gothic window with a pointed arch at the top.

lantern A fenestrated superstructure on the roof of a building, often on a dome.

lapis lazuli A semiprecious stone that is blue in color.

lararium A shrine or small chapel in a Roman home designed for worship of the household gods.

latilla Small-diameter poles laid across vigas to form a web to support roof finishing materials. Spanish.

Latin cross A cross form with three relatively equal length arms and one longer arm.

lattimo Opaque milky-colored glass.

layette Small chest designed to store women's accessories such as gloves.

lectern A stand with a sloping top designed to support a book or to be used as a writing surface.

lectica *pl. lecticae* A Roman bed designed to be carried and used for funerals, by women, or by ill or wounded individuals.

Often highly decorated, it has four posts covered by animal skins for shade, and sometimes surrounding curtains.

lectus *pl. lecti* A Roman bed used for dining or sleeping. Various types were made. A fulcrum was used at one or sometimes both ends to provide support.

lectus adversus The Roman nuptial bed. Named for its location opposite the entry to the atrium.

lectus cubicular *pl. lecti cubiculares* A Roman sleeping couch that was higher than the dining couch, or lectus triclinaris, and required a footstool for use.

lectus triclinaris Roman dining couch designed for three people. Usually arranged in threes around a central table in the triclinium.

lepel bortie Traditional Dutch spoon board made of wood to hold 12 spoons.

lesenes Narrow strips of stone without bases or capitals used to form panels.

letto *pl. letti* Italian bed.

library chair English reading chair with a low seat and an angled backward-projecting shelf on the top of the back to hold a book.

lierne rib A rib that does not begin or end at a capital or ridge but that is used to connect other ribs.

linenfold Medieval motif, usually carved in wood, having the appearance of cloth folded vertically.

lit à colonnes A French four-poster bed with a tester.

lit à couronne French bed with a centered round or oval canopy with the appearance of a crown from which draperies extended to the corners of the bed.

lit à duchesse Type of French bed with a partial tester attached to the wall. Also called a lit d'ange. Called an angel bed in England.

lit à la Polonaise French bed with a round or oval canopy supported by curved metal posts and from which curtains were hung.

lit clos Cupboard bed. Also called *clos* and *mi-clos*. French.

lit d' ange Type of French bed without columns but with a suspended tester.

lit de repos French Renaissance daybed with a head and footboard of the same height. Eighteenth-century examples also had a back.

lit en bateau Bed with rolled over ends of equal height and narrowed toward the top. Concave sides curved into the ends. French.

lit en housse Renaissance bed with curtains that can be raised.

liu xian zhou Six Chinese immortals table placed in front of a tang hua an.

livery cupboard A ventilated medieval cupboard that was used to store food.

load-bearing construction A type of wall construction in which each part of the wall supports the weight of the wall above it.

loggia Italian exterior covered passageway.

lohan chair Chinese chair. Also called a quanyi or saint's chair. Armchair whose arms are formed by a crest rail that curves around three sides of the chair. The seat is high and the front stretcher is often used as a footrest.

Lombard band Bands of short arcades just beneath the roofline or to visually divide the walls at each story. Typical in Germany and northern Italy.

long gallery A room in Renaissance homes located above the entrance that often spanned the entire width of the structure. Used for entertaining.

loper A vertical board that pulls out horizontally from the base of a desk to support a writing surface.

lotiform column The Egyptian column that incorporates a capital decorated with a lotus flower with associated calyxes.

low relief A type of relief carving in which the design is cut from the top only. Same as bas-relief.

lowboy An American colonial innovation used as a dressing table consisting of three side-by-side drawers supported by legs sufficiently high to sit beneath. Usually matches the base section of a tallboy.

lozenge Diamond-shaped figure.

lucunaria See *coffer*.

lüftmalerei A type of buon fresco painting used on houses in Northern Italy and Southern Germany during the Baroque period. Designs include architectural features such as window and door surrounds, religious scenes, and scenes from fairy tales.

lunette A crescent shape.

luohan chuang Chinese platform for sitting on that is surrounded by low railings.

lu-tou A board or capital placed over the beam located in a notch in a Chinese building.

macellum *pl. macella* Roman building in which markets were located.

machicolation A horizontal projecting battlement at the roofline with openings in the floor to allow defenders to fend off attackers.

madrassa Islamic school, usually a theological college, associated with a mosque.

majolica Italian Renaissance ceramic product with a white glaze. Other colors were used to form the pattern.

Majorca chair See *cadeira de sola*.

maki-e A type of Japanese lacquer work.

makura Traditional Japanese pillow filled with buckwheat hulls.

Maltese cross A cross form with four V-shaped arms.

manara Tower associated with early Islamic mosques. Evolved into more slender minaret in most areas.

manchette Pad for the wooden arm of a French seating unit.

manta de techo A cloth stretched beneath a ceiling to prevent the infiltration of dust.

marquetry A type of veneering that makes use of a variety of materials fit together to form a thin sheet.

martyrium *pl. martyria* Memorial structure, usually centrally planned, for a Christian martyr.

maru Bailey of a Japanese castle.

mascaron An ornamental face, usually human and often frightening and intended to ward off evil spirits.

mashrabiyyah Wooden lattic or pierced screen used over windows in Islamic design. Same as Spanish mesherabijeh.

mastaba A type of Egyptian tomb shaped like a flat-topped mound with sloped sides.

masu A small, square wooden Japanese box originally used to measure rice portions.

mausoleum *pl. mausolea* A structure designed as a monument and that has space inside for burial.

mechanical desk A type of bureau plat with an adjustable writing surface in the center drawer and hinged covers on side drawers. A brass gallery rail or wood lip around the top prevented objects from rolling off.

megaron *pl. megara* A building plan consisting of a main room preceded by a covered porch with supporting columns.

menhir A single standing stone in prehistoric architecture.

mensa *pl. mensae* A Roman table.

mensa delphica *pl. mensae delphicae* A round-topped table supported on three separate legs.

mensa vasaria *pl. mensae vasariae* Roman occasional table.

méridienne Daybed with scrolled ends of unequal height and a back panel that matched the heights of the ends.

merlon The vertical projection of a crenellated wall that served as a shield for an individual behind it.

mesa Spanish table.

mesherabijeh Spanish term for Arabic mashrabiyyah.

metope The panels between triglyphs in the frieze of certain architectural orders. Usually has high-relief carving.

mi-clos See *clos*.

micro mosaic Technique used to create detailed pictures using pieces of glass or enamel only slightly wider than a human hair.

mihrab A niche or small alcove in the qibla, or wall facing Mecca, in an Islamic mosque.

minaret Tower associated with Islamic mosques. Used for announcing times for prayer

minbar (also **mimbar**) Monumental pulpit in Islamic mosque.

minka House of a member of the non-ruling class in eighteenth-century Japan.

minster English term for an abbey church.

minstrel gallery Balcony above the entry to an English great hall during the Medieval period.

mirador Moorish and Spanish windows without coverings that looked onto a pleasing view.

misericord A short folding apron on the seat of a choir stall chair in medieval churches.

misión *pl. misiones* Spanish complex with a mission church, living quarters, reception rooms, and other structures surrounding a courtyard. Much like medieval castles, misiones were often self-supporting.

mitesaki The third bracket in a Japanese three-step bracket complex.

mizuya-dansu Japanese kitchen chest. Ranges in size from one-door units to much larger ones. Usually has drawers in various sizes and multiple storage compartments. Most modern examples are in two sections.

mocarbe Spanish term for muqarna.

modillion Decorative projecting brackets that support the overhang of a cornice or roof.

mokoshi A type of pent roof in Japanese Zen architecture.

molding A type of relief carving in which sharp edges are rounded, or a patterned design cut in a long surface by removing material. Also, the shaping of materials during manufacture to result in a three-dimensional design.

monastery chair Type of X-shaped armless Italian Renaissance chair used in monasteries.

monk's chair A chair with a back that pivoted downward to form a table. Called a chair table in America.

monk's table A settle with a back that pivoted downward to form a table.

monopodium A furniture support that features an animal's head and feet. Roman examples frequently separated the lion's head and paws with an eagle's breast, wings, and legs.

monoprostyle A porch with a single row of columns.

monopteral A circular temple with only columns and a roof. Also called a *cyclostyle*.

moon gate Opening consisting of a partial circle greater than 180 degrees in Chinese architecture.

mosque Islamic religious structure designed for daily prayers.

mouse-tooth brickwork Brick set in a zigzag pattern at the roof rake or angle. Used especially by the Dutch who called it muisetanden.

Mudejar Spanish term for Moslems who remained in Spain after the Moors were expelled from the country in 1492.

moya The center section of a Japanese hall defined by posts that support the roof.

muisetanden See *mouse-tooth brickwork*.

mule chest A type of Jacobean chest with a large upper section accessed through a hinged lid and having one or more drawers beneath the upper section. Also called a blanket chest.

mullion Stone or timber separation between the lights of a window.

mulqaf A ventilating shaft that projected through the roofs of ancient Egyptian buildings.

multifoil Designs with more than five foils.

münster German term for an abbey church.

muqarnas Islamic and Moorish design feature employing multiple very small domes that met at points that projected downward. Mocarbe in Spanish.

musalla Prayer hall within an Islamic mosque.

muxarabi Spanish grilles made of wood lattice in geometric designs.

naijin Sacred area in a Japanese temple hall in which only initiates are allowed.

nailhead Three-dimensional square motif with the appearance of a pyramid.

nanguan mao yi Chinese official's chair with arms that turn downward to form the arm post as well as the arm. The back curves into the back uprights.

naos *pl. naoi* The most sacred part of ancient temples in which the cult statue was housed.

narthex Vestibule across the entry end of a church.

naturalistic A pattern that has the appearance of a natural object such as a flower or animal but that has been somewhat simplified to meet the requirements of the material used.

nave The central portion of a basilica or church that is separated from side aisles by a colonnade or other structure. The nave is wider than the aisles flanking it.

neck 1. In the Roman Doric and Tuscan orders, a horizontal band around a column between the astragal molding at the top of the shaft and the bottom of the echinus. In Roman and later columns, often decorated with relief carvings. Equivalent in location to the Greek hypotrachelion. 2. A projecting horizontal course or courses of brick near the top of a chimney.

nicho Spanish for niche.

niello A technique used with metal objects in which engraved depressions are filled with a black substance formed from silver and other materials.

nijiri-guchi Low entry to a Japanese tea house.

nimbus *pl. nimbi* Halos or circles behind the head on a depiction of an individual to indicate saintly status.

noeud Knot on top of the crossing of an X-shaped stretcher during the Baroque and Rococo periods.

nogging Brick, rather than wattle and daub, used between timber framing members in medieval buildings.

nomen-dansu Small Japanese chest with square drawers used for storing masks used in dramas.

nulling Short vertical flutes with at least one curved end used as a band pattern.

obelisk A tall, square-based monument with a small pyramid at the top.

octastyle A building façade with eight columns across the front.

oculus A circular opening at the top of a dome.

odanoma Room in a Japanese building that is raised on a platform.

odeion Ancient Greek roofed theater in which poetry was read and music performed.

odeum A small completely roofed theater designed for reading of poetry or plays for small audiences. Roman.

oecus *pl. oeci* The main section of a Greek house, or a large open room in a Roman home designed for receiving guests.

oecus Corinthius An opening in the roof of a Roman or Greek house supported by a peristyle.

oecus tetrastylos An opening in the roof of a Roman or Greek house supported by four columns—one at each corner.

oeil-de-boeuf Baroque bull's-eye window, usually a horizontal oval.

ofuro Room for bathing in a Japanese house.

ogee arch Arch with S-shaped curves on each side that meet at a point. Also called a keel and ogive arch. Persian. Islamic.

ogive arch S-curved pointed arch.

open pediment The entablature beneath a pediment that is interrupted to allow an opening to be included.

opisthodomos The room behind the naos in a Greek temple that was usually used to store valuables.

opus sectile A type of mosaic in which large pieces of stone are usually cut and fit into geometric or abstract shapes.

orchestra A circular area on the floor of a Greek theater where singers and dancers performed. From the Greek *orchesina,* meaning "dancing space."

orders Layers of jambs in openings of Romanesque and Gothic buildings.

oriel window A projecting window supported by one or more brackets.

ormolu Gilded bronze figures or mounts often used to protect corners and edges of furniture.

ornamentation The deliberate treatment of a surface or object to provide decoration and interest.

oshiire Japanese closet in which the futon is stored when not in use.

Osiride pillar A sculpture of the Egyptian god Osiris identifiable by crossed arms that is used in front of a square support.

ostium *pl. ostiae* The passageway leading from the entrance of a Roman home into the first courtyard, usually the atrium.

ottoman Nineteenth-century round or oval seating unit with a truncated cone serving as a backrest.

outshot house A type of American colonial house plan in which rooms were added to create an L-shape at the back.

ovolo A molding with an approximate quarter-circle convex curve. The reverse of cavetto.

padercita A stepped adobe wall often associated with a corner fireplace. Spanish.

pagoda Introduced to China with Buddhism, pagodas housed sacred relics and writings. These multistoried structures are typically circular, square, or octagonal in form with multiple-tiered roofs.

paintbrush foot See *Braganza foot.*

palaistra *pl. palaistrai* Wrestling area in ancient Greece. Usually part of a gymnasium and surrounded by colonnades or buildings.

palampore Cotton fabrics from India with painted designs.

palanquin A chair mounted on poles to enable it to be carried.

palisade A wall or fence constructed with side-by-side vertical posts.

palmate column The Egyptian column that incorporates a capital decorated with palm fronds that appear to be tied with bands to the shaft.

palmette A motif composed of palm fronds that radiate from a central motif or curve.

panache A feather plume mounted on the top of a bedpost.

panchetto Small Italian chair with a tall, narrow back supported on three splayed legs.

panel pattern A nonrepeating pattern covering a fixed area.

pantile S-shaped fired clay roofing tiles used especially by the Dutch.

papelera Spanish cabinet similar to the vargueño but without a drop front. This small cabinet was designed to set on a table or stand.

papier mâché Material made of small pieces of paper or textiles glued together in layers.

papyriform column The Egyptian column that incorporates a capital decorated with a papyrus flower with associated calyxes.

paradise Islamic garden.

parapet The extension of a wall above the roofline.

parcel gilt Selective gilding of an object so that only parts are gilded.

parcheman A carved motif with the appearance of folded fabric but that bulged outward at intervals.

pargetry Carved or molded plaster designs. English.

parlor stand A nineteenth-century square table designed to support a lamp or bric-a-brac. Four splayed legs supported the table.

parlor suite Victorian suites of seven or more seating units for use in parlors or living areas. Usually consisted of an armchair, a sofa, a rocker, and a number of parlor (armless) chairs.

parterre Flower gardens arranged in formal, often symmetrical, patterns with separating paths.

pastas A courtyard with columns ranged along one side only.

pastiglia A technique that uses gesso to form raised designs that may be painted or gilded.

pastophoria Medieval rooms in churches that correspond to the Byzantine diaconicon and prothesis.

patera *pl. paterae* Circular motif.

patio Spanish courtyard.

pattern An orderly arrangement of motifs.

pediment The triangular end of a building that includes the moldings and the recessed area between the moldings.

peinures-vivantes Naturally lit three-dimensional sculptural forms such as cherubs that might spread over architectural features.

pelta A crescent-shaped shield used as a motif by the Romans.

Peñasco door A Spanish door made of numerous panels, moldings, and jigsawn boards.

pendentive A method used to connect a dome to a square base in which a portion of a sphere larger than the dome is cut through by arches on each of four sides. The triangular sections between the arches curve upward and inward to meet the base of the dome.

pent roof An unsupported overhanging shed roof projecting from a point on a wall other than an eave.

pentice An unsupported shed roof used over an entrance in Pennsylvania Dutch buildings. Sometimes also used in Dutch buildings.

pepper pot tower In Tudor architecture, a small turret with a conical roof.

Pergamene capital A late Greek capital decorated with palm fronds.

peribolus Wall that surrounded an ancient Greek temple complex to separate sacred and profane areas.

peripteral A classical building with columns around it.

peripteros A type of circular structure with a cella that was usually domed and surrounded by a colonnade.

peristyle From "peri" meaning "around" and "stylos" meaning "column," a building that has a single row of columns on all sides.

peristylium The courtyard in a Roman home surrounded by colonnades. In the city, the peristylium was behind the atrium; in villae, it was the first courtyard entered.

Persiana Early blinds in Moorish Spain made of narrow wood slats that could be opened and closed. Modern version is the Venetian blind.

Philadelphia chair American version of Windsor chairs.

phoenix Chinese motif symbolic of the empress.

Phrygian bonnet Type of close-fitting conical cap worn during the French Revolution as a symbol of liberty. Also called a liberty cap.

piano nobile Level above ground level in an Italian structure.

piéce-sur-piéce A type of squared log cabin construction used in French colonial areas.

pier glass Tall, narrow mirror designed to be mounted above a pier table.

pier table A table designed to be located beneath a pier glass. The table had an apron but no drawers.

piercing Designs that extend through a surface. Often used for ventilation.

pierrotage A material used to fill the interstices in French poteaux-sur-sole construction that consisted of a mixture of clay and rubble stone.

pietre dure A surface such as a floor or furniture top made of polished stones cut and fit to form a picture or pattern.

pilaster A squared vertical decorative projection with the appearance of a column that has a base, shaft, and capital.

pilastrade A series of side-by-side pilasters.

pilotis Ground-level piers or columns that support a structure raising it above grade level. Used to build structures on the water or above ground.

pinacotheca *pl. pinacothecae* A room used in ancient Rome for the display for artwork including sculptures and pictures.

ping Chinese ornamental screen.

pintle A wooden pin that fits into a socket in a door frame that allows the door to pivot. Used instead of hinges.

pinyonet Literally pine seed. Spanish inlay using very small pieces of bone.

pishtaq Monumental entry with a tall arched façade within a rectangular frame on the front of some Islamic buildings.

pithos *pl. pithoi* Large storage jars. Usually terra-cotta.

placet See *escabelle*.

placita A small courtyard. Spanish.

plate tracery Medieval tracery formed by cutting openings in a large stone. Plate tracery resulted in thick stone partitions between glass areas.

plaza 1. A large open public area surrounded by buildings. Spanish.

plinth A square or rectangular block or base used beneath a statue, column, pilaster, or door frame. May be inscribed or have relief carvings and often has its own set of moldings. 2. The base of an exterior wall when treated differently than the wall above.

pluteus *pl. plutei* Short wall or railing used to prevent individuals from falling from a height. Roman.

podium A raised platform with stairs only in the front on which Etruscan and Roman buildings were constructed.

pointed arch An arch with a point at the apex rather than a curve. Pointed arches differ from curved arches in that they have no keystones.

polis *pl. poleis* Greek city.

poppy head An ornament used as a finial. Medieval.

porta (Always used in the plural form.) A monumental gate in a Roman wall.

portal *pl. portales* A colonnaded and covered porch in Spanish architecture. Also called corredor.

portcullis A vertical movable gate made of heavy timber or metal that moves in tracks or grooves at the sides.

porte cochere Covered passageway, usually attached to a structure.

portico A porch on a gable end that has columns across the front.

porticus A colonnaded and covered Roman walkway open on at least one side. Comparable to the Greek stoa.

portón *pl. portones* A Spanish double door designed for the passage of carriages and livestock.

portrait chair A chair with a picture of an individual on its back, usually consisting of a porcelain plaque.

portula A small gate for pedestrians that was often cut into a larger one. Spanish.

post and lintel A method of spanning space that employs two or more vertical posts supporting a horizontal lintel.

postern A small unobtrusive gate.

posticum The room behind the cella in a Roman temple. Equivalent to the Greek opisthodomus.

postigo A small, Spanish pedestrian door set within or beside a portón.

poteaux et pièce coulissante Meaning "posts and sliding piece" in French. A type of French building construction in which planks or squared tenoned logs are fit into grooved uprights.

poteaux-en-terre A type of building technique used by the French in which vertical posts are set into a trench.

poteaux-sur-sole A type of building construction that uses a horizontal sill or stone foundation on which posts are set vertically. Used in French architecture where spaces between the vertical members are filled with bousillage or pierrotage.

pouf Nineteenth-century upholstered bench with visible wooden legs. Usually round.

pozzetto Upholstered Italian sofa or love seat designed to be placed permanently against a wall.

predella Platform. Italian.

presbytery An area within a church used only by the clergy.

presidio Spanish fort.

press bed A seventeenth-century bed that folded into a cabinet closed by a door hinged at the top and that when open was supported by posts and became a tester.

press cupboard A large two-tiered cupboard used to store clothing or linen. The upper section is enclosed with doors and divided into compartments. Drawers or shelves are used in the lower section. The top features a cornice supported by colonnettes or split spindles.

prie-dieu A small desk with a sloping top and a padded kneeling piece near the floor.

prodigy house Large Tudor mansion constructed around a quadrangle with associated parks, gardens, and lawns.

prodomos The vestibule of a Greek house. Equivalent to the pronaos of a Greek temple.

pronaos The Greek term used for a vestibule or entry porch of a temple. Used for both Greek and Egyptian temples.

propylon A building located before a ceremonial gateway.

propylum *pl. propyla* The ceremonial gateway leading into temple precincts in ancient Rome.

prostyle Temple form with a colonnaded porch or portico on the front only.

prothesis In a Byzantine church, a room located on the north side of the sanctuary used to store the Eucharist and to prepare it for use.

prothyron A recessed porch at the entrance to a Greek house.

protomai capital Column capital with projecting high-relief animal forms, usually on at the front.

pseudo-dipteral A peripteral structure with space for a second row of columns.

pseudo-peripteral A structure in which engaged columns or pilasters surround the building but in which no freestanding columns are used around at least three sides of the building.

psyche Long mirror supported by a frame in which it pivoted. Also called a cheval mirror.

pteroma The walkway between the wall of a Greek temple and the columns surrounding it.

puddled adobe Clay, sometimes mixed with a binder, piled up to make walls without first making bricks.

pueblo Spanish for town.

puente "Bridge," in Spanish. A type of Spanish Renaissance stand to support a vargueño. Trestle ends were connected by a stretcher with a colonnade or arcade.

pulvinus The side of a volute on a column capital with the appearance of a rolled scroll or cushion.

puncheon Hand-hewn wood board or a door made of puncheons.

purlin A support that runs perpendicular to rafters and to which rafters are attached between the ends.

putto *pl. putti* A chubby, nude figure of a child, sometimes with wings. Also known as amorini or cherubs. Italian.

pylon A structure that is battered on all sides. Used in pairs to flank entrances to Egyptian temples and complexes.

pyramidion The small pyramid shape on top of an obelisk or pyramid.

pyrtaneium Building in ancient Greek cities that represented the homes of citizens. The building enclosed the public altar.

pyxis A small lidded box in a spherical or cylindrical form. Usually made of expensive materials, it was designed to store jewelry.

qibla The direction of Mecca.

Qing-style armchair Chinese chair with lattice work or "steps" on the sides or back.

quadrant vault A vault formed by half an arch.

quadratura Paintings that created the illusion of extending architecture beyond the actual space of the buildings.

quadriga A chariot pulled by four horses.

quadripartite vault A vault divided into four triangular sections by diagonal ribs.

quanyi See *lohan chair*.

quatrefoil A motif with four foils

quincunx Cross in square plan employing four arms of equal length, each of which was surmounted by a dome.

quoin Masonry units used at corners and sometimes around openings to reinforce the visual strength of the structure.

raden Type of Japanese lacquer work that employed powdered mother-of-pearl or small pieces of the same material applied to lacquer while it was still wet.

rail A horizontal member of a framework for a panel.

rainbow roof An American colonial roof with a convex curvature along the diagonal creating additional room beneath the roof. Also called a whaleback roof.

raised ranch A two-story house that appears to be a single story on the front, but in the back, both stories can be seen.

ramada Navaho Indian pavilion designed to provide shade. Roof of poles and branches supported on four vertical poles.

ratona Low circular table with a brazier located in the center. Spanish. Moorish.

Récamier bed Type of French Neoclassical daybed with rolled ends.

reeding A convex curve in a linear direction. Compare with flute.

refectory table Long, narrow table used for dining in monasteries. Later used in residences. Typically, trestles served as supports.

rejas Decorative iron grilles used in Spanish Gothic churches to separate the choir and the nave.

relief carving A type of carving in which the background is removed so that the finished design is raised above it. See *low relief, bas relief, alto relief*, and *high relief.*

relieving arch An arch located above an opening or ceiling to carry some of the weight above the opening horizontally to vertical supports.

reliquary Container for sacred relics such as a piece of the true cross, the bone of a saint, or a portion of a saint's garment.

remate A parapet wall at a gable end with a curved profile and no piercings.

repoussé A method of decorating metal by hammering out the design from the back so it is raised on the front.

reredos The screen behind an altar. Spanish.

ressaut The projection of an entablature to cover a column placed in front of a structure and that returns to the building itself on both sides of the projection. Also used to describe building projections that include an entablature.

retable Altarpiece decorated with a painting or sculpture.

reticulated A type of Roman masonry façade in which similarly sized stones are laid diagonally. The resulting design has the appearance of a net.

retrochoir The choir in a church located behind the altar. Typical of English churches.

rhythm Repetition of a design or component.

rhyton A type of Greek drinking vessel.

ribbed vault A vault subdivided by masonry arches that cover the joints.

rinceau *pl. rinceaux* A linear panel pattern consisting of branching vines in S-curves and spirals.

riven Wedge-shaped timbers cut by splitting a log from the outside to the center.

riwaq Covered walkway around a courtyard. Islamic.

rock-cut church Ethiopian church hewn from natural rock.

Romayne work Carved human head motifs often surrounded by foliage.

rondavel African mud houses that are circular in form and have a thatched roof with a metal cap.

rose window A circular window divided into segments by mullions with glazed openings.

rosette A circular motif whose design radiates from a center point and has the appearance of a stylized flower.

rostral column A column on which the beaks of captured ships have been mounted.

rostrum A raised platform from which speeches were given in ancient Rome.

rowell See *corona.*

royal portal Medieval cathedral doorways on which sculptures of royal personages appeared.

running dog See *Vitruvian scroll.*

rusticated Stonework that employs blocks that are cut on four faces to fit together easily with the front and back faces left in their natural state or textured in some way.

Saber leg A concave furniture leg that has no separate foot.

sabot A type of ormolu mount designed to fit over the foot of a piece of furniture to protect it.

saddled seat A wooden furniture seat with a slight concave curve to fit the human body.

sala Room in a Spanish house.

saltbox house An American colonial style house with an extended roofline in the back that often reaches almost to the ground. Original examples had a change in the pitch of the roofline indicating where the house was added onto. The roof is also called a catslide roof especially in the South.

san cai ti jui Chinese chair similar to the zuiwengyi. The chair folded and had a headrest, and a footstool could be extended from beneath the seat.

sanctuary Sacred area in which the altar is located in a church. Typically describes area in Catholic and some Orthodox churches. The term chancel is used for Protestant churches.

santo Statue of a saint. Spanish.

Saracenic A type of metalwork made in Venice by immigrant Oriental artisans using Arabic script and Islamic designs. Architectural influences of the Islamic religion on buildings in their area of influence. Characterized by geometric motifs, bulbous domes, minarets, and foiled horseshoe arches.

sardivan Fountain in the courtyard of a mosque.

sashikake Japanese roof that slopes in one direction.

Savonarola chair A type of Italian Renaissance X-shaped chair with five or seven legs arranged from front to back that curved upward to form arms.

scaena frons The architectural backdrop of the stage of a Roman theater equivalent to the Greek skene.

scagliola Faux marble made of gypsum, ground alabaster or ground selenite, glue, and pigments. Worked like clay to form table tops and other decorative features.

scarab An Egyptian decorative motif that resembles the dung beetle.

scoop See *nulling.*

scotia Molding that employs a concave curve. May be a semicircle or a part of an ellipse.

scraffito Decorative technique in which lines are scratched through various layers of colored or textured material beneath.

scratch carving A pattern in which incised lines are used to outline the components. Material between the lines is not disturbed.

screens passage In the English medieval great hall, a passage that was shielded from view by a screen.

scriptorium *pl. scriptoria* The writing room in a medieval monastery.

secrétaire à abattant A fall front desk with a vertical rather than sloped front.

secrétaire en dos d'âne French double desk formed of a pair of bureaux en pente that were attached at the backs so users faced one another.

sedia Italian armchair with a tall back and upholstered seat.

sediolum A four-legged backless stool common in Rome.

segmental arch An arch that forms less than half a circle.

sekkaidan A portion of the floor in a Japanese emperor's living quarters that was covered with dirt so the emperor could participate in certain rituals that required his contact with the earth without being exposed to inclement weather.

sella *pl. sellae* The general term for a Roman seating unit. With another term, used for specific types of seats.

sella curulis An X-shaped stool that usually folded and that was a seat of honor in Etruria and Rome used only by those with political importance.

sella gestatoria A Roman sedan chair with the general appearance of a cathedra. The chair was mounted on poles or rods to make it portable and was usually enclosed by curtains.

semicircular arch An arch that forms half a circle.

seqt Egyptian ratio equivalent to Golden Mean: 1:1.618. Used as the basis of proportions for buildings and art.

serdab A small hidden room in Egyptian tombs.

serekh An early type of Egyptian house that used vertical boards laced together with leather strips.

serpentine Tops of furniture having complex curves.

settle A bench with a solid back, wings at the sides, and sometimes a curved or straight hood.

sexpartite vault A vault divided into six parts by two diagonal ribs and one central rib.

sgabello *pl. sgabelli* Type of small Italian Renaissance chair typically with an octagonal seat under which are shaped aprons. A tall, narrow wood slab forms the back including the back leg. The front leg is also formed with a slab.

shaft The vertical post between the base and capital of a column.

shaping A method of removing materials from a surface. Outside edges are modified so they conform to a specific shape. Also, a method of piercing a surface.

shawabty Sculptural figures that substituted for an individual in Egyptian tombs.

shell keep A stone keep.

shellac An alcohol-based finish made from the secretion of the lac beetle. Color can be added to shellac.

shepherd's bed A raised shelf designed for sleeping. Often a part of a Spanish colonial fireplace surround.

shibayama Ivory plaque used on export furniture from Japan in the nineteenth century.

shikibuton Japanese cushion.

shikifu Sheets used to cover a Japanese shikibuton or cushion.

shikinen-sengu Japanese tradition of rebuilding shrines every 20 years.

shimashira Central pillar in Buddhist shrine under which sacred relics are buried.

shiro Japanese fortified castle.

shitomido Japanese vertical wood lattices that could be swung upward to open a wall.

shodana Asymmetrically arranged Japanese display cabinet with drawers, compartments, and shelves.

shoe A wedge-shaped furniture foot used mostly on tables.

shoin Formal Japanese room with a window overlooking a garden or view. Often used as an office. Also house with a shoin.

shōji Translucent sliding panel covered with paper.

shonk A large piece of storage furniture that differed from the Dutch kas in that the feet were attached to the drawer base for a total of three pieces rather than four: a drawer base with feet, a large upright storage cabinet closed by doors, and an overhanging cornice. Used in German areas of Europe and in German colonial areas.

shouldered architrave A decorative door surround in which the header extends beyond the vertical posts.

show-frame A nineteenth-century seating unit with exposed wood framework.

shu gui Chinese wardrobe cabinet with two doors and interior shelves and drawers.

shutter dog A decorative iron piece that rotated to keep shutters in place.

sideboard Medieval shelf on which food was placed prior to serving. Superseded by the credence.

siège courant French furniture that could be moved from one location to another. Ususaly sat in the middle of a room.

siège meublant French furniture designed to remain in one location against a wall.

sigma A semicircular or crescent-shaped couch used by the Romans for dining around a round or oval table.

siheyuan Chinese house built around a courtyard.

silla Spanish Renaissance armless upholstered chair with a low seat.

sillon de cadera Moorish X-shaped folding chair.

sillon de cajon Type of Spanish chair with a gondola back.

simianping Legs of Chinese furniture that are attached at the corners of furniture.

singerie Monkey motif.

sistrum A rattle used in Egyptian religious ceremonies.

skene The backdrop in a Greek theater.

slant-front desk An early type of desk developed during the William and Mary period. The first examples were supported by a frame; later examples were supported on a drawer base. The top section contained cubbyholes and drawers and was closed by an angled lid that could be let down and used as a writing service.

slat-back chair See *ladder-back chair.*

slaw bed An American colonial folding bed hidden by curtains when not in use. When open, two posts at the head support a tester from which the curtains are supported.

sleigh bed American bed with an outscrolled headboard. The footboard curved either outward or inward.

slipper chair English and American chair with a low seat.

slope See *Bible box.*

smalti Tesserae used for mosaics that were made of glass in which air bubbles are trapped.

solarium *pl. solaria* A roof terrace on which was located an area for relaxation or a garden.

solium *pl. solia* The Roman chair similar to the Greek thronos, which usually had solid arms and was sometimes solid to the floor. A chair for an important person that was larger than other seating units and always required a footstool for use. See *subsellia.*

solominic column Column with twisted shaft.

soportales *sing. and pl.* A covered Spanish porch enclosed by an arcade.

sotto in su Type of trompe l'oeil painting used on ceilings during the Baroque period. Italian term means "up from under." The illusion created was often one of the heavens opening up.

speculum *pl. specula* A Roman hand mirror.

sphinx A mythical creature with a lion's body and the head of a human or another animal. See *cryosphinx* and *androsphinx.*

spina A short wall running down the center of a Roman circus.

spinapesce Brick laid in a spiral pattern to form a dome.

spiral A design that begins with a sharp curve and that winds outward away from the central point in an ever-lessening curve.

splat A flat vertical board, usually shaped, in the center of an open-backed seating unit.

splint A type of material used for weaving inexpensive furniture seats. Coarser than rush and usually woven in a basket weave.

split spindle A long turned piece with a flat back that encompasses half a circle.

split-entry A home without a living area at the entry level.

split-level A house with a single living level on one side and two stories on the other side all connected by half flights of stairs.

springline The imaginary line between two springpoints on the same arch.

springpoint The point at which an arch begins to curve.

squab Cushion.

squinch A method used to connect a dome to a square base in which an arch or beam is carried diagonally between two sides to first form an octagonal base on which the dome is constructed. Multiple layers are often needed with each projecting slightly over those below.

stabadium Roman outdoor couches designed for dining. Made of concrete or stone.

stain A finish material that adds color to a material without hiding inherent properties of the material.

stele *pl. stelae* A type of upright monument often with a rounded top that is either inscribed or decorated. Used as memorials as well as records of events and political treaties.

stellar vault A vault divided into parts by ribs that form a star shape.

stereobate Steps in a Greek crepidoma other than the one at the top.

stile A vertical member of a framework for a panel.

stippone Italian cabinet with numerous drawers and compartments. Most important furniture piece in Baroque homes.

stoa *pl. stoae* A covered walkway with a wall on one side and a colonnade on the other. The wall may front a building.

stoep A type of raised covered porch used at the entry of Dutch homes. Usually in rural areas, and frequently featuring a pair of built-in benches. The roof was supported by posts.

strapwork Flat, very low-relief carved interlaced bands.

stretcher A piece of material that connects two furniture legs.

string course A row of masonry of a different color or material or on a different plane used to visually identify on the exterior the various interior levels of a building.

stube Room with a heating stove in a Pennsylvania German house.

studiolo Italian Renaissance study located in homes of the wealthy.

stump bed English bed with short posts.

stumpwork Raised appliqué needlework.

stupa Originally, a moundlike structure used in the Buddhist religion that housed relics of Buddha including his ashes. Later, stupas were objects of veneration. The stupa evolved into the pagoda.

stylized A pattern inspired by nature but simplified in such a way that only an impression of the real object is given.

stylobate The top step of the crepidoma on which a Greek structure was located.

su gui Enclosed Chinese bookcase on a wide base.

subsellium *pl. subsellia* A footstool used with the solium. Roman

sudare Bamboo shades that roll up. Japanese.

summer beam A ceiling support beam that rested on an exterior wall at one end and on the masonry chimney unit at the other end.

superimposition Stacking of objects including orders of architecture and arcades.

Sussex chair Chair named for the area in which it was made by local carpenters. A simple type of chair requiring no special expertise. Usually had a rush seat.

swastika A cross form with four equal arms that intersect at a center point. Each arm has a 90-degree angle halfway along its length.

ta Chinese platforms designed for sitting.

tabako-bon Japanese tobacco box.

tabby A primitive type of concrete used by the Spanish in colonial America in areas where shells were numerous. The mixture consists of ground or loose shells with lime mortar, sand, and water. It is necessary to use forms until the material is set. Also called tapia.

taberna *pl. tabernae* A Roman shop.

tablas Spanish for boards.

table à dèjeuner Small, portable French table used for serving small meals or drinks that had a gallery rail around the top to prevent objects from falling.

table à fleurs See *jardinière*.

table à écrire Small French desk similar to the bureau plat. The apron had a single drawer and the writing surface was covered with leather.

table à l'Italienne Italian Mannerist refectory table with an ornamental stretcher connecting the slab ends. French.

table dormant Medieval term for a table designed to remain in one place.

tablero A vertical rectangular panel on the front of each layer of a stepped pyramid in Mesoamerican architecture.

tablinum *pl. tablina* The room or recess directly behind the atrium in a Roman home that served as the office and in which important papers and genealogical portraits and records were kept.

tabouret Drum-shaped upholstered stool.

tabularium Ancient Roman building in which the written laws were stored.

taenia A flat molding in Greek architecture used as a transition between the architrave and frieze.

tainoya Less important rooms in Japanese dwellings of the ninth through fourteenth centuries.

tallboy American term for highboy.

talud The sloping section beneath a tablero in Mesoamerican architecture.

tamagaki Fence around a Japanese sacred site.

tang hua an Long, tall table placed beneath a painting often with another table in front of it.

tang xiang Long Chinese chest used for storing fur-lined garments horizontally. Made it unnecessary to fold garments across seams.

tansu Japanese chest. When used in a compound word, tansu is altered to dansu.

tapia See *tabby*.

taquillón A Spanish chest with drawers, compartments, or a combination of the two designed to support a vargueño.

taruki Rafters in a traditional Japanese building.

tatami Japanese mats laid in geometric patterns on the floor.

tateana Early Japanese pit dwelling.

technology The application of knowledge or science to achieve a practical purpose.

tejas Curved roofing tiles made of fired clay. Spanish.

telamon *pl. telamones* A male figure used for support. Unlike the Atlas, the figure was not bowed. Roman.

temenos The sacred precinct of a temple that is enclosed by walls. Greek.

tempera A type of painting that uses pigments mixed with egg yolk.

templum *pl. templa* A sacred area surrounded by a wall and entered through a monumental gateway, or propylum. Roman equivalent of the temenos.

tenjô Japanese ceiling.

tenju Japanese tower in a castle with multiple stories.

tenshukaku Keep or defensive tower of a Japanese castle.

tent-pole column Egyptian column with a simple capital shaped like an inverted bell.

tepidarium The warm room in a Roman bath where guests could bathe in tepid water from a container or relax in the moist heat.

term *pl. termes* A tapered pillar with a bust emerging at the top. Sometimes had feet at the base. Same as gaîne.

terrace A group of connected English row houses.

terrazzo Marble chips mixed with cement and ground smooth to form a flooring material.

tessera *pl. tesserae* Small shaped pieces used in mosaics.

tester Framework over a bed from which curtains could be hung.

testudo A type of Roman ceiling that had a large cove or quarter circle curve at the wall and ceiling angle. It was called testudo after the back of the tortoise, which shape it resembled.

téte-à-téte Nineteenth-century double chair made in an S-shape so that the seats were separated by the back. Also called a courting chair or vis à vis.

tetraconch A centrally planned building with four conchs surrounding a central section.

tetrapylon A monumental gateway with openings on all four sides.

tetrastyle A building façade with four columns across the front.

thakos *pl. thakoi* A Greek seat composed of a boxlike unit.

thalamos The nuptial chamber of a Greek house located in the oecus.

thermae Monumental Roman baths in which there were rooms for bathing in hot, tepid, or cold water as well as saunas. Usually included other facilities such as libraries, picture galleries, conversation areas, and even classrooms.

tholos *pl. tholoi* A round structure. May be underground. May be made only of columns without an enclosed room (see *monopteral*).

thronos *pl. thronoi* A chair for an important person in ancient Greece. Usually has arms.

thrown chair A chair made with turned pieces.

thyron The hallway between the entrance to a Greek house and the courtyard or aule.

ti hong Chinese red lacquer that employs multiple layers of lacquer. Some layers might be of a different color so that when the surface is carved, the design is multicolored. Also known as Peking lacquer.

t'iao Tiers of brackets supporting a Chinese roof.

tie beam A horizontal beam that connects two side walls.

tierceron rib Ribs that begin at the springpoint or capital and connect to the ridge rib.

tierra amarillo A yellowish clay that contains flakes of mica.

tierra blanca A type of gypsum that has reflective mica chips in it.

tipi A type of cone-shaped tent structure used by American Plains Indians.

tô Also *tope*. Japanese pagoda.

tokonoma An alcove in a traditional Japanese-style room that contains a scroll. Often a flower arrangement or bonsai is also located within the tokonoma.

tondo *pl. tondi* A round frame in which there is a painting or carving.

tope A Buddhist monument with a dome shape.

torii Traditional Japanese gate located at the entrance to a shrine or temple that serves as the transition between sacred and profane areas. Characterized by a pair of upright supports with two crossbars.

torreón *pl. torreones* A large, fortified Spanish tower.

torus *pl. tori* Molding that employs a convex curve. May be a semicircle or a part of an ellipse.

tou-kung Clusters of brackets in Chinese architecture. Also known as dougong.

toupie Top-shaped furniture leg.

tracery Decorative stonework in Gothic structures often used in windows to support glass.

trachelion The fluting located between the annulets and hypotrachelion on a column shaft.

transept A portion of a structure that crosses the main structure at a right angle and extends beyond the side walls of the main structure.

transverse arch An arch across the width of a bay.

transverse rib A rib on the long side or ridge of a vault.

trapeza *pl. trapezai* A Greek table.

trapezophoron *pl. trapezophora* A table pedestal that featured addorsed animals.

trastero A freestanding Spanish cupboard enclosed by doors.

travertine A type of limestone used by the Romans for building construction. It was not affected by environmental factors.

travois An arrangement of poles covered with skins on which belongings could be carried. Pulled by dogs, horses, or other animals.

trefoil A design that employs three foils.

trelliage Nineteenth-century term for decorative metal grilles used outdoors.

tremido Type of Portuguese ornament with wavy parallel grooves.

trenail Wooden pegs used as nails in Medieval construction.

trencadis The technique of using broken tiles to create mosaics.

trespoli Small Italian table used to support a mirror while dressing.

trestle table A table supported by trestles at each end and, when very long, in the middle as well.

tribunal An area in a Roman basilica where judges and advocates were seated during legal proceedings. Usually located opposite the entrance to the building.

triclinium *pl. triclinia* A formal dining room in a Roman home.

triglyph A block with three grooves carved in it. In ancient Greece, there were often two central grooves with a half groove (hemiglyph) on either side.

tripos Metal tripods used in Rome for supporting incense trays, wine craters, and pots for boiling meat.

tripteral A classical building with three rows of columns around it. Rare.

triptych Three panels hinged together.

triumphal arch A temporary or monumental arch through which soldiers passed after returning from campaigns and that was believed to remove their aggressive tendencies in preparation for life at home.

trompe l'oeil Literally "fool the eye." Perspective paintings that give the impression the depictions are real objects rather than painted ones.

troneca Loopholes through a parapet wall through which Spanish defenders could fire at attackers.

trundle bed A short bed that could be rolled beneath a higher bed when not in use.

truss A triangular-shaped device that is used to span space. Very stable if at least one corner is solidly attached.

trussing bed A Medieval folding bed that was tied or trussed for travel.

trussing chest A medieval chest small enough to be carried.

tsuitate A movable opaque Japanese screen with a single panel.

tuckaway table A space-saving table designed so the top tilts to vertical when not in use.

Tudor rose Five-petaled rose motif. English.

tufa A lightweight volcanic stone available in several colors. Deteriorates when exposed to the air around the sea and if frozen.

tumulus *pl. tumuli* A mound of earth formed above a tomb with a domed or vaulted roof.

tunnel vault See *barrel vault*.

turkey work Needlework that produced a wool pile on a textile base. Designs imitated those of carpets from the Near East.

turning A method of carving by mounting the piece so that it can be turned while carving is being accomplished. Usually done on a lathe, a machine that constantly turns the piece during carving.

tympanum The recessed area between the moldings surrounding a pediment.

udjat An Egyptian motif that uses a human eye with the markings of a falcon's eye.

under eave bed An American colonial bed with short posts designed to fit in the angle beneath the roof.

uraeus *pl. uraei* In ancient Egypt, the royal symbol that uses the form of a rearing asp or snake ready to strike.

vargueño Spanish writing cabinet with a vertical fall front that conceals pigeon holes and drawers. The top is also hinged. On each end, there is a handle for carrying.

velarium *pl. velaria* An awning supported by posts that provided shade for spectators at outdoor events in Rome.

veneering The application of a thin sheet of material to another, usually less expensive material.

vergeboard See *bargeboard*.

vernis martin French Renaissance version of japanning.

vestibulum *pl. vestibule* The outdoor area in front of the entrance to a Roman domus or villa where guests awaited entry.

viga A large timber used as a roof framing member. May project at both ends or be cut off flush with the wall.

villa *pl. villae* Ancient Roman domestic structure built around a courtyard.

villa rustica A Roman villa in the countryside designed for farming. It often also contained living quarters for the owner's family.

villa urbana A suburban or rural domestic building that differed from the villa rustica in that the villa urbana was not designed for farm-related activities.

vis-à-vis See *téte à téte*.

vitreae camerae A Roman room in which small pieces of glass were mounted on structural components.

vitrine Cupboard with glazed doors that enclosed shelves. Used for display of objects.

Vitruvian scroll A variation of the wave pattern in which the curved lines spiral and double back on themselves.

volute A spiral ornament. Employed on the front and back of Ionic capitals.

voussoir A wedge-shaped unit used to form an arch by placing the narrow end toward the center.

voyeuse French chair with a low seat designed to be straddled. Has a padded shelf on the top of the back on which the occupant's arms could be rested. Called a conversation chair in England.

voyeuse à genoux French lady's chair with a low seat and a padded shelf across the back. Designed so users could kneel in the seat and rest their arms on the shelf while watching games being played. Called a conversation chair in England.

wachseinlegen A seventeenth-century decorative technique used on furniture by the Dutch in which incised lines were filled with a yellow mixture of sulfur and either wax or putty.

wainscot chair A type of chair with a solid paneled back and a hinged seat that covered a storage box.

waisted leg Type of Chinese furniture leg used on ceremonial furniture. The leg was attached to the apron of the furniture recessed from the edges.

wall hutch Wall-mounted ventilated livery cupboard.

wall-pillar Churches in German-speaking areas during the Baroque period and later that had a series of open chapels separated by pillars flanking the nave.

watadono Wide Japanese corridor.

water leaf A band pattern consisting of leaves with a prominent midrib.

wattle Interlaced branches forming a web between two supports.

weatherboard Sawn boards of uniform thickness.

westwerk The western front of a medieval church with the entry flanked by towers.

whatnot Nineteenth-century shelving unit, sometimes with a mirror.

wheel window Type of circular window used during the Gothic period.

whiplash Flowing lines popular during the Art Nouveau period that curved back on themselves.

whitewash A lime-based medium applied to give a surface a white color.

window of appearance An upper-story window with a balcony, a balustrade, and a baldachin from which an appearance can be made to the public.

Windsor chair A type of chair made with a saddled seat, turned splayed legs and stretchers, and usually spindles beneath the back.

wing chair A high-backed chair with wings that angled forward from the top of the back to shield users from drafts.

xiang qian Chinese lacquer technique in which recesses were made in dried lacquer and the spaces filled with ivory, metals, mother-of-pearl or other materials.

xystus *pl. xysti* A Roman garden associated with a villa. Often located away from the villa itself with porticus leading to it and surrounding it. Large xysti featured pools of water and topiary. Most had flowers.

yagura Japanese tower.

yan ji Chinese draw-leaf table.

yang ci Also called Canton enamel. Metal plaques painted with enamels in Chinese design.

yesería Moorish all-carved carved plaster decoration.

yin ping tuo Chinese lacquer technique in which other materials such as metals or ivory are applied to an object before the lacquer dries. The entire piece is then lacquered again and burnished to reveal the inlaid design.

yosemune-zukuri Japanese hipped roof.

yurt See *ger*.

zaguán A covered passageway associated with a Spanish building that led to a large double door through which carriages and livestock could be driven. See also *portón*.

zakomara *pl. zakomary* Semicircular gables traditionally used on Russian buildings often with a shell design.

zanjas Spanish aqueduct made of fired clay tiles.

zapatas Shaped, wooden Spanish corbels, often chip carved.

zhedievi Chinese X-shaped folding chair.

zhuan lun hing chang Chinese rotating octagonal bookcase with interior shelves and pigeonholes.

ziggurat An ancient Mesopotamian tomb form that incorporated a number of stepped-back platforms.

zimbabwe African stone structure with surrounding walls enclosing groups of individual buildings. The term dzimbadzemabwe from which the name Zimbabwe is derived means "big house of stone" in the indigenous Shona language.

zuiwengyi Deep-seated Chinese chair with an adjustable back. Known as a drunken lord's chair.

Endnotes

CHAPTER 1

1. From the Greek *eurythmia* (eu–well; rhythmos–rhythm) meaning harmony.
2. For the translation of these principles, see *Vitruvius: The Ten Books on Architecture,* Translated by Morris Hicky Morgan, Dover Publications, Inc., New York, 1960, pp. 13–16.
3. In ancient Greece, every male took a turn at serving as a priest so there was no class of priests as was typical in other cultures.
4. Also known as palissandre.
5. In Renaissance Italy, the term intarsia was used, although usually to describe a picture done in this manner that was used as veneer.
6. The counterclockwise swastika called *suavastika* is extensively used in India.
7. The original "diaspros" (Greek) denoted a fabric with a pattern woven in monochrome showing two textures that reflected light differently.

CHAPTER 2

1. By definition, civilization requires that a culture have a system of writing.
2. Memphis is located about 12 miles north of modern Cairo.
3. All dates are approximate partially due to the lack of a definitive date for the beginning of the Egyptian calendar. When available, dates given by Durant have been used. See Durant, Will, *The Story of Civilization: Part 1: Our Oriental Heritage,* New York: Simon and Schuster, 1954.
4. An evergreen that grows up to 45 feet tall.
5. *Zizyphus spina-christi.* Also called "Christ's thorn" and "Chinese date." Yields the jujube fruit. The wood is hard. One hieroglyphic text speaks of a coffin of sidder and gold.
6. Dom palm reaches over 32 feet in height.

CHAPTER 4

1. Durant, Will, *The Life of Greece,* New York: Simon and Schuster, 1966, p. 21.
2. Heinrich Schliemann (1822–1890) excavated Mycenae and Tiryns, another Mycenaean city, and claimed to have discovered Troy. Modern archaeologists conclude that Schliemann went beyond the layer of Homeric Troy in his diggings but that the site probably was that of Troy.
3. The term tholos can be applied to most round structures.
4. The term naos is sometimes used as synonymous with "cella." Cella is Latin; naos is Greek. Some authors stipulate that the term cella incorporates all three of the spaces within the Greek temple: the pronaos, the naos, and the opisthodomos.

CHAPTER 5

1. The Cloaca Maxima was constructed by Lucius Tarquinius Priscus c. 578 BC to drain the marshy area near the narrow Tiber crossing and became the main drain of Rome.
2. The plural "porta" was used for gates and often doors because it usually required two leaves to close the opening.
3. Latin for "island."
4. The term balneum was used for the vessel into which water was poured for bathing and later for the room in which bathing occurred.
5. Domus is both singular and plural.

CHAPTER 6

1. Dates, especially those of ancient China, vary according to source. When possible, the dates used in this chapter are from Durant. (Durant, Will, *The Story of Civilization: Part 1: Our Oriental Heritage,* New York: Simon and Schuster, 1954.
2. Ibid, p. 641.

CHAPTER 8

1. Charles-Alexis-Adrien Duhérissier de Gerville (Gerville-la-Forêt) (1769–1853) first used the term Romanesque in a letter to De Caumont in 1820, although in reference to the Romance languages. Caumont subsequently used the term in his book *Essaie sur l'architecture du moyen âge, particulièrement en Normandie* in 1824.

CHAPTER 9

1. Early practitioners of the craft were known as upholderers.

CHAPTER 11

1. Spain's Philip II had gained control of the Netherlands when his father, Holy Roman Emperor Charles V, abdicated in 1555 and divided Hapsburg possessions among his three sons. In 1579, what is now Belgium negotiated peace with Spain. In 1581, the Protestant William of Orange of what is now the Netherlands repudiated Philip's control.

2. Durant, Will, *The Reformation: A History of European Civilization from Wyclif to Calvin: 1300–1564,* New York: Simon and Schuster, 1957, p. 307.

CHAPTER 14

1. Several different spellings of Viking names occur. This Viking's name is often spelled Bjorne Herjólfsson.

2. Morison, Samuel Eliot, *Admiral of the Ocean Sea: A Life of Christopher Columbus,* Boston: Little, Brown and Company, 1942.

3. Garraty, John A., & Peter Gay, Editors. *The Columbia History of the World,* New York: Harper & Row, Publishers, 1972, p. 655.

4. The first lasting Spanish settlement in Puerto Rico was established in 1521. While the French and English made some earlier attempts at settlement, the first permanent English settlement was that of Jamestown in 1607, and the first lasting French settlement was in Quebec beginning in 1608.

5. Although there were six known Spanish expeditions to California beginning with Cabrillo in 1542–1543 and ending with Carreri in 1696, the Spanish did not establish any settlements in California prior to 1769. California, was a Spanish colony until 1821 and did not become a state associated with the new United States until 1849.

6. Also called Spanish New Mexico style.

7. This construction method was similar to the **columbage** construction of northern France during the same period.

Some differences occurred in the materials used to fill the interstices.

CHAPTER 15

1. The Mayflower set out with 102 passengers. Five died en route and two were born.

2. Garraty, John R. and Peter Gay, Eds., *The Columbia History of the World,* New York: Harper & Row Publishers, 1972, p. 679.

3. The region of the colonial South included the Chesapeake Bay region (Virginia and Maryland) and Carolina, which was later split into Georgia and North and South Carolina.

CHAPTER 17

1. The spelling of the name was changed later. The name consisted of two German words: "bieder," meaning common or plain, and "meier," which was a common surname.

CHAPTER 18

1. Like the Crystal Palace in London, the New York Crystal Palace was designed for an international exhibition in 1853. It, too, was constructed of wrought iron and glass. The New York builders enameled the glass and vitrified it to avoid the problem with heat that had plagued the London building.

2. Although he was already selling the device, Otis did not receive a patent on it until 1861.

CHAPTER 19

1. The term bungalow comes from India, where it refers to single-story houses in the region of Bengal. The Bengali huts are known as bangala and are especially suited to the hot, humid climate.

Resources

ATLASES, DICTIONARIES, AND ENCYCLOPEDIAS

Astley, S. (1990). *Border Designs: A Treasury of Hundreds of Decorative Designs in Colour and Black and White.* London: Studio Editions.

Boyce, C. (1999). *Dictionary of Furniture.* New York: Henry Holt and Company.

Curl, J. S. (1999). *Oxford Dictionary of Architecture.* Oxford: Oxford University Press.

Fleming, J., and Honour, H. (1977). *Dictionary of the Decorative Arts.* New York: Harper & Row.

Guralnik, D. B., ed. *Webster's New World Dictionary of the American Language.* New York: Popular Library: The World Publishing Company.

Jones, Owen. (1989). *The Studio Library of Decorative Art: The Grammar of Ornament.* London: Studio Editions.

Lewis, P., and Darley, G. (1986). *Dictionary of Ornament.* New York: Pantheon Books.

Oliphant, M. (1998). *The Atlas of the Ancient World: Charting the Great Civilizations of the Past.* New York: Barnes & Noble Books.

Osborne, H., ed. (1989). *An Illustrated Companion to the Decorative Arts.* Ware, Hertfordshire, UK: Wordsworth Editions.

—. (1985). *The Oxford Companion to the Decorative Arts.* Oxford: Oxford University Press.

Parker, J. H. (1986). *Classic Dictionary of Architecture: A Concise Glossary of Terms Usd in Grecian, Roman, Italian, and Gothic Architecture, Fourth Edition.* London: New Orchard Editions. (Originally published in 1875.)

Pevsner, N., Fleming, J., and Honour, H. (1976). *A Dictionary of Architecture.* Woodstock, NY: The Overlook Press.

Saylor, H. H. (1952). *Dictionary of Architecture.* New York: John Wiley & Sons.

GENERAL HISTORY

Black, J., ed. (2005). *World Historic Events.* Bath, UK: Parrago Publishing.

Breasted, J. H. (1935). *Ancient Times: A History of the Early World.* Boston: Ginn and Company.

Cooke, J., Kramer, A., and Rowland, T. (2005). *History's Timeline.* New York: Barnes & Noble Books.

Derrik, M., ed. (2000). *Millennium Year by Year: A Chronicle of World History from AD 1000 to the End of 1999.* London: DK Publishing.

Durant, W. (1954). *The Story of Civilization, Part I: Our Oriental Heritage.* New York: Simon & Schuster.

Garraty, J. A., and Gay, P., eds. (1981). *The Columbia History of the World.* New York: Harper & Row.

Haywood, J. (2002). *Atlas of Past Times.* Ann Arbor, MI: Borders Press.

Kagan, D., Ozment, S., and Turner, F. M. (1979). *The Western Heritage.* New York: Macmillan.

Mycrs, B. S., and Copplestone, T., eds. (1985). *The History of Art: Architecture, Painting, Sculpture.* New York: Dorset Press.

Oliphant, M. (1998). *The Atlas of the Ancient World: Charting the Great Civilizations of the Past.* New York: Barnes & Noble Books.

Reader's Digest Association. (2004). *Reader's Digest Illustrated History of the World: The Dawn of Civilisation: Prehistory to 900 BC,* London: Reader's Digest Association.

Tillier, A. (2000). *Paris.* London: DK Travel.

ART HISTORY

Adams, L. S. (1999). *Art Across Time: Volume I, Prehistory to the Fourteenth Century.* Boston: McGraw-Hill College.

Atkinson, A. (2002). *Lost Civilizations: Rediscovering Ancient Sites through New Technology.* New York: Watson-Guptill Publications.

Bazin, G. (1959). *A History of Art from Prehistoric Times to the Present.* (F. Scarfe, trans.). New York: Bonanza Books.

Chase, G. H., and Vermeule III, C. C. (1963). *Greek Etruscan and Roman Art.* Boston: Museum of Fine Arts.

Cheney, S. (1939). *A World History of Art.* New York: The Viking Press.

DK Publishing. (1998). *Art: A World History.* London: DK Publishing.

de la Crois, H., Tansey, R. G., and Kirkpatrick, D. (1991). *Gardner's Art through the Ages: Volume I, Ancient, Medieval, and Non-European Art.* New York: Harcourt Brace Jovanovich.

Gardner, H. (1959). *Helen Gardner's Art through the Ages.* Fourth edition. (S. M. Crosby, ed.) New York: Harcourt, Brace & World.

Johnson, P. (2003). *Art: A New History.* New York: Harper-Collins Publishers.

Marceau, J., ed. (1997). *Art: A World History.* London: DK Publishing.

Scranton, R. L. (1964). *Aesthetic Aspects of Ancient Art.* Chicago: The University of Chicago Press.

ARCHITECTURE AND STRUCTURE

Caffin, C. H. (1929). *How to Study Architecture.* New York: Dodd, Mead and Company.

Camesasca, E. (1971). *History of the House.* New York: G. P. Putnam's Sons.

Cichy, B. (1964). *The Great Ages of Architecture from Ancient Greece to the Present Day.* New York: G. P. Putnam's Sons.

Cole, E., ed. (2005). *The Grammar of Architecture.* New York: Barnes & Noble Books.

Crouch, D. P. (1985). *History of Architecture: Stonehenge to Skyscrapers.* New York: McGraw-Hill.

Field, D. M. (2001). *The World's Greatest Architecture Past and Present.* Edison, NJ : Chartwell Books.

Field, W. (Oct., 1942). "A Reexamination into the Invention of the Balloon Frame," *The Journal of the American Society of Architectural Historians,* Vol. 2, No. 4, pp. 3–29.

Glancey, J. (2006). *Architecture.* London: DK Publishing.

—. (2000). *The Story of Architecture.* London: DK Publishing.

Hamlin, T. (1953). *Architecture through the Ages.* New York: G. P. Putnam's Sons.

Höcker, C. (2000). *Architecture.* Hauppauge, NY: Barron's Educational Services.

Jordan, R. F. (1968). *A Concise History of Western Architecture.* London: Harcourt Brace Jovanovich.

Kostof, S. (1985). *A History of Architecture: Settings and Rituals.* New York: Oxford University Press.

Lloyd, S., Rice, D. T., et al. (1963). *World Architecture: An Illustrated History.* New York: McGraw-Hill.

Lloyd, S., Müller, H. W., Martin, R. (1974). *Ancient Architecture: Mesopotamia, Egypt, Crete, Greece.* New York: Harry N. Abrams.

Mark, R. (1994). *Architectural Technology up to the Scientific Revolution.* Cambridge, MA: MIT Press.

Musgrove, J., ed. (1987). *Sir Banister Fletcher's A History of Architecture.* Oxford: Architectural Press.

Norwich, J. J., ed. (1982). *Great Architecture of the World.* New York: Bonanza Books. (Originally published in 1975. London: Mitchell Beazley Publishers.)

Parker, J. H. (1989). *A Concise Glossary of Architectural Terms.* London: Studio Editions. (Originally published in 1896.)

Pevsner, N. (1983). *An Outline of European Architecture.* Harmondsworth, Middlesex, UK: Penguin Books.

Pothorn, H. (1983). *A Guide to Architectural Styles.* Oxford: Phaidon Press.

Priess, P. (1973). "Wire Nails in North America." *Bulletin of the Association for Preservation Technology,* Vol. 5, No. 4, p. 87.

Robertson, D. S. (1969). *Greek and Roman Architecture.* Cambridge, UK: University Printing House.

Scarre, C., ed. (1999). *The Seventy Wonders of the Ancient World: The Great Monuments and How They Were Built.* London: Thames & Hudson.

Schoenauer, N. (2000). *6,000 Years of Housing.* New York: W. W. Norton & Company.

Statham, H. H. (1912). *A Short Critical History of Architecture.* London: B. T. Batsford.

Strickland, C. (2001). *The Annotated Arch: A Crash Course in the History of Architecture.* Kansas City: Andrews McMeel Publishing.

Sturgis, R. (1989). *Sturgis' Illustrated Dictionary of Architecture and Building,* Volume 1. New York: Dover Publications. (Unabridged reprint of 1901–1902 edition).

—. (1989). *Sturgis' Illustrated Dictionary of Architecture and Building,* Volume 2, New York: Dover Publications. (Unabridged reprint of 1901–1902 edition.)

—. (1989). *Sturgis' Illustrated Dictionary of Architecture and Building,* Volume 3. New York: Dover Publications. (Unabridged reprint of 1901–1902 edition.)

Vitruvius. (1960). *Vitruvius: The Ten Books on Architecture.* (M. H. Morgan, trans.). New York: Dover Publications.

Watkin, D. (1986). *A History of Western Architecture.* London: Barrie & Jenkins.

Wodehouse, L., and Moffett, M. (1989). *A History of Western Architecture.* Mountain View, CA: Mayfield Publishing Company.

Wright, G. R. H. (2000). *Ancient Building Technology: Volume 1, Historical Background,* Leiden, The Netherlands: Brill Academic Publishers.

DESIGN

Ball, V. K. (1980). *Architecture and Interior Design: A Basic History through the Seventeenth Century.* New York: John Wiley & Sons.

Harwood, B., May, B., and Sherman, C. (2002). *Architecture and Interior Design through the Eighteenth Century.* Upper Saddle River, NJ: Prentice Hall.

Pile, J. (2000). *A History of Interior Design.* New York: John Wiley & Sons.

Whiton, S. (1974). *Interior Design and Decoration.* New York: HarperCollins.

Whiton, S., and Abercrombie, S. (2001). *Interior Design and Decoration.* Upper Saddle River, NJ: Prentice Hall.

FURNITURE

Boger, L. A. (1997). *The Complete Guide to Furniture Styles.* Prospect Heights, IL: Waveland Press.

Charlish, A., ed. (1976). *The History of Furniture*. New York: Crescent Books.

Davidson, M. B, ed. (1967). *The American Heritage History of Colonial Antiques*. New York: American Heritage Publishing Co.

Fitzgerald, O. P. (1995). *Four Centuries of American Furniture*. Iola, WI: Krause Publications.

—. (1982). *Three Centuries of American Furniture*. Englewood Cliffs, NJ: Prentice Hall.

Gloag, J. (1966). *A Social History of Furniture Design from BC 1300 to AD 1960*. New York: Crown Publishers.

Huntley, M. (2004). *History of Furniture: Ancient to Nineteenth Century*. Lewes, East Sussex, UK: Guild of Master Craftsman Publications.

Litchfield, F. (2006). *Illustrated History of Furniture from the Earliest to the Present Time*. El Paso, TX: El Paso Norte Press. (Originally published in 1893.)

Lucie-Smith, E. (1985). *Furniture: A Concise History*. New York: Thames & Hudson.

Mcrccr, E. (1969). *Furniture 700–1700: The Social History of the Decorative Arts*. New York: Meredith Press.

Miller, J. (2005). *Furniture: World Styles from Classical to Contemporary*. London: DK Publishing.

Quantum Publishing. (2000). *Encyclopedia of Furniture*. London: Quantum Books.

Richter, G. M. A. (1966). *The Furniture of the Greeks Etruscans and Romans*. London, The Phaidon Press.

Riley, N., ed. (1989). *World Furniture*, Secaucus, NJ: Chartwell Books.

Sassone, A. B., et al. (2000). *Furniture: From Rococo to Art Deco*. Köln, Germany: Benedikt Taschen Verlag GmbH.

Sparke, P. (1986). *Furniture: Twentieth Century Design*. New York: E. P. Dutton.

Watson, F. (1982). *The History of Furniture*. New York: Crescent Books.

Wanscher, O. (1966). *The Art of Furniture: 5,000 Years of Furniture and Interiors*. New York: Reinhold Publishing Corporation.

ORNAMENT

Glazier, R. (1983). *A Manual of Historic Ornament*. New York: Van Nostrand Reinhold.

Hamlin, A. D. F. (1921). *A History of Ornament: Ancient and Medieval*. New York: The Century Co.

Jones, O. (1989). *The Grammar of Ornament*. London: Studio Editions.

Speltz, A. (1936). *Styles of Ornament: Exhibited in Designs and Arranged in Historical Order with Descriptive Text*. New York: Grosset & Dunlap.

EGYPT AND THE NEAR EAST

Adams, L. S. (1999). *Art Across Time: Volume I, Prehistory to the Fourteenth Century*. Boston: McGraw-Hill College.

—. (2007). *Art Across Time*. Boston: McGraw-Hill.

Badawy, A. (1968). *A History of Egyptian Architecture: The Empire (The New Kingdom) from the Eighteenth Dynasty to the End of the Twentieth Dynasty 1580–1085 BC,* Berkeley, CA: University of California Press.

Crawford, H. E. W. (1977). *Mesopotamia Copenhagen Studies in Assyriology: Volume 5, The Architecture of Iraq in the Third Millennium BC*. Copenhagen: Akademisk.

Durant, W. (1954). *The Story of Civilization Part I: Our Oriental Heritage*. New York: Simon & Schuster.

Garraty, J. A., and Gay, P., eds. (1981). *The Columbia History of the World*. New York: Harper & Row.

Gilbert, K. S., ed. (1976). *Treasures of Tutankhamun*. New York: The Metropolitan Museum of Art.

Killen, G. (1980). *Ancient Egyptian Furniture: Volume 1, 4000–1300 BC*. Warminster, Wilts, UK: Aris & Phillips.

Seidel, M., and Schulz, R. (2005). *Egypt*. New York: Barnes & Noble Books.

Smith, E. B. (1968). *Egyptian Architecture as Cultural Expression*. New York: American Life Foundation.

AFRICA

Afolayan, F. (2004). *Culture and Customs of South Africa*. Westport, CT: Greenwood Press.

Denbow, J., and Thebe, P. C. (2006). *Culture and Customs of Botswana*. Westport, CT: Greenwood Press.

Garlake, P. (2002). *Early Art and Architecture of Africa*. Oxford: Oxford University Press.

Long, D. E. (2005). *Culture and Customs of Saudi Arabia*. Westport, CT: Greenwood Press.

Mair, L. (1977). *African Kingdoms*. Oxford: Clarendon Press.

Njoku, R. C. (2006). *Culture and Customs of Morocco*. Westport, CT: Greenwood Press.

Olukoju, A. (2006). *Culture and Customs of Liberia*. Westport, CT: Greenwood Press.

Owomoyela, O. (2002). *Culture and Customs of Zimbabwe*. Westport, CT: Greenwood Press.

Salm, S. J., and Falola, T. (2002). *Culture and Customs of Ghana*. Westport, CT: Greenwood Press.

Sobania, N. (2003). *Culture and Customs of Kenya*. Westport, CT: Greenwood Press.

Taylor, S. D. (2006). *Culture and Customs of Zambia*. Westport, CT: Greenwood Press.

CRETE AND GREECE

Akurgal, E. (1966). *The Art of Greece: Its Origins in the Mediterranean and Near East,* New York: Crown Publishers.

Index